# CLASS, &RACE, GENDER, &CRIME

*Sixth Edition*

## THE SOCIAL REALITIES OF JUSTICE IN AMERICA

**PAUL LEIGHTON**
*Eastern Michigan University*

**GREGG BARAK**
*Eastern Michigan University*

**ALLISON COTTON**
*Metropolitan State University of Denver*

**CARRIE L. BUIST**
*Grand Valley State University*

**K. SEBASTIAN LEÓN**
*Rutgers University*

**ROWMAN & LITTLEFIELD**
*Lanham • Boulder • New York • London*

Acquisitions Editor: Alyssa Palazzo
Acquisitions Assistant: Hannah Eveland
Sales and Marketing Inquiries: textbooks@rowman.com

Credits and acknowledgments for material borrowed from other sources, and reproduced with permission, appear on the appropriate pages within the text.

Published by Rowman & Littlefield
An imprint of The Rowman & Littlefield Publishing Group, Inc.
4501 Forbes Boulevard, Suite 200, Lanham, Maryland 20706
www.rowman.com

86-90 Paul Street, London EC2A 4NE

British Library Cataloguing in Publication Information Available

**Library of Congress Cataloging-in-Publication Data**
Names: Leighton, Paul, 1964– author. | Barak, Gregg, author. | Cotton, Allison M., 1969– author. |
    Buist, Carrie L., author. | León, K. Sebastian, author.
Title: Class, race, gender, and crime : the social realities of justice in America / Paul Leighton, Gregg Barak,
    Allison Cotton, Carrie L. Buist, K. Sebastian León.
Description: Sixth edition. | Lanham : Rowman & Littlefield, [2025] | Includes bibliographical
    references and index.
Identifiers: LCCN 2024027931 (print) | LCCN 2024027932 (ebook) | ISBN 9781538173275 (cloth) |
    ISBN 9781538173282 (paperback) | ISBN 9781538173299 (epub)
Subjects: LCSH: Criminal justice, Administration of—United States. | United States—Social conditions.
Classification: LCC HV9950 .L455 2025  (print) | LCC HV9950  (ebook) | DDC 364.973—dc23/eng/20240812
LC record available at https://lccn.loc.gov/2024027931
LC ebook record available at https://lccn.loc.gov/2024027932

*To our families*

# Contents

# Preface

The Founding Fathers wrote in the Declaration of Independence, "We hold these truths to be self-evident, that all men are created equal, that they are endowed by their Creator with certain unalienable Rights, that among these are Life, Liberty and the pursuit of Happiness." It is ironic that many of those talking about liberty and equality were slave owners, leading some to wonder exactly how "self-evident" these truths really were. In her Pulitzer Prize–winning essay, Hannah-Jones (2019) bluntly says: "The United States is a nation founded on both an ideal and a lie."

Indeed, the Declaration contains a list of grievances against England to justify violent rebellion, and the original Declaration attacked the king for waging "cruel war against human nature itself, violating its most sacred rights of life & liberty in the persons of a distant people who never offended him, captivating & carrying them into slavery in another hemisphere, or to incur miserable death in their transportation thither" (Christianson 1998: 66). The capture and transportation of African people into slavery was similar to the British policy of transportation, whereby convicts—as well as poor people kidnapped for cheap labor—were put on boats bound for indentured servitude in Australia or the American colonies. At the request of Southern men, this passage was deleted and replaced with the more general "long train of abuses and usurpations." The Declaration hid the issue of the Founding Fathers owning slaves while using rhetoric to "claim that they were the slaves—to Britain" (Hannah-Jones 2019). The Founding Fathers not only had slaves but also prohibited all women and many poor men from voting for a government supposedly "of . . . by . . . and for the people."

Former Supreme Court justice William O. Douglas reminds us, though, that the Declaration still had an "enduring appeal" because it stated that "the throwing off of chains by an oppressed people is a noble project; and second, that all men have a common humanity, that there is a oneness in the world which binds all men together" (1954: 3). A modern expression of that sentiment would more explicitly include women and a term inclusive of nonbinary people as well. The larger point, though, is that the ideals of equality, even while not fully practiced by the Founding Fathers, were articulated in a way that allowed marginalized groups to secure increasing legal rights and recognition. Hannah-Jones (2019) also notes the power of the ideal that went with the lie about equality: "Through centuries of black resistance and protest, we have helped the country live up to its founding ideals. And not only for ourselves—black rights struggles paved the way for every other rights struggle, including women's and gay rights, immigrant and disability rights."

The authors of this book believe there is still an important gap between our ideals and the reality of inequality—and it shapes this book. We strongly value the ideals of freedom and equality. Yet, at the same time, we are all too aware of the numerous current inequalities and ways in which the United States is not living up to those ideals. History too frequently overlooks oppression as well as the intense struggles it took to get the country from the limited notions of equality at its founding to the better, but still incomplete, understanding of it today. There are also powerful forces at work today that obscure the extent of inequality.

Because freedom and inequality are such broad topics, this book focuses on the areas of crime and criminal justice, which are where state power is most acute. The criminal justice system has a monopoly on the use of force through the coercive powers of the police to detain, arrest, and use deadly force against people suspected of committing crimes; the court system's power to find guilt and pass sentence against people convicted of crimes; and the prison system's ability to deprive people of their freedom and to execute condemned citizens. The law defines what actions are harmful and thus gives direction to the formidable powers of the criminal justice system. Thus, ideas about "law and order" can be an oppressive mechanism employed to protect the privileged class (and their property) in an unequal and exploitative society, or it can be the call of conscience reminding the country about its promises of equality and liberty for all.

While this book focuses on law and criminal justice, our method is to connect those topics to social structures of inequality that systematically deny liberty to many people. A key to linking these is through class, race, and gender/sexuality. These categories represent some, but certainly not all, of the ways that people's life experiences can be arbitrarily and negatively impacted in the contexts of criminal law and criminal justice. Indeed, Marx argued that all of human history was a class war that involved the struggle between the haves and have-nots; law and criminal justice are tools wielded by the wealthy in this struggle. Feminist scholars point out that Marx's analysis of the workers and owners of the means of production left out women doing unpaid housework; there are also issues of sexuality, sexual access, and reproductive control. Finally, race has also been a defining issue throughout U.S. history in terms of conquest and empire, and any honest telling of U.S. history should start with white settlers taking land from Native Americans and then building the wealth of the country through the use of African slaves; other immigrant groups have also been exploited for cheap labor to build America's capitalist economy.

Of course, it is important to understand not only how class, race, and gender/sexuality work separately but also how they work in combination in people's lives. For example, people often say that the Fifteenth Amendment codified the right to vote for the formerly enslaved. But it only gave former *enslaved men* the right to vote (if they could overcome the many barriers to political participation that white society erected for them, such as physical barricades, poll taxes, and literacy tests); Black women had to wait for the passage of the Nineteenth Amendment in 1920 before they, and white women, could vote.[1] This book emphasizes the integration of class, race, and gender/sexuality to create a more realistic and candid analysis that comes from looking at multiple aspects of identity.

For example, consider the story of Doug Glanville, a former professional baseball player and ESPN commentator. One day Glanville (who is a Black man) was shoveling snow on his driveway, and a white police officer passed by several whites shoveling their driveways and approached Glanville. The officer was enforcing an ordinance prohibiting door-to-door solicitations, like asking people to shovel their driveways for money. Glanville thought the officer treated him "without respect" as Glanville explained he owned the home and was not a poor Black person looking for work in an affluent neighborhood (in Reiman and Leighton 2023). The officer left without an apology. Glanville's wife, an attorney, emailed a state senator who lived in the neighborhood about "shoveling while Black." Glanville subsequently had a meeting at the town hall with city officials. While race is clearly a factor here, the trajectory of the encounter was very different from those of poor Black people who come under suspicion of the police, highlighting the importance of class.

In drawing other examples, we do not always see whites as "bad" or other groups as always "good." No one race, class, or gender/sexuality group holds a monopoly on decency or deviance. However, some race, class, and gender/sexuality groups receive extra scrutiny and reprimand for deviance than others, and this discipline comes from the groups that hold disproportionate power in society. Likewise, privilege may make some groups feel more virtuous than others, even if their amount of drug use, crime, and social harm are similar (or greater).

This book seeks to raise awareness and challenge some of the beliefs, policies, and procedures that undermine social justice because of oppression based on class, race, and gender/sexuality. And while those terms are typically reserved for the poor, minorities, women, and the LGBTQ+ population, everyone fits into a class; whites have race, men have a gender, and heterosexuals have a sexual orientation. Too often, people see middle- and upper-class heterosexual white men as not having class, race, gender, or sexuality because their positions are the privileged positions that are constructed as "normal," while all other positions are "other"—and less than. These biases are reflected and recreated in the administration of criminal justice but also in criminology, law, and the mass media. In short, our effort here is to show that "crime" and "criminals" are socially constructed phenomena, meaning that law, policing, prosecution, and punishment focus on a relatively small number of many morally blameworthy harmful acts. Criminal justice and criminology are like a carnival mirror that throws back a distorted image of harms done by certain groups rather than reflecting true dangers (Reiman and Leighton 2023). But what is a "crime" and who are "criminals" seems natural and inevitable (rather than the result of social and political processes) because they are reproduced daily through various discussions in the streets, the corporate-owned media, the governing bodies, the courts, and other cultural bodies. Moral agents, social movements, political interests, media, and policy makers usually reinforce the prevailing notions of crime and criminals, so criminal justice—and the injustice it does—becomes accepted and normalized; ideologies convince people that the patterns are inevitable and just, when in fact they are created and can be changed when unjust.

For reasons like this, concepts of "equal protection" and "due process" are important but limited. Although the police might not coerce a suspect into confessing and the defendant might have a lawyer for representation in court, the late Judge David L. Bazelon once noted, "It is simply unjust to place people in dehumanizing social conditions, do nothing about those conditions, and then command those who suffer, 'Behave—or else!'" (in Leighton and Reiman 2001: 39). Supreme Court justice Louis Brandeis would have agreed, because he noted that the Founding Fathers "knew that order cannot be secured merely through fear of punishment for its infraction" (*Whitney v. California*, 274 U.S. 357 [1927]: 375).

The narrow legalistic conceptions of crime are valid and pragmatic, but they are not sufficient by themselves for a full understanding of justice. Instead, the analysis of criminal justice needs to include broader social, cultural, and historical conceptions of crime and justice. This kind of inquiry sheds more light on important (but frequently neglected) questions of *social* justice. In the spirit of critical pedagogy, we believe that this type of integrative analysis and its implications can help move the administration of justice closer to the ideals of peace, equality, and human liberation.

# About the Sixth Edition

This edition has taken a while—too long, to be honest—to produce. It reflects not just the challenges of starting work during the depths of the pandemic and its hang-over, but some changes in authorship as well. To help better cover the diverse issues raised in this text, we have added two authors for this edition. One is Carrie L. Buist, who brings her knowledge of gender and LGBTQ+ issues. The other is K. Sebastian León, who brings expertise on Latino studies, immigration, and white-collar and corporate crime.

The new authors provided many fresh ideas and challenges to existing material. We welcomed the ideas, and they have resulted in a significant revision. Indeed, we have substantially updated the text throughout the book (without adding much to the overall word count), and we have made some modest adjustments to the structure. Although taking significant time, we believe this new edition fills an important need in the discipline to help students understand the realities of justice in the 2020s.

While adding new authors and restructuring some aspects of the book, however, we have kept what we believe to be the strengths: it is the only authored (rather than edited) book in the field to systematically address class, race, gender/sexuality, and their intersections in relationship to crime and justice. We have kept a structure that systematically covers important ideas and topics, while having authors with diverse expertise sharing their knowledge and passions in that outline. Specifically, in part II, "Inequality and Privilege," we have kept the chapters that provide substantive introductions to class (chapter 3), race (chapter 4), gender/sexuality (chapter 5), and their intersections (chapter 6). The chapters in part III, "Law and the Administration of Criminal Justice," on criminal law (chapter 7), policing (chapter 8), prosecution and courts (chapter 9), and punishment (chapter 10) all share a common structure, with headings for class, race, gender/sexuality, and intersections. As with the previous edition, each chapter starts with an opening narrative of interest that sets the tone for the chapter.

Readers who have used previous editions will note that the single chapter covering law enforcement and prosecution has now been split into one chapter for law enforcement and another for prosecution and the courts. We no longer have a chapter on victimology, but the key material from that chapter has been moved to the chapters in part II, where we cover class, race, gender/sexuality, and intersectionality. With discussion of victimization and material about justice in chapters 3 (class), 4 (race), 5 (gender/sexuality), and 6 (intersections), we hope to connect the sociological understanding of those concepts with criminological content to help the reader make connections and set up later chapters.

In a few other places, too, we have moved and cut material based on input from the new authors, extensive feedback solicited by our publisher, our own use of the book, and issues we believe needed more emphasis based on events since the fifth edition. We have, of course, also updated statistics, events related to the themes of the book, and theoretical and empirical developments in the areas of policy inquiry and justice practice.

*Some notes on language* seem important, because preferred language changes, and terms are often contested. We have generally tried to use people-first language, like "people in prison" rather than "prisoners." Given the roughly 150,000 words in the book (not including references) and our efforts to integrate new material, there are some places that we have unfortunately missed. But sometimes the perfect is the enemy of getting finished with a significantly improved, overdue new edition.

Further, this book now has contributions from six authors, not all of whom use the same language. Where there has not been consensus, we have opted to respect the language of individual authors, even if that makes the text inconsistent within a chapter or between them. Perhaps most noticeable is the interchangeable use of "criminal justice system" and "criminal legal system." Discussions about the "justice system" have been the common wording through most of the twenty years the previous editions of this book have been in print, so references to it are numerous. However, we appreciate that the system delivers results that are often far from just—a main point of this book—and that "legal system" is a more accurate characterization.

Finally, the use of "gender/sexuality" does not mean to suggest that the two concepts are always related, although they are often discussed together. Indeed, "LGBT+" captures issues of gender ("T" for trans) and sexuality (lesbian, gay, and bisexual). Similarly, our use of "gender/sexuality" is meant to be a practical shorthand to indicate that within this book, discussions of sex, gender, and sexuality tend to be found in the same places. Those discussions clarify the connections and distinctions among the terms, and "gender/sexuality" is a convenience. It is another place where the perfect is the enemy of getting finished with a significantly improved and overdue new edition.

## Note

1. Native Americans were not considered citizens until the Indian Citizenship Act of 1924, which gave them the right to vote. This is not an intersectional issue, because Native men and women were both legally prohibited from voting, but does speak to the importance of understanding race beyond Black and white.

# Acknowledgments

*Acknowledgments are due to many people who helped make this edition a reality when it easily might not have happened.* First and foremost, we were fortunate to have Adrienne McCarthy, of the University of Kansas, to work as a research assistant for this edition and help us do right by it. During the fog of COVID, Adrienne started updating statistics, gathering articles, and curating articles on key topics. She also synthesized material on Asian Americans that was edited and used in several chapters. She also offered some helpful critiques that we took to heart—even when we thought we were (finally) finished with a chapter. We further thank Adrienne for her thoughtful and diligent work on the ancillary instructor materials (chapter summaries, outlines, test questions, and PowerPoint decks), which are available from the publisher.

Alyssa Palazzo, of Rowman & Littlefield, picked up this project during the pandemic when it was very bogged down. Alyssa did great work in resolving many administrative issues that set the stage for progress. She was responsive and set up a supportive foundation that helped move the project forward.

Thanks to Alyssa's support, we were able to have Kaitlyn Selman, of Illinois State University, write a draft of the abolition section of the conclusion. We are pleased to have a thoughtful discussion of abolition in the book given how much it is on the minds of people as they see the damage done by the criminal justice/legal system, and we believe that students studying criminal justice at this historic juncture need to at least understand what abolition is about. Kaitlyn wrote a strong and thoughtful section in response to a discussion about how the material would fit the book and the chapter. We have edited her work and added material to help make it connect with other parts of the book as well.

Dayanara Sanchez and Brittany Mason, both of Eastern Michigan University, also helped move this project along through their work on the references. Dayanara started the first few chapters before handing it off. Brittany did the majority of the work and read through the book to check that we had all the references we needed and helped sort out ones from the one-hundred-page double-spaced reference document that were no longer necessary. Heather Mooney, who has been helpful with multiple editions, stepped up again for the final push, and her support enabled the completion of the manuscript. Finally, the authors would like to thank founding author Jeanne Flavin for her contributions to the early editions of this book. We also appreciate the efforts of some of the previous students whose work lives on in this edition, especially Emily Flores, Cortney Riggs, Heather Mooney, Natalie Morin, Jennie Brooks, Maya Pagni Barak, and Dana Horton.

*P. L., G. B., A. C., C. L. B., and K. S. L.*

# Introduction
## Crime, Inequality, and Justice

The standard view of criminal justice is that criminal law is built on a consensus about harmful acts that reflects social norms, that police investigate crime and arrest wrongdoers, that prosecutors weigh the strength of the evidence and then decide when to press charges, that juries decide on guilt or innocence, that judges sentence according to guidelines that eliminate disparities, and that people objectively study crime and criminals to ultimately reduce the amount of victimization. That view is not wholly incorrect, but the standard view is problematic because, in the bigger picture, changing social, political, and economic conditions shape the formation and application of the criminal laws of the United States. Crime and criminal justice are shaped by the political economy, which refers to how politics, law, and economics influence one another. As such, official crime rates do not explain the dynamics of the criminal justice system as much as they explain social stratification, the surplus population—those who are unemployed or unemployable and are thus considered the "dangerous class"—technology, and prevailing beliefs and anxieties. In this way, the realities of crime and justice reflect, and usually recreate, inequalities in class, race/ethnic, and gender/sexuality relations.

For example, slavery rather than prison had been the dominant form of social control for African Americans before the Civil War. When the Thirteenth Amendment (ratified in 1865) freed the enslaved people, it removed that system of control and created serious anxiety among the white population. Enslaved people went from property to economic competition; Black men were freed at a time when many Southern white women were widowed or single because of the large number of young white men killed during the war. Southern whites wanted another system for social control, but building prisons at that time was impossible. The war had been fought primarily in the South, and that was where most of the destruction had occurred. The repairs required labor, which was in short supply, again because of the large number of young men killed in the war. Additionally, labor-intensive crops grown on plantations still required attention. Thus, Southern states passed Black codes that penalized many behaviors by Black people that whites found rude, disrespectful, or threatening. After the Black people were convicted, they would be leased for labor to serve their sentence. Plantation owners could now lease "convicted criminals" rather than own slaves.

Because crime and justice are shaped by the political economy, crime and crime control are also inseparable from the changing relations of inequality, hierarchy, and power. Crime and crime control are thus important locations where inequality is recreated or challenged. Domestic violence, rape, and fraud by financial institutions to enrich executives while devastating millions—each crime, while committed by different types of offenders for very different reasons, recreates an aspect of privilege and inequality. Such inequality and privilege can be challenged both by the explanations given for these different crimes and by the decision of whether the perpetrators are to be pursued or not by the criminal justice system.

This book argues that there are a wide variety of morally blameworthy acts that harm real people, but the law chooses to criminalize only certain ones. Manslaughter is a death because of negligence, but it applies only to individuals; there is no corporate manslaughter law in the United States. Great Britain, Canada, and Australia all have various corporate manslaughter provisions that apply to workplace and other deaths caused by negligent conduct of supervisors or executives. The social reality of crime and crime control is further shaped by the decisions of police about who is arrested, by prosecutors' decisions about whether to pursue a case and which charges are most appropriate, by judicial processes that find certain offenders guilty, and by judicial decisions about who goes to prison (Reiman and Leighton 2023). Statistics appear to be objective measurements about crime but are the result of decisions and processes that are influenced by class, race, and gender/sexuality. Media decisions about what to report and which "frame"—or "spin"—to put on a story add to the ways that the reality of crime and justice is socially created. So too do criminology books and journals.

These relations are dynamic, subject to the changing needs of the dominant groups in the prevailing political economy. For example, criminal prosecutions and punishments first appear with the simultaneous decline of feudalism and the rise of capitalism, which ushered in the early developments of the modern state, capital, labor, private property, and mercantilism (wealth from trade).

Another example is that the "crime of bankruptcy" was punishable by death in the English courts in the late 1700s because it was defined as an "act of debtor fraud, de facto theft by absconding with property and avoiding judicial process and the paying of just debts" (Pomykala 2000). While it was never treated as a capital offense in the United States, the framers of the Constitution did add bankruptcy to the list of federal powers used to prevent fraud. Now, bankruptcy for individuals is still stigmatized, and student loan debt can only be discharged with proof that paying it back would involve hardship. In contrast, corporations routinely engage in strategic bankruptcy, which is legal and encourages "firms to use bankruptcy to avoid lawsuits; to decrease or eliminate damage awards for marketing injurious products, polluting or other corporate misconduct; [and] to abandon toxic waste sites" (Delaney 1999: 190). Even in bankruptcy that involves reorganization rather than liquidation, "financial risk can be shifted away from more powerful institutional creditors and the corporation itself and onto the backs of more vulnerable" and less organized groups, meaning workers and consumers (Delaney 1999: 190).

By contrast, many criminal laws that first emerged to control poverty, street crime, and the disorder of the dangerous classes in mercantile England are still with us today in one form or another. But like the evolution of bankruptcy law, these long-standing criminal laws operate to control the marginal and powerless classes. In fact, criminal justice policies are the preferred method for managing rising inequality and the surplus populations of the United States rather than managing the misbehavior of the powerful. *Surplus populations* refer primarily to economically marginal persons and those who are unemployed or unemployable; they are people with little attachment to the conventional labor market and little "stake in conformity" (Anderson 1974). Because of this status, surplus populations are also called "marginal classes" or "dangerous classes." Of course, the war on crime is not publicly discussed as an explicit war on the poor and "down-and-out" or as the enforcement of inequality and privilege. But the result of the current war on crime has been to fill the prison system with the poor and a disproportionate number of young minorities (who are most likely to be poor and discriminated against in the labor market).

These dynamics are not new, and a historical overview of social control reveals that on the frontier as well as in the industrial United States, the administration of justice was about regulating and controlling the "dangerous classes." Freed Black slaves were subject to harsh Jim Crow laws, and the Chinese were highly criminalized after they finished work on the transcontinental railroad (Auerbach 1976; Barak 1980; Harring 1983; Walker 1980). The political and legal apparatuses of the United States were dominated by the organized power of wealthy, white, and male interests to the detriment of slaves, freedmen, workers, nonworkers, women, and people of color.

Still, over time, the criminalizing of behavior has been subject to periods of legal and constitutional reform that have gradually expanded the meanings of "due process" and "equal protection" for a wider and more diverse group of people. Since our nation's beginnings, then, the various struggles for justice, inside and outside the administration of criminal law, have included the goal of empowering the marginalized. As the notion of struggle suggests, history is not a linear progression of ever-greater equality. Achievements can result in backlashes, and those who are "more equal" always resist the gains of the "less equal." Moreover, new forms of inequality often arise to take the place of old forms, and being granted a right in law does not make it a reality.

In the first part of the introduction, we wanted to explain how criminal justice was embedded within larger social systems of class, race, and gender/sexuality. Critical thinking about criminal justice requires examining the biases of the society for which it provides "law and order." The next part of the introduction reviews some points that guide our analysis of class, race, gender/sexuality, and their intersections. The third part of the introduction discusses some frames of reference for understanding criminal justice and crime control as a "system" so that readers can have a fuller sense of the complexities of criminal justice.

With this book, we hope to encourage critical thinking and help the reader develop their own point of view. We do this by highlighting some assumptions that often go unexamined, both within criminology and more generally. We discuss the workings of power and privilege that are too often accepted as "the way things are." Even without thinking fully about the extent of problems with the current system, public opinion polls reveal that only 14 percent of people had "a great deal" or "quite a lot" of confidence in the criminal justice system (Jones 2022; Washburn 2023). That is a stunning rejection of current practices, what has passed for reform, and mainstream criminology and criminal justice (which studies crime and educates criminal justice workers). The study of crime and the workings of criminal justice need to be rethought. We hope this book helps with that rethinking by systematically exploring class, race, and gender/sexuality and by helping readers imagine alternatives (even considering what can be done now in order to be able to do tomorrow what we are unable to do today).

## The Social Relations of Class, Race, Gender, and Crime

Class, race, and gender/sexuality all have important unique histories, and their intersections provide lessons about power, privilege, and inequality. At any given moment, class, race, or gender/sexuality may "feel more salient or meaningful in a given person's life, but they are overlapping and cumulative in their effect on people's experience" (Andersen and Collins 1998: 3). Class, race, and gender/sexuality are all required in order to begin to describe an individual's experience in the world, and they are likewise all required to understand crime and criminal justice. For example, rape generally leads to few arrests and convictions, but that statement also needs to acknowledge the hyper-enforcement of rape laws against Black men when white women were thought to be involved.

Attending to combinations of class, race, and gender/sexuality draws attention to women of color. Black women, for example, are often rendered invisible because "Black" tends to mean "men" and "women" tends to mean "white" (Roberts 1993). Further, the combination of race and gender yields something new, like how the stereotypes of Black men and white women would not predict those of Black women—especially in the areas of sexuality and parenting. The stereotypes have long driven policies of control of Black women's bodies that discourages procreation, subordinates groups, and regulates fertility (Roberts 1993). These processes continue today (Flavin 2009; Potter 2015), and intersectional analysis clarifies that they also apply to poor white women. Appreciating that all white women are not middle class opens up a history of the forced sterilization of poor white women, and we note in chapter 9 a study showing that criminal cases against pregnant women were almost exclusively against *poor* women. While the report noted the significant criminalization of women of color, "the racist carceral tactics established during the war on drugs . . . are now being extended to target poor white communities in the midst of the opioid and methamphetamine epidemics" (Kavattur et al. 2023: 4).

While readers will have differing levels of interest in, and concern about, the various groups discussed in the book, the approach of studying class, race, and gender/sexuality in various combinations can yield important insights about social control more generally. For example, an increasing number of states have enacted severe abortion restrictions (or bans) and fetal personhood laws (that bestow rights on the "unborn"), both of which require the policing of a wide range of women's behavior in a way that threatens their right to privacy. Police routinely subpoena (from a data broker) women's locations, search history, browsing history, DMs, etc.; they can also request so-called tower dumps, which identify all devices in a location on a certain day and time (Cahn and Manis 2022). The executive director of the Surveillance Technology Oversight Project notes:

> None of the tactics we will see used to target pregnant people will be new. We've seen these same surveillance techniques developed in the name of immigration enforcement, national security, combating drugs, and so many other law enforcement priorities. And the truth is that when you develop those techniques, you are at the whim of those in power and whatever they next decide to call a crime. (in Newman 2022)

Only by studying and integrating the combinations of class, race, and gender/sexuality can one come to fully appreciate how bias undergirds the construction of what will and will not become criminal, as well as the effects of biased rules. This bias also shapes the construction of individual experience and identity, including experience with crime and the criminal justice system. More specifically, we bring several assumptions to the study of class, race, gender, and crime control:

- First, these categories of social difference all share similarities in that they confer privilege on some groups and marginalize others, so they relate to power resources in society. Ideology works to naturalize privilege, making people less aware of their privilege so that they are more likely to believe there is a "level playing field" and not see systemic or structural inequality.
- Second, few people are pure oppressors or victims, so it is a complex matrix in which all people are more aware of their victimization than of their privilege. For example, many poor white men do not understand how they can have white, male, and heterosexual privilege because what they see most is their economic hardship and exploitation.
- Third, systems of privilege and inequality derived from the social statuses of class, race, and gender/sexuality are overlapping and have interacting effects that can be more than the sum of their parts. Here, 1 + 1 is more than 2, or gendered racism is much more powerful than simply adding gender and race.
- Fourth, while class, race, and gender privilege all tend to be similarly invisible because of ideology, the experience of those oppressions will vary considerably depending on the specific nature of the prejudice and stereotypes. Class, race, and gender/sexuality are not interchangeable, even if they all confer privilege on some and oppression on others. We are not interested in trying to establish if one is "worse" than the others. They are all real and impact people's lives in combinations that are important to understand.
- Fifth, understanding marginalization also requires appreciating the diversity within categories—American Indians represent hundreds of different tribes; Hispanics and Asians represent dozens of different countries and cultures. In addition, other countries have marginalized minority groups, so the experience in the United States of a Chinese minority group can be different from that of another Chinese person of the same class, gender, and sexual orientation. Colorism—a privilege accruing to lighter-skinned people—means that lighter- and darker-skinned people of the same group will have different experiences.

Subsequent chapters unravel the complexities of class, race, and gender/sexuality as they interact with crime, justice, inequality, and popular culture. These chapters expose how what people see as unacceptable crime and acceptable social control are shaped by these inequalities. We are not talking about conspiracies of elites and decision makers here, but rather how "commonsense" understandings are limited and distorted by power. Crime and criminals are restricted primarily to tabulations and representations of the conventional criminal code violations: murder, rape, burglary, robbery, assault, and face-to-face larceny-theft. Almost all crimes in the suites, if not ignored, are typically downplayed rather than focusing on human decisions and harms done to society (Reiman and Leighton 2023). There are no databases or publications for corporate crime like the FBI has for street crime; white-collar corporate fraud and offenses against the environment, workers, and consumers are not captured in FBI press releases about "Crime in America." Reporters and authors, including academics, analyze data that are more readily available, and those findings get reported in textbooks on criminal justice that focus on street crime.

Culturally produced images of crime and criminals reinforce one-dimensional notions that criminality and harmful behavior are predominantly the responsibility of the poor and minority groups. Common stories of crime and criminal justice appear and reappear in the news, in films, on television, in literature, and in criminal justice textbooks that reinforce these ideas. It is no wonder that when most people try to picture the typical American crime, the common image that emerges is one of young, urban male victimizers. There are also the numerous police-action reenactments that can be viewed regularly on television programs that recycle images of these young men as dangerous drug dealers whose dwellings must be invaded during the early hours of dawn by militarized law enforcement personnel in order to repress the dangerous faces in the "war on crime." Even a show like *White Collar*—which features art theft, counterfeiting, and high-end racketeering—still does not present corporate crime or the ways in which elites victimize employees, consumers, and the environment (Buist and Leighton 2015). (However, Showtime's *Billions* depicts elite wrongdoing in both the financial sector and government.)

For many decades, politicians have appeared before the media talking about a "get tough" platform that criticizes the "leniency" of previous election cycles. Even efforts to get "smart" on crime do not reduce sentence length or consider the possibility of reuniting the offender, the victim, and the community in some kind of restorative form of justice. As part of the inherited politics of a war on crime, the political economy of incarceration, and the privatization of penal services ("bodies destined for profitable punishment"), the language and images of dangerousness and retribution continue to contribute to the United States' criminal justice–industrial complex (Leighton and Selman 2018).

## Criminal Justice Theorizing

Among other important assumptions that undergird this work is that the administration of criminal justice may be viewed as both a "system" and a "nonsystem" (Bohm and Haley 2004); it may also be viewed as an "apparatus" involving both public and private sectors (Duffee 1980; Kraska 2004). Compared with theories of crime/criminality, theories of crime control and criminal justice are underdeveloped. In *Theorizing Criminal Justice* (2004), Peter Kraska has identified eight essential orientations or theoretical metaphors that attempt to explain the workings and expansion of "criminal justice." He notes that four of these orientations are primarily concerned with the formal criminal justice system and that four are concerned with criminal justice as a broader apparatus. The first group views criminal justice as *formal models of the administration of criminal justice as a system*. These include rationalism/legalism, system, crime control versus due process, and politics. The second group views criminal justice as *informal models of a criminal justice apparatus as a nonsystem*. These include socially constructed reality, growth complex, oppression, and late modernity. In reviewing these orientations here, we suggest that readers identify their own perspective on criminal justice as well as any additional helpful perspectives for understanding this field.

The *rational/legal* theoretical orientation is less "a well-defined area of scholarship" than "a way of thinking dispersed throughout various literatures in criminology/criminal justice" (Kraska 2004: 19). These models argue that criminal justice operations are the product of rational, impartial decision making based on the rule of law, at least in the ideal if not in practice. The *systems* theoretical orientation has been considered the dominant paradigm in criminal justice studies for more than fifty years. Both the rational/legal and systems models view the recent expansion and growth in size and power of the criminal justice system as a "forced reaction" to a worsening (real or imaginary) crime problem rather than a policy choice. The next two orientations, crime control versus due process and politics, require different explanations.

The crime control versus due process and the politics models view these developments as a matter of human will subject to different ideological values, political preferences, and material conditions. These models contend that crime and crime control are not some kind of inevitability or natural phenomenon. The *crime control versus due process* orientation indicates whether policy and court decisions favor the police and crime control or due process ("rule of law"). This general perspective is good at identifying one's preference for due process, which sees the criminal justice system as an obstacle course to make it difficult for the well-resourced government to deprive usually poor citizens of their liberty, or a crime control model, which assumes the guilt of those identified by police and wants to efficiently and cheaply punish them (Packer 1964).

The *politics* orientation to criminal justice expands the two models by assuming that politics "is at play at all levels of the criminal justice apparatus—from the everyday actions of the corrections officer or police practitioner, to the political influence of local communities, to agencies involved in criminal justice policy formulation and implementation, and to lawmaking at the national and state levels" (Kraska 2004: 206). In short, these two orientations view all criminal justice activity and thinking as interest based, involving inherent conflicts, power struggles, influence building, and hardened ideological positions. They both argue that the strategies of criminal justice result from a complex mix of political and social interests.

The next four models, with their focus on the criminal justice apparatus, broaden the object of criminal justice study to include "1) crime control practices carried out by state and non-state entities; 2) the formal creation and administration of criminal law carried out by legislators, the police, courts, corrections, and juvenile subcomponents; and 3) others involved in the criminal justice enterprise, such as the media, academic researchers, and political interest groups" (Kraska 2004: 7–8). The *apparatus*-oriented models view crime control as involving more than the activities of state agencies and political negotiations over the appropriate means of carrying out the administration of criminal justice. These four models regard criminal justice administration not only as a nonsystem but also as part of the larger culture and entities that sustain the legitimacy of the prevailing political, economic, and social arrangements.

In the context of the larger culture and society, these apparatus-oriented models view the police, courts, and corrections agencies as promoting various myths of crime and crime control for the purposes of establishing and maintaining their legitimacy and the prevailing hierarchical order. For example, the *socially constructed reality* orientations, including moral panics, adopt interpretative approaches where criminal justice is the result of an intricate process of learning and constructing meanings. Similarly, the *growth complex* orientations to criminal justice are about believable stories of "crime fighting" and the legitimacy of the criminal justice bureaucracy's survival and growth as an industry.

Some *oppression* orientations argue that the criminal justice apparatus is simply a tool of the economically powerful to control the behavior of the poor, the disadvantaged, and the threatening classes. The social roots of other oppressive models emerged with the struggles for social justice and the critical theories of class, race, and gender/sexuality inequality. These models argue that the selective enforcements and differential applications of the law are a representation of the dominant economic, ethnic, and patriarchal interests interacting.

Finally, the *late modernity* orientations to criminal justice explain changes in crime and punishment as adaptations to late modern social conditions or risks, such as the rise in economic globalization, telecommunications, and privatization and the decline of state sovereignty relative to corporate power. Applied to recent criminal justice trends, these models locate crime and crime control within a rapidly changing world, and they attempt to explain how the various responses to crime and injustice over time have occurred.

According to Kraska, none of the eight theoretical metaphors are capable of standing alone or of being more than partial explanations for the developing changes in criminal justice behavior. Indeed, fuller accounts would also include similar theorizing about immigration systems, which have become more intertwined with the harsh administration of criminal justice. Further, the criminal justice system has also become more intertwined with welfare, public housing, child protective services, school, juvenile justice, and health care in the social control of the poor, and especially minority women. All of these systems are increasingly linked, necessitating an understanding of "regulatory intersectionality: the means by which social welfare systems collect and transmit evidence of purportedly deviant conduct from social welfare systems to child welfare and criminal systems, resulting in escalating risk of harm and escalating harms for poor women who seek support" (Bach 2019: 819).

What is important to keep in mind from this review is that, first, a number of these metaphors draw attention to how the criminal justice system reflects and recreates our unequal society. It does this despite seemingly class-, race-, and gender/sexuality-neutral laws, as well as police with body cameras and judges bound by sentencing guidelines. Second, although the repression of marginalized groups is a constant, crime, law, and police constantly change as society changes. Many of these changes, described as late modernity or neoliberalism, involve reductions in the social safety net for marginalized groups, government downsizing and deregulation, privatization (public services provided by for-profit companies), increasing corporate power, tax cuts for the wealthy, growing inequality, globalization, and climate change. There are also social movements against these trends and problems—and (sometimes slow and uneven) progress toward racial and gender equality. By providing "law and order" to a society struggling with—and hopefully toward—equality, the criminal justice system will also be a site of struggles. It is only by understanding class, race, gender/sexuality, and intersectionality in society, criminology, the criminal justice system, and the intertwined systems of social control that people can call out problems and work toward the promise of equality found in our country's founding documents and noblest ideals.

# PART I

## Crime Control and Criminology

# CHAPTER 1

# The Crime Control Enterprise

*In his farewell address as president, Eisenhower warned of a military-industrial complex, which is helpful in thinking about the criminal justice–industrial complex. The Republican World War II general was concerned that defense policy was being driven by businesses, politicians, and military officials. Insulated from public view and accountability, they could make policy in their best interest rather than the nation's. He noted (1961) that until World War II, "the United States had no armaments industry"—other businesses converted to manufacture them during wars—but having a permanent armaments industry with millions of employees and substantial military spending was new and troubling: "The potential for the disastrous rise of misplaced power exists and will persist. We must never let the weight of this combination endanger our liberties or democratic processes. We should take nothing for granted."*

*Similar to the military-industrial complex is a criminal justice–industrial complex born from the drastic buildup of the criminal justice system starting in the 1970s. While prisons and the criminal justice system have historically had contracts with businesses for supplies and consultants, the nature of these relationships and the amount of money involved reached a critical mass because of the wars on crime and drugs. Prisons and the prison-industrial complex have been the most visible aspect, with private prison companies created to profit from the incarceration binge and regular Las Vegas–style conventions for businesses selling goods and services (Selman and Leighton 2010). This phenomenon was recognized in the 1990s:*

> *The United States has developed a prison-industrial complex—a set of bureaucratic, political, and economic interests that encourage increased spending on imprisonment, regardless of the actual need. The prison-industrial complex is not a conspiracy, guiding the nation's criminal-justice policy behind closed doors. It is a confluence of special interests that has given prison construction in the United States a seemingly unstoppable*

*momentum. It is composed of politicians, both liberal and conservative, who have used the fear of crime to gain votes; impoverished rural areas where prisons have become a cornerstone of economic development; private companies that regard the roughly $35 billion [$89 billion in 2017] spent each year on corrections not as a burden on American taxpayers but as a lucrative market; and government officials whose fiefdoms have expanded along with the inmate population. (Schlosser 1998)*

*The industries push for more "bodies destined for profitable punishment" (Leighton and Selman 2018), which create larger businesses that lobby for more of the same, creating profits for some and "grave implications" for justice. Reform becomes more difficult when people profit widely from the existing system and its practices.*

*The criminal justice– and military-industrial complexes share more than a common idea. By the mid-1980s, the Cold War against Russia—called the "evil empire" by then-president Reagan—was winding down, and defense firms were looking for new markets to bolster revenue. The Department of Defense signed a memorandum of understanding with the Department of Justice for technology development and commercialization, and products from the defense industry have become regularly available to local law enforcement since 1997 through what's known as the 1033 program. The drug war served to fuel the growth of militarization of police, especially the expansion of special weapons and tactics (SWAT) teams across small and large urban areas. Indeed, police deployed a wide range of such technology against Black Lives Matter protestors, who, ironically, have been protesting the use of force that is an outgrowth of wars on crime and drugs that are really wars against minority communities (German 2020; Grinberg 2019; Toor 2018).*

*After the tragic terrorist attacks of 9/11, the criminal justice complex developed stronger ties with intelligence agencies, the Department of Homeland Security, and Immigration and Customs Enforcement (ICE). What has emerged is a security-industrial complex (SIC) that includes criminal justice, private security, and military and intelligence operations. It is fed by fears of crime, minorities, and immigrants. It also includes a troubled teen industry, which is twice the size of the juvenile justice system and ensnares middle- and upper-class teens with wilderness camps, military-style boarding schools, drug rehab, "last chance" ranches, therapeutic boarding schools, Christian "emotional growth" schools, and conversion therapy for LGBTQ+ youth (Mooney and Leighton 2019). These largely unregulated businesses have a long history of being abusive (Government Accountability Office 2007; Szalavitz 2006) and came to wider public awareness after celebrity Paris Hilton disclosed her own experiences with them (Hilton 2020), fueling #BreakingCodeSilence and #ISeeYouSurvivor.*

*Industry and politicians, aided by the media, have created an "era of punitive excess" (Travis and Western 2021): beyond those under correctional supervision, today's landscape of punishment also includes the extensive criminalization of social problems such as homelessness and mental illness, intrusive policing policies such as stop and frisk, the imposition of fines and fees that exacerbate poverty, the legislatively defined collateral sanctions that close off opportunities for a full life to millions with criminal records, and the new technologies that place the entire public under a form of state surveillance.*

*The COVID pandemic disrupted patterns of crime and aspects of the criminal justice system, but not the militarization of law enforcement, the punitive excess of criminal law, or the criminal justice–industrial complex. Sadly, COVID exposed how separate the worlds of criminal justice and public health are "at a time when hundreds of thousands of lives, the socioemotional development of millions of children, and billions of dollars in economic activity directly depended on questions about control measures, enforcement methods, the organization of the health system, and the many ways in which law was immediately influencing vulnerability, resilience, and social behavior" (Burris et al. 2021).*

*As public health measures to save lives became equated with oppression, some law enforcement chiefs stepped up to say they would not enforce masking or maximum occupancy orders (Chammah 2020). Low-paid retail and service employees were left to enforce mask mandates, frequently becoming targets for verbal and physical abuse. As the pandemic progressed, they also had to become "vax bouncers" who enforced vaccine mandates at businesses and learned to detect fake vaccine cards so their employer did not face fines (Spivack 2021). As governors stopped local mask mandates, school districts refused to comply, making school officials the target of threats of violence. It's serious enough that the "kind of FBI involvement in local school board security hasn't been seen since the civil rights movement and the infamous opposition to school integration in such places as Little Rock, Arkansas" (Figliuzzi 2021).*

## Introduction

The conventional view is that the criminal justice system is composed of police, courts, and corrections, all working to fight crime and administer justice. While that is not inaccurate, it is still only a partial understanding of the work, mission, problems, issues, and career opportunities related to criminal justice. Seeing the system as a criminal justice enterprise or criminal justice–industrial complex reveals another understanding of an entity spending $305 billion per year and employing almost 2.5 million people.

Unlike a traditional business, the criminal justice system does not have a CEO but instead is comprised of thousands of federal, state, territorial, tribal, county, and city agencies having roughly similar operating procedures. Like many industries, criminal justice generates social problems even as it tries to do good. For example, social media companies try to be beneficial by connecting people, but they also spread divisiveness, misinformation, and extremism because that content is engaging and profitable (Zuboff 2021). Facebook "can be quicker at recommending groups built around child predation than it is to remove them" for the same reason (Putnam 2022). Oil companies and the fossil fuel industry allow people to be warm, have electricity, and travel, but greenhouse gas emissions threaten climate collapse and human extinction (Kramer 2020). Chemicals are used in 95 percent of manufactured goods, but their production exceeds the "planetary boundary"—a "safe operating zone" for life on earth and beyond which processes that sustain life on Earth are destabilized (Persson et al. 2022; Steffen et al. 2015). As with other industries, people need to see the problems, benefits, and potential for reform in criminal justice.

Further, just as business and political decisions often make sense by "following the money," criminal justice policy can often be better understood by looking at who benefits from a policy rather than at evidenced-based decision making or discussions about retribution, deterrence, incapacitation, and rehabilitation. The amount of money and number of employees, shown in table 1.1, underscores how important it is to understand criminal justice as an industrial complex. (The totals do not include expenditures or workers in the troubled teen industry, private security, private detective work, or other related security occupations.) Sometimes, the people profiting from the system, its injustices, or excessive fear of crime—or who are comfortable in their routines—have little interest in reforms.

"Following the money" is one aspect of a larger strategy for thinking critically about criminal justice policies—and their failures—by identifying who benefits and who loses. These benefits are not always financial and may involve the criminal justice system reinforcing privilege and power along the lines of class, race, and gender/sexuality,[1] to name only a few.

## Trends and Power Dynamics

Before the next chapter starts the systematic review of class, race, and gender/sexuality and their intersections, the remainder of this chapter discusses some

TABLE 1.1 **Criminal Justice Expenditures, Payroll, and Employees**

| | Total Expenditures (in Billions of US$) | Employee Payroll (in Billions of US$) | Total Employees |
|---|---|---|---|
| Criminal justice system total | 304.6 | 13.7 | 2,447,000 |
| Police | 149.0 | 7.1 | 1,192,000 |
| Judicial and legal | 66.4 | 3.0 | 497,000 |
| Corrections | 89.2 | 3.6 | 758,000 |

*Source:* BJS 2021d: tables 1 and 4.

*Note:* Detail may not add to total because of rounding. Payroll as of March 2017 (the latest available from BJS at the time of publication). Employment rounded to nearest thousand.

larger trends. These trends both reflect power dynamics and reinforce inequalities produced by these dynamics. Some of these trends impact the criminal justice enterprise, while others are trends within it. These trends include climate change, globalization and neoliberalism, immigration, militarization, privatization and revenue enhancement, and cybercrime and security.

## Climate Change/Climate Crisis

One of the most important justice issues is global warming and climate change, a problem that highlights the marginalization of youth as well as class, race, and gender/sexuality. Greenhouse gases released by burning fossil fuels are causing—and will continue to cause—increased human deaths, illness, injury, and damage to ecosystems that sustain life (Intergovernmental Panel on Climate Change 2022). These effects are felt disproportionately by those who are marginalized, both within the United States and globally. That pattern is expected to intensify as climate change–related natural disasters become worse, social support systems become more stressed, and the criminal justice system becomes more punitive toward the marginalized in the face of more disorder. But it is youth in general who will suffer the consequences as governments and corporations continue to pursue a course of conduct usually described as "catastrophic" and "apocalyptic" (Atwoli et al. 2021; Whyte 2020).

In the short to medium term, climate change will bring about more heat waves, drought, war, sea-level rise, pandemics, ocean acidification, and severe storms and flooding (Masters 2022). Of growing concern is how problems of food shortages, infrastructure destruction, disease, and climate refugees interact, amplify each other, and create cascading harmful impacts (Kemp et al. 2022). Climate change already disproportionately impacts the marginalized. For example, poor neighborhoods have fewer trees to provide shade during heat waves, and more asphalt and concrete contribute to a heat island effect. "Urban heat islands, often located in the neighborhoods occupied by lower-income residents and people of color, can be up to 20 degrees hotter than adjacent areas on summer days" (Sandoval 2022).

Reviews of research about the effects of natural disasters related to climate change describe "mental stress, substance abuse, economic hardship, food insecurity and poor social infrastructure." Additionally, "weather events were linked to various forms of gender-based violence, from physical and sexual assault to forced marriage, trafficking and psychological abuse" (Rodrigues 2022). The gender-based violence included the aftermath of Hurricane Katrina: "there was a backlash against gay communities because others blamed them for the disaster" based on the story of God destroying Sodom and Gomorrah for immorality. In other cases, "transgender people have been threatened in relief shelters or barred from access to them" (Rodrigues 2022). Unfortunately, neoliberalism (discussed in the next section) has meant cuts in social supports but expanded resources for criminal justice and other "security" agencies. So, it is likely that "social control mechanisms that already predominantly punish the powerless and those at the margins of society will be aggravated. In the growing climate emergency, more punitive societies will have even less tolerance for minor criminal behavior caused by desperation" (Twyman-Ghoshal et al. 2022).

Although the worst consequences are in the future, climate change is one factor that is already causing serious harm to the mental health of young people. A survey of ten thousand people aged sixteen to twenty-five years, one thousand from each of ten countries, found that almost 60 percent said they felt "very" or "extremely" worried about climate change (Hickman et al. 2021). At least half of the young people said they felt helpless, afraid, angry, and powerless—and 75 percent of young people said they think the future is frightening. Young people also felt a strong sense of betrayal, with more than 60 percent saying the government was dismissing people's distress, was not doing enough to avoid a climate catastrophe, could not be trusted, and was "lying about the effectiveness of the actions they are taking." The combination of these feelings meant that "more than 45% of respondents said their feelings about climate change negatively affected their daily life and functioning" (Hickman et al. 2021).

Further, 83 percent of youth said that "people have failed to take care of the planet," and a majority agreed with items stating that they wouldn't have the same opportunities their parents did, and "the things I most value will be destroyed" (Hickman et al. 2021). In an effort to assert their rights, a group of young people in the United States sued the federal government over its contribution to global warming, arguing that it violated the constitutional rights of the youngest generations by failing to protect public trust resources. This suit, *Juliana v. U.S.*, was not just about the enforcement of certain environmental laws but the assertion of important constitutional claims within a context of extensive scientific knowledge about the processes and harms of climate change (*Juliana v. U.S.* 2015; Niehaus 2022).

The suit claimed that "the Constitution recognizes and preserves the fundamental right of citizens to be free from government actions that harm life, liberty, and property." Further, "in the Preamble of the Constitution, these rights belong to present generations as well to our 'Posterity' (or future generations)" (*Juliana v. U.S.* 2015: 84). The government, through affirmative actions involving the subsidizing and issuing of permits for the fossil fuel industry, "directly caused atmospheric $CO_2$ to rise to levels that dangerously interfere with a stable climate system required alike by our nation and Plaintiffs" (*Juliana v. U.S.* 2015: 85). The government actions that have destabilized the climate system have harmed the young people's "capacity to provide for their basic human needs, safely raise families, practice their religious and spiritual beliefs, maintain their bodily integrity, and lead lives with access to clean air, water, shelter, and food" (*Juliana v. U.S.* 2015: 86). And, "after placing Plaintiffs in a position of climate danger, Defendants have continued to act with deliberate indifference to the known danger they helped create and enhance" (*Juliana v. U.S.* 2015: 86).

An additional claim is that the U.S. Constitution guarantees equal protection of the law, and "the harm caused by Defendants has denied Plaintiffs the same protection of fundamental rights afforded to prior and present generations of adult citizens" (*Juliana v. U.S.* 2015: 88). Specifically, "defendants have a long history of deliberately discriminating against children and future generations in exerting their sovereign authority over our nation's air space and federal fossil fuel resources for the economic benefit of present generations of adults" (*Juliana v. U.S.* 2015: 89).

Unfortunately, a majority of a federal court of appeals denied the suit on procedural grounds by deciding that the youth did not have standing. Although they agreed that the youth had stated an injury and harm and had showed causation, the majority did not believe that the courts had the power to compel Congress and the executive agencies to fix the problem. (The dissent stated: "Seeking to quash this suit, the government bluntly insists that it has the absolute and unreviewable power to destroy the Nation," but "the Constitution does not condone the Nation's willful destruction" [*Juliana v. U.S* 2020: 33].) In spite of not granting relief to the young people, the court still noted: "A substantial evidentiary record documents that the federal government has long promoted fossil fuel use despite knowing that it can cause catastrophic climate change, and that failure to change existing policy may hasten an environmental apocalypse" (*Juliana v. U.S.* 2020: 11).

The court of appeals in *Juliana* found that the record "conclusively establishes that the federal government has long understood the risks of fossil fuel use and increasing carbon dioxide emissions" (*Juliana v. U.S.* 2020: 15). Indeed, the court notes that "as early as 1965, the Johnson Administration cautioned that fossil fuel emissions threatened significant changes to climate, global temperatures, sea levels," and the EPA issued reports in 1983 and the 1990s that the court says "implored the government to act before it was too late" (*Juliana v. U.S.* 2020: 15). However, the government's blameworthiness does not arise just from knowledge, or even knowledge combined with omissions or neglect. The appeals court noted that the government "affirmatively promotes fossil fuel use in a host of ways, including beneficial tax provisions, permits for imports and exports, subsidies for domestic and overseas projects, and leases for fuel extraction on federal land" (*Juliana v. U.S.* 2020: 15–16). Remember that the court issuing these conclusions is not favorable to the young people, whose claims it dismisses, and "the government by and large has not disputed the factual premises of the plaintiffs' claims" (*Juliana v. U.S.* 2020: 16).

While *Juliana* was just against the government, the larger fossil fuel industry and its trade associations have committed numerous morally blameworthy harmful acts. As early as 1954, leaders of the American Petroleum Institute (API) were aware of the research linking their products to $CO_2$ pollution in the atmosphere with potentially dangerous consequences (Franta 2018). In *Carbon Criminals, Climate Crimes*, criminologist Ronald Kramer reviews how companies in the energy industry monitored academic research starting in the 1950s, then developed their own research teams, and by the 1970s, "Exxon strove to be on the cutting edge of inquiry" (2020: 69; Franta 2021).

However, as oil companies acquired knowledge that their business model would wreak havoc on the planet, Kramer notes that "they used this knowledge to plan for future explorations of oil" in the Arctic as it warmed. They also "climate-proof[ed] their facilities, all the while doing nothing to reduce the resulting carbon pollution and climate disruption" (Kramer 2020: 59). While research was originally intended to help companies like Exxon participate meaningfully in discussions about greenhouse gas regulation, they later "engaged in a concerted effort to deny that global warming was occurring at all" (Kramer 2020: 59). The industry funded politicians who denied climate change and various organizations that created doubt about the reality and severity of climate change, which they knew would strategically delay reforms that would hurt their profitability (Oreskes and Conway 2012). They also "lobbied effectively to prevent government regulation of carbon emissions and to block the development of renewable energy" (Kramer 2020: 59–60).

## Globalization and Neoliberalism

*Globalization* refers to the growing interdependency among events, people, and governments around the world that are increasingly interconnected through finance, trade, communications, and transportation. Goods, labor, and money move more freely around the world, leading to some widespread benefits but also to a "race to the bottom" as nations accommodate corporations looking for the cheapest labor, along with the least restrictive environmental, labor, and other regulations. The price for the benefits of globalization, then, is increased environmental destruction, exploitation of people for labor, tax avoidance by the rich and corporations, and concentration of corporate power.

Further, globalization creates expanded opportunities for criminals as well as "legitimate" capitalists. "Free trade" is not meant to include illicit goods, but expanding the free flow of goods and money also inevitably encourages trafficking in persons (for sex and labor), drugs (prescription and illicit), organs for transplant, counterfeit goods, weapons, toxic waste, and exotic wildlife. It also encourages large financial institutions to profit from the laundering of money from illegal activities. As crime becomes transnational, crime control must do the same, requiring workers who are fluent in different languages and who understand other regions of the world where the United States must collaborate.

Globalization has also meant increases in the size of corporations and their power, as well as in their criminal and legal-but-harmful behavior. Corporate lobbying weakens protections for consumers, workers, and the environment, and "dominant firms today take laws as mere suggestions" (Stoller 2022). Many chapters in this book will expose corporate crime and wrongdoing, which are neglected in criminology, but it is important for now to note a shift from government to corporate power. For example, while big technology companies like Facebook, Twitter (now X), YouTube, and Instagram sometimes censor content under pressure from the government, frequently they use their vague terms of service to determine what political viewpoints and sexual expressions are acceptable (York 2022). PayPal, Mastercard, and Visa do the same, so Pornhub, OnlyFans, GoFundMe, and other websites will remove content the payment processors find objectionable (Taibbi 2022). And "it's an open secret within energy circles that the eventual death of oil and thermal coal won't come from environmentalists or even directly from renewable energy, but rather when big banks decide to stop financing it, rendering it 'unbankable'" (Kimani 2022).

The rise of corporate power relative to government power has several other aspects that are collectively known as *neoliberalism*: deregulation, privatizing government services by contracting out to for-profit businesses, reducing taxes (especially for the wealthiest), and cutting social spending for public goods and social safety nets for the poorest. Many neoliberal policies are justified by reference to the "free market" in ways that prioritize profit (usually for a few) at the expense of the wider public. References to the "free market" also obscure how few markets are actually free: they are usually dominated by a few large firms that want to further secure their position rather than deal with the competition of an actually free market (Stoller 2019).

Globalization and neoliberalism directly contribute to inequality, making it important for the study of class, race, and gender/sexuality. Inequality is also important for criminology because it contributes to crimes of the poor driven by need and crimes of the wealthy driven by greed and feelings of unaccountability (see chapter 2). As far back as 2006, the chief economist of Wall Street investment bank Morgan Stanley noted, "Billed as the great equalizer between the rich and the poor, globalization has been anything but." Surely, "the rich are, indeed, getting richer but the rest of the workforce is not" (Roach 2006). This contribution to inequality is not new, because earlier forms of globalization like colonialism and imperial processes—such as the trans-Atlantic slave trade—laid a foundation of inequality that today's globalization builds on (Hawkesworth, 2018).

Increasingly, inequality is not just between nations but between the rich and poor within a nation, including the United States. Sadly, the COVID pandemic has "delivered a windfall to billionaire wealth" (Kaplan 2021). Oxfam (2022), the global human rights organization, notes that "the world's ten richest men more than doubled their fortunes from $700 billion to $1.5 trillion—at a rate of $15,000 per second or $1.3 billion a day—during the first two years of a pandemic that has seen the incomes of 99 percent of humanity fall and over 160 million more people forced into poverty." (The organization believes that "extreme inequality is a form of economic violence.")

Neoliberalism thus creates a variety of social problems, but another feature of neoliberalism is creating beliefs that such problems are the result of individual failings—not having enough hustle, bad choices, poor culture, etc. This dynamic is seen in many "feel good" stories and "perseverance porn." For example, the *New York Times* ran the story of an eight-year-old chess champion who has been homeless for a year, saying it "will make you smile." His talent is getting recognized in spite of being homeless, but the unasked question is about "how it was possible for a child in one of the richest cities in the world to be homeless" (Macleod 2019). Stories of kids recycling to pay for college are "uplifting" and circulate through the media and social media, but the critical question not raised in the corporate- and billionaire-owned media is why children have to literally wade through garbage to get a decent education in the richest country in world history. Children sell lemonade to pay for a parent's chemotherapy without an awareness that in no other developed country would it be necessary for child labor to pay for medical bills because of universal health care. (And many nations subsidize or make college free as an investment in the future of the country, so student loans are not the crisis they are in the United States.) These stories paint the world as one where "every problem is understood through an individualist lens, and not as a result of systemic forces that dominate society" (Macleod 2019). Such forces include the existence and importance of class, race, gender, and sexuality.

## Immigration

The history of U.S. immigration has been of tension between anti-immigrant sentiment (often based on prejudice about race or national origin), the need for labor, and our ideals about being a land of opportunity (the plaque on the Statue of

Liberty says, "Give me your tired, your poor, your huddled masses yearning to breathe free, the wretched refuse of your teeming shore"). What emerges is known as racialized mobility regimes, meaning that a person's race, ethnicity, and national origin have a significant impact on their ability to legally enter, remain, work, and receive the rights of a citizen. (Having wealth also helps.) Mobility is also affected by the need for specific types of labor, for example with the capture and forced immigration of Africans as slaves, the use of Chinese to build the transcontinental railroad, and mass deportations of Latin populations after the financial crisis of 2008–2009 reduced the need for homebuilding and construction workers (Golash-Boza 2016b).

Some important current issues arise because of the expansion of the immigrant population since 1990, a shift from European to South and Central American immigrants, the spread of tough-on-crime attitudes to immigration enforcement, and a growth in U.S. Border Patrol. There has also been deeper involvement by many local police in immigration enforcement. The result is a large, high-tech, militarized immigration control complex that is heavily focused on the southern border of the United States. It is deployed against a greatly exaggerated "Latin threat," when the reality is consistent findings that immigrants have lower crimes rates than people born in the U.S. and that aggressive race-based immigration enforcement causes many community problems.

Since 1990, the immigrant population more than doubled—from 20 to over 45 million (Ramos and Wenger 2018: 1100). Immigrants and their U.S.-born children together total approximately 86 million people, which is 26 percent of the U.S. population (Batalova et al. 2021). During this time, Customs and Border Protection (CBP) became the largest civilian police force in the country (Martínez 2022). As part of the Department of Homeland Security (DHS), they oversee thousands of contracts worth billions of dollars for surveillance and intelligence. Another part of DHS, Immigration and Customs Enforcement (ICE), has been "reaching into the digital records of state and local governments and buying databases with billions of data points from private companies." They have, without judicial, legislative, or public oversight, "created a surveillance infrastructure that enables it to pull detailed dossiers on nearly anyone" through "datasets containing personal information about the vast majority of people living in the U.S., whose records can end up in the hands of immigration enforcement simply because they apply for driver's licenses; drive on the roads; or sign up with their local utilities to get access to heat, water and electricity" (Wang et al. 2022).

Anti-immigration measures are often based on fears of crime, which contribute to the exaggerated perception of a "Latin threat." This belief, which stokes hostility and hate crimes toward "foreigners" and "migrants," is perpetuated by media (Silber Mohamed and Farris 2020) and politicians, but research finds that *increases in immigration lead to decreases in crime* (Chouhy and Madero-Hernandez 2019; Zatz and Smith 2012). Indeed, during the period starting in 1990, Latin immigration increased while rates of street crime fell dramatically. Research reviews written by the Sentencing Project (Ghandnoosh and Rovner 2017), the American Society of Criminology (n.d.), and the conservative Cato Institute (Nowrasteh 2015) all agree that the *crime rates for immigrant populations are lower than those for people born in the United States.*

Research even finds that increases in undocumented immigrants does not increase crime (Light and Miller 2017), and undocumented immigrants in the state of Texas are less likely to be involved in serious crimes (i.e., felonies) compared to legal immigrants *and* native-born U.S. citizens (Light et al. 2020). Across the United States, undocumented immigrants are, on average, *half* as likely to be arrested for a violent crime as U.S.-born citizens (Moyer 2020). In reality, there is an "immigrant or Latino paradox" because they "tend to perform better than natives across a range of social issues, such as crime, mental health, and alcoholism, despite their disadvantaged status" (Ramos and Wenger 2018: 1104).

Many immigrants are simply trying to work to send money back home to support their family, so they try to stay out of trouble. Established immigrant communities have "social, cultural, and economic institutions in place that spur higher levels of informal social control and reduce crime" (Ramos and Wenger 2018: 1102). There is also a "context of reception" effect, where a welcoming attitude may reduce crime and "immigration enforcement policies may actually increase crime by undermining relationships between the police and local community" (Ramos and Wenger 2018: 1113; Provine et al. 2016). Some cities have asserted themselves as "sanctuary cities" that will refuse to turn over undocumented immigrants for deportation over minor offenses and traffic violations, practices that research finds "do not threaten public safety" (Hausman 2020). In spite of these realities, escalating immigration enforcement has been an aspect of the movement to be tough on crime—a trend known as "crimmigration." This includes a "growing number of grounds for deportation, lessened due-process protections, long terms of imprisonment for border crossers, fewer exceptions to removal decisions, and weakened judicial discretion to offer relief from removal" (Provine et al. 2016: 5; Golash-Boza 2016b). Where the "New Jim Crow" (Alexander 2012) refers to the racialized impact of mass incarceration on Black people, "Juan Crow" refers to the impact of those processes on the Latin population (Isom Scott 2020).

Criminalizing immigration makes immigrants more vulnerable to being victims of a range of crimes and exploitation. If immigrants—both legal and undocumented—are afraid to report crimes against them, others are more likely to commit sexual assault, theft, wage theft and labor violations, and other crimes against them. Family members, even those with legal status, can be less likely to report victimization to the police out of fear of possible immigration enforcement actions for themselves or their loved ones (Ricks 2017). In short, current policies can be criminogenic in that they incentivize victimization and hinder the accountability of perpetrators. Who is a better crime target than someone who won't dial 911 for fear of deportation?

We realize that some of these observations may seem inconsistent with media content, especially unrepresentative and statistically rare cases involving gangs like MS-13 that associate criminality with Latino migrants. Mara Salvatrucha, or MS-13, is a transnational gang with U.S. origins that often makes headlines for gruesome and exceptionally violent homicides. Two things can be true at the same time: that such violence is unacceptable and deserving of corrective justice, but also that such cases are disproportionately sensationalized and used to stoke anti-immigrant sentiment—particularly toward Central American and Latino men (Kopan 2017; León and Barak 2023). Undocumented migrants are not a public safety threat, but we must also respect the sober and grisly reality that there are instances, however rare, where immigrants participate in violent crime.

Many law-abiding immigrants are longtime residents of the United States who have built businesses and families here. Deportation tears families apart and disrupts communities. Some people might feel that is appropriate for "illegal aliens," who seem by definition to be criminals. But crossing the border without documentation is a civil (not criminal) offense because the procedure leading to deportation is simpler and the government does not need to pay for a public defender (Sheehan 2017). Being undocumented is thus analogous to status offenses like underage drinking or violating anti-vagrancy statutes—but the label of being "illegal" exaggerates the threat from that person's conduct and conveys a stigma reducing (or flattening) their entire personhood into that label.

## Militarization

Although law enforcement has always been a quasi-military organization, when Sir Robert Peel created what is considered the first modern police force in London in 1829, his "principles of policing emphasized crime prevention, public approval, willing cooperation of the public, and a minimal use of physical force" (Bickel 2013). In the United States, the civil unrest of the 1960s led to the modern escalation in the militarization of the American police (Strauss 2007). *Militarism* is "a set of beliefs, values, and assumptions that stress the use of force and threat of violence as the most appropriate means to solve problems. It glorifies the use of military power, hardware, operations, and technology as its primary problem-solving tools" (Kraska 2007: 164–65). The "similarities between a police paramilitary drug raid [at home in the United States] and the latest Iraq war" represent "the cultural, organizational, operational, and material blurring of the line between war and law enforcement, on the one hand, and between U.S. military and civilian criminal justice, on the other hand" (Kraska 2007: 166).

Police departments across the United States have experienced dramatic growth in specialized units such as SWAT teams and special response teams (SRTs) that are based on similar units within the military. In 1983, only 13 percent of towns with populations between twenty-five thousand and fifty thousand had a SWAT team, but thirty years later almost 90 percent did (Balko 2013; *Economist* 2014). Further, these units were once thought of primarily as *reactive* units for handling hostage standoffs and other unique situations, but the war on drugs transformed these units into *proactive* forces, specifically trained to execute police raids in poor, urban communities. Then their mission expanded further to break up poker games and wagering on college football games ("illegal gambling"), underage drinking in bars, suspected cockfighting, and "Tibetan monks who had overstayed their visas while visiting America on a peace mission" (Balko 2013; *Economist* 2014).

Military personnel train and assist these specialized units, and veterans of conflicts in Iraq and Afghanistan find that they can become consultants to train local SWAT teams. These practices have been an economic boon to suppliers of these paramilitary law enforcement teams (in weaponry, body armor, training, and vehicles, for example), who have been fortified by asset seizure laws and stereotypes of criminal minorities.

The militarization of policing has been accompanied by an escalation in violence, lethal and otherwise. No-knock or quick-knock paramilitary raids—used to collect evidence, such as drugs, guns, or money—naturally surprise citizens and put both citizens and police in potentially volatile situations. Dealing with these potentially dangerous situations justifies further extraordinary measures because the raid includes

> a rapid entry into the residence using specialized battering rams or sometimes entry explosives, the use of flash-bang grenades designed to temporarily disorient the occupants, a frantic room-by-room search of the entire residence where all occupants are expected to immediately comply with officers' screamed demands to get into the prone position. If a citizen does not comply immediately because he or she is confused, dazed, obstinate, or doesn't know that the people raiding the house are police, more extreme measures are taken. Finally, the police ransack the entire residence for contraband. (Kraska 2007: 167)

The commonality of these types of tragedies is not known because data on SWAT teams gone wrong are not officially recorded.

The militarism of the police has also been apparent in reaction to protests, especially (BLM) protests about police violence against minorities. Of particular concern is research suggesting that unnecessarily forceful police responses to protests can contribute to the escalation of the situation and crowd violence, which is then taken as confirmation of the madness of the crowd (Schweingruber 2000). Both leading up to the BLM protests and thinking back on those that have occurred thus far, it is important to remember that most crowds are peaceful, although people are more likely to tell stories and remember examples of crowd violence.

The scattered examples of protesters clashing with police and doing property damage may also be remembered because they confirm people's implicit or explicit stereotypes about the unruliness or threatening nature of African Americans. Indeed, there is already a class bias in the study of collective behavior because of the early works on "mobs" by the educated elite that became classics, like the still-popular 1841 book, *Extraordinary Popular Delusions and the Madness of Crowds* (Mackay [1841] 1932). The thought that crowd dynamics are "contagion" effects suggests disease and has a negative connotation, and when combined with variations on "madness," it serves to delegitimize collective action and the validity of issues that are the basis for collective protest.

Many of these negative evaluations of crowds are still present in a number of introductory sociology books despite several decades of research suggesting that crowds should not be seen as any more irrational, emotional, suggestible, destructive, or spontaneous than average individuals (McPhail 1991; Rheingold 2002; Schweingruber and Wohlstein 2005). Individuals are drawn to demonstrations and events because of common predispositions or values, and the "collective support enables people to put their beliefs into practice in broad daylight, even in the face of opposition from the police. In short, the crowd empowers" (Drury 2002).

Evaluations about the values and beliefs of collective demonstrations tend to be based not only on crowd behavior but also on an observer's agreement or disagreement with the goals of a protest. Stereotypes and privilege can make it difficult to see that even crowds engaged in violence can have legitimate collective grievances. And Hinton, in her thoroughly researched book *America on Fire*, notes that Black Americans who participated in collective protests "were rebelling not just against police brutality. They were rebelling against a broader system that had entrenched unequal conditions and anti-Black violence over generations" (2021: 7). But many see these as "an attack on existing American institutions rather than an appeal for inclusion within them" (Hinton 2021: 7).

While crime and disorder can stoke fears that seem to legitimize police militarization, especially when it is glamorized in popular culture, community policing that shares the values of Sir Robert Peel is marginalized:

> If after hiring officers in the spirit of adventure, who have been exposed to action oriented police dramas since their youth, and sending them to an academy patterned after a military boot camp, then dressing them in black battle dress uniforms and turning them loose in a subculture steeped in an "us versus them" outlook toward those they serve and protect, while prosecuting the war on crime, war on drugs, and now a war on terrorism—is there any realistic hope of institutionalizing community policing as an operational philosophy? (Bickel 2013)

## Privatization and Revenue Collection

*Privatization* refers to the process of government outsourcing certain tasks to for-profit businesses, with frequent and ongoing conflict between high profits for the business and honest, quality services for the government. While prisons have frequently contracted out food service and health care ("nominal privatization"), privatization escalated in the 1980s with the creation of businesses that built, owned, and managed prisons ("operational privatization"). A number of private prison companies later had initial public offerings in which they raised money by selling shares to the public and became traded on the stock exchange (Selman and Leighton 2010). As the industry has grown, so too have concerns about the number of (poor, Black) "bodies destined for profitable punishment" (Leighton and Selman 2018).

The movement to private prisons started in order to offset the high correctional expenses resulting from the incarceration binge in the United States. With the expansion of prisons, jails, parole, and probation, the number of companies involved in delivering services has expanded, and they have diversified into providing more services. For example, the privatization of punishment is not solely found in the construction and management of prisons but also includes housing undocumented people (including families), juvenile offenders, and the mentally ill; contracting to provide health-care and food services for incarcerated persons; contracting to provide community-based forms of surveillance, including electronic monitoring; and contracting for reentry services for the formerly incarcerated (Selman and Leighton 2010).

The reality of contemporary corrections is that it includes several multinational prison businesses with billions of dollars' worth of stock and billions more in debt to Wall Street banks. The money from investors and banks allowed private businesses to build many facilities and thus continue the unprecedented expansion of the prison population—an example of understanding the political economy of punishment, or how politics and economics exert influence on punishment more significantly than on arguments about retribution, deterrence, and sentencing guidelines (Rusche and Kirchheimer [1939] 1968). At each stage of history, the reliance on imprisonment in its different forms was tied up in a political economy of punishment:

> When society was manual-labor based and dependent on the production of goods and cheap labor, imprisonment included prison labor. It was not until the use of prison labor was no longer economically viable and politically advantageous that reforms were instituted. . . . With the advent of new technologies that reduced the demand for manual labor, imprisonment served to warehouse the surplus labor supply. As capitalism became more service oriented, imprisonment became a *service* to be provided. As capitalism becomes a combination of technology, service and information, so too does punishment, in the forms of electronic monitoring and GPS tracking. (Killingbeck 2005: 169, emphasis in the original)

With outsourcing and globalization, wages of most workers go down while those at the top do much better, leading to an overall situation of greater inequality. In private prisons, guards tend to be paid less and have fewer benefits than government workers, and the antiunion stance of private prisons makes it difficult for workers to substantially improve work conditions (Bauer 2016). Median earnings for correctional officers employed by states is higher than for similar positions in private prisons, but the chief executive officer (CEO) of a private prison company makes more than the average head of a similarly sized department of corrections. The end result is staff turnover, apathy, and poor judgment—which can combine to precipitate riots, unconstitutional conditions of confinement, or inmate abuse (Bauer 2016; Carceral 2005). These concerns are amplified when considering members of marginalized communities like LGBTQ+ incarcerated folks, or more specifically transgender and gender-nonconforming individuals who are often incorrectly and improperly housed and surveilled.

As more companies generate revenue from corrections, there is more potential for misplaced power in the multibillion-dollar prison-industrial complex to distort sentencing and criminal justice (and mental health and immigration) policy: the interests of corporate shareholders become increasingly important, causing increased corporate lobbying and campaign donations, while public safety and public accountability become less relevant. Basic free-market principles dictate that companies with shares traded on a stock exchange have a duty to make money for their shareholders. Thus, businesses involved in incarceration have no duty to balance their desire for ever-increasing profits with the larger public good that would come from, say, crime prevention funding or money for schools. Indeed, sentencing reform and declining crime rates are "risk factors."

The expansion of criminal justice fines and fees is an important development within the criminal justice–industrial complex. By 2011, the Conference of State Court Administrators issued a policy paper, "Courts Are Not Revenue Centers," where they state that the use and structure of fees "has recast the role of the court as a collection agency for executive branch services" (2011: 9). The process frequently involves aggressive policing of submisdemeanor infractions and issuing citations that carry a fine plus a court fee—what's called "cash register justice" (Natapoff 2019). People who cannot afford to pay often do not show up, whereupon the court issues an arrest warrant, which carries another fee (Reiman and Leighton 2023). These policies create a new generation of individuals encountering debtors' prison, unable to restore their freedom because they simply cannot afford to pay their fines and fees. These policies disproportionately impact people of color, women, and LGBTQ+ folks who often experience higher rates of unemployment or underemployment.

In response to the police shooting of an unarmed Black teenager in Ferguson, Missouri, a Department of Justice (DOJ) investigation found that the city finance director and city manager asked the police chief to aggressively issue citations so that revenue from court fees could be increased because of other budget shortfalls. Management carefully monitored police "productivity" (number of citations issued), so the DOJ found that "many officers appear to see some residents, especially those who live in Ferguson's predominantly African-American neighborhoods, less as constituents to be protected than as potential offenders and sources of revenue" (DOJ 2015: 2). It also found that the municipal court worked to "advance the City's financial interests" and "does not act as a neutral arbiter of the law or a check on unlawful police conduct" (DOJ 2015: 3). These practices especially harm the poorer residents, because "minor offenses can generate crippling debts, [and] result in jail time because of an inability to pay" (DOJ 2015: 4).

Unfortunately, the problem is not confined to Ferguson, and the government also helps businesses collect revenue in hidden ways from unfair practices. In one southern jurisdiction, for example, being released on bail required wearing an electronic monitoring device that cost $300 a month, and while the fee was payable directly to the monitoring company, the company shared part of its revenue with the government. Trial can take a year or more, so fees pile up and strain the budgets of already poor households. The failure to pay means a return to jail, so "people are pleading guilty because it's cheaper to be on probation than it is to be on electronic monitoring" (Markowitz 2015). Thus, the government and the criminal justice system itself are part of the problem of distorting policy and public safety by trying to increase revenue, largely by engaging in predatory finance and abusive collection practices. And they contract out functions so that there is a "vast network of private companies profiteering from the criminalization of poverty and communities of color" (Kornya et al. 2019).

## Cybercrime and the "Pre-Crime" Society

The current world, with nations separated by a defined geographical border, government agents at border crossings, and national laws, does not fit with how cybercrime functions. People in one country use computers in many countries to attack targets all over the world, then launder money electronically through additional other countries. This situation makes it challenging for jurisdictions where people are victimized by cybercrime to investigate and prosecute, even if they had the tools to do so. But the scale of losses—money, information, and the security of critical infrastructure—makes it too large to ignore (Geller 2017).

The "Stuxnet" computer virus, widely attributed to the United States and Israel, ushered in a new era of cybercrime (Arthur 2013). Until that point, cybercrime and terrorism were limited to attacking and potentially damaging other computers, but Stuxnet attacked industrial controls so that Iran's centrifuges to refine uranium would operate in a way that broke the machines. The objective of crippling Iran's nuclear power program was achieved, but it ushered in a model of cyber attacks on any computer-controlled critical (and not so critical) infrastructure, much of which is also connected to the internet: power plants, the electric grid, traffic lights, emergency response systems, water processing, elevators, cell towers, hospitals, the stock exchange, gas pipelines, cars, billboards, subways, implantable medical devices, and an increasing number of devices upon which people have come to depend. Leveraging a series of hacks can easily result in chaos in a city or across a nation.

Former president Obama brought some of the functions and responsibilities for the nation's digital security to the White House when he announced in late May 2009 that he would appoint the nation's first cyber security czar. The Pentagon also has a "Cyber Command," and the Secret Service, which developed high-tech laboratories to investigate counterfeit currency, took on the investigation of credit card breaches and other attacks on financial infrastructure.

As cybercrime has become more widespread, it has also become more professional. While hackers living in their parents' basement are still part of the scene, "80 percent of hackers are now working with or as part of an organized crime group" (Goodman 2016: 222). Those who develop malware (malicious software) are specialized in that business and sell or rent their product for others to distribute. The malware developers allow their customers "to file bug reports, propose and vote on new features for upcoming versions of the software, and even submit and track trouble tickets" (Goodman 2016: 233). In many other ways, organized cybercrime mimics the organization and business models of Silicon Valley technology companies.

Cybercrime also involves an expanding assortment of "virtual dark markets"—underground sites that auction or sell hard drugs, child pornography, fraudulent passports, counterfeit dollars, military weapons, and stolen identities. The dark web is the place "that's distinguished by that increasingly rare commodity: complete anonymity." Although most people do not browse the dark web, "the software you need to access it is free and takes less than three minutes to download and install" (Grossman and Newton-Small 2013: 28).

The dark web has thus become a tool for criminals, political dissidents, hackers, intelligence agents, law enforcement, and anyone who needs or wants to conduct their online affairs in private. Thus, some prosecutors and government agencies regard the dark web as a potential nightmare, an electronic haven for thieves, human traffickers, and peddlers of state secrets. Dark web markets resemble eBay for criminal goods and services, but often with some limits—see figure 1.1—that reflect the morals of the owner and/or a desire to avoid too much law enforcement scrutiny. Increasingly, though, such activities are being moved to the Telegram messaging app, to which people are directed from advertisements on Facebook, Instagram, and other social media (which do not aggressively police such ads because they represent revenue for the company).

The dark web also has digital payment systems called cryptocurrencies that may be used for both legitimate and illegitimate dealings. Bitcoin, Monero, and Zcash have no physical form, and their worth is "determined by supply and demand and is valuable only insofar as individuals and companies have agreed to trade it" (Grossman and

You may be shocked to find listings here that are outlawed in your jurisdiction. That doesn't mean Abacus is lawless. In fact, we have a very strict code of conduct that, if given a chance, we believe most people would agree wtih our rules are based in treating other as you would like to be treated, do not try to scam others on market and mind your own business. In the spirit of those rules, there are some things you will never see here, and if you do please report them. We do not allow child pornography or any resources that might lead to, selling humans or their parts, services to harm other (physical or mental including assassination, threatening, arson, surveillance, harassment etc), fentanyl or analogues, poisons, selling guns, explosives or any items which may lead to any terroristic actions (some exceptions are tasers, pepper sprays), just to name a few.

Abacus Market is totally against the War on Drugs, which today is questioned around the world, has only brought deaths, abuses of power, spending on public money. We are against of limit people's access to controlled substances that they decided to get. The will be able to get it from streets without knowing what they are buying and eliminating the simplicity of sharing information with other people in the same situation.

We have lot of plans related with harm reduction, some of our closest friends died due to an overdose from a substance they bought adulterated and they did not know it. We encourage to all our buyers to learn what are lethal doses of each substance and to not trust in nobody, buy your own testing kits or send some samples to your nearest testing laboratory to be sure about what you are going to take. If we find that some seller is selling adulterated substances they will banned forever from our platform and all their customers will be immediately warned.

The old saying, "with freedom comes responsibility", couldn't be more true here. You will find easy access to things that could get you in trouble with your authorities and are downright terrible for your health. So, just because you can, doesn't mean you should. However, You are owner of your life and it's your job to judge what is good and bad for you. No one else can do that.

**FIGURE 1.1** Rules for a Dark Web Market
While many media and government reports emphasize the child pornography and murder for hire that is available in darknet markets, many have a more modest scope. The items prohibited on this website are available on other dark web markets, though buyers may need to wade through many scams to find the real deal. Still, often vendors have a personal morality that overrides their desire to make money on some items, and they have an interest in keeping a lower profile to avoid being the target of occasional law enforcement takedowns.

Newton-Small 2013: 29). No governments back these currencies; they are completely decentralized, and users can transfer such cryptocurrencies from one digital wallet to another without banks brokering the transactions or imposing fees. With no central authority, these digital assets are not subject to frozen accounts or blocked payments.

Although Bitcoin was intended to be digital cash for anonymous transactions, it is no longer anonymous. Bitcoin relies on a different privacy mechanism than credit cards and checks, where a person's name and account number are public but the account balance is private (banks authorize a transaction but do not disclose a balance or credit limit). With Bitcoin, wallet numbers and balances are available through the public blockchain, but that information was originally separated from a person's identity. However, as Bitcoin became more popular, regulators required people selling Bitcoin to comply with "Know Your Customer" (anti–money laundering) requirements, so wallets could be linked with people's identities. Thus, technologists who wanted to have the equivalent of digital cash for anonymous transactions have created "privacy coins" like Monero and Zcash, which use different cryptology to obscure the sender, receiver, and amounts of transactions from the public blockchain while still having mechanisms against fraud and double spending of coins.

The advances in technology may facilitate crime, but they also expand the ability of law enforcement and security agencies to undertake surveillance and collate information into a form that may or may not be "intelligence." The traditional criminal justice system that reacted to crime becomes a "pre-crime society" (Arrigo and Sellers 2021), which tries to "forecast and prevent crime before it occurs through the algorithmic calculation of risk, institutional dataveillance, preemptive policing, crime mapping, crime analytics, and the digital tracking and monitoring of citizens all in the service of securitization" (Arrigo et al. 2021). Such hopes rely on "big data"—"vast amounts of information to be collected on individuals for the purpose of strategic 'life mining.'" As this happens, "our humanity is reassembled into quantified 'data-doubles' to be viewed, measured, and sorted according to potential dangerousness or risk" (Arrigo et al. 2021). For some people, this is a positive development to create a more orderly society without needing the most explicitly coercive forces of criminal justice. For others, this represents a dystopian society of surveillance, always on and everywhere, resulting in decisions that people cannot review or challenge. Indeed, philosopher Michel Foucault noted that while there was a utopian dream of a "perfect society," there was also "a military dream of society; its fundamental reference was not to the state of nature, but to the meticulously subordinated cogs of a machine, not to the primal social contract, but to permanent coercions, not to fundamental rights, but to indefinitely progressive forms of training, not to general will, but to automatic docility" (1979: 169).

## Implications

This chapter has highlighted such factors as climate change, neoliberalism and globalization, immigration, militarism, privatization, and cybercrime/surveillance that are affecting the criminal justice enterprise. The challenge for the criminal justice enterprise with climate change is to be on the side of trying to stop carbon criminals and climate crimes, not criminalizing people protesting to stop human extinction. Each other area has a similar challenge, where the criminal justice enterprise can be used for public good or corrupted to dispense injustice. But a theme of this book is that the criminal justice enterprise can be no fairer than the society for which it provides "law and order," so sometimes justice requires changes to society rather than criminal justice reform.

Part II of this book looks at the fairness of society in terms of class (chapter 3), race (chapter 4), gender/sexuality (chapter 5), and intersections (chapter 6). Part III explores how these inequalities play out in lawmaking (chapter 7), policing (chapter 8), prosecution and the judicial process (chapter 9), and punishment (chapter 10). In setting up those chapters and closing this one, we note that while criminal justice workers are becoming more diverse, diversity in the administration of justice is important for at least two reasons. The first issue is of fairness and confidence in the system: the more closely the criminal justice labor force represents the distribution of diverse groups in society, the more the system appears to represent "we the people." If equality and justice are to happen within the United States, then it is especially important that in the justice system, an important core of democracy, women and minorities should be included and in positions of authority (Álvarez and Urbina 2015).

The second issue is of incorporating substantively different group backgrounds into the criminal justice enterprise, including those who study crime and teach criminology: women and people of color are more likely to bring experiences and insight into the field that generations of white men may not, while highlighting the importance of the application of intersectionality in our discussions of these experiences. On this point, "decades of research by organizational scientists, psychologists, sociologists, economists and demographers show that socially diverse groups (i.e., those with a diversity of race, ethnicity, gender and sexual orientation) are more innovative than homogeneous groups" (Phillips 2014). To accomplish change, those with minority status cannot be token representations for diversity, a "Society of One"—or even a "Society of Few" (Álvarez and Urbina 2015).

## Review and Discussion Questions

1. What is meant by the criminal justice–industrial complex? Why do the authors advocate "following the money" as a way to understand criminal justice policy?
2. What are some ways that this idea, and seeing criminal justice as an industry, shifts the analysis of criminal justice practice and policy?
3. Why does this chapter in a book about class, race, and gender/sexuality discuss climate change? What are the justice issues involved with carbon criminals and climate crimes?
4. According to this chapter, what are the concerns about globalization? What is neoliberalism, and what impact does it have on the criminal justice enterprise?

5. To what extent do immigrants contribute to the crime problem, and what is the effect of anti-immigrant policies?
6. What is militarization of the police and why is it a concern? Why do the authors criticize the idea that crowds, like those at protests, are "mad" or irrational? Why are they skeptical of the idea that Black Lives Matter protests led to increases in the crime rate?
7. How does the escalation of criminal justice fines and fees affect policing, courts, and justice?
8. Why is cybercrime such a challenge for the criminal justice system? What is the "pre-crime society" and why is it a concern?

## Note

1. This book uses "gender/sexuality," but they are not one and the same. As noted in the introduction, they are not always interconnected, but our examinations of gender lead to discussions of sexuality. See chapter 5.

# CHAPTER 2

# Criminology and Class, Race, and Gender/Sexuality

*The history of criminology is the story of three schools of thought: reason, science, and power. These classical (1764), positivist (1876), and critical (1976) paradigms gained popularity roughly one hundred years apart. All these perspectives are still present in contemporary criminology, so it's important to know their merits, limitations, and historical context.*

*The classical school focuses on the rewards and punishments that can shape people's choices, while the positivist school focuses on the traits and characteristics that differentiate offenders from nonoffenders. Critical criminology questions the underlying structures, like the "criminal justice logic" (Coyle and Schept 2018) that simply aims at getting people to obey the law and enforces "law and order" in a very unequal society. "Critical" means perspectives of justice beyond criminal justice and studying harms beyond what the political process defines as crime. It argues that sometimes the criminal justice system is a social problem because it both reflects and recreates power—including classism, sexism, racism, homophobia, and more—and it challenges us to take action.*

*For most of early Western history, the "demonic perspective" (Pfohl 1985) saw crime as sinful behavior and an offense against God (or the gods). People engaged in crime because evil forces possessed them or they had succumbed to the temptations of Satan. Brutal methods, including torture, were used to discover and to punish those who were possessed by, or had surrendered to, the devil. In the middle of the eighteenth century, classical criminologists challenged the demonic perspective. Characteristic of the Enlightenment, classical theory argued that crime was the result of observable "worldly" forces, such as the absence of swift, certain, and effective punishments. According to the classical perspective, all people were basically rational and had free will, so crime was a rational choice they made when trying to maximize their pleasure and minimize* their pain. The response to the pursuit of self-interested criminal behavior, therefore, became the rational employment of "swift, certain, and proportional" punishment to deter potential offenders who calculated the pleasure of crime versus the pain of punishment. This criminology was developed in reaction to the harsh, corrupt, and often arbitrary nature of criminal justice in the 1700s and was inspired by a desire to bring about rational legal reforms—and not be subject to the moods or excesses of any given ruler.

In the late 1800s, the classical perspective was challenged by the scientific approach of the positivist school. Its biological, psychological, and sociological orientations to the study of criminal behavior argued that criminals are not in fact normal, rational human beings who choose to engage in crime to maximize their pleasure and minimize their pain. Instead, criminals are viewed as different from noncriminals—and it is their differences that compel them to engage in crime. Such "criminogenic properties" call for intervention, reform, and treatment to socially engineer individual criminals and their surroundings to make deviance less likely.

While still the dominant perspective in criminology today, positivism has been challenged by the emergence of the critical school of criminology in the 1970s, which was part of a larger, feminist philosophical critique of "value-free, objective, and neutral" social science (Whittingdale 2021). Critical criminology in the United States reflected the reality that with racism, sexism, imperialism, and other types of inequality, justice required more than criminal justice reform and professionalism. Both classical and positivist criminologies ignored, and thus left unchallenged, the powerful interests that benefit from the attention paid to crime in the streets rather than the wilding of a deregulated Wall Street, financial weapons of mass destruction, and unchecked corporate power (Barak 2017). Both classical and positivist criminologies lacked concern about racial and gender inequality, and so recreated it. In contrast, critical criminologies—feminist, peacemaking, queer, green (environmental), prison abolition, survivor (Cook et al. 2022), etc.—focus on the "justice" part of criminal justice by striving to bring about more equitable and peaceful societies, locally and globally.

## Introduction

Criminology is the study of the nature and causes of crime as well as the treatment of offenders. It includes theories of criminal behavior and the operation of criminal justice systems. Criminology is very much a part of the criminal justice enterprise because it is a field of academic inquiry that shapes the attitudes, beliefs, and knowledge of people who take criminology classes and may go on to work in the system. Criminological research helps shape people's understanding of what the "crime problem" is, who is causing it, why they are criminal, and what responses society should take to it. Criminological research is used to support new laws and policies. Criminologists appear in the media to offer perspectives on events, trends, and problems.

Because criminology is embedded in the criminal justice enterprise, it does not always see the problems it causes or appreciate their seriousness. Students of criminology should think through how they feel about "criminal justice logic" and ask, "Is criminology a discipline of freedom or one of captors?" (Friedman 2021: 1). While many may respond that they would like to see violent and dangerous people locked up, there is nevertheless a problem of mass incarceration—also referred to as the "carceral state"—that must be studied and challenged. Police and punishment are too often seen as the solution, even when a variety of crime prevention programs are effective but lie outside of the criminal justice system and too often are not part of criminological study.

Criminological research within the criminal justice–industrial complex is dominated by the classical and positivist schools, which together make up mainstream criminology. The mainstream perspectives focus criminologists on a limited number of theories, which shape decisions about what constitutes a problem worthy of study (or publication), what method is appropriate for the study, and what the results mean (León 2021). Mainstream criminology emphasizes individual-level theories (Pratt and Cullen 2005) rather than structural factors. Published papers frequently involve quantitative methods, which cannot get to the how or why of phenomena, and often control for class, race, and gender/sexuality (to study other dynamics) rather than explore their impact.

Unfortunately, "information and knowledge are formed by unequal power relations based on class, race, gender, and sexuality" (Stockdale et al. 2021), which shapes what is viewed as "authoritative" knowledge in criminology. Indeed, Stockdale and colleagues (2021) asked students to name criminological researchers and theorists they knew on a sticky note, assign them a race/gender combination, then post it on a board divided into sections for whites and nonwhites, males, females, and nonbinary. Students were surprised when they saw almost all the notes placed in the white male box. This bothered them because "through their degree they want to increase their awareness and understanding of a range of perspectives for personal growth as well as to have a more rounded world view" (Stockdale et al. 2021).

The situation represents a problem for the growth of criminology as well. An article from the natural sciences noted a process that applies to criminology as well: "Examining 1.8 billion citations among 90 million papers across 241 subjects, we find a deluge of papers does not lead to turnover of central ideas in a field, but rather to ossification of canon" (Chu and Evans 2021). "Ossification" refers to the process of bone formation, and in this context to an idea becoming fixed or unable to change. The authors suggest that "fundamental progress may be stymied if quantitative growth of scientific endeavors—in number of scientists, institutes, and papers—is not balanced by structures fostering disruptive scholarship and focusing attention on novel ideas."

Critical criminology tends to be the disruptive force, and it is the perspective from which this book is written. While it has helped foster many novel ideas, we also recognize that it has been slow and sometimes limited in recognizing its whiteness, maleness, heteronormativity, and colonialism (Shah 2021). Still, it is important to critically evaluate the limits of the information and theories that are deemed "authoritative," to be aware of how mainstream criminology can reinforce inaccurate stereotypes, and to understand the impact on those who find little helpful knowledge about their communities in criminology. So, the call is to develop ways to diversify criminological knowledge in ways that challenge existing power structures and ideas.

Critical criminology concerns itself with power and understands that humans lead their lives "in social structures which are largely not of their own making" (Young 2011: 222). For example, nobody chooses to be born into a poor, high-crime neighborhood. While they do exercise choices within it, understanding neighborhood crime requires examining economic policies about employment, public assistance benefits, education, resource allocations, and taxes. Individual choice needs to be examined within the histories and ongoing forms of structural racism and class-based inequality that create such neighborhoods in the first place. Factors such as the distribution of income, wealth, and economic power shape these policies and the context within which individuals make choices. Focusing on individual-level factors reinforces that crime is a problem of individuals, not the social structure, and it conveniently avoids raising questions about who benefits and who bears the burdens of contemporary social arrangements (Reiman and Leighton 2023).

This chapter explores how criminological theory, as well as the researcher's own class, race, and gender/sexuality, often shape criminological knowledge and the taken-for-granted assumptions about the field. Thus, the first part of the chapter elaborates on the opening narrative by further exploring the classical, positivist, and critical perspectives on criminology. The second part of the chapter explores the roles that class, race, and gender/sexuality have played in the field of criminology. It also discusses the importance of intersectionality.

## Classical, Positivist, and Critical Criminologies

*Classical criminology* emerged during the late 1700s and early 1800s during the Enlightenment in Europe. It was a reaction to both rebellions and the harsh and arbitrary punishments administered by the state, so it set out to study the relationship of citizens to the state's legal structure. Classical criminology emphasized reforming the state's unjust systems of administering punishment, which would result in increased legitimacy for the state and its rule of law. Influenced by two new doctrines, the *social contract* and *free will*, classical criminologists adopted the view that "reason and experience, rather than faith and superstition, must replace the excesses and corruption of feudal societies" (Beirne and Messerschmidt 1991: 286).

Classical criminology builds on the idea of the social contract, which is based on the assumption that people pursuing their own self-interests leads to a perpetual unproductive "war of all against all." People thus "surrender some measure of their individuality so that government [can] enact and enforce laws in the interests of the common good; the government, in return, [was to] agree to protect the common good but not to invade the natural, inviolable liberties and rights of individual citizens" (Beirne and Messerschmidt 1991: 287). The social contract is not a historical event but a theory of an agreement (a contract) that men, at least those who were free and who possessed property, rationally and voluntarily chose to participate in.

The two principal classical theorists, Cesare Beccaria (1738–1794) and Jeremy Bentham (1748–1832), both applied the doctrines of free will and rational, pleasure-maximizing choices to the study of crime and punishment. They objected to the inequities in the administration of the criminal law and proposed reforms of penal justice that sought to balance the good of society with the rights of the individual. Human beings were rational and free to engage in rightful or wrongful behavior, so the punishment was to fit the social harm caused by the crime (instead of reacting to demonological possession). Classical theory has been and remains an integral part of legal and economic thought, and it has influenced the nature of punishment and sentencing.

While classical theorists advanced reforms, the aristocrats also worked to secure and legitimize a social order in which they had privilege. Consider the following quotation taken from Beccaria's book, *Essay on Crimes and Punishments*. In trying to reason through the appropriate punishment for an offender, he takes the imagined voice of the criminal:

> What are these laws that I am supposed to respect, that place such a great distance between me and the rich man? He refuses me the penny I ask of him and, as an excuse, tells me to sweat at work he knows nothing about. Who made these laws? Rich and powerful men who have never deigned to visit the squalid huts of the poor, who have never had to share a crust of moldy bread amid the innocent cries of hungry children and the tears of a wife. Let us break these bonds, fatal to the majority and only useful to a few indolent tyrants; let us attack justice at its source. I will return to my natural state of independence; I shall at least for a little time live free and happy with the fruits of my courage and industry. The day will perhaps come for my sorrow and repentance, but it will be brief, and for a single day of suffering I shall have many years of liberty and of pleasures. (in Vold and Bernard 1986: 29)

The revolutionary implication behind this passage is obvious; it shows the logic of crimes driven by need and how redistribution of wealth could reduce crime and enhance justice. Instead, Beccaria argues the "humanitarian" position that the death penalty is an ineffective deterrent that should be replaced by the more protracted suffering of life imprisonment.

Positivism emerged in the late 1800s and turned its focus away from law to begin a scientifically based study of crime as a social phenomenon. Borrowing from the methodology of the natural sciences, *positivist criminology* sought to analyze crime through systematic data collection and analysis to uncover, explain, and predict the ways in which observable facts occurred in regular patterns.

While the systematic collection of data is a crucial step for deeper understanding, there are unacknowledged power dynamics behind it. For example, Francis Bacon—who laid the foundation for the scientific method—called

for nature to be "bound into service" and made a "slave" of mankind. (The sexual nature of these descriptions of "natural domination" is no coincidence; [author Carolyn] Merchant proposes that the conceptualization of the Earth as female in no small part contributed to its ultimate subjugation—and that the legacy of the Scientific Revolution can be seen in the contemporary subordination of women). (Byju 2021)

Further, positivism, in mimicking the natural sciences, emphasized statistical data that a researcher took from "subjects" in a sometimes "parasitical" way (Whittingdale 2021) for publications inaccessible to those who contributed knowledge. While some feminist research uses positivist methodology, it also used and legitimated a wider range of methods. It did not just claim that women's voices were also authoritative but used qualitative, "unstructured interviews as a means of making room for alternative voices, experiences, and meanings" (Whittingdale 2021). Further, "in recounting acts such as helping interviewees 'with the demands of house-work and motherhood' where conducting interviews conflicted with these, or committing to answer 'all personal questions' that interviewees asked, Oakley's work disrupted the illusory ideal of 'hygienic research' and the mythological conception of objective data production" (Whittingdale 2021). Finally, feminist methodologies can involve sharing results with research informants and strategizing for advocacy.

Positivist criminology tried to uncover the biological, psychological, economic, and social forces that propelled individuals into engaging in crime, and it began to assert that the "treatment should fit the criminal" rather than the "punishment should fit the crime." But the aristocratic men who engaged in positivist criminology "scientifically" explored types of criminals and theories of crime that reinforced class, race, and gender-based inequalities. The father of modern criminology is Cesare Lombroso (1835–1909), who also founded the positivist school of criminology. Though Lombroso was an advocate for scientific measurement, record keeping, and data-driven claims, his overall research design reflected unacknowledged privilege. Lombroso took measurements of the skulls of Italian prisoners, which he used to assert a connection between head shape and criminality. But those in prison reflected the biases of the criminal justice system, so Lombroso's work "scientifically" validated the existing biases of his society and the criminal justice system against the poor and minorities. He never scrutinized his fellow aristocrats for criminal traits.

Lombroso's work argued that "born criminals" were "atavistic" throwbacks to earlier stages of evolution, and he noted "how closely" criminals' skulls "correspond to [the] . . . normal skulls of the colored and inferior races" that he viewed as subhuman (in Arford and Madfis 2022). Lombroso developed the view that Black people were the missing evolutionary link between white people and apes. He is also given credit for studying female criminality, because his contemporaries did not and modern criminology still neglects it, but Lombroso believed that

> the criminal woman is a true monster. Honest women are kept in line by factors such as maternity, piety, and weakness; when a woman commits a crime despite these restraints, this is a sign that her power of evil is immense. (in Arford and Madfis 2022)

His belief that female criminals were more masculine remained with criminology well into the 1900s and continues to be researched and examined today.

With Lombroso's museum and treatment in criminology books, his "white supremacism and misogyny are characterized as scientific 'flaws' rather than symptomatic of dominant ideology. His beliefs are frequently individualized as 'mistakes' he would come to regret, while the harm and violence spawned by the colonialist logic at the core of European 'civilization' go virtually unrecognized" (Arford and Madfis 2022). Lombroso's knowledge claims supported "the needs of slavery and sustaining the dispossession of indigenous communities by colonial expansion" (in León 2021: 17). His ideas spread through Latin America, where they were used to criminalize Indigenous and Black people (León 2021) and became popular with fascist regimes and eugenics movements. (Eugenics involves strategies to supposedly improve the racial quality of a nation or population through extermination, limitations on migration and marriage, and the forced sterilization of peoples seen as inferior.)

Saying "the science was good" and "the racism was bad" avoids the need to explore scientific racism—validating the belief that white men were the most evolved and civilized. The lesson is not to disregard the systematic collection of knowledge but to appreciate that Lombroso was not reflexive about his position and the power relations with those he studied. Indeed, "virtually all European intellectual spaces were imbued with self-serving notions of superiority, whereby sexism, racism" and capitalism "were laundered into concepts of 'modernity' and 'progress'" (León 2021: 17). While contemporary society is less overtly racist and sexist, avoiding the discussion about scientific racism (and sexism) blocks an opportunity to question how the criminology of our day helps to justify our current society's unjust structures.

During the 1900s and into the early 2000s, positivist criminology has continued to develop. But its shortcomings include its overemphasis on the individual level and relatively little research at the ecological or macro level: why crime varies across neighborhoods, cities, and larger areas. One of the most in-depth reviews of the research concluded that "resource/economic deprivation theory" was "well supported" with "relatively strong effects" that "remain stable across various methodological conditions" (Pratt and Cullen 2005: 412–13). Such ecological analysis is important because many criminals say they got into crime because it was what was going on in their neighborhood, so the important criminological question is why those neighborhoods have so much crime.

The newest school is *critical criminology*. Nearly fifty years old, this school first emerged as radical (i.e., Marxist) criminology and helped incubate feminist, left-realist, peacemaking, news-making, cultural, green (or environmental), queer, anarchist, and prison abolition perspectives, to name a few. Despite the diversity of critical criminologies, they have in common an agreement on the limitations of criminological knowledge and seek to challenge the unacknowledged recreation of unequal power inherent in the classical and positivist criminologies.

For example, critical criminologists are skeptical of the rational and positivist belief about objectivity and point out that there are no "value-free" standpoints—everyone has some assumptions and values. Certain assumptions and points of view may seem "natural" or "objective" because they are widely shared by the dominant groups, but they contain hidden values that can reproduce existing inequalities. Critical criminologists therefore acknowledge their subjectivity and that they are part of a moral and political endeavor (to make a better, less harmful society).

Critical criminology in part represents a departure from the traditional practices of criminology that have focused attention on changing the behavior of the lawbreakers either through punishment (classical criminology) or individual treatment (positivist criminology). Critical criminology is concerned with punishment, treatment, and reforming the administration of criminal justice, but it prefers to locate these changes within the contexts of social, political, and economic justice. Critical criminology is thus concerned not so much with "law and order" but with "whose law?" and "what order?" (Chambliss and Mankoff 1976)—that is, with the power relations involved in the law, the fairness of the social order that law is protecting, and solutions that promote a just society rather than simply repress criminals.

In sum, unlike classical and positivist criminologists, critical criminologists are scholars of power and perspective, meaning they question the privilege that goes with having one's viewpoint be seen as "objective" and how such privileged standpoints and "knowledge" contribute to inequality. They have turned the activity of explanation back on itself: in the process of reflection and introspection, critical criminology asks about the basic assumptions and thought processes of criminological inquiry that generate our "knowledge" about crime. Morally and politically, critical criminology questions the status quo, official versions of reality, and prevailing ideologies about the "solutions" in crime control. Even while advocating for better pathways to human liberation and crime reduction in all its forms, critical criminology also remains committed to empirically supporting its scholarship and interventions in policy formation.

## Class and Criminology

Social and economic class are discussed less than race and gender. Unfortunately, both income and wealth are unequally distributed, and class mobility is more limited than most people would like to believe. These assertions are developed in chapter 3, and this section reviews some of the important ways that understanding class, inequality, and economic power relates to criminology. For example, criminological theory is frequently based on an unquestioning acceptance of how the criminal law defines crime. But class is related to political power and lawmaking, so it is also deeply implicated in understanding what has been defined as crime and why fifty years of being "tough on crime" has not applied to white-collar crime. Economic resources also play a role in the working of the legal system. The first part of this section provides an overview of these issues, followed by a discussion of the link between inequality and crime and the relative neglect of white-collar, corporate, and governmental crime.

Crime theory frequently assumes that criminal law reflects consensus rather than the outcome of a political process that includes class conflict and class biases. (Chapter 7 discusses the disproportionate number of legislators who are millionaires.) Indeed, "criminology is in the unusual position of being a mode of social inquiry whose central concept is defined officially, by governments," so "politics openly, necessarily, insinuates itself into the heart of criminology. Political systems hand criminology a ready-made research agenda" (Reiman and Leighton 2023: 256). Large corporations and wealthy individuals lobby lawmakers to ensure that harmful behavior of the powerful is minimally criminalized, so when criminologists focus on street crime and the crimes of the poor, it seems like a "natural state of affairs" rather than an expression of inequality and privilege. Criminology develops theories about the criminality of the poor rather than examining harms of the rich.

In turn, the criminal law controlling the offenses of the poor rather than the offenses of the rich appears to reflect the legitimacy of an agreed-on definition of "dangerous" crime and typical criminals.

When crime theory unreflectively takes the criminal law as a given, the fiction of crime as neutral law sets in (Platt 1974). Working within the confines of "crime" as defined by the law cedes control of criminology to lawmakers and the political process that produces criminal law. Thus, many social harms—environmental pollution, workplace injuries, defective products, neocolonialism, and crimes against humanity—are excluded from study, even though they present more of a threat to people's well-being and security than much of what is officially designated as crime (Barak 1991; Reiman and Leighton 2023).

Among the main theorists exposing the myth of neutral criminal law were the nineteenth-century philosophers and political economists Karl Marx and Friedrich Engels, who noted that the law helps uphold a very unequal distribution of property and resources. Marx and Engels thus "insisted that the institutions of the state and law, and the doctrines that emerge from them, serve the interests of the dominant economic class" (Beirne and Messerschmidt 2000: 110). For them, crime was not about the defects of morality or biology, but rather about the defects of society and the product of the exploitation and alienation caused by the repressive conditions of industrial capitalism (Chambliss and Seidman 1982; Quinney 1977).

Research on the link between social disadvantage and crime is no longer a priority as it once was for a brief period during President Johnson's "Great Society" of the 1960s. Inequality is rarely an explanatory factor, and reducing inequality is even less frequently a recommended policy. By not being studied, or considered appropriate for policy recommendations, the current level of inequality becomes taken for granted and seen as natural.

Among those who look at issues related to class, an important finding is that poverty itself is not the key, because "if that was the case, then graduate students would be very dangerous people indeed" (Currie 1998: 134). The important concepts in varieties of strain theory thus relate to inequality, relative deprivation, and blocked opportunities. As Elliott Currie points out, the important contribution to crime and violence is "the experience of life year in, year out at the bottom of a harsh, depriving, and excluding social system [that] wears away at the psychological and communal conditions that sustain healthy human development" (1998: 134).

Braithwaite discusses the importance of poverty, but within the context of inequality. High levels of inequality mean that there are more poor and destitute than would exist under a more equal distribution. Thus, "there are criminals motivated by the need for a decent standard of living, where 'decent' can mean what they perceive most people in their community enjoy, what whites but not blacks enjoy, what they used to enjoy before they lost their jobs, or what they were led to expect to enjoy by advertising and dramatization of bourgeois lifestyles on television" (Braithwaite 1992: 82). Inequality also produces more structural degradation—the experience of being poor when supposedly anyone can make it if they try hard enough—which Braithwaite argues is important because humiliation is linked with rage and violence.

Further, a "classless" criminology does not apply strain theory to the rich. They, too, want more money but have limited legitimate opportunities to make additional millions or billions. They can innovate with their wealth to create novel and sophisticated illegitimate opportunities. Crime is also more likely if inequality means that the wealthy are unaccountable for their harmful actions and if inequality leads the wealthy to have less respect for the poor. The wealthy develop an ideology, a system of beliefs that justifies inequality and their exploitation as natural, inevitable, and ultimately fair. Ultimately, the "propensity to feel powerless and exploited among the poor and the propensity of the rich to see exploiting as legitimate . . . enable crime" (Braithwaite 1992: 94).

Class also distorts criminology when people assume that the poor are the most criminal and only study them in spite of numerous studies dating back to the 1940s showing that serious criminal behavior is widespread among middle- and upper-class individuals, even if they are rarely arrested (Reiman and Leighton 2023). In his underappreciated book on the troubles of middle-class youth, Currie notes that the "long tradition of research on juvenile delinquency had shown us again and again that the problems of drugs and violence among middle-class youth were both widespread and surprisingly severe, though mostly absent from our official statistics" (2005b: 5). The standard operating procedure in criminology is to uncritically assume that higher social class is a protective factor against delinquent behavior rather than protective against being arrested, charged, and convicted.

However, Luthar researched peer support for substance abuse among inner-city (minority) youth and realized she needed a comparison group to draw meaningful conclusions. So she conducted similar investigations among affluent (white) suburban youth, finding that delinquency rates were "comparable" and "substance use levels among affluent, suburban teenagers were significantly higher than among their inner-city counterparts," as was peer support for it (in Mooney and Leighton 2019). She started to investigate why and subsequently reported on "The Problem with Rich Kids" (Luthar 2013). She found in affluent families an "overemphasis on status and wealth," as well as pressure for perfection and accomplishment that took precedence over the development of moral character. "Scheduled hyperactivity" led to a work hard–party hard environment, with emotionally and physically absent parents. Money and privacy led youth to have easy access to alcohol, fake forms of identification, pharmaceuticals, and other illegal drugs.

Currie's book *The Road to Whatever* (2005b) argues that middle-class youth have substantial problems with drug addiction, anger, desperation, and delinquency. Poverty and race cannot be the cause of these issues, and Currie argues that they are reflections of larger cultural problems. He sees the middle class as having internalized a "harsh and neglectful individualism," producing a "high demand, low support environment" that is "quick to punish and slow to help."

When problems appeared with middle-class youth, insurance made it easy to systematically overprescribe drugs in a "reflection of a cultural predilection for the quick fix, an unwillingness to grapple with difficult issues" (Currie 2005b: 137). Instead of nonjudgmental listening and pragmatic support, Currie finds that "the withdrawal of support" is regarded as an acceptable and laudable way of dealing with problems. In addition to a "tendency to give up on kids who could not overcome their problems," there was also "a readiness to shame, isolate, and punish them in the name of 'treatment'" (Currie 2005b: 155). Many who have grown up in these environments recognize these dynamics from friends, family, and classmates, but criminology still manages to focus their attention on crimes of the poor.

Other notable wrongdoing by the wealthy involves white-collar and corporate crime. Sutherland (1939) coined the term "white-collar crime" in a talk about how a major deficiency of criminological theory was that it could not explain crime by the rich. In coining the term, Sutherland did not claim this was a new phenomenon, which he traced back to the early days of the United States. But the term and his work helped focus a small number of scholars on crimes where the perpetrator was an upper-class person, the crime was committed in the course of the criminal's occupation, and the crime was a violation of trust. Criminology was slow to follow up on Sutherland's research, and its primary focus still remains on street crime, although crimes by the upper class exact a far heavier toll in terms of dollars and lives (Reiman and Leighton 2023). The criminological literature spends little time trying to explain or understand financial fraud. An analysis of 4,878 articles in fifteen criminology journals showed that only 6.3 percent were about white-collar crime—and only 3.4 percent in the ten journals ranked highest in prestige (McGurrin et al. 2013: 9).

Further, "white-collar crime" includes crimes committed by both the powerful and the relatively powerless. For example, embezzlement and improper use of a credit card qualify as types of "white-collar" crime, but they should not be confused with those crimes of the powerful committed by large corporations, financial institutions, or governments. A careful examination of these acts thus requires looking at the relative power of the criminal and victim. The most frequently discussed white-collar crimes are employee pilfering and credit card fraud, in which businesses, corporations, and financial institutions are the victims. The least frequently discussed are corporate and government crime, in which the powerful are the perpetrators who are victimizing employees, consumers, taxpayers, or the environment. "Insurance fraud" usually means false claims against the industry, not improper denials of claims by insurance companies; likewise, workplace theft usually means stealing by employees but should also include improper withholding (wage theft) from paychecks. Accordingly, studies of white-collar crime should pay attention to crimes of the powerful whose actions and practices violate the rights of groups of people or cause harm to workers, consumers, communities, and the environment.

Individuals in a corporation who violate the law in the corporation's interests, who also benefit themselves individually through bonuses and promotions, perpetrate *corporate crimes*. These involve a range of practices that victimize employees, consumers, the environment, stockholders, and creditors. Acts also may include fraud against the government, which victimizes taxpayers. Anticompetitive practices cause higher prices for consumers and put downward pressure on wages and working conditions. *Corporate violence* refers to acts that inflict physical and emotional suffering rather than simply monetary losses, as in the case of dangerous or defective products, unsafe working conditions, and health problems caused by pollution or toxic exposure to chemicals and unsafe food. These harms, injuries, and violations may be national or transnational in scope. *Environmental crimes* are perpetrated by corporations and government actions that add to environmental degradation and the climate crisis. *Crimes of globalization* may involve the exploitation of workers in developing countries as well as the related policies and practices of global financial institutions such as the International Monetary Fund, the World Bank, and the megabanks of developed nations.

Public officials who are trying to perpetuate a specific administration, exercise general government power, or accomplish undue influence on behalf of large campaign contributors perpetrate *state crime*. The victims can be as widespread as all taxpayers who are forced to pay for corruption, fraud, and sweetheart deals. Victims can also be a specific political group—or even its leaders—who are denied basic political rights through surveillance and harassment. Finally, *state-corporate crimes* represent hybrid forms of state- and corporate-organized crimes working together.

With all these various forms of crime and white-collar crime, collectively referred to as "crimes of the powerful," class biases operate in the social construction of "perpetrators" and "victims." Serial killers who commit street crimes are a trendy topic of study for criminologists, but criminology devotes little attention to trafficking in human beings or to mass slaughter, including genocide.

## Race and Criminology

*Race* is a problematic concept that is often used to categorize physical characteristics, while *ethnicity* typically refers to national origin, language, culture, and religion. Though race *seems* to be a coherent and stable concept, it is socially constructed: the creation of racial categories and their placement in a hierarchy was done by white people to maintain their power. Calling race socially constructed is meant to draw attention to the very real social, legal, and political consequences of categorizing people. Consider that no other nation uses the same categories as the United States, which has changed the categories over time. "Hispanic" is an ethnicity rather than a race because of lobbying by the Mexican government, which did not want Mexicans categorized as nonwhite given the legal discrimination against Black people historically. These issues are explored in chapter 4, while this section reviews some of the connections between criminology and the racial hierarchies that privilege some and disadvantage others.

Historically, research on crime has consciously and unconsciously reproduced the racism of prevailing social attitudes, while also being a site for resistance. For example, Lombroso wrote, "The white races represented the triumph of the human species, its hitherto most perfect advancement" (in Miller 1996: 185). As discussed above, this belief influenced his criminal anthropology and became the basis for policies that repressed nonwhites throughout the world. In contrast, Willem Bonger wrote *Race and Crime* in 1943 as a critique against the growing fascist movement in Europe and arguments about the superiority of Nordic peoples (Hawkins 1995: 23).

American criminology and social science have generally been characterized by a "liberal political tone and assumptions" that sees Black disadvantage as attributable to white prejudice rather than biological inferiority (Hawkins 1995). Hawkins starts his analysis with W. E. B. Du Bois (1868–1963), a prominent Black intellectual who is typically omitted from criminology texts. He is important because "many of the most virulently racist, social Darwinist critiques of black life were published during the period he wrote [and] Du Bois was among the first to provide a retort to their argument" (Hawkins 1995: 13). Du Bois seemed to accept the higher rates of Black (street) criminality; he ascribed them to the social disruption and urban migration that occurred after the end of slavery as well as to the legacy of physical, sexual, and emotional abuse that accompanied the enslavement of Africans.

Sellin shared some of Du Bois's analysis of crime, recognizing that Black crime rates might be higher than whites' because "it would be extraordinary, indeed if this group were to prove more law-abiding than the white, which enjoys more fully the advantages of a civilization the Negro has helped to create" (1928: 64). Sutherland and Sellin did theorize about the importance of culture for criminality, but they saw culture as somewhat different from nationality (based on political boundaries) and race. Important data for them included the observation that immigrants from the same culture would have different rates of criminality, depending on the age at which they arrived in the United States and the number of generations their family had been here—data that cannot be explained by reference to biology or genetics.

Shaw and McKay's study of social ecology in Chicago neighborhoods also questioned the importance of biology and genetics because "no racial, national or nativity group exhibits a uniform, characteristic rate of delinquents in all parts of Chicago" (1942: 153). The key factor for them in explaining delinquency was social disorganization rather than the racial traits of those who lived in certain areas. Wolfgang and Cohen (1970) later elaborated on the persistence of high rates of criminality among Black folks while other immigrant groups had moved out of socially disorganized communities and zones of transition. In particular, they noted that these Black residents faced more blocked opportunities because of racism than white immigrants and that the legacy of racial oppression creates pessimism among the Black community, whereas white immigrants remained optimistic about achieving the American dream.

Wolfgang and Cohen's *Crime and Race* (1970) also critiques biological determinism and a genetic predetermination to general criminality. Like Bonger, they argue that criminality is not a specific trait like eye color:

> According to Mendel's rule of inheritance of specific traits, if criminality were genetically determined, we should inherit specific tendencies for embezzlement, burglary, forgery, etc. And if we inherited specific criminal forms of behavior, and some of us were genetically destined to be burglars or stock embezzlers, rapists or check forgers, we would also have to inherit specific noncriminal occupations, which would mean some of us would be genetically destined to become police officers or truck drivers or school teachers, as to have red hair. (Wolfgang and Cohen 1970: 92)

The critique in the preceding paragraphs does not mean that criminology should exclude the disciplines of biology, physiology, and genetics from a comprehensive and integrated approach (Barak 1998). Our concern is that because racial classification is based on political factors, the link between race and crime is problematic.

This liberal tradition in criminology tries to balance a recognition that racial bias inflates the officially counted criminality of minorities with an awareness that minorities frequently live in criminogenic conditions where overpolicing also occurs. Thus, Hawkins argues for the development of a conflict perspective, which examines official records of minority crime as an index of social control that shows "how the criminal justice system is used by the dominant ethnic and racial groups to maintain their status" (1995: 34). This perspective contends that contact with the criminal justice system (which begins with police interactions) has as much to do with social standing as it does with criminal conduct, and perhaps more because of overpolicing in some neighborhoods coupled with racial profiling.

Currently, mainstream positivist criminology is developing "general theories" of crime, which do not account for the oppression of minority groups. Indeed, "a foundational assumption of the general theories is that causes of crime are racially invariant—that is, African Americans and Whites commit crimes for identical reasons" (Unnever et al. 2019: 3). By extension, they assume "that 'Blackness' is interchangeable with other racial categories" (León 2021: 21). The criticism is that "these general approaches largely erase the country's racial history and its role in both causing crime and criminalizing race" (Unnever et al. 2019: 3; Steffensmeier et al. 2010; Wright et al. 2016). Thus, such general criminological theories and theorists presume that the history of racial oppression and its current structural reality is unimportant for understanding crime, as is understanding race as a reason why some people's actions are criminalized more than others. Ultimately, the racial invariance thesis is a neutral-sounding assumption that covers up power dynamics whereby criminological theories made by white men to explain the criminality and deviance of minorities erases the racial oppression of that society and its link back to crime by minorities.

Even though general strain theory (GST) seems to be a general theory, it has been adapted to recognize the unique strains of Black and Latino/a/x people—and women. GST recognizes that strain can involve losing something valuable, failing to achieve a goal, or experiencing something unpleasant. These strains lead to depression, anger, and frustration, and the reaction to these negative emotions can involve crime. Rather than assuming that life's strains fall equally on everyone—"add and stir" approaches—a race-centric GST suggests that

> Blacks experience race-specific strains such as disadvantaged social positions, racial discrimination, economic shortcomings, and injustices which are conducive to crime. Given a relative lack of social support and access to legitimate coping resources due to their structural position in American society, Blacks are more likely to cope with strains and the induced negative emotions with crime compared to Whites. (Isom Scott et al. 2020: 3)

Latinx general strain theory (Isom Scott et al. 2020) notes that while the Latino/a/x population does not face the same level of discrimination as Black people, immigration and deportation concerns are additional sources of strain. Real and presumed abilities with English are reasons for discrimination, and many face "acculturation-related strains, or the stresses that may arise from trying to reconcile cultural differences" (Isom Scott et al. 2020: 4; Rabin et al. 2022).

Going beyond GST are efforts to build a Black criminology and a Latino/a/x criminology (LatCrim). Both explore how experiences with "injustice at the hands of criminal justice officials support existing societal inequalities" and the ways in which "ethnoracial inequalities in the United States in education, employment, and health are exacerbated by the disproportionate imprisonment of groups of color" (Krivo and Peterson 2009: 9–10). While Black criminology can be traced back to W. E. B. Du Bois, its modern origins are Russell's work (1992). Today, "the premise of Black Criminology is that race is a central organizing theme in understanding African American offenders, African Americans victims, how the judicial system criminalizes African Americans and treats them more punitively" (Unnever et al. 2019: 5). Works such as *A Theory of African American Offending* recognize that centuries of subordination have created a worldview—one "continually being reaffirmed and shaped as African Americans confront everyday racism" (Unnever and Gabbidon 2011: xvii)—that is related to offending. Factors such as unjust treatment at the hands of criminal justice system employees can also weaken respect for the law and are public degradation ceremonies that can incite anger. The theory also recognizes that Black people are disproportionately poor and have higher exposure to environmental toxins such as lead, which can increase criminality.

While LatCrim shares many of the same general goals, it starts from the premise that "the lived experiences of Latinxs in America are still not fully incorporated into the understanding of their pathways into and resilience against crime and the criminal justice system" (Isom Scott et al. 2020: 4). Among many issues is that data are frequently broken down into white/Black or white/nonwhite categories, thus erasing the Latino/a/x population (León 2021). LatCrim is also more conscious about how criminological research and theorizing comes from the Global North and can carry support for colonialism (Grewcock 2018). As one of the founders of postcolonial studies explains, colonialism involves the belief that "'they' were not like 'us,' and for that reason deserved to be ruled" (Said 1994: xiii). Thus, LatCrim recognizes the "impact of colonization on the different areas of knowledge production" (Maldonado-Torres 2007: 242).

As Cunneen (2014) writes, "current criminal justice processes (including risk assessment) continue to single out indigenous peoples as a 'crime-prone' population," and empirically informed discourse largely excludes the "broader framework of the effects of colonization." Some scholars do emphasize colonialism (Agozino and Pfohl 2003; Monchalin 2016), but these are exceptions to the dominant trends in criminological research. Scholars of race and injustice have to compellingly show how supposedly race-blind institutions are racist, instead of mainstream scholars having to compellingly show that they are not.

## Gender/Sexuality and Criminology

Sex, gender, and sexuality refer to people's biology, identification, and sexual orientation. As we explore in chapter 5, society and criminology are sites for patriarchy, a system that privileges men and perpetuates their unequal power. Women are subjected to stereotypes, control of reproductive functions, and gender violence, from street harassment to sexual assault to intimate partner violence. Another main concern is that gender roles and social expectations carry a strong expectation of heterosexuality, and *heteronormativity* promotes the belief that heterosexuality is the only normal and natural way to be. LGBTQ+ people raise questions about that belief, and the bullying, harassment, hate crimes, and legislation to legalize discrimination reveal how much effort goes into maintaining a supposedly natural system. This section reviews how these issues are reflected, recreated, and challenged in criminology.

Historically, gender has not been the explicit focus of research in mainstream or "malestream" criminology: research conducted by males, on males, for males. On the surface, the marginalization of gender results because men have been the majority of criminal offenders, especially serious violent offenders, and have dominated the criminal justice system from lawmakers to parole officers. Women have made up a smaller percentage of offenders and have tended to commit less serious crimes than men. But in addition, criminology reflects and recreates a larger view that women's lives, experiences, and thoughts are not as important as men's. The data from women is seen as not worth theorizing about, and theory based on men is "universal" and can be applied to women and people who are nonbinary or queer.

Further, criminology reflects and reproduces patterns that fail to consider the connection between masculinity and the higher rates of crime—especially violence—that men commit. For example, men are the majority of homicide victims, and the perpetrators are overwhelmingly other men rather than women. Women also suffer significant victimization, overwhelmingly from men known to them rather than other women. So why isn't the fact that men are the predominant perpetrators more central to criminological analysis? If the proportion of men and women killing, doing school shootings, spree killing, and becoming serial killers were reversed, would more focus be on *women and femininity*?

In taking all of this into account, the message has been that women do not especially matter as victims, within the criminal legal system, within the discipline of criminology, or as employees in male-dominated agencies. When women were studied, historically theorists considered women as being particularly determined by their biology. Lombroso, for example, studied women offenders to support his theory that criminals were physically anomalous. After taking extensive measurements, he concluded that the born-female offender was closer to a normal man than a normal woman. However, he also sought to distinguish between different types of female criminals: "Unlike the 'semi-masculine, tyrannical and selfish' born criminal who wants only to satisfy her own passions, the occasional [female] offender puts trust in her male protectors and regains confidence in men—especially her lawyer, and in some cases that Lombroso is fond of relating, her executioner" (Hart 1994: 23).

Another failure of early positivist theorists, especially those with a psychological or psychoanalytic approach, was the perception that women's deviance was peculiarly sexual. For example, Pollak (1950) argued that women's tendency toward deceit stemmed from their physiological ability to hide their true sexual feelings and the social expectation that they will conceal menstruation and menopause. Freud stated that women had "penis envy," and W. I. Thomas believed that women had a biological need to feel loved and that this need could lead to prostitution. Thomas also believed that women were the property of men (Belknap 2020).

While those are no longer mainstream beliefs, there are residuals of those beliefs in current social expectations about what some deem "appropriate" gender behavior and the pressure for conformity they generate. Further, "as an official agent of social control, the criminal justice system responds not only to crime but also transgressions against gender norms" (Flavin 2009: 4). One important way the criminal justice system achieves this end is by becoming weaponized in matters of reproductive choice:

> By restricting some women's access to abortion and obstetric and gynecological care, by telling some women not to procreate and pressuring them to be sterilized, by prosecuting some women who use drugs and become pregnant, and by failing to support the efforts of incarcerated women and battered women to rear their children, the law and the criminal justice system establish what a "good woman" or "fit mother" should look like and how conception, pregnancy, birth and child care and socialization are regulated. (Flavin 2009: 4)

Generally, the women prosecuted are poor and/or minority women, which highlights the importance of looking at intersections [chapter 6] and has become crucial to understanding the impact of the 2022 Supreme Court case declaring that there is no constitutionally protected right to abortion.

In the twentieth century, criminologists moved away from viewing deviant behavior as inherently abnormal and pathological. Models started to examine external sources of crime, such as poverty, social structure, and racial discrimination. Despite this trend, most studies of crime continued to look exclusively at men and boys. But in the 1970s, with the advent of feminist criminology, research on gender—specifically girls and women—became more important. However, male-centered criminology maintained that their existing research could apply to women and the findings would be the same. This "add women and stir" approach was challenged by feminist scholars such as Chesney-Lind (Belknap 2004) and many others who continue to draw attention to the importance of methodological frameworks that focus on gender. Criminological theories including (but not limited to) strain, differential association and learning, control, labeling, and life course were not focused primarily on gender in their initial development. However, in time, these more traditional theories have been applied to girls and women by moving beyond the "add women and stir" mentality and instead having women and girls as the subject matter of the research.

For example, strain theories have evolved since the 1930s when Merton discussed social goals and the means of achieving them. For instance, some people will use innovation and illegitimate means like crime to achieve goals of success when legitimate opportunities are blocked. The theory is rooted in class struggle but fails to recognize that women are disproportionately poor and that gender discrimination leads to fewer legitimate means for success—yet women commit *less* crime than men do (Belknap 2020). Other strain theories that examine emotional responses to negative stimuli find that "gender differences appear to emerge because males are more likely than females to respond to strain and negative emotions through illegal behavior" (De Coster and Heimer 2018: 1887).

At present the increased interest in testing, challenging, and creating new research projects to explore the experiences of girls and women in the criminal legal system has moved away from the application of these historically male-centered theories. For example, research on pathways into crime finds extremely high percentages of sexual abuse in the lifetimes of women: 86 percent of girls, 71 percent of women, and 60 percent of women in jails experienced sexual violence, partner violence, or caregiver violence (Vera Institute of Justice 2016). Feminist pathways thus holds that

> early experiences of physical child abuse, sexual abuse, and other forms of trauma, as well as financial marginality and relational difficulties (e.g., familial drug use, intimate partner violence), start women on a trajectory toward criminal offending. In response to these traumatic and abusive experiences, some women develop mental health difficulties and attempt to cope and survive by engaging in behaviors such as running away, sex work, misbehavior at school, and substance use. (Sutton and Simons 2021: 27)

Awareness of this victimization has led to criticism of the criminalization of survival behaviors and advocacy for a trauma-informed approach for those who have survived crime (Cook et al. 2022), including within queer criminology (Buist and Semprevivo 2022; Katz 2022).

As an established body of feminist theory and feminist criminology research grows, feminist research has begun to contribute to our understanding of crime and men's high incidence of criminality. This speaks to the importance of recognizing gender as being more than a women's issue and working toward feminist standpoints that include a theoretical and analytical focus on multiple relations of class, race, and gender (Megan and Brunsma 2017). Among these challenges is the fact that inherited ways of thinking obstruct our ability to imagine alternative ways of viewing crime and punishment. In other words, the existing biases built into our knowledge base make it difficult to imagine what a fully inclusive and transformed body of knowledge, gendered and otherwise, will be like.

Among the most significant existing biases is to see gender as binary (masculine and feminine) and to assume heterosexuality (that is, to make heteronormative assumptions). Just as "malestream" criminology emphasized research conducted by males, on males, for males, it has reinforced heteronormative institutions and thus also contributed to the marginalization of LGBTQ+ people and a distortion of gender when it does study them. Feminist criminology's focus on gender-related issues as well as critical criminology's interest in power has been integral to the development of what is called "queer criminology," which centers research on the LGBTQ+ population. (The authors of *Queer Criminology* note that "the word *queer* makes some people cringe" [Buist and Lenning 2016: 3], and its use will be explained more in chapter 5.)

Understanding the marginalization of the LGBTQ+ population more fully develops a critique of how history and the current operation of the criminal legal system have historically criminalized marginalized populations. Queer criminology studies the experiences of LGBTQ+ folks in the criminal legal system who have been targets of victimization, who have justice system involvement whether convicted of crimes or not, and who are working within the system (Buist and Lenning 2023). Criminology has limited its study of these populations to the deviance literature and as victims of hate crimes, and it needs to "come out of the closet." One example is Panfil's study of gay men who are in street gangs: "In a discipline thoroughly interested in peer networks and group dynamics, it is only logical to investigate how primarily-queer, primarily-heterosexual, or mixed peer groups influence delinquency and criminality" (2013: 108).

Queer criminology also investigates why states want to make it a felony for a transgender person to use a bathroom that does not correspond to what is listed on their birth certificate. The point is not to "add queer and stir" but to transform theory and justice by recognizing "sexuality and gender identity as integral to one's experiences in the same manner in which we recognize the significance of race or social class"—as "an inherent part of one's self and something that has bearing on experiences and outcomes in the criminal legal system" (Buist and Lenning 2016: 120). Further, as pathways theory has been integral to feminist-centered approaches to criminological research, queer criminology has explored the impact victimization has on the criminal justice involvement of LGBTQ+ people.

## Intersectionality and Criminology

Discussions of intersections and intersectionality refer to overcoming the limitations of "adding a variable and stirring"—or ignoring marginalized people and their experiences on both micro and macro levels. Social science often tries to hold "all else equal" to model the influence of one variable (e.g., class *or* race *or* gender/sexuality) on another. While each is important in its own right, by themselves they provide an incomplete description of a person's life experiences and "social location." A person may be white, but multibillionaires are different from those considered "white trash" or "rednecks"; rich and poor white women will have some different experiences and concerns than their male counterparts.

Intersectionality is sometimes illustrated by picturing each class having its own color or pattern—and the same with race, ethnicity, and national origin, as well as each combination of sex, gender, and sexuality. The intersection of these would reflect a wide variety of patterns and shades of color. The larger reason for highlighting people's patterns is "understanding how multiple social identities such as race, gender, sexual orientation, SES [socioeconomic status], and disability intersect at the micro level of individual experience to reflect interlocking systems of privilege and oppression (i.e., racism, sexism, heterosexism, classism) at the macro social-structural level" (in Harris and Leonardo 2018: 2).

The term "intersectionality" and its status as a subject of explicit study is recent, but the tensions behind the intersections of class, race, and gender are long-standing. For example, the women's suffrage movement and the feminist movement were criticized for mostly benefiting white women, especially middle-class white women. Black women have been told that the Black civil rights movement was about race, not gender, which effectively means it centered on the interests of Black men. Black feminism called out such problems and was thus instrumental in the development of an intersectional approach to social oppression. Although the development of Black feminism evolved for many years, the Combahee River Collective ([1977] 2015) is often attributed with its development, and their 1977 statement noted,

> The most general statement of our politics at the present time would be that we are actively committed to struggling against racial, sexual, heterosexual, and class

oppression, and see as our particular task the development of integrated analysis and practice based upon the fact that the major systems of oppression are interlocking.

Feminist and other critical scholars continue to demand an intersectional approach that must include class, race, gender, sexual identity, and more. Globally, Gomes (2021) has examined the importance of decolonizing the field to include diversity and move beyond whiteness, masculinity, and binary gender expectations. She further argues "that how we understand gender depends on how we understand race and class and vice versa." That starts with critiquing the construction of "categories of whiteness and blackness, masculinity and femininity" (Gomes 2021: 96).

Kendall's book, *Hood Feminism*, brilliantly explores the importance of multifaceted feminism to include gun violence, hunger, education, housing, and more. Kendall notes that since mainstream feminism rhetoric has been

> rooted in biases like racism, ableism, transmisogyny, anti-Semitism, and Islamophobia, it automatically works against marginalized women and against any concept of solidarity. It's not enough to know that other women with different experiences exist; you must also understand that they have their own feminism formed by that experience. (2020: 7)

While it may seem obvious to use class and race and gender to get a "fix" on a person's social location, it is easier said than done. One of those dimensions may be more important than the others in a specific situation, but that factor will not always be most important—and theorists have not created good models to understand whether class or race or gender or sexuality will be most important (and why). Further, the combination of factors does not work in a simple additive way like 1 + 1. Combining devaluation because of gender with devaluation because of race creates gendered racism, which can be far more powerful because of the interacting dynamics. Adding further marginalized statuses—poor, lesbian, immigrant, non-Christian—dramatically escalates oppression further in ways that are multiplicative (Collins 1990).

Intersectionality is further explored in chapter 6, and its development in criminology reflects the tensions and trajectory described above. For example, the *radical* perspective in criminology that emerged in the late 1960s and early 1970s drew heavily from Marx's ideas about capitalism, so it emphasized how class conflict was at the root of most crime and crime control. In examining the historical male bias in criminology and the importance of class for early critical criminology, Cook notes: "Yes, it is important to study social class and crime and we need to expand our conceptualizations of crime . . . as to examine gender, race, socioeconomic class, heteronormativity, and their impacts on crime" (2016: 335).

Marxist feminist criminology advanced intersectionality by analyzing how class and capitalism differentially impact women and contribute to gender inequality. Separately, Black criminology (Russell 1992) sought to understand and explain crime committed by Black people, and it advocated the analysis of how the criminal legal system impacts the Black community. Thus, the almost exclusive focus on class broadened to include fuller intersectional consideration of how people act, how others respond to and define those actions as criminal, how certain actions are viewed as more or less serious or as more or less "criminal" and deviant, and how the law and legal systems are organized to control behavior in highly stratified and unequal societies (Potter 2013).

Intersectionality in criminology can be applied in two main ways. First, it primarily suggests "centering the margins" (Shah 2021), which means investigating the experiences of and oppressive dynamics on populations that have been marginalized and rendered invisible. The focus of many of these efforts is thus on women of color (Miller 2008; Potter 2013). For example, as Lissa Yellowbird investigated the disappearance of an oil worker, readers see the impact of class as the Indigenous people in the area of the oil boom continue to struggle to make ends meet—especially Indigenous women—while corporations and a handful of individuals profit from the pain inflicted by poor safety regulations (Murdoch 2021). In addition, research centering the margins reveals that the criminal legal system is just one of several strong systems of social control that operate especially harshly on Black women. There is also the welfare system and the child welfare system that result in sustained surveillance and judgments about the women's work, reproduction, and mothering practices (Gurusami 2019). Centering the margins also includes the LGBTQ+ population (Buist and Lemming 2023).

The second application of intersectionality to criminology is to create a more purposeful examination of certain intersections, even if they are not the most marginalized. For example, chapter 8 opens by describing Paul Butler's *Chokehold* (2017) about the policing of Black communities and his belief that a "Black + male" intersectional approach is important to understanding the role of masculinity. Butler does not say Black men are the most abused group—just that "intersectionality teaches us that gender matters for black men as well, and ignoring gender undermines the chances of making things better" (2017). In a different way, examining the violence of working-class adolescent males against girlfriends and gay people revealed their feelings of powerlessness, despair, and humiliation regarding their future economic prospects because those feelings were related to anxiety about living up to the masculine ideal of "breadwinner" as well as their heterosexuality (Totten 2000).

Both applications of intersectionality to criminology have a foundation in critical legal studies. For example, critical race theory starts with the recognition that racism is an ingrained aspect of American society that cannot be readily remedied by law, and that laws and legal frameworks are not race-neutral concepts. Developed in the late 1970s through the efforts of scholars who were discontent with the slow pace of achieving racial justice (Delgado 1995), critical race theorists argue that the racism that permeates society is part of a socially constructed reality that promotes the interests of men and women in elite groups. While critical race theory assumes the reality of structural racism, not everyone who believes in structural racism is a critical race theorist. In fact, critical race theorists are critical of many strategies and ideas advanced by liberals, and they believe that racial progress, like "civil rights gains for communities of color[,] coincide with the dictates of white self-interest" (Delgado and Stefancic 2012: 22). For example, the *Brown v. Board of Education* desegregation case had less to do with the recognition of Black people's rights than with how the United States was "locked in the Cold War, a titanic struggle with the forces of communism for the loyalties of uncommitted emerging nations, most of which were Black, brown or Asian." So, the United States had to soften its stance toward minorities. "The interests of whites and Blacks, for a brief moment, converged" (Delgado and Stefancic 2012: 23). (Historians have found many communications from U.S. ambassadors around the world that support this position.)

Similarly, critical race feminism emerged from critical race theory to address the gap between what tended to be white feminism and critical race theories focusing on men (Wing 1997). Specifically, critical race feminists have objected both to feminist approaches that presume white middle-class women's experiences are representative of all women's experiences and to critical race scholarship that presumes minority women's experiences are all the same and can be represented by the experiences of their minority male counterparts. The effect of what are called "essentialist perspectives" has been to "reduce the lives of people who experience multiple forms of oppression to addition problems: 'racism + sexism = straight black women's experience'" (Harris 1997: 11). In other words, racial and ethnic minority women—as victims, offenders, and workers—are not simply subjected to quantitatively "more" disadvantage than white women; their oppression is of a qualitatively different kind.

In a similar fashion, critical white studies (Delgado and Stefancic 1997) considers what it means to be white in the United States. Far from being a safe haven for white supremacists, critical white studies prompts whites and nonwhites alike to consider the legacy of whiteness and to ask questions like, How do whites as members of the dominant race benefit (or not) depending on their place in the social order of stratification? What does white privilege mean to the poorest whites—sometimes called "white trash"—and to the poorest white women especially? How has our culture constructed "whiteness" and "Blackness" such that they are not neutral descriptors but laden with meaning, value, and status? Thus, critical white studies underscores that whiteness is not an objective position or natural default position for looking at the world but a racialized perspective with consequences for all racial groups.

The various critical theories inform an intersectional criminology that investigates how power shapes people's lives and behavior, whether by making victimization, crime, and deviance more likely or by simply making it more likely that they will be labeled as criminals and deviants. Intersectionality is an antidote for times when "everyone has the same risk of victimization" is comforting but wrong. It explores the very power dynamics that need to be explored and understood to create a fairer criminal legal system—and it explores why those power dynamics are obscured. Understanding that some groups are privileged because of their class, race/ethnicity, and gender/sexuality is also important because privilege is the unifying concept underlying these three variables.

## Implications

The criminal law furnishes the basis for much of criminology and criminal justice study as though the law were objective or neutral. However, while some laws serve the interests of most people, most laws reflect the special or partisan interests of elected people who have conscious and subconscious desires in maintaining the privileged orders or status quo of which they are obvious benefactors. Reiman asserts that criminology needs philosophical reflection on the nature of crime "to establish its intellectual independence of the state" and thus declare "its status as a social science rather than an agency of social control, as critical rather than servile, as illumination rather than propaganda" (Reiman and Leighton 2023: 256). Similarly, criminology also needs reflection on and independence from class, race, and gender constructs if it is not to become simply another tool of social control and propaganda for an unequal status quo.

This reflection on the nature of crime and crime control is especially important because the definition of crime drives the resources of policing and the rest of the criminal justice system. It also becomes the basis for theorizing about crime as well as for the collection of official data that are used for research about crime and presented in criminology books to explain crime. Without critical reflection, the criminal law appears neutral and above question because its values seem reinforced by police activity that is focused on, say, street crime rather than white-collar crime and by criminological theory, data, and books that also have the same emphasis or focus as the criminal law.

The discipline of criminology—which is the study of the causes of crime and the treatment of offenders—is part of the criminal justice enterprise. Studies that define what the crime problem is and what to do about it also draw on and reinforce hierarchies of status and power along the lines of class, race, and gender/sexuality. Consider this summary of research about COVID and crime (Piquero 2021), published in a prestigious journal, which stated that "the most significant findings" indicated:

> (1) a steady increase in specific forms of violence, including primarily homicides/community gun violence and domestic violence; (2) reductions or stability in virtually all property crimes, but the acceleration of certain types of offending, such as fraud and cybercrime, due in large part to increased reliance on the internet and related platforms; (3) the emergence of new crime types, such as public health violations for breaking COVID-19 safety protocols; (4) a reduction in prison and jail populations—especially in the first 6–9 months of the pandemic; (5) a rapid spread of viral infections in jails and prisons; (6) a substantial increase in opioid use and fatalities; (6) the creation of gaps in the delivery of needed medical and mental health screening and treatment; and (7) an initial reduction in police stops, citations, and arrests—particularly in the first few months of the pandemic as many departments pulled back on patrol and limited contact with the public in large part due to viral spread, lockdowns—leading to fewer persons out in public, and a lack of protective equipment.

The areas of criminological research of the COVID era identified above are certainly important, but research on hate crimes against Asian Americans is notably missing, consistent with how criminology often overlooks Asians (Zhang et al. 2022). The omission of hate crimes against Asians is surprising because, in a rare display of bipartisan agreement, Congress passed the COVID-19 Hate Crimes Act. Its preamble bears witness to hate crimes and violence against Asian Americans and Pacific Islanders, including a killing in Atlanta, Georgia, where six of the eight victims were Asian women. Not only were hate crimes against them increasing before the pandemic (Ren and Feagin 2021), but violent crimes against Asian Americans nearly doubled from 2015 to 2018, and they were the only racial group that has experienced increased victimization across all offense types between 2008 and 2019 (Zhang et al. 2022). Into this environment, then-president Trump fueled animosity by talking about the "Chinese virus" (Gover et al. 2020: 655). So, by April 2021, over a third of Asian adults in the United States "feared someone might threaten or physically attack them" (Ruiz et al. 2021).

These problems reflect what has been called "Orientalism," which refers to attitudes seeing Western people and culture as superior to "the Orient" (the Middle East, Africa, and Asia) (Moosavi 2019). Orientalism justified the colonial extraction of wealth, the exploitation of Asian laborers, the internment of Japanese people in the United States during World War II, and other forms of marginalization—including forms that spill into criminology (Wu et al. 2021).

In addition, the article (Piquero 2021, quoted above) reviewing the "significant findings" notes the reduction in police stops because of COVID, but not the continued police violence and shootings of Black people. The 2020 killing of George Floyd in Minneapolis, for example, sparked another round of widespread global protests (Shanahan and Kurti 2022). The protests, in turn, led to widely circulated but unsupported claims that the protests demoralized the police, causing the increase in the violent crime rate in 2020 and 2021 (Reiman and Leighton 2023). The ongoing police violence against minorities, the Black Lives Matter protests, and the causes of increased violent crime are all important criminological issues, but the racial ones are not raised.

Even if criminologists were still studying why violent crime increased in 2020–2021, the "de-policing" argument—that officers feel demoralized and fear liability, which leads them to engage in less proactive enforcement measures—is the same as the "Ferguson effect" (named for the city where people protested the police killing of Michael Brown in 2014) (Pyrooz et al. 2016). The Ferguson effect, too, was the same as earlier claims for "obedient acquiescence" in which "police policy and practice is not to be challenged or questioned, else officer well-being and public safety is at risk" (Marier and Fridell 2020: 712).

Research using different time frames and geographic areas has found no evidence of a systemic Ferguson effect whereby protests lead to increases in crime (Marier and Fridell 2020; Pyrooz et al. 2016; Rosenfeld and Wallman 2019; Skoy 2021). The Ferguson protests had a "negligible" effect on already high levels of burnout and cynicism among police (Marier and Fridell 2020: 693). When police do withdraw, the impact was on very minor crimes where police have high discretion, and "arrests for the more serious crimes were unchanged" (Marier and Fridell 2020: 698; Rosenfeld and Wallman 2019). So, it is unlikely that the Black Lives Matter protests, like those for George Floyd, resulted in the alarming increase of violent gun crime in 2020–2021.

Indeed, why was it not important to raise the issue that some increased crime can result when police brutality has reduced the legitimacy of the police in the eyes of many minorities? In the face of police misbehavior, "people are less willing to cooperate with police in investigations, less willing to report crimes or other problems to the police and more willing to take matters into their own hands" (Dawson 2018; MacFarquhar 2021; Rosenfeld 2016). Further, gun sales started climbing dramatically at the start of the pandemic, before the Floyd protests (Levine and McKnight 2020). They hit record levels, and "previous spikes in purchasing, such as those following mass shootings and political elections, have been associated with increased firearm violence" (Kravitz-Wirtz et al. 2021). Indeed, the pandemic caused more people to carry guns and to leave guns loaded and unlocked; increased mental health problems, drinking, and drug use; and reduced criminal justice operations aimed at incarcerating gun offenders (Cook 2020; Kravitz-Wirtz et al. 2021; Ludwig 2021).

Some readers may see it as unfair criticism to bring up race issues because that was not what the author (Piquero 2021) was trying to do. But the question is why the review of "significant findings" that leaves out racial issues is the authoritative account of pandemic criminology.

## Review and Discussion Questions

1. What are the key points espoused in the classical, positivist, and critical theories of criminology? How are all three still relevant to contemporary discussions of crime and justice?
2. What are the strengths and weaknesses of classical, positivist, and critical criminologies?
3. Why do the authors believe that reflection and critique, of the type provided by critical criminology, is so important for criminology and criminal justice?
4. From this chapter, what is your understanding of class, and what are several ways that it shapes criminology?
5. What are some of the ways that criminology has spread racism, and what are some ways it has challenged racism? What is the concern about racially neutral-sounding "general theories"?
6. How has criminology traditionally seen women? What does "add women and stir" mean and why is it criticized? What does queer criminology add to our understanding?
7. What is the basic idea of intersectionality? What are the important influences on the development of intersectional criminology? How does criminology benefit from an intersectional perspective?
8. From reading the "Implications" section, what do you think are the strengths and weaknesses of the authors' critique of the significant findings about COVID?
9. The text mentioned a classroom exercise where students listed the criminology theorists and authors they know. They identified them as male, female or nonbinary, and whether they were white or minority. They drew a grid with male-female and white-minority as boxes, with nonbinary in the middle, then placed the criminology theorists and authors in the box appropriate for their characteristics. What was the result for them and why was it a problem? What would be the result if you did this? (For more information on the exercise, see Stockdale et al. [2021].)

# PART II

## Inequality and Privilege

# CHAPTER 3

# Understanding Class and Economic Privilege

The novel Snow Crash (Stephenson 1992) is set in an alternative United States when the four things we do best are music, movies, software, and high-speed pizza delivery. Hiro lives in a twenty-by-thirty-foot U-Store-It, formerly intended for people with too many material goods. Hiro is a free-lance computer hacker; he also belongs to the elite order of Deliverators, entrusted with the task of thirty-minute pizza delivery for Mafia-owned businesses (specifically, CosaNostra Pizza franchise #3569). In contrast with his own residence, deliveries are to the "burbclaves"—suburban enclaves, gated communities. Some of them are Apartheid Burbclaves: "WHITE PEOPLE ONLY: NON-CAUCASIANS MUST BE PROCESSED." As he approaches the gate, a laser scans his bar codes and he rolls through the immigration gate and past "customs agents ready to frisk all comers—cavity search them if they are the wrong kind of people."

Hiro's partner, a skateboard courier, gets arrested in the burbclave by MetaCops Unlimited ("DIAL 1-800-THE-COPS All Major Credit Cards"), who also enforce traffic regulations for one of the major companies that operate private roads. Many of the franchise-organized quasi-national entities prefer to have their own security force rather than engage a general contractor. Security is a big deal because they're "so small, so insecure, that just about anything, like not mowing your lawn, or playing your stereo too loud, becomes a national security issue." The burbclave doesn't have a jail, but "any half-decent franchise strip" has one, either the cowboy-themed Hoosegow or The Clink, Inc. The MetaCops quickly see the sign: "THE HOOSE-GOW: Premium incarceration and restraint services. We welcome busloads!"

While Snow Crash is considered science fiction, its author considers it an "alternative present." Indeed, the world in the novel satirizes many features of the present day, including the shift from manufacturing to a service-based economy, rising income inequality, residential segregation, the *popularity of gated communities, the privatization of justice functions, the predict-able, franchise-based world George Ritzer describes in* The McDonaldization of Society *(2004), and the growth in corporate power to rival the resources of states and many nations in the global village.*

*Inequality also plays out in climate change fiction like* The Waterknife *(Bacigalupi 2016). A waterknife is a person who cuts off water to towns and subdivisions in the increasingly drought-stricken southwestern United States. In current real life, water flow down the Colorado River is sharply declining (Flavelle 2023), and in the novel, the river has stopped flowing into Texas. "Denial. Collapse. Acceptance. Refugees" (Bacigalupi 2016: 26). When water is cut off, relief workers show up to provide drinking water, "but sewage treatment isn't working anymore, since they got no water going through the system," so disease becomes a problem (Bacigalupi 2016: 354). Next, "businesses go away. And then jobs dry up." Renters go first, then homeowners: "A whole city getting the fuck out" (Bacigalupi 2016: 354).*

*To control the flow of Texas refugees and preserve their own water resources, neighboring states passed laws to control their borders. The wealthy and people with the right job skills could get permits to live in other states, but regular people had to hire coyotes (traffickers) to get past Border Patrol, drones, and militias. Border crossers were shot and sometimes hung out on display; they became "piled corpses who had tried to buy their way north to places with water and jobs and hope" (Bacigalupi 2016: 110). Even if they were successful in illegally crossing a border, the Texans were not welcome. They would suffer abuse, and the Texas "bangbang girls, they'll do pretty much anything for a shower" (Bacigalupi 2016: 136).*

*Many regular people in Arizona had makeshift dust masks to protect them-selves from brutal dust storms, and drank out of "Clearsacs": pieces of plastic that people peed in one end of and drank filtered water out of the other. Nearby, the rich live in an "arcology" with air-conditioned "triple-filtered apartments. Clean air. Perfectly recycled water, their own farms, everything they needed to live, even if Phoenix was going to shit right outside" (Bacigalupi 2016: 89): "You know, nice splashing waterfall to drink an espresso next to" (Bacigalupi 2016: 104).*

*Back in contemporary real life, climate change has a disproportionate impact on the poor and already most vulnerable. Meanwhile, "those who have done the most harm to the environment through their astonishingly high levels of conspicu-ous consumption—operating super-yachts, building mega-homes, running luxury cars, and flying private jets—are now among those most alarmed by the signs of disruption and damage affecting global ecosystems, and the first planning to escape disaster" (South and South 2021: 234).*

## Introduction

The Constitution claims that everyone is entitled to equal protection under the law. The statues of Lady Justice show her blindfolded so that she can impartially weigh the claims on her scales. But most Americans know that being rich has its advantages in the areas of crime, punishment, and law. Death-row inmates joke that people who have capital do not get capital punishment, and the data support their observation. Being wealthy makes it more likely that someone can literally or figuratively get away with murder.

Discrimination against people of color, women, and the LGBTQ+ population means they are disproportionately poor and thus also subject to class bias. Too frequently, intersectionality does not include class, so the amount and type of economic bias exerted on the marginalized is not fully recognized. And because people generally underestimate the amount of economic inequality that exists, the extent of class bias in criminal justice is not fully appreciated. Indeed, "if you grew up well-off, you probably don't know how easy it is for poor people to end up in jail, often for the same dumb things you yourself did as a kid. And if you're broke and have limited experience in the world, you probably have no idea of the sheer scale of the awesome criminal capers that the powerful and politically connected can get away with" (Taibbi 2014: xxiii).

Some observers see this pattern and argue that the criminal justice system is about controlling the poor and keeping them in their place (Chambliss and Seidman 1982; Quinney 1977; Shelden and Vasiliev 2018). Indeed, "crime" means "crime in the streets" rather than "crime in the suites," or white-collar crime, which is more prevalent and more costly to society (Reiman and Leighton 2023). Roadblocks to achieving the "American dream" are key concepts in strain theory, although few texts note that the wealthy also desire more money and may turn to (white-collar) crime because they have a limited number of legitimate ways to achieve additional millions or billions of dollars. Thus, understanding class is important for gaining insight into many facets of criminology and criminal justice.

Fundamentally, class revolves around questions of the distribution of income, wealth, and status. (These questions clearly are related to racial and gender identity since many women, minority men, and gender-nonconforming and other queer folks tend to occupy the lower levels of income distribution.) Yet, despite its importance, class is less frequently discussed than race and gender/sexuality. Indeed, while "class remains a primary determinant of social life," most public "discourses about modern society have been largely de-classed" (Mooney 2008: 68). The neglect of class occurs in a context where "the scale of this inequality is almost beyond comprehension, perhaps not surprisingly as much of it remains hidden from view" (Mooney 2008: 64).

Conversation about class is more muted because the government produces less vital information about class than race or gender, and the corporate- and billionaire-owned media are less likely to explore it. Further, discussions of class and information about the distribution of income and wealth can potentially disrupt deeply held beliefs about a United States where everyone is middle class and anyone can get ahead if they try hard enough. It is easier to talk about "working families," which include people of all classes, rather than acknowledge the hardships faced by many and the class privilege of those with higher incomes. Box 3.1 has some statements that help further identify class privilege.

---

BOX 3.1

### You Know You're Privileged When . . . (Part 1)

In 1988, Peggy McIntosh's frustration with men who would not recognize their male privilege prompted her to examine her own life and identify ordinary ways in which she experienced white privilege. "I think whites are carefully taught not to recognize white privilege, as males are taught not to recognize male privilege" ([1988] 1997: 292). Since then, the idea of privilege checklists has spread, and people have applied the idea to many different types of privilege.

This box covers the issue of class privilege, and each of the next three chapters will have a similar box to cover white privilege (chapter 4), male and heterosexual privilege (chapter 5), and intersections (chapter 6).

I know I have class privilege when

- I can buy things for my comfort and because they are fashionable.
- I do not fear being hungry or homeless, and I have not had to decide whether to pay rent or buy food with my limited money.
- I have the time and money to take care of my body (if I choose).
- I do not worry about my access to medical care.
- I can advocate for my class without being seen as looking for a handout.
- Whenever I've moved out of my home it has been voluntary, and I had another home to move into.
- I hunted for sport, not because of food insecurity.
- I can employ people to help with household tasks and child care.

*Source:* Adapted from Pease 2010: 77–78.

---

Describing the distribution of economic resources in the United States is straightforward: since the mid-1970s, the distribution of wealth has become more unequal (Ritholtz 2022). But saying that "the rich are getting richer and the rest of us are getting taken" is seen as inciting "class warfare" (Hightower 1998: 105), even though that term is not applied to policies that empower businesses at the expense of workers, many of whom are experiencing downward mobility. It is also not applied to policies that further empower large financial institutions over customers and borrowers.

This chapter investigates class to explain important concepts and introduce facts about inequality. The first sections provide an overview of what class means, how people would like to see wealth distributed, how income and wealth are distributed, and what studies say about the ease of mobility between classes. After that, the chapter turns to address how class relates to criminology and criminal justice issues. First it explores class and victimization, then finishes with a review of how class has historically played a role in the administration of justice.

## Social Class and Stratification in Society

*Class* refers to divisions concerning status, sometimes conceptualized as a hand of cards, with the suits representing education, income, occupation, and wealth

(Scott and Leonhardt 2005). But primary attention should be placed on economic power and resources, which are also more important than other aspects of class for understanding the nature of crime control and the functioning of the criminal justice system. Money is ultimately the primary factor involved in motivations and opportunities (of both the rich and the poor) to commit crime as well as in the responses of the criminal justice apparatus. Wealth means political influence to lobby for more favorable laws and less oversight; it allows people to hire better lawyers and shapes assumptions about whether one is a reputable member of the community. Thus, the focus of our discussion of class is economic because it is a convenient shorthand for understanding the larger issues that relate to crime, power, law, and justice.

Many social thinkers have tried to devise meaningful ways to divide up the spectrum of income and wealth. Karl Marx identified the *bourgeoisie*, who owned the means of production (factories, banks, and businesses); the *petit bourgeoisie*, who do not have ownership but occupy management or professional positions; and the *proletariat*, or workers, who need to sell their labor to make a wage. Marx also identified the surplus population, or *lumpenproletariat*, who have no formal ties to the system of economic relations because they are unemployed or unemployable (Lynch et al. 2000). In developing his theory, Marx contributed a useful critique of capitalism, involving his belief that history could be described as an ongoing war of the rich against the poor for control of wealth—and that law was a tool in this war. The criminal justice system also becomes a tool to manage the surplus population, and under this view, reforms of police to stop brutality are destined for failure because their purpose is to control the poor (Shanahan and Kurti 2022).

One interesting effort to take Marx's framework and apply it to the contemporary labor situation is the *precariat* (Standing 2014), which combines the notion of the proletariat with the sense of precariousness that many workers experience with ongoing low-wage contract work, no benefits, and no career path. This group are not "romantic free spirits" (Standing 2014: 15) and are in this situation because globalization, outsourcing, and business demand for "flexible" labor have reduced wages, security, and job training. The precariat have no "bargain of trust or security in exchange for subordination" (Standing 2014: 14) that helps define the proletariat. Over the precariat are a salatariat of those with longer-term jobs with decent salaries, although they are a shrinking group.

No doubt the precariat captures something of the flavor of modern society when 64 percent of U.S. households say they are living paycheck to paycheck—and that includes people with incomes over $100,000 (Sforza 2023). While some upper-income families do live on the edge because of student loan and/or medical debt, others have a low bank account balance because they make investments, take vacations, engage in conspicuous consumption, pay for private school tuition, and have other indicators of economic privilege. Thus, to be most helpful in understanding class, the idea of living paycheck to paycheck should be supplemented by measures of luxury consumption, as well as ownership of financial assets and businesses "that give a person distinct advantages in a capitalist society" (Brouwer 1998: 13).

Other attempts to describe the class system are less useful because they are not tied to a theory of power relations, and they offer less insight into law, crime, and justice. For example, this description is true, but it does not explicitly place people in hierarchies of power: "Class is your understanding of the world and where you fit in; it's composed of ideas, behaviors, attitudes, values, and language; class is how you think, feel, act, look, dress, talk, move, and walk" (in Dunn 2019: 9). Often descriptions outline criteria for upper, middle, and lower classes. For example, "the working class in the United States consists of people with little to no college education who are paid by the hour or by the job as opposed to receiving a salary" (Dunn 2019: 8). In contrast, a description more tied to power is that "the working class fulfills the largest labor-intensive role of any group in producing economic goods" but is "defined by their lack of power at work and in society at large. The working class receives much less support from the U.S. capitalist economy than the significant amount of work they put into it" (Dunn 2019: 8).

This lack of power and support has been noted since industrialization accelerated in the 1800s in the United States and Europe, especially its impact on the health of the poor and working class. Observers who do not have an analysis of class power suggested that reforms should include better sanitation, morals, and some workplace safety. While some reforms have been helpful, the chair of a 2013 National Institute of Medicine report called "Shorter Lives, Poorer Health" told Congress: "The lower people's income, the earlier they die and the sicker they live" (in Introcaso 2021; Reiman and Leighton 2023: 105–7). In contrast, an analysis that includes class and power, from Marx's collaborator Engels, argues that

> the lives of working-class people were foreshortened by avoidable injustices upon which capitalism was premised and which were expressed in wagelabour practices. In Engels's analysis, social murder through such violence could have been prevented through a different economic structure and social relations. The bourgeoisie knew this, but they benefited from the use of working-class people as the "means of profit." (Grover, 2018: 340)

*Underclass* refers to the poorest of the poor, who are locked into poverty, and usually refers to minority populations. "*White trash*" is used for the poorest whites who have none of the power and prestige of most whites. They have resources equal to or even less than minorities but have white skin, so "white trash studies" can potentially shed theoretical light on issues of race and class (Dunn 2019; Wray and Newitz 1996). White skin, for example, has not protected poor white women from forced sterilization that also aimed to prevent poor Black and Native American women from having children (Isenberg 2016). More generally, many working-class whites do not believe they experience white privilege because of class-based exploitation and powerlessness.

Further, many schemes for understanding class have difficulty placing women. Feminists argue that women's relationship to class structure is mediated by "the configuration of the family, dependence on men, and domestic labour" (in Gamble 1999: 206). While minorities are disproportionately poor because of discrimination, some analysts of racial capitalism suggest that "race exists as a form of class domination, even if it is not neatly reducible to this relationship" (Shanahan and Kurti 2022: 84; Austin 2023). In this analysis, race should not be seen as an explanation for social outcomes because the question instead is about how race is used to justify exploitation for profit. For example, "Why would slaveholders import Africans if they were motivated by a hatred of Africans?" (Austin 2023). Instead, "colonialism and slavery did not exist because of race; the merchants and statesmen who benefited from these forms of rapacious exploitation produced racial arguments as a justification" for brutal practices that allowed them to accumulate wealth (Shanahan and Kurti 2022: 85).

The study of class is also part of a larger question about *stratification*, which is concerned with the stability of the distribution of social goods such as income, wealth, and prestige. Because most of these goods have an unequal distribution, part of stratification attempts to explain how small minorities maintain control over a disproportionate share of social resources. Part of the explanation involves the role of the criminal justice system and the phenomenon of how *The Rich Get Richer and the Poor Get Prison* (Reiman and Leighton 2023), a book that has been in print through thirteen editions since 1979.

## Economic Distributions—Ideals and Reality

While equality of the rich and the poor under law is a goal, most people do not want everyone to have the same amount of income and wealth. But how much inequality is fair, and what would a just distribution of economic resources look like? The first section below reviews a thought experiment and some questions to help readers think about their own preferences before sharing the results of a wide-scale survey. The second section examines the distribution of income, as in how much people earn over a year, and how that compares to corporate persons. The third section examines wealth, which is the assets or debt that people accrue over their lifetime. The concluding section contains a short discussion of mobility and the ease with which people can or cannot be upwardly mobile in the class system.

### Income and Wealth Distributions—Ideals

One important answer to the question of what constitutes economic justice is from Rawls (1971), who argued that justice is the result of decisions that people would make about society from behind a "veil of ignorance." That is, people would design a fair society if they had to make choices not knowing their position in that society, whether they would be rich or poor, white or minority, male or female or nonbinary, and so on. So, if you were going to be randomly placed in a society, what would you want the distribution of income and wealth to look like?

Researchers have explored this philosophical question by asking people which of three countries they would want to be placed into based on information about the distribution of wealth in each country (Norton and Ariely 2011). For example, imagine there were one hundred people in the country and the total wealth was $100. In country A, the poorest twenty people would split $20, as would the richest twenty people. In country B, the poorest twenty people would split $11, while the richest would share $36. In country C, the poorest twenty people would share ten cents, while the richest twenty would share $84.

Knowing that you were going to be randomly placed in the wealth distribution—bottom, top, or one of the groups in between—which country would you choose to be a citizen of?

Within the confines of this forced choice, most people (47 percent) choose country B, which is actually the distribution of wealth in Sweden. Only 10 percent choose the level of inequality in country C, which is the United States. This result tracks closely with Rawls's analysis, in which he outlined a strategy of maximizing the minimum levels of wealth. Even though some level of inequality helps motivate people and reward them for their talent and efforts, high levels of inequality make many people worse off to enhance the wealth of the top few percent. Because those with little wealth are more numerous than the very wealthy, someone randomly placed in society will more likely have little wealth, so most people want to allow some inequality but maximize the prospects of the least well-off.

Researchers also asked respondents to create a just distribution of wealth by dividing up wealth themselves and choosing how much wealth went to the top and bottom. In addition to asking about this "ideal" distribution of wealth, they asked people what they believed the distribution of wealth to be. The researchers conclude that

> Americans also construct ideal distributions that are far more equal than they estimated the United States to be—estimates which themselves were far more equal than the actual level of inequality. Second, there was much more consensus than disagreement across groups from different sides of the political spectrum about this desire for a more equal distribution of wealth, suggesting that Americans may possess a commonly held "normative" standard for the distribution of wealth despite the many disagreements about policies that affect that distribution, such as taxation and welfare. (Norton and Ariely 2011: 12)

The full results are available in table 3.1, which indicates that Americans believed the top 20 percent should own 32 percent of the wealth, when in fact they owned 84 percent at that time. On the other side of the distribution, Americans believed the bottom 60 percent should own 45 percent of the wealth, when in reality they owned less than 5 percent.

**TABLE 3.1 Actual, Perceived, and Ideal Distributions of Wealth in the United States**

|  | Wealth of Poorest 60 Percent (% of all wealth) | Wealth of Richest 20 Percent (% of all wealth) |
|---|---|---|
| Actual amount of wealth | 5 | 84 |
| Perceived amount of wealth (what people believe) | 20 | 59 |
| Ideal amount of wealth (what people would choose) | 45 | 32 |

*Source:* Calculated from Norton and Ariely 2011, based on 2007 wealth data.

The other striking aspect of this research is that Americans substantially under-estimate the amount of inequality. People believed the top 20 percent own 59 percent of the wealth when they really own 84 percent; people believed the bottom 60 percent own 20 percent of the wealth when they really own less than 5 percent. These mistakes about economic facts hide the true amount of inequality and thus support the unequal status quo.

### Income Distribution—Real

Because people tend to underestimate inequality, the next sections provide data about the actual distribution of income and wealth in the United States. The facts about economic distributions are important for furnishing a concrete picture of inequality and concepts such as relative deprivation, which focuses on people's evaluations of their place relative to what others have and what they believe they are entitled to. As discussed in chapter 2, Braithwaite argues that "inequality worsens both crimes of poverty motivated by *need* for goods for *use* and crimes of wealth motivated by *greed*" (1992: 81, emphasis in the original). Crime can be related to the powerlessness and exploitation of those at the bottom of the class system as well as to the unaccountability of, and manipulation by, those at the top. Strain theory involves the notion of blocked opportunities, yet it is seldom discussed in terms of class mobility, stratification, and greed by the wealthy—but these would be helpful contexts.

While the thought experiment in the last section used accumulated wealth, this section is about income, which consists of people's salary and other sources of money paid to them in a year. For most people, income takes the form of paychecks, although it can also include interest, dividends, rents from property, royalties from intellectual property like patents, and capital gains (when someone sells assets like property or stocks for more than they paid for it). Table 3.2 illustrates the distribu-tion of income in the United States.

**TABLE 3.2 Percentage of Income Earned and Income Limits in the United States, 2022**

| Population Share | Share of Total Income (%) | Highest Income in Group ($) |
|---|---|---|
| Lowest (poorest) 20 percent | 3.0 | 30,000 |
| Second | 8.2 | 58,020 |
| Third | 14.0 | 94,000 |
| Fourth | 22.5 | 153,000 |
| Top (richest) 20 percent | 52.1 | 2,800,000,000 |
| Top 5 percent | 23.5 | 295,000 |

*Sources:* Guzman and Kollar 2023: tables A-3 and A-4a; Taub 2024.

*Note:* The highest-paid hedge fund manager in 2022 made $2.9 billion, and the $2.8 billion in the table reflects the highest-paid American-based manager.

The first column of table 3.2 illustrates that the richest 20 percent of the population take more than half the income earned in the United States, while the poorest 20 percent share 3 percent. In some ways, there does not seem to be much income inequality: 80 percent of the population is making less than $153,000 a year. Indeed, 95 percent of the population makes less than $295,000, although households at that level are more likely to have some degree of wealth and better health insurance than households with lower incomes. Still, in spite of economic privileges, they may not feel rich in comparison to the multimillion-dollar salaries of CEOs, athletes and celebrities, and the multibillion-dollar incomes of hedge fund managers. (The top income of $2.8 billion is equivalent to a paycheck of almost $108 million every two weeks.)

Since 2010, the federal minimum wage has been $7.25 and is not indexed to inflation. About half of the states set higher minimum wages, although no state has endorsed the idea of a "living wage" (Glasmeier 2017) or supported a $15 an hour wage for urban fast-food workers. Business groups lobby state governments for laws that prevent cities from setting minimum wages higher than the state minimum wage, blocking both progressive localities and areas with high cost of living from helping workers.

The poverty level for a single person in 2024 was $15,060 a year (Department of Health and Human Services, n.d.). The poverty level for a family of three was $25,820, meaning that a single person needs to earn close to $15 an hour to keep themselves and two children above the poverty level. This is more difficult for many minorities, and twice as many female-headed households are in poverty (25 percent) compared to male-headed households (13 percent).

While women and many minority groups are overrepresented in the lowest segments of the income distribution, table 3.3 shows wide variation in median household income among minority groups (the median is the middle value, with half of the distribution above it and half below). The census data used for the table

**TABLE 3.3 Income and Poverty Rates by Race and Sex, 2022**

| Race and Sex Groups as Reported by Census | Median Income ($) | Poverty Rate (%) |
| --- | --- | --- |
| White, non-Hispanic | 81,060 | 8.6 |
| Black | 52,860 | 17.1 |
| Asian | 108,700 | 8.6 |
| American Indian and Alaska Native | 52,810 | 25.0 |
| Hispanic | 62,800 | 16.9 |
| Male | 52,770 | 10.5 |
| Female | 41,320 | 12.5 |

*Sources:* Guzman and Kollar 2023: table A-2, figures 1, 4, and 6; U.S. Census Bureau 2023: table A-2.

*Note:* The median income for racial groups is for households, which can reflect the combined income of multiple wage earners, while the income by sex is for individuals. When comparing full-time, year-round employees, median earnings of men were $62,350 compared to $52,360 for women.

does not allow for intersectional analysis, for example, how women of different racial groups compare to their male counterparts or to women in different racial groups.

The numbers in tables 3.2 and 3.3 are for years when the economy had supposedly recovered from the pandemic. The economic recession from the pandemic affected lower- and middle-income households more than richer ones. Lower-income households were more likely to have jobs that ended during the pandemic and little savings to fall back on. Women disproportionately dropped out of the labor force to take care of children because day care was closed and kids needed supervision, including for online school. But these trends were a continuation of a larger historical movement to greater inequality, so "the long-running shift in the distribution of U.S. household income towards upper-income families stayed on track during the coronavirus pandemic" (Kochhar and Sechopoulos 2022).

For example, in 2022, the median pay of CEOs for the five hundred largest public companies was $14.5 million, down slightly from 2021. The highest-paid was the CEO of Alphabet (Google) at $226 million, comprised of $2 million in salary, $6 million for personal security, and $218 million in stock awards (Fernandes 2023). (For CEOs, salary tends to be a small part of the overall pay or "compensation package," which includes stock options, spending allowances, and generous pensions that are frequently protected even during company bankruptcy proceedings.) CEO pay grows faster than employee salaries—and faster than profits and other company performance measures. Indeed, an important comparison is the ratio of CEO pay to that of an average worker in the company. This metric was first proposed by Cotton, a lawyer who argued that CEO pay needed to be contextualized with information on the wages of an average worker so that shareholders could make a better judgment about whether executive pay was excessive and "tantamount to the looting of the corporation" (Cotton 1997: 182). He also thought it was hypocritical for well-paid executives to speak out against increases in the minimum wage: "Fifty cents an hour poses threats to employment while several billion dollars spread over a small class of executives is never discussed in terms of threats to employment even though workers are frequently laid off" (Cotton 1997: 162).

In 1980, CEOs of the largest companies were paid 40 times as much as the hourly wage earners at their companies (Smith and Kuntz 2013). When Cotton wrote, it was 85 times the pay of the average worker (1997: 182), but in 2021 the average S&P 500 CEO made 324 times the pay of the median employee (Ockerman 2022). The Securities and Exchange Commission did adopt Cotton's proposal to report the ratio, which they said was 193 times the median employee pay. That is lower than the 324:1 ratio because Securities and Exchange Commission (SEC) rules allow companies to "apply certain exclusions, make estimates and assumptions" (Janney and Lutz 2022).

Saying that the CEO-to-worker pay ratio "has increased" and the shift in the income distribution toward the rich "stayed on track" are written in the passive voice, which obscures who is responsible for the result. Nobel Prize–winning economist Joseph Stiglitz notes that "inequality is the result of political factors as much as of economic ones" (2012: 30). Congress enacted numerous tax cuts for the wealthy and refused to raise the minimum wage; it deregulated industry and allowed concentrated corporate power, which raised prices and depressed wages. In other words, the rich use their disproportionate political and other influence to enact policies that ensure themselves more money, which increases their influence to enact policies that ensure themselves more money. Sometimes this sentiment is put more bluntly by saying that there is a class war and only the rich are fighting. Perhaps that sounds provocative, but billionaire investor Warren Buffett said, "There's class warfare, all right, but it's my class, the rich class, that's making war, and we're winning" (Stein 2006). Current fronts in the class war include businesses fighting against increasing interest in unionization, which may be recovering from historically low levels. For example, "SpaceX, Amazon, Trader Joe's, and Starbucks are trying to have the NLRB [National Labor Relations Board] declared unconstitutional—after collectively being charged with hundreds of violations of workers' organizing rights" (Rhinehart and McNicholas 2024).

To be clear, the growing inequality is because those at the top of the income distribution are taking it from those who have less. Research finds that if the more equitable income distributions of the 1940s to 1970 were applied to today, all Americans earning below the ninetieth percentile would have higher incomes— "enough to more than double median income—enough to pay every single working American in the bottom nine deciles an additional $1,144 a month. Every month. Every single year" (Hanauer and Rolf 2020). Instead of a median household income of $50,000 in 2018, the household would have had $92,000 if the income distribution from 1975 held steady. Because many 2018 households are working more hours than 1975 households, part of the analysis focused on full-year, full-time, prime-aged workers. For them, "in 2018, the combined income of married households with *two* full-time workers was barely more than what the income of a single-earner household would have earned had inequality held constant" (Hanauer and Rolf 2020).

The study noted that minorities and women have made gains compared to white men, but this was in the context of stagnant or declining wages overall, especially for nonurban men without a college education. White people are still better paid than minorities or women with the same level of education, so white privilege remains. But many white people do not feel white privilege because of class, and a report on income inequality noted that "the majority of white men have benefited from almost none of this growth isn't because they have lost income to women or minorities; it's because they've lost it to their largely white male counterparts in the top 1 percent who have captured nearly all of the income growth for themselves" (Hanauer and Rolf 2020). Indeed, 88 percent of those in the top 1 percent of household incomes are white, and 85 percent of those households do not rely on women's income to be in that group (Yavorsky et al. 2020).

Inequality gets considerably worse if corporations are factored in. This should be done because American law treats corporations as "persons"—although protest signs often comment, "I'll believe corporations are persons when we execute one." The intense concentration of economic resources in corporations generates considerable political power and social harms but makes accountability increasingly difficult, although criminological theory is blind to all of it.

For example, Victoria's Secret is number 480 on the 2022 list of *Fortune* magazine's five hundred largest companies (*Fortune* 2022), with revenue (income) of almost $6.8 billion. Walmart is the largest of the Fortune 500 companies, with revenue of $573 billion, compared with the median household income of $74,580 (in 2022). Such incomes make them gargantuan in relation to not only individuals but also cities, states, and the federal regulatory agencies that are supposed to police and control corporations.

Indeed, rather than comparing modern corporations with individuals, they can instead be compared with countries. Specifically, the revenue of a corporation can be compared with the gross domestic product (GDP) of a country, which is the total value of all the goods and services that it produces (Leighton 2013). With this analysis, Walmart would be the twenty-fourth largest economy in the world, right behind Belgium and larger than Thailand (World Bank 2022).

### Wealth Distribution—Real

While income is an easily understandable way of examining inequality, wealth is more important. Wealth looks at accumulated assets and debt over a lifetime: bank accounts, stocks and bonds, retirement accounts, houses, cars, and ownership of businesses; it also includes debts such as car loans, student loans, mortgages, medical debt, and credit card balances. Wealth provides security for setbacks in life, such as job loss, employment transition, and medical hardship. It can provide money to start a business to build even more wealth. At still higher levels, wealth generates political power.

Wealth is even more unequally distributed than income. Through intergenerational transfers, wealthy parents are able to give their children gifts, set up trust funds, and leave inheritances (Bhutta et al. 2020). The transmission of wealth also happens less directly, when parents buy a home in a neighborhood with better schools, thus conferring benefits to their children. Wealthier families invest in their children's health, like braces for straight teeth that help secure many higher-paying jobs later in life. Half the population has no dental coverage, so the full costs need to be paid out of pocket, leading many to skip visits and suffer not only physical pain but also "the psychological hell of having poor teeth in a rich, capitalist country" (Smarsh 2014). Networks of other wealthy people can provide opportunities for summer jobs or internships that look good on college applications. Through a variety of mechanisms, "wealth (or a lack thereof) can persist across generations and reflect, among other factors, a legacy of discrimination or unequal treatment in housing, education, and labor markets" (Bhutta et al. 2020). Because intergenerational transfers involve more than just the current generation and their parents, current wealth inequality reflects many generations of wealth transfers, and the country's history of slavery has a direct bearing on current economic inequality.

Table 3.4 provides a summary of wealth and the distribution of stocks in the United States. More than two-thirds of all wealth is held by the wealthiest 10 percent, while the poorest 50 percent—a group five times as large—holds less than 3 percent. Although many Americans own stocks through retirement accounts, the top 10 percent own about 87 percent of all stocks; the top 1 percent own about half, while the bottom 50 percent own 1 percent. Ownership of privately held businesses is even more concentrated.

TABLE 3.4 **Shares of Net Worth and Business Ownership, 2023**

| | Wealth Percentile Groups | | |
| --- | --- | --- | --- |
| | 0–50 (Poorest 50 Percent) | 90–100 (Richest 10 Percent) | 99–100 (Top 1 Percent) |
| Percentage of all net worth owned | 2.5 | 66.9 | 30.3 |
| Percentage of all shares of corporations owned | 1.0 | 86.9 | 49.4 |

*Source:* Federal Reserve Board, n.d., data for Q4 2023.

Like income, wealth inequality has been worsening over the last several decades, and Stiglitz notes that "the riches accruing to the top have come at the expense of those down below." He further notes that much of the wealth distribution is about laws and policies as much as individual effort and that "incentives [are] directed not at creating new wealth but at taking it from others" (2012: 6).

About 10–15 percent of people have negative net worth (more debt than assets), which erases the small amounts of wealth held by others in the bottom 50 percent. For these families, credit card debt tends to be high, along with auto loans that exceed the value of the car. Almost $1.8 trillion in student loans contributes to the negative segment of the wealth distribution. For many individuals, that debt is larger and paid off later in life, but education provides an increase in human capital, which can generally lead over time to better income and jobs. (The next section on mobility provides more detail.)

Below the median wealth, assets tend to be in the form of checking and savings accounts plus vehicles. People own a home, although large mortgage balances mean the house does not contribute greatly to wealth (the sale price of the house minus the mortgage debt is the amount of wealth/equity from the house). Ownership of businesses is negligible, reflecting both low levels of ownership and relatively small businesses. Above the median, families have not just bigger checking and savings accounts, but they are more likely to own stocks, bonds, and mutual funds, and they are more likely to have retirement accounts that are better funded (Bhutta et al. 2020). They have less debt and own capital-appreciating assets such as rental property or second homes.

Although lists of people with high salaries tend to include minorities and women who are athletes or entertainers, the lists of those with the largest wealth are record label owners, movie producers, and those who own media and technology companies (means of production) rather than actors, entertainers, or celebrities. For 2023, there were only sixty women on the *Forbes* 400, a list of the four hundred wealthiest Americans, and in many cases the money came from inheritances or divorce (Peterson-Withorn 2023). Only three of the four hundred were Black men (Williams 2023), and one of them—basketball star Michael Jordan—"is the first pro athlete to make the 400" (Peterson-Withorn 2023). There are no Black women since Oprah Winfrey dropped below the minimum for the list (although she is still a billionaire).

For 2023, membership in the *Forbes* 400 required $2.9 billion in wealth. The list collectively has $4.5 trillion in wealth, but even within these four hundred households, there is a substantial distance between those at the bottom (with $2.9 billion) and those at the top of the list ($251 billion). As with income, those at the top have gained a disproportionate share. In 1982, the top of the list made $2 billion (less than $7 billion in 2023 dollars), while in 2023 the top person made $251 billion (Peterson-Withorn 2023).

In addition to controlling the means of production (the factories and businesses from which people buy goods), the wealthy also own the "means of mental production"—the media and technology platforms—and thus control over the dominant narratives about inequality, big business, and other issues of justice. Table 3.5 shows the media businesses and their ownership by corporations (themselves controlled by the wealthy) or directly owned by billionaires. Because most Americans get their "commonsense" view of the world from news and entertainment media, the wealthy use their ownership of media to "justify their privileges and disguise social injustice by shaping popular sentiments" (Winlow et al. 2021: 39).

Although the media feature talking heads with differences of opinion shouting at each other, there is rarely questioning whether unfettered capitalism is really the best choice for America. Problems tend to be portrayed as localized or the result of "bad apples," so reforms can be limited and not change the

**TABLE 3.5  Media Ownership by the Wealthy**

| Media Company | Owner |
|---|---|
| NBC (including MSNBC, CNBC), USA Networks, Fandango, Hulu, Universal Pictures, Telemundo | Comcast |
| ABC, ESPN, Lifetime, History, A&E, FX, Marvel Studios, Lucasfilm, FiveThirtyEight | Disney |
| CBS, Paramount Pictures, Showcase Cinemas, MTV, Nickelodeon, VH1, Showtime Networks, BET, and Computer Curriculum Corp. | Billionaire Redstone family (via ownership of National Amusements and ViacomCBS) |
| CNN, HBO, Warner Bros., Turner Broadcasting System, Otter Media | AT&T |
| FOX, *Wall Street Journal*, HarperCollins | Billionaire Murdoch family |
| *Washington Post* | Billionaire Jeff Bezos (Amazon CEO) |
| Bloomberg, *BusinessWeek* | Billionaire Michael Bloomberg |
| *New Yorker*, *Vogue*, *Wired*, *Vanity Fair*, *GQ*, Reddit, newspapers in 24 cities | Billionaire Newhouse Family (via Condé Nast Publications) |
| Reuters News | Billionaire Thompson Family |
| Meta (Facebook), Instagram | Billionaire Mark Zuckerberg |
| Twitter | Billionaire Elon Musk |

*Sources:* Future of Media Project 2022; Peterson-Withorn 2022; Reference for Business 2022a, 2022b; Sherman 2020.

domination of society by big business or the continued accumulation of wealth by billionaires at the expense of everyone else (Reiman and Leighton 2023). Other ideological influences—ones that "distort reality in a way that justifies the prevailing distribution of power and wealth, [and] hides society's injustices" (Reiman and Leighton 2023: 200)—make people believe that any changes will only make the economic system worse and thus limit their capacity to imagine alternatives to the current society.

As with income, the median wealth conceals wide differences by race as detailed in table 3.6 from a survey done before the pandemic. The concept of relative wealth means that for every dollar of wealth a white household has, a Black one has eight cents. The racial pattern of wealth inequality is rooted in racialized policies that have stood in the way of people of color earning wealth and passing it on to the next generation: the appropriation of Native American lands and establishment of reservations; the sanctioning of uncompensated slave labor for people of African origin and the use of housing, educational, and economic segregation to perpetuate their isolation; the use of occupational and educational segregation and the denial of citizenship status to marginalize Latinos; and the adoption of exclusionary laws in the twentieth century to keep people of Asian origin from purchasing land, owning businesses, or obtaining citizenship (Tippett et al. 2014: 2). Another factor currently slowing wealth accumulation is that "many communities of color have a greater array of family members in poverty, which, through an altruistic motive, reduces their resources to save" (Tippett et al. 2014: 8).

Because women are disproportionately in poverty and suffer wage discrimination, their wealth is also low. Measuring exactly how much lower is challenging because married women share their partner's assets, which are reported as belonging to the family. Single women who respond to the wealth survey are a smaller group, which makes generalizations difficult. However, the Federal Reserve, which conducts the wealth survey, notes important deficits in women's wealth across all the ways they analyze the problem. That makes those families "less resilient to unexpected shocks (e.g., income loss), less prepared for retirement and less able to help children achieve upward economic mobility" (Kent and Ricketts 2021; Zaw et al. 2017).

### TABLE 3.6  Median and Relative Wealth by Race

|  | Median Wealth ($) | Relative Wealth ($) |
| --- | --- | --- |
| White | 187,300 | 1.00 |
| Black | 14,100 | 0.08 |
| Asian | 206,400 | 1.10 |
| Hispanic | 31,700 | 0.17 |

*Source:* Based on calculations from data in Bennett et al. 2022.

### Economic Mobility—Real

Inequality is less of a concern where there is a high degree of mobility, so many people express less concern for widespread poverty or concentrated disadvantage if the people could easily improve their position. However, people tend to believe there is more mobility than actually exists, just as people believed wealth was distributed more fairly than it is. Anecdotal stories of self-made millionaires and billionaires are popular because they confirm the idea of mobility and the American dream, and the billionaires who own the media want to promote stories about how anyone can make it if they are smart and work hard.

The reality is that high levels of inequality—like the United States has—means less economic mobility (Corak 2020: 231). Inequality produces strong "inequality of opportunity":

> Socioeconomic status influences a child's health and aptitudes in early years—indeed even in utero—which in turn influences early cognitive and social development, and readiness to learn. These outcomes and the family circumstances of children, as well as the quality of neighborhoods and schools, influence success in primary school, which feeds into success in high school and college. Family resources and connections affect access to good schools and jobs, and the degree of inequality in labor markets determines both the resources parents have and ultimately the return to the education the children receive. This entire process then shapes earnings in adulthood. (Corak 2013: 85; Chetty et al. 2020)

Having a society that makes it difficult to escape poverty "can stifle upward social mobility, making it harder for talented and hard-working people to get the rewards they deserve" (Corak 2013: 79). This situation also hurts the nation and economy since the talents of the poor are not fully realized (Corak 2020). With law enforcement and criminal justice focused on those at the bottom, criminal records are also more likely, which adds to social exclusion and limits a person's earning potential.

We recognize that mobility happens, just less frequently than people think. For example, compared to several peer nations, U.S. children born to parents in the poorest 20 percent of the income distribution are least likely to make it to the top 20 percent and are most likely to remain in the bottom 20 percent; children born to parents in the top 20 percent are most likely of the nations to stay in that top category (Corak 2013, 2020). Specifically, if the parents are in the bottom 20 percent of the income distribution, there is only an 11 percent chance that their child will earn enough to get into the top 20 percent of the income distribution. (Note that the top 20 percent, according to table 3.2, currently starts at $153,000, so the chance of becoming a millionaire is smaller.) The chance of a child born to parents in the bottom 20 percent staying in that category is about 34 percent, and the chances of a child born into the highest income category remaining there is about 37 percent (Corak 2020: 236).

Much of the research on mobility is based on studies of men's mobility. Drawing conclusions about everyone based on studies of men is a common problem in social science, medical, criminological, and other research (see chapter 6). Because of generational changes in women entering the workforce and breaking some glass ceilings (that limit upward mobility), the picture of their upward mobility is different but important to understand as well.

Examining college degrees and student loans is another way to help understand economic mobility. Several decades ago, college was easier to pay for through part-time and summer jobs, along with financial aid in the form of grants. But college costs have increased, and more financial aid is in the form of loans—and paychecks are from an increasingly insecure, low-wage environment. So college became less affordable just as it was becoming increasingly important for maintaining or improving one's economic prospects. Further, the federal financial aid website reports an expected family contribution that is less than the bills students actually face (Goldrick-Rab 2016). This means that those without family wealth to support their education must work more and/or take out more loans, which has significant effects on a student's GPA, the likelihood of completing the degree, and the future effects of their indebtedness on their life's choices.

For example, community colleges are a relatively affordable way for diverse people to get, or start, a college degree. But a 2021 nationwide survey of community college students found that 14 percent of community college students were housing insecure, meaning they had an inability to pay rent or needed to move frequently ("couch surfing") (CCCSE 2022: 13). In addition, the survey found that about 29 percent of community college students had food insecurity, with 15 percent answering yes to the question, "Were you ever hungry but didn't eat because there wasn't enough money for food?" (CCCSE 2022: 8). A 2020 survey found higher levels of food insecurity, with 38 percent of community college students and 29 percent of four-year university students experiencing food insecurity in the last thirty days (Goldrick-Rab 2016; McCoy et al. 2022).

Students who are hungry are less likely to engage fully with class material, and many work long hours at low-wage jobs, which makes them too tired to study and attend classes. Work and school schedules often conflict. All these factors make successful completion of the degree, or transfer to a four-year college, less likely. (Having several years' worth of debt but no degree is worse for many students than if they had not attended college [Goldrick-Rab 2016].) Even when students successfully completed a four-year degree, they often had to go to great lengths to find money to stay in school, which meant "a lower likelihood of participating in extracurricular activities, visiting professors during office hours, and spending time on campus." Such students have "fewer opportunities to build relationships that could pave the way for social networks yielding greater returns to the college degree," including information about jobs and opportunities (Goldrick-Rab 2016: 33). In contrast, families with some wealth can make contributions that confer a number of advantages. Family wealth can expand the options for students to wider geographical areas with more economic opportunities, opening the possibility of attending more expensive, elite educational institutions. Having food and secure housing does not make college easy, but it does remove several formidable barriers.

Finally, "low-income families hold student debt amounting to about 70 percent of their income, while wealthier families have student debt amounting to around 10 percent of their income" (Goldrick-Rab 2016: 94). The lower levels of debt put fewer constraints on life after a bachelor's degree—there can be more options for graduate school or additional training, moving away from parents and in with a partner, or starting to save for a house and building their own wealth.

None of this is to say that students from wealthy families do not have struggles in college. Rather, the point is that family wealth reduces some serious barriers to completing a college degree and has the potential to set up conditions for them to build social networks that can help in the future. This wealth privilege combines with advantages from better schools, money for SAT preparation, lower debt-to-income ratios after graduation, and inheritances. The combination of these factors allows children of the wealthy to accumulate wealth more easily than those with less class privilege.

## Class, Victimization, and Justice

This section of the chapter starts to connect the general overview of class with criminology and criminal justice. By looking at victimization and then some historical patterns of class-based justice, the remainder of the chapter sets a foundation for later chapters that systematically explore how class impacts each stage of the criminal justice system, from lawmaking to prisons. Specifically, the first section on victimization reviews official data and critically reviews both criminal harms by corporations that are not included in the data as well as morally blameworthy harms (Kramer 2020) that are not part of the criminal law. The second section provides a broader look at class and justice, including criminal justice.

### Victimization and Class

Researchers have found that the overall rates of victimization in urban criminal violence are due largely to racial inequality and poor socioeconomic conditions. Unfortunately, victimization data from crime surveys reveal little about the structural context of victimization in terms of income, wealth, class, or even home ownership. The National Crime Victimization Survey (NCVS) does have several tables on victimization by income level, but the United States chooses not to collect additional data about the inconvenient truth of class bias (Leighton and Reiman 2014).

Table 3.7 reports the effect of income on violent victimization. The clear conclusion is that those who have less than $25,000 suffer violent victimization at a rate at least three times as great as those making more than $200,000. The overall pattern is clearly that violent victimization declines as income rises, and the pattern is even clearer when focusing on serious violent crime. This pattern has been found historically in the Bureau of Justice Statistics (BJS) data about income and victimization.

The BJS information on victimization by income presents an incomplete picture in several respects. The victimization survey does not ask about crimes committed by business or government, like whether someone in the household has experienced wage theft or false advertising. Further, many harmful acts of business and government are excluded from the FBI's Uniform Crime Reports, which aggregates and standardizes local police reports. Reiman and Leighton (2023) recalculate figures from the FBI's Uniform Crime Reports on how Americans are murdered to include workplace hazards, occupational diseases, and preventable medical errors to arrive at "How Americans Are Really Murdered." This does not include other crimes of the powerful that result in death, but it suggests that while the FBI reports

**TABLE 3.7  Violent Crime Rates by Household Income (per 1,000 Aged Twelve and Older)**

| Type of Crime | <$25,000 | $25,000–$49,999 | $50,000–$99,999 | $100,000–$199,999 | $200,000+ |
|---|---|---|---|---|---|
| Violent crime | 29.6 | 16.9 | 14.6 | 12.2 | 9.7 |
| Serious violent crime | 11.7 | 5.9 | 4.3 | 3.9 | 2.9 |

*Source:* BJS, 2021a, table 3.

*Note:* Violent crime includes rape or sexual assault, robbery, aggravated assault, and simple assault; it excludes homicide because the NCVS is based on interviews with victims and therefore cannot measure murder. Serious violent crime excludes simple assault. The data for 2022 were highly unusual in showing higher rates of violent and serious violent crime for households with income above $200,000 than for households with $50,000–$99,999 and $100,000–$99,000. The data in the table are from 2021 and show the pattern of declining victimization rates for higher incomes that is generally shown in the NCVS.

information on 13,927 murders where the weapon is known, "How Americans Are Really Murdered" includes information on 173,299 murders (Reiman and Leighton 2023: 98). The category "occupational hazard and disease" contributes significantly to the revised estimate, and because the victims in this category work in blue-collar manufacturing and industrial jobs, these victimizations are disproportionately located in the lower-income groups. As noted in chapter 4, toxic waste facilities also tend to be in poor and especially minority areas, increasing the likelihood of a range of diseases.

Too much of the data on white-collar crime is collected by businesses to show how they are victimized, while few sources try to track harms committed by corporations against workers, consumers, communities, and the environment. Insurance companies may also produce information on fraud related to false claims by patients and doctors, but not their wrongful denial of claims for profit. Workplaces collect data on employee theft, but not wage theft against employees.

Further, the victimization for any year would not pick up the mass financial victimization caused by corporate fraud by the savings and loan industry in the 1990s that required a $500 billion bailout, or the more destructive fraud of the Enron era in the early 2000s and the 2008–2009 financial crisis. The exclusion of these types of victimization from crime surveys and most discussions in criminology adds to the sense that these harms do not amount to "real" crime. Indeed, during the collapse of Enron and other companies in 2001—when accounting fraud cost investors 70 to 90 percent of their money and top officials of those companies "were getting immensely, extraordinarily, obscenely wealthy" (Reiman and Leighton 2023: 149)—the Department of Justice reported that "property crimes had continued their downward trend and fallen to an all-time low" (Barak 2012: 73). The bipartisan Financial Crisis Inquiry Commission that reported on the 2008–2009 financial crisis "uses variants of the word 'fraud' no fewer than 157 times in describing what led to the crisis" (in Reiman and Leighton 2023: 159).

But no major financial institution faced criminal charges, so officially no criminal victimization happened.

The victims' rights movement has generally not been concerned about victims of white-collar and corporate crimes, even though the impact of these losses includes people delaying retirement, living in poverty, taking additional jobs, and scaling back on college education for their children. Impacts also include psychological harms like increased cynicism, reduced trust, depression, and suicide (Leighton and Reiman 2002; Reiman and Leighton 2023).

In conclusion, although official sources supposedly summarize "crime," they send the ideological message that street crime is "real" crime and that crimes are committed by the poor. Such reports trivialize the serious harm done by the wealthy and corporations even as they present great detail on even the minor wrongdoing of the lower classes. Shouldn't crime and victimization reports cover the violations of law by rich and poor, thus presenting comprehensive information about criminal harms and the threats citizens face (Leighton and Reiman 2014; Reiman and Leighton 2023)?

## Class Justice

Along with providing facts about the distribution of wealth and income, this chapter has emphasized that the high level of inequality in the United States is the result of choice through economic and social policies. That wealth brings with it power is likely not a surprise to readers, even if they would not fully endorse Marx's notion that history is primarily a struggle between the wealthy and the poor. But analysis of campaign donations and spending by political action committees (PACs) is largely consistent with Marx's statement that "the modern State is but a committee for managing the common affairs of the whole bourgeoisie" (in Reiman and Leighton 2023: 196). The argument is not that all the wealthy and large corporations have the same interests, but that government policies generally favor the continued accumulation of wealth by relatively few, while allowing for increasing exploitation of workers, consumers, and the natural environment. As befitting the notion of class struggle or class war, there are also times of notable organized social movements and protest, which usually turn social crisis into some "reform." But in spite of decades and centuries of reforms, the United States has high levels of inequality historically and in comparison to peer nations.

This section provides a partial and brief review of this history and its impact on justice, which provides some context for understanding our current situation. We would start by noting that throughout most of the 1800s and well into the 1900s, a blatant kind of class justice prevailed (Auerbach 1976; Barak 1980). The law was heavily influenced by a reverence for private property and laissez-faire social relations, which means "let them do as they will" and entails few regulations beyond the protection of private property. (Laissez-faire economics is the foundation of current neoliberalism, introduced in chapter 1.) Businesses sometimes produced dangerous goods or misrepresented their products, thus using their "freedom" to accumulate wealth in exploitative and unethical ways. By contrast, labor was highly regulated. Until the 1930s, unions were an illegal interference with "freedom of contract" and an unlawful conspiracy that limited an employer's property rights.

In spite of many companies amassing large fortunes from the Industrial Revolution, they fought attempts at minimum wages for employees. They often required employees to live in a company town, rent dwellings from the company, and shop at company stores. The prices charged by the company were more than the wage, so the debt bound families to the company as indentured servants. Fatigue, combined with the employers' indifference to workplace safety, created "an appalling record of industrial accidents" (Gilbert 1998: 57).

In other areas, exposés of the meatpacking industry shocked the public and motivated legislators to enact the first food and drug acts. Certain journalists, called muckrakers, believed that "big business was 'bad business' insofar as it was more concerned with profit than human life" (Lynch and Frank 1992: 13). Congress passed the Sherman Act in 1890, with Senator John Sherman emphasizing,

> If we will not endure a king as a political power, we should not endure a king over the production, transportation, and sale of any of the necessities of life. If we would not submit to an emperor, we should not submit to an autocrat of trade, with power to prevent competition and to fix the price of any commodity. (Khan 2017)

Lawyers like Louis Brandeis, who would later become a Supreme Court justice, shared their concerns about the "curse of business" and the problems of companies becoming large in the interest of becoming a monopoly—one that violated public trust rather than worked in its interests. "No country," he wrote, "can afford to have its prosperity originated by a small controlling class" (in Douglas 1954: 187). Justice Douglas (1954) explained, "Brandeis did not want America to become a nation of clerks, all working for some overlord." Further, the concentrated economic power of large corporations yields concentrated political power. Thus, antitrust law was intended to prevent "enabling a small minority to amass outsized wealth, which they could then use to influence government" (Khan 2017). That influence can come at the expense of workers, consumers, and the environment.

By the turn of the twentieth century, the buying of justice that had prevailed earlier was threatening the very legitimacy of criminal justice in the United States (Cantor 1932). Political corruption became widespread, and political machines dominated urban areas: "The machines controlled city governments, including the police and the courts" (Edelstein and Wicks 1977: 7). Graft and other forms of bribery contributed not only to the buying of justice by those who could afford it but also to a changing national morality. "Rackets," "pull," and "protection" were common antidotes for stubborn legal nuisances. And "the ability to 'make good' and 'get away with it' offsets the questionable means employed in the business as well as professional world. Disrespect for the law and order is the accompanying product of this scheme of success" (Cantor 1932: 145).

The working classes aggressively resisted exploitation through on-the-job actions and social movements. To combat challenges to the emerging monopoly or corporate order of industrial capitalism, the wealthy and ruling classes initially employed illegal violence, such as the hiring of private security to brutalize protesting workers.

The discontent of those who were not benefiting from the expanding economy threatened the growing prosperity of those who were. As a response to the growing resentment of the lower and working classes and to the middle-class Progressives who believed in the "perfectible society," the ruling strata sought to stabilize the social order. Roosevelt's New Deal sought to save capitalism from itself (Leighton 2018; Pearce 1976), or, in the words of Mark Twain, the president "persisted in attacking the symptoms and letting the disease carefully alone" (in Seybold 2017).

As the number of violent incidents increased, as the contradictions of American democracy became more apparent, other methods for regulating and controlling the masses were needed—methods reflective of a modern, rational system of crime control and a criminal justice system based on a more equal-appearing application of the rule of law (Barak 1980). The Progressive Era ushered in "hard" and "soft" reforms to the administration of criminal justice (Center for Research on Criminal Justice 1975). Examples of the harder, more technical, reforms included the formation of systems of state policing, the initiation of truancy laws, and the forced sterilization of some "mentally defective" persons, poor people, and sex offenders. Examples of the softer, or humane, reforms included the development of the juvenile justice system, the public defender system, and, a bit later, systems of treatment and rehabilitation. Each of these soft reforms aimed at a fairer, more objective, scientific, and humane administration of criminal justice. In combination, these reforms helped secure and legitimate the needs of an emerging corporate capitalism as they contributed to more rational, bureaucratic, and efficient systems of criminal justice. That, in turn, legitimized greater state intervention into the lives of those marginalized on the basis of their class, race, or gender/sexuality. The practice of forced sterilization, for example, continued until as recently as the 1970s and provided the foundation for policies aimed at getting women who receive welfare to agree to be implanted with the contraceptive Norplant.

As the size of corporations grew through the 1900s, the large concentrations of wealth they held translated into political power that is currently exercised through corporate lobbyists and political action committees. PACs that donate thousands—or even millions—of dollars can achieve considerable clout, especially because only 1.44 percent of the adult population gave more than $200 to a political party or candidate during the 2020 election cycle (OpenSecrets.org, n.d.). Many corporate interests donate heavily to both political parties to ensure access to legislators and favorable action on their legislation, regardless of which party wins the election. Further influence and consideration comes from the corporate use of "the high-paying job offer from industry, the lavish parties and prostitutes, the meals, transportation, housing, and vacation accommodations, and the many other hustling enticements of money" (Simon 1999: 24).

The result of this influence can be tax breaks, less regulation and policing, and limits on the extent of punishment (harms are misdemeanors rather than felonies, are civil matters rather than criminal, or have limits on the size of damages juries are allowed to award against businesses). For example, even after the savings and loan crisis of the late 1980s and early 1990s required a half-*trillion*-dollar bailout, the authors of *Big Money Crime* note that Congress went on a spree of "cavalier" financial deregulation, spurred on by lobbying and political donations. This created the "paradox of increasing financial deregulation coming on the heels of the most catastrophic experiment with deregulation in history" (Calavita et al. 1997). In turn, this deregulation created the conditions for the string of corporate corruption in 2001–2002 that included Enron, WorldCom, and many others (Leighton and Reiman 2002). Congress passed the Sarbanes-Oxley Act to correct some of the systemic causes of widespread fraud, but some of this correction has been undermined by subsequent corporate lobbying (Reiman and Leighton 2023).

Further, the financial services industry then lobbied to deregulate many aspects of their business, which resulted in the financial crisis of 2008–2009 (Barak 2012). Indeed, Barry Ritholtz—the CEO of an investment research firm and author of *Bailout Nation* (2009a)—argues that the financial crisis was "wasted": the "smoldering resentment" among people because of the "massive taxpayer wealth transfer to inept, corrupt, incompetent bankers" provided the "best chance to clean up Wall Street in five generations." But "what we got instead, was the usual lobbying efforts by the finance industry. They own Congress, lock stock and barrel, and they throttled Financial Reform" (2009b). So, even after a series of financial crises, financial institutions aim their sights both at putting loopholes in new rules and at reducing the budgets of enforcement agencies.

The abandonment of antitrust enforcement starting in the 1980s and the acceleration of globalization has meant that corporations became larger and more powerful, creating the world that Sherman hoped to avoid: having "king[s] over the production, transportation, and sale of any of the necessities of life" and "autocrat[s] of trade, with power to prevent competition and to fix the price of any commodity." The Biden administration has made some steps to stop some mergers, although it is too early to know how serious this effort will be. Optimistically,

> experts on both sides [of the political spectrum] have come to recognize that there is a serious monopoly crisis in America, with a lack of competition across the board in sectors as diverse as search engines, agribusiness, and airlines. This concentration crisis fosters inequality, damages innovation and productivity, harms incomes, and transforms entire industries into "kill zones" where no one will invest. (Stoller 2023)

Once, corporate charters were meant to limit and control corporations, but they now act as a shield from the public and give corporations permission to act in the best interests of shareholders rather than the larger public good. Thus,

> the corporation is now a superhuman creature of the law, superior to you and me, since it has civil rights but no civil responsibilities; it is legally obligated to be selfish; it cannot be thrown in jail; it can deduct from its tax bill any fines it gets for wrongdoings; and it can live forever. (Hightower 1998: 34)

While many of the individual men and women who work in the corporation make good neighbors, the corporation itself can be a problem because "the corporation's legally defined mandate is to pursue, relentlessly and without exception, its own self-interest, regardless of the often harmful consequences it might cause to others" (Bakan 2004: 2). Indeed, Bakan asked Robert Hare, a noted expert on psychopaths, to apply his diagnostic checklist to corporations and found a close match: they are irresponsible by putting others at risk; manipulative of everything, including public opinion; lacking in empathy for others and unable to feel remorse;

unwilling to accept responsibility; and superficial in relating to others (Bakan 2004: 56–57). Just as psychopaths are known for their superficial charm, corporations may "act in ways to promote the public good when it is to their advantage to do so, but they will just as quickly sacrifice it—it is their legal obligation to do so—when necessary to serve their own ends" (Bakan 2004: 118).

Thus, protecting citizens, workers, consumers, communities, and the environment from the excesses of corporate behavior is an important function of law. But this social control is brought into question by donations and strategic lobbying on the part of corporations. When the size of corporate actors is combined with their institutional personality, the dark side of big business becomes visible. Obviously, not all businesses are bad, and the point is that there is a problematic antisocial tendency that must be kept in check, but the control mechanisms to regulate and hold corporations accountable have become less powerful relative to the corporations themselves (Barak 2015, 2017).

Generally, with the crimes of the powerless, the governmental legal agents wage "wars" like the ones on illicit drugs or undocumented families and have "zero tolerance" for a range of petty crimes. Such acts receive disproportionate priority with investigations, surveillance, arrest, and prosecutions. The poor and powerless are disproportionately represented as "common criminals" or the "dangerous class," and they are treated accordingly.

By contrast, many crimes of the very powerful are "beyond incrimination" or not subject to the criminal law in the first place because of lobbying and donations to politicians. Thus, the possibility of criminal liability and prison does not even exist. Policing is done through regulatory agencies that are "defective by design" (see chapter 8) and resolve issues through tax-deductible fines—large-sounding dollar amounts that are like parking tickets to multibillion-dollar corporations.

## Implications

This chapter began by noting the reluctance in our society to discuss issues of economic class. It has made class more visible by reviewing the economic facts and setting a foundation for how inequality impacts criminology and criminal justice. The criminal law focuses on the crimes of the poor, and criminology ignores white-collar and corporate crime, so people (including criminologists) believe it is the poor who are the worst threat to society (Reiman and Leighton 2023). Even when criminology studies the causes of crime, wealth and inequality are rarely considered, despite their importance. Indeed, a twenty-five-year retrospective on the 1967 President's Crime Commission stated, "While evidence shows that criminal justice procedures are more evenhanded than in the past, it is also painfully obvious that the growing gap between rich and poor, and white and black, continues to make criminal justice a social battleground rather than a mechanism to increase social peace" (in Conley 1994: 66).

Because of the long history of racism, Blacks, Hispanics, and Native Americans are disproportionately poor, so issues of class and race are tied together in ways that will be explored in other chapters. The current and evolving problem is that criminal justice is contributing to the differences between rich and poor and between white people and minorities. Current domestic policies of crime control operate as if "Americans have concluded that the problems of the urban poor are intractable and therefore they [apparently agreed to have their money] spent on a vast network of prisons, rather than on solutions" (in Welch 1996: 101) that include basic social and educational services for the poor. Some of these programs are cheaper than prisons and have the potential to reduce crime by preventing child abuse, enhancing the intellectual and social development of children, providing support and mentoring to vulnerable adolescents, and doing intensive work with juvenile offenders (Currie 1998: 81).

A statement of this problem more than twenty years ago is still relevant:

> On the one hand, we are expending a greater portion of our public dollars on incarcerating, punishing, treating and controlling persons who are primarily from the lower economic classes in an effort to reduce crime. On the other hand, we have set in motion economic policies that serve to widen the gap between the rich and poor, producing yet another generation of impoverished youths who will probably end up under control of the correctional system. By escalating the size of the correctional system, we are also increasing the tax burden and diverting billions of dollars from those very public services (education, health, transportation, and economic development) that would reduce poverty, unemployment, crime, drug abuse and mental illness. (Irwin and Austin 1997: 10–11)

While the levels of inequality and economic mobility have important implications for the American dream and for criminological theories such as strain or conflict theory, criminology does not pursue these ideas in a way that would increase consciousness of class, inequality, and stratification. Sadly, the criminal justice system reflects the class biases in society—and helps to reinforce them. The United States has enlarged its apparatuses of criminal justice and crime control against the poorest members in society while the rich, especially corporations, continue to gather more wealth and feel unaccountable for the adverse consequences of their morally blameworthy harms.

## Review and Discussion Questions

1. The threat of global warming and ecological crisis is often described as human extinction, which suggests it threatens everyone equally. What are the ways this is true, and what are some of the ways that the burden falls on the poor?
2. What do you see as the most important harms of inequality?
3. What are some of the ways to define class? How are descriptions that are tied to a theory of power relations different from other descriptions?
4. If you were going to be randomly placed in a society, what level of inequality would you choose for it—how would you distribute wealth to the top and bottom 20 percent? Would it look like the current strata in the United States today?
5. Does the United States have more or less inequality than you thought? Why don't Americans know the actual levels of inequality between classes?
6. How is wealth transmitted intergenerationally? What historic practices affect current intergenerational transfers of wealth?
7. How do the intersections of race and gender/sexuality impact class inequality?

8. How does student loan debt factor into your economic mobility, meaning your likelihood of doing better or worse than your parents? Are there other debts or economic privileges that play an important role?

9. What are some ways that inequality has an impact on justice and criminal justice? Do you think this impact is larger or smaller than in past times? How successful were the various reforms to make criminal justice (appear) more fair?

# CHAPTER 4

# Understanding Race and White Privilege

*In Plessy v. Ferguson (163 U.S. 537 [1896]), the Supreme Court set the precedent of "separate but equal": separate facilities for Black folks did not offend constitutional provisions about equal protection so long as they were equal to those provided for whites. The 1890 Louisiana Separate Car Act required separate railway cars, and Plessy was part of a civil rights group that challenged it (Rojas 2021). When Plessy sat in a car designated for whites only, the conductor told him to leave. As the Court described it, on Plessy's "refusal to comply with such order, he was, with the aid of a police officer, forcibly ejected from said coach, and hurried off to, and imprisoned in, the parish jail."*

*The Court found that separate cars were a reasonable regulation, made "with reference to the established usages, customs, and traditions of the people, and with a view to the promotion of their comfort, and the preservation of the public peace and good order." Social prejudices cannot be overcome by legislation, and if the races "are to meet upon terms of social equality, it must be the result of natural affinities, a mutual appreciation of each other's merits, and a voluntary consent of individuals." Although Plessy argued that enforced separation "stamps the colored race with a badge of inferiority," the majority said it is "not by reason of anything found in the act, but solely because the colored race chooses to put that construction upon it."*

*The Court recognized that Plessy "was seven-eighths Caucasian and one-eighth African blood; that the mixture of colored blood was not discernible in him." Indeed, Plessy was chosen by the civil rights group because he could pass as white (Rojas 2021). The suit involved a claim "that he was entitled to every right, privilege, and immunity secured to citizens of the United States of the white race." Plessy argued, "In a mixed community, the reputation of belonging to the dominant race, in this instance the white race, is 'property,' in the same sense that a right of* action or of inheritance is property." The Court conceded it was for the purposes of the case but argued that the statute did not take his property: either he was a white man who was entitled or a Black man who was not.

But who decides, and how?

The train conductor seemed to have power to make racial classifications, which would result in arbitrary decisions, but the Court did not see that issue as properly before it. The state legislatures could guide decisions on racial classifications, but some said "any visible admixture of black blood stamps the person as belonging to the colored race; others, that it depends upon the preponderance of blood; and still others, that the predominance of white blood must only be in the proportion of three-fourths."

Justice Harlan was the sole dissenter, claiming that the decision would prove to be as "pernicious" as the Dred Scott case, which declared that escaped slaves who traveled north to freedom were still property and should be returned to their Southern masters. For Harlan, the statute seemed inconsistent, for example, in allowing Black nurses to attend white children but not a white adult in bad health. Harlan also pointed to another group that "is a race so different from our own that we do not permit those belonging to it to become citizens of the United States" and are, "with few exceptions, absolutely excluded from our country." But under the law "a Chinaman can ride in the same passenger coach with white citizens," yet Blacks, "many of whom, perhaps, risked their lives for the preservation of the Union, who are entitled, by law, to participate in the political control of the state and nation, who are not excluded, by law or by reason of their race, from public stations of any kind, and who have all the legal rights that belong to white citizens, are yet declared to be criminals, liable to imprisonment, if they ride in a public coach occupied by citizens of the white race."

Unlike the majority, Harlan argued that the purpose of the law was to compel Black people to "keep to themselves" rather than to keep whites out of Black areas, and "no one would be so wanting in candor as to assert the contrary." He acknowledged that whites were the dominant race and said that while "every true man has pride of race," the Thirteenth Amendment abolished slavery and "prevents the imposition of any burdens or disabilities that constitute badges of slavery or servitude." Even though whites were the dominant race and "will continue to be so for all time," he was clear that

> in view of the Constitution, in the eye of the law, there is in this country no superior, dominant, ruling class of citizens. There is no caste here. Our Constitution is color-blind, and neither knows nor tolerates classes among citizens. In respect of civil rights, all citizens are equal before the law. The humblest is the peer of the most powerful. The law regards man as man, and takes no account of his surroundings

*or of his color when his civil rights as guaranteed by the supreme law of the land
are involved.*

*In 2021, the Louisiana Board of Pardons voted to clear Plessy's criminal record.
The descendants of Plessy and Ferguson have formed a joint nonprofit to link his
activism to the nonviolent protests of the civil rights movement. An article on his
pardon suggests that "the racial disparities and discrimination that extended from
that ruling ultimately were at the heart of the protests that erupted last year after
the death of George Floyd" (Rojas 2021).*

## Introduction

The previous chapter reviewed inequalities in income and wealth to establish the
foundations of how economic bias undermines the ideal of equality before the law,
such that the poorest is not the peer of the most powerful. This chapter reviews how
race undermines the ideal of equality before the law under a system that should be
color-blind. But doesn't being color-blind erase hundreds of years of oppression and
current inequalities?

Too often, "seeing race" means discussing Black people when there are many
racial groups that live under systems of white supremacy. Though there are dynamics and experiences unique to Black people in the United States, white supremacy
harms all racial minority groups because it is the dominant system that shapes their
collective opportunities and outcomes. However, all oppressed groups do not experience racism and discrimination in the same way. Each minority group also has its
own unique history, strengths, contributions, and struggles that often differ from
dominant narratives and portrayals. Further, just as there is wide variety within the
white population, diversity also exists in other minority groups. Among Hispanics
or the Latino/a/x population (which are terms that vary in usage across regions and
generations), wide variations exist to the point where entire nationalities and migra-
tory waves are associated with drastically different outcomes. Gender and darkness
of skin color also combine in ways that provide advantages and disadvantages to
people within the same racial identity.

While exploring the differences between racial groups is critical, it is the system of white supremacy they have in common. For many, this term is politically
loaded, but it must be understood as an ideological package—a system of beliefs
and "sincere fictions" (Bonilla-Silva 2018: 2)—that justifies present racial inequalities. These beliefs transcend individuals and exist independently from individual
actions. Thus, our interest is not in trying to identify who is a racist or seeing
racism as a property of individuals. Instead, we emphasize how white supremacy
is found in the default *structure* of society so that it is perpetuated regardless of
whether or not individual doctors, bankers, police officers, and managers are racist (Golash-Boza 2016a).

The system of white supremacy is not just about racial groups but also colorism, which describes a preference for lighter-skinned members of minority groups.
Colorism suggests that there is a "pigmentocracy" where skin color is the basis for

an evolving "tri-racial system with Whites at the top, a new group of Honorary Whites in the middle, and a Collective Black group at the bottom" (Hargrove and Gonzalez 2022). The "Black group" does not just mean African Americans but darker-skinned members of all racial and ethnic groups, who tend to have less education and income than lighter-skinned members of the same group.

Colorism does not deny the importance of racial classifications but suggests that people see skin color as well. In addition, colorism helps reveal the diversity within racial categories by highlighting how not all African Americans see themselves as dark (even though lighter-skinned African Americans, like former biracial president Obama, identify as African American). Although colorism is underexplored in criminology, the limited findings suggest that darker-skinned people have worse outcomes with, and perceptions of, the criminal justice system (Carter and Talley 2022). Further, lighter-skinned people wanted to work in the criminal justice system because of their interest and passion, as well as for the compensation and status of working in law enforcement; darker-skinned individuals wanted to work in the system because they experienced trauma or wanted to make a change (Carter and Talley 2022).

Whether discussing racial categories or colorism, our emphasis on white supremacy disrupts power-neutral understandings of race and multiculturalism that suggest diversity is like a salad bowl or a collection of different fruits that have no hierarchical ordering. While that may be a goal, race currently serves to sort opportunities concerning employment, education, housing, law, criminal justice, and many others. However, part of the ideology of white supremacy presents social institutions as race neutral, and "color-blind racism" presents inequality as the product of "market dynamics [and] naturally occurring phenomena." For example, housing segregation is explained as the result of nonracist "natural tendencies among groups" to be with their own race (Bonilla-Silva 2018: 2) when the United States has a long history of housing discrimination (Rothstein 2018).

Indeed, this chapter follows up on the idea of racial capitalism (introduced in chapter 2), which suggested that race was less an explanation for unequal social outcomes than what needed to be studied in relation to the changing needs of capitalism. Thus, understanding the political economy of an era and the influence of wealth, the demand for cheap labor, and the surplus population are a starting point for discussing race, white supremacy, and criminal justice. Historically, for example,

> the African slave trade began in earnest only after large-scale Native American slavery proved impractical in North America. The abolition of slavery led to the importation of low-wage labor from Asia. Legislation banning immigration from Asia set the stage for the recruitment of low-wage labor from Mexico. The new racial categories that emerged in each of these eras all revolved around applying racial labels to "nonwhite" groups in order to exploit them while at the same time preserving the value of whiteness. (Lipsitz 2005: 68)

The criminal justice system has played a significant role in these processes of exploitation and marginalization. In each era, laws and the gears of criminal justice were tailored to coerce, punish, or otherwise control nonwhite segments of society, which allowed white-administered capitalism to extract profits from racialized bodies while denying their humanity. This process continues today, when neoliberalism increasingly marginalizes the poor, especially minorities, and expands economic exploitation: "The lowest tiers of the workforce represent the class fraction, or fractions, for whom the carceral state has been deployed, not as a response to crime but to manage daily life, tightly regulating how they are allowed to congregate, support themselves when consigned to informal economies, shop, and even drive their cars" (Shanahan and Kurti 2022: 74).

Such systems of oppression generate substantial resistance, and "few whites realize the huge amount of energy and talent that whites themselves have dissipated in their construction of anti-black attitudes and ideologies and in their participation in social discrimination" (Feagin and Vera 1995: 2). These attitudes also prevent white people from "seeing clearly their own class exploitation and . . . organizing effectively with black and other minority workers" (Feagin and Vera 1995: 15; see also Ignatiev 2008). The racism that criminal justice both reflects and recreates is thus part of the "sociology of waste" that squanders the talent and potential of minority groups (Feagin and Vera 1995).

A similar waste happens with class and gender/sexuality, and examining these systems of power, oppression, and privilege makes it easier to imagine and build systems that protect people, respect human dignity, and advance a more equitable system of public safety. To help get there, this chapter covers the relationship between race and (in)justice. It is divided into four sections. First, we discuss how race and ethnicity are socially constructed concepts, meaning that they are manufactured for political purposes despite robust attempts to make them seem "objective" and scientific. Second, we explore the meanings and connections among key terms such as *racism*, *stereotypes*, *discrimination*, and *prejudice*. Of particular importance is the idea of privilege and understanding that whiteness itself is a racial category, despite whiteness often being seen as a "normal" position or default raceless standpoint. Finally, like the last part of chapter 2, this chapter addresses how race relates to criminology and criminal justice issues. It first explores race and victimization, then finishes with a brief review of how race has historically played a role in the administration of justice.

We understand that many whites and lighter-skinned people find it stressful to deal with material on white privilege and white supremacy. While everyone should have some space to process their feelings about this material, we hope it will not displace ongoing efforts to learn about race. Sometimes even small amounts of stress trigger defensive moves that shut down conversations about racism, thus having the effect of maintaining systems of white supremacy and privilege—a concept known as "white fragility" (DiAngelo 2018). For example, even when the discussion is about structural racism, white people sometimes turn the conversation back to racism being an individual-level problem about false beliefs—then they credential themselves, through stories about minority friends, as being nonracist. Other reactions, like guilt, anger, and silence, are so strong that the conversation comes to be about the harm they are feeling from reading about racism rather than the harms of racism. We hope white students can focus less on "Am I racist?" and more on "What does it mean to be white?" so they will not "continue to enact policies and practices—intentionally or not—that hurt and limit" minorities (Bergner 2020).

One final note on the terminology for racial groups is necessary because language evolves, labels are political and contested, and there is never consensus in the way identities are labeled or referenced. For example, some use *Black* and *American Indian*, while others prefer *African American* and *Native American*. Of necessity, we use the language of resources we consulted for this book, as well as the individual preferences of different authors of this book when there was not a consensus.

Readers should keep in mind, though, that *Native American* refers to American Indians, and the capitalization designates their status as First Peoples on the land before it became the United States. (Others born in the United States are Native Americans.) Asian Indians are from India. *Latinx* is used as a gender-neutral term that includes men (Latinos), women (Latinas), and all those who do not identify with the gender binary (discussed more in the next chapter). *Latino/a/x* also captures gender beyond the binary while acknowledging that some people have chosen masculine and feminine identities. At times, to capture the history of racism or someone's prejudice, we include quotations containing words that may be offensive to contemporary readers. We do not endorse these attitudes or the use of racial epithets but believe it is important to acknowledge that those attitudes have and continue to exist.

## The Social Construction of Ethnicity and Race

*Race* is a collection of physical traits. *Ethnicity* refers to national origin, language, culture, and religion. Race and ethnicity overlap because people in certain regions of the world share certain physical features, cultures, and religions, but, in general, *race* more often refers to biological features, whereas *ethnicity* more often refers to geography and behavioral features.

While physical differences exist between people and the effects of racism are real, racial and ethnic categories are socially constructed, meaning categories are fluid over time and can be best understood in terms of politics and power. There are no genetic markers for the identification of race. Scientists agree that modern humans originated from a population that emerged out of Africa and migrated around the globe, so there is a continuum of genetic variation that makes the concept of race meaningless. Genetic tests examine those differences to find clues about ancestry by identifying similarities to genetic populations in different geographic regions (Fullwiley 2014). But mapping those geographic regions onto race—deciding, for example, that a European with a single African ancestor is "Negro"—shows the social construction of race.

Indeed, the U.S. Census Bureau (2022) itself notes that "the racial categories included in the census questionnaire generally reflect a social definition of race recognized in this country and not an attempt to define race biologically, anthropologically, or genetically." The idea that the census "reflects" definitions of race recognized in the country obscures how politics and scientific racism have played into changing definitions. This section tries to briefly capture how some of the changes in racial categories, as well as the willingness of people to claim those identities, are not based on science or objective criteria.

The first U.S. Census in 1790 had just three categories: (1) free white men and women, (2) all other free people, and (3) slaves (Brown 2020). Recently, the Census Bureau has used five categories of race:

- White
- Black or African American
- American Indian or Alaska Native
- Asian
- Native Hawaiian or Other Pacific Islander

The census has allowed more opportunities for people to specify a background nationality within these categories, although the borders of many countries are based on social, political, and military circumstances and are sometimes unstable political compromises.

The census treats race and ethnicity as separate concepts, so "Hispanic or Latino" refers to a person of Cuban, Mexican, Puerto Rican, South or Central American, or other Spanish culture or origin, regardless of race (Lopez and Wu 2022). Back in the 1930s, in response to congressional debate about immigration restrictions, the census created a category of "Mexican." As an additional racial category, it officially made Mexicans nonwhite, even though they had been slipped in with white people for purposes of school segregation and Jim Crow laws because their blood did not have "Negro ancestry." After the census, the Mexican government and Mexican Americans successfully lobbied to have the classification changed: "Although having their whiteness restored did not lessen discrimination, the Mexican government and Mexican Americans fully understood the implication of being officially recognized as a non-White group" (Foley 2005: 60). When Congress again called for the creation of statistics on people of Spanish culture, origin, and descent in the 1970s, political lobbying resulted in the current system of ethnicity being separate from race so that Hispanics would not automatically be nonwhite.

Currently, people from the Middle East and North Africa (MENA) are classified as white, even though they face discrimination closer to what people of color experience (Wang 2022). The fear and stereotypes after September 11, 2001, widened the gap between the privilege most people in the white category have and the discrimination and harassment targeted against those who identify as MENA. The census is considering a proposal to add MENA as a category, and it is taking comments on whether MENA is a race or ethnicity (Wang 2022, 2023).

Census policies about counting mixed-race people reinforce that race is not objective. The category of "mulatto" appeared in 1850 to capture information about people who were not "pure" Black or white because "some scientists believed these groups were less fertile, or otherwise weak; they looked to census data to support their theories" (Parker et al. 2015). At that time, the census workers were instructed to mark as mixed "all persons having any perceptible trace of African blood" (Parker et al. 2015), thus reserving the "white" category at the top of the racial hierarchy for those who were "pure." While "blood" is used in a figurative sense to mean ancestry, white people have also been concerned about actual blood transfusions from people of color (see box 4.1).

## BOX 4.1

### Race and Blood

In 1935, a doctor in Germany had a patient who needed a blood transfusion, which required a live donor rather than stored blood. Unable to find a suitable donor quickly, the doctor donated his own blood. Instead of receiving praise, the Jewish doctor was sent to a concentration camp for "defiling" the blood of the German race. German scientific racism about blood "purity" fed claims of Aryan supremacy but set back serious scientific research on blood. Laws severely limited the availability of blood for transfusions because of the possibility of being charged with "an attack on German blood" if the donor could not prove it was pure Aryan blood (Starr 1998: 26).

In the United States, the topic of "colored" versus "white" blood also stirred up controversy during World War II. The Red Cross knew that "blood was blood" but nevertheless followed the wishes of the military and refused to collect blood from African Americans. When the attack on Pearl Harbor created a large demand for blood to treat wounded soldiers, the Red Cross collected blood from Black folks but labeled and processed it separately. As historian Douglas Starr notes, "the policy proved offensive to many Americans because the country was, after all, fighting a racist enemy" (1998: 108). In the late 1950s, Arkansas passed a law requiring the segregation of blood. Louisiana, home of the *Plessy v. Ferguson* case, "went so far as to make it a misdemeanor for physicians to give a white person black blood without asking permission" (Starr 1998: 170). The segregation of blood ended during the 1960s, more because of the civil rights movement than further advances in science.

Reinforcing the concern in the census about mixed-race people were antimiscegenation laws that prohibited whites from marrying members of a different race, although members of minority groups could marry outside of their race without legal consequences. Antimiscegenation laws required specific definitions of race in order for state registrars to certify a person's racial composition so the marriage could be deemed legal. In Virginia, *white* meant "no trace whatever of any blood other than Caucasian; but persons who have one-sixteenth or less of the blood of the American Indian and have no other non-Caucasian blood shall be deemed to be white persons" (*Loving v. Virginia*, 388 U.S. 1 [1967]). The fraction of Native American blood was based on the "desire of all to recognize as an integral and honored part of the white race the descendants of John Rolfe and Pocahontas." The Supreme Court declared antimiscegenation laws unconstitutional because of individual rights to association in 1967 in the case of *Loving v. Virginia* (388 U.S. 1 [1967]).[1]

The recording of "mulattos" gave way to "other" as a category, and the census started allowing people to self-report identities important to them rather than having the census worker decide. But when people used the "other" option to record themselves as mixed race, the census recorded the first race someone listed (so someone who recorded white-Black would be recorded as white). Starting with the 2000 Census, people could select "mixed race" and report what they feel are the important racial identities in their background. The number of people claiming multiple races has increased dramatically since then.

These changes have allowed people to better express their racial identities, but politics and power affect choices. For example, between 1960 and 2000, the Native American population doubled, then doubled again between 2010 and 2020 (Hampton 2023). Some of this was actual Natives being more willing to identify themselves on the census because officially recognized tribes encouraged members to do so, as federal aid is based on tribal population. Further, "older generations would either avoid the census or lie on it (leaving Native blank) out of fear that social services would take their children. It's sobering to see how many people have mentioned this" on discussion forums (Hampton 2023; Brune 1999).

However, much of the more recent growth has been driven by whites choosing the mixed-race white–Native American option. Some white people using genealogy websites have found a small fraction of Native American ancestry—and they are more willing to claim it than a small fraction of Black. Ancestry websites send emails advertising, "You're related to Pocahontas!" and often use questionable records to satisfy customers that they have a Native princess in their background (Hampton 2023). When white people engage in "ethnic shifting" or "ethnic shopping" (Hitt 2005), Native American is one of the most popular, leading to many "Pretendians." Indeed, a survey found that 34 percent of whites falsely claimed an ethnic identity on their college applications, and half of those chose Native American (Spencer 2021). (And 85 percent of those were accepted and believed it helped.)

No one links claims of race on the census with college applications and actual tribal membership, where reliance on "blood quantum" rubrics determines membership eligibility. Blood quantum is the percentage of Native American ancestry a person has, calculated on the basis of records about other formally recognized tribal members. Blood quantum is thus important because tribal membership can confer certain benefits, and the tribes also want to exercise sovereignty over standards for membership. But this way of measuring "Indian-ness" also meant that, "over time, Indians would literally breed themselves out and rid the federal government of their legal duties to uphold treaty obligations" (Chow 2018).

The social construction of race is further exemplified by the international diversity of racial categories (Stevens et al. 2015). No other country uses the same categories as the U.S. Census. This issue has important consequences for what criminal justice data are collected, how they are analyzed, and what "knowledge" is produced. For example, Canada collects criminal justice data only about "natives" and "nonnatives." The government there is concerned that "'black' citizens have originated from many different countries over the last century, including the U.S., the West Indies, India, and Africa" (Lauritsen 2004: 70). Combining this diverse group into a single category makes analysis problematic, especially when there is no record of the country of origin or time of arrival in Canada. Criminologists then try to interpret white-black differences, even as "new 'white' immigrants continue to arrive from places as diverse as Russia or middle-eastern countries" (Lauritsen 2004: 70).

Thus, one general concern is that analysis using official data cannot be "objective" knowledge about race if race itself cannot be objectively and consistently defined (Gabbidon and Greene 2005: 40). Another general concern is that diversity within groups is masked by the broader categories. For example, "Native American" includes 566 federally recognized tribes, although there are actually more because the federal government has stringent requirements for recognition, which is the basis for certain grants, entitlements, and casinos. Likewise, "wide ethnic diversity may exist in large Latino neighborhoods, as ethnic minorities come from places like Mexico, Cuba, Puerto Rico, and other Central and South American countries, each of which have distinct cultural practices and use of Spanish language." Thus, "residents may be quite different from Latino officers that have been assigned to patrol their neighborhoods" (Álvarez and Urbina 2015: 155).

Stating that race and ethnicity are socially constructed does not deny that some differences exist among people or that people experience very real oppression based on their (claimed and perceived) race and ethnicity. But far from reflecting inherent or essential racial identities, these racial categories reflect the social, economic, and political power of the society that creates them. Power and privilege are reflected in the schema of racial classification, which shapes people's lives and identities through stereotypes, prejudices, discrimination, and racism.

## Stereotypes and Power

*Stereotypes* are preconceived notions about the behavior, attitudes, looks, feelings, and motives of a group of people. These notions are held by individuals, communities, and societies. They serve to further reinforce the categorization of people, but they have the additional properties of being fixed and negative generalizations. Many definitions stress the inadequate or problematic basis of stereotypes in personal experience—such as when people hold stereotypes about groups they have never personally encountered but "know" about them from friends or the media.

Embracing racist stereotypes can be a way for groups to secure a better place in the racial hierarchy: "Like wave after wave of newcomers to this country before, Asian immigrants and refugees learned that absorbing and repeating anti-Black racism helps in the assimilation process" (V. T. Nguyen 2021). The book *How the Irish Became White* (Ignatiev 2008) documents how Irish immigrants in the 1800s competed for the same jobs and housing as Blacks; people saw "Negroes as smoked Irish." But they learned to "become white" by embracing anti-Black racism.

The idea of Asians as a "model minority" might seem like a positive rather than negative evaluation, but being "a paragon of hard work and docility carries a negative undercurrent" (Feagin and Feagin 1996: 404). It came about in the 1960s to critique civil rights protests and is meant to tell other minority groups to work harder and complain less. These stereotypes are also negative for Asians because they include high expectations and a low tolerance for deviance, among other debilitating pressures. Further, "while 'model minorities' are characterized as diligent, it is thought that they lack the strong persona to make effective leaders" (Yee 2023). Views of Asian women as "exotic" tend not to be truly positive and are a way to communicate that they are submissive sex objects, appropriate for conquering and fetishizing.

The idea of Asians being a "model minority" homogenizes a diverse group, making it seem as if all Asian groups are high achieving and none need help. For example, chapter 3 noted that Asians have a higher median income than whites, but the high incomes of Asian Indians counterbalances the poverty of other Asian groups. The "model minority" also exists in tension with depictions of Asian "enemies" in World War II, the Korean and Vietnam Wars, and a variety of times (especially with car manufacturing) when the United States had "Asian enemies that were economic in nature" (Gover et al. 2020: 648). When COVID hit, Asians quickly went from being the model minority to being seen as "culturally uncivilized, physically inferior, and hygienically backward" (Ren and Feagin 2021: 748).

*Prejudice* refers to a negative or hostile attitude toward another social group. It is an attitude that exists before any action against the social group is performed. Psychologically, people project onto the minority group many of the negative attributes they wish to deny in themselves, such as a propensity toward violence, criminality, promiscuity, or immorality. Prejudice literally means prejudging someone, usually on the basis of a stereotype. While prejudice is a thought or attitude, *discrimination* occurs when people act on the basis of stereotypes and prejudice, such as denying people housing, employment, or promotions. Prejudices coupled with discrimination in the workplace, for example, can propel members of the dominant race to promotions because of their assumed positive traits. Persons who subscribe to white supremacy (even subconsciously), that is, might assume their white colleagues are smart and hardworking and that any mistakes were made in "good faith." Members of minority groups may not get the same benefit of the doubt, so mistakes and problems are more likely to be interpreted as reflecting less integrity, work ethic, motivation, or intelligence.

Because whites still have the vast majority of the power in society, they have the greatest ability to discriminate, so much of this chapter focuses on the problems associated with white prejudice and discrimination. In other words, people of all races can have prejudices or excessive pride of race, referred to as *individual* or *individualized racism*. But members of minority groups generally do not have the power that can translate prejudice into substantial and recurring discrimination against whites in areas such as employment, business contracts, classrooms, systemic police violence, and criminal justice harm. The term *institutional* or *structural racism* acknowledges that racist behavioral patterns or consequences have structural aspects that systematically stratify society, shape identity, and produce substantive differences. For example,

> when white terrorists bomb a black church and kill five black children, that is an act of individual racism, widely deplored by most segments of society. But when in that same city—Birmingham, Alabama—five hundred black babies die each year because of lack of proper food, shelter and medical facilities, and thousands more are destroyed and maimed physically, emotionally, and intellectually because of conditions of poverty and discrimination, that is a function of institutional racism. (Carmichael and Hamilton 1967: 65)

A lack of understanding about race is perpetuated through the belief that race is about people of color and that whites do not have race. But being white involves having a race. That race (being white) affects identity and opportunity, even if white people have little race consciousness: "In the same way that both men's and women's lives are shaped by their gender, and that both heterosexual and lesbian women's experiences are shaped by their sexuality, white people *and* people of color live racially structured lives. In other words, any system of differentiation shapes those on whom it bestows privilege as well as those it oppresses" (Frankenberg 1993: 1).

## White Privilege

Because whites are the dominant group, this social position and its privileges are naturalized through ideology so that being white seems neither privileged nor socially constructed. Ideology serves to naturalize the racial hierarchies by describing society as the result of people's natural tendencies and the operation of free markets. Not only are white traits valued and minority traits devalued, but *white privilege* is created when whiteness becomes the norm. One aspect of this is that white people are not seen as speaking for whites but from and for a universal point of view:

> There is no more powerful position than that of being "just" human. The claim to power is the claim to speak for the commonality of humanity. Raced people can't do that—they can only speak for their race. But nonraced people can, for they do not represent the interests of a race. (Dyer 2005: 10)

To be clear, the author of the quote believes whites have race, and he is speaking to the popular perception of whites instead having no race. The point of studying the race of whites is to make that point of view clearer:

> White people have power and believe that they think, feel and act like and for all people; white people, unable to see their particularity, cannot take account of other people's; white people create the dominant images of the world and don't quite see that they construct it in their own image; white people set standards of humanity by which they are bound to succeed and others bound to fail. (Dyer 2005: 12)

Because the majority group position is naturalized, members have few occasions to reflect on the "property interest" they have in being white. Box 4.2 contains a series of questions to provoke thoughts about naturalized or unrecognized privilege. The next step is for white people to explore the question, "What are some of the ways your race has shaped your life?" (Bergner 2020).

---

### BOX 4.2

### You Know You're Privileged When . . . (Part 2)

As we noted in box 3.1 on class privilege, Peggy McIntosh's frustration with men who would not recognize their male privilege prompted her to realize that whites "are carefully taught not to recognize white privilege, as males are taught not to recognize male privilege" ([1988] 1997: 292). We have adapted and updated these, as well as some by Wildman ([1996] 1997: 325) and Wildman and Davis (1997):

- When I am told about our national heritage or about "civilization," I am shown that people of my color made it what it is.

- Whether I use checks, credit cards, or cash, I can count on my skin color not to work against the appearance of my financial reliability.

- I can do well in a challenging situation without being called a credit to my race.

- If I declare there is a racial issue at hand or there isn't a racial issue at hand, my race will lend me more credibility for either position than a person of color will have.

- I can take a job without having my coworkers suspect that I am not qualified and got it because of race.

- I can go shopping and be assured that I will not be followed or harassed by security because of my skin color.

- I do not have to educate my children to be aware of systemic racism for their own daily physical protection. I do not have to have intense discussions with my kids about how to behave when stopped by police so they do not get shot.

- I can think over many options—social, political, imaginative, or professional—without asking whether a person of my race would be accepted or allowed to do what I want to do.

- People will not be surprised if I speak English well.

- People seeing me will assume I am a citizen of the United States; they will never assume that my children or I are illegal immigrants.

- If I am late, people will assume that I have an individual, personal reason for being late. My lateness will not be dismissed as a joke about white time.

- People will pronounce my name correctly or politely ask about the correct pronunciation. They will not behave as if it is an enormous imposition to get the name right.

Tim Wise is more pointed about white privilege, writing about the willingness of whites to tell racial and ethnic minorities to stop dwelling on past injustices while simultaneously continuing to celebrate the past, as they want to remember it on holidays like the Fourth of July. He describes the origin of white privilege in this way:

> From nearly the second that Europeans first stepped onto the shores of this continent, our identity mattered. It allowed us to feel superior to the native peoples whom we began to kill, subordinate and displace from their land almost immediately. It allowed us to take advantage of land-giveaway programs in the colonies—which we created, of course—like the head right system which provided fifty acres of land to males from England who were willing to settle in the so-called New World. Within a few decades, classification as a white person would become the key to avoiding enslavement; it would determine who could hold office, who could sit on juries, who had rights of due process; and by the time the republic was founded, being considered white would become the key to citizenship itself. (Wise 2012: 4)

In this way, Wise sums up the unearned benefit package that was first bestowed on European settlers and was subsequently enlarged through generations of human trafficking (slavery) that transferred gifts of land, power, status, money, and education to the descendants of those settlers for the next 350 years. Whites also have the privilege of writing this history, so the contributions of entire races of people to the development of the "American" way of life are ignored in textbooks and omitted from the news.

Andrew Hacker (1995) has created a classroom exercise to help students understand the value of being white. In "The Visit," an embarrassed official comes to a white person to say he (or she) was supposed to have been born to Black parents. At midnight, they will become Black and will have the features associated with African ancestry, so they will not be recognizable to current friends but inside will be the same person they always have been. The white man is scheduled to live another fifty years as a Black person, and the official's organization is willing to offer financial compensation, as the mistake is the organization's fault.

Hacker notes that white students do not feel out of place asking for $50 million (1995 dollars), or a million dollars a year, which is a good indication of the value— the property interest mentioned in *Plessy v. Ferguson*—of being white. Students who say that because of affirmative action they would be better off as a Black person still come up with a figure to "buy protections from the discriminations and dangers white people know they would face once they were perceived to be black" (Hacker 1995: 31–32). As social indicators of all kinds reveal, African Americans and Hispanics occupy the least favored positions. Indeed, Michael Tonry summarizes the situation as one in which "mountains of social welfare, health, employment, and education data make it clear that black Americans experience material conditions of life that, on average, are far worse than those faced by white Americans" (1995: 128; Johnson and Leighton 1999).

## Race, Victimization, and Justice

This section of the chapter starts to connect the general overview of race with criminology and criminal justice. By looking at victimization and then some historical patterns of race-based justice, the remainder of the chapter sets a foundation for later chapters that systematically explore how race impacts each stage of the criminal justice system from lawmaking to prisons. Specifically, the first section on victimization reviews official data and critically reviews harms that are not part of the criminal law. The second section provides a broader look at race and justice, including criminal justice.

### Victimization and Race

As the data on class and victimization indicated, crime victims are disproportionately from the lower economic classes. While white people make up the majority of the poor, minorities are disproportionately poor and thus disproportionately victims of crime and many noncriminal social harms. The figures that follow illustrate some of the racial differences, but official statistics, as noted earlier, do not capture the structural violence experienced by minorities (Brown 1987). Nor do they expose the impact racial inequality has on the patterns of victimization.

Table 4.1 presents the official data on violent victimization rates by race. The data generally show that Black people were the most likely to suffer violent victimization. Native Americans tend to have high rates of victimization as well, although meaningful analysis is difficult when the BJS adds everyone who identifies as mixed race into the Native American–only category. The only justification for creating this heterogeneous category is that the sample sizes for the separate categories were small, which is also the reason for combining Asians with the category Native Hawaiian or Other Pacific Islander.

Most victimization involves offenders and victims of the same race and is thus *intraracial* crime, although Native Americans are the most likely of any racial group to experience a violent victimization (especially rape) by someone of a different

**TABLE 4.1 Rate of Violent Victimization, by Victim Demographic Characteristics, 2021 (per 1,000 Aged Twelve and Older)**

| Race | Violent Crime | Serious Violent Crime |
|---|---|---|
| White[a] | 16.1 | 5.4 |
| Black[a] | 18.5 | 7.7 |
| Hispanic | 15.9 | 5.4 |
| Asian/Native Hawaiian/Other Pacific Islander[a, b] | 9.9 | 2.9 |
| American Indian/Alaska Native/two or more races[a, c] | 45.1 | 9.6 |

*Source:* BJS 2021a: table 3.

*Note:* Violent crime includes rape or sexual assault, robbery, aggravated assault, and simple assault; it excludes homicide because the NCVS is based on interviews with victims and therefore cannot measure murder. Serious violent crime excludes simple assault. The data for 2022 were highly unusual in showing higher rates of violent and serious violent crime for white people than Black people. The data in the table are from 2021 and show the pattern of victimization by race that has been historically shown in the NCVS.

[a] Excludes persons of Hispanic origin (e.g., "White" refers to non-Hispanic white persons and "Black" refers to non-Hispanic black persons).

[b] Includes persons who identified as Asian only or as Native Hawaiian or Other Pacific Islander only. Categories are not shown separately due to small numbers of sample cases.

[c] Includes persons who identified as American Indian or Alaska Native only or as two or more races. Categories are not shown separately due to small numbers of sample cases.

race. For 2022, out of the homicides for which the FBI had data on the race of victims and offenders, 3,127 homicides were white-on-white, and 3,644 were Black-on-Black (UCR 2022: expanded homicide data table 6). The absolute number of Black-on-Black homicides is slightly lower than that for whites, but Black folks make up about 13 percent of the population, so the proportion is very high, and the problem is compounded because the homicides are concentrated among Black men (as victims and perpetrators). These data contradict the continued media over-representation of minorities as the perpetrators of violence against whites and the simultaneous overrepresentation of whites as victims of all crimes.

One subset of crimes involving different races, or *interracial* crimes, is "hate crimes," or bias-motivated offenses. Box 4.3 covers some of the controversy about these acts and the punishments that may or may not accompany them. (Remember that most crimes officially counted as hate crimes are not prosecuted that way.) The FBI defines "hate crimes" or "bias crimes" as crimes against persons or property "motivated, in whole or in part, by the offender's bias against a race, gender, gender identity, religion, disability, sexual orientation, or ethnicity." They range from murder down to vandalism. Hate crime statistics should be interpreted with caution. First, the number does not reflect all hate crimes but simply those that were recorded as such by the police, making these statistics more a measure of police activity and concern than actual hate crime. The number of police departments participating in reporting hate crime statistics changes from year to year. And some that do report do not report fully. For example, for 2022, the state of Mississippi officially recorded thirty-two hate crime incidents (UCR 2022: table 11A). Any biases present in the police force will affect the likelihood of officers being willing to record the offense as bias motivated and fill out the additional paperwork. For example, white privilege may make some white officers more sensitive to aspects of bias in crimes involving white victims and minority offenders; at the same time, they may be less likely to see bias in crime involving minority victims and white offenders. Also, future increases in the number of reported hate crimes might be viewed cautiously as they could be due to more complete reporting practices or greater sensitivity on the part of police.

---

## BOX 4.3

### The Controversy over Hate Crime Legislation

Hate speech typically involves actual speech or writing that expresses hostility to a group, including symbolic speech such as burning a cross. In *R.A.V. v. St. Paul* (507 U.S. 377 [1992]), the Supreme Court struck down a law making it a crime to display objects such as a burning cross that "arouses anger, alarm or resentment in others on the basis of race, color, creed, religion or gender." The majority of the court found that it violated free speech rights guaranteed by the First Amendment. In a subsequent case, *Virginia v. Black* (538 U.S. 343 [2003]), the Court modified its position somewhat by upholding a Virginia law prohibiting the burning of crosses where it was done with an attempt to intimidate.

Sentencing enhancement laws for bias-motivated crimes, by contrast, add additional penalties to personal or property crimes because of the bias or hate shown in victim selection. For example, the Supreme Court unanimously upheld sentencing enhancement for bias-motivated assaults in *Wisconsin v. Mitchell* (508 U.S. 476 [1993]). There, a Black teenager had been watching the civil rights film *Mississippi Burning* with friends. Later, the group saw a young white boy, and Mitchell asked the group whether they felt "hyped up to move on some white people." He added, "You all want to fuck somebody up? There goes a white boy; go get him" (in *State v. Mitchell* [485 NW2d 807, 809, (1992)]). The court held that the Wisconsin statute was not aimed at punishing protected speech or expression and that motive could be considered in court. Previous speech by defendants ("I wish you were dead") is frequently admitted into evidence in court to establish motive and is not considered to have an impermissible "chilling effect" on free speech. The Supreme Court also found that the state provided an adequate basis for singling out bias crimes for enhanced penalties because they are "more likely to provoke retaliatory crimes, inflict distinct emotional harms on their victims, and incite community unrest" (*Wisconsin v. Mitchell* 508 U.S. 476 [1993]).

---

In 2022, race/ethnicity/ancestry accounted for almost 60 percent of bias crime incidents (UCR 2022: table 1). The largest category was anti-Black (3,421 of 6,567 incidents), followed by anti-white (966 incidents) and anti-Hispanic (738 incidents); anti-Asian hate crimes (499 incidents) have come down from higher levels when they became scapegoats for the COVID pandemic (discussed in chapter 2). When Asians wore masks, they were "racialized as diseased and framing them as source of pandemic (63 percent), portraying them as particularly weak or sickly individuals

(15 percent), and generally asserting Asian groups' foreignness or inherent socio-racial inferiority (12 percent)" (Ren and Feagin 2021: 749; Yee 2023).

The FBI does not record incidents of anti-immigrant hate crimes, which are likely scattered throughout the racial categories and concentrated in anti-Hispanic hate crimes. Most legal and illegal immigration is from Mexico (Golash-Boza 2016b), and "being Mexican is being equated to illegality" (Urbina et al. 2014: 39). But as noted in chapter 1, research reviews all agree that the crime rates for immigrant populations are lower than those for people born in the United States. Unfortunately, hate crimes increased as former president Trump's popularity grew (Potok 2017). He called Mexico an "enemy" (Trump 2015) and instituted what he intended to be a "total and complete shutdown" of Muslims entering the United States because he believed they had "great hatred towards Americans" (Johnson 2015; Ali 2017).

Ultimately, the climate created by such statements and widespread hate crimes against immigrant groups makes them feel unwelcome and fearful of the government, including—and especially—law enforcement. Immigrant communities withdrew from health care, for example, including prenatal checkups, childhood nutrition programs, medication for attention deficit hyperactivity disorder (ADHD), and the management of chronic diseases like diabetes (Hoffman 2017; Rabin et al. 2022). The fear, stress, anxiety, depression, and retriggering of trauma are concerns in themselves and add to physical health problems, especially in families separated at the border by policies of the Trump administration (Rabin et al. 2022).

When immigrant groups become isolated, they are more vulnerable to victimization from within their community as well as from outside individuals, groups, and businesses seeking to oppress and exploit them. Battered women are less likely to seek help, as are those immigrants who are raped or robbed (many immigrants use cash because they do not have bank accounts). Immigrant workers can be exposed to more toxic and unsafe work environments, as well as subjected to wage theft with less likelihood they will complain (Barak and Leighton 2013). While the era of mass deportations started under President Obama took on a harsher reality under President Trump, in both cases, "deportation sends a message to their communities" that they should be "willing to work in dead-end, low-wage jobs that barely ensure their subsistence" (Golash-Boza 2016b: 19). Deportation mainly targets Latin American and Caribbean men of color, and thus "mass deportation shares many similarities with mass incarceration" (Golash-Boza 2016b: 10).

In addition, structural violence—sometimes called "slow violence" or a "state of violence"—causes ongoing victimization that is not recorded in official statistics. One of many examples of structural violence is that Black Americans are more likely than whites to live in toxic physical environments. Research in the 1980s found that "three of every five Black and Hispanic Americans live in a community with uncontrolled toxic-waste sites" (Austin and Schill 1991: 69). Although poverty is an important factor, "the racial composition of a community was found to be the single variable best able to explain the existence or nonexistence of commercial hazardous waste facilities in a given community area" (Lee 1992: 14; Bullard 1994). Hazardous wastes were examined because nationally comprehensive data were easily available: "Many other problems in minority communities, such as air pollution, workplace exposure, pesticides, lead poisoning, asbestos, municipal waste and others, are equally or more serious" but not subject to ready assessment (Lee 1992: 16; Bullard 1994; Lynch and Stretesky 1998).

The problem has not changed in the forty years since these findings. For example, a study of air pollution from 2014–2018 found that

> census tracts where the majority of residents are people of color experience about 40% more cancer-causing industrial air pollution on average than tracts where the residents are mostly white. In predominantly Black census tracts, the estimated cancer risk from toxic air pollution is more than double that of majority-white tracts. (Younes et al. 2021)

Unfortunately, it isn't just air pollution. Robert Bullard, one of the founders of environmental racism analysis (Buckley 2022), notes that "for over 40 years and in 18 books," his basic message has been that "communities of color and low-income communities get more than their fair share of things that other people don't want" (Bullard et al. 2022).

Problems in Flint, Michigan, are an ongoing example. The city is made up of mostly poor and Black residents who were—and still are—subjected to high levels of lead, a neurotoxin, in their drinking water. The problem came from a switch in drinking water supplies to the Flint River, whose water was known to be significantly more corrosive than the existing water source. Government officials refused to spend small sums of money for chemicals to reduce corrosion, which ultimately caused many minerals—including lead—to leach from water pipes (Fasenfest 2017). Government officials ignored Flint residents when they showed up at meetings with visibly yellow-brown water from their taps and complained of their skin burning after showers. Automaker General Motors complained of "visible corrosion damage" on metal parts exposed to the water (Colias 2016), but government officials maintained that the water was safe. Residents wondered, "If it's too corrosive for an engine, what's it doing to the inside of a person?" (Colias 2016).

Lead is a significant concern, especially for children, because even at low levels it can result in delayed puberty, hearing problems, reduced cognitive performance, lower IQ scores, decreased academic achievement, and behavioral problems, including ADHD (National Institute of Health 2013: 2). High levels of lead in people's bodies are associated with crime, and the removal of lead from gasoline is one of the factors contributing to the declining crime rate in the United States in the 1990s (Reiman and Leighton 2023: 28). It is an open question whether the children of Flint will receive long-term support to recover from the effects of lead, or whether the "solution" will be a build-out of the juvenile and criminal justice system to punish the children who were harmed by negligent government officials. Although Flint is no longer in the news, the problems remain, and it is but one of many poor and minority communities lacking clean drinking water (Bullard et al. 2022).

The Biden administration has promised to do something about environmental racism, except that they fear getting sued, so they are not using race as a factor in policies about environmental racism/justice (Buckley 2022; Friedman 2022). Some see this as a practical strategy given how the current Supreme Court reviews equal protection claims. Others feel that there is no way to deal with environmental racism in a color-blind way. Bullard notes:

When you look at the most powerful predictor of where the most industrial pollution is, race is the most potent predictor. Not income, not property values, but race. If you're leaving race out, how are you going to fix this? (in Friedman 2022)

## Racial Justice

This chapter has noted large-scale injustices that have been perpetrated on minority groups. The consistencies in the practice of racial injustice in the Americas date as far back as Christopher Columbus's ill treatment of the Indigenous peoples, followed by the early colonists' treatment of American Indians and the enslavement of Africans. This intense and sustained history of mistreatment has raised questions about genocide in the United States with respect to both Native Americans (Weyler 1992) and African Americans (Johnson and Leighton 1999; Patterson [1951] 1970, 1971).

Not only were Africans enslaved, but after the Civil War, the criminal justice systems swept the newly freed slaves off the streets and leased them back to plantation owners, who could continue to amass wealth from labor-intensive crops (Oshinsky 1996). The Chinese were exploited to build the transcontinental railroad but were denied citizenship and then excluded from the country after the work was done. In addition, the dominant white culture's desire for land and natural resources led to the forced relocation of Native Americans and the wholesale violation of *all* treaties signed by the U.S. government and sovereign tribes (Lazarus 1991).

This analysis goes back to the classic work on "punishment and social structure" by Georg Rusche and Otto Kirchheimer ([1939] 1968), which revealed that the relationship between the type and form of punishment in society changes with the political economy. Important aspects of the analysis are the notions of surplus labor and the costs of production. While the idea of surplus labor can be used in a class-based analysis, minorities are disproportionately poor and the first to be fired in any downturn, so they are a key part of the labor pool that is regulated through punishment. Other aspects of the political economy go beyond labor to include access to cheap resources and strategies for dominant groups to accumulate wealth.

One striking example is the rise of Black people under jurisdiction of the criminal justice system after the Civil War. The Civil War abolished involuntary servitude and freed the enslaved people, although "the transition from bondage to freedom was more theoretical than real" (Gorman 1997: 447). Millions of Black people were "suddenly transformed from personal property to potential competitors" (Tolnay and Beck 1995: 57). Southern whites had to compete with Black people for jobs, and plantation owners would now have to compete with one another for good help with higher wages. In addition, many white people feared "domination" by the newly freed Black folks (who outnumbered the whites); they also feared Black men having sex with white women, especially since there was a shortage of young white men because they were killed in the war. In addition,

this ideology—that black people belonged to an inferior, subhuman race—did not simply disappear once slavery ended. If the formerly enslaved and their descendants became educated, if we thrived in the jobs white people did, if we excelled in the sciences and arts, then the entire justification for how this nation allowed slavery would collapse. (Hannah-Jones 2019)

In the late 1800s, there were few prisons, and the Civil War had destroyed many buildings in the South. The solution lay in leasing inmates out to the plantations from which they had just been freed. After all, the economic base of the South was the same—labor-intensive crops such as tobacco and cotton. Leasing the former slaves to plantation owners meant the owners had cheap labor, Black people were back under control, and—as a bonus—agents of the criminal justice system took a share of the money involved in the leases. The threat of plantation prisons kept many other Black people in servitude under labor contracts that recreated the conditions of slavery: "The horror of the ball and chain is ever before [Blacks], and their future is bright with no hope" (in Gorman 1997: 71).

Worse still, under the lease system, owners no longer had the same economic interest in Black people as property, which removed some restraints against brutality. If a slave died, the owner had to buy another, but leased Black people who died were easily and cheaply replaced: "One dies, get another" (in Johnson 2002: 43). The situation is summarized by the title *Worse Than Slavery*, whose author notes that in Mississippi in the 1880s, not one leased convict lived long enough to serve a sentence of ten years or more (Oshinsky 1996: 46). However, because of the social control, cheap labor, and fees generated by the leases, the system expanded to include a variety of grueling and dangerous jobs like mining, building roads, clearing swamps, and making turpentine.

The nominal basis for arrests was laws based on slave codes: "The slave codes of the antebellum period were the basis of the black codes of 1865–1866 and later were resurrected as the segregation statutes of the period after 1877" (Gorman 1997: 447). When able-bodied Black men had not actually done anything wrong, the police would falsely charge them with crimes. When the men could not pay off the court fees, they were forced to go to work to "pay back their debts." These bogus arrests were sometimes orchestrated by "employers working hand-in-glove with local officials to keep their [work] camps well stocked with able-bodied blacks" (Oshinsky 1996: 71).

Black prisoners were essentially slaves, and the state functioned as a slave master (Gorman 1997). Black "criminality" was "less a product of their conduct than their social standing" (Hawkins 1995: 34)—a sentiment so strong today that many prefer to use the term "justice-involved people" rather than "offenders." The folk song "Standin' on de Corner" captures this dynamic:

> Standin' on de corner, weren't doin' no hahm,
> Up come a 'liceman an' he gab me by d'ahm.
> Blow a little whistle an' ring a little bell;
> Heah come 'rol wagon a-runnin' like hell.
> Judge he call me up an' ast mah name
> Ah tol' him fo' sho' Ah weren't to blame.
> He wink at 'liceman, 'liceman wink too;
> Judge he say, "Nigger, you got some work to do."
> Workin' on ol' road bank, shackle boun'.
> Long, long time fo' six months roll aroun'.
> Miserin' fo' my honey, she miserin' fo' me,
> But, Lawd, white folks won't let go holdin' me.
> (in Franklin 1989: 104–5)

Variations on this pattern occur for other minorities at different points in history. For example, many Chinese immigrated in response to the need for workers on the transcontinental railroad. "Chinese" appeared on the census, and the government restricted naturalization processes for citizenship to whites only. (Justice Harlan noted in *Plessy* that the Chinese, although being able to ride in the railcar for whites, were of "a race so different from our own that we do not permit those belonging to it to become citizens of the United States.") After the transcontinental railroad was completed, Chinese labor was no longer needed, so the Chinese Exclusion Act of 1882 prohibited immigration—"the first time federal law proscribed entry of an ethnic working group on the premise that it endangered the good order of certain localities"—and a succession of measures maintained a near ban until the 1960s (National Archives 2023). To control the surplus population that was already in the country, the United States passed new criminal laws that selectively prohibited "Orientals" from possessing drugs or that differentially applied existing drug laws against them. At the same time, both moral panics and the criminalization of minorities could occur for reasons other than political economy; bigotry and racism on their own were enough.

Although Japanese immigration amounted to a relatively small number of people on the Pacific Coast, they fell into patterns of labor exploitation and prosperity: "By 1920, Japanese immigrant farmers controlled more than 450,000 acres of land in California, brought to market more than 10 percent of its crop revenue, and had produced at least one American-made millionaire" (Library of Congress, n.d.). Out of concern about this rising influence and affluence, in the early 1900s many of the concerns raised about the Chinese were repeated with the Japanese. In 1913, California "passed the Alien Land Law, which barred all aliens ineligible for citizenship, and therefore all Asian immigrants, from owning land in California, even land they had purchased years before." Earlier calls for a "Japanese Exclusion Act" resulted in the Immigration Act of 1924, which "imposed severe restrictions on all immigration from non-European countries, and effectively ended Japanese immigration, supposedly forever" (Library of Congress, n.d.).

The appropriations of Japanese and Japanese-American wealth continued with their internment in "relocation camps" during World War II. After the Japanese bombed Pearl Harbor, President Roosevelt issued an executive order that allowed the secretary of war to establish areas "from which any or all persons may be excluded" to protect national interests "against espionage and against sabotage." The whole West Coast of the United States was declared such a zone, and all people of Japanese ancestry, whether citizens or not, were excluded. About 120,000 subsequently lived behind barbed-wire fences in camps guarded by armed soldiers. This executive order and the actions because of it subjected the Japanese to numerous hate crimes from the community before they were sent to live in the camps. White people took over their houses and businesses with little to no payment. One man, a U.S. citizen born in Hawaii, commented,

> I have never been to Japan. We would have done anything to show our loyalty. . . . My wife and I lost $10,000 in that evacuation. She had a beauty parlor and had to give that up. I had a good position working as a gardener, and was taken away from that. We had a little home and that's gone now.

And, referring to the other countries the United States was fighting, he asked, "Where are the Germans? Where are the Italians? Do they ask them questions about loyalty?" (Opler 1943).

The camps were hastily built with few amenities and strict rules—far from the resorts and "pioneer communities" they were portrayed as (Reeves 2015: xv)—so those held there experienced breakdowns and suicides. An American citizen of Japanese ancestry challenged his removal, but the Supreme Court upheld the orders. The Court deferred to military judgment that these acts were necessary (*Korematsu v. U.S.* 323 U.S. 214 [1944]), although the government later noted that it made some false claims in Court arguments (Katyal 2011). One of the dissents was dismayed that it was necessary to explain the violation of constitutional rights in a "case of convicting a citizen as a punishment for not submitting to imprisonment in a concentration camp, based on his ancestry, and solely because of his ancestry, without evidence or inquiry concerning his loyalty and good disposition towards the United States" (*Korematsu v. U.S.*, 323 U.S. 226 [1944]).

The *Korematsu* majority claimed that it was only deciding the issue of exclusion from an area, not the forced isolation in a camp. But the Court also cooperated with the president to delay those challenges until the war ended, at which time the cases were dismissed (Reeves 2015). Korematsu's conviction was overturned in 1983, and in 1988 then-president Reagan signed the Civil Liberties Act of 1988 that formally apologized and offered token monetary compensation. But Reagan's Justice Department fought against efforts to overturn *Korematsu*, and it was finally struck down in 2018 in the case upholding then-president Trump's travel ban on people from Muslim nations (*Trump v. Hawaii*, 17-965 [2018]: 38) (see chapter 7).

Native Americans have also been exploited for the benefit of the white population, but the benefit was about land and the resources on it rather than labor. The thefts of land and the government's subsequent breaking of treaties have left many Native Americans on small, isolated reservations (Lazarus 1991; Weyler 1992). When comparing historical tribal lands to current reservation boundaries, research found that "the amount of land shrank by 98.9 percent," and 160 of 380 tribes no longer had a current recognized land base (Flavelle 2021). In addition, "most tribes were pushed far from their historical lands," so they lost access to traditional ways of providing for themselves (hunting, fishing) and plants important for cultural practices. Compared to traditional lands, reservation lands "also have less hospitable climates" and have "left Native Americans significantly more exposed to the effects of climate change" (Flavelle 2021). Also, the lands were less likely to have oil and gas resources that could provide an economic base for the tribe (Eichstaedt 1994).

Although the tribes are supposedly sovereign nations, the federal government still acts like a colonial power that leaves them with little control or resources. For example, the Standing Rock Sioux tribe has been engaged in ongoing litigation and protest over the Dakota Access Pipeline. Although discussion of the oil pipeline is often in terms of climate change, for the tribe it is part of a long history of the government disregarding their treaty rights to land and water (Ostler and Estes 2017). The tribe wants to protect its own drinking water from spills where the pipeline goes under the river. Also, the tribe claims that some of the land on which the pipeline will be built is sacred, but there is no respect for that, even though "we would never put a native pipeline underneath Arlington Cemetery" (Jaffe 2016).

This section has tried to explain why many minorities picture themselves as profoundly marginal and expendable, leaving them with a sense of alienation perhaps best captured in Derrick Bell's "Chronicle of the Space Traders" (1989). In this story, Black people as a group are sacrificed to aliens for gold needed to retire the national debt, a chemical to clean up pollution, and a limitless source of clean energy. Following a national referendum and a Supreme Court decision, Black folks are lined up and turned over to the aliens—in chains, just as they entered the country hundreds of years ago. The moral of this story for Bell is that we have made no racial progress; whites would sacrifice Black lives for their own gain today just as they did four hundred years ago with the institution of slavery. Among the Black community, the chronicle "captures an uneasy intuition" that Black Americans "live at the sufferance of whites—that as soon as our [Blacks'] welfare conflicts with something they [whites] consider essential, all our gains, all our progress, will turn out to be illusory" (Delgado and Stefancic 1991: 321).

## Implications

This chapter earlier quoted Bullard as saying: "Communities of color and low-income communities get more than their fair share of things that other people don't want" (Bullard et al. 2022). That was in the context of pollution and toxic waste, but also poverty—and less of the things people want, like wealth (see chapter 3). Global warming brings increasing environmental disasters, which "widen racial wealth gaps" because money gets sent "to rich White communities that can recover quickly. Communities of color generally lose." Minority communities also get more "flooding and an inadequate government response after a disaster" (Bullard et al. 2022).

Minorities also have more illness and disease, including asthma, respiratory disease, strokes, and diabetes. Further, "heat-related deaths among Black people occur at a 150% to 200% greater rate than for White people" (Bullard et al. 2022), and climate change will make the ratio worse. One cause of these problems is the lack of health insurance and having worse health insurance, which also makes medical conditions worse. People have fewer doctor visits, childhood immunizations, dental visits, preventive health care, and cancer screenings to name a few (Reiman and Leighton 2023); they also have less access to drug treatment (Hoffman 2023). And when disease hits, people go to the doctor later and sometimes cannot afford treatment. Not surprisingly, minorities generally have shorter life expectancy (Flagg 2021) and higher infant mortality rates.

Many of these factors came together during the pandemic when research found that "Black and Latinx people and Indigenous Americans are roughly three times as likely to be hospitalized and twice as likely to die from COVID-19 as are white, non-Hispanic people in the United States" (Maxmen 2021). Table 4.2 breaks this figure down more by racial group in the context of children who lost a parent. This outcome was the result of preexisting health issues, being coerced to show up for jobs that exposed them to COVID because of economic insecurity and jobs with

TABLE 4.2 **Children Who Lost a Parent or Caretaker to COVID, by Race and Ethnicity**

| Race or Ethnic Group | Proportion of Children Who Lost a Parent or Caregiver |
| --- | --- |
| White | 1 in 753 |
| Black | 1 in 310 |
| Latino | 1 in 412 |
| Native American | 1 in 168 |

*Source:* Coker et al. 2023.

no sick leave, and worse health care (Maxmen 2021). These factors and more led Native Americans to have some of the highest death rates from COVID, a death toll described as having "no modern precedent" (Lopez and Wu 2022).

Outside of the COVID pandemic, the stress of living in an unequal society has been studied as "weathering." It is not just poor health insurance or worse medical care, but the stress of racial and economic discrimination itself causes worse health outcomes (Gupta 2023), and "blacks are, biologically speaking, older than whites of the same chronological age" (Blitstein 2009: 56). Weathering erodes the systems of the human body, fueling the progression of disease, aging, and death. As stressors ranging from environmental pollution to high crime to racism-induced anger accumulate and feed on one another, they alter the behavior of a community, which can lead, for example, to higher rates of smoking, drinking, and drug use. The medical field initially rejected Geronimus's ideas when she first presented them in 1990, but it has come around as more data links discrimination and poor health outcomes. For example, income does not fully protect Black people from health problems, even though they get better health care, and similar problems show up in extremely poor white populations in Appalachia (Geronimus et al. 2006a, 2006b; Gupta 2023). But the "high-effort coping" found to underlie weathering appears most pronounced in minority populations.

The stress of discrimination can also be seen in MRI scans, according to a neuroscientist at Harvard Medical School: "Even in kids as young as 9 to 10 years old, the disparities faced by certain groups of people have a clear impact on how the brain develops in areas that can lead to trauma and stress-related disorders such as PTSD" (in McFarling 2023). He further notes that "if we're going to treat the world as colorblind, we're not going to create mental health solutions that are effective for all people." We noted this same concern with environmental justice—race-neutral policies will not deal with problems caused by race. And this issue is not just with pollution and health. As this chapter has shown, an important source of current U.S. wealth is the historic exploitation of minorities, but currently people say they "don't see race" or don't want to. For some people, this sentiment comes from a well-meaning desire to treat everyone equally, although there are also organized efforts to minimize discussions of race and to delete "systemic" when it appears before words like "racism" and "oppression" (Alter and Harris 2023; Mervosh and Goldstein 2023).

Further, the ways that white people write history erase both the racial injustices of the past as well as the activism of minority communities fighting racial injustices. The common view of history is that *Plessy*'s separate-but-equal doctrine was overruled by *Brown v. Board of Education*, a tired Rosa Parks refused to give up her seat to a white person, there were some marches, Martin Luther King Jr. gave his "I Have a Dream" speech, and then Congress passed civil rights legislation. But this view of history as having happened and the white majority as having decided to end discrimination does a disservice to the tireless organizing of the Black community and those who were killed in the struggle for equality.

For example, before *Brown*, the Black community challenged policies that denied them admission to state law and medical schools. If there was not an equal institution for Black students, then the Courts would allow them to enroll in white professional schools. Once in professional schools, Black students challenged policies that required them to sit in the back of the classroom and that segregated parts of the library. By the time the Court heard *Brown*, activist Black lawyers had done much to undermine *Plessy*.

History has also rewritten Rosa Parks from a militant, lifelong activist into a woman acting out of personal reasons—she was tired and did not want to stand. Although "quiet" was frequently used in her obituaries, her history of activism earned her repeated death threats. At one point early in her life, Parks told her grandmother, "I would rather be lynched than live to be mistreated and not be allowed to say 'I don't like it'" (Theoharis 2015). She had repeatedly refused to give up her seat to whites on the bus, part of her efforts to survive but not accept racism. That day, she said, "I had been pushed around all my life and felt at this moment that I couldn't take it anymore." While the bus driver usually kicked her off the bus, that day he called the police, who arrested her.

The subsequent boycott of the bus system required a high level of organization and commitment for the Black community to get where they usually went with buses. Likewise, the boycott of segregated lunch counters required individual sacrifices and community support to replace the meals normally purchased at the restaurants. Further, many communities directed violence at Black protesters, and local police—who were sometimes KKK members—supported and escalated the violence against protesters. Protesters had to endure not just attacks by dogs and fire hoses, but beatings and lynchings as well. But they continued to organize and fight.

In the 1960s and 1970s, Black power groups like the Black Panthers became more outspoken about the necessity and morality of using violence in the face of violent racist oppression. Some local Black Panther chapters organized to provide food and health care to their communities, and they built social movements that the police and white power structure found threatening. A number of Black Panther leaders died in police shootouts, like Fred Hampton in Chicago. Although the police described it as a twenty-minute long "wild gun battle," the grand jury report "found evidence that 76 expended shells were recovered at the scene, and that only one could be traced to a Panther" (Grossman 2014). To many, this action seemed like an execution.

During this time, there were also many less spectacular cases of police using deadly force against unarmed Black protestors and those near protests and almost never being held accountable for wrongdoing. "These were 'normal' cases, endlessly repeated in the history of the country, coming randomly but persistently out of a racism deep in the institutions, the mind of the country" (Zinn 2003: 463). In 1973, Rosa Parks commented, "The attempt to solve our racial problems nonviolently was discredited in the eyes of many by the hard-core segregationists who met peaceful demonstrations with countless acts of violence and bloodshed. Time is running out for a peaceful solution" (Theoharis 2015).

## Review and Discussion Questions

1. What is meant by the social construction of race? What are some of the examples the authors give to support this point?
2. Highlight the distinctions between the following related terms: *stereotypes*, *prejudice*, *discrimination*, and *racism*. How are institutional and individual racism different?
3. What is meant by the term *white privilege*? Why should we study white supremacy as a system and not just white supremacist groups? What is white fragility?
4. Why does this chapter argue that whites have race and why does it matter?
5. What are some ways that all minority groups share similar experiences in the United States?
6. What races have the highest official rates of victimization? What are the limits of official data?
7. What are some examples of slow or structural violence?
8. When looking at punishment and social structure, what relationships are important? How does it apply to Black people, Asians, and Native Americans?
9. How can race-neutral policies replicate institutional racism?

## Note

1. Hollywood also reinforced racial purity by prohibiting leading white stars from kissing minority actors, thus limiting roles for minorities (Karlamangla 2022). (The first white-Black interracial kiss was on *Star Trek* in 1968 [Jim Crow Museum 2007].)

# CHAPTER 5

# Understanding Gender/Sexuality and Male/Heterosexual Privilege

On his podcast America First, *white supremacist Nick Fuentes announced that he is a "proud incel." The term "incel" is short for "involuntary celibate," which the Anti-Defamation League (ADL) defines as "young, heterosexual men who blame women and society for their own inability to form romantic or sexual attachments" (in Center on Extremism 2023). The ADL has a definition of that term because men who identify as incels have reportedly been connected to a number of acts of terrorism in the United States and abroad. Take for example the Uvalde, Texas, elementary school mass shooting in 2022.*

*On the morning of May 24, 2022, Salvador Ramos shot his grandmother in the face and headed off to a nearby elementary school where he killed nineteen students and two teachers and injured seventeen others. Although popular media sources did not indicate the possibility that Ramos identified as an incel or with the incel community, reports have indicated his hatred of women, including online threats to rape and kill them. Threats such as these are not uncommon in the incel world, and one report found that 89 percent of incel online users support rape, and 53 percent "[voice] support on threads about pedophilia" (Shapero 2022).*

*Unfortunately, this phenomenon is found all over the world. For example, in 2021 Jake Davison of Plymouth, UK, killed five people, including his mother and daughter, before killing himself. Reports have indicated his allegiance to the incel community as he recorded his intention on YouTube (Center on Extremism, 2023; Kent and Ritchie 2021). In Toronto, Canada, Alex Minassian killed eleven people and injured five after posting on his Facebook page, "Private (Recruit) Minassian Infantry 00010, wishing to speak to Sgt. 4chan please. C23249161. The Incel Rebellion has already begun! We will overthrow all the Chads and Stacys! All hail the Supreme Gentleman Elliot Rodger!" (BBC News 2018). The "Supreme Gentleman" Elliot Rodger is* another incel who uploaded multiple videos to YouTube espousing his beliefs before killing six (shooting three and stabbing three), including two women and four males (three of Asian descent). He also penned a 141-page manifesto, in part documenting his hate for women and his plan to kill women in the Alpha Phi sorority in California in 2014. In the document, Rodger referred to himself as the "ideal magnificent gentleman," and his "fans" began referring to this in their own videos, posts, and forums. Later, online stores sold merchandise with his picture and the moniker "Supreme Gentlemen" (BBC News 2018). Rodger concluded his manifesto by stating that he was the real victim. (4chan is an unmoderated internet site, so users post material that includes hate speech and derogatory material about many minority groups. "Chad" and "Stacy" are names that incels use to refer to people who are the antithesis of themselves—think Barbie and Ken. The numbers possibly represent something related to his military service.)

Further exploration of the incel movement reveals that what began as a group solely for those considered involuntarily celibate has evolved into a social media movement comprised of misogynists, and the hatred of women has expanded to include hatred toward many other marginalized groups—although many of these participants (like Rodger) would argue that they are the ones being marginalized. The Southern Poverty Law Center has identified about one hundred white nationalist organizations and hundreds of additional general hate groups in the United States, which include the Proud Boys (commonly seen at the same protests, rallies, and riots attended by white nationalists and other hate groups). Christian identity and neo-Confederate groups contain a variety of hateful ideologies, while groups that are predominantly anti-immigrant, anti-LGBTQ+, and anti-Semitic are still interconnected with other groups. But a common thread is male supremacy, which includes but is not limited to homophobic, transphobic, anti-women, and sexist sentiment.

Award-winning documentarian Louis Theroux's series Forbidden America shows white supremacist and Holocaust denier Nick Fuentes with pistols in each hand, looking into the camera and saying, "America first, bitch," before rapidly firing each handgun like he is John Wick after his dog is murdered. The show exposes a new breed of hate-mongers who are so far right they are banned at Republican events. Therefore, when Fuentes and his followers are rejected from buying tickets to the Conservative Political Action Coalition (CPAC) event, he replies, "CPAC sucks; it's gay." In turn, Fuentes responds to his ban by forming his own version of CPAC, the America First Political Action Committee (AFPAC).

The documentary shows Fuentes, at eighteen years old at the 2017 march in Charlottesville, Virginia, where "far-right," "alt-right," "white supremacist," and "white nationalist" groups—largely made up of white men—marched with Nazi *symbolism, assault rifles, and riot gear. Images of these men carrying tiki torches were both laughable and chilling, harkening back to the days of lynch mobs. During the rally that turned riot, James Alex Fields drove his car into a crowd of folks protesting the hate march, killing Heather Heyer (a civil rights activist) and injuring multiple others (Fieldstat, 2019). Four years later, Fuentes stood on the steps of the U.S. Capitol Building on January 6, 2021, telling the crowd to "break down barriers and disregard the police" (Doerer 2022). His social media posts and speeches try to recruit incels as part of the wide net of hate he throws. For instance, Fuentes has said:*

- *"We are anti-gay, anti-woman, anti-Black, antisemitic."*
- *"When a bitch going crazy sometime you got to grab her, sometimes you have to control yo' bitch. Listen I would defer to Blacks on this. They've got it figured out."*
- *"Hitting women is sometimes necessary."*

*Fuentes has also commented on eliminating feminism and incentivizing monogamy to make it difficult for women to become "whores" (Doerer 2022).*

*The focus on incels should not obscure the larger pattern of spree and mass shootings by men. If women were the vast majority of shooters, wouldn't the focus be on "What's wrong with women?" Instead, the concern is about guns and mental health, which is not misplaced, but it fails to take into account that it is men's mental health problems that are so destructive, and men who are disproportionately attracted to the empowerment of guns to resolve grievances. The focus on incels, though, highlights how misogyny often accompanies white supremacy, so it is important to look to new frameworks like patriarchal violence (discussed later in the chapter) that embrace the intersection of race, religion, and misogynistic violence.*

## Introduction

The previous chapters reviewed inequalities in class and race to establish the foundations of how those biases undermine the ideal of equality before the law. This chapter reviews how gender undermines the ideal of equality before the law, an ideal most people say they want even if they resist using the word "feminism." But what does equality mean when men and women are different biologically in ways that go far beyond racial differences like skin color and hair texture? An obvious important area of difference is reproductive systems, and in male-dominated societies, women's bodies and reproductive capacities have often been seen as the property of men or an area that men especially want to control. Society thus has battles over reproductive rights (abortion, birth control, maternal health care, and sex education) and larger issues of reproductive justice (the ability to secure reproductive rights is influenced by structural and systemic barriers such as race, class, immigration status, and other intersecting identities).

In taking up the task of analyzing gender, we recognize that within the criminal legal system, men are the majority of offenders and victims. But in addition, as chapter 2 discussed, women and girls have gone understudied in these areas: "Criminology theories were constructed 'by men, about men' and explain male behavior rather than human behavior" (Belknap 2007: 3). This chapter provides some background on the marginalization of women more generally, which highlights the importance of feminist criminology in centering the experiences of women and girls with the coercive power of the criminal justice system. After all, women are 51 percent of the population but are considered a minority and part of diversity, equity, and inclusion plans.

Further, sexuality is an important aspect of gender, which is examined through queer studies and queer criminology. "Queer" is used here as an inclusive term meant to encompass any number of identities (i.e., LGBTQ+). It also recognizes that not all members of the LGBTQ+ community will identify with the use of "queer" because of its long history of being synonymous with hate toward the community (Buist and Lenning 2023). This chapter also provides background on the very long history of marginalization of LGBTQ+ folks that includes the present day. We review the tenets of queer criminology as important to efforts to *queer* criminology—to correct deep-seated assumptions of heterosexuality and the invisibility of the LGBTQ+ community (Ball 2014; Buist and Lenning 2023; Dwyer et al. 2016; Woods 2015).

Because people's treatment within the administration of justice is shaped by what takes place outside the criminal justice system, this chapter, like the previous two, locates its discussion—this time on gender and sexuality—in terms of the relevant terminology. The point from the previous chapter about racial privilege is revisited in terms of male, cisgender, and heterosexual privileges. A subsequent section describes the variety of gendered and patriarchal violence necessary to maintain a system based on male, cisgender, and heterosexual privilege. Finally, like the last parts of chapters 2 and 3, this chapter addresses how gender and sexuality relate to criminology and criminal justice issues. It first explores gender, sexuality, and victimization, then finishes with a brief review of how they have historically played a role in the administration of justice.

As we noted in chapter 1, the use of "gender/sexuality" is not to imply that they are one and the same. They are not always interconnected, although our examinations of gender often lead to discussions of sexuality. In spite of this shorthand to be able to expand coverage of sexuality in a book about class, race, and gender, we remind readers that gender and sexuality are not the same, but both are necessary for understanding criminology, crime, and justice within our criminal legal system.

## Gender, Sex, and Society

This section defines and discusses some key terms that will lay a foundation for better understanding the implications of gender and sexuality for crime and justice issues. As a reference source for terms that go beyond what is in this chapter, we recommend the glossary posted by the Centers for Educational Justice & Community Engagement at UC Berkeley.[1] And as with the previous chapter on race, language changes and evolves; it can be contested and political. When we are not using the language of our sources, we try to use language preferred by members of various communities at the moment, but that may change over time.

The words "sex" and "gender" are often used interchangeably in everyday discussion and in research (Weisshaar and Casey 2022). But, simply stated, *sex* relates specifically to people's bodies and biology (i.e., genitals), while *gender* relates to how that person identifies. A person born with a penis and identifying as a man is usually considered *cisgender*, as is the person born with a vagina who considers themselves female. Someone born with a penis but identifying as a woman is usually considered *transgender* or *gender nonconforming*, as is a person born with a vagina who identifies as male. How a person feels about who they are is their *gender identity*, and it is something only that person can reveal about themselves. *Gender expression* is how that person presents themselves to others, and it may or may not reflect their identity.

While sex tends to be thought of as a binary limited to male or female, that framework does not fit everyone. Some are born "intersex," a general term used for a variety of situations in which a person is born with a reproductive or sexual anatomy that does not fit the typical criteria used to classify someone as female or male (Intersex Society, n.d.). Other people do not fit the classification criteria because they are transgender and are taking hormones or having surgeries to transition between the two categories. Characteristics are not fixed, and identity can be fluid: "We may choose, for instance, to modify specific biological traits. Our biology is clearly not our destiny" (Renzetti 2013: 7).

Sex does not determine gender identity, so no one, whether assigned male or female at birth, is born masculine or feminine. Gender involves social processes through which people learn and are socialized into identifying and acting according to the notions of what an "appropriate" role is for men and women in our society based on their social location. *Masculinity* and *femininity* describe these roles, and although they are also presented as an either/or binary, gender is very much a continuum, as people can have various mixtures of traits. Gender roles and expectations are not universal and permanent but change with time, race, and class. But what has been consistent over time has been that higher status and more desirable qualities have been attached to male gender roles, and qualities thought to be associated with females and the feminine have been devalued.

While gender roles are changing somewhat, women who are unapologetic about sexual pleasure and their own sexuality are still called "sluts" and are subject to "slut shaming" more than men are shamed for the same behavior. Women who are ambitious and as assertive as their male colleagues are more likely to be called "bitches" or other terms that make it more challenging for them to exercise effective leadership. Media messages are more likely for women than men to reinforce that the most important qualities are their looks, bodies, and sexual availability, so physical beauty, fashion, and weight are taken more seriously than with men. Social judgments are more likely to lead women than men to have low self-esteem and higher rates of cosmetic surgery. To be sure, men also have low self-esteem, eating disorders, and cosmetic surgery—largely for their failure to live up to dominant ideals of masculinity. But these still occur within the context of male privilege, even if it is not fully felt because of class, sexuality, and race. (Remember from previous chapters that privilege does not mean life is easy; it just means that, *overall*, being male is not what causes difficulties and is more likely to help them get the benefit of the doubt compared to being female or nonbinary.)

*Patriarchy* is the term for societies that organize around male privilege or a hierarchy with males at the top. Patriarchal societies vary in form and expression depending on whether they are agricultural, industrial, or service societies—although it is significant that patriarchy has been a constant through many economic systems in Western society. Part of patriarchy is *misogyny*, the "organized, institutionalized, normalized hostility and violence toward women" (in Humm 1990: 139). Misogyny is expressed through s*exism*, which describes beliefs and social relations holding that men are superior to women, and is present both at the individual and institutional levels.

In contrast to overt hostility, "benevolent sexism" takes the form of *paternalism* and *chivalry*. While these forms of sexism appear to treat women kindly, they ultimately reinforce patriarchy by viewing women as needing protection from stronger and dominant men. Women are placed in a passive and dependent position, sometimes implying that women owe something in return for the acts of courtesy and protection, rather than promoting equality and respect. Chivalry has generally been limited to white women and includes values and attitudes that placed "women on a pedestal," representing "the idea that women need male protection and that they should be more virtuous than men" (Scully 1990: 79). Indeed, historically, "the pedestal" prevented white women from working outside the home, participating in sports, and voting, as well as many other privileges reserved for men. White men have always been expected to deal with the "public sphere" outside the home, which was seen as competitive and corrupt. White women have been expected to seek protection and guidance from men and to make the home (the "private sphere") a pleasant refuge for men. These expectations were serious enough that women were prohibited from opening their own bank accounts (without their husband's signature) until 1974.

However, these traditional notions of the pedestal and "proper" feminine behavior never included women of color. Women of color have always worked outside the home, for example, on the plantations in the South or on the fruit and vegetable farms for Latina migrant workers. Women of color have always been expected to protect and defend themselves and their children in the absence of a man in the home, whether in times of slavery or in homes where migrant/seasonal workers are left home for long periods of time.

Taken together, these values, norms, and beliefs of patriarchy devalue women in society, setting them up for unequal treatment and punishment when they deviate from expectations (including when they fall off the pedestal by failing to live up to unattainable standards of virtue). Often people do not see how roles and expectations are socially constructed because ideology tries to make the differences seem natural, including through *biological* essentialism, which refers to the idea that there exist some innate qualities and personality traits that would exist in each sex that go beyond cultural conditioning. The issue here is not to point to biological differences in, say, reproductive function, but whether men or women have inherent traits that exist across cultures and throughout time. Feminists are generally skeptical about claims of essentialism because they tend to be used to justify inequality and male privilege. Such assumptions appeared historically in research from men explaining crime and women's deviance: women were not as evolved as men (Lombroso and Ferrero), had a desire for love (Thomas), had penis envy (Freud), and were deceitful by nature (Pollack) (Belknap 2007, 2020).

Although one might scoff at these inaccurate generalizations about women, essentialism gives rise to stereotypes that have contributed to denying women the right to vote and the ability to get professional licenses in law and medicine (women were viewed as too emotional or were seen as unable to handle the logic of the field). Further, essentialism (whether based on sex, race, class, or anything else) homogenizes a group of people; that is, it denies differences and diversity within a group of people (e.g., women, minorities, the poor). Just as with racial stereotyping, this process is dehumanizing, and it normalizes power relations so that inequality is not questioned because it appears to be the result of natural differences.

Gender is thus a social construction, and part of the process is gender being "done" or "performed" through routine interactions with other people. For example, by being aggressive and unemotional, males can assert claims to masculinity. The use of force, like committing hate crimes against LGBTQ+ folks, reinforces the heterosexual aspect of masculinity, as does sexual aggression against, and domination of, women. By making themselves up to look attractive to men, being sensitive to others, downplaying their accomplishments, and being quiet and nonassertive, women perform femininity. In both cases, men and women "do gender" by handling situations in such a way that the outcome is considered gender appropriate. Still, masculinity and femininity are never accomplished and secure in a final way; they are something that must be continually "done" and (re)accomplished; that is, men and women are expected to continuously demonstrate their "gender" throughout their lives.

In this way, gender has several levels: individual/psychological (identity), interactional (expression, "performing" gender), and institutional (roles, expectations) (Weisshaar and Casey 2022). These levels interact in ways that are shown in Victor Rios's ethnographic study, aptly titled *Punished: Policing the Lives of Black and Latino Boys* (2011). He found that masculinity, and specifically hypermasculinity, develops in the context of males who perceive that they have no access to traditional avenues of success and who have experiences of repression from the criminal legal system:

> Whereas race determined how a young person was treated in the criminal justice pipeline, masculinity played a role in whether they desisted or recidivated as they navigated through the system. One of the outcomes of pervasive criminal justice contact for young Black and Latino men was the production of a hyper-masculinity. Angela Harris defines hyper-masculinity as an "exaggerated exhibition of physical strength and personal aggression," which is often a response to a gender threat "expressed through physical and sexual domination of others." Drawing on this definition, we contend that the criminal legal system encourages expressions of hyper-masculinity by threatening and confusing young men's masculinity. This, in turn, leads them to rely on domination through violence, crime, and school and criminal legal counterculture. In essence, detrimental forms of masculinity are partly

developed through youths' interaction with police, juvenile hall, and probation officers. (Rios 2011: 130)

*Feminism* comprises both a basic doctrine of equal rights for women and an ideology for women's liberation from patriarchy. Feminism's basic goals are consciousness raising about oppression, wage and labor fairness, representation in politics/legislation, and an end to the violence and harassment that women face. A wide diversity of perspectives are contained under this umbrella term, indicating that *feminisms* is more appropriate by not suggesting a singular woman's point of view. Liberal feminism, for example, tends to seek equality for women within the existing political and economic system. In contrast, socialist and more radical feminisms tend to seek equality for men and women but under a different system, usually one that is less hierarchical and stratified than currently exists.

Historically, though, many varieties of feminism were developed by middle- to upper-class cisgender white women for middle- to upper-class cisgender white women. This dynamic has led to criticism of feminism for excluding and alienating innumerable women from different classes, races, and sexualities. The excluded women felt like feminism did not see their problems and advocate for solutions that helped them. So new feminist concepts and theories have and continue to develop to represent these concerns. For instance, recent developments in intersectional feminism, including intersectional criminology, have been integral in moving the discussion forward. (Intersectionality is explored in chapter 6.)

Another important aspect of gender is *sexuality*, which is a site for patriarchal control as it is tied to men's control over women's reproduction and reproductive rights, standards of beauty and body objectification, and attempts to ensure sexual access or availability. Both masculine and feminine gender roles carry a strong expectation of *heterosexuality*. To be sure, someone born male and who identifies as masculine (thus cisgender) can be gay, although societal expectations for being a "real man" or woman is a sexual orientation that is heterosexual. *Sexual orientation* includes "emotional attractions and sexual attractions, practices, desires, and fantasies" (Silva 2018).

In the United States and beyond, the standard of sexuality is heterosexuality, and therefore many aspects of gender roles and social expectations are constructed through that lens. Heterosexuality is thus the privileged orientation, and *heteronormativity* promotes the belief that heterosexuality is the only normal and natural way to be. All identities and other sexual orientations suffer oppression in heteronormative societies, although they experience it in different ways—much like different races experience racism under white supremacy differently. These orientations include lesbian, gay, bisexual, transgender, queer, questioning, asexual, and two-spirit (LGBTQ+). "Two-spirit" is a modern word for a variety of gender-nonconforming people in some (but not all) Native American tribes who often had a position of spiritual leadership. It is not the same as being gay and is "more about the embodiment of two genders residing within one person" (Enos 2018).

Research on the LGBTQ+ population is often referred to as *queer studies* and, as especially relevant to this book, *queer criminology*. (The word "homosexual[ity]" is an antiquated medicalized term that should not be used in current research.) The authors of *Queer Criminology* note that "the word *queer* makes some people cringe but others prefer the use of a word as a means of deconstruction and inclu-sivity" (Buist and Lenning 2016: 3, emphasis in the original). The term attempts to be inclusive because it covers everyone who is not cisgender. The deconstruc-tion applies because people in this group raise questions about the naturalness of heterosexuality, and those who are not cisgender raise questions about the fluid-ity of identity that many people take for granted as fixed. The extent of hostility directed toward those who are not cisgender or heterosexual exposes how much effort society puts into policing supposedly natural aspects of gender and sexuality. That hostility also reveals the privileges that heterosexuals have in terms of safety, nondiscrimination, acceptance, and not having one's gender and sexual orientation questioned. ("What do you think caused your heterosexuality?" "Do you think it could be a phase because you're confused?")

While we have tried to present LGBTQ+ viewpoints and issues throughout the chapters of this book, we remind readers that much of the discussion is nevertheless based within a heteronormative lens. Research about men and women often assumes heterosexuality and makes no note that the experiences of LGBTQ+ could be differ-ent in terms of influences on their criminality, desistance from crime, levels of victim-ization, trust in police, experiences of punishment, and much more. This observation applies to much present research, as well as research of the past, so findings are most prevalent about cisgender and heterosexual individuals regardless of age, race, or class. While there is more research being done on the LGBTQ+ population, it is vital to include queer criminology and the unique experiences of those justice-involved folks to have a full understanding of the impact of criminal justice practices. Also, people who deliver services or exercise power within the criminal justice system have a special obligation to understand the populations they work with.

Chapter 4 noted that people of all races could be prejudiced and have stereo-types, but *discrimination* implied a position of power to act on those prejudices, so the chapter emphasized discrimination against minorities by the white majority. Similarly, while men and women can both buy into stereotypes and harmful gender-role expectations, men will be the primary initiators of various types of discrimina-tion because they tend to have the positions of power. Likewise, cisgender males and females, and heterosexuals generally, will be in more of a position to discriminate against the LGBTQ+ population.

## Male, Cisgender, and Heterosexual Privileges

The chapter on race quoted Dyer about how whites had power because they could claim to speak for all people, while people of color were normally considered to speak for their race alone. The same concept applies to gender, with men being seen as having no gender—and thus speaking for all ("mankind")—while women are seen as speaking only for women, a "special interest group." To further illus-trate this point, substitute "men" for "whites" in Dyer's quote: "Men have power and believe that they think, feel and act like and for all people; men, unable to see their particularity, cannot take account of other people's; men create the dominant images of the world and don't quite see that they construct it in their own image; men set standards of humanity by which they are bound to succeed and others bound to fail" (based on Dyer 2005: 12).

Men do not usually see this privilege because it is the purpose of gender roles and stereotypes to make the inequality of current society seem natural, inevitable, and just. But

> men's physiology defines most sports, their needs define auto and health insurance coverage, their socially designated biographies define workplace expectations and successful career patterns, their perspectives and concerns define quality in scholarship, their experiences and obsessions define merit, their objectification of life defines art, their military service defines citizenship, their presence defines family, their inability to get along with each other—their wars and rulerships—defines history, their image defines god, and their genitals define sex. (in Forell and Matthews 2000: 5)

The law is an important example, and it tends to see women as men see them because most laws are written, enforced, and judged by men. For many years the legal standard used in law was that of the "reasonable man" because historically women were not allowed to sue in court or sign contracts, so questions about negligence or duties of care were based on a "reasonable man." But the standard remained even after women achieved more civil rights and were better integrated into the workforce, where the development of sexual harassment law exposed the problem of applying the reactions of a "reasonable man" to behavior that victimizes a woman. While most jurisdictions now formally use the term "reasonable person" for legal analysis, it is not always clear how much the standard has changed even though the name is different.

For example, an early case involving a hostile work environment involved a female manager in an office with widespread pornographic pictures and a coworker the Court majority described as "extremely vulgar and crude" who "customarily made obscene comments about women" (in Forell and Matthews 2000: 37). The majority, applying a "reasonable person" standard, found the environment to be "annoying" but not hostile in a way that raised sex discrimination issues. In the Court's view, the pornographic posters had minimal effect "when considered in the context of a society that condones and publicly features and commercially exploits open displays of written and pictorial erotica at the newsstands, on prime-time television, at the cinema, and in other public places" (in Forell and Matthews 2000: 37). For the majority, that such environments existed was a given, and the woman had "voluntarily entered" it; by showing intolerance of such conditions, the Court implied that the woman was being hostile—not the environment. Besides, the law was "not meant to—or can—change" such workplaces, nor did the majority think it was "designed to bring about the magical transformation in the social mores of American workers" (in Forell and Matthews 2000: 37).

Here, the neutral-sounding "American worker" is "men who hold values allowing them to talk crudely about women and look at degrading pornography whenever they want to, including at work" (Forell and Matthews 2000: 38). The dissenting judge noted how the "reasonable person" worked to uphold the "prevailing male prerogative" (in Forell and Matthews 2000: 42). For this judge, the appropriate standard was not a gender-neutral reasonable person, and "unless the outlook of the *reasonable woman* is adopted, the defendants as well as the courts are permitted to sustain ingrained notions of reasonable behavior fashioned by the offenders" (Forell and Matthews 42, emphasis added).

The same question about the appropriateness of gender-neutral standards also applies to the crime of stalking, where the question is whether the behavior of the stalker causes a "reasonable person to experience fear or substantial emotional distress" (BJS 2021b: 1). Data on victimization rates that we present later in this chapter show that transgender people have higher rates of violent victimization than do cisgender people, and the LGBTQ+ community has higher rates than straight/heterosexual people do. (Consider that straight men had a victimization rate of 18.7 per 1,000 people, while bisexual women had a rate of 151.2 [BJS 2022a: 7].) But should the reasonableness of fear in people with *very* different rates of violent victimization be evaluated against the same gender-neutral, probably cisgender and heterosexual, "reasonable" person?

The law has also been reluctant to define women as victims when the crimes committed against them take place in their homes or as part of a relationship, especially with a man. For centuries, men benefited from not being held accountable for their crimes against women. The failure to recognize domestic violence as criminal behavior reinforced the patriarchal idea that "a man's home is his castle" (expressed currently as "my house, my rules"). Since the 1970s, however, violence against women in the home has been considered a crime. Likewise, what was originally viewed as a "private matter," such as acquaintance rape, marital rape, and stalking, is now being treated more frequently as a criminal offense, even if police investigations, arrests, and convictions leave much to be desired. While women are gaining the right to be treated like other assault victims and have their battering husband, for example, arrested and punished, the reality is that many women still face social, economic, and cultural barriers that further victimize and humiliate them when they seek equal protection under the law.

Indeed, male privilege is clearly demonstrated when people ask, "Why does she stay?" rather than "Why does he batter?" or "Why did he say, 'If I can't have you, no one can'?" Those questions and the societal views behind them privilege men by taking violence and possessiveness for granted, and they simultaneously oppress women by scrutinizing their behavior for something to find fault with. Even many criminology students do not know that most battered women do leave abusive intimate partners several times and work to minimize the violence that they—and their children and pets—face. Not only are there many barriers to leaving, but leaving is also the most dangerous time period because batterers want control of their partners, and leaving the relationship threatens that control, so it is met with increased violence. Male privilege is also present in how society views sexual assault, especially with drinking: "He was drunk" tends to excuse sexual violence for men, and "She was drunk" invites blame for women.

When people try to blame women's behavior for gendered violence and argue that the remaining violence is because of a "few bad apples," masculinity and male power go unexamined. Instead, sexual assaults should be seen as "an extension of normative male behavior, the result of conformity to the values and prerogatives that define the male role in patriarchal society" (Scully 1990: 49). Sexual assaults and coercion are not just the result of misogyny but also of men's desire for amounts of heterosexual sex that will bolster their social standing and allow them to have close male friends without being seen as gay. Further, male power makes it less likely that they will engage in role-taking, like trying to see the situation from the woman's point of view, whereas for women understanding the attitudes of men in a situation and "role-taking is a survival strategy" (Scully 1990: 116).

The power and role-taking dynamic explains how, in a survey of college students at an elite college, researchers found "many instances [where] we saw heterosexual men who were acutely aware of their own sexual needs but less attuned to their partners' rights to sexual self-determination" (Glennon 2020). So "people committing assaults thought they were having consensual sex." The researchers also note that

> we heard from many young women who told us that they were in a room with a man and they didn't really want to be there anymore, and so they just performed oral sex on him to get out of there. And those young men didn't force those women to have sex, but I think that they fundamentally didn't recognize what it was that the person that they were with wanted to do. (Chang 2020)

The researchers note that it is not just gender and that many other forms of power are at play, including race: "Every single one of the Black women that we spoke to had experienced unwanted, nonconsensual sexual touching. *Every single one*" (Chang 2020, emphasis in the original).

Another important area of male privilege is the reliance on white males as the primary subject for medical and biological research in the United States. At the founding of medicine, "Hippocrates and other well-known doctors considered the female body an inferior variant of the male body," so "there was a fundamental assumption that the female body was 'lesser,' and therefore didn't need rigorous examination" (Loudin 2023). After World War II, scientists started collecting data on what they called the "standard man" for the purposes of knowing how much radiation a worker could be exposed to. In 1974, the project was still ongoing, and the now renamed "reference man" was used for a variety of purposes through medicine and physiology, and fields that build on those (Yu 2023). Outside of reproductive organs, women were seen as "small men."

This legacy still exerts an influence, even though in 1993 the National Institutes of Health required women (and minorities) to be included in research it funded. But there are still substantially more single-sex medical studies on men than women. The legacy of the "standard man" also affects athletic training for women. A 2023 editorial in one of the *British Journal of Medicine* series was titled "Underrepresentation of Women Is Alive and Well in Sport and Exercise Medicine" (Anderson et al. 2023). Although women make up about half of current Olympic teams and a large number of elite athletes, "if you look at the research papers between 2016 and 2020, only six percent is focused on female athletes" (Loudin 2023). Most of the evidence base for exercise was developed on men, leaving female athletes with less information to build their own training programs on.

Moving forward, "the key is asking what the female body can do, not what makes it different. We haven't even approached that full potential yet" (Loudin 2023).

Finally, male privilege is also shown in the pay gap between men and women. Although the gap has closed slightly in the last twenty years, women employed full time, year-round, are paid about 84 percent of what men are paid (Department of Labor 2023). On average, women have more years of education, and the U.S. Department of Labor explains that "women's labor is undervalued. Most of the disparity in women and men's pay cannot be explained by measurable differences between them" (2023). When considering race and ethnicity, "in 2022 Black women earned 70% as much as White men and Hispanic women earned only 65% as much" (Kochhar 2023). Since women are less likely to work year-round and full time, other measures of the wage gap are larger. Further, family caregiving responsibilities "can reduce women's earnings, while fatherhood can increase men's earnings" (in Aragao 2023). Men's earnings may increase because, even in 2022, women are still more active in households with children than are men, and fathers are more active in the workplace when they have children at home (Kochhar 2023). During the COVID pandemic, women "disproportionately left the labor force entirely compared to men; they have disproportionately taken on the work around the house, the child care, and the child's education," noted the author of a study published in the *Journal of the American Medical Association* (in O'Connor 2021). The survey found that because of these dislocations, women increased their alcohol consumption more and had more mental health problems.

Wage data also reveal cisgender and heterosexual privilege. A report conducted by the Human Rights Campaign (n.d.) found that

LGBTQ+ White workers earn 97% for every dollar the typical worker earns; LGBTQ+ Latinx workers earn 90 cents for every dollar the typical worker earns, and LGBTQ+ Black workers earn 80 cents for every dollar the typical worker earns, LGBTQ+ Native American workers earn 70 cents for every dollar the typical worker earns, and finally LGBTQ+ Asian/Asian Pacific Islanders workers earn $1.00 for every dollar the typical worker earns.

While this is a helpful look at how LGBTQ+ status interacts with race, the LGBTQ+ category is diverse, and some groups within it fare better than others. For example, while about 16 percent of straight and cisgender adults live in poverty, and 22 percent of LGBTQ+ adults overall, 29 percent of cisgender bisexual women live in poverty. In addition, 29 percent of transgender adults live in poverty, but 40 percent of Black and 45 percent of Latinx transgender adults live in poverty (Human Rights Campaign, n.d.).

Clearly there are more examples of male, cisgender, and heterosexual privilege. This section has presented an outline of the basic concepts to push against the various ideologies that hide these forms of power and oppression. Consistent with previous chapters on class and race, box 5.1 provides a privilege checklist as another way to understand these ideas.

## BOX 5.1

### You Know You're Privileged When . . . (Part 3)

As we noted in box 3.1 on class privilege, Peggy McIntosh's frustration with men who would not recognize their male privilege prompted her to realize that whites "are carefully taught not to recognize white privilege, as males are taught not to recognize male privilege" ([1988] 1997: 292). Her list of forms of male privilege, though, needs to be updated, and it should also be expanded to include cisgender privilege and heterosexual privilege. This list also uses adaptations from Deutsch (n.d.), Killermann (2011), and Community Peacemaker Teams (n.d.), all of whom note that they borrow from McIntosh.

Male privilege

- People are more likely to praise me as a good father for not meeting other responsibilities because of my children, while people are more likely to believe that a woman in the same situation needs to get her act together.
- I do not have to worry about the message my wardrobe or demeanor sends about my sexual availability.
- If I work at a service job such as a waitress or barista, my effort to provide good and friendly service will not be seen as an expression of romantic or sexual interest.
- My ability to make important decisions and my capability in general will never be questioned depending on what time of the month it is.
- I do not need to plot my movements through public space in order to avoid being sexually harassed or assaulted, or to mitigate sexual harassment or assault. If I am assaulted, no one is likely to blame me or talk publicly about how I deserved it.
- I have the privilege of being unaware of my male privilege.

Cisgender privilege

- I can use public restrooms without fear of verbal abuse, physical intimidation, or arrest.

- I am not required to undergo an extensive psychological evaluation in order to receive basic medical care.
- I can purchase clothes that match my gender identity without being refused service or mocked by staff.
- Strangers don't assume they can ask me what my genitals look like and how I have sex.
- People do not use me as a scapegoat for their own unresolved gender issues.

Heterosexual privilege

- I will receive public recognition and support for an intimate relationship: people will congratulate me for an engagement, and wedding planners will not refuse to work with me.
- I can easily find a neighborhood in which residents will accept how I have constituted my household and family.
- I can raise, adopt, and teach children without people believing that I will molest them or am "grooming" them for something inappropriate.
- I can go wherever I wish knowing that I will not be harassed, beaten, or killed because of my sexuality.
- I will not be fired from a job nor denied a promotion based on my sexuality.

As a final note, straight and cisgender people do not have to check online travel guides when they travel abroad for family vacations so that they and their partners are not potentially arrested, charged, and sentenced to prison or executed for their relationship. Queer folks are actively discriminated against across the globe, and when the United States chooses to participate in events such as the 2022 FIFA (soccer) World Cup in Qatar, where "homosexual" activity is illegal and can be punished with execution (Human Rights Watch 2022), it sends a loud and clear message to the LGBTQ+ community that life and liberty are not guaranteed to every citizen.

## Gender Violence and Patriarchal Violence

As with class and race, the criminal legal system plays a role in policing gender and sexuality. But this is also true of gender violence, which involves acts of violence, abuse, or harm that are specifically targeted at individuals based on their sex, gender identity, or sexuality. (It also affects those who are *perceived* to be non-conforming, as for example someone who identifies as cisgender or is heterosexual but has an expression that others interpret to be LGBTQ+.) Gendered violence is rooted in power imbalances and reinforces patriarchy, as well as cisgender- and heteronormativity.

Important forms of gendered violence include intimate partner violence (IPV) (Belknap 2020), hate crimes against women and LGBTQ+ people, rape/sexual assault, stalking, and sex trafficking. (*IPV* is often preferred over "domestic violence," which can involve acts of family violence like siblings abusing each other, child abuse, parental abuse by children, and elder abuse.) Other forms of gender violence include street harassment, involving acts in public spaces like catcalls, sexual comments or propositions, derogatory language, following people, and invading their personal space. While many people try to minimize the seriousness of these acts as "flirting" or "joking," it is an exercise of power that normalizes objectification and hostility. Many similar acts occur in the workplace, where institutions and agencies sometimes protect powerful men who engage in misconduct. Increasingly, people are using artificial intelligence programs ("nudification" apps) that remove clothing to create nude images of high-school-aged females. Such images "harass, humiliate and bully young women[,] can harm their mental health, reputations and physical safety as well as pose risks to their college and career prospects" (Singer 2024).

A significant example of gender violence is IPV, and the Power and Control Wheel was developed to explain patterns in abusive relationships. While physical violence is an important aspect of those relationships, not all violence is physical, and the goal of many abusers is power and control over their victims. One section of the wheel includes "using male privilege" and provides examples including "treating her like a servant, making all of the big decisions, acting like the 'master of the castle,' and being the one to define the men's and women's roles" (Domestic Abuse Intervention Programs, n.d.). Other parts of the wheel include economic abuse, threats, intimidation, emotional abuse, isolation, minimizing, denying, blaming, and using children. In many ways, the other tactics support male privilege and the ability of the abuser to reap benefits from the relationship through the abuse and exploitation of his partner.

While this has been a helpful tool, it is important to also consider other models, including ecological models that include community and social dynamics to help develop intervention and prevention efforts. Criticism of the wheel includes that it uses male and female pronouns, thus reinforcing the gender binary, and that it was developed by interviewing women in heterosexual partnerships. Research since the 1990s has shown that IPV is just as prevalent, if not more so, in LGBTQ+ relationships, so advocates developed a lesbian/gay and more recent trans-specific version of the wheel.[2] Recent research, from a more queer criminological framework, has focused on the experiences of justice-involved queer folks who encounter violence in relationships (BJS 2022a; Guadalupe-Diaz 2019; Kurdyla et al. 2022; Messinger 2017).

A heteronormative patriarchal society encourages violent behavior and hostility against women and those who do not conform to heterosexual cisgender roles. Violence is even more disproportionately inflicted on LGBTQ+ women of color, for who they are and not what they have done (Buist and Lenning 2023). This intersectional awareness contributes to research on frameworks like patriarchal violence (PV), which allows people to

> better understand the dynamic, interconnected system of institutions, practices, policies, culture, beliefs, and behaviors that supports and causes violence against women and girls (cis and trans), and other gender oppressed people and protects, normalizes, and condones the dangerous behavior of those who do harm, most often men and boys. PV disproportionately harms Black girls, women, intersex, gender non-conforming, and other gender oppressed people. Patriarchal violence upholds, reproduces, and enacts patriarchy and other systems of oppression. (Black Feminist Future, n.d.)

This concept provides a framework for merging white supremacy with gender violence in ways the opening narrative started to explore. Even for those less extreme than the people highlighted there, we know that the political climate in the United States for the last decade or so has helped to embolden mostly white men to unleash violence on any number of marginalized communities.

## Gender, Victimization, and Justice

This section of the chapter starts to connect the general overview of gender/sexuality with criminology and criminal justice. By looking at victimization and then some historical patterns of gender- and sexuality-based justice, the remainder of the chapter sets a foundation for later chapters that systematically explore how gender/sexuality impacts each stage of the criminal justice system from lawmaking to prisons. Specifically, the first section on victimization reviews official data and critically reviews harms that are not part of the criminal law. The second section provides a broader look at gender/sexuality and justice, including criminal justice.

### Gender and Victimization

As with class and race, some victimization caused by gender inequality will not be seen as crime and will thus be excluded from official statistics. And making sense of official statistics requires a critique of masculinity and the problematic values— emotional detachment, the sexual objectification of women, aggression, etc.—that are revealed in the data. Understandings of crime and violence up until recently did not consider why men have such high rates of offending relative to women, nor were theorists giving much attention to the roles of gender, socialization, and masculinity (Katz 2022).

The clearest indication of men as disproportionately involved in violent offending is the homicide data reported in table 5.1. The largest category is male offender and male victim, and the next largest is male offender and woman victim. The much

**TABLE 5.1 Murder by Sex of Victim and Sex of Offender, 2022**

| Sex of Victim | Sex of Offender | |
| --- | --- | --- |
| | Male | Female |
| Male | 5,680 | 653 |
| Female | 2,099 | 241 |

*Source:* UCR 2022, expanded homicide data table 6.

*Note:* For single-victim/single-offender homicides.

**TABLE 5.2 Rate of Violent Victimization, by Gender (per 1,000 Aged Twelve and Older)**

| Sex | Violent Crime | Serious Violent Crime |
| --- | --- | --- |
| Male | 17.5 | 4.9 |
| Female | 15.5 | 6.2 |

*Source:* BJS, 2021a: table 3.

*Note:* Violent crime includes rape or sexual assault, robbery, aggravated assault, and simple assault; it excludes homicide because the NCVS is based on interviews with victims and therefore cannot measure murder. Serious violent crime includes rape or sexual assault, robbery, and aggravated assault. The data for 2022 were highly unusual in showing nearly equal victimization rates for males and females, so the data are from 2021 and show the more typical pattern of victimization in the NCVS.

smaller third-largest category is female offender and male victim, although some of these are battered women killing abusive men. Certainly, violent women do exist, and some women batter some men, although these examples are exceptions to general trends despite their prevalence in media and feminist backlash. Overall, "girls and young women are far more often the victims of violence than the perpetrators of it" (Kendall 2020: 51).

For 2021, BJS victimization statistics showed a slightly different pattern from FBI and earlier BJS trends. Table 5.2 presents the data, which indicate that while men experienced a slightly higher overall rate of violent victimization, women experienced a higher rate of serious violent victimization. Some of this difference is because the data in table 5.1 were from police reports of homicides, and the data in table 5.2 are from the National Crime Victimization Survey (NCVS), which is self-reported victimization (and thus excludes homicide). But consistent with the FBI, the BJS reports that victims perceived their offenders to be male 77 percent of the time and female about 8 percent of the time (BJS 2022a: 10). Further, "of violent incidents with male victims, a greater number involved male offenders (1,837,040 incidents) than female offenders (193,840)," and "of violent incidents with female victims, a higher number involved male offenders (1,354,920 incidents) than female offenders (530,370)" (BJS 2022a: 12).

One other area of official data is stalking, which also has a distinct gendered pattern. According to the BJS, "stalking is repeated unwanted contacts or behaviors that either cause the victim to experience fear or substantial emotional distress or that would cause a reasonable person to experience fear or substantial emotional distress" (2021b: 1). Stalking victimization is more likely to be perpetrated by men toward women. Women are more than twice as likely as men are to be stalked. Most women (outside of celebrity stalking) knew their stalkers, and they are three times as likely to be stalked by an ex-intimate partner.

As noted in the previous chapter on race, the FBI collects some limited and problematic statistics on hate crimes, and these also include incidents based on gender, sexual orientation, and identity. When looking at the statistics in table 5.3, keep in mind that many states do not have hate crime laws that fully include gender, sexual orientation, and gender identity. Many LGBTQ+ people—especially minorities—are reluctant to contact the police, and police may not see incidents as hate crimes worth recording. Rather than presenting facts about the amount of hate crime against the LGBTQ+ population, table 5.3 should be taken as a measure of police activity and concern. Were there really less than 500 incidents of anti-trans and anti-gender-nonconforming hate crimes across the country at a time of inflamed culture wars and many states enacting legislation to strip trans and other gender-nonconforming people of their rights?

**TABLE 5.3 Numbers of Hate Bias Incidents by Sexual Orientation, Gender, and Gender Identity**

|  | Incidents |
|---|---|
| **Sexual Orientation:** | **1,944** |
| Anti-gay (Male) | 1,075 |
| Anti-lesbian (Female) | 190 |
| Anti-lesbian, gay, bisexual, or transgender (mixed group) | 622 |
| Anti-heterosexual | 22 |
| Anti-bisexual | 35 |
| **Gender:** | **95** |
| Anti-male | 18 |
| Anti-female | 77 |
| **Gender Identity:** | **469** |
| Anti-transgender | 338 |
| Anti-gender-nonconforming | 131 |

*Source:* FBI, "Hate Crime Statistics Annual Reports," table 1.

Indeed, consider the reaction to Anheuser-Busch's 2023 decision to put Dylan Mulvaney, a white transgender woman, on a Bud Light can celebrating her "365 days of womanhood." TikTok videos from mostly white straight men showed them shooting at Bud Light cans and running over twelve-packs with their large pickup trucks. Musician Kid Rock posted a video on Twitter in which he used an assault rifle to destroy several cases of Bud Light, then turned to the camera and announced, "Fuck Bud Light and Fuck Anheuser-Busch." The number and intensity of these incidents raise doubts about the level of officially reported hate crimes and the impact of these videos on the LGBTQ+ population. Many have not forgotten the 2016 shooting spree at Pulse nightclub that left forty-nine people dead and fifty-three wounded, making it at the time the worst mass shooting in U.S. history.

Another notable issue with the official data is how the FBI recorded twenty *single-bias* hate crimes involving rape. But only one was recorded as anti-female and two more were anti-transgender. But ten of the single-bias incidents were about race, and two more were about religion. Why were these not considered multiple bias and also anti-female? For example, one rape was classified as anti-Sikh, but those attackers did not simply commit an assault or engage in property damage. They engaged in sexual violence and chose to attack a woman to make a point about her religious beliefs. Certainly the choice of women as a target evidenced a certain level of misogyny that should be recognized as hate bias at the intersection of religion and sex.

One final source of official statistics is a BJS (2022a) report, *Violent Victimization by Sexual Orientation and Gender Identity from 2017–2020*. Figure 5.1 clearly indicates that transgender people (51.5 victimizations per 1,000) have substantially higher rates of violent victimization than cisgender people (20.5 victimizations per 1,000). Also clear is that straight (heterosexual) people have the lowest rates of victimization, while bisexual people have the highest. Within each category, women had higher rates of victimization. For example, bisexual women had a victimization rate of 151.2 per 1,000, and bisexual men had a rate of 64.5 per 1,000 (BJS 2022a: 7). The analysis also found that domestic violence was eight times as high among bisexual persons and more than twice as high among lesbian or gay persons as it was among straight persons. Such statistics bolster the findings of the National School Climate Survey conducted by GLSEN, which found that nearly 82 percent of the 22,298 student participants reported feeling unsafe at school because of their actual or perceived LGBTQ+ identities. Approximately 405 students also reported avoiding bathrooms, locker rooms, and physical education and gym classes. Additional findings in this report highlight LGBTQ+ students being threatened (76 percent) or physically harmed (31 percent) based on their sexual orientation or gender expression (Kosciw et al. 2022).

The FBI reports on simple and aggravated assaults but does not break out intimate partner violence. (There is an incident-based reporting system that captures this data, but few police departments use it.) The BJS reports on aggregate rape and intimate partner violence but does not break out victimization rates by gender in its main victimization report, although it has some other specific publications reporting those data. Although not "official" data sources, there are legitimate and reliable resources used to fill in the picture of victimization when it comes not just to gender but to marginalized populations like people of color, LGBTQ+ folks, and

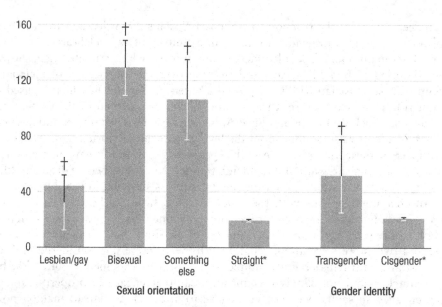

**FIGURE 5.1** Rate of Violent Victimization, by Sexual Orientation and Gender Identity (per one thousand aged sixteen and older)

*Source:* BJS 2022a: figure 1.

*Note:* The lines going from within the bars to above them represent a 95 percent confidence interval. All surveys, including the National Crime Victimization Survey used in this figure, contain possible errors in making generalizations from the survey sample to the larger population. The 95 confidence interval indicates a 95 percent likelihood that the victimization rate of the larger population is within this range.

† There is a statistically significant difference between the group and the reference group at the .05 level (a 5 percent risk that there is no difference between the victimization rates of these groups).

foreign-born individuals living in the United States (this is especially dependent on their legal status).

Another example of alternative, reliable data is the Association of American Universities' (AAU) Campus Climate Survey on Sexual Assault and Sexual Misconduct (Westat et al. 2020), which reports increases in sexual assault on college campuses and increases in reporting. This is consistent with other research finding that the #MeToo movement led to increases in the reporting of sex crimes and arrests for sexual assault (Levy and Mattsson 2022). The AAU found that 13 percent of women reported nonconsensual sex contact by physical force or inability to consent, with rates higher for women than men, and higher for undergraduate students than graduate or professional students. For transgender and gender-nonconforming students, the AAU survey uses "TGQN" to encompass "transgender woman, transgender man, nonbinary/genderqueer, gender questioning, or gender not listed." Among undergraduate TGQN students, 65.1 percent reported experiencing harassing behavior since first enrolling at the school, 21.5 percent with partners reported intimate partner violence, and 15.2 percent stalking (Westat et al. 2020).

Reinforcing the picture of widespread abuse are reports and settlements for periods of months and years where men in institutions were engaged in pervasive sexual abuse. More than 330 athletes, mostly female gymnasts, settled with

Michigan State University for $500 million because of its role in continuing to support Larry Nasser as he abused girls and women on the Olympic and other national teams for years (Levenson 2018). The prestigious "University of Michigan has agreed to a $490 million settlement with more than 1,000 people who say they were sexually assaulted by a former sports doctor during his nearly four-decade career at the school" (Associated Press 2022). The University of Southern California in 2021 paid $852 million to settle cases with 710 women who were sexually abused when they were treated by a former campus gynecologist; in 2018, the university paid another $215 million to settle cases brought by more than 18,000 women who had also been treated by him (Romo 2021). A 2022 report about U.S. women's soccer, done by a former U.S. deputy attorney general, focused on three coaches and highlighted "a history of sexual misconduct allegations against them and executives' failure to investigate and act on the accusations. It also warned that girls face abuse in youth soccer" (Jiménez 2022). Also in 2022, the CEO of Hockey Canada and the entire board of directors resigned after criticism for its handling of accusations of sexual assault by players (Shoalts 2022).

## Gendered Justice

The differential treatment of men and women—and of boys and girls—reflects a gendered double standard that dates back to the chauvinistic sexual customs and conceptions of private property first articulated in ancient Greek and Roman laws (Posner 1992). Until recently, these customs explicitly prevailed in U.S. law. Women were considered chattel or possessions of their fathers or husbands and were forbidden from holding property or bank accounts in their own names or from entering into business deals or contracts. Women were treated as "second-class" citizens, and they were subject to the patriarchal rules of family, usually under the paternalistic guise of protecting and controlling them "for their own good." Whether in the public or private sphere, gendered justice denied women equal protection under the law. In fact, it was not until the 1980s that husbands could be charged with the crime of raping their wives.

Early European feminists worked to raise awareness of women's oppression, a tradition that continued in spite of social revolutions in Europe and passionate discourses about equality and brotherhood. Indeed, in the late 1700s, Mary Wollstonecraft, in the name of "sisterhood," observed "the inconsistency of radical males who fought for the freedom of individuals to determine their own happiness and yet continued to subjugate women, leaving them to 'procreate and rot'" (Kandal 1988: 12). In the United States, few advocates of abolishing slavery saw any connection with women's suffrage. For example, the Grimké sisters used their status as part of a prominent Southern family to argue that female slaves "are our sisters" and have a "right to look for sympathy with their sorrows and effort and prayer for their rescue." But the New England Abolition Society chastised them for forgetting "the great and dreadful wrongs of the slave in a selfish crusade against some paltry grievance" and "trifling oppression" of their own (Kandal 1988: 214).

The Progressive Era saw the enacting of laws that tried to suppress abortion, pornography, contraception, and sex work. The Mann Act of 1910 outlawed the importation of contraceptives, the mailing of obscene books and other materials, and the interstate traffic in sex workers. The selective enforcement of those laws disproportionately against the female sellers rather than the male purchasers of sex remains a component of the social relations of gendered justice and social control.

Final ratification of the Nineteenth Amendment occurred in 1920 and finally gave women the right to vote, fifty years after the Fifteenth Amendment granted newly freed male slaves the right to vote. African Americans used their political voice to pursue a federal antilynching law, while white women pursued issues related to child labor and laws about women's working conditions. Women were united in the goal of getting the right to vote, but once they had it, "the lines that divided women—class, race, age, ideology—became more significant" (DuBois and Dumenil 2005: 483). The National Women's Party introduced an equal rights amendment in 1923, which immediately exposed different views of equality. At a time before a minimum wage law and a mass of New Deal legislation that many now take for granted, women had worked to pass laws that protected them from exploitation in the workplace before unions, collective bargaining, and occupational health and safety laws. They feared that equality would mean that hard-won protections would be repealed, while others "countered that such legislation treated women as invalids and could limit their economic opportunity" (DuBois and Dumenil 2005: 483).

One area in which patriarchy impinges on women through social, economic, and political forces is reproductive rights, as women's bodies have historically been subjected to oppression through control of their reproductive processes. According to the World Health Organization, *reproductive rights*

> rest on the recognition of the basic right of all couples and individuals to decide freely and responsibly the number, spacing and timing of their children and to have the information and means to do so, and the right to attain the highest standard of sexual and reproductive health. They also include the right of all to make decisions concerning reproduction free of discrimination, coercion and violence. (2005)

The United States has a history of coerced sterilization, particularly of Black and Native American women. As late as the 1990s, some states considered mandating the use of Norplant or Depo-Provera (long-acting contraceptive implants) to control younger, inner-city women on welfare and poorer women of color. "The consequences of this extend beyond the biological question of 'Who procreates?' It speaks to the question of 'Who matters?'" (Flavin 2009).

That question took on renewed importance in 2022 when the Supreme Court overturned the almost fifty-year ruling of *Roe v. Wade* that provided women a constitutional right to abortion. *Roe* expanded the ability of women to get access to not only abortion but *safe, legal* abortion. With the 2022 ruling in *Dobbs v. Jackson Women's Health Organization* (19-1392), individual states have greater ability to limit and even ban the availability of abortion in what is one of the few instances where the Court has taken away such a significant right that it previously recognized. As of summer 2024, fourteen states had a total ban on abortion, and many more had a ban after six weeks of pregnancy, which is often before a woman knows she is pregnant (Center for Reproductive Rights, n.d; *New York Times* 2024).

While reproductive rights in the United States are often associated with the right to abortion, they encompass a much wider array of women's (and men's) reproductive processes and a woman's right to choose or refuse treatments such as abortion, sterilization, contraception, family planning, and infertility treatment. Reproductive rights also include the right to be free from illnesses or other conditions that might interfere with sexual and reproductive functions. They encompass the right to provide for healthy children by meeting not only their physical needs but also their educational, emotional, and social needs (Flavin 2009). Reproductive rights are "fundamental rights" that should receive the highest level of protection because they are related to "the right to bodily integrity, the right to privacy (including the right to an abortion), and the right to procreate" (Flavin 2009: 39). The right to privacy is frequently explained as "the right to be let alone" or "to have government off our back" and establishes a personal sphere free from government intrusion.

Reproductive rights are also grounded in the right to bodily autonomy, which means an individual's authority and control over their own body and the decisions concerning their own physical and mental well-being. The right to bodily autonomy and integrity is strong enough that organs cannot be taken from the dead without their prior permission. Indeed, "if a person cannot be forced to have criminal evidence removed from his body, or a father cannot be compelled to donate an organ to [save] his child['s life], then it follows that forcing a woman to be sterilized or take contraceptives similarly violates her right to bodily integrity" and privacy (Flavin 2009: 40). But the Court in *Dobbs*, when striking down abortion, stated that "attempts to justify abortion through appeals to a broader right to autonomy" were wrong because they could allow "fundamental rights to illicit drug use, prostitution, and the like" (*Dobbs v. Jackson Women's Health Organization*, 19-1392 [2022]: 32).

While individual and reproductive rights are important, reproductive justice is the larger issue. It looks at how being able to exercise one's rights depends on a person's identity and the social, economic, and political conditions that affect a woman's autonomy over her own body and her reproductive health. Thus, the role of poverty, racial discrimination, gender violence, abuse of technology, pharmaceutical and/or medical coercion, and family planning programs should be considered. This is true for all women regardless of how one was assigned at birth.

Current gender/sexuality issues also include as many as six hundred anti-LGBTQ+ bills introduced as of spring 2023 (Choi 2023; Movement Advancement Project 2023b). While some of these bills carry over from previous years, in 2018 there were a total of forty-two bills introduced, which increased to 417 bills in 2023 (Choi 2023). Most of these proposed bills would impact education, while others affect health care, civil rights, legal identification, and public accommodations (such as bathroom access). Some of the newly introduced bills include proposed bans of drag performances (39), although there is no evidence that drag performers or other members of the LGBTQ+ community are any danger to others.

Another example involves the ongoing debates regarding bathroom and locker room usage, although again there is no valid evidence that queer folks are victimizing anyone in these locations—but what we do know for certain is that "more U.S. congressmen have been convicted of assaulting someone in a public bathroom than trans people have" (Bird 2017; Wicks 2016). One final example of legislation that targets the queer population in the United States is the 2023 law of Florida's Governor DeSantis that is commonly referred to as the "Don't Say Gay" bill (Parental Rights in Education Bill). This hate legislation, which was extended to include elementary and high schools, is couched within the argument that parents should be the decision makers "regarding the upbringing of their children," and it bans "classroom discussion about sexual orientation or gender identity in certain grade levels" (in Johnson 2019). By depriving young people of basic knowledge about gender identity and sexual orientation, this law will have a deep and detrimental impact on children, teens, and adults (Parris et al. 2021).

## Implications

Studying gender, or how men and women accomplish masculinity and femininity, entails a consideration of how social structures constrain and channel behavior, which in turn may influence a person's criminal or law-abiding behavior or one's actions in the workplace (Messerschmidt 1997). Sexuality entails the same consideration, although patriarchy and heteronormativity make them challenging to see. While women and the LGBTQ+ population have made some social, political, and economic gains, they experience periods of intense backlash as well. And men (particularly white, cisgender, and heterosexual) still control all of the key institutions of power, such as the military, government, business, academic, and financial institutions of the United States.

Women have made significant advancements in education, workforce participation, and political representation. The #MeToo movement as well as reports and settlements about pervasive sexual misconduct shed light on the prevalence of sexual harassment and assault that would have been invisible decades ago. This has led to increased awareness and conversations about consent and gender-based violence. However, gender inequalities persist, particularly in the form of the gender pay gap, and the COVID pandemic exposed how quickly workforce participation gains could be rolled back. While women are slowly making gains in leadership positions, they are still underrepresented through politics, business, finance, and law. While men's sexual misconduct against women is more visible and publicized, it is not yet clear how much that will impact the extent of it, especially with regular men (as opposed to men in powerful positions who are protected by their institutions). Reproductive rights and justice face intense challenges.

LGBTQ+ people have also made some significant gains. They are more visible in culture, politics, and other areas of society. According to Gallup, LGBTQ+ identification keeps increasing, especially among younger people—almost 16 percent among Generation Z (born 1997–2002), compared with 2 percent for baby boomers (born 1946–1964) (Jones 2021). Same-sex marriage was legalized nationwide in 2015, and some antidiscrimination laws have been passed in some states to protect LGBTQ+ individuals in employment, housing, and health care. However, as the victimization data show, discrimination, violence, and harassment against LGBTQ+ individuals persist, particularly for transgender and gender-nonconforming individuals. Gains with antidiscrimination laws face backlash, as does access to gender-affirming care.

Scholars continue challenging the treatment of gender and heteronormativity in existing theory and research. Women and the LGBTQ+ community are less frequently treated as anomalies and are being located more at the center of research. With the advent and application of queer criminology, *all* women—regardless of sex assigned at birth—will be included in research that continues to wrestle with the exploration of how race and ethnicity, class, and other social characteristics such as age intersect with gender. However, as with the problems of racial color blindness, superficially appealing "gender-neutral" policies conceal years of oppression, and they still often do not identify the most appropriate standard for comparison.

## Review and Discussion Questions

1. How are *sex* and *gender* different? What is meant by *cisgender*, and why is that term important?
2. What is patriarchy? How are misogyny and benevolent sexism similar and different?
3. How are the various identities in the LGBTQ+ acronym similar and different?
4. What is heteronormativity? What is the point of queer studies and queer criminology?
5. Drawing from the text and box 5.1, what do you think are the best examples of male, cisgender, and heterosexual privilege?
6. If it is not triggering for you, review some forms of gendered violence. How does patriarchal violence differ as a framework?
7. Go to the National Center on Domestic and Sexual Violence (http://www.ncdsv .org/ncd_articles.html) and look at the original Power and Control Wheel. Choose another variation that interests you (gender, race, ethnicity, youth, etc.). What do you see about how power works in abusive relationships?
8. How would you summarize the patterns of offenders and victimization discussed in this chapter? How do sexuality and gender interact?
9. What are reproductive rights and reproductive justice? Why are they important?

## Notes

1. Available at https://cejce.berkeley.edu/geneq/resources/lgbtq-resources/definition-terms.
2. These, along with dozens of other variations for race, ethnicities, immigrants, teens, and more, are available through the National Center on Domestic and Sexual Violence: https:// www.ncdsv.org/ncd_articles.html.

# CHAPTER 6

# Understanding Intersections and the Nuances of Privilege

*The intersecting relations of class, race, gender, and crime are captured in an increasing amount of research by and about women of color and the LGBTQ+ community. It is also captured in some research about Black men, whose intersectional challenges are captured in a book written by a former gang member who has become a university professor.*

*The account is Victor Rios's (2011) book* Punished. *It is a nuanced treatment of the criminalization of urban and marginalized male street youths and their resistance to the cultural mainstream, inside and outside of the criminal justice system. In one of Rios's anecdotal reflections, he tells of an encounter between a white female potential employer-manager and a young Black man seeking unsuccessfully to bridge the cultural gap and find legitimate work:*

> *Ronny was called in for a job interview at Carrows, a chain restaurant that served $9.99 sirloin steak and shrimp. He called me up, asking for help. I lent him a crisp white dress shirt, which I had purchased at a discount store when I worked as a server at a steak house during my undergraduate years. I convinced Ronny to wear fitted khakis, rather than his customary baggy jeans. He agreed, with the condition that he would wear his white Nike Air Force Ones, a popular basketball shoe at the time. . . . Famous basketball players such as Kobe Bryant wore these shoes during games and advertised for Nike. Black and Latino youths in Oakland gravitated to these shoes, sometimes even wearing them to more formal events such as high school proms and weddings. I asked Ronny why he insisted on wearing these shoes in a professional setting. He replied, "Because professionals wear them."*
>
> *Many of the boys believed that they had a clear sense of what courteous, professional, and "good" behavior was. Despite their attempts to present themselves with good manners and good morals, their idea of professional behavior did not match mainstream ideas of professional behavior. This in turn created what I refer to as misrecognition. When the boys displayed a genuine interest in "going legit," getting a job or doing well in school, adults often could not recognize their positive attempts and*

*sometimes interpreted them as rude or malicious acts and therefore criminalized them. (Rios 2011)*

*With these observations, Rios describes some of the traps within which many poor Black and Latino boys become ensnared by a society that closely resembles a caste system of immobility based on ranks of class, race, and gender. The boys' socialization in poor urban neighborhoods has taught them to survive by being aggressive and charismatic, by being willing (and able) to fight at a moment's notice, by being able to run from danger, and by maintaining a stylish appearance at all times.*

*For that reason, Air Force One shoes by Nike are part of an inner-city uniform—some might even call it a cloak of protection or power signifying elite status. So, when these boys think about trying to get respect from the mainstream society while maintaining readiness and respect in their own neighborhoods (which is where they will have to return after working a shift at a restaurant), their first inclination is to wear their best sneakers to a job interview. And although the message received by employers might be one of disrespect, the employers usually don't understand the life that these boys have to navigate.*

*In short, living in a poor neighborhood and being Latino or Black and being male is an intersectional problem: the difficulties that some people face just for being poor (indecent housing, inadequate clothing, poor diet, crowded living conditions, limited transportation, etc.) are compounded by the difficulties of being Black or Latino (prejudice, discrimination, stereotypes, police brutality, mass incarceration, hopelessness, etc.) and with being male (hypermasculinity standards, toughness, independence, the role of sexual aggressiveness, etc.). With all of this stacked against them, it is very hard for a young man like Ronny to believe that he should wear a pair of wingtip shoes to a job interview at a restaurant when the people in his neighborhood will think he is "soft" or "ripe" for victimization while he is walking to and from his job. Besides, Ronny already believes that "professionals" wear Air Force Ones because highly paid rappers and sports figures wear them. Rios continues:*

> *The boys attempted to use the resilience skills they had learned on the streets, their organic capital, in spaces that could not value the respectability and morals that they brought to the table. These morals and values were often rendered deviant, and the boys were excluded or criminalized. Ronny's story is indicative of how many of the boys attempted to tap into mainstream institutions but failed. As they encountered rejection, they returned to the resilience and survival strategies that they had developed in their neighborhoods. (Rios 2011)*

*The day of the interview, Rios prepared Ronny by helping him to develop the "acceptable" cultural capital. He also located himself in the restaurant and ordered a meal so that he could observe the interaction between Ronny and his potential* manager. During the interview, "Ronny tried to use his charisma to connect with the manager, but she kept her distance and did not look at Ronny the entire time he answered questions, seemingly uninterested in what he had to say. At the end of the interview, Ronny abruptly stood up and walked away from the manager, with no handshake or smile. He went outside."

Rios had decided to take his food to go, and as he was leaving the restaurant to meet up with Ronny, he noticed that the manager "was greeting a White male youth. She smiled, gave him her hand, and offered him a place to sit down. Ronny's first contact with her was not this friendly."

At the debriefing following the interview, Ronny told Rios that "he had a good feeling and that the manager had seemed to like him." In turn, Rios asked Ronny to walk him through the interview, confirming that Ronny had followed the plan flawlessly. Rios wrote,

> I was proud of him. "You followed the plan. You did a great job," I told him. "Why didn't you shake her hand when you left?" I asked. "Cause," Ronny replied. "Why not?" I scolded. "Because it was a White lady. You not supposed to shake a White lady's hand. They be scared of a nigga. They think I'm a try to take their shit or fuck 'em. I just said thanks and walked out." Ronny did not get the job. (Rios 2011)

Rios captures the drive that many Black and Latino boys have in trying to gain legitimate employment by being willing to enter into work spaces as low-level employees, showing enthusiasm for the job, and seeking out mentors to help prepare them for the interview. But the stereotypes abounding in the United States that criminalize Black and Latino boys are brought into the interview, not from the mainstream side (in this case) but from the outsider's point of view. Ronny is well aware of the stereotypes of people who look like him, and his knowledge of those stereotypes all but compelled him to practically sabotage his own attempt to gain employment. Certainly, it is unclear whether Ronny didn't get the job because of his shoes or his unwillingness to shake the manager's hand, but Rios is purposeful with his description of the job candidate who came in after Ronny, that is, making a point to mention the welcoming behaviors that were absent during Ronny's interview and yet so obvious to Rios at the beginning of the second boy's interview. Such are the kinds of "niceties" that many whites face in interviews with people of their same race, where they may take for granted that someone will be welcoming to them when they appear for an interview. This is, in part, one example of the unearned benefit package that exists in white privilege and class privilege: not having to wonder whether interviewers will view you as someone who will try to rob or rape them.

# Introduction

Imagine standing in the middle of an intersection with a view down several streets that run in different directions. If a friend stands at the end of one of those streets, she can share some of the same view, but her perspective will also be different: the features that are closest will be different, and she will have a view down different side streets. Now think of those streets as being social dimensions such as class, race/ethnicity, and gender/sexuality. To add to the analogy, imagine class as being represented by the height of the buildings and the floor one is standing on (including, perhaps, being in a basement or subbasement). The view of those streets represents a person's "social location." Describing a person's social location based solely on race, for example, would be incomplete and possibly confusing; it would be like saying "Main Street" or "Third Street" in a large, diverse city without specifying a cross (intersecting) street. An indication of whether the location was in a penthouse or lower floor would also have value in describing both the location and the view (perspective). Thus, an accurate description requires other markers, such as gender and class, to get a "fix" on the location.

While this analogy is a helpful starting point to conceptualize intersections, it also has some limitations. While intersections and the floor of a building sort of capture class, race/ethnicity, and gender/sexuality, there are many more aspects of identity. Most intersections try to limit the number of roads crossing through at one time, so the analogy breaks down if we were to try to add religion, citizenship/immigration status, physical (dis)ability, body type, mental health diagnoses/neurodivergence, and more. Further, the recognition of new racial/ethnic and gender/sexuality categories may be like adding new "lanes" on the street, but they all have somewhat different histories. Chapter 4 noted that different racial and ethnic groups have different experiences—not just different lanes, but different roads that are not nicely parallel like a city grid. Finally, the notion of roads suggests something fixed—Main Street has a permanent location, with known starting and ending points. However, aspects of race and gender/sexuality are more dynamic and contested in the construction of categories and people's willingness to claim identification. Episodes from the past are still being uncovered and interpreted, and people in the present are consciously and unconsciously building the future.

Rather than pushing the street analogy further, this chapter will shift to discussing various meanings of intersectionality. While we have grounded intersectionality as an everyday reality of how people live, this chapter explores the processes of power that can obscure aspects of intersectionality. We want readers to recognize that all people are at the center of multiple intersections of power, inequality, and privilege as shaped by their class, race/ethnicity, and gender/sexuality (just to name some of the main ones). Nobody fits into any *one* category; instead, everyone exists simultaneously at the intersection of *many* categories that shape not only their view of the world and the actions they take but also other people's view of them. The overlapping of two or more of these classifications (e.g., race, class, and gender/sexuality), however, is often unobserved in discussions about any one individual classification. So when researchers talk about "Latinas" or "women" or "poverty," they very rarely acknowledge the large number of people who experience the world as all three. That is, poor Latina women experience the disadvantages of all three groups simultaneously. And if that same Latina is undocumented and bisexual, her attempts to navigate the world that everyone else inhabits can be fraught with difficulties that are not apparent to people with fewer layers of marginalized identity.

Even the widely used phrase "women and minorities" does not consider that approximately 25 percent of the population are *women of color* (see box 6.1). They are—and will always be—both, although race may be more important in some situations and gender in others. The point here is not to "add up" identities but rather is to understand that we are talking about a single person with many aspects of identity that combine into complex identities and expressions of them—and thus they experience complex combinations of privileges and oppression.

## BOX 6.1

### Ask a Simple Question . . .

Fact: Men are more likely than women to be murdered in their lifetime. Black people are more likely than whites to be murdered in their lifetime.

Question: Who is more likely to be murdered, a white man or a Black woman?

Fact: Black non-Hispanic folks constitute about 12 percent of the U.S. population but make up nearly 32 percent of people who are currently incarcerated in state or federal prisons. Women make up over half of the U.S. population and around 7 percent of those incarcerated in state or federal prisons.

Question: Are Black women overrepresented or underrepresented in correctional facilities?

Having trouble answering these questions?

Answers: To take the first example, logic probably made it relatively easy to figure out that Black men face the highest likelihood of being murdered relative to Black women and whites. The conclusion that white women face the lowest likelihood of being murdered relative to white men and Black folks was probably also straightforward. But to answer the question posed with any degree of confidence requires more information on race *and* gender. This information ultimately reveals that Black women actually face a higher likelihood of being murdered than white men.

The second question is probably best answered "Both." Black women are both overrepresented

(by race) and underrepresented (as women) in prisons. The difficulty in answering this question illustrates how much more progress needs to be made in understanding intersectionality since the early 1980s book *All the Women Are White, All the Blacks Are Men, but Some of Us Are Brave* (Hull et al. 1982) set the foundation for creating Black women's studies as an academic discipline for university students. The authors meant the book to serve as a "reference text and pedagogical tool" for people interested in creating a discipline that would reduce the "extremely negative ways in which Afro-American women have been portrayed in literature, scholarship, and the popular media" and would expand "opportunities for Black women to carry out autonomously defined investigations of self in a society which through racial, sexual, and class oppression systematically denies our existence" (Hull et al. 1982: xviii).

The subsequent forty years have seen some of that promise fulfilled, but more work needs to be done to undo the multiple overlapping privileges of researchers. Ultimately, the issues raised by these two questions go beyond mere semantics and wordplay. This exercise speaks in a small way to the importance of considering characteristics such as race and gender not as separate constructs but as interlocking ones that have real consequences.

Ignoring someone's multiple experiences frequently leads to invisibility or missed connection. For example, during the Women's March on Washington, DC, in 2017, many white feminists converged on the nation's capital in the largest single day of protest in U.S. history. At issue were former president Trump's statements during the general election campaign about reversing the gains of the previous decades of women's rights, repealing the Affordable Care Act ("Obamacare"), eliminating funding for Planned Parenthood, restricting access to abortions, banning transgender folks from military service, and more. Many women of color who shared those interests also marched for fairness in hiring and accountability in policing, among other seemingly nonwhite concerns. Oftentimes, white feminism fails to address the additional concerns of marginalized groups who also identify as feminists, and who must shoulder the burden of multiple fights for equality.

As straightforward as this perspective seems, scholars of crime and justice have been slow to embrace the idea of "intersectionalities" and the complexities it raises. Researchers tend to focus on one social dimension at a time, controlling for everything else to the best of their ability, to produce a clear understanding of that one dimension. Further, some research that tries to discuss more than one dimension of life still lacks an understanding of privilege. Many studies that look at race differences do not acknowledge white privilege and how that can shape patterns of behavior, research questions, methods, and conclusions. Likewise, many studies of gender differences do not acknowledge male privilege and how that can shape patterns of behavior, research questions, methods, and conclusions. Many criminologists, in other words, still assume that gender is relevant only when discussing women, race is relevant only when discussing people of color, and class is relevant only when talking about the very rich or the very poor. Similarly, many people assume that sexuality is relevant only when applied to the LGBTQ+ community. The point is, on the contrary, that everyone has a social class, ethnic/racial identity, and gender/sexuality, and they bring this identity to what they study. That identity shapes what theories make sense to them, what questions seem worth exploring, how they should study those questions, and how others will react to that research.

The intersections of class, race, and gender thus describe a way of viewing social inequalities and privileges as interrelated and interacting. So, for example, sometimes Black and Latina women make decisions about how to respond to abusive intimate partners based on how they believe the police will treat their abusive partner because he is a poor Black or Latino male. That decision may not seem intuitive for people who grew up learning and believing that police officers are their friends and should be called to help. But marginalized populations may have experienced generational trauma from government officials, so they are often distrustful of criminal legal professionals like the police. Police are not always responsive to minorities as crime victims, and they search for drugs or demand identification from people even if it is not relevant to the reported crime. As is clear from the news, there is also some chance for police violence and shooting, so while many white people who are middle class and above do not hesitate to call the police, those folks who have a history of horrors with the system are not quick to welcome a group whom they may see as predatory into their neighborhoods, families, and homes.

Thus, this chapter explores some of the challenges to understanding intersectionality. Toward this end, the rest of the chapter is divided into two sections followed by a section on the implications. The first section centers intersectionality; it moves beyond the brief mentions of intersectionality in previous chapters to focus on the development of the concept and some ways to understand it. The other parts of this section explore whether there is a "master status," meaning that one aspect of identity is always more important than others; privilege in its increased complexity; and data and techniques for modeling intersectionality that present challenges to the development of intersectional knowledge. Finally, like the last parts of the previous chapters on class, race, and gender, this chapter addresses how intersections relate to criminology and criminal justice issues. It first explores victimization, then finishes by highlighting a few examples from history and current social movements where an intersectional analysis is important.

## Centering Intersectionality

Kimberlé Crenshaw of Columbia Law School is credited with coining the term *intersectionality* in the early 1990s. She originally meant it as a critique and explainer to the legal profession about a discrimination case. The judges had decided that Black women were not discriminated against by an employer: there was no gender discrimination because they hired white women, and no racial discrimination because they hired Black men. While reversing the invisibility of women of color is still an important goal of intersectional research and advocacy, the ways in which we understand intersectionality has evolved. In a 2017 interview, Crenshaw noted that:

> Intersectionality is a lens through which you can see where power comes and collides, where it interlocks and intersects. It's not simply that there's a race problem here, a gender problem here, and a class or LBGTQ problem there. Many times that framework erases what happens to people who are subject to all of these things. (Columbia Law School 2017)

Here, Crenshaw recognized the importance of understanding that by separating race issues from gender issues from LGBTQ+ issues, we miss how those groups intersect and there are people affected by all of those issues simultaneously. Further, intersectionality is encountered at both the individual and group level: a *woman* who identifies as bisexual may face heightened domestic violence victimization, and bisexual *women* experience the most domestic violence victimization in the LGBTQ+ community.

Not only has Crenshaw's definition of "intersectionality" evolved over time, but different interviews, in light of different events that were happening, bring out different aspects of what intersectionality means. Readers who find an interview with her, or others who do intersectionality research, should avoid feeling like there is a single truth about intersectionality to be discovered. For example, in another interview, Crenshaw discussed some different but equally important ideas about intersectionality:

> Intersectionality is about capturing dynamics and converging patterns of advantage and disadvantage. Those are going to change from context to context. Our way of thinking about what discrimination looks like is flattened, and it says, race discrimination is the same for everyone. We're thinking Black women experience racism the same way Black men do or that Latinas experience sexism the same way that white

women do, but there are millions of different ways that power converges. We're telling some of those stories to disrupt the false assumption that there is only one story, or a couple, and that intersectionality is just a number. It's not a number. It's a set of experiences. (in Moffitt 2021)

Within criminology, the origins of intersectionality are best located in *Black criminology*, perhaps first introduced in 1992 by Katheryn Russell. She advocated for more Black criminologists, in part to draw more attention to issues of race that had long been ignored by mainstream (and thus white) criminology. Later, Russell wrote that "the call for a Black Criminology was a call for expanding the theoretical framework for race and crime research. Done properly, a Black Criminology would work the same way that feminist criminology works to fairly represent women's experiences in criminology scholarship" (Russell 2019).

For example, Black criminology calls for more in-depth analysis of race, just as feminist criminology argues for more in-depth analysis of gender, because mainstream criminology "can't add women and stir" and assume it will get the same results as it did with men. (Buist and Lenning [2023] argued similarly for queer criminology.) While Russell uses feminist criminology as an analogy, it started largely as a white female response to a white male criminology, and it later incorporated more intersectionality. As a Black woman, Russell backed intersectionality in her call for Black criminology and all the work she did developing it over the subsequent years. Black criminology has been slow to attract the attention it so rightly deserves within the discipline.

Additionally, while historically criminology ignored intersectional frameworks, some criminological research has indeed done important intersectional work without explicitly acknowledging it as intersectional. Some examples of this include work within feminist criminology that examines pathways to crime that expose the importance of victimization and trauma (Paik 2017). Furthering this insight, Paik highlights the 1999 work of Elijah Anderson's Code of the Street that delved into experiences of Black men in urban Philadelphia and in doing so highlighted many times over the effects of race, class, and gender as related to crime. Indeed, Rios's work in the opening narrative of this chapter captures similar findings to Anderson's research. Additional examples include Panfil's (2017) detailed qualitative study of gay gang members, most of whom were men of color, or Kahle's (2020) research on bullying victimization of LGBT students in schools. In short, students and researchers do not need the word "intersectionality" in the title for it to be intersectional—and conversely, sometimes research claiming to be intersectional does not mean that intersectional concepts are being applied in any significant way.

As we noted in chapter 2, intersectionality in criminology can be applied in two main ways. First, it primarily suggests "centering the margins" (Shah 2021; Potter 2015), which means investigating the experiences of and oppressive dynamics on populations that have been the most marginalized and thus rendered invisible. Women developed feminist criminology because they were marginalized by androcentric (male-centered) criminology (Cook 2020), LGBTQ+ and queer folks developed queer criminology in response to heteronormative criminology (Ball 2014; Buist and Lenning 2023; Dwyer et al. 2016; Panfil 2017; Woods 2015), and Black people started the development of Black criminology to counter their invisibility within mainstream white criminology. Intersectionality can take people who have multiple marginalized identities and explore their realities. The point is not to create "generalizable knowledge" but to focus on a group to reveal a more complete picture of crime and what society's response to it says about that society.

The second application of intersectionality to criminology is to create a more purposeful examination of *certain intersections*, even if people have a mix of marginalization and privilege—or mostly privilege. For example, chapter 8 opens by describing Paul Butler's book *Chokehold* (2017) about the policing of Black communities, and he believes that "intersectionality teaches us that gender matters for Black men as well, and ignoring gender undermines the chances of making things better." Although *Dorm Room Dealers* does not describe itself as intersectional, it is an ethnography of economically privileged men—sons of mayors, businesspeople, doctors, and accounting executives for major firms—who have a "never go to jail in the first place" card even though they were dealing drugs during a drug war (Mohamed and Fritsvold 2011).

An important avenue for exploring intersectionality is colorism, which chapter 4 introduced. *Colorism* is a term used to describe the preferential treatment that lighter-skinned individuals in nonwhite cultures receive. Some of this research is already intersectional, although outside of criminology and the criminal legal system. Lighter-skinned women from India, for example, are sometimes afforded privileges that darker-skinned Indians do not enjoy. In her book *The Global Beauty Industry: Colorism, Racism, and the National Body*, Meeta Rani Jha (2016) describes how the Westernized image of beauty is disseminated in advertisements around the world. They push idealized images of happiness and prosperity with images of white women attached to their products. When companies sell these products globally with images of Westernized beauty (a slender, tall, white female with blond hair and blue eyes, for example), the image is sold along with the product. Darker-skinned, shorter, rounder women are pushed to the outside of this market. Colorism, by seeking light-skinned women, becomes ingrained not only in the goals of womanhood but also in the expectations of manhood in brown-skinned wives (Rani Jha 2016).

In the United States, the impact of colorism was evident during slavery and factored into what job a slave was assigned: "Black slaves with darker skin tones were subjugated to more physically demanding jobs such as fieldwork while those with lighter skin tones were given more desirable jobs that were less strenuous" (Barideaux et al. 2021: 184). These stereotypes persist in the criminal legal system in any number of ways, including how juries judge darker-skinned defendants, especially if their victims are white, how the media portrays crime, and how people are punished. Indeed, understanding the effect of race and colorism can literally be a matter of life and death: research finds that when a Black male defendant whose victim was white is faced with a death penalty sentence, Black defendants are twice as likely to receive the death penalty if they are "dark-skinned and [have] more Afrocentric facial features" (Barideaux et al. 2021: 185).

## No "Master Status"

Attempting to examine the interacting effects of class *and* race *and* gender/sexuality is difficult, so a logical step to getting a handle on it is to ask which is the most important. If, for example, gender consistently had the most significant impact, then it could be described as the *master status*. Unfortunately, though, neither class nor race nor gender/sexuality is always the most important consideration. In some situations, one may be more important than the others in shaping the social reality of a situation, but existing theory is not sufficiently developed to predict which factor will be most important under which conditions:

> If an accident happens in an intersection, it can be caused by cars traveling in any number of directions and, sometimes, from all of them. Similarly, if a Black woman is harmed because she is in the intersection, her injury could result from sex discrimination or race discrimination. (Potter 2015: 67)

Her harm could also be because of class or sexuality (or many other aspects of identity that are beyond the scope of this book). This complexity, though, does not undermine the advantages of trying to examine all of them rather than settling for a simpler, inaccurate analysis.

Theorists who focus primarily on class or race or gender can make a strong claim about the importance of the attribute they study. Marxists, for example, point to class and argue that history is defined by the struggle between the rich and poor, the haves and have-nots. Law is a tool used by the rich, who make the law in this class warfare. But law often also has a patriarchal bias because cisgender and heterosexual white men tend to make the law and they are the majority of judges and prosecutors. The control of sexuality, sexual access, and reproductive functions has also been a major site of contention throughout history. Others would argue that race is fundamental because it has been the basis of genocide in the United States of African Americans and Native Americans—and chapter 4 noted that American history has included a succession of minority groups who were exploited and excluded through laws. Laws made by the white majority defined the slave owner's property rights, reaffirmed segregation, and established the basis for the criminal justice system to police minorities, especially to maintain control over excess labor.

All three positions make an important and strong claim, which is why this book highlights class, race, and gender/sexuality. Yet, when combined, the arguments do not support a claim that one factor is *always* the most important, so the emphasis must be on understanding how they work together. Indeed, while the quote above noted how discrimination against a Black woman could be because of race *or* gender, often it is because of the combination. For example, stereotypes about Black women do not clearly follow from stereotypes about Black men or white women, and likewise the types and intensity of discrimination against Black women might not be predicted by treatment of Black men or white women.

Intersectionality is an important antidote to *essentialism*, which refers to the idea that all people in a category—like women or Black people—share some "essential" characteristic. Recognizing the different combinations of gender, sexuality, and class within a racial category increases skepticism about essentialism. Essentialism, then, serves as a deterrent to understanding people individually and collectively with any accuracy at all. Further, if one begins an analysis with the belief that a group of people "just are" or "naturally do" certain things, then the analysis is likely to contain power dynamics that are simultaneously obscured (because "that's just the way things are"). For example, in his essay "Blessed Are the White Trash," Wilkey writes,

> When poor Appalachian people are reduced to being white trash, it seems, in a rather twisted way, more reasonable that their resources can be exploited and extracted without adequate compensation. When hardworking men and women in central Appalachia are portrayed as dumb hillbillies, it is easier to pretend that coal companies are benevolent saviors rather than plunderers treating the region as a sort of internal colony. It seems more plausible, when Appalachian people are stripped of their humanity, that they should be sent down mine shafts to break their bodies and their hearts for the benefit of out-of-town coal barons making a mint on the backs of the working poor, while such exploitation is heralded as a bootstraps-up opportunity. (2017)

Capturing diversity and complexity is challenging, especially when people often communicate through short social media posts and media use click-bait headlines that simplify and sensationalize. But a helpful conceptual starting point is Maxine Baca Zinn and her colleagues, who use the analogy of a prism to capture this idea: light is made up of many colors that appear to be the same, but it "is not an infinite, disorganized scatter of colors. Rather refracted light displays an order, a structure of relationships among the different colors—a rainbow" (2003: 1). Currently, there are quite a few studies of individual groups, and the next major task is to build better understandings of the larger structure of relationships so that the "patchwork" of studies can be transformed into something even more understandable.

## Privilege

As pointed out in each of the chapters on class, race, and gender/sexuality, privilege is the flip side of oppression, and ideology makes both seem "natural." The rich are less likely to appreciate structural barriers to class mobility, economic exploitation, and the seriousness of corporate crime. Male privilege will affect how men view gender equality, including but not limited to professional equity, harassment, and sexual violence. White privilege will affect how whites view and understand racial progress and racial stereotypes and how they evaluate minorities. Studying intersections adds to this understanding that middle-class *whitemaleness* (Potter 2015: 7) tends to be the unspoken default, making this position seem universal—much like heteronormativity. Instead, intersectional criminology "acknowledges that both the man in the 'hood (urban neighborhood) and man in the hood (a Ku Klux Klan member) do manhood" and calls for "a critical analysis of how each man's identity is formed, is responded to by others, and affects his reactions in the social world" (Potter 2015: 145).

While middle-classness may be a default, the real power is with white, affluent, cisgender, heterosexual men. Consider that currently about $82 trillion is invested in venture capital and private equity. (Private equity is a type of fund where pooled investment money is used to buy businesses and change practices to be able to extract more profit, in ways that often involve job losses, gouging consumers, and a focus on the short term instead of sustainable business development.) Out of that

$82 trillion, "less than 1.3 percent of that money is invested in firms run, owned or founded by women and people of color combined. So that means 98.7 percent of all venture capital and private equity goes to white men" (Coleman 2023). In spite of this immense privilege and power accruing to a small group, many people have some degree of privilege—including those afforded by colorism—that can coexist with marginalized ones.

People can be privileged in some ways but not in others, and they are usually more aware of the identities that result in them being discriminated against rather than the ones that afford them privilege. Indeed, many white people, including many white men, who grew up poor have a difficult time understanding privilege because they experienced food and housing instability. Police were less likely to give them the benefit of the doubt than a more affluent white person. McIntosh's article on white privilege ([1988] 1997) did not always ring true for them. For example, *"'If I should need to move, I can be pretty sure of renting or purchasing housing in an area, which I can afford and in which I would want to live'* is more a statement of middle-class white privilege than just white privilege. So is: *'I can go shopping alone most of the time, pretty well assured that I will not be followed or harassed'"* (Crosley-Corcoran 2017). Box 6.2 further explores some of these intersectional privileges.

---

## BOX 6.2

### You Know You're Privileged When . . . (Part 4)

In keeping with this chapter's focus on intersectionality, we build on the forms of class privilege discussed in chapter 3, white/color privilege discussed in chapter 4, and male/cisgender/heterosexual privilege discussed in chapter 5. Intersectionality is a "nuanced concept of privilege" (Crosley-Corcoran 2017), so we will discuss and unpack the statements of privilege.

• *People who meet me for the first time will assume that I have a regular job and no criminal record.*

This statement was originally meant to be about white privilege because of the criminality that is often associated with Black men. However, many poorer white people may not benefit from this assumption, so it also contains some class privilege. Further, while Black people are the targets of stereotypes of being on welfare and criminals, they generally have the privilege of citizenship. People are more likely to see the Latino/a/x population as being "illegal," even though many are citizens and relatively few are undocumented—and being undocumented is a civil rather than criminal offense.

• *When I wear expensive clothing or jewelry or drive an expensive car, I will be treated as though I obtained these goods through the fruits of my own legitimate labor rather than through illegal activity or my association with a sexual intimate.*

The first part of this statement about "legitimate labor" largely reflects white privilege. The second part about "association with a sexual intimate" reflects male privilege because people are more likely to think that a woman's most valuable qualities are her appearance and sexuality rather than competence.

• *I can think over many options—social, political, imaginative, or professional—without asking whether a person like me would be accepted or allowed to do what I want to do.*

This statement is used to get at racial privilege as minorities enter largely white occupations, especially prestigious ones, and take on leadership positions. It has also been used to reveal male privilege as women enter male-dominated professions, especially prestigious ones, and take on leadership positions. However, it also applies to cisgender people entering a wide variety of occupations, especially ones that involve working with youth.

- *When I learn about the civil rights movement and the Black power movements, most of the leaders that I will learn about will be Black men. I will be taken more seriously as a political leader than black women.*

This statement noted that because of white privilege, many Black males do not see themselves as privileged as males (Woods 2008). It was meant to redirect to a similar point for white men about recognizing themselves in how history is written. But the statement is heteronormative in that an LGBTQ+ Black man would not see themselves in that history and would have even greater challenges than a cisgender heterosexual Black man in gaining credibility as a political leader.

While this book has focused its analysis of intersectionality around class, race, and gender/sexuality, intersectionality also incorporates many more dimensions. Although we have made a trade-off by going into depth on some aspects rather than being comprehensive about all aspects of identity, privilege, and oppression, we would encourage readers to use our discussion as a basis for incorporating other identities.

The focus of box 6.2 is on the idea of *privilege* rather than classism, racism, or sexism. Rather than having people ask questions like, "Am I racist? Am I sexist? Am I homophobic?" they should be asking instead, "To what extent do I have race/color, gender, cisgender, and heterosexual privilege?" This shift is not meant to induce guilt because privileged identities are rarely chosen: people are not responsible for their sex, gender, sexual orientation, or race; class has a great deal to do with family background and stratification. The question of "Am I a . . . ?" diverts attention from systemic oppression and individualizes the problem—and does so with a question where it is easy to come up with reasons to say, "No, I'm not a . . . ." Asking about privilege should help focus attention on the cultural, social, and legal mechanisms that support and reinforce expressions of classism, racism, and sexism. The discussion about privilege is meant to avoid a situation where whites, men, heterosexuals, and more affluent people focus on how to avoid the respective labels of racist, sexist, and homophobic while simultaneously benefiting from their privileged position.

Because privilege is an unearned benefit at the expense of other people, there are some obligations to learn about it and undo it (Pease 2010). These forms of systematic discrimination would not exist if some people in the social order and hierarchy did not benefit from them, so people who have privilege can use that privilege to speak out against it. Further, the Social Work Code of Ethics includes cultural competence standards that state: "Social workers must take action against oppression, racism, discrimination, and inequities and acknowledge *personal privilege*" (National Association of Social Workers 2021, emphasis added). They further add that

> social workers should obtain education about and demonstrate understanding of the nature of social diversity and oppression with respect to race, ethnicity, national origin, color, sex, sexual orientation, gender identity or expression, age, marital status, political belief, religion, immigration status, and mental or physical ability. (National Association of Social Workers 2021)

While the social work code of ethics is not binding on criminology and people in criminal justice professions, our experience is that many students enter criminology and criminal justice because they want to help people—and social work says its purpose is to "enhance human well-being." That includes "individual well-being in a social context and the well-being of society" (National Association of Social Workers 2021). These similarities reinforce a larger point that to work with people in ways that do not reinforce privilege and oppress others, workers *must* recognize personal privilege. And the demonstration of understanding about social diversity can only be achieved through intersectional analysis.

With criminology and criminal justice, it is important to incorporate the views of marginalized groups into theories, policies, and procedures because the point of law enforcement, for example, is to protect and serve *all* people within a particular jurisdiction. Being marginalized means that your views, interests, and rights have been pushed to the edge, overlooked, or met with hostility. A view that incorporates the perspective of only the dominant groups is not equal justice under the law and cannot serve all the interests of a diverse community, even though some people in privileged positions may prefer (and even advocate for) the simpler (and traditional) views from their social location.

Returning to the analogy that opened this chapter, problems arise when policy is made for a whole city based on the view from a skyscraper in a wealthy white neighborhood and made to serve their interests. This view captures the details of only their reality to the exclusion of many others who may be viewing the world from the windowless basement floor of a building at a different intersection of the city. If coercive force by the criminal legal system is really going to be done for "justice," then it must equally enforce the interests of everyone (Reiman and Leighton 2023). The injustices that arise from providing "law and order" for a society marked by economic inequality, white supremacy, and male cisgender heteronormativity apply also to their intersections.

## Data and Modeling

A final challenge to studying intersections relates to the limitations of many models used to study social dynamics and sparse data about intersectionality. Government and other publications present a table on race and then another table on gender, but too often there is not one on race and gender. In this way, race and gender are treated as separate variables rather than as overlapping social locations—and class is usually not considered. Even when race data are fully collected, some of the five categories are relatively small, so they get collapsed into the category "other" or are even completely omitted (for example, in some of the victimization data in previous chapters). Various chapters have already noted how internally heterogeneous racial categories can be, and adding together Native Americans, Pacific Islanders, and non-white Latinos creates a category so diverse that it defies interpretation. Even some racial categories such as Black, Hispanic, white, Asian, and Native American mask great variations along the lines of generation/age, class, language, gender, sexuality, culture, national origin, and religion.

Another barrier to understanding intersections in relation to crime and justice is that most research retains the single-category variables of class, race, and gender, so the findings are about how a certain variable interacts with race, where the results combine the effects for males and females or all classes and sexual orientations. These mostly quantitative attempts to look at the effect of each variable separately come at the expense of understanding how these structuring factors interact with one another to yield, for example, *gendered racism* in a myriad of forms and shapes.

Furthermore, the emphasis on quantitative methods and statistical analyses has resulted in a tendency among academics to conduct research from the assumption that they can "hold all else constant." But even though it is common knowledge that racial discrimination means Black folks have lower income, researchers "control" for income to estimate the amount of racial discrimination, and the results of this sophisticated statistical control end up minimizing the amount of discrimination.

Much of the scholarship that provides the best understanding of how intersections play out in the social world tends to be qualitative, descriptive, and narrative, emphasizing the contextual aspects of people's day-to-day existence. This research does not assume that the usual survey questions cover all the important topics, nor does it assume that the multiple-choice answers in a survey capture everyone's experience. Surveys are doing a better job with allowing participants to put in a wider range of options for race and moving beyond binary heteronormative categories, but progress is limited if questions themselves still reflect various privileges. Luckily, as more people do intersectional research and it is read and cited by others, the knowledge base builds.

Box 6.2 described intersectionality as a "nuanced concept of privilege" (Crosley-Corcoran 2017), and intersectional understandings of crime and the operations of the criminal legal system also become nuanced. For example, disproportionate minority contact (DMC) with, and penetration into, the criminal legal system is well established. But here is the nuance afforded by an intersectional analysis that simply tries to look at different racial groups and binary sex categories:

> The vast majority of studies (64 percent) found mixed evidence of race effects in juvenile justice processing, meaning one minority group may have been disadvantaged at a certain decision point but not another, that minority groups may have been disadvantaged at one stage and not another, that minority males may have been affected but not minority females, etc. These complicated mixed findings provide a more precise and accurate picture of DMC, but also highlight the increasing difficulty of trying to address the issue of disparate treatment of minority youth while accounting for differences across races, gender, and other factors that account for mixed results on DMC. (Spinney et al. 2018: 586)

## Intersectionality, Victimization, and Justice

This section of the chapter starts to connect the general overview of intersections with criminology and criminal justice. By looking at victimization and then some historical patterns of justice through an intersectional lens, the remainder of the chapter sets a foundation for later chapters that systematically explore how complex identities interact with each stage of the criminal justice system from lawmaking to prisons. Specifically, the first section on victimization reviews official data and important alternate concepts of harm and victimization that provide better insight into the experiences of some groups. The second section provides a broader look at how intersections can change people's understanding of history and why they are important for contemporary social movements.

## Victimization and Intersectionality

Box 6.1 asked about the relative rates of victimization for white men and Black women. Men have higher victimization rates than women, but the rates for Black folks are higher than for whites, so the question reinforces the importance of understanding intersections. Indeed, policy makers and practitioners increasingly say they want to look at data-driven proposals and evidence-based interventions, which requires intersectional data to do correctly. But the Bureau of Justice Statistics publishes very little intersectional data as part of its public reports on the National Crime Victimization Survey. Given the obvious increased interest in intersectionality, we found it frustrating that some of the victimization data we used in a previous edition has not been routinely updated.

The data we published in the last edition was not as current as we would have liked, but the general summary is instructive about general patterns that are important to understand. For example, official statistics at the time generally supported the contention that men are more likely to be victimized than women and that minorities generally had higher rates of victimization than whites—but some groups of men are less likely to be victimized than some groups of women. This matters because criminology and policy should ideally put greater emphasis into studying acts that cause the greatest harm.

The BJS (2011) broke down victimization data by race, ethnicity, and gender. The men in each category had higher victimization rates than women in the same racial or ethnic category. Black men had higher victimization rates than men of other races, and Black women had higher rates of victimization than other women. But Black women had generally higher rates of violent victimization than white men (with the exception of robbery). Indeed, the category of completed violence (as opposed to "threatened and attempted violence") showed that Black men had the highest victimization rate, followed by Black women and Hispanic men.

Given the strong pattern of people with low income experiencing greater victimization, part of this dynamic may be class based because minority women have the least income. Unfortunately, the data are not published in a form that breaks down victimization by gender and income. However, the BJS (2011) presented victimization rates by race (limited to white and Black) and selected levels of income. The poorest Black people in the survey (income less than $7,500) had higher rates of overall violent victimization, and it seems likely that Black folks had higher levels of victimization from completed violence than whites at the same income level. Black people experienced more burglaries than whites of the same income and were probably the victims of theft of more than $250 more than whites of similar incomes.

In criticizing the BJS and other sources for the lack of intersectional data, we realize that limitations of sample size make it hard to do a robust analysis that covers race and gender, or race, income, gender, and sexual orientation. However, this problem can be somewhat resolved by combining multiple years of victimization data, as the BJS has done for any number of publications. While this breaks the convention of reporting what victimization was like the previous year and how that compared to other recent years, pooling years of data provides other important aspects of victimization, especially intimate partner violence, sexual assault, and victimization of people of color and the LGBTQ+ population.

While the use of pooled data is helpful for some types of analyses, we also advocate for data that provide insight into the likelihood of repeat victimization. Indeed, part of what would be helpful to know is someone's cumulative lifetime chances of being a victim. Being at higher risk of victimization because of class, race, or gender/sexuality is rarely a one-year event, and it generally increases the likelihood of being a victim of multiple crimes. The effect of multiple victimizations, especially violent ones, has effects that quickly escalate into posttraumatic stress disorder (PTSD) and complex PTSD. Victimization researchers are starting to explore the effects of generational and historical trauma on current individuals of minority groups, especially women who have experienced extended periods with high rates of official and unofficial victimization.

For example, Native American women experience high levels of violence in addition to other generational traumas. A dated but comprehensive government study found that in the previous year, about 40 percent of American Indian and Alaska Native women had experienced violence, including 14.4 percent who had experienced sexual violence. Sadly, that increased to 84.3 percent who had experienced violence in their lifetime, including 56.1 percent who had experienced sexual violence (Bureau of Indian Affairs, n.d.). This victimization comes on top of hundreds of years of trauma from seizures of land and forced dislocations that disrupted tribal social structures and cultural practices. Forced relocations like the infamous Trail of Tears exposed Native Americans to harsh weather conditions, inadequate food and supplies, and outbreaks of disease, so many died along the way. The establishment of reservations led to the loss of sovereignty and economic stability. The white governments of the United States and Canada set up boarding schools where Indigenous children were forcibly separated from their parents; were punished for speaking tribal languages and practicing cultural traditions; and were subjected to physical, sexual, and emotional abuse (McDiarmid 2019; Monchalin 2016; Weyler 1992). (But white culture depicts the Native Americans as savages [Ross 1998].)

For other groups, too, the lifetime chances of criminal victimization need to be added to the probability of victimization from other acts not formally labeled as crimes, like the chances of increased exposure to toxic waste, unsafe workplaces, and brutality at the hands of the criminal justice system (to name just a few). For women, the victimization rate for, say, acquaintance rape (where the rapist is known to the victim) needs to be added to the likelihood of a relationship involving domestic violence, sexual harassment at work, and street harassment. Women of color have additional factors beyond those articulated for white women and also experience victimizations that relate to racial stereotyping. Teachers and other adults "see black girls as more adult like than their white peers," so they "don't give black girls the care and protection they need" (Cottom 2017).

Further, perceptions of victims and their "worthiness" shape the reaction to these individual and lifetime profiles of victimization in ways that vary by class, race, and gender/sexuality. For example, when a Black man is assaulted, some may be inclined to assume he was doing something that precipitated the violence, perhaps by being involved in the drug trade or some other illicit business. The same misguided assumptions hold true for minorities who go missing in the United States—that is, the assumption is that minority women and girls are runaways or sex workers or that minority men and boys are somehow involved in illegal activities. Consequently, missing persons cases involving racial minorities rarely receive national media or federal law enforcement attention, thereby making it less likely that the abducted minorities (least of all minority men and boys) will be located and their abductors brought to justice. Hence, a white middle-class woman may be seen as the "true/ideal victim," deserving of the most sympathy, especially when her behavior was consistent with the "pedestal values" (described in chapter 5).

For example, research focused on how women who are victims of crime are portrayed in newspaper media found that Black women victims of crime were portrayed as being "bad" compared to white and Latina women. Black women victims of crime were more likely to be subjected to victim blaming, such as when news stories discussed the "unsafe environments" the women were in when victimized (Slakoff and Brennan 2020). In contrast,

> stories about White female victims were the most likely to produce sympathetic overall narratives, even after we controlled for other variables. This finding was unsurprising given the "ideal" victim stereotype, White privilege, and minority devaluation. (Slakoff and Brennan 2020: 173)

This research found that minority female victims were portrayed similarly to other minority victims, and "no significant differences emerged in the likelihood that a story would result in an overall sympathetic narrative (versus one that was unsympathetic overall) for Black versus Latina victims" (Slakoff and Brennan 2020: 173).

A final limitation of official data is that they do not reveal the experience of victimization and the barriers to getting help. For example, while the physical experience of being battered is the same for all women, a victim's ability to obtain help in escaping the abuse is strongly related to class, race/ethnicity, and sexuality. Battered Latinas, for example, find a shortage of bilingual and bicultural advocates, both within the system and in nonprofits. This problem also exists for many immigrant women from Asian countries. In addition, minority women such as Latinas and Asians are often stereotyped as docile and domestic, and as sensual and sexually available. Both groups can hold low status in the traditional family hierarchy, and there can be a culture-based emphasis on maintaining harmony.

The economically marginalized position of many women of color also means they have limited resources to fill the gaps in available support services to assist them (e.g., by procuring an attorney, seeking counseling, hiring a translator, or telephoning family and friends who reside outside the United States). An immigrant woman may face additional challenges seeking help. If she doesn't speak English, police officers may rely on the batterer to provide the translation. Immigrant women's families may be far away, contributing to the experience of isolation. Some immigrant women are basically held hostage by their boyfriends or husbands, who threaten the women with deportation if they report their abuse. Even if such threats are unfounded, they may still intimidate women with no independent access to information.

For Black women in particular, an emphasis on racial solidarity and not "airing dirty laundry" has often meant placing the needs of collectivity (family, church, neighborhood, or race) over their own individual needs. This emphasis promotes individual sacrifice that is a barrier to escaping abuse. But at the same time, they may be reluctant to seek help from the police because they fear the police will do little. Or they may fear that the police will deal with the abuser too harshly, thus compounding the problem of minority overrepresentation in prison (see chapter 10). Police brutality against minorities may be seen as the dominant issue in minority communities, hindering women from calling the police. Although this quote is twenty-five years old, it sadly still has relevance: "Women of color fear that the protections they seek could result in their men being beaten or even killed by cops. And if the batterer, often the sole source of support for the victim and her children, is charged with a felony, he could spend his life behind bars under the 'three-strikes-and-you're-out' mandate" (Swift 1997).

## Intersections and Justice

Through the 1800s and 1900s, prisons were about 95 percent male and 5 percent female (Rafter 1990). The social control of girls and women also included the patriarchal institutions of marriage and family, and other recalcitrant and wayward women were subjected to medicalization and mental health institutions for their problems (Foucault 1980; Platt 1969). When the first wave of organized imprisonment of women occurred between 1870 and 1900, many reformatories were opened as alternatives for white women. White women benefited from this chivalry—a form of "benevolent sexism" discussed in chapter 5—because they were regarded as in need of moral reform and protection. While the reformatory movement "resulted in the incarceration of large numbers of white working-class girls and women for largely noncriminal or deportment offenses" (Chesney-Lind 1996: 132), African American women continued to be warehoused in prisons, where they were treated much like male inmates (Butler 1997). In the South, Black women often ended up on chain gangs and were expected to keep up with the men in order to avoid beatings (Rafter 1990). The last states abolished chain gangs in the 1990s, in part because equal protection requirements meant that men and women, white and Black, could be put on them (Gorman 1997). The idea of putting white women on the chain gang was enough to end the practice for all.

Contemporary analyses of imprisonment includes more attention to the pathways through which people end up there. For example, the school-to-prison pipeline has long explored how the educational system shuttles boys of color into the criminal legal system based on zero-tolerance policies. But scholars are also highlighting the discrimination and harassment that Black girls encounter and applying the broader concept of *school-to-confinement pathways* (Morris 2018). Rather than being limited to prison, this approach encompasses other restrictive practices that punish Black girls, like surveillance and confinement, even if they are not physically located in jail or prison. This is an important distinction to make and one that clarifies how gender itself is policed, perhaps especially when taking race, class, and gender into consideration. For instance, consider the importance of access to education:

> Few curricula taught in elementary and secondary schools were designed with Black girls in mind, especially those who are living in racially isolated, high-poverty areas. If the curriculum being taught does not even consider the unique needs and experiences of Black girls seeking to climb out of poverty and the ghetto, as is most often the case, do they *really* have equal access to education? (Morris 2018: 26, emphasis in the original)

Intersectionality is not just important for understanding crime and social control, but also social movements and protest. For example, three queer Black activists created Black Lives Matter and the associated movement that has become global in reach. It was originally created in response to the 2013 acquittal of George Zimmerman for killing Trayvon Martin. One of those activists, Patrice Cullors, emphasized, "We're talking about all black lives; we weren't just talking about black men dying in the hands of the police. We're talking about black women, black trans people, black queer people" (Segalov 2015). Black Lives Matter wanted to "maximize our movement muscle, and to be intentional about not replicating harmful practices that excluded so many in past movements for liberation," so they recognized the need for leadership by women, queer, and trans activists: "Black liberation movements in this country have created room, space, and leadership mostly for Black heterosexual, cisgender men—leaving women, queer and transgender people, and others either out of the movement or in the background to move the work forward with little or no recognition" (Matthews and Noor 2017).

Further, although the focus of the media and many lists of victims has been on Black men, transgender people of color and Black women also have been victims of police brutality, including rape and sexual abuse. Families of Black women killed by police are less frequently asked to speak and tend to get less support. The hashtag #SayHerName arose as a complement to #BlackLivesMatter to help highlight that all Black lives matter and that the problem is systemic (Crenshaw and Richie 2015). At the same time, police violence against Black women, trans people, and gender-nonconforming people reveals additional aspects of policing Black sexuality and how the "toughness" of Black women becomes a reason to ignore pain in ways that would clearly be unacceptable with middle-class white women.

## Implications

Challenges remain in sorting out the complex ways in which class, race, and gender/sexuality (and more) simultaneously structure people's actions and others' reactions to them. Hierarchies like these either sustain or resist the prevailing systems of inequality and privilege. To the extent that the "isms" discourse (racism, sexism, etc.) remains necessary, people should realize that patterns of domination and subordination are not interchangeable. Someone subordinated under one form of discrimination or oppression is not similarly situated as someone under another form. For example, there is a difference between a Black or Brown male subject to racial prejudice and a white, or a Black, or a Brown woman subject to sexual stereotypes; cisgender white women who are oppressed under sexism are in a privileged position based on heterosexism and racism. Drawing attention to a matrix of privilege and oppression highlights the benefits of the current system for different groups as well as the ideological blinders that may prevent individuals from seeing those benefits.

Because of any number of dynamics, many intersections scholars like Potter (2015) advocate centering minority women in the discussion—because they have been most marginalized, silenced, and subjected to unflattering stereotypes. While all people exist at the intersections of many categories, there is a concern that intersectionality without race is a *whitening of intersectionality* that does not engage the "relevance and toxicity of the social relations of race" (Potter 2015: 70). This is not meant to limit intersectionality to studies of Black women but requires that criminology pursuing intersectionalities include critical studies of whiteness, masculinity, and heteronormativity to represent a fuller spectrum of human experience and explain more of the intersectional causes of crime. Queer criminology endeavors to pursue these concerns and approaches to research as well and could use more in-depth research and recognition of the violence Black transgender women face in their everyday lives. Indeed, at times,

> queer policies actively avoid being tied to Blackness and poor/working-class people, despite queer progress being made on the backs of low-income Black queer and trans activists. Separating increasingly criminalized Black people from decreasingly stigmatized queer lifestyles has resulted in the erasure of Black queer people, especially those who are transgender or gender-nonconforming, from LGBTQIA+ narratives. (Mikell 2023)

Among the most promising developments has been a focus on how class, race, and gender are not only social constructs but also are processes involving creative human actors. Structured action theory (Messerschmidt 1997) in particular highlights the ways in which our dominant cultural conceptions of doing masculinity and femininity intersect with the physical body, racial categories, and social classes and how these relations, in turn, shape crime and justice. Hence, whether addressing the needs of victims, offenders, or criminal justice workers, the "same" treatment is usually not "fair" treatment because, too often, equal treatment is defined by a male norm or reflects white middle-class biases and ignorance of the challenges faced by poor men and women of color.

In evaluating proposed policies and legislation, for example, we should take care to consider their impact on people occupying a range of social locations rather than, for instance, assuming that all women face the same challenges in leaving an abusive partner. Ask, "What is this program, policy, or law supposed to accomplish? How will it actually be implemented? What are the ramifications for historically marginalized groups? On what assumptions is it based? Who is included, and who is left out? What can be done to improve on this effort?" (Miller 1998; Renzetti 1998).

# Review and Discussion Questions

1. In the opening narrative, how did class, race, and gender play into Ronny's experience with trying to get a job at Carrows?
2. What are some analogies to help understand intersections and what are the limits of them? After reading this chapters, what analogy would you use to help explain this idea?
3. Explain how the intersectionalities of class, race/ethnicity, and gender apply to everybody, including men and women, whites, people of color, straights, and gays.
4. What is meant by "master status"? Is there one?
5. What are the origins of intersectionality? What are some of the ways it can be used and understood?
6. Why is "Am I a [racist, sexist, etc]?" not the right question to ask? What is? Why?
7. What privileges do you think are most important for you to understand in approaching the study of class, race, and gender? What other types of privilege discussed in the chapter may also be important? Why?
8. What are some problems with data and trying to create mathematical models of intersectionality? What types of data do the authors indicate are helpful? Why?
9. How would you describe the general patterns of victimization from an intersectional perspective? Why is it important to use an intersectional perspective with victimization? Why include lifetime and generational trauma?
10. What are some ways that intersectionality is important to the Black Lives Matter movement and media coverage?
11. What are the advantages of viewing society, crime, and criminal justice from an intersectional perspective? What are the disadvantages of failing to view society, crime, and criminal justice from an intersectional perspective?

# PART III

## Law and the Administration of Criminal Justice

# CHAPTER 7

# Lawmaking

*In 1964, a court sentenced Rummel to three years in prison for the felony of fraudulently using a credit card to obtain $80 worth of goods. Five years later, he passed a forged check for $28.36 and received four years. In 1973, Rummel was convicted of a third felony—obtaining $102.75 under false pretenses by accepting payment to fix an air conditioner that he never returned to repair. He received a mandatory life sentence under Texas's recidivist statute, and challenged it for violating the Eighth Amendment's prohibition of cruel and unusual punishment by being grossly disproportionate to the crime.*

*In Rummel v. Estelle (445 U.S. 263 [1980]), the Supreme Court upheld his life sentence for the theft of less than $230 that never involved force or the threat of force. One justice noted, "It is difficult to imagine felonies that pose less danger to the peace and good order of a civilized society than the three crimes committed by the petitioner" (445 U.S. 263 [1980]: 295). However, the majority opinion stated there was an "interest, expressed in all recidivist statutes, in dealing in a harsher manner with those who by repeated criminal acts have shown that they are simply incapable of conforming to the norms of society as established by its criminal law" (445 U.S. 263 [1980]). After "having twice imprisoned him for felonies, Texas was entitled to place upon Rummel the onus of one who is simply unable to bring his conduct within the norms prescribed by the criminal law" (445 U.S. 284 [1980]).*

*The Rummel case was not a quirk of Texas law, and the Supreme Court affirmed the precedent several times, including a California "three strikes" law that led to a fifty-year sentence for two acts of shoplifting videos from a retail chain. The law was written so that Andrade's residential burglary convictions from 1982 covered the requirements for two serious or violent felonies, and the two 1995 shoplifting offenses could be charged as felonies even though the value in one was $84.70 and the second was $68.84. The Supreme Court quoted the presentence report as saying he admitted he stole them* *to sell so he could buy heroin. He has been a heroin addict since 1977. He says when he gets out of jail or prison he always does something stupid. He admits his addiction controls his life and he steals for his habit. (Lockyer v. Andrade, 538 U.S. 63 [2003])*

The Supreme Court, *citing* Rummel v. Estelle, *held that the California law resulting in a fifty-year sentence was neither disproportionate nor unreasonable.*

*No states or the federal government have similar laws to punish repeat wrongdoing by corporations. However, as far back as 1949, Sutherland analyzed the records of seventy large corporations and found that each of them had been found guilty of wrongdoing by at least one criminal, civil, or administrative tribunal. Although not all of these were criminal violations, Sutherland found that 97 percent of the corporations had at least two adverse decisions, with an average of fourteen per company. (Sutherland's publisher pressured him not to name the companies, but his work was reissued after his death with the names [Sutherland 1985].)*

*Sutherland found that corporate crime was rational and deliberate. This finding still holds, and while corporations are larger and more criminal, the law has not taken any steps to increase punishment for rational, deliberate, and repeated wrongdoing. Consider that from 2000 to 2023, Bank of America racked up 283 settlements and paid almost $84 billion in penalties and settlements (Violation Tracker, n.d.).[1] Why doesn't the law treat Bank of America as "incapable of conforming to the norms of society"? In comparison with the three offenses that triggered repeat offender laws for poor thieves, Bank of America had 116 violations just in the category of "investor protection violation." Even if these are civil offenses, why isn't there a twenty-five strikes—or a hundred strikes—and you're out law, meaning they can no longer engage in that line of business?*

*Only a few of the nearly three hundred Bank of America violations are criminal offenses, but most are nevertheless more serious than the crimes of Rummel and Andrade. And other companies have more criminal violations than Bank of America but are still not subjected to habitual offender penalties. Johnson & Johnson, for example, had ten criminal settlements between 2005 and 2015. This is a shorter time frame than Andrade's criminal cases and more of them. In terms of seriousness, Violation Tracker notes that one case involved "one of the largest health care fraud settlements in U.S. history."*

*Some questions for lawmakers and about lawmaking: Why is it that after twice imprisoning Rummel, Texas was "entitled" to sentence Rummel to life in prison because he is "unable to bring his conduct within the norms prescribed by the criminal law," but corporations can commit an unlimited number of criminal offenses without concern for their ability to bring their conduct within the norms prescribed by the criminal law? Why does fifty years of war on crime only apply to crimes of the poor? How is it that policy choices pushed Andrade into a long prison sentence rather than drug rehab, like so many other people in prison who are there because of substance abuse (and mental health) issues but who do not get treatment? More generally, how have policy makers continued to pursue failed policies so that "after decades of war on drugs, they remain cheap and available— only drug treatment is difficult to obtain—with the United States continuing to have a higher rate of drug overdose deaths than comparable nations"? (Reiman and Leighton 2023: 12).*

## Introduction

Legal scholar Black states, "Law itself is social control, but many other kinds of social control also appear in social life, in families, friendships, neighborhoods, villages, tribes, occupations, organizations, and groups of all kinds" (1976: 6). However, law is a special form of social control because it represents "governmental social control" (Radcliffe-Brown [1933] 1965). The government has a monopoly on the "legitimate" use of coercion—stop, arrest, imprison, and execute—and the law serves to identify the acts (crimes) and actors (criminals) that power is to be used against. Even laws that are not "commonly accepted by the people still ha[ve] the power to shape behavior through sheer force of the punishments handed down for violations of it" (Miller and Browning 2004: 6).

The criminal law thus represents the first stage at sorting through behavior that is annoying, troublesome, harmful, and deviant to see what blameworthy harms should be crimes and subject to governmental social control. The criminal law, by what it includes and how seriously it punishes, signals to the police and prosecutors how to prioritize their efforts. Sentencing guidelines, while advisory, shape the behavior of judges by indicating which defendants should be sent to prison and for how long. The sorting of other harms into civil offenses and administrative rules is also important because it sends a message about how serious the behavior is and how it will be policed.

The criminal law not only shapes the priorities of those in the criminal justice system but also plays an important role in shaping people's attitudes about what is dangerous and harmful behavior (Reiman and Leighton 2023). The criminal law reflects consensus that rape, robbery, and street crime are serious harms, but it also helps create the consensus that these are the worst harms and that many white-collar and corporate harms are not really serious. This effect is magnified through the media, which uses the criminal law as the basis for reporting on "crime," including story frames about the "crime problem" and "crime waves."

This chapter examines law and lawmaking in the context of class, race, and gender/sexuality; it points out, where possible, how law has challenged inequality as well as how it serves to recreate power and privilege. Discussion of lawmaking is unusual in mainstream criminology texts because they assume there is consensus around the harms of street crime, so there are no issues to discuss. But we believe that critical thinking requires exploring how power plays a role and distorts the criminal laws from being a "natural" or "objective" reflection of harm. Laws outside of the criminal law are also important to understand because they simultaneously reinforce privileges of class, race, and gender/sexuality—or promote equality.

All these laws reflect a system of campaign donations and lobbying sometimes described as "legalized bribery" (Friedrichs 2010: 148).

To explore these issues, the next section of the chapter provides an overview of sources of law and the demographics of lawmakers (to what extent do those making the laws look like the nation they are making laws for?). Subsequent sections look at class, race, gender/sexuality, and intersections and lawmaking. The class section elaborates on the opening narrative by exploring how similar blameworthy harms by the rich and poor are not equally reflected in criminal law. The section on race discusses the history of overtly racist laws and the problem of current laws that seem racially neutral but lead to disparities. The gender/sexuality section explores how different versions of feminism (feminisms) understand equality differently and how that shapes policy advocacy, and it further discusses some of the current controversies in this area. A final section is about intersectionality and some of the ways these laws come together to impact those who live in the margins.

## Lawmaking and Its Workers (Legislators)

Readers are most likely to be familiar with state criminal law and the criminal procedure—like the *Miranda* warnings ("You have the right to remain silent . . .")—that comes from Supreme Court interpretations of the Constitution. Together, these sources furnish the basis for investigations and arrests by the state and local police, as well as charges by local prosecutors. The people convicted of these crimes fill local jails and state prisons. These crimes are most of the content for police shows and criminology books. While aspects of criminal law have a great deal of similarity across states, important areas of difference include the criminalization of abortion, LGBTQ+ issues, marijuana, and some psychedelic drugs.

Similar offenses exist in federal criminal law, but they are used when elements of the crime happen in different states. Many white-collar and corporate crimes tend to be prosecuted at the federal level because victims can be scattered over states, and corporate offices and victims are in different jurisdictions. With cybercrime, too, perpetrators and victims are in different jurisdictions, often with a chain of computers or financial institutions in still other jurisdictions.

Federal and state governments also make a variety of laws that expand the inequalities of neoliberalism (see chapter 1) or promote equality: laws dealing with the minimum wage, social assistance, taxation, and discrimination. Although these are not criminal laws, they shape the society for which the criminal justice system provides "law and order." Other state and federal laws protect people—or not— from predatory financial institutions, corporate polluters, the fossil fuel industry, defective products, unsafe workplaces, and adulterated food and drugs.

With both federal and state governments, most law is made by elected officials in Congress and state legislatures. But, "as the scope and complexity of matters regulated by the government have expanded, Congress has tended to pass acts that provide only a framework for responding to a problem; the appropriate regulatory agency is then authorized to create the detailed, relevant rules" (Friedrichs 2010: 261). Many of these agency rules regulate businesses, which have increasingly been attacking whether agency authority was explicitly and properly delegated, with the goal of limiting the government's ability to police businesses.

In addition, executive orders of the president manage operations of the federal government and have the force of law. Executive orders do not create new laws or amend existing laws, so they are limited to interpreting or implementing existing laws, managing the operations of the executive branch, or exercising inherent presidential powers. This authority encompasses areas such as national security, foreign policy, and the administration of federal agencies.

Finally, courts are involved in making law. State courts have the final say on whether state laws violate the state constitution, and they provide an authoritative interpretation of state laws (although the state legislature can amend the law if a majority does not like the court's interpretation). Federal courts and the Supreme Court decide if state and federal laws, executive orders, and agency decisions violate the Constitution. In doing so they decide what rights people—and businesses—have against the government. They also interpret federal law, although Congress can amend the law if a majority does not like the court's interpretation.

The previous chapter on intersections noted that it would be a problem if decision-making power were held by a group in a penthouse at an intersection in one particular area of town, especially if it was used for their own benefit. Unfortunately, this is very much the case because legislators are predominantly wealthy cisgender white men: "Even as the share of nonwhite Americans has grown, a Politico analysis of data from the National Conference of State Legislatures finds that most state legislatures are lacking in diversity, with nearly every state failing to achieve racial and gender parity with their own population data" (Rayasam et al. 2021). The same applies to Congress: non-Hispanic white Americans account for 75 percent of voting members in Congress but only 59 percent of the U.S. population, and women are about 25 percent of voting members but 51 percent of the population. Further, 2 percent of voting members identify as lesbian, gay, or bisexual compared to 6.5 percent of the population; there have been no openly transgender members yet (Schaeffer 2023).

Lawmakers are also predominantly members of the upper classes, if not at birth then by the time they take office. Because Congress reports assets in ranges, the best guess is that between 39 and 48 percent of Congress are millionaires, compared with about 8 percent of the U.S. adult population, so millionaires are five to six times more prevalent in Congress than among the people they represent (Sherman 2020). And "while most of the public is estimated to be part of the working class [household income less than $60,000], the percent of congressional members who have spent part of adulthood in the working class has remained stagnant at two percent" (Sorensen 2021).

These gaps in representation matter a great deal in terms of laws that get passed and policy initiatives that fail:

> Can we pass equal pay laws and give women control of their own health care decisions when women represent just 20 percent of Congress? When just 8 percent of Congress is Hispanic, is it no wonder that even the most "balanced" and "fair" immigration bills include stratospheric increases in border security and funding for deportations? With only 9 African American senators in the nearly 240-year history of our country, and just one black woman (Sen. Carol Moseley Braun over

two decades ago), will we tackle successfully the issues of education equity, criminal justice reform, and the chronic lack of investment in communities of color? (Reingold et al. 2021: 2)

In addition, trust in government is higher when people have representatives who share their life experiences.

## Class, Crime, and the Law

The rich and powerful use their influence to keep harmful acts (from which they profit) from becoming crimes, even though these acts may be more socially injurious than those labeled criminal. The concept of *analogous social injury* "includes harm caused by acts or conditions that are legal but produce consequences similar to those produced by illegal acts" (Lanier and Henry 2004: 19). Much of the harmful and illegitimate behavior of the elite members of society has not traditionally been defined as criminal, unlike behavior perpetrated by the poor and the powerless, the working and sometimes the middle classes. Thus, basing crime control theory and practice on the assumption of consensus and a neutral criminal law ignores the fact that the legal order and the administration of justice reflect a structural class bias that concentrates the coercive power of the state on the behaviors of the relatively poor and powerless members of society.

This observation is consistent with Black's highly acclaimed analysis in *The Behavior of Law* (1976). Black discovered that the law varies directly with hierarchy and privilege, meaning that greater inequality in a country accompanies more law. He also applied his proposition to disputes between two parties of unequal status and wealth. Based on a wide variety of cases, Black concluded that there is likely to be "more law" in a downward direction, such as when a rich person is victimized by a poorer one. This means the use of criminal rather than civil law, for example, and a greater likelihood of a report, investigation, arrest, prosecution, and prison sentence. In contrast, when the wealthier harms the poorer, Black argued that there is less law—meaning civil law, monetary fines rather than jail, and therapeutic sanctions rather than punitive ones. Further, Black argued that there is likely to be "more law" in the downward direction when an individual victimizes a *group* high in social organization, such as a corporation or the state. Conversely, "less law" results when a corporate body or the state victimizes individuals (or groups of individuals) that have lower levels of social organization, such as poor communities.

For example, the criminal law applied to a man in California who went into a Walgreens, filled a garbage bag with merchandise, and left the store without paying. The goods he stole from Walgreens drug store (a large corporate chain) were worth between $200 and $950, and he was charged with fifteen counts of "grand theft, second-degree burglary and shoplifting" (Legum 2021); he ended up spending sixteen months behind bars. Just a few months earlier, Walgreens itself had settled a class-action lawsuit alleging that it stole wages from more than 2,600 of its employees in California between 2010 and 2017. Among other concerns, Walgreens had rounded down employees' hours on their time cards and failed to pay wages to employees who were denied legally required meal breaks. The result of a company stealing from its employees was a $4.5 million settlement—$2.8 million going to the employees, which was just a fraction of the potential damages (Legum 2021). This was a civil case, so there was no threat of prison for anyone or criminal consequences for Walgreens. Indeed, wage theft, even in the amounts of millions of dollars, is considered a civil offense, and employees are generally left on their own to find a lawyer to sue for back pay and damages (Leighton 2018).

One of the most important advantages of corporate criminals lies "in their ability to prevent their actions from becoming subject to criminal sanctions in the first place" (in Braithwaite 1992: 89), so the harms are "beyond incrimination" (Kennedy 1970). Technically, the definition of *crime* is "an act prohibited by a criminal law," but the point of prohibiting an act by the criminal law is to protect society from injurious or dangerous actions. Criminological theorist Agnew explains that crime means "unjustifiable and inexcusable" harms that involve "voluntary and intentional behavior with intention broadly defined" as involving "purposeful, knowledgeable, reckless, and negligent behavior" (2011: 35). While this definition includes acts that are crimes, it also includes "unrecognized blameworthy harms" that are not crimes (but perhaps should be, and should be of interest to criminologists). Further, "much state and corporate harm falls into this category, since the power of state and corporate actors makes it easier for them to justify and excuse harm, hide blameworthiness, and prevent state sanction" (Agnew 2011: 38). (And, making "the public and state aware of unrecognized blameworthy harms" should be "a major mission" of criminologists [Agnew 2011: 43].)

These unrecognized blameworthy harms may cause widespread damage, but the criminal law does not forbid abuses of power in the realm of economic domination, governmental control, and denial of human rights (Simon 1999). Great Britain, for example, has a corporate manslaughter law that makes criminal manslaughter provisions applicable to companies where a gross failure of supervision leads to a worker's death; Canada and Australia have similar laws, but not the United States (Reiman and Leighton 2023). Even when the law recognizes corporate harm as belonging to the criminal law, repeated criminality is not punished through habitual offender or "three strikes and you're out" laws (as discussed in the opening narrative). In general, getting tough, waging wars on crime and drugs, and "zero tolerance" have characterized lawmaking for harms done by the poor. Legislators have imposed mandatory minimum sentences, toughened penalties, and appropriated money for police and prisons. In contrast, the general approach to business activity—even harmful and dangerous acts—has been deregulation. Legislators have rejected new laws to punish corporate crime, and lobbyists for corporations and billionaires have used the lawmaking process to reduce the power and budgets of enforcement agencies so that they have fewer resources with which to write new regulations, fight for them in court against challenges by well-funded businesses, and investigate wrongdoing.

In some cases, harmful actions (like wage theft) are civil offenses rather than criminal ones, and the difference is significant because civil actions are not punishable by prison and do not carry the same harsh stigma. A plea to civil or administrative charges usually does not require an admission of guilt and thus cannot be used against a business in other related litigation, such as suits by customers, workers, communities, or shareholders. Civil fines and judgments are tax deductible as a business expense. Whether civil or criminal, laws and rules can be written with exceptions and loopholes or use language that is vague so actual prosecution is difficult.

*The Rich Get Richer and the Poor Get Prison* suggests that the result of these relations is that law is like a carnival mirror. It magnifies the real harms from street crime, and it minimizes the real harms done by crime in the suites. As a consequence, both the criminal law and the administration of justice do "not simply *reflect* the reality of crime; [they have] a hand in *creating* the reality we see" (Reiman and Leighton 2023: 78, emphasis in the original). Thus, to say that the criminal law appropriately focuses on the most dangerous acts is a problematic statement because the criminal law shapes our perceptions about what is a dangerous act.

While the carnival mirror has been an apt analogy for a long time, the wars on crime and drugs have made its distortions more pronounced. For example, causing the death of a worker by willfully violating safety laws is a misdemeanor with a maximum sentence of six months in jail. This level of punishment was established in 1970 by Congress, which has repeatedly rejected attempts to make it tougher, so harassing a wild burro on federal lands carries twice the maximum sentence of causing a worker's death through willful safety violations (Barstow 2003). In contrast, for street crimes, Congress continued to be "tough on crime" over decades by enacting three-strikes laws, expanding the number of "strikable" offenses, increasing the number of criminal acts covered by a mandatory minimum sentence, increasing the mandatory minimum sentences, and making more offenses eligible for the death penalty.

Likewise, the level of fines set in 1970 stayed in place until it was increased in 1990, and only in 2015 did Congress allow OSHA fines to be automatically adjusted for inflation on an annual basis. Further, the maximum fine for a serious violation ("those that pose a substantial probability of death or serious physical harm to workers") was $16,131 in 2024, and the penalty for "willful or repeated" violations increased to $161,323. At these levels, OSHA fines are the same as parking tickets, or even less of a concern, to multibillion-dollar businesses. It can be profitable to expose workers to unreasonable risks and pay the fines, if they get caught. Worse still is that in 2021, the average penalty actually paid for a serious violation was $4,460 for federal OSHA (less for state OSHA) enforcement, and the median penalty for killing a worker was $9,753 for federal OSHA (less for state OSHA) enforcement (Reiman and Leighton 2023: 95–96).

The analysis provided here also applies to financial crimes, including several episodes of massive and widespread fraud. In each case, Congress and regulators created conditions for control fraud, the name given when top executives work together to undermine financial controls and engage in collective embezzlement. They loot the business, which reports record profits until suddenly it declares bankruptcy (Barak 2013). This is a type of fraud where people should be intolerant of corruption because it redistributes wealth from the poor and middle classes to the wealthy. It also hinders economic growth by misallocating money away from productive, beneficial investments into financial bubbles and scams (Ramirez and Ramirez 2017).

The first example of Congress creating criminogenic (crime-producing) conditions is the savings and loan (S&L) crisis, which occurred because of financial deregulation. Because banking deposits by regular people were backed by the Federal

Deposit Insurance Corporation (FDIC), lawmakers and regulators wanted to make sure banks did not take foolish risks that would cause the insurance to pay up. When S&Ls were deregulated, executives realized they could make risky loans that would make them rich if they paid off—and if they did not, then the FDIC would cover the losses. It was like gambling with other people's money and being allowed to keep any profit. From there, executives realized it was easier to make fraudulent loans to companies they controlled and to get kickbacks from fraudulent loans to crooked business associates. Fraud was a central factor in 70–80 percent of the failed S&Ls (Reiman and Leighton 2023: 148).

Some executives personally stole tens of millions of dollars, and others were responsible for the collapse of financial institutions that needed government bailouts to the tune of $1 billion (Binstein and Bowden 1993; Calavita et al. 1997; Pizzo et al. 1991). The total cost of the S&L bailout ultimately climbed to about $500 billion (Day 1993), yet few S&L crooks went to prison (Pizzo and Muolo 1993), and the ones who did received an average sentence of two years compared to an average of nine years for a bank robber (Reiman and Leighton 2023: 148–49).

After such expensive and widespread fraud, Congress briefly decided to "get tough" but soon removed regulations put in place to safeguard against similar fraud taking place. These actions during the 1990s set the stage for the 2002 financial scandals involving Enron, WorldCom, Global Crossing, Tyco, and others. For example, auditors like Arthur Andersen were sued by shareholders of failed S&Ls after Andersen certified financial statements showing the S&Ls were financially solid. Congress passed the Private Securities Litigation Reform Act (1995) that made it harder to sue auditors, giving them more freedom to not do proper audits and not expose fraud.

The economic meltdown and Great Recession of 2008–2010 had similar origins in legislative and executive branch decisions to deregulate. In an article explaining the crisis, Barry Ritholtz, author of *Bailout Nation* (2009a), writes in the voice of the financial industry, "D.C.: We could not have done it without you. We may be drunks, but you were our enablers: Your legislative, executive, and administrative decisions made possible all that we did. Our recklessness would not have reached its soaring heights but for your governmental incompetence" (2008b: 100). But the result was less from governmental incompetence than from the financial industry lobbying to deregulate itself.

First Congress repealed a law passed during the Great Depression that separated commercial banking activities (checking and savings accounts and loans) from investment banking activities (helping corporations issue stocks and bonds, mergers and acquisitions, managing assets, and advising on complex financial transactions). This repeal allowed banks to become bigger and allowed commercial banks to engage in riskier investment activities.

In addition, Congress passed a law that deregulated certain derivatives and exempted them from regulation by the Securities and Exchange Commission (SEC). This lack of oversight contributed to the growth of complex mortgage-backed securities and credit default swaps, which were not subject to the same regulatory oversight as traditional securities. Thus, larger financial institutions increasingly created, sold, bought, and held complex but lightly regulated financial products. This led to systemic risks that were not well understood by the financial institutions or those who did business with them.

Ritholtz also notes that a consistent element of the problem was "an abdication of responsibility from the various entities assigned to supervise and regulate" our financial system (2008c). For example, the complex securities were based on mortgages given to borrowers who were without the resources to repay them—people so poor "they did not have a pot to piss in" (*This American Life* 2008). The Federal Reserve had power to regulate mortgage underwriters (the people who approve mortgage loans) but failed to do so. It could have limited or prohibited mortgages where borrowers did not verify income or assets (a "liar's loan"). But mortgages were in great demand by investment banks that made large profits pooling and reselling the mortgage-backed securities.

Another problem was that the SEC waived its leverage rules for five big Wall Street firms. "Leverage" is essentially how much a firm can borrow (debt) for the amount of assets (capital) it has. Before 2004, the permitted debt-to-capital ratio was twelve to one, but after lobbying by investment banks, the SEC allowed these firms to use whatever leverage they wanted. Firms increased their leverage to thirty and even forty to one, essentially borrowing $30 and even $40 for each dollar of assets (Ritholtz 2008b: 101). With more leverage, firms can generate large profits with little of their own money when the market is right, but it also means that losses more quickly involve losing other people's money.

Financial institutions borrowed to invest in the complex, risky, and unregulated securities described above. Thus, as the housing market declined and the value of these products dropped, Wall Street firms did not know the extent of the losses they and their trading partners were exposed to. The lack of transparency caused a lack of trust that froze up the credit system because no one wanted to lend money in case the borrower turned out to be in deep financial trouble.

The financial crisis did produce sweeping legislation, known as the Dodd-Frank Act (2010). The financial institutions that received taxpayer bailouts worked to undercut serious financial reform by putting loopholes in new rules and also by reducing the budgets of enforcement agencies. The smaller budget does not save taxpayers because the SEC is funded by fees paid by the firms they regulate. Thus, financial institutions pay less to the government and have a weaker watchdog on the beat.

## Race, Crime, and the Law

Chapter 4 discussed how laws were used against various racial and ethnic groups to help provide cheap labor and resources. This section expands on that analysis to look more broadly at how criminal and other laws explicitly targeted racial and ethnic groups in ways that clearly violated equal protection guarantees but were still upheld by courts. Indeed, some people mark Black people's freedom not from the end of the Civil War, but from the end of "separate but equal" with the 1954 *Brown v. Board of Education* case or the civil rights legislation of the 1960s (Hannah-Jones 2019). While more recent laws have been facially neutral (there is no wording to indicate that they apply only to certain racial or ethnic groups), many have a disparate impact on minorities.

Black people arrived as slaves in what would become America in 1619, and they have spent most of the time since living under a legal system that explicitly oppressed them. One constant remained as the slave codes became the Black codes and the Jim Crow segregation statutes: "Blackness itself was a crime" (Russell 1998: 22). Slave codes, from 1619 to 1865, were the criminal law and procedure for enslaved Africans (Gorman 1997; Oshinsky 1996). The codes regulated slave life from cradle to grave and were virtually uniform across the states in upholding the institutions of chattel slavery. "Under the codes, the hardest criminal penalties were reserved for those acts that threatened the institution of slavery (e.g., the murder of someone White or a slave insurrection). The slave codes also penalized Whites who actively opposed slavery" (Russell 1998: 15).

The slave codes recognized the problem of maintaining a population in slavery who resented it—and who ran away and rebelled when they could. Indeed, "despite all the self-congratulatory kudos for 'civilizing' Africans and trying to anesthetize whites with the myth of Black docility and complacency, Southern plantation owners actually understood not only that slavery 'bred insurrection' but that those revolts 'threatened the entire social structure of white Southern communities'" (Anderson 2021: 12). The Second Amendment right to keep and bear arms obviously did not apply to slaves, who were forbidden to own weapons. Meanwhile, in some states, "white men were required to own a 'good gun or pistol' to give them the means to 'search and examine all negro houses for offensive weapons and ammunition'" (Anderson 2021: 5). Enforcing slavery was also done through the notorious slave patrols, which were the precursors to the first American forms of policing. Slave patrollers, working in conjunction with state militias, were allowed to stop, search, and beat slaves who did not have proper permission to be away from their plantations.

Slave codes also established where slaves could go and what activities they could engage in. They established separate tribunals and procedural practices that did not give enslaved people the same rights as free white men: no rights to a jury trial, to be presumed innocent, or to appeal a conviction. Nor were slaves permitted to serve as jurors or to act as witnesses against whites. Slave laws also sanctioned "plantation justice," which permitted slave owners to impose sanctions, including lashes, castration, and hanging, and to hire bounty hunters to catch runaway slaves (Russell 1998). In short, slaves were not citizens, so they could be assaulted and killed by their owners with no consequences, and—under threat of punishment—they had to be extremely deferential to white people.

Punishment for crimes involving interracial relations also involved racial double standards: "A Black man who had sex with a White woman faced the most severe penalty, while a White man who had sex with a Black slave woman faced the least severe penalty" (Russell 1998: 16). In fact, more Black men were executed for raping white women than for killing white persons. Georgia's law allowed capital punishment for Black men for the attempted rape of a white woman, which it kept after the Civil War (Scully 1990). Similarly, in Virginia, the only law carrying the punishment of castration was the rape of a white woman by a Black man. According to most slave codes, however, the rape of a Black woman by a white man or by a Black slave was not a crime.

After the Civil War and emancipation, newly freed Black men and women were given the right to enter into contracts and to marry. At the same time, the first Black codes adopted in 1865 created a new system of involuntary servitude (discussed in chapter 4). For example, the adoption of vagrancy laws allowed Black people to be arrested for the "crime" of being unemployed, and licensing requirements were imposed to bar them from all but the most menial of jobs in the South. Black codes were enforced by police and courts, but the newly granted rights for Black people served to mobilize white vigilantes, including the Ku Klux Klan (KKK). This led to the "lynching ritual," an extreme form of vigilante racial justice that between 1892 and 1964 claimed the lives of three to ten thousand Black Americans (Tolnay and Beck 1995). While lynchings are often depicted as spontaneous events done by small groups, they were often planned and attracted large crowds, including white families. Photographs and lynching postcards became a small industry that sold mementos to spectators, who would then send them to family members with inscriptions like "token of a great day" (Florido et al. 2022).

Jim Crow laws began to take hold in the early 1900s following the *Plessy v. Ferguson* decision (see opening of chapter 4). These laws mandated separate public accommodations for Black and white people and applied to cemeteries, hospital wards, water fountains, public restrooms, churches, swimming pools, hotels, movie theaters, trains, phone booths, lunch counters, prisons, courthouses, buses, orphanages, parks, and prostitution (Myrdal 1944). They also dictated where "whites, coloreds, and Negroes" could rent or buy property, which spoke to how extensively these laws sought to regulate both the private and public lives of Black folks.

In addition to laws explicitly regulating race, racial stereotypes and fears were used to influence lawmaking. Drug laws are one clear example of this. For example, the San Francisco Ordinance of 1875 was the first prohibitionist drug law to ban the operation of "opium dens" by Chinese immigrants, who were viewed as threatening to the purity of white women. Also, a 1910 report detailed "the supposed superhuman strength and extreme madness experienced by Blacks on cocaine, and [which] explained that cocaine drove Black men to rape" (Lusane 1991: 33). Rumors circulated that cocaine made Black people, specifically Black men, bulletproof, and an article in the *New York Times* ("Negro Cocaine 'Fiends' Are a New Southern Menace") reported that southern police were switching to larger-caliber weapons to protect themselves from drug-empowered Black men (Lusane 1991: 34).

The modern war on drugs was similarly inspired by racism. Then-president Nixon declared in 1971 that drug abuse was "public enemy number one," but he and his administration had a hidden agenda. Nixon's advisor Ehrlichman later explained that the President felt that protestors of the Vietnam War and Black people were his enemies:

> We knew we couldn't make it illegal to be either against the war or black, but by getting the public to associate the hippies with marijuana and blacks with heroin, and then criminalizing both heavily, we could disrupt those communities. We could arrest their leaders, raid their homes, break up their meetings, and vilify them night after night on the evening news. Did we know we were lying about the drugs? Of course we did. (in Reiman and Leighton 2023: 19)

So the drug war was built on a lie, which perhaps explains its success at disrupting and oppressing minority communities while failing to reduce the availability of drugs, drug use, and overdose deaths.

Another significant example of racism influencing criminal law is the Anti-Drug Abuse Act of 1986, which penalized the possession of crack cocaine (thought to be more common in the inner cities) one hundred times more heavily than powdered cocaine. This meant that "the same sentence would be applied to a dealer holding 50 grams of crack as the one selling 100 times that amount in cocaine, enough to fill a briefcase, privileging the high roller who sold powder to [Wall Street] bond traders . . . and crushing the corner hustler who funneled its cheaper derivative to the poor" (Bellafonte 2023). The sentence for first-time crack offenders (without possession of a weapon or other aggravating factors) was longer than the sentence for kidnapping and only slightly shorter than the sentence for attempted murder.

This law is like many others passed since Jim Crow that are "facially neutral." That means that the words in the text should apply to everyone equally, because the law does not explicitly refer to groups of people or racial classifications. In practice, though, about 85 percent of those sent to prison under the crack provisions have been Black (Bureau of Justice Statistics 2001: 11). That outcome does not reflect racial differences in usage, because the U.S. Department of Health and Human Services reported that 2.6 percent of whites, but only 0.2 percent of Black folks, ages eighteen to twenty-five had done crack cocaine during their lifetime; 0.6 percent of whites and 0.1 percent of Black people had done it in the previous year (SAMHSA 2012: table 1.36B). Indeed, a former drug czar acknowledged that the typical crack smoker was a white suburbanite despite the stereotypes of urban crack houses filled with Black people (Lusane 1991).

Congress knew about the disproportionate impact of this law from protests, reports, and recommendations from the U.S. Sentencing Guidelines Commission. In 1995, 1997, and 2002, the Sentencing Commission recommended ending the 100-to-1 disparity, and, in an unusual display of bipartisanship, Congress rejected their recommendation (Hinojosa 2008; Smothers 1995). In 2007, the chair of the Sentencing Commission stated, "The Commission believes that there is no justification for the current statutory penalty scheme" and it "remains committed" to its 2002 recommendation that any ratio "be no more than 20 to 1." The Fair Sentencing Act of 2010 reduced the 100:1 disparity to 18:1. Sociologist Nikki Jones (2011) says, "What the Act suggests is that it's better for our criminal justice system to be somewhat racist rather than very racist."

Although Nixon associated marijuana with hippies, the association of Mexican field workers with marijuana "was at the center of the argument for criminalization" (Ahrens 2020: note 45). Racism is also present in depictions of the need to protect white youth from the drug (Earp et al. 2021). However, acknowledging the racism of the drug war is a less compelling argument for legalization than opening up new areas of business from which largely white entrepreneurs could benefit. Legalization campaigns also tend to feature whites as responsible users, and when states legalize marijuana, they do not always enact social equity programs that are designed to undo some of the harm of marijuana enforcement that disproportionately fell on minorities. Indeed, the situation in the United States is similar to Canada: "We had this situation where Black and Indigenous people were being overly criminalized.

Now they're being left out of what is a multibillion-dollar industry" (Austen 2021). If governments do not properly redress the harms done to the poor and minorities by the drug war, and they decriminalize marijuana in ways that allow whites and people with capital to profit from new business opportunities, then injustice is compounded; decriminalization doubles down on inequality, even if it seems like a progressive advance in freedom. As one commentator noted, "that people of color are largely shut out of the legal cannabis industry, after paying the heaviest price for it, is the definition of white privilege" (King 2018).

Overall, the most powerful contemporary indictment of the racial effect of facially neutral legislation is Michelle Alexander's *The New Jim Crow* (2012). She argues that the discrimination against Black people of the Jim Crow era, which was struck down by the Supreme Court in the *Brown v Board of Education* case, has been replaced by legal discrimination against (Black) "criminals." Once the criminal justice system labels someone a "criminal," then whites can "engage in all the discriminatory practices we supposedly left behind," because Black people with criminal records are subject to "legalized discrimination in employment, housing, education, public benefits and jury service, just as their parents, grandparents and great-grandparents once were" (Alexander 2012: 1–2).

Laws in many states strip convicted felons—as well as minor criminals whose poverty makes it impossible to repay fines and court costs—of the right to vote. For example, Clinton Drake had $900 in fines due after being in prison for five years because of two marijuana possession charges. As a Vietnam veteran, "I put my life on the line for this country," he notes—and his two sons have also served in the military: "But I'm not able to vote" (Alexander 2012: 159). To him, the fines "are like a poll tax. You've got to pay to vote," just like with the Jim Crow laws that restricted Black voting after the Fifteenth Amendment gave the freed male slaves the right to vote.

In addition, presidential executive orders are also lawmaking, and their racial impact was especially evident with former president Trump's reshaping of immigration. In announcing his 2015 candidacy for president, Trump had called Mexico an "enemy" and said

> They're sending people that have lots of problems, and they're bringing those problems with them. They're bringing drugs. They're bringing crime. They're rapists. And some, I assume, are good people. (Trump 2015)

His 2017 order, "Enhancing Public Safety in the Interior of the United States," called for stricter enforcement and increased deportations, the hiring of ten thousand additional agents, and increased use of local law enforcement in immigration enforcement (so-called 287[g] agreements). It also declared that sanctuary cities that "attempt to shield aliens" have "caused immeasurable harm to the American people and to the very fabric of our Republic," although research does not support that claim (see chapter 8).

Although the titles and language of such orders seem facially neutral in applying to all undocumented immigrants, as Trump's earlier statements indicate, they were intended to apply to Mexicans and the Latino/a/x population. In this respect, Trump followed a pattern set by the Obama administration: "Nearly all deportees—97 percent—are from Latin America and the Caribbean. DHS rarely deports any of the approximately 25 percent of undocumented migrants in the United States that are from Asia and Europe" (Golash-Boza 2016b: 8).

The policy of separating immigrant parents from their children resulted from a "zero tolerance" policy announced by then–attorney general Jeff Sessions in 2018, which aimed to prosecute all adults crossing the border illegally, including those seeking asylum because they have been persecuted or fear it. The policy directed the Department of Justice (DOJ) to criminally prosecute adults apprehended for unauthorized entry, even if they arrived with children. As a consequence, when parents were detained and faced criminal charges, their children were separated from them and placed in separate facilities. But a Pulitzer Prize–winning article noted that "a mountain of evidence" shows that "separating children was not just a side effect but the intent. Instead of working to reunify families after parents were prosecuted, officials worked to keep them apart for longer" (Dickerson 2022). The policy traumatized those separated as well as those responsible for the children: "Though they were experts in caring for severely traumatized children, this was a challenge to which they did not know how to respond" (Dickerson 2022).

Although at various points before and after assuming the presidency Trump called for a "Muslim ban," his executive orders had facially neutral-sounding titles, like "Protecting the Nation from Foreign Terrorist Entry into the United States" and "Enhancing Vetting Capabilities and Processes for Detecting Attempted Entry into the United States by Terrorists or Other Public-Safety Threats." In all the versions of the orders, most of the listed nations had populations that were majority Muslim, with early versions listing nations that were more than 90 percent Muslim (*International Refugee Assistance Project v. Trump*, 17-1351 [2017]: 13).

When people challenged the order because it separated them from relatives, the Trump administration claimed that the order represented a finding about national security and was unreviewable by the courts. However, all courts up to and including the Supreme Court found that presidential executive orders could be reviewed by the courts. The question, then, was what to do with an executive order that had racially neutral language "but in context drips with religious intolerance, animus, and discrimination" (*International Refugee Assistance Project v. Trump*, 17-1351 [2017]: 12).

The Supreme Court majority upheld Trump's executive orders. They noted that candidate Trump had posted to his website a "Statement on Preventing Muslim Immigration" that remained there after he became president. But they felt that they should "consider not only the statements of a particular President, but also the authority of the Presidency itself" (*Trump v. Hawaii*, 17-965 [2018]: 29). Under that analysis, the immigration law passed by Congress gave Trump the power to issue the order, and it was backed by sufficient findings by security agencies about the "identity-management information" systems in various countries.

A minority of justices argued that Trump's order violated the Constitution, which required the government to be neutral to religions so it does not "send messages to members of minority faiths 'that they are outsiders, not full members of the political community'" (*Trump v. Hawaii*, 17-965 [2018]: 3). They argued that courts have historically looked at the context of an executive order and speeches by those who made it. Applying that process to the full record of Trump's statements painted a "harrowing picture, from which a reasonable observer would readily conclude that the Proclamation was motivated by hostility and animus toward the Muslim faith" (*Trump v. Hawaii*, 17-965 [2018]: 4). Indeed, "Trump justified his proposal during a television interview by noting that President Franklin D. Roosevelt 'did the same thing' with respect to the internment of Japanese Americans during World War II" (*Trump v. Hawaii*, 17-965 [2018]: 5). (See chapter 4.) He later tweeted: "People, the lawyers and the courts can call it whatever they want, but I am calling it what we need and what it is, a TRAVEL BAN!" (*Trump v. Hawaii*, 17-965 [2018]: 9).

More generally, harmful immigration laws and policies continue regardless of which political party is in power (Kubrin 2014; Martínez 2008; Pickering et al. 2014; Turnbull et al. 2020). The systematic caging of individuals and families who have done nothing but seek refuge in the United States from systemic violence and inhumane living conditions—sometimes caused by U.S. foreign policy—has resulted in critiques that federal immigration policy inflicts a form of legal violence (Menjívar and Abrego 2012).

Immigration policy in the United States governs (1) who is eligible to be admitted *into* the United States and under what conditions, and (2) who is eligible to be detained and expelled *from* the country. In the former arena, immigration controls have relied on pretexts of public health and safety to enforce racialized notions of human worthiness. By the turn of the twentieth century, a series of immigration amendments targeted the "diseased," "lunatics," "idiots," "epileptics," the "insane," and "homosexuals" for exclusion (Schrag 2010). At Ellis Island, doctors commissioned by the U.S. Public Health Service (PHS) screened all immigrants to ensure they met entrance criteria, although in the "eyes [of PHS officers], the goal was to prevent the entrance of undesirable people" into the country (Bateman-House and Fairchild 2008). Following medical inspection, Immigration Service officers also sought to weed out those who might be an "anarchist, bigamist, pauper, criminal, or otherwise unfit" (Mullan 1917: 736) for admittance.

Policies and examinations were influenced by scientifically legitimized racism and eugenicist values of the era (see chapter 2), with examination procedures varying for European, Latin American, and Asian immigrants (Bateman-House and Fairchild 2008). In practice, these racialized discourses of public health surveillance are part of a multi-century legacy of associating "otherness" with disease and dehumanizing human beings as pests to be expelled or controlled (Cohn 2012; Gutin 2019; Markel and Stern 2002).

A final issue related to lawmaking and race is the imposition of state and federal criminal justice systems on Native American reservations. The Indian Law and Order Commission noted, "Because the systems that dispense justice originate in Federal and State law rather than in Native nation choice and consent, Tribal citizens tend to view them as illegitimate; these systems do not align with Tribal citizens' perceptions of the appropriate way to organize and exercise authority" (2013: 4). Tribes generally focus on "restoring balance and good relations among Tribal members," which is usually not the focus of state and federal criminal justice systems. Because of stereotypes,

> prosecutors may be more skeptical of Indian victims. Judges might award harsher sentences to Indian defendants because of assumptions they make about Indian

country crime and those individuals involved. In the case of Federal courts, criminal sentences for the same or similar offenses are systemically longer than comparable State systems. (Indian Law and Order Commission 2013: 5)

Further, trials—usually in courthouses far from reservations—do not involve a jury of the Native Americans' peers.

Such systems are thus seen as lacking legitimacy and generate distrust, so victims do not come forward, and witnesses may be reluctant to cooperate. Under these conditions, public safety suffers. The Indian Law and Order Commission, created by the Tribal Law and Order Act of 2010, argued that respecting Native sovereignty and self-determination on issues of tribal justice can best attain public safety on reservations. This means allowing tribes to select whether to have a system of federal law or state law or to use their "inherent authority" to create a system of tribal justice that reflects all defendants' constitutionally guaranteed rights (Indian Law and Order Commission 2013: 23).

## Gender/Sexuality, Crime, and the Law

One of the main themes of this text is examining inequality, while realizing that the path to equality is complex. With class, people generally want less inequality but not perfect equality. Racial equality is an important goal but cannot happen by people simply being color-blind and ignoring centuries of racial oppression. Gender/sexuality is also complex because feminists have different perspectives on equality, even if many people equate feminism generally with a specific white, middle-class liberal form of feminism.

What feminisms have in common is a concern with women's oppression and marginalization; all feminism makes women's experiences central to social, political, and economic analysis. But feminisms differ in where they locate the source of oppression, what they consider to be the most important issues, and therefore what kinds of laws and criminal justice reforms are needed to correct the problems. Thus, there is no single analysis of gender discrimination or of how to reconcile sexual differences with equal protection. So this section reviews the main strands of feminist legal thinking and politics of change that are helpful in understanding gender issues related to law and the administration of justice. While it attempts to identify and articulate core beliefs of different feminisms, they have overlap. Also, individuals may think in terms of liberal feminism on one issue but be more radical or socialist on another.

*Liberal feminism* tends to be what many people mean when they refer to feminism. It has focused on reducing discrimination to ensure that women and men have equal civil rights and equal opportunities in work and business within the current economic structure and work conditions. Their project for change revolves around achieving sexual and gender equality through equal opportunity and nondiscrimination policy. This advocacy has included trying to fulfill the promise of the Civil Rights Act of 1964, where "sex" was added late in deliberations to the racial categories in prohibiting employment discrimination in an attempt to kill the act. Instead, it passed with the new prohibitions against sex discrimination. Nevertheless, President Johnson focused on race during implementation and ignored sex discrimination until repeatedly being called out by feminists (National Archives 2022).

The emphasis on equal opportunity and nondiscrimination can also be seen in Title IX of the Education Amendments of 1972, which prohibits sex discrimination in any educational program or activity receiving any type of federal financial aid. Title IX offices at colleges and universities investigate harassment and discrimination on the basis of sex, gender, pregnancy, sexual orientation, and identity. And Title IX reshaped sports by providing more resources for women's sports and teams (U.S. Courts, n.d.; Women's Sports Federation 2019).

Critical feminists of whatever strain—Marxist, socialist, or radical—object to liberal approaches not only for failing to question the existing economic system but also for wanting equality in it: "Do we really want equality with men in this nasty competitive capitalist system? Do we want to be equally exploited with men? Do we want a piece of the pie or a whole different pie?" (Redstockings 1978: 94). These groups challenge the idea that feminism should be about having more female billionaires in an increasingly unequal society. Is the point of feminism to have more female executives of companies that exploit workers, fleece customers, pollute communities, and cause ecological collapse? While critical feminists want women to do better in different social and economic arrangements, they differ in the emphasis they place on economic, biological, racial, and sexual sources of oppression, privilege, and inequality.

*Marxist feminism* is concerned with the way the criminal legal system under capitalism serves the interests of the ruling class at the expense of the lower classes. Marxist feminists view the oppression of women as an extension of the oppression of the working class. They argue that it is impossible for anyone to obtain genuine equal opportunity in a class society in which the wealth produced by the powerless mainly ends up in the hands of the powerful few. These powerful few are disproportionately male, which makes it even harder for women, as the privileged men have a vested interest in maintaining their higher status. Hence, they maintain that if *all* women are to be liberated—not just the middle class and affluent—then the laws of the capitalist system must be replaced by a system of "people's laws."

*Socialist feminism* argues that women are oppressed not only because of their subordinate economic position but also because of their "class" as women. Socialist feminists were among the first of the feminist theorists to recognize exploitation rooted in racism and heterosexism. Like Marxist feminism, socialist feminism clarifies how economic conditions alter labor market demands for women. In addition, socialist feminism highlights how sexist ideology legitimates women's "place" in the domestic sphere and their exclusion from higher-paying men's jobs. Patriarchal ideologies and exclusionary practices produce pools of marginal women who resort to crimes of survival, such as minor fraud, transporting drugs, or exchanging sex for money.

Thus, socialist feminists call for widespread economic and cultural changes to dismantle the twin problems of capitalism and patriarchy. They place special emphasis on the needs of the poor and working women—women who suffer the consequences of a system that not only exalts men over women but also exalts the wealthy over the poor. They advocate equal work opportunities for men and women as well as policies that would alleviate women's "second shift" by increasing child-care and family-leave programs while at the same time increasing men's involvement in domestic work.

*Radical feminists* argue that the source of the problem is male-dominated society. They criticize liberal and Marxist feminists for not going far enough because those feminisms

> focus on how women's choices within patriarchy can be "empowering." In contrast, radical feminism offers a blunt assessment of patriarchy and demands that we work for dramatic changes, not only in public policy but in our personal lives and ways of thinking about ourselves. The radical feminist goal is revolutionary: it does not advocate liberal accommodation but an end to the cultural normalization of the gender/sexual hierarchy. (Brunskell-Evans 2017: 2)

Thus, it is not sufficient to overturn society's male-dominated legal and political structures; transformation must also happen to all the social and cultural institutions (such as the family, the church, the educational system, and entertainment) that reinforce women's roles in devalued activities such as childbearing and nurturing—as well as devaluing women's activities. (Teaching and nursing, for example, are important professions, but the vast majority of workers are women, so those professions are "feminized" and devalued.)

Radical feminists focus attention on how men attempt to control women, which means examining female victims, particularly survivors of gendered violence such as intimate partner violence and sexual assault (see chapter 5). They argue that one of the pathways to women's liberation involves self-determinism inside and outside their sexual and parental roles. That includes, for example, permitting each woman to choose for herself when to use or not use reproduction-controlling technology (e.g., contraception, sterilization, abortion) and reproduction-aiding technologies (e.g., artificial insemination, in vitro fertilization, surrogate or contract motherhood).

Some radical feminists have contributed to the anti-transgender rhetoric and become known as TERFs (trans-exclusionary radical feminists). These anti-trans ideologies are in part based within gender-critical movements, which recognize how the social construction of gender contributes to women's subordination. But TERFs emphasize the significance of biological sex as a primary determinant of one's identity, and thus they reinforce the binary understanding of male and female genders. This feminism has gained attention because of supportive comments from celebrities such as J. K. Rowling (author of the Harry Potter series), singer Macy Gray, comedian Dave Chappelle, and conservative politicians—although not all anti-transgender celebrities or politicians would define themselves as TERFs. For example, J. K. Rowling has stated, "[TERFs] aren't even trans-exclusionary— they include trans men in their feminism, because they were born women" (in Urquhart 2020). But the focus on sex and gender expectations that are assigned at birth narrows the ability of transgender folks to obtain their own human agency as transgender folks face barriers that most other people do not.

*Transfeminism* seeks to center the transgender experience, and it developed out of a need to include transgender perspectives within feminism because both grow partly from

> Simone de Beauvoir's observation that "one is not born, but rather becomes, a woman." Transgender studies extends this foundation, emphasizing that there is no

natural process by which anyone becomes woman, and also that everyone's gender is made: Gender, and also sex, are made through complex social and technical manipulations that naturalize some while abjecting others. (Enke 2012: 1)

Transfeminism disrupts the heteronormative assumptions where "men" and "women" refer only to how a person was biologically born or what they were assigned at birth. But transfeminism is not an "add-on" to feminism—the point is not to add trans people and stir: "Transgender studies is about everyone in so far as it offers insight into how and why we all 'do' gender" (Enke 2012: 2). However, transfeminism also seeks to understand the experiences of trans people as part of centering the margins and securing trans folks greater civil rights.

Feminist thinking generally adopts three approaches to gender inequality: the sameness perspective, the difference perspective, and the dominance perspective. Advocates of the *sameness perspective*, also referred to as the "gender neutral" or "equal treatment" perspective, support a single standard governing the treatment of women and men. This approach avoids perceptions of "special treatment" for women and tends to accept a male standard that is then applied to women as well. But in addition to concerns about advocating for equality within the existing system with justice, the sameness approach may actually harm women through "equality with a vengeance"—like when sentencing for women is based on the "get tough" standard that applies to men. Further, gender bias in sentencing cannot be eliminated simply by stipulating (as is done in the Federal Sentencing Guidelines) that gender is not to be considered. The pretense of gender neutrality masks males' domination and patriarchal values.

Advocates of the *difference perspective* call for differential treatment of women and men. After all, some very real differences exist in the situations of men and women, such as women's capacity to bear children. Critics of this perspective view it as both patronizing and necessary (MacKinnon [1984] 1991). Others talk about how women might be seen as getting "special treatment" or receiving "special rights," while other critics raise concerns about reinforcing gender stereotypes. For example, a policy of permitting single parents to receive a "downward departure" from sentencing guidelines would primarily benefit women and would likely be seen as a special right for those playing a traditional gender role.

Both the sameness and the difference approaches assume a male norm. As MacKinnon has argued, "gender neutrality" is simply the male standard, and the "special protection" rule is simply the female standard, "but do not be deceived: masculinity, or maleness, is the referent for both" ([1984] 1991: 83). Further, both perspectives reflect a preoccupation with gender differences while ignoring the role of power and domination. In contrast, the *dominance perspective* recognizes that men and women are different and that the sexes are not equally powerful. Most differences between men and women can be attributed to a society in which women are subordinate and men are dominant. Advocates of the dominance perspective maintain that the solution to gender inequality is not to create a single standard (sameness) or a double standard (difference) but to address the inequality in power relations between the sexes.

The dominance approach has been criticized for its failure to acknowledge that "legal rights are sometimes overshadowed by social realities" (Chesney-Lind and

Pollock 1995: 157). For instance, while women have the legal right to be treated like any other assault victim and to have their battering husband arrested and punished, the reality is that women also face social, economic, and cultural barriers that may impede or prevent them from taking full advantage of their legal rights.

The point in reviewing these perspectives has been to help readers locate their own values, keeping in mind that many people have different approaches to different issues. Regardless of what approach one takes to trying to fix gender/sexuality inequities in the law, there are some important limitations on the legal protections, even while there are also gains. For example, the Supreme Court recognized that "sex," within the meaning of the 1964 Civil Rights Act, applied to employment discrimination because of sexual orientation and gender identity (*Bostock v. Clayton County*, 17-1618 [2020]; EEOC, n.d.). The opinion noted that the law prohibited an employer from discriminating against "an individual" because of sex, and "it is impossible to discriminate against a person for being homosexual or transgender without discriminating against that individual based on sex" (*Bostock v. Clayton County*, 17-1618 [2020]: 8–9).[2] While Justice Gorsuch's reasoning has been attacked from many perspectives, the 6–3 decision asked readers to

> consider, for example, an employer with two employees, both of whom are attracted to men. The two individuals are, to the employer's mind, materially identical in all respects, except that one is a man and the other a woman. If the employer fires the male employee for no reason other than the fact he is attracted to men, the employer discriminates against him for traits or actions it tolerates in his female colleague. Put differently, the employer intentionally singles out an employee to fire based in part on the employee's sex, and the affected employee's sex is a but-for cause of his discharge. Or take an employer who fires a transgender person who was identified as a male at birth but who now identifies as a female. If the employer retains an otherwise identical employee who was identified as female at birth, the employer intentionally penalizes a person identified as male at birth for traits or actions that it tolerates in an employee identified as female at birth. Again, the individual employee's sex plays an unmistakable and impermissible role in the discharge decision. (*Bostock v. Clayton County*, 17-1618 [2020]: 9–10)

Although the Court recognized LGBTQ+ rights in this case, overall they have a mixed record. The Court has generally allowed, but not required, states to include LGBTQ+ language in civil rights protections extending to public accommodations. Public accommodations include hotels, restaurants, and many places of business engaged in sales to the public—rights of access that are practically important and that the Supreme Court has said "vindicate the deprivation of personal dignity that surely accompanies denials of equal access to public establishments" (in *303 Creative v. Elenis*, No. 21-476 [2023]). However, they have limited or struck down such laws when the Court felt speech or expression was at stake. So, the Court held that

> Massachusetts's public accommodations statute could not be used to force veterans organizing a parade in Boston to include a group of gay, lesbian, and bisexual individuals because the parade was protected speech, and requiring the veterans to include voices they wished to exclude would impermissibly require them to "alter

the expressive content of their parade." And in *Boy Scouts of America v. Dale*, when the Boy Scouts sought to exclude assistant scoutmaster James Dale from membership after learning he was gay, the Court held the Boy Scouts to be "an expressive association" entitled to First Amendment protection. (*303 Creative v. Elenis*, No. 21-476 [2023])

With respect to LGBTQ+ weddings, the Court held that antidiscrimination laws meant a cake maker had to make a gay couple a cake over his religious objections (because the cake was not expression), but a web designer's work was expression so that she did not have to design LGBTQ+ wedding websites against her religious convictions.

While some states have included LGBTQ+ protections in antidiscrimination law, many do not and are hostile to LGBTQ+ interests in ways that impact liberties, quality of life, and agency. For example, Tennessee lacks legal protections regarding employment nondiscrimination, housing nondiscrimination, public accommodations (bathrooms, locker rooms, etc.), credit and lending nondiscrimination, and nondiscrimination for state employees, and it has even banned cities and counties from passing nondiscrimination laws (Movement Advancement Project 2023a, 2023b). Tennessee has fewer protections than other states, but many states lack at least some of those protections and/or nondiscrimination laws protecting LGBTQ+ students, anti-bullying policies, state curricular standards to be LGBTQ+ inclusive, and conversion therapy bans (coercive "therapy" to make LGBTQ+ youth heterosexual). Chapter 5 noted a number of other examples such as "Don't Say Gay" laws.

Some of the legislation hostile to LGBTQ+ interests are so-called religious liberty or religious freedom laws that allow "public and private servants to deny Queer citizens assistance based on religious objections to homosexuality and gender nonconformity" (Buist and Lemming 2016: 31). While some acts have nondiscrimination clauses about race and sex, they less frequently include protections for LGBTQ+ populations: "imagine that you are eating lunch at the counter of a local restaurant, and between your bites of burger, the owner asks you to leave. You ask why and the owner replies that they don't serve 'your kind'—your kind meaning, gay" (Buist and Lenning 2016: 31–32). This situation would be similar to Black people being refused service at a segregated lunch counter, which happened and led to boycotts as part of the civil rights movement (see chapter 4). But because of Indiana's Religious Freedom Restoration Act (passed before then-governor Mike Pence became vice president), "fifty-five years later, here we are again, for if you are gay and in Indiana . . . this similar bigotry could happen to you" (Buist and Lenning 2016: 31–32).

In 2021, the Equality Act was introduced in Congress and passed by the House to protect the rights of LGBTQ+ people. The Equality Act "prohibits discrimination based on sex, sexual orientation, and gender identity in areas including public accommodations and facilities, education, federal funding, employment, housing, credit, and the jury system" (Equality Act 2021). This bill expands the definition of public accommodations to include "places or establishments that provide (1) exhibitions, recreation, exercise, amusement, gatherings, or displays; (2) goods, services, or programs; and (3) transportation services." It also prohibits an individual from being denied access to a "shared facility, including a restroom, a locker room, and a dressing room, that is in accordance with the individual's gender identity" (HR 5—Equality Act).

The Equality Act is important because the hundreds of proposed anti-LGBTQ+ bills (see also Equality Federation 2023) send a clear message to the LGBTQ+ community that they are less-than. The various proposed legislation can only exacerbate mental health concerns for queer youth, including suicide ideation (thoughts, wishes, and preoccupations concerning suicide and death). Nearly 50 percent of LGBTQ+ youth aged thirteen to seventeen considered suicide in the previous year, and 18 percent of LGBTQ+ youth in the same age range attempted suicide (Trevor Project 2022). The national survey also found that almost three-quarters of LGBTQ+ youth reported experiencing anxiety, while 58 percent reported symptoms of depression. The findings also report that Native/Indigenous survey participants reported the highest percentages of anxiety (83 percent), depression (70 percent), and attempted suicide (21 percent)—and Middle Eastern/Northern African youth had the next highest percentage at 20 percent.

Finally, even before the Supreme Court revoked the right to abortion (see chapter 5), many states had started to give legal status to embryos and fetuses (Paltrow and Flavin 2013: 323). Laws like the federal Unborn Victims of Violence Act of 2004 "and most state fetal homicide laws treat the fetus as an independent second victim that has legal rights distinct from the pregnant woman harmed by the criminal act: that is, when a pregnant woman is murdered or injured, two victims are claimed—the woman and her fetus—not one" (Flavin 2009: 99). The recognition of fetal "rights" has important implications for women's bodily sovereignty by giving fetuses a legal cause of action *against* mothers and turning them into "baby carriers" or "bystanders to their own bodies" (Flavin 2009). In addition, "questions of fetal personhood reach far beyond just abortion to our rights to IVF, most forms of birth control, emergency contraception, and fundamental privacy rights" (Cheung 2022). Fetal personhood also raises questions about care for women who have ectopic pregnancies (a life-threatening condition for the woman because the fertilized egg implants outside the uterus [American College of Obstetricians and Gynecologists 2022]) and for miscarriage care in general (Pregnancy Justice 2022).

Most immediately, fetal protection laws give the state the ability to assert the rights of the "unborn person" against the pregnant woman, often by criminalizing her for using drugs (even where treatment was not available), alcohol, or cigarettes; being the victim of abuse (which had health implications for the fetus); failure to obtain prenatal care; having HIV; refusing to undergo cesarean surgery; or giving birth "at home or in another setting outside a hospital" (Paltrow and Flavin 2013: 316). Concern about "chemicals" is limited to drugs the woman may take and not the misapplication of pesticides in proximity to pregnant women or industries that pollute neighborhoods containing pregnant women. Thus, "enshrining 'equal protection' for fertilized eggs and embryos necessarily decimates rights for living American women" (Cheung 2022). The laws criminalize women rather than more directly confronting domestic violence, universal health care, environmental toxins, or a drug war that has not made treatment a priority.

The Supreme Court's ruling that abortion is not a constitutionally protected right has made abortion a significant topic for lawmaking in at least some states.

States that have abortion bans and wish to be aggressive about enforcing them will look to criminalize people in other states who "aid and abet" (help) women in the state in getting an abortion; they may also try to criminalize a woman in a state with an abortion ban for leaving to go to a state where abortion is legal to get one. In response, twelve states (as of 2023) have passed "shield laws" to protect providers in the state

> and those that assist them, from another state's investigations of reproductive healthcare that is legal in the shielding state. Likewise, shield laws foreclose the extradition of a provider not fleeing from justice, and prohibit in-state medical boards from recognizing the disciplinary suits from out-of-state entities when related to the provision of legal reproductive health care. (Rebouché 2023: 1633–34)

## Intersectionality, Crime, and the Law

The introduction to this chapter noted that legislators do not look like the people they represent. They are richer and disproportionately male, white, and heterosexual. The data there did not examine intersections, like the number of Black women or Latinas compared with the population, because that data is not regularly reported in an accessible way. One study noted that women of color are about 20 percent of the population, but after the "record-breaking 2018 elections," they held 8.8 percent of seats in Congress and 7.4 percent of seats in state legislatures (Reingold et al. 2021: 1–2). The problem of low representation has been complemented by "single axis" studies in which "political scientists have often assumed that there are no gender differences among minority representatives, and no racial differences among female representatives" (Reingold et al. 2021: 5).

Representation matters because lawmakers from marginalized backgrounds have different life experiences, which shape their priorities—although generalizations should be careful not to essentialize (and suggest that all women or all Latinas have the same perspective). For example, while everyone in Congress and state legislatures are committed to representing their districts, women in general felt that they "gave voice to the voiceless" in ways that included "representing children, the economically disadvantaged, immigrants, people of color, the unborn, and others whose interests have not been adequately represented in Congress" (Dittmar et al. 2017: 16). Having to face numerous barriers as women seems to have made them more aware of barriers others face, but the specific focus that takes is shaped by generation/age, political party, class, race, sexuality, religion, and so on.

Further, women of color had different interests depending on the racial or ethnic group of their constituents and themselves. For example, "immigration is likely to be more salient to Latinas than to Black women in Congress, whereas the reverse may be the case with some housing and economic issues" (Dittmar et al. 2022). But because they have faced multiple barriers, women of color are more likely to propose policies with intersectional (rather than "single axis" race or gender) impact (Reingold et al. 2021: 19). In addition to sponsoring legislation, they help educate other members about the life experiences of those with less privilege. Such education can happen in informal settings, meetings, and committee hearings and through suggestions of witnesses and experts who testify at hearings.

Other important intersectional analyses of lawmaking follow from ideas about class and race mentioned earlier in the chapter. We noted that the criminal legal system does not criminalize morally blameworthy harms of the rich, and the crimes of the poor are the main focus of criminal law. That makes criminal justice a tool in class warfare to control the poor, especially the unemployed surplus-labor pool that contains a disproportionate number of minorities. The class analysis focuses on the poor, while the race analysis equates the controlled "dangerous classes" with racial minorities and Latino/a/x immigrants. Given that racialized minorities are disproportionately poor and are excluded from conventional avenues of upward economic mobility, the class and race analyses are intertwined even as social scientists often try to isolate these concepts and assess them as separate constructs. This serves as a reminder that race and gender/sexuality categories often correlate with class. Nevertheless, racism and racist assumptions are frequently behind "moral panics" ("Black men on cocaine are bulletproof!") or other situations thought to justify increased social control (e.g., drug and immigration laws).

The widespread misperception that Black men are engaged in criminal activity, for example, is reinforced by the inundation of images and sensational news coverage of Black boys and men, resulting in what Russell (1998) refers to as the *criminalblackman* (written as one word to reinforce how strongly "criminal" and "Black man" are connected in popular imaginations). But racial stereotypes of Black women and girls also feed criminalization as well. Indeed, the 100:1 crack-to-cocaine sentencing disparity was also driven by concerns about Black women: "As has been compellingly argued by historians, sociologists, legal scholars, and others, the willingness to believe that cocaine, and especially crack cocaine, required uniquely punitive responses was derived in large measure from racist assumptions about African Americans in general and African American mothers in particular" (Paltrow and Flavin 2013: 334). Such assumptions are still very much present in the commentary about BLM "riots" and "looting." Consider the sight of Black women in the remains of a Dollar General store burned during protests:

> Now, on first read, you would assume it's looting. But if you took time to listen, we're watching mothers trying to discover baby formula and diapers because they knew that there's going to be no place to be able to provide for their children. You could hear the conversations—"Is that baby formula?" They were passing it to each other—"I found some." And it broke my heart to witness mothers trying to get baby formula because now there is no place for several miles to get baby formula. Without the nuance, we frame the mother as a looter. Knowing the story, you frame the mother as a good mother. (Bennett 2020)

But it is on the basis of racist stereotypes that laws often get passed, and while they may be facially neutral, the stereotypes and context of concern that drove the law leads to disparate enforcement.

Chesney-Lind (2006: 10) argues in "Patriarchy, Crime, and Justice" that "to fully understand the interface between patriarchal control mechanisms and criminal justice practices in the United States, we must center our analysis on the race/gender/punishment nexus." She explains how media demonization, the masculinization of female offenders, and the criminalization of women's victimization—all part of the feminist backlash starting in the 1980s—have resulted in greater increases in rates of arrest and incarceration for both women and girls compared to those of men and boys. (While men and boys make up the majority of people in the system, the *rates* of arrest and incarceration have grown more quickly for women and girls.) And this increased rate has disproportionately and negatively affected girls and women of color.

The unnecessary concern about the criminality of immigrants has been noted throughout this book, with Trump's remarks about Mexicans (and, by extension, Latinos) being drug dealers and rapists as the latest chapter. His rhetoric led to harsh facially neutral policies that also applied to others in the Latino population. Policies under Trump and Biden have even tightened restrictions on asylum seekers—people who typically have fled their home countries because of persecution or fear that they will suffer persecution due to race, religion, nationality, membership in a particular social group, or their political opinions (Department of Homeland Security 2023; Immigration Equality 2020). The category "particular social group" has been interpreted by court cases and other authoritative sources to include victims of domestic violence and people in the LGBTQ+ community (although the Department of Homeland Security [2019] uses LGBTI, with "I" being for intersex people). Asylum seekers who have fled their countries because they fear they will be punished with prison or with death because of their identities as members of the LGBTQ+ community are impacted by these restrictions.

## Implications

Ideally, the study of lawmaking, criminal law, and the administration of justice should take the intersectionality of class, race, gender, sexuality, and age into consideration. This is difficult on the one hand because the law does not take into account or define crimes based on the class, race, and sex or gender of the offender. The criminal law is most obviously biased in a class-based way, while it is more race and gender neutral on its face. But what the law regards as a crime and whom society sees as criminals reflect the statuses of class, race, and gender/sexuality. Indeed, the problem is that facially neutral laws still result in disparate treatment because the stereotypes behind some laws, and the privileges they protect, are shared by others who arrest, charge, and sentence.

While the main examples of law explicitly targeting racial minorities are older, there is a clear and problematic recent history. For example, Blumstein (1995) found that 20 to 25 percent of the Black incarceration rate (representing about ten thousand Black people annually at the time) is not explained by disproportionate offending. As the *Harvard Law Review* noted, "substantial underenforcement of antidiscrimination norms" and "increasingly sophisticated empirical studies indicate disparities in the treatment of criminal suspects and defendants that are difficult to explain by reference to decisional factors other than racial discrimination" (1988: 1476). The National Academy of Sciences panel on incarceration noted that "racial disparities in imprisonment have worsened substantially since the early 1990s relative to racial patterns of involvement in serious crime" (Travis et al. 2014: 94). This finding applies to both men and women, with the absolute number of minority men involved in the criminal justice system at very high levels and the number of minority women at relatively lower levels but increasing at the fastest rates.

The concerns about disparities raise issues regarding the implementation of facially neutral laws, and lawmakers try to claim that they enacted the law in good faith. Rather than trying to debate the character of legislators and whether or not they are personally racist, we believe it is important to understand the moral status of facially neutral lawmaking by applying the distinction between direct and oblique intention:

> To intend some consequence directly one has to desire it. To intend it obliquely one has only to foresee it. . . . We have the duty to avoid bringing about consequences that we ought not bring about, even if we do not desire those consequences in themselves, provided only that we know they will be consequences. I am to blame if I knowingly bring about someone's death in the course of some plan of mine, even if I do not desire his death in itself—that is, even if I intend the death only obliquely and indirectly. . . . This is very relevant to the decisions of legislators (many of whose intentions are oblique), in that they have a duty to consider consequences of their legislation that they can foresee, and not merely those that they desire. (Hare 1990: 186)

To help legislators foresee the likely consequences of proposed laws, they can require racial, gender, or LGBTQ+ impact statements that are modeled after current environmental and financial impact statements (Urban Institute 2021). Such statements can assist them as they are considering the law and also provide ongoing feedback on the fairness and justness of the administration of those laws. Lawmakers might still pass laws that would make the situation worse for victims or offenders based on class, race, or gender/sexuality, but they would have to work harder to defend the importance of those laws in the face of evidence that the law would contribute to inequality. Moreover, public officials would have to dialogue with and answer to an empowered community armed with the knowledge of how class, race, and gender/sexuality impact the differential administration of justice in the United States.

While Hare highlights the moral responsibilities of legislators for the foreseeable results of laws, the larger point for the purposes of this book is that disparities can arise from facially neutral legislation because of the administration of justice. This includes the police, courts, and especially sentencing. Laws are written in categorical language that calls for the arrest and processing of persons engaged in legally prohibited acts, but police officers and other agents of crime control do not apply these laws uniformly. Rather, when deciding whether or not to give a traffic violator, for instance, a warning, a ticket, or an intensive search, law enforcement will exercise a certain amount of discretion. The question becomes to what extent discretion is exercised as a reflection of institutionalized (rather than individualized) racial bias against nonwhites, over and above any bias created by enforcing laws that have a disproportionate impact on minorities.

## Review and Discussion Questions

1. What do you consider to be the most important lessons about lawmaking from the opening narrative comparing and contrasting Rummel, Andrade, Bank of America, and Johnson & Johnson?

2. Why doesn't criminology focus more on lawmaking? Why should it?
3. What are some important sources of law, both criminal and noncriminal? Why are the noncriminal laws important?
4. How do the demographics of Congress and state legislatures compare to the larger population? Why is that important?
5. What do Reiman and Leighton (2023) mean when they say the criminal law is like a carnival mirror in terms of class-based harms? What examples support their claim?
6. In what ways has the criminal law been explicitly used to control minorities? What does it mean to say that law is "facially neutral," and what are some seemingly neutral laws that have had a disproportionate impact on minorities?
7. What are the differences between liberal and more critical feminisms? Which of these models/approaches do you ascribe to for what issues, and why? What are some of the ways that law protects women and the LGBTQ+ community, and how does it oppress on the basis of sex/sexuality?
8. Why is it important to have women of color—not just white women and Black men—as lawmakers in proportion to their population?
9. What does Hare say about the responsibility of lawmakers for the foreseeable results of their laws? What is their responsibility for fixing facially neutral laws that have a well-documented disparate impact on minorities?

## Notes

1. Violation Tracker is a searchable database, open to the public, of companies and settlements against them by state and federal agencies, as well as some private litigation. The data for this introduction comes from their list of the top one hundred most penalized companies (https://violationtracker.goodjobsfirst.org/top-100-parents) and some follow-up searches.
2. Chapter 5 noted that "homosexual" is an antiquated term and should not be used, and we stand by that in spite of its use by the aging justices on the Court.

# CHAPTER 8

# Law Enforcement

*While every group has prejudices, chapter 4 noted that white people have more power to act on their biases and create discrimination. The protection of white privilege through these actions has important consequences for the treatment of minorities by the criminal justice system. Legal scholar Butler elaborates on this point in* Chokehold *(2017). For him, a chokehold is not only a controversial and sometimes prohibited police practice for bringing suspects into compliance through pressure to their airway, but it is also a metaphor for a "self-reinforcing" system of control—people resist the chokehold when they cannot breathe, which is taken as resistance that necessitates more force—that operates on Black folks more generally.*

*Butler combines a Harvard Law School education with years as a federal prosecutor, which he admits made him a "perpetrator" of the chokehold. Personally, he says, "I am a black man who at times is afraid of other black men. And then I get mad when people act afraid of me." He does not wear hoodies (hooded sweatshirts), less because of the police than "when I put on a hoodie, everybody turns into a neighborhood watch person."*

*Butler's focus is on the criminal justice system. He notes some of the actions of police against African Americans during the presidency of an African American:*

> *In Ferguson, Missouri, arrested a man named Michael for filing a false report because he told them his name was "Mike." Locked up a woman in Ferguson for "occupancy permit violation" when she called 911 to report she was being beaten up by her boyfriend and the police learned the man was not legally entitled to live in the house. Killed a seven-year-old girl in Detroit while looking for drugs at her father's house. Shot Walter Scott in the back in North Carolina after stopping him for a traffic infraction. Severed Freddie Gray's spinal cord in Baltimore. Unloaded sixteen bullets into a seventeen-year-old Laquan McDonald while he lay cowering on a Chicago street. Pushed a teenage girl in a bikini to the ground*

*in McKinney, Texas. Shot twelve-year-old Tamir Rice in Cleveland within two seconds of seeing him in a public park. Pumped bullets into Philando Castile in Minnesota while his girlfriend livestreamed it on Facebook, with her four-year-old daughter in the backseat. (Butler 2017)*

Butler argued that Trump may have emboldened a few overtly racist cops, but "most police officers are decent working-class men and women with no more racial hang-ups than teachers, doctors or anyone else." The problem goes deeper— that "virtually every objective investigation of a U.S. law enforcement agency finds the police, as a policy, treat African Americans with contempt." Whites would not tolerate their neighborhoods being policed in the way described in the previous paragraph—at least middle- and upper-class whites who have the power to make sure that does not happen. But even in seemingly extreme cases of mistreatment of minorities, there is rarely a criminal indictment or convictions of a police officer (with the possibility that Black officers may be disciplined more harshly for mistreatment of minority civilians than white officers).

Further, one Baltimore resident commented that they caught Freddie Gray because of cameras placed all over the city. But when allegations arose that the police van drove in a way that threw Gray around the back of the van and caused life-ending injuries, there was no video footage: "They could have watched that van, too, but no—they missed that one. I thought the cameras were supposed to protect us" (Reel 2016). Instead, Baltimore hired a company called Persistent Surveillance Systems to fly over the city in "a small Cessna airplane equipped with a sophisticated array of cameras." For as many as ten hours a day, the cameras "continuously transmitted real-time images to analysts on the ground. The footage from the plane was instantly archived and stored on massive hard drives, allowing analysts to review it weeks later if necessary" (in Reel 2016; see also Grinberg 2019).

Moreover, a leaked 2017 memo from the FBI's Domestic Terrorism Analysis Unit reveals that despite a surge in white supremacist violence, the FBI was going to target "black identity extremists" (German 2020), which really meant Black Lives Matter protestors who were exercising their constitutional rights (Toor 2018). Subsequently, Attorney General Garland testified that, "in the FBI's view, the top domestic violent extremist threat we face comes from racially or ethnically motivated violent extremists, specifically those who advocate for the superiority of the White race" (Senate Appropriations Committee 2021: 7). But the FBI has consistently overemphasized the threat from minorities and downplayed the threat from the far right (Castle 2021).

For Butler, "cops are rarely prosecuted because they are, literally, doing their jobs." What police do when they keep law and order is maintain a racial order, a hierarchy where African American men are seen as a threat. The chokehold serves *to restrict Black men from many locations, and it brings in money from their fines and fees. It is "something like an employment stimulus plan for working-class white people, who don't have to compete for jobs with all the black men who are locked up, or who are underground because they have outstanding arrest warrants, or who have criminal records that make obtaining legal employment exceedingly difficult." So "efforts to fix 'problems' such as excessive force and racial profiling are doomed to fail. If it's not broke you can't fix it."*

## Introduction

Policing is the most visible form of state power within criminal justice. Police stop, detain, arrest, and use deadly force. More than "50 million Americans have contacts with the police, about half of which are officer initiated" (Pickett et al. 2022: 292). In addition, police kill 900–1,200 people a year. Minorities are overrepresented, with male American Indian/Alaska Natives killed at a rate more than six times that of white males, and Black males killed 2.4 times as frequently; Hispanic men overall were slightly more likely than white men to suffer a police killing (Liu et al. 2023). Viral videos that have captured unnecessary police killings of Black men have brought wider support to Black Lives Matter protests, including outside of the United States in countries that also have issues with race and policing (Shanahan and Kurti 2022). At times, police seem more concerned with preventing video dissemination than with preventing brutality, and some police have taken to playing Disney music loudly in the background of deployments so the footage will be removed from YouTube or other platforms because Disney militantly blocks unauthorized use through copyright law (Wegner 2022).

Further, police and the Border Patrol have been visible in the lives of the Latino/a/x community, but immigration enforcement has historically been a "side topic" in criminology and law enforcement research because immigration offenses have been administered as matters of *civil* (not criminal) law. In spite of repeated findings that immigrants—whether "documented" or "undocumented"—do *not* contribute to higher crime rates, significant challenges face immigrant communities and public safety professionals. Indeed, as southern border security and immigration policy have been weaponized by politicians, criminal justice systems and immigration enforcement are increasingly blended. The result is called "crimmigration" to capture the idea of criminalizing immigration by using "get tough" methods of criminal justice policy to deport Latino/a/x immigrants, regardless of whether they have committed a serious or violent crime (Stumpf 2006).

For some minority populations, police stops have public health consequences, including extreme stress and PTSD (Jackson et al. 2021). Crimmigration, too, has resulted in a wide range of harms. Americans who are not directly affected by aggressive policing increasingly understand some of these problems, and only 45 percent express confidence in the police—with some measures of trust and confidence at all-time lows (Washburn 2023).

The statutes that create and direct policing agencies place some limitations on their authority, and others are imposed by procedural law, derived mainly from

Supreme Court decisions. However, the trend has been to erode Fourth Amendment rights by giving the police greater freedom to stop and search as part of the war on crime and drugs. So, "what distinguishes policing from other contexts is not that officers have some unique insensitivity to racial stereotyping, but rather that they have unparalleled discretion, legal authority, qualified immunity, and weapons" (Pickett et al. 2022: 311). That combination often results in unequal treatment according to class, race, gender/sexuality, and their intersections.

## Policing and Its Workers

The United States has about fifteen thousand public law enforcement agencies with one million full-time personnel, including seven hundred thousand sworn personnel (with the power to arrest) at the local and state levels of government. (Private security are not included in these figures, but they are a multibillion-dollar industry that would like the power to transport people to jail [Cushing 2021].) While this section paints a general picture, virtually no two police agencies in the United States are structured alike. Even neighboring agencies can differ greatly:

> Some residents of Allegheny County are served by police officers working full-time, earning an average of $71,000 a year. Other residents in this same county are served only by part-time officers who are paid around $10 an hour—less than employees at the nearby Walmart. The best-staffed police departments in the county have ten times as many officers per capita than the county's poorest communities. And perhaps most importantly, the communities with the highest crime and greatest need for public-safety services are often the ones with the fewest and least-paid officers. As this Article's analysis shows, Allegheny County is not the exception but the rule. (Rushin and Michalski 2020: 284)

Most policing is done at the local level by city agencies and (less commonly) sheriff's departments. The word "sheriff" comes from the United Kingdom, where a "shire reeve" was elected to oversee local government functions (including crime-related responses) in geographic units known as shires. In the United States, the word "county" has replaced "shire," but sheriffs remain directly elected and thus sensitive to both constituent needs and partisan politics. Municipal police department chiefs are also sensitive to politics, but in a more indirect way because they are appointed by the mayor.

The salary and resource differences have a substantial impact on the quality of officers, resources and equipment, and support (like specialized units for sexual assault as well as crime analyst positions). Some of these differences are also based on the size of the department, and while large metropolitan police departments are commonly featured in fiction and news media, most police agencies at the municipal and county level are small.

Local police perform functions that include investigating crimes, enforcing the criminal and traffic laws of the state, and supervision of jailed inmates. Chiefs and sheriffs, especially those who oversee jails, have a seldom acknowledged power to "exercise significant control not merely over conditions but also over both the supply of and demand for jail bedspace: how large they should be, how many people they should confine, and who those people should be" (Littman 2021: 862). Often their advocacy to build larger jails increases the number of people under control of the criminal justice system, and it is funded by new taxes, increases in court fines and fees, and contracts with private companies that shift costs to people held in jail or their families.

In addition to jails, there is "a hidden scaffolding of financial incentives [that] underpins the policing of motorists in the United States, encouraging some communities to essentially repurpose armed officers as revenue agents searching for infractions largely unrelated to public safety" (McIntire and Keller 2021). About twenty states evaluate police on the frequency of traffic stops, and many more localities evaluate on the basis of fee-generating citations issued mostly to minorities for pedestrian and bicycling violations (Boddupalli and Mucciolo 2022; see discussion of Ferguson in chapter 1).

Educationally, the vast majority of local police departments only require a high school degree or GED, and a small minority require a two- or four-year degree. Federal law enforcement, especially the FBI, has higher educational requirements. Police cadets on average spent 833 hours training in academies, then doing extra hours in the field (BJS 2021c). Being a cosmetologist or plumber each require more than three thousand hours of training—and all other developed nations require substantially longer training (Institute for Criminal Justice Training Reform, n.d.). For those interested in police reform, it is also important to think about how time is spent *within* this critical training period. In the United States, "the highest average number of hours of instruction was dedicated to firearms skills (73 hours), followed by defensive tactics (61) and patrol procedures (52)" (BJS 2021c: 3). Other significant blocks of time were spent with emergency vehicle operation (40 hours) and health and fitness (50), with less time spent on cultural diversity (14), conflict management/mediation (13), ethics and integrity (12), sexual assault (7), and sexual harassment (4) (2021c: 10–11).

The median salary (half make more and half make less) for police was $74,910 in 2023, with 80 percent of police and detectives making between $45,790 and $117,100 (Bureau of Labor Statistics 2024b). Pay varies with geography, seniority, rank, and many other factors, but the federal government paid police and detectives more than local governments.

The larger the police agency, the more likely it is to employ women and officers from diverse racial/ethnic backgrounds. While white men remain highly overrepresented, this has been slowly declining. From the early 1900s until 1972, policewomen were responsible for protection and crime prevention work with women and juveniles, particularly girls. While women engage in virtually all of the duties that men do, in 2020 they accounted for only 14 percent of local police, including 11 percent of first-line supervisors and 4 percent of police chiefs (BJS 2022b: 4, 6). Unfortunately, "the percentage of female officers employed full time in 2020 was not significantly different from the percentage in either 2016 or 2013" (2022b: 4). Women were 15 percent of federal law enforcement, although the FBI was 21 percent women (BJS 2022c: 8–9). Racial and ethnic diversity is detailed in table 8.1 and shows that federal law enforcement is more diverse. The high level of Hispanic people at the federal level is because Customs and Border Patrol (CBP) is the largest

TABLE 8.1 **Diversity in Local and Federal Law Enforcement**

|  | Local Police (%) | Federal Law Enforcement (%) |
|---|---|---|
| White | 69 | 61 |
| Black | 12 | 10 |
| Hispanic | 14 | 21 |
| Other | 4 | 3 |

*Sources:* BJS 2022b: 5; 2022c: 8.

employer of federal law enforcement, and 38 percent of its officers were Hispanic, including about half of Border Patrol agents (Cortez 2019).

In making sense of the statistics and the overall environment, several points are important. First, women and racial minorities interested in working in most areas of criminal justice share the challenge of entering overwhelmingly white male work environments, with women of color being doubly disadvantaged. Sexual and racial discrimination happen and act to preserve law enforcement—and other criminal justice professions—as disproportionately white male domains. Sexual harassment is still very much a problem, notes a researcher who interviewed many women officers:

> I assumed that we would find harassment had fallen off the radar, but that has not been the case. Women in the 2000s describe fairly heinous experiences with sexual harassment and discrimination. Covert, yes, but still experiences we would associate with the 1980s. I think (that's) one of the reasons that the number of women in policing is actually starting to drop now. (in Hadley 2018)

Interviews with female officers published in the journal article "Suck It Up, Buttercup" (Angehrn et al. 2021) noted:

> Reports from women included feeling unsafe with a colleague or a superior officer, being groped between their legs in a patrol car by their training officer, being sent pornographic images, receiving a message from a colleague mentioning that he was masturbating while thinking of her, and having sexual objects (i.e., sex-toys) put in their workspace by their colleagues.

An investigation of more than ten thousand employees of Department of Homeland Security (DHS) agencies found that more than one-third had experienced sexual harassment or sexual misconduct at work. A draft report, heavily censored by DHS officials, found "more than 1,800 employee allegations of sexual harassment and sexual misconduct perpetrated by other federal employees" from 2011 to 2018 throughout Homeland Security agencies, "including instances of 'surreptitious videotaping in bathrooms, unwelcome sexual advances and inappropriate sexual comments.'" Agencies used cash payouts to settle complaints, often without investigation or discipline of the perpetrators, even in a case where "an employee alleged that her supervisor made inappropriate sexual remarks, solicited sex from her and then withheld job and training opportunities when she refused his advances" (Cameron 2022).

Harassment can be based on race or sex or combined in the form of "racialized sexual harassment" that serves to keep some women of color from entering, advancing, or remaining in a predominantly white male occupation. The lack of access to the predominantly white "all-boys club" (Rabe-Hemp 2018) can be a catch-22 state of affairs: if women do not socialize (either by choice or exclusion), they risk not learning information related to their job or promotion opportunities and may be labeled as aloof or "cold." But if women socialize with men at work, they may be perceived to be sexually available, which reflects negatively on their professionalism. Gay and lesbian officers working in this male-dominated field experience a sense of marginalization and harassment at least as severe as other minority groups on the job. And "since officers distrust the public and put an immense amount of trust in their fellow officers, being shunned by your colleagues can have potentially dangerous, even life-threatening results" (Buist and Lenning 2016: 57).

Third, racial and/or ethnic minorities not only have to deal with having their work devalued by their white peers, but they find that their community identities or loyalties are subject to questioning. They must prove to their communities that they are not "sellouts" while also demonstrating to white officers that they are strictly enforcing the laws against their community and behaving toward minorities as the white officers are. This dynamic is especially pronounced with Hispanic officers (Álvarez and Urbina 2015), and it became especially stark under Trump, who called Mexican immigrants criminals and rapists while also hiring many CBP agents (chapter 7). Some Latino/a/x recruits and agents are descendants of people who made an unauthorized entry, and most realize their job is to stop people looking for a better life or crossing to see their family (Mejia 2018). But in Texas, the Latino/a/x population makes up 51 percent of those living in poverty, so the decision "to apply for and accept a Customs and Border Protection job that offers a starting salary of nearly $56,000 a year and generous benefits is not a complicated one" (Cortez 2019). Officers then feel that they are being paid to do a job, and they want to hang on to the job to support their families.

In cases of police brutality or when excessive force is used by Black police officers against those in the Black community, some see it as evidence that the incident was about the nature of police, not race. But people should not jump to that conclusion without considering that the occupational culture and training of police outweighs the race of a police officer. That both white and Black police kill Black and Latino/a/x community members is not a sign to relax about racism because policing is still a white paramilitary endeavor with an overreliance on militarized policing in poor and minority communities. Indeed, "white male officers were the most likely to harass and use force against Black civilians," and research "results strongly suggest that diversification [of police] can reshape police-civilian encounters" (in Pickett et al. 2022: 313). Finally, undercover work requires the involvement of detectives whose brown skin permits them to blend into certain neighborhoods, but they sometimes fear that a white officer will accidentally shoot them.

In conclusion, there are significant limitations on essentializing gender relations or police-race relations in an occupational setting. "Essentializing" is the idea that "all women are oppressed by all men in the same ways or that there is one unified experience of dominance experienced by women" or minorities (Buist and Lenning 2016). The social reality is that people are influenced not only by their personal attitudes and experiences but also by the context in which they live and work. But the contributions of women, minorities, and women who are minorities should be both valued and incorporated into the ways that law enforcement agencies operate today so as to eliminate racism, minimize discrimination, and maximize fairness in the administration of justice.

## Policing and Class

Class bias in policing takes two main forms. The first is that for street crimes and drugs, poor people are more likely to be investigated by the police and arrested (and prosecuted and sentenced to prison). The second is that policing systems are weak and "defective by design" for many corporate crimes. Acts like wage theft, worker safety violations, unsafe food, and predatory financial institutions are policed by agencies that tend to be understaffed and have weak enforcement powers (Reiman and Leighton 2023).

Chapter 2 noted that numerous studies dating back to the 1940s show that serious criminal behavior is widespread among middle- and upper-class individuals, but arrests are concentrated among the poor. People thus see the poor as the criminal class and believe that middle-class and affluent people commit less crime, when the reality is that they are simply less likely to be arrested. Indeed, Chambliss's classic study, "The Saints and the Roughnecks," documents the extensive deviance and criminality among upper-class youth and the biases of police. Chambliss called the upper-class group the Saints ironically, because they "were constantly occupied with truancy, drinking, wild driving, petty theft and vandalism. Yet not one was officially arrested for any misdeed during the two years I observed them" (1973: 28).

Chambliss noted that the lower-class Roughnecks also committed crimes, but "in the sheer number of illegal acts, the Saints were more delinquent." Nevertheless, the police saw the Roughnecks as more delinquent and thus watched them more carefully for crimes and arrested them frequently. While the Saints did have a better demeanor with the police—being respectful and apologetic—Chambliss argues that the differences in arrests were because of the "class structure of U.S. society":

> If the police treat middle- and upper-class delinquents (or cocaine-snorting college students) the same way they treat lower-class delinquents (or black, ghetto crack users), they are asking for trouble from people in power. If, on the other hand, they focus their law enforcement efforts on the lower classes, they are praised and supported by "the community," that is, by the middle- and upper-class white community. (1973: 30)

Both a police chief (appointed by a mayor) and a sheriff (who is directly elected) will be responsive to the concerns of wealthy citizens, who have money to donate in elections and have networks of other wealthy people who have influence in a community. The deference to wealthy residents is not just about arrest but is also seen in the likelihood of using force and in general respect. For example, table 8.2 shows that those with higher incomes are more likely to believe that the police are there to protect people like them from crime. Those with lower

TABLE 8.2 **Views of Police by Income**

| Income | Protect People Like You from Crime (%) | Knows Someone Physically Abused by Police (%) |
| --- | --- | --- |
| <Less than $30,000 | 50 | 32 |
| $30,000–49,999 | 54 | 24 |
| $50,000–79,999 | 65 | 20 |
| $80,000 and higher | 64 | 16 |

*Source:* Ekins 2016.

incomes are more likely to know someone who has been physically abused by the police and less likely to feel that the police are there to protect people like them (see also Jackson et al. 2021). Low-income people also *fear* the police: "Personal fear is higher among low-SES respondents, both Black and White, because they have greater exposure to aggressive policing in high-crime areas but feel less in control of police-contact outcomes (e.g., less able to hire a lawyer)" (Pickett et al. 2022: 305).

Research also confirms the picture of police deference to the wealthy, even when they are engaged in crimes. The authors of *Dorm Room Dealers* report on the "antitargets" of the drug war—affluent, mostly white college students who sold marijuana (before California legalized it) and other drugs. One student, for example, sold $80,000 to $160,000 a month of drugs and made $10,000 to $20,000 in profit. Almost all the dealers were from "middle-upper class to affluent/upper class" and "had parents of considerable economic standing"—mayors, businesspeople, doctors, and accounting executives for major firms (Mohamed and Fritsvold 2011: 11–12). Because of their class status, they operated with relative impunity despite "the near absent or, perhaps more accurately, pathetic risk-minimization strategies" (Mohamed and Fritsvold 2011: 6).

The authors, while fully aware of class bias, write, "We were still taken aback by the lack of criminal justice and university administration attention paid these dealers, despite the brazenness, incompetence, and general dearth of street smarts." At times, "it almost seemed as if our network's dealers were deliberately trying to draw attention to themselves or test social and legal boundaries." Many dealers described encounters where the dealers' wealth and status served not as a "get-out-of-jail-free" card but as a "never-go-to-jail-in-the-first-place" card (Mohamed and Fritsvold 2011: 132).

Indeed, in one especially striking example, the wealthy college dealers were selling from a room in their house that had visible quantities of drugs, cash, and expensive consumer electronics. When some customers came back after a purchase to rob them, the dealers called the police to say someone took cash and electronics from them (Mohamed and Fritsvold 2011). The dealers indicated to the researchers that the police totally knew what was going on, but the officers found the customers who had robbed the dealers, returned the cash and electronics to the dealers, and announced a drug bust of the arrested customers who stole the drugs. Having the police be responsive and respectful when called by people who have been victimized while engaged in a crime—a drug crime in the middle of a drug war no less—is a significant privilege, especially when other citizens fear police and are violated by them even when the citizens have done nothing wrong.

Because wealthy people are less likely to be arrested, they are less likely to appear in police or "commonsense" profiles of drug dealers or criminals. These profiles, as well as the "intuition" police develop by arresting people, shape where they look for possible criminal activity and who the "suspicious" people are. The effect of being rewarded for arresting and controlling poor people rather than those with wealth and political power is a self-reinforcing cycle: arresting poor people creates a profile of poor criminals, which means surveillance and investigations are focused there to maximize resources, and then arrests confirm the profile. If the arrests and profile had been of rich college students (or college students in general) or Wall Street traders, subsequent surveillance and investigation would have yielded arrests to validate those profiles.

In addition to all the research showing that the wealthy engage in regular crimes as much as everyone else (Reiman and Leighton 2023), a long history of research shows criminality among the largest corporations—which is ignored in criminal profiles, as well as in discussion of career criminals, habitual criminals, and recidivism (see chapter 7). Sutherland noted this long-standing problem in his 1949 study of corporate crime:

> The records reveal that every one of the seventy corporations had violated one or more of the laws, with an average of about thirteen adverse decisions per corporation and a range of from one to fifty adverse decisions per corporation. . . . The "habitual criminal" laws of some states impose severe penalties on criminals convicted the third or fourth time. If this criterion were used here, about 90 percent of the large corporations studied would be considered habitual white-collar criminals. (in Reiman and Leighton 2023: 131)

Other studies confirm the high prevalence of repeat criminality and habitual corporate crime, even after they successfully prevent many of their harmful actions from becoming categorized as crimes in the lawmaking process. For example, a Department of Justice (DOJ) study examining 1975–1976 found that half of the six hundred corporations they examined were charged with a serious violation during that year. From 1975 to 1984, almost two-thirds of the Fortune 500 "were involved in one or more incidents of corrupt behavior such as price fixing, bribery, violation of environmental regulations and tax fraud" (Etzioni 1990: C3).

Since that time, corporations have become larger and engage in more extensive violations of civil and criminal law. In contrast to the average of thirteen violations Sutherland found, chapter 7 noted that Wells Fargo by itself had about three hundred. And of course there is a larger volume of corporate crime that goes undetected. A *Harvard Business Review* article, focused on three of the one hundred largest corporations, found that "none of [them] has faced a recent civil or criminal charge," but, "on average, each firm had experienced a violation that could lead to regulatory sanctions (such as a bribe or financial fraud) once every three days" (Soltes 2019b). A follow-up article asserts that "the vast majority of corporate offending—even in serious financial matters such as reporting fraud or bribery—is not publicly detected, sanctioned or reported" (Soltes 2019a: 925).

Corporations are sites of so many violations in part because the "corporate structure itself—oriented as it is toward profit and away from liability—is a standing invitation to such conduct" (Hills 1987; see also Bakan 2004). In addition, though, researchers since Sutherland have noted that white-collar and corporate crime are persistent because they are rational strategies given the lax policing and minimal penalties. Policing in the case of white-collar and corporate crime is not just done by agencies like the FBI but also by regulatory agencies. In addition to the rule-writing functions they have (see chapter 7), agencies are also responsible for a variety of inspections and enforcement activities (often with the FBI or other law enforcement that has the ability to arrest). Many agencies call themselves the "cop on the beat," so the policing of white-collar and corporate crime is done by agencies like the Securities and Exchange Commission (SEC), the Environmental Protection Agency (EPA), the Occupational Safety and Health Administration (OSHA), the Consumer Financial Protection Bureau, etc.

This policing system has a number of weaknesses. For example, few state-level agencies make white-collar and corporate crime a priority, leaving substantial aspects of the problem to the federal government. With state and federal enforcement, the first limitation on policing the crimes of the powerful is that businesses use their resources to lobby to limit the powers of agencies that police them. For example, wage theft involves nonpayment of wages due to employees by the employer and is a problem experienced by 17 to 34 percent of workers (Kim 2021: 977; Kim and Allmang 2021: 535). Workers might expect robust policing to fight this crime wave, but several state wage and hour divisions (the agencies responsible for policing wage theft by employers) only have the ability to respond to individual requests for help rather than actually initiate investigations (Leighton 2018). Investigations are an especially effective strategy for industries where wage theft is most likely. States often try to empower workers to sue for back wages—in effect making them the police and prosecution—but many workers do not understand minimum wage and overtime laws (Lee and Smith 2019). Many also lack the knowledge to file a suit in court or find an attorney who would file for low-wage workers, where their fees may be small.

In addition, regulatory agencies are underfunded and understaffed, which means they do not have the resources to fulfill their policing mandates. For example, "six states did not even have a single investigator in their state WHD [wage and hour division] offices, and 26 states had less than 10 investigators" to police wage theft (Kim and Allmang 2021: 540). Beyond wage theft, the Occupational Safety and Health Administration reached the lowest number of inspectors in its history (since 1970) in January 2019 (before the pandemic), caused by both budget cuts and a deliberate failure to fill agency vacancies by the Trump administration (Berkowitz 2019).

Another problem is that agencies have a conflicting dual mandate: they should be promoting business while also performing a policing function. The SEC, for example, is supposed to promote capital formation and police investment fraud. Because of business lobbying and neoliberalism (see chapter 1), promoting business takes precedence over enforcing rules. Worse still, "agency officials may fear the negative political consequences, such as cuts in future agency funding from enforcing the law too vigorously against businesses" (Lee and Smith 2019: 797). Even when agency officials do not fear business, they may rely heavily on industry for expertise, which causes the agency to have the industry's viewpoint rather than regulating for the public good. Regulators also know that if they cooperate with industry, they have a better chance of landing a lucrative job with the industry after they finish working for the government. After getting additional industry experience, they are more valued as regulators, and that regulatory experience and connections increases the chance they can land a better-paying job with the industry. This revolving door is described as *agency capture*, which refers to the process by which regulatory agencies—supposedly the police on many white-collar crime beats—come to be dominated (from the inside) by the industries they regulate.

Thus, despite the impressive record of habitual criminality on the part of the corporations, presidents have all consistently worked to get government "off the backs" of (e.g., to deregulate) corporations as they ratcheted up their war on the crimes of the poor. Such strategies of crime control are actually policies of class control. They are the equivalent of removing police from a high-crime area.

Crimes of the powerful are also prevalent because agencies like the FBI do not make them a priority. White-collar crime task forces of the FBI are understaffed and underfunded, and they focus on such wide-ranging schemes as internet, insurance, and Medicaid fraud. Further, white-collar crime includes acts where middle- and upper-class perpetrators victimize those who are more powerful (people who embezzle from corporations), as well as corporations who victimize those who are less powerful. Consistent with Black's *Behavior of Law* (chapter 7), the FBI and other policing agencies have been more involved with sanctioning middle managers who embezzle from institutions and executives of small companies than with executives of large companies that cause mass victimization.

This long-standing pattern was made worse by the reassignment of agents from white-collar crime—but not the war on drugs—to the war on terror. Thus, the "limited resources for white-collar crime" masks a decision to prioritize fighting the drug war rather than costly white-collar and corporate crime that physically and financially hurt a wide range of citizens. At the close of the Bush II presidency, the FBI was devoting so few resources to white-collar crime that companies had to turn to private investigators to prepare "courtroom-ready prosecutions" that they could take to the FBI because they were unable to get the agency's attention, even in cases of multimillion-dollar cases of loss (Lichtblau et al. 2008).

These collective patterns can be clearly seen in the area of financial crimes. In the wake of Enron, the DOJ did convene specialized task forces, like the Enron task force. It was a successful model because their cooperative interagency investigations laid the foundation for dozens of convictions. The task force ultimately secured the conviction of CEOs Ken Lay and Jeffrey Skilling. As these trials were winding down, FBI officials in 2004 said that mortgage-related problems had "the potential to be an epidemic" (Schmitt 2008), but they were ignored.

An investigative report of the SEC after the Enron-era frauds found that regulators, "while determined and well trained, are so understaffed that they often have to let good cases slip away" (Leaf 2005: 38). In the immediate aftermath of the scandals, President Bush created a new Corporate Fraud Task Force, although the official responsible for this "financial SWAT team" directed a credit card company that had paid more than $400 million to settle consumer and securities fraud suits. The task force reports in 2003 and 2004 were lists of cases and settlements, with no effort to discuss larger problems or make policy recommendations. From 2005 to 2007, the task force did not issue a report, and the 2008 report largely reviewed the 2003–2004 reports. The 2008 report was issued just before the financial crisis, but it did not indicate an awareness of corporate misconduct that would cause a global financial crisis in 2008–2009. The DOJ ultimately disbanded Bush's Corporate Fraud Task Force for a more narrowly focused Financial Fraud Enforcement Task Force that quickly lost focus on corporations and investigated individuals who victimized financial institutions (Barak 2012).

By 2008, the former lead prosecutor of Enron's Ken Lay and Jeffrey Skilling commented that "most sitting U.S. Attorneys now staring at the subprime crisis find scant resources available to pursue sophisticated financial crimes" (Schmitt 2008). Then–attorney general Mukasey repeatedly rejected calls for an equivalent of the Enron task force (Lichtblau et al. 2008). If there are no investigations, there can be no prosecutions—and there were no criminal prosecutions of big financial institutions or the executives at the center of the financial crisis. While some may see this as a "bug in the system," from the point of view of big financial institutions, keeping agencies "defective by design" (in Reiman and Leighton 2023: 160) is a feature of the system.

## Policing and Race

Race-based policing is a problem because it reduces the legitimacy of the police to the extent that it upholds white privilege rather than being used for the public safety of all. Further, overpoliced minority communities feel like they are underserved by the police when they call for help (Rios 2011), adding to the alienation and frustration that some communities feel toward police. Police stops are also more likely to result in verbal disrespect and physical aggression, including lethal encounters over trivial events. The fear of police causes stress and trauma to minority communities, and the continuous stream of videos has fueled Black Lives Matter protests and calls to defund the police. Many of the same issues apply to the Latino/a/x community because increasing "crimmigration"—the criminalization of immigration and Latino/a/x immigrants—has involved the local police (although there is also backlash to this use).

In looking at race and policing, it is helpful to keep in mind what other chapters have said about the history of the criminal justice system being used against minorities. Indeed, "there is not a single era in the United States history in which the police were not a force of violence against Black people" (in Pickett et al. 2022: 295). This observation lies at the heart of sentiments—like the ones Butler expressed in the opening narrative—that current police violence against Black people does not expose a "broken" system that needs another round of reform. As abolitionists note, "after decades of attempts to tinker with the institution of policing, it is becoming impossible to ignore that no amount of police reform seems capable of stopping cops from killing Black people" (Shanahan and Kurti 2022: 24).

To examine the problems of race and policing, this section starts by looking at surveys about confidence in, and fear of, the police. Significantly, one of the best done and most important recent surveys indicated, "It would be difficult to overstate the Black–White divide in police-related fearfulness" (Pickett et al. 2022: 302). It is not driven by media or differential involvement of Black people in crime, and part of this section looks at disproportionate minority contact with police. Those who dismiss it as exaggerated responses to a few tragic police shootings miss the point about "the habitual manner in which officers harass and treat Black Americans as suspects through pedestrian and traffic stops" (Pickett et al. 2022: 311). A part of this section looks at police behavior once a stop or encounter happens, the preference many minorities have for crime victimization over police encounters, as well as the stress the stops can produce. A final part of this section on race examines the policing aspect of immigration enforcement.

The results of surveys about confidence in the police are important because trust helps create a sense of security and fosters cooperation; confidence is fundamental for belief in the legitimacy of the criminal justice system and respect for the law. The results of recent surveys are reported in table 8.3. The table, and this section, focuses on white and Black responses because with law enforcement they are the extremes, with other minorities in between. White and Black responses tend to be reversed images—10 percent of whites have very little confidence in the police (lowest category), and 8 percent of Black people have a great deal of confidence (the highest category). White people are twice as likely to believe that police are properly trained in the use of force, and four times as likely to believe that they treat everyone equally, but only a minority of white people express confidence in either statement.

Some of the lack of confidence in law enforcement comes from personal experience and knowledge of how others have been treated. For example, 71 percent of Black people know someone treated unfairly by the police, compared with 34 percent of whites—and 51 percent of Asians and 48 percent of Hispanics (Pickett et al. 2022: 296). These experiences not only undermine confidence, but they cause fear, which is a separate aspect of race and law enforcement. Measures of fear are less common but important because "perceiving that the police are ineffective or illegitimate is fundamentally different than being afraid that they will hurt or kill you" (Pickett et al. 2022: 293). Fear drives much of the current crisis about the legitimacy of policing and the intensity of Black Lives Matter protests.

Pickett et al.'s survey found that 42 percent of Black respondents said that they were *very* afraid police will kill them in the next five years, compared with 11 percent of whites and 30 percent of the mostly Hispanic "other" category (2022: 302). (Black and white responses of "very afraid" and "very unafraid" were "mirror opposites," as with the confidence data in table 8.3.) Further, Black respondents were more afraid of being murdered by the police than by criminals. In addition, while "fear of police . . . should not replace fear of crime" (in Pickett et al. 2022: 310), it has for many, as indicated in table 8.4.

Chapter 2 noted that higher rates of arrest for Black people were best explained by a combination of biased policing and higher rates of involvement in crime due to the effects of living in a racist society. The key idea in analyzing race and policing is that contacts and arrests are *disproportionate to involvement in crime*, and race-based policing affects many innocent minorities. Some earlier studies did not

TABLE 8.3 **Confidence in Police and Police Training, by Race**

|  | White (%) | Black (%) |
|---|---|---|
| Great deal of confidence in police | 25 | 8* |
| Very little confidence in police | 10 | 29* |
| Confident police are trained to avoid the use of excessive force | 46 | 20 |
| Confident police treat Black and white people equally | 48 | 12 |

*Sources:* Supplemental data of Gallup Poll available from Jones (2022) and *Washington Post*–ABC Poll (Berman and Clement 2023).

* This data is from a Gallup Poll, which used "white" and "non-white" as categories, so it likely understates the Black-white difference by including responses from other minority groups whose views fall between those of white and Black people.

TABLE 8.4 **Preferences for Crime Victimization or Police Encounters, by Race**

|  | White (%) | Black (%) |
|---|---|---|
| Prefer to be robbed or burglarized rather than questioned by the police "without good reason" | 18 | 45 |
| Prefer crime victimization (robbery or burglary) over being searched by police | 36 | 52 |

*Source:* From Pickett et al. 2022: 310.

fully examine disproportionate contact, even though they produced clear evidence of discrimination. For example, the *Harvard Law Review* (1988: 1496) stated, "The argument that police behavior is undistorted by racial discrimination flatly contradicts most studies, which reveal what many police officers freely admit: that police use race as an independently significant, if not determinative, factor in deciding whom to follow, detain, search, or arrest." The racially based profile of the typical criminal that grows out of such policing is then used to justify the belief that "race itself provides a legitimate basis on which to base a categorically higher level of suspicion" (*Harvard Law Review* 1988: 1496).

As driving while Black (DWB) and related issues of race-based stop-and-frisk policies grew in prominence, researchers demonstrated that police contact was disproportionate—minorities were not exaggerating or overly sensitive. Data in 1988, for example, showed that, of vehicles on the New Jersey Turnpike, African American motorists with out-of-state plates accounted for fewer than 5 percent of the vehicles but 80 percent of the stops. A decade later, in Illinois, Hispanics made up less than 8 percent of the population and took fewer than 3 percent of the personal vehicle trips, but they made up approximately 30 percent of the motorists stopped for discretionary offenses, such as failure to signal a lane change or driving one to four miles over the speed limit (Harris 1999). To control for differences in driving violations, observers in Maryland watched an interstate near Baltimore and recorded information on 5,741 cars. They found that 93.3 percent were violating traffic laws, and of this group 17.5 percent were Black and 74.7 percent were white. However, the Maryland State Police reported that 72.9 percent of the vehicles they stopped had Black drivers (Harris 1999).

Another major finding came from New York's attorney general (NYSOAG) based on the "Stop, Question and Frisk Report Worksheet" filed by New York Police Department (NYPD) officers. These data go beyond driving to include stops related to the Supreme Court's decision in *Terry v. Ohio* (392 U.S. 1 [1968]), under which a police officer can detain a civilian if the officer can articulate a "reasonable suspicion" that criminal activity is "afoot." The NYSOAG analyzed 4.4 million stops between 2004 and 2012 and found that 83 percent of those stopped by the NYPD were Black or Hispanic, even though these groups made up about 50 percent of the population (Goldstein 2013). In response to police arguments that these groups committed a disproportionate amount of crime, a federal judge noted: "Nearly 90 percent of the people stopped are released without the officer finding any basis for a summons or arrest."

Further, the judge found that "weapons were seized in 1.0% of the stops of blacks, 1.1% of the stops of Hispanics, and 1.4% of the stops of whites." Contraband of other types "was seized in 1.8% of the stops of blacks, 1.7% of the stops of Hispanics, and 2.3% of the stops of whites" (*Floyd v. City of New York*, 08 Civ. 1034 [2013]: 7). The stops that found contraband—known as the "hit rate"—are important because they show that stops of white people were most likely to find evidence of lawbreaking.

Recently, Stanford University did a nationwide analysis of one hundred million traffic stops by geographically diverse state and municipal police. Compared to whites, Black folks and Hispanics were more likely to be stopped, and "stopped black and Hispanic drivers were searched about twice as often as stopped white drivers." But the "hit rate" for finding contraband was highest for white drivers. Marijuana legalization reduced the overall number of stops, but "with black and Hispanic drivers still more likely to be searched than white drivers post-legalization" (Pierson et al. 2020).

While having a lower hit rate for stops of Black people than whites does not prove racism, it shows that police stop minorities on the basis of less evidence and often unnecessarily. The further problem, noted in early driving-while-Black research, was that the consequences of the stops were more severe: police were more likely to search, to dump the contents of vehicles by the side of the road, and to be verbally and physically aggressive with minorities in the car (Engel and Calnon 2004: 69–72). Research by the Bureau of Justice Statistics found "evidence of black drivers having worse experiences—more likely to be arrested, more likely to be searched, more likely to have force used against them—during traffic stops than white drivers" (BJS 2005: 9). Other stops involved officers who were quick to unholster firearms. The judge in the NYPD case also found that "once a stop is made, blacks and Hispanics are more likely to be subjected to the use of force than whites, despite the fact that whites are more likely to be found with weapons or contraband" (*Floyd v. City of New York*, 08 Civ. 1034 [2013]: 13). Indeed, "one NYPD official has even suggested that it is permissible to stop racially defined groups just to instill fear in them that they are subject to being stopped at any time for any reason—in the hope that this fear will deter them from carrying guns in the streets" (*Floyd v. City of New York*, 08 Civ. 1034 [2013]: 14).

Police interactions with minorities more often include "pushing, shoving, punching, kicking, and the use of mace," which are "often combined with belligerent and antagonistic language, with the perceived intent of provoking community members so that officers can use violence" (Pickett et al. 2022: 311). People who try to dismiss the fear that Black communities have because police shootings of minorities are (regrettable but) few in number miss the point that physically intrusive and degrading stops are "routinized for Black Americans" (Pickett et al. 2022: 311). That many minorities preferred criminal victimization over police stops "makes the fact that some Americans are handcuffed and searched multiple times per year only to be released without charge each time all the more concerning" because, "in their psychological effects, these repeated police searches may be similar to robbing civilians repeatedly" (Pickett et al. 2022: 310).

We emphasize here that "the great majority of black people who are subjected to these humiliating and difficult experiences . . . have done absolutely nothing to deserve this treatment—except to resemble, in a literally skin-deep way, a small group of criminals" (Harris 1999). Because the majority of those stopped are innocent but the stops themselves are legal, Blackness is, in effect, criminalized. In addition, racially disproportionate stops and citations for trivial infractions matter by distorting the social world, by imposing a "spatial restriction on African-Americans, circumscribing their movements" and basically ensuring that Blacks stay out of areas where whites and the police feel they "do not belong" (Harris 1999; see also Butler 2017; Withrow 2006).

To help see the racial privilege in this area, imagine that the police "seized televisions, furniture and cash from fraternity houses based on an anonymous tip that a few joints and a stash of cocaine" were there. Or, white "suburban homemakers could have been placed under surveillance and subjected to undercover operations to catch them violating laws regulating the use and sale of prescription" drugs (Alexander 2012: 124) such as opiates. To be clear, we do not believe such enforcement would be a wise way to achieve equality. But the police harassing injured white athletes on painkillers or trying to goad white people going to a café into a fight would be an example of how whites, especially those with wealth, would not tolerate the kind of policing Black communities routinely experience.

A further issue involving race and policing involves computerized "predictive policing," which uses current data about crime and policing to create algorithms and databases to help police make "smart" decisions about the future deployment of resources. Brayne (2017) observed the Los Angeles Police Department (LAPD) implement such a system and add numerous other databases to it (automatic license plate reader databases, foreclosures, social media, electronic toll passes, etc.). While noting that data have the potential to make the system fairer and hold police accountable, she raises concerns that the software "hides both intentional and unintentional bias in policing and creates a self-perpetuating cycle: if individuals have a high point value, they are under heightened surveillance and therefore have a greater likelihood of being stopped, further increasing their point value" (Brayne

2017: 21), because each contact with police is data loaded into the program that raises that person's score.

Further, certain place-based aspects of the algorithm reflect race-based policing patterns, but "once they are inputted as data, the predictions appear impartial; human judgment is hidden in the black box under a patina of objectivity" (Brayne 2017: 22). Also, because the system analyzes networks of people and engages in data "dragnets" in certain neighborhoods, it widens the net of surveillance. Individuals whom the police search for in the database get extra points, regardless of whether they have done anything.

In addition, people wary of surveillance may avoid social institutions that generate data linked to the police database. However, Brayne suggests that such individuals will be disadvantaged in their health, employment networks, education, and general economic mobility. This process exacerbates "any pre-existing inequalities for an expanding group of already disadvantaged individuals" because of "cascading disadvantages" (2017: 23). As other government databases link to the police one, the stigma is not just of arrest but also of being in the database and being the subject of queries:

> From electronic ankle monitors and predictive-policing algorithms to workplace surveillance systems, technologies originally developed for policing and prisons have rapidly expanded into nonjuridical domains, including hospitals, schools, banking, social services, shopping malls, and digital life. Rooted in the logics of racial disparity and subjugation, these purportedly unbiased technologies not only extend prison spaces into the public sphere but also deepen racial hierarchies and engender new systems for social control. (Benjamin 2019)

Specific issues in this area include the overclassification and misclassification of people as being gang affiliated, along with the difficulties of undoing or correcting these records once entered (Jacobs 2009; Petering 2015). Gang databases have also contributed to the expansion of policing strategies aimed at primarily Latino immigrant communities to facilitate immigration enforcement (Conway 2017; Hufstader 2015).

Immigration and the politics of border security are increasingly central to understanding race and policing. Historically, immigration and immigration-related violations have been outside the scope of criminal justice. While "improper entry" into the country is a misdemeanor for a first offense (8 U.S.C. § 1325), existing here without authorization is a civil violation punishable by deportation. (Not everyone who is currently undocumented committed improper entry because people might remain in the United States beyond the terms of their visas.) Although deportation is a serious event, the civil nature of the proceeding means there are fewer due process rights than those given to criminal defendants (e.g., right to counsel [Barak 2023]).

Although immigrants tend to be less involved in criminal activity than persons born in the United States, phrases like "illegals" or "criminal aliens" reinforce criminal identity by framing a status offense (like being underage at a bar or having an expired license) as a criminal threat and national security concern. Still, the growth of crimmigration has resulted in an expansion of surveillance and deportability for immigrant communities. Federal programs enlist local enforcement to help identify deportable immigrants. The "287(g)" partnerships deputize local police to screen people for immigration status and hold them, but local police are diverted from their regular duties and are not compensated for their time or jail space (Akins 2013). The Secure Communities program has local police transmitting fingerprints of arrested individuals to the DHS to see if the person is deportable by reason of being an immigration violator, terrorist, criminal alien, etc. By focusing on those arrested for a crime, this program sought to connect deportation efforts to a broader crime control strategy. But according to one rigorous evaluation, "the program ha[d] no discernible impact in medium- and large-sized U.S. cities" on either serious or more common crimes (Treyger et al. 2014: 310). The evaluation noted a number of concerns with the Secure Communities program, including that it may incentivize more intense policing of immigrant communities and anyone who might appear to be an immigrant (Barak et al. 2020; León and Cervantes 2022). In counterproductive fashion, the aggressive policing of immigrant communities *paired with* the looming threat of deportation for members of that community produce strong incentives to avoid police and not call them to report a crime or other victimization. Immigrants do not want to be witnesses or cooperate with police to arrest those who might be causing harm in their community (Kubrin 2014: 292).

Many jurisdictions have pushed back on the punitive nature of immigration enforcement. Some jurisdictions (primarily medium- and large-sized cities) have embraced the label "sanctuary city," a term that originated in the 1980s to build support for Central Americans who were fleeing systemic violence in civil wars that were partly supported by the United States. Being a sanctuary city is not a formal or legal condition but a political orientation where city leaders signal that they do not intend to cooperate with federal law enforcement agencies on deportations for nonviolent offenses. Today, despite research showing that sanctuary cities have no more crime attributable to immigrants, the term "sanctuary city" has become increasingly weaponized in debates about whether a politician or political party is being "too soft" on border security or immigration policy.

From a public safety perspective, however, there are reasons to be a so-called sanctuary city. Immigrant populations, including undocumented or unauthorized residents, have lower crime rates while bringing significant benefits like workforce participation, as well as contributions to local and regional economic and social activity. Some cities are home to undocumented residents who have spent decades in the United States and who have raised families, built community businesses, and participated in their communities. Being a sanctuary city might mean, then, that local leaders recognize that deportation can be understood as a civic death penalty for those who have established their lives in the United States. Indeed, deportations for minor wrongdoings break up families or force children (who may be U.S. citizens) to go with a parent to a country that is not their home or birthplace, or to remain in the United States without the economic and emotional support of an immediate family member.

## Policing and Gender/Sexuality

In the 1970s, explanations of women's lower level of criminal involvement were often based on the assumption that women have benefited from police officers' and judges' paternalistic and chivalrous attitudes. As a result, the argument went, women were less likely to be arrested, convicted, or incarcerated. Over the past quarter century or more, assumptions of paternalism have been criticized on a number of grounds. First, most studies asserting paternalism have not empirically evaluated whether it is in fact responsible for the differences. Second, Black women and minorities have not benefited from paternalism by police, and chivalry is "a racist and classist concept . . . reserved for the women who are least likely ever to come in contact with the criminal justice system: the ladies, or white middle-class women" (Klein ([1973] 1995): 10, 13). Moreover, Black women have been characterized by racist segments of society as "welfare queens," "mammies," "Jezebels," and tough, masculine "Black Amazons." Chivalry is not bestowed on such women, and the terms function as a tool of dehumanization that situates Black women as nonworthy subjects of police and community protection.

In contrast to the widely held but false belief in chivalry is the long-standing denial of police services to women victims of male intimate partner violence by the mostly male police force. Indeed, there has been a historical reluctance to define women as victims when crimes have been committed against them in their homes or as part of a relationship. The police have had a key role in using their discretion to not hold men accountable for their crimes against women (Gross 2015). For example, in recent interviews, "a survivor described police questions as: 'Why didn't I listen to [the perpetrator]? Why didn't I do what he said?' Another survivor explained: 'One time [police] got called out, and [the officer] asked what I had done to deserve [the abuse]'" (Gezinski 2022).

To combat this problem, legislatures passed mandatory arrest laws, which require police to make an arrest in situations where the officer has probable cause to believe domestic violence has occurred. Such policies reinforce the message that battering is a serious crime and make police the complaining witness so the case is not dropped even if the victim does not want to press charges. Such actions taken against a woman's wishes may further disempower her and cause economic problems if the family is dependent on the batterer's income, but they were supported by many liberal and some radical feminists. However, other radical feminists and women of color doubted that the tough-on-crime approach would bring women safety and believed it would further criminalize communities of color. As it turned out, the unfortunate result of these policies has been greater arrest rates of battered women because the police go into a situation and simply arrest both parties if there is evidence that women have fought back physically. In this sense, "dual arrests force women to choose between personal safety and a potential arrest, a major problem given the severity of the domestic violence epidemic" (Hodges 2021). For example:

> The police officer told me he was handcuffing me. I said, "Why are you handcuffing me?" [The officer] said, "Because you hit [the perpetrator]." I said, "Do you understand he was killing me?!" And [the officer] was like, "I don't need to know anything. You can tell the judge about it." (Gezinski 2022)

In this sense, "many victims of ongoing battering have ended up with less protection and fewer services and have been labeled as a defendant" (Miller and Meloy 2006: 92; Sherman 2012). The negative consequences of mandatory arrest policies fall most heavily on women of color because they are seen as more likely to fight back and are stereotyped as aggressive. The perceived gender neutrality of the policy hurts domestic violence victims who need to contend not just with the abuse but also with an arrest for an assault, which may lead to denial of access to shelters and victim assistance, child custody issues, difficulties with employment or housing, and being mandated to attend a batterer intervention program (Miller and Meloy 2006). Ultimately, many battered women fear being criminalized, so they are less likely to call the police.

While there is a high rate of abuse in LGBTQ+ relationships, those being abused face barriers to help seeking that other populations do not experience—starting with police and extending to shelters, temporary housing, legal advocacy, and more (Buist and Lenning 2023). Additionally, there are unique concerns in LGBTQ+ relationships such as the process of outing their partner if their partner has not disclosed their LGBTQ+ status to their families, friends, employers, churches, and so on. The threat of being involuntarily outed by police reports creates pressure to stay in these relationships and not get the police involved.

Further, mandatory arrest policies create additional challenges for police officers who are typically not trained on any LGBTQ+ issues. In response to dual-arrest problems, some jurisdictions require police to identify a primary aggressor and only arrest them, but identifying the primary aggressor is based on gender stereotypes. Arresting the more masculine partner in an LGBTQ+ relationship may not be appropriate. Further, women are not seen as the aggressors in heteronormative relationships, so when police arrive at a scene where two women have been fighting, the officers may mistake it for family violence between members of an extended household or simply not recognize the queer relationship because of heteronormative assumptions. When police see two men fight, they may take it as a common fight between guys and not as part of an intimate relationship where one person needs protection and services.

Another significant issue with the policing of gender is the Supreme Court's decision in *Dobbs v. Jackson Women's Health Organization* that there is no constitutional right to an abortion (see chapter 7). States that have enacted abortion restrictions (or bans) and fetal personhood laws require the policing of a wide range of women's behavior, with serious implications for their right to privacy. While some of these issues are not new, the combination of new, more restrictive laws, an escalation in enforcement, and technology will create novel developments in the policing of women. The executive director of the Surveillance Technology Oversight Project notes:

> None of the tactics we will see used to target pregnant people will be new. We've seen these same surveillance techniques developed in the name of immigration enforcement, national security, combating drugs, and so many other law enforcement priorities. And the truth is that when you develop those techniques, you are at the whim of those in power and whatever they next decide to call a crime. (in Newman 2022)

In order to police abortion restrictions, stillbirths and miscarriages are often treated as potential criminal activity. Policing abortion restrictions can also involve monitoring women's menstrual cycles for irregularities that might indicate pregnancy to ensure that any fertilized egg is carried to term. Severe abortion restrictions that criminalize "aiding and abetting" mean that if a woman is suspected of getting an abortion—or attempting to get one—people in her cell phone contacts list and social media DMs can become suspects. Finally, laws giving rights to fetuses and fertilized eggs allow for policing of pregnant women's decisions. In practice, "healthcare provider or police suspicion of drug use during pregnancy frequently triggers criminal charges against individuals who deliver healthy infants" (Beety and Oliva 2023: 35).

One of the ways that police receive information about possible violations of these laws is health-care providers. They call the police when pregnant women seek medical attention for injuries in states with severe abortion restrictions. Hospitals administer drug tests to pregnant women, sometimes without their consent, then turn the results over to police (Walter 2023). These referrals are especially likely to result in charges for Black women because of stereotypes about who the "bad moms" are. Enforcement strategies that involve police deter pregnant women from seeking medical care, especially when (as is the case in most places) drug treatment is not easily available. Thus,

> The American Medical Association, American Academy of Pediatrics, American College of Obstetricians & Gynecologists, and American Psychiatric Association have issued position statements explaining that they are staunchly opposed to the criminalization of pregnant people for drug use because such tactics undermine the health of the very people that those laws are allegedly designed to "help" and "protect" from harm: pregnant people and their children. (Beety and Oliva 2023: 45)

Another important change in enforcement is Texas crowd-sourcing the enforcement of its restrictive abortion law (SB 8) to citizens of the state and providing them with a monetary bounty if they are successful. The law prohibits doctors from performing an abortion after they can hear a heartbeat (about six weeks) and anyone from "'aid[ing] or abet[ting]' the performance of an abortion—apparently including nurses, receptionists, people providing transportation, and anyone who paid for the abortion" (Strauss 2023: 85). (Does someone who repairs an abortion clinic, or cleans it, or provides medical equipment "aid and abet"? [Reagan 2022: xxiv].) But the bill prohibits state and local officials from taking action and says it "shall be enforced exclusively through . . . private civil actions" (in Strauss 2023: 84–85; Dorf 2023).

Private citizens do not have to allege any injury to themselves or show any connection to the abortion, and they do not need to be in the county where the woman lived or the abortion happened. If they are successful, "the court is required to award the plaintiff a bounty of 'not less than' $10,000 for each abortion, plus costs and attorney's fees" (in Strauss 2023: 84–85). However, no recovery of costs is allowed when someone successfully defends themselves. Several states have subsequently copied the enforcement part of the Texas law, thus opening up a new era where states "grant members of the public a mandate to investigate, collect evidence and initiate civil suits" to enforce laws (Reagan 2022: xxiii–iv).

Whether enforcement is done by police or private citizens, it requires personal knowledge of the woman and information about her health-care choices. Unlike the citizens in private civil suits, police have access to technology platforms that women use to monitor their cycles, search for information, chat/DM with others, and make payments. Further, our electronic devices not only hold a repository of our communications and purchases, but create a log of our every movement, allowing police to reconstruct a pregnant person's visit to a pharmacy, shipping facility, or abortion clinic. Police can track cellphones and cell-enabled smart devices using cell-site location information from phone providers, though a warrant is required for prolonged searches of individuals or so-called "tower dumps," which identify all devices in a location. (Cahn and Manis 2022)

For example, was a pregnant woman falling down the stairs a deliberate act to miscarry (Beety and Olivia 2023: 46)? Even if the incident did not result in a miscarriage, if police are suspicious, they can subpoena technology companies to see if the woman searched for information about abortion or inducing a miscarriage (Cahn and Manis 2022).

While compelling a person to turn over their cell phone and electronic devices requires a judge's approval for a warrant, a subpoena for "business records" of the tech company is easier. While companies say they are strict about their standards for giving police information, that seems unlikely because it costs the companies time and money; it is cheaper and easier to go along with even overly broad police requests. Accepted police warrants can already be very broad, such as the use of "tower dumps" (noted above) or "geofence warrants," which require "Google and other companies to produce information on all the users in a specified time and place, whether one room or virtually an entire town" (Cahn and Manis 2022). (Such warrants can also be used to investigate crimes during protests like Black Lives Matter demonstrations.) Other data is simply for sale by data brokers who collect it from apps and websites people visit, so some advertising databases contain "the names and addresses of women seeking abortion care" (Cahn and Manis 2022).

If those who oppose abortion win control of federal power (the presidency and Congress), any antiabortion ban or restriction could bring the police powers of the FBI, the Food and Drug Administration, the U.S. Postal Service, and banking regulators to bear on women seeking abortions as well as all those who aid and abet.

A final issue with gender/sexuality and policing is police violence. Although 96 percent of police killings are of men (Liu et al. 2023), police—especially male officers—engage in sexual violence against women and trans people, as well as intimate partner violence. The best source of data on the lifetime prevalence of police violence against women is displayed in table 8.5. The physical violence category includes police using a weapon (gun, baton, Taser) or if they had "ever hit, punched, kicked, dragged, beat, or otherwise used physical force." Police sexual violence asked about "forced inappropriate sexual contact on you, including while conducting a body search in a public place." Psychological violence asked if a police officer ever engaged in "non-physical aggression toward you, including threatening, intimidating, stopping you without probable cause, or using slurs." Neglect asked if "the police either did not respond, responded too late, or responded inappropriately" when called. The final category of positive policing was "one question asking whether police had ever provided assistance, protection, or any other service to the participant" (Fedina et al. 2018: 151). The intimate partner violence (IPV) row includes physical or sexual violence by a romantic or sexual partner, while the

## TABLE 8.5  Lifetime Prevalence of Police Violence by Women

| | Physical (%) | Sexual (%) | Psychological Violence (%) | Neglect (%) | Positive (%) |
|---|---|---|---|---|---|
| Overall lifetime prevalence of police violence | 4 | 3.3 | 14.4 | 17.2 | 46.6 |
| Lifetime prevalence of police violence by those who also experienced intimate partner violence | 8.9 | 4.6 | 28.2 | 35.6 | 62.3 |
| Lifetime prevalence of police violence by those who also experienced sexual violence | 12.8 | 5.5 | 35.4 | 40.9 | 59.8 |

*Source:* Adapted from Fedina 2018: 152.

sexual violence (SV) row measured unwanted sexual activity by someone other than a romantic or sexual partner.

The results are not broken out by race or sexual orientation but include all racial groups and some foreign-born women; about 11 percent of the sample was LGB, although several trans respondents were dropped. The lifetime prevalence is in the context of women whose median age is thirty-five. Women who had experienced either IPV or SV were at substantially higher risk of also suffering from police violence in all forms, even while they were more likely than the general sample to have had a positive experience.

The International Association of Chiefs of Police, in a publication about responding to LGBTQ+ sexual assault, notes that in a transgender survey, "of the survey respondents who interacted with law enforcement the year prior to the survey, four percent reported having been sexually assaulted by the officer or forced to engage in sexual activity to avoid arrest" (n.d.: 4). They also say agencies "should consider": "Prohibiting all forms of on-duty sexual contact and include language inclusive of LGBTQ+ communities in agency directives regarding officer sexual misconduct" (International Association of Chiefs of Police: 7). LGBTQ+ youth also report inappropriate pat downs by police, which can be retraumatizing for a population that disproportionately suffers from childhood sexual abuse.

In addition, "studies have found that 40 percent of police families have dealt with domestic violence. This number stands in stark contrast to the 10 percent of nonpolice families that report domestic violence" (Hodges 2021). (The 40 percent number is widely cited, although the original source of this number is rarely noted, making it difficult to evaluate its context or generalizability.) However, higher rates of IPV are expected given the identification many officers have with aggressive and dominant masculinity, the power imbalances with their partners, their training on tactics, and the likelihood that they will be believed and other police will not hold them accountable.

## Policing and Intersectionality

People imagine the typical criminal to be a Black man because of a false but self-fulfilling profile that focuses police resources on them and takes arrests as verification of the profile. While men are the majority of offenders, certain crimes that could qualify as "white men's crimes" are neglected in profiles and enforcement. The serious underrepresentation of women and minority men as CEOs and in other executive positions of large corporations effectively blocks them from the access necessary to engage in large-scale white-collar crimes. A review of 436 defendants from work done by the Corporate Fraud Task Force from 2002 to 2009 found only thirty-seven women, about 9 percent (Steffensmeier et al. 2013). "Paralleling gendered labor market segmentation processes that limit and shape women's entry into economic roles, sex segregation in corporate criminality is pervasive, suggesting only subtle shifts in gender socialization and women's opportunities for significant white-collar crimes" (Steffensmeier et al. 2013: 448). While 156 men were identified as ringleaders, only three women were—and two were married to another ringleader.

Indeed, while white men with power are not held accountable for a number of harms, including an ecological crisis that may drive humanity to extinction, the focus of law enforcement is on the poor, and disproportionately minority women and the minority LGBTQ+ community. The race section discussed driving while Black, for example, and this concept has been adapted for the transgender community: "walking while trans" refers to anti-loitering laws that have historically targeted sex workers, a widespread problem in spite of New York and California recently repealing them (McKinley and Ferré-Sadurní 2021). Functional variations of walking-while-trans laws persist as anti-loitering laws, anti-solicitation laws, manifestation ordinances, and/or crimes against nature by solicitation (CANS in Louisiana).

Regardless of the name, these laws are the "'female version' of stop-and-frisk laws" (McKinley and Ferré-Sadurní 2021) that police use against minority men. Data from the New York State Division of Criminal Justice Services indicated that in 2018, about 90 percent of people arrested under the statute were Black or Latinx, and 80 percent identified as women (Diaz 2021).[1] Transgender women of color, while not visible in that statistic, are disproportionately affected by such laws because they are falsely stereotyped as sex workers. The CANS law, in particular, is used to arrest and harass members of the LGBTQ+ community, even though the "crimes against nature" are oral and anal sex, which are widely practiced by cisgender heterosexuals as well (Buist and Lenning 2023; Center for Constitutional Rights 2023).

Further, because LGBTQ+ youth are more likely to have experienced family conflict, abandonment, or child abuse, they are most likely to be homeless and engage in survival crimes that bring them into contact with the police. This population, especially the minority LGBTQ+ youth, reported high levels of disrespect and derogatory comments from police about their appearance and gender nonconformity (Dank et al. 2015). Police refused to call trans individuals by their preferred name, reinforcing that trans individuals are imposters or a fraud rather than respecting the identity they have chosen and are working toward through hormones and surgery. (The International Association of Chiefs of Police [n.d.] confirms that calling people by their preferred names and pronouns is the best practice.)

Minority youth also reported inappropriate strip searches and pat downs that seemed designed to humiliate and harass. One youth commented, "It happened too often actually. Sometimes when I'm just out there smoking a cigarette or I'm walking down the street the way [they will put me] up against the wall and they be like feeling me . . . like not frisking me it will be feeling me up" (Dank et al. 2015: 24). A Black transgender woman echoed the problem: "[There] is a difference between a pat and a rub. They just rub you down. And it is just filthy" (Dank et al. 2015: 24). The gay, lesbian, and trans populations discussed having sex with police, sometimes for money and sometimes using their positions as police to get it for free (Dank et al. 2015: 27).

In addition to minority LGBTQ+ people, both the public and the police need to be more aware of the violence that happens to minority women, even though the emphasis has been on minority men. Minority women and girls are also subjected to heightened attention from police. For example, "after excessive force, sexual assault is the most common complaint against the police, and African American women are the most likely victims" (Butler 2017). If there is a girl who had a temper tantrum and is in handcuffs for "punching" a teacher, it is a Black girl (Ritchie 2017). If Tasers are used against girls on a playground, it is safe to bet they are Black girls. Further, researchers studying this topic report male officers requiring girls to remove clothing for unsupervised searches for minor wrongdoing (Ritchie 2017). The protocol should be to wait for a woman officer to minimize the potential for inappropriate situations and retraumatizing someone who has experienced sexual abuse. This applies not just to Black and Asian girls but is especially an issue with Muslim girls. Indeed, one noted, "For some of us it's about: 'You're not covered up enough'; for us it's like, 'You're covered up too much'" (Ritchie 2017).

Butler's *Chokehold*, the subject of the opening narrative, focuses on Black folks, but he notes that the idea of chokehold also applies to Muslim Americans through national security interventions, "surveillance of poor women receiving government benefits," Native Americans, the "exploitation and deportation of undocumented Latino workers," "police and private violence against transgender women of color," and the "sex trafficking of Asian women" (2017). Ultimately, though, Butler uses an intersectionality approach to study how the chokehold applies to Black men, because "intersectionality is about the difference that gender makes for race, and that race makes for gender" (2017). When Black men were lynched, the act often involved cutting off their penis, thus requiring an analysis of gender and sexuality in racist violence. Butler likewise believes that masculinity is implicated in the current treatment of Black men, thus necessitating a "Black + male" intersectional approach: "intersectionality teaches us that gender matters for Black men as well, and ignoring gender undermines the chances of making things better" (2017).

The unique nature of immigration enforcement also requires an intersectional analysis that focuses on men because deportation functions as a "gendered racial removal program" (Golash-Boza and Hondagneu-Sotelo 2013) whereby Latino and Caribbean men are disproportionately targeted for arrest and eventual deportation (Hernández 2008). Latino masculinities, immigration status, and racial-ethnic identity all converge to shape the biographical trajectories of both Border Patrol agents and those who are deported because of their work, and a range of scholarship has examined how Latino law enforcement view their own role in the deportation machine (Cortez 2020).

With so much of police violence being directed against Black men, Black Lives Matter is needed to reaffirm the lives that are being too frequently taken—and taken without criminal consequences (which signals an acceptance of the situation). But even here, #SayHerName is necessary because violence against Black women and trans people often gets lost, even by those trying to affirm the value of Black lives (Crenshaw and Richie 2015). Certainly #AllLivesMatter is also an important sentiment, but there is no debate that wealthy white lives matter. Abusive men who kill their women intimate partners face less harsh consequences than abused women who kill their abuser. The lives of white sex workers seem to matter little, even if their loss might attract more concern than the murder of a Black sex worker.

## Implications

In so many ways, the proposed "Cop City" in Atlanta is a sign of the times, as is the resistance to it. Originally approved in 2017 in a secret session, the project for a $90 million, eighty-five-acre police training ground for urban policing became known as Cop City. Those acres are part of one of the largest urban forests in the United States, and they are located in a largely Black area of the city, which has fewer parks than richer, white areas (Wingfield 2023). The land was originally settled by the native Muscogee Creek people, who were driven out by white settlers in the early 1800s, after which the place developed into the "finest plantation in the county," and later a prison farm (Bethea 2022). Three hundred faith-based leaders, many of whom have ties to the civil rights movement, protested the proposed training facility and summed up the concerns with a letter to end "police militarization, as well as ecological destruction and systemic violence rooted in legacies of genocide and enslavement" (Wingfield 2023).

The killing of George Floyd in Minneapolis sparked intense Black Lives Matter protests across the country, including Atlanta. After a "brutal police response from Atlanta police," six officers were charged with excessive force (Budds 2023). Although those charges were later dropped, the city promised to institute additional police training to reform the police. Cop City became the training—a place where police supposedly could practice doing better by training in a realistic city setting. But many residents were skeptical that this was the needed reform, and others suggested it allowed police to "practice urban warfare" or that it was "a police murder playground" (Bethea 2022; Jones 2023). A local Baptist minister said the city planned to "destroy the nation's largest urban forest and replace it with the largest militarized police training facility in North America" (Jones 2023). An activist named Twig was more blunt that Cop City was going to be a training ground for "doing even more brutal crowd control, even more brutal *SWAT* raids, even more brutal murder. And a lot of us were, like, 'Oh, fuck that'" (Bethea 2022).

Through 2022, forest defenders tried to prevent the clear-cutting of the land, and police allege the tactics included Molotov cocktails and the destruction of construction machinery. Five protestors were arrested and charged with "domestic terrorism" (Georgia Bureau of Investigation 2023; Robinson 2023). The situation became worse with the police killing of a nonbinary activist named Tortuguita, who died with fifty-seven gunshot wounds. Police fired after an officer was shot in the leg, although there are conflicting accounts about whether it was Tortuguita or friendly fire from the police (Cheney-Rice 2023; Valencia et al. 2023). "Police are now stationed around the construction site, like a crisis scene out of the tactical village being built there. The City Council asked the department to reconsider the decision, saying that allocating officers to stand guard is hurting crime-fighting efforts elsewhere" (Budds 2023). As activists occupied the forest and refused to leave, "law enforcement has arrested over 40 Stop Cop City demonstrators under the state's domestic terrorism statute, which carries a penalty of up to 35 years in jail" (Robinson 2023). Those charged included a legal observer from the Southern Poverty Law Center, perhaps as punishment for trying to help the activists ensure that their rights were not violated. Police also organized a militarized SWAT raid on the state-registered charity Network for Strong Communities that helped the activist group Defend the Atlanta Forest, including with a bail fund. "The cops used PayPal data to bring money-laundering charges" (Hardcastle 2023) and charity fraud charges. A former federal prosecutor of white-collar crime told the *New York Times*: "It's a stretch to use what are white-collar financial fraud claims to charge these individuals, but obviously they want them charged" (Rojas and Keenan 2023).

The city's concessions seemed to mirror the problem with police reforms that never get at the heart of the problem: authorities agreed not to test explosives there, to move a gun range farther from residences, and to plant more trees. Critics say the deeper problem is that Atlanta—along with Minneapolis, where Floyd was killed—is among the cities with the most inequality. Building Cop City and "building a bigger police state is how Atlanta appeases both its corporate tenants—Delta, Home Depot, and Coca-Cola are among the project's donors—and its wealthiest tax base" (Cheney-Rice 2023). Corporations are paying for two-thirds of the cost, and they include: "Studies/Shadowbox Studies, Carter Accenture, CNN, Chick-Fil-A, Coca-Cola Company, Cox Enterprises, Cushman & Wakefield, Delta, Equifax, Georgia Pacific, Georgia Power, Home Depot, Inspire Brands, Koch Brothers, KPMG International Limited, the Loudermilk Family, McKesson, Norfolk Southern, United Parcel Service, Waffle House, [and] Wells Fargo" (Mowatt 2023: 513).

The then-mayor promised that Cop City would provide "21st century training, rooted in respect and regard for the communities they serve." But residents of poor and minority neighborhoods see the police training from Cop City being used against them to protect the wealthy, and to keep order in a city where residents want to protest systematic cuts for services and infrastructure for the poor and minority communities. In 2023, Georgia considered HB 505, which "would increase the penalty for 'riot' from a misdemeanor to a felony punishable by up to 20 years in prison." The momentum is certainly to increase penalties for protest: "Since 2017, 21 states have enacted at least 41 anti-protest laws, mostly in response to racial justice and environmental demonstrations" (Robinson 2023).

Cop City is supported partly by a moral panic about crime and false narratives about policing crime (see chapter 1). (The Cox Enterprises listed above as a corporate sponsor owns the largest newspaper in Atlanta.) Indeed, the George Floyd protests inspired many cities and states to propose new police training facilities like cop city. The stakes are high because biased law enforcement can "undermine the legitimacy of the use of coercive power and can make the criminal justice system no better than the criminals it pursues." It can "erode trust in the system of justice, create public cynicism and hostility, and make police work more difficult and dangerous" (Cole 1999; see also Harris 1999). That was written more than twenty years ago, and the question is how policing will respond in the next 20 years.

## Review and Discussion Questions

1. Why do some people think that police violence is not evidence of a broken system?
2. What is crimmigration? What are the concerns for race and policing that it raises? What are the effects on public safety of aggressively policing immigrants? Of being a sanctuary city?
3. What are some important aspects of the job of policing? What issues arise because policing is mainly a white, male, and heterosexual workforce?
4. What are the two main forms of class bias? What are some examples of each?
5. Why is racial bias in policing important? How do confidence in, and fear of, police differ by race? What are "hit rates" and what do they say about race-based policing? What does the chapter say has been routinized in police encounters with racial and ethnic minorities? Why are algorithm-based decisions not as neutral and objective as they may seem?
6. What are mandatory arrest laws and what are the problems of dual arrest? What are some issues with how abortion and fetal personhood are policed? What are the forms and extent of police sexual violence against women and LGBTQ+ people?
7. What is "walking while trans," and why is this issue in the "Intersections" part of the chapter? What are some other intersectional concerns with the policing of women? Of men?
8. What is Cop City and why is it controversial? What are some developments since this chapter was written? If you were going to design a training program and place for police to practice "21st century training, rooted in respect and regard for the communities they serve," what would it look like?

## Note

1. An HBO documentary titled *The Stroll* (Allen 2023) exposes the violent forms of sexual and physical abuse suffered by Black trans women at the hands of NYPD police in the 1990s and indicates how those trans people who were not sex workers were, and are, treated.

# CHAPTER 9

# Prosecution, Plea Bargains, and Deportation

*As an eighteen-year-old, Nicolas Gomez was a member of Mara Salvatrucha, or MS-13, a transnational gang (see chapter 1). His involvement with MS-13 is a tragically familiar story (Barak et al. 2020; León and Barak 2023). Young Central American youth fled political instability and state-sanctioned violence, some of which resulted from U.S. foreign policy, and relocated to Southern California. Youth gangs were proliferating, and to protect themselves, these youths formed what would become MS-13 and the Eighteenth Street Gang. Preemptive and retaliatory violence between these and other gangs are part of a broader culture of fear. Gangs provided protection because youth who live in mixed-status or undocumented-status households do not call police or seek formal assistance after victimization because they fear immigration-related enforcement actions, like deportation, for themselves or their family.*

*At fourteen years old, Gomez found himself as a teenager of a single mom in a neighborhood with competing gangs. Within four years, he would be the youngest defendant in a six-person drive-by shooting and the only person to face prison time. Gomez thought he was shooting a rival member of the Eighteenth Street Gang. He was mistaken, and the victim, Richard Sheridan, tragically died at the hands of six teenagers and young adults. The prosecutor in this case originally offered twenty years in exchange for pleading guilty. Gomez refused. The prosecutor offered a second plea deal, this time for twenty-five years. Gomez again refused. Gomez's case then went to trial, where he was found guilty of second-degree homicide and first-degree assault.*

*At sentencing, the court threw the book at him, figuratively speaking: twenty-five years to life for second-degree murder and an additional twenty-three years for first-degree assault. His sentences were to be served consecutively, meaning he would finish his twenty-five years and then remain incarcerated to serve the additional twenty-three years. In essence, what could have been twenty years under the first plea offer became a de facto life sentence.*

*Was Gomez treated unfairly and punitively for not taking the plea deal? After all, the offers were twenty years, then twenty-five years, and then forty-eight to life. In practice, Gomez experienced what legal scholars call the "trial tax" where Gomez might have otherwise secured the "guilty plea discount." This trial tax varies, but defendants who reject a negotiated plea experience a two- to six-times increase in the odds of imprisonment, and a 15–60 percent increase in average sentence length for exercising their constitutional right to a trial by jury (Johnson 2019). In short, defendants who are convicted at trial consistently face substantially longer and more punitive sentences than those who plead guilty in a way that makes it easier, cheaper, and faster for the system. The severity of the trial tax illustrates why the prosecutor is the most powerful person in the courtroom: they decide the initial charges, the plea bargain, and what charges to bring at trial (which largely determines the sentence guidelines range judges will apply if the person is found guilty).*

*At the time of writing, Nicolas Gomez remains incarcerated in New York State and has aged into his forties. He is expected to be deported to Honduras if he ever steps out of prison—back to a place his family fled because of the violence and conditions there. In writing about his case, we note that Gomez unequivocally accepts responsibility for his actions. And we do not mean to excuse his action that violently ended Sheridan's life, but it is also important to explore the ripple effects of harsh and harmful policies that have a multi-decade history, and which created conditions favorable to interpersonal violence.*

*While some may believe life in prison for taking a life is fair, this option is expensive and unnecessary for public safety. Criminologists have shown, for decades, a relationship between crime involvement and age. Men and boys are most likely to engage in interpersonal violence between the ages of fifteen and twenty-five, with sharp and continued decreases in the likelihood of violent and property crime as individuals age. Mr. Gomez is no longer the same person and is no longer at risk for engaging in interpersonal violence. Is Gomez more than his (deadly) mistake as a teenager?*

*Further, Gomez's offense took place just four months after his eighteenth birthday, and if the same crime had taken place before that, his case could have gone through the juvenile justice system. That outcome was not assured because part of the decades-long process of getting tough entailed "waiving" more juvenile cases into the adult system. However the idea of "adult time for adult crime" flies in the face of emerging neuroscience research finding that the brain of an eighteen-year-old still has up to seven years of remaining growth and development, particularly in the area where advanced reasoning, impulse control, and delayed gratification primarily occur. This brings up a range of philosophical and practical questions for legal scholars and juvenile justice practitioners.*

*Indeed, the U.S. Supreme Court has used arguments based on neuroscience to inform decisions like* Roper v. Simmons *(2005; unconstitutional to execute people for crimes committed when they were juveniles),* Graham v. Florida *(2010; unconstitutional to impose a life sentence without parole for a nonhomicidal crime committed as a juvenile), and* Miller v. Alabama *(2012; unconstitutional to impose mandatory life in prison without the possibility of parole for juvenile homicide offenders) (Johnson et al. 2009). Robust empirical scholarship points to the mismatch between legal adulthood (eighteen in most contexts) and the age of full brain development (approximately twenty-five years) (Mercurio et al. 2020), raising further questions about the proper judicial processing of these cases.*

## Introduction

While the police are the most visible representatives of the criminal justice system, the judicial process—charging, bail, plea bargaining, and sentencing—has serious and far-reaching consequences for those entangled in it. Media highlight courtroom drama, but many consequential decisions occur in private and in ways that belie the adversarial nature of courtroom dramas. For instance, the prosecutor's decisions about whether to charge someone with a crime and what crimes to charge them with are dramatic and significant events that do not necessarily make compelling TV. Only about 3–5 percent of criminal cases go to trial, so cases are mostly resolved through a plea-bargaining process with gut-wrenching decisions that happen as part of assembly-line process outside of the public view.

Courtroom dramas usually make the judge seem like the most powerful actor, banging the gavel and putting lawyers in their place as they battle each other. But the reality of plea bargaining is different. The prosecutor, defense attorney, and judge form a "courtroom workgroup," which relies on cooperation, compromise, and shared norms for how cases are approached (Gould and León 2017). Efficiency, to facilitate high caseloads, shapes how individual cases are negotiated, and the reality is "far from adversarial" (Gould and León 2017: 652). The members of the group create cooperative understandings and an "occupational subculture specific to that court." The members even come to agree on penalty ranges and the practical meaning of a "reasonable" versus "excessive" request or position.

Within this group, the prosecutor emerges as the most powerful actor. Their decisions shape which cases come before the work group, and their choice of initial charges shape the final plea, and thus the sentencing guidelines range the judge can impose. One of the few pieces of research to intensively explore the power of prosecutors noted that

> over the 1990s and 2000s, crime fell, arrests fell, and time spent in prison remained fairly steady. But even as the number of arrests declined, the number of felony cases filed in state courts rose sharply. In the end, the probability that a prosecutor would

file felony charges against an arrestee basically doubled, and that change pushed prison populations up even as crime dropped. (Pfaff 2017: 127)

But, for all their power, "there is almost no data or research on what drives them" (Pfaff 2017: 134), so few scholars regularly study prosecutors—and reform proposals rarely mention them.

Immigration enforcement is not typically included in discussions of the criminal justice system. Technically, immigration law is a *civil* and administrative matter, but criminal convictions for immigrants can lead to deportation (Tosh 2019), which the Supreme Court recognizes as "banishment or exile" (*Padilla v. Kentucky*, 08-651 [2010]: note 11). Also, the systems used to detain and deport migrants are, like prisons and jails, inherently punitive and traumatic (Barak 2023). So the immigration regime—immigration laws, courts, and processes—should be understood as a partner to the criminal justice system, intertwined coercive systems in the service of formal social control. But because officially the immigration system is "nonpunitive," immigrant detainees do not have the same protections and procedural safeguards that have been constitutionally guaranteed to criminal defendants. There is no right to counsel (Sixth Amendment), protection from self-incrimination (Fifth Amendment), or presumption of innocence until proven guilty (Fifth Amendment). Judicial review is largely absent, unlike criminal justice–related detention, because immigration law and hearings exist under a doctrine known as plenary power, where the regular courts are deferential to the discretion of the executive and legislative branches of government.

The judicial and immigration processes are like conveyor belts that move some people quickly to the end (prison, deportation) and provide off-ramps for others (Reiman and Leighton 2023: 123–24). These processes contain many different possible steps with implications for class, race, gender/sexuality, and intersectionality. To set a foundation, the next section explores the judicial process, the immigration regime, and their workers. The chapter then examines the effect that class, race, gender/sexuality, and intersections have on the judicial and immigration processes.

## The Judicial Process, Immigration Regimes, and Their Workers

The judicial process involves a number of steps, so the next section discussing it is longer than the comparable sections for the lawmaking and policing chapters. The extended overview highlights the many ways that discretion, coercion, and efficiency lead to unjust outcomes in general. As with the previous two chapters, part of this section explores demographics and dynamics about the class, race, and gender/sexuality of the workers.

### The Judicial Process and Immigration Regimes

The court subsystem consists of four basic stages: charging, pretrial, plea bargaining (or trial), and sentencing. After the suspect is arrested and booked, a prosecutor reviews the facts of the case and the evidence with total discretion about what to do:

Let's say that a person has been arrested for possessing five pounds of weed (in a jurisdiction where marijuana possession and selling is criminalized). The prosecutor can choose not to charge that person (no sentence, obviously), charge them with simple possession (usually a sentence of limited duration or severity), or charge them with possession with intent to distribute, which can require—by statute—several years in prison. Most prosecutor offices are not transparent about what factors would lead them to which charging decision—and that's assuming that the office even has uniform standards. Many don't, and they decide these issues on an ad hoc basis, which risks allowing inappropriate considerations like race to influence who gets charged. (Butler 2021)

Prosecutors are not transparent about which cases they drop and why, so there is no accountability if that discretion is used in a biased way. (The lack of transparency around dropped charges, or a lack of charges, is especially frustrating to many people in cases where they believe video clearly shows police brutality.) If a prosecutor files charges and "a case reaches the courtroom, the prosecutors need not provide a public explanation of why they chose that case over others" (Krieger 2023).

The Sixth Amendment to the Constitution guarantees defendants the right to counsel to people charged with a crime. The 1963 *Gideon v. Wainwright* decision (372 U.S. 335), among other twentieth-century decisions, extended the right to an appointed lawyer to misdemeanors where the punishment includes the possibility of jail time. The right is to "effective assistance of counsel" and also extends to other critical stages: police lineups, custodial interrogations, preliminary hearings, first appeal of a negotiated or postconviction sentence, sentencing hearings, and probation and parole revocation hearings.

Defense attorneys can sometimes receive a "bad rap" for defending obviously guilty (or unpopular) clients or for winning their case through technicalities. However, the right to effective assistance of counsel—and other constitutional rights—would be meaningless if lawyers refused to defend their clients on the grounds that they knew (or believed, or the community generally believed) that a defendant was guilty. Instead, defense attorneys play a critical part of the administration of justice by ensuring evidentiary rigor and procedural justice. They ensure that the prosecutor can make the case beyond a reasonable doubt and thus are an important check on state power (Gould and Barak 2019).

With less serious crimes such as misdemeanors or ordinance violations, the prosecutor prepares a *complaint* specifying that the named person has committed an offense. If the offense is a felony (where the punishment entails a minimum of twelve months of incarceration), then either the prosecutor prepares an *information* or gets the grand jury to issue an *indictment*. After the charge(s) have been filed, the pretrial stages begin, when the suspect becomes a defendant and is brought before a lower-court judge for an *initial appearance*. The defendant is presented with the formal charge(s) and advised of their constitutional rights.

For a misdemeanor or an ordinance violation, a *summary trial* without a jury may be held. For a felony, a *probable cause hearing* is held to determine whether or not there is enough evidence to make a "reasonable person" believe that, more likely than not, the proposed action is justified. In practice, the probable cause standard is "very easily met, allowing prosecutors to 'pile on' charges that they may not be able to prove at trial. This phenomenon, known as 'overcharging,' gives the prosecutor an advantage at the plea-bargaining stage of the process" by incentivizing (scaring) the defendant into pleading guilty to a smaller subset or less serious charge rather than risk a trial on the full set of charges (Davis 2019: 5; Kipnis 2001). Overcharging can and does lead to miscarriages of justice, including both lengthy sentences and innocent defendants taking guilty pleas.

The probable cause hearing also decides whether or not *bail* is appropriate and how much it should be. If bail is denied or set higher than a defendant can afford, they stay in jail even though they have not been convicted. Of the 663,100 people in jail in 2022, 70 percent (466,100) were *not* convicted, and this percentage has increased over the last ten years (BJS 2023a: 3). While a few people are a danger or a flight risk, most people remain in jail because they cannot afford relatively small amounts of bail. Bail is a situation where money quite literally buys someone's freedom (if temporarily), so the poor get punished by remaining incarcerated. (Chapter 3 noted that women, minorities, and the LGBTQ+ community are all disproportionately poor, so bail is class-based policy that leads to intersectional injustice.) That bail so clearly perpetuates class-based injustice makes it a target for reform movements. One progressive prosecutor, for example, "announced that her office would support the release of individuals charged with nonviolent offenses who were detained pretrial because of their inability to post bonds of $1,000 or less" (Davis 2019: 9). While this reform may seem straightforward or even common sense, it requires fighting a profitable bail-bond industry.

Besides keeping people locked up because of their poverty, the bail decision has many significant consequences. If people have a job and do not make bail, they may lose their job, which can also mean losing the place where they live and custody of their children. Also, people who do not make bail cannot help out with their defense by contacting witnesses and gathering evidence, so they are more likely to be convicted or take a bad plea offer (Jones 2013). Research in the *Stanford Law Review* found that "compared to similarly situated releasees, detained defendants [who could not make bail] are 25% more likely to be convicted and 43% more likely to be sentenced to jail, and commit future crimes" (Heaton et al. 2017: 717–18). The "future crimes" happened because "even short-term detention has criminogenic effects," both because of jail conditions and reduced employment options (Heaton 2020: 369).

If the judge finds probable cause, then an indictment or information is filed with the court, and the defendant is scheduled for an *arraignment*. The arraignment informs the defendant of the charges against them and requires them to enter a plea in open court. While defendants plead "not guilty" at early stages, upwards of 95 percent ultimately plead guilty to some charges against them under a *plea bargain*. Although plea bargains are the most common way to resolve cases now, for much of American history they were explicitly prohibited (Kipnis 2001). Gradually, plea bargaining became accepted because of its efficiency, and in a series of cases, the Supreme Court has extended the right of effective assistance of counsel to plea bargaining. In a 2012 case, the defendant's lawyer did not communicate plea offers to him, and the government argued there was no harm done since he had no right to receive a plea offer. But the Court decided that was ineffective assistance of counsel, saying that plea bargaining is "not some adjunct to the criminal justice system; it is the criminal justice system" (*Missouri v. Frye*, No. 10-444 [2012]: 7).

Plea bargaining is necessary to process large numbers of cases, because giving people trials takes more resources—prosecutors, public defenders, judges, and jurors. Of course

> many Americans want government to be efficient and keep costs down. But efficiency in the criminal-justice system has a serious downside: The more easily and cheaply it can be run, the more people end up in it, so it becomes an efficient way to put large numbers of poor and minorities behind bars. (Hessick 2021b)

In contrast, the Supreme Court has generally approved of plea bargains and believes that "properly administered, they can benefit all concerned" (*Bordenkircher v. Hayes* 434 U.S. 357 [1978]: 7).

While the Supreme Court believes that having a lawyer makes the plea knowing and voluntary, they overlook concerns about coercion (Kipnis 2001). For example, in the case where the Court said pleas can benefit all, Hayes tried to pass a bad check for $88 and was offered a plea deal where the prosecutor would recommend five years in prison. The prosecutor said if Hayes did not take the deal, the prosecutor would "seek an indictment under the Kentucky Habitual Criminal Act, which would subject Hayes to a mandatory sentence of life imprisonment by reason of his two prior felony convictions" (*Bordenkircher v. Hayes* 434 U.S. 357 [1978]: 2). (Hayes had a rape conviction from when he was seventeen and a subsequent robbery, for which he was placed on probation.) Hayes, asserting his innocence (*Bordenkircher v. Hayes* 434 U.S. 357 [1978]: 26), went to trial and was convicted and sentenced to life imprisonment with a possibility of parole.

The Court majority upheld the sentence. They said precedents limiting "the evil of prosecutorial vindictiveness" (*Bordenkircher v. Hayes* 434 U.S. 357 [1978]: 6) did not apply to Hayes. Because it was within the prosecutor's discretion to charge under the habitual offender law, Hayes was not being punished for exercising his constitutional right to a jury trial: "in the 'give-and-take' of plea bargaining, there is no such element of punishment or retaliation so long as the accused is free to accept or reject the prosecution's offer" (*Bordenkircher v. Hayes* 434 U.S. 357 [1978]: 10). The majority, citing an earlier case, said that while the risk of more serious punishment at trial "may have a 'discouraging effect on the defendant's assertion of his trial rights, the imposition of these difficult choices [is] an inevitable'—and permissible—'attribute of any legitimate system which tolerates and encourages the negotiation of pleas'" (*Bordenkircher v. Hayes* 434 U.S. 357 [1978]: 12). Others, however, note that there is no right to discovery of evidence with plea bargaining, and the inability to see the prosecution's evidence before deciding increases the risk of coercion and mistakes (Pfaff 2017: 133). Indeed, the inevitability of a public trial was a safeguard on the prosecutor "command[ing] the vast resources of the state" and "the danger that he might bring those resources to bear against an innocent citizen—whether on account of honest error, arbitrariness, or worse. But the plea bargaining system has largely dissolved that safeguard" (in Butler 2013: 2184).

In practice, people confined in jail are most likely to take a plea, even if they are innocent. Defendants also can save additional fees they would have to pay for the court trial. But their guilty plea creates or adds to their criminal history, which can impact their future employment and other areas of life. If they are arrested in the future, that criminal history can increase their bail amount and future sentencing guidelines.

An alternative to a plea bargain is a deferred or nonprosecution agreement, where the prosecutor agrees to drop charges if the defendant stays out of trouble or successfully completes rehabilitative activities. This option is seldom used for poor street criminals but has become a common way to resolve corporate cases, with the agreement involving a fine and promises to implement corporate reforms. Indeed, the Department of Justice (DOJ) has expanded their use, even in the face of criticism that reforms in such promises "are often little more than window-dressing" (in Reilly 2015: 317; Government Accountability Office [GAO] 2009). Even where a negotiated settlement is preferable to a trial, plea bargains can achieve the same reforms and involve some public accountability by being approved by a judge and recorded by the court (Uhlmann 2013). Deferred and nonprosecution agreements are essentially private contracts between prosecutors and defendants.

Defendants found guilty or who take a plea go on to the *sentencing process*, which is done by the judge and/or jury, depending on the jurisdiction. That sentence is based on statutory law and sentencing guidelines. Options here usually consist of *incarceration* in prison (for sentences greater than one year), jail (for sentences less than one year), or some type of community-based sanction like *probation* or GPS monitoring. Once offenders have served out their whole sentence in one form or the other, they will still be subject to "invisible punishments," including exclusion from public housing, denial of student loans, and loss of the right to vote—what are referred to as "collateral consequences." They may also have substantial fees and fines due for their hearings, plea, public defender, incarceration, and probation. These fees can be detrimental to establishing a noncriminal life after incarceration and conviction.

Although largely ignored by mainstream criminology, how the immigration regime works is a reflection on U.S. democracy and is hugely consequential for the twenty-three million people (about 7 percent of the U.S. population) who are noncitizens. Immigration courts make decisions to allow people to stay in the country or be "removed" (deported). These courts are housed within the Department of Justice, which has an Executive Office for Immigration Review (EOIR), and the vast majority of cases are deportation hearings (Barak 2023: 37). Some see this structure as problematic because immigration judges are appointed by the nation's top prosecutor—the attorney general. Indeed, "the Attorney General may vacate any decision of the Board [of Immigration Appeals] and issue their own decision in its place" (Department of Justice 2023). Also, "at the discretion of the Attorney General (AG), cases assigned to one judge can be withdrawn and assigned to another" (TRAC, n.d.). Since the attorney general serves at the pleasure of the president, immigration courts are more political, and proposed legislation like the Real Courts, Rule of Law Act of 2022 seeks to create independent immigration courts similar to tax courts, bankruptcy courts, and the Court of Appeals for Veterans Claims (American Immigration Lawyers Association 2023).

In immigration court, the U.S. government is represented by an attorney from a division of the Department of Homeland Security or the DOJ. But unlike criminal courts, where a defense attorney is appointed at government expense for the poor, "immigrants—even unaccompanied children—have no legal right to an attorney if they cannot afford to hire one" (TRAC, n.d.). In other ways, too, immigrants typically have far fewer due process protections and legal resources to advocate on their behalf (Barak 2023). Indeed, even immigrants filing for asylum because they are fleeing violence must provide their own interpreters (8 C.F.R. § 208.9[g]). For example, Deisy was an unaccompanied child from Central America who had a nonprofit organization help her with an asylum petition, but the nonprofit could not find a professional interpreter given the short notice of the hearing:

> Frantic, they contacted me, a non-native and non-professional Spanish speaker, to ask if I could help. I agreed, and met Deisy at the Asylum Office. During the three hours of her interview, Deisy dutifully responded to the asylum officers' questions. As she articulated the violence that she fled, her eyes never wavered from mine. The intensity of her gaze seemed to carry a pleading, insistent message: "Please be my voice. Please get this right." (Mellinger 2022)

## Judicial Process Workers

The criminal court process relies on lawyers and nonlawyers. The nonlawyers are primarily bailiffs, stenographers, and court administrators, but they also include occupations like victim and domestic violence advocates. With the exception of bailiffs, the other nonlawyers (especially stenographers) are primarily women and white. The educational backgrounds of these nonlawyers vary greatly, from those with a high school diploma or GED to those with undergraduate and postgraduate degrees. These judicial workers' annual incomes place them in the working and middle classes.

The lawyers—prosecution, defense, and judges—are more consequential for the process. These key players have overwhelmingly graduated from a four-year college or university as well as a three-year law school and have passed a state bar examination to be certified to practice law. The larger legal profession from which these criminal justice workers are drawn is still largely white and male, although gender representation is changing. In 1970, only 3 percent of lawyers were women, but that increased to 39 percent by 2023 (American Bar Association [ABA] 2023). In 2022, women were 56 percent of law school students, so the percentage of female lawyers should continue to increase.

Women are underrepresented among senior partners of law firms, and the ABA (2023) survey found "virtually no women among the very highest-compensated law firm attorneys in 2020. Only 2 percent of law firms said their highest-paid attorney is female—and that number actually dropped from 8 percent in 2005. Women were advocates involved in arguing before the Supreme Court in 12 to 22 percent of the cases, but most were "public interest lawyers, public defenders representing the criminally convicted or government lawyers. Translation: Women are doing the same work but for less pay" (Liptak 2022).

People of color were 21 percent of the legal profession in 2023 (ABA 2023). The ABA survey found that the "number of Black lawyers is virtually unchanged," from 4.7 percent in 2012 to 5 percent of the profession in 2023. Minorities who are senior partners increased slowly over decades, from less than 3 percent in 1993 to 11.4 percent in 2022 (ABA 2023). Asians were the largest share of law firm partners of color, while they represented 6 percent of all lawyers overall—about the same percentage as Hispanics. "One-half of 1% of all lawyers (0.5%) were Native American in 2022—nearly unchanged from 0.6% a decade earlier" (ABA 2023). In 2022, 4.2 percent of lawyers working at surveyed law firms reported being LGBTQ+, about double the level of ten years earlier (ABA 2023).

Within the criminal justice system, prosecutors may be called the district attorney (or DA), county attorney, or state's attorney. They are generally elected and employed by a county to prosecute violations of state laws, and most crimes violate state law. Regardless of the name, the prosecutor holds the most power relative to the judge and the defense attorney. Not surprisingly, then, women, Blacks, Hispanics, and other minorities have been highly underrepresented as prosecutors. So the reality is a substantial gap between the majority of white, middle-class prosecutors and the overwhelmingly indigent white and minority defendants.

Importantly, a study of wrongful convictions involving African American men reported that prosecutorial misconduct was a factor in 36 percent of the wrongful murder convictions and 15 percent of the rape and sexual assault cases (Free and Ruesink 2012). Overall, they concluded, "the lack of diversity among actors in the criminal justice system makes it easier for nonwhites to be processed through the system without the necessary safeguards to minimize the probability of a wrongful conviction" (Free and Ruesink 2012: 196). However, Butler—the Black former prosecutor who wrote *Chokehold* (2017) that opened the last chapter—indicates that it is not so easy. He took the prosecutor's job "hoping I could create change from within" and "help keep Black people as safe as possible in a racist criminal justice system" (Butler 2021). What he found was that "rather than changing the system, the system was changing me" because "the way for a young lawyer to move up in the prosecutor's office was to lock up as many people as possible, for as long as possible."

Because chief prosecutors for each county are elected, partisan politics is important in the recruitment of prosecutors, both county and federal. For attorneys with any political ambitions, choosing to work as a district attorney is a wise decision. People standing up for victims and engaged in the "war on crime" are well positioned to run for higher office, although many run unopposed after getting elected and serve for decades (Pfaff 2017: 139). While federal prosecutors oversee a much smaller percentage of cases, they involve significant issues like corporate crime, internet crime, and political corruption. Violations of federal law are prosecuted by ninety-three U.S. attorneys (one assigned to each of the federal district court jurisdictions), all nominated by the president and confirmed by the Senate. They supervise assistant U.S. attorneys and are part of the DOJ, overseen by the attorney general.

Although the attorney general and the U.S. attorneys are political appointments, "overtly political prosecutions are the purview of non-democratic countries" (Krieger 2023: 34). While far from absolute, Congress and most presidents have not tried to direct prosecutors to indict their perceived enemies and generally respect a norm of prosecutorial independence. However, "the strength of this norm has been tested by President Donald Trump's efforts to thwart it" and his belief that "I have absolute right to do what I want with the Justice Department" (Krieger 2023: 34). (His subsequent claims that the criminal indictments against him represent the "weaponization" of the Justice Department suggest that he sees himself as the victim of what he believes he had a right to do, and Trump has threatened to prosecute Biden if he wins the presidency while claiming absolute immunity for any wrongdoing he did as president [Feuer and Haberman 2024].[1])

Prosecutors work closely with defense counsel, who may be privately retained attorneys, court-appointed lawyers, or public defenders. Criminal defense lawyers (except for white-collar criminal defense) tend to have less status than prosecutors or judges. Current Supreme Court justice Ketanji Brown Jackson (the first Black woman justice to sit on the high court) is the first justice with defense attorney experience (Savage 2022). The knowledge and skills of defense attorneys are increasingly recognized as important to those who want to reform the criminal justice system (Lowell 2022). However, most people tend to see them as sympathetic to criminals and criminal interests, although white-collar and corporate criminal defense firms tend to be high prestige. Many federal prosecutors become highly paid corporate defense attorneys, and their firms are influential in policy making about business regulation (Krieger 2023).

Although the backgrounds of criminal defense attorneys are similar to those of prosecutors, defense attorneys are generally less connected to the local political scene. Unlike prosecutors and judges, criminal defenders of all types are not elected public officials (whose employment is based on approval ratings). They are all private citizens whether they are self-employed or salaried employees of local government's public defender service, so their chief alliances are with the vagaries of the legal marketplace or the civil service system to which they belong. Because 80 percent of state prison inmates were too poor to afford their own attorneys, they relied on one of three types of criminal attorneys: a court-appointed lawyer, a public defender, or a contract lawyer. Most criminal defense attorneys practice for many years as career civil servants in the public defender's offices, justifying their roles "as mediators between the poor and the courts, resigned to seeking occasional loopholes in the system, softening its more explicitly repressive features, and attempting to rescue the victims of blatant injustices" (Platt and Pollock 1974: 27).

Compared with the funding for prosecutors' offices, public defense is underfunded and perpetually in crisis. Because the public defender system has been in crisis for decades (Gross 2023), the situation feels more normal than problematic. The underlying problem is that "consistent underfunding of indigent defense has regularly led to excessive caseloads that hinder the quality of representation" (Gottlieb 2021). In 2022, the average annual salary of a public defender was $59,700, which is lower than it was in 2004 when inflation is taken into account (Gross 2023). Assigned counsel do not fare much better: "in the State of New York, the hourly rate paid to assigned counsel has not increased since 2004, which has caused a shortage of lawyers willing to accept appointments" (Gross 2023).

Studies based on the time use of private attorneys on criminal cases indicate that "the typical public defender had two to three times the workload they should have in order to provide an adequate defense" (Oppel and Patel 2019). An ABA workload project in Oregon "found that the 592 attorneys with whom the state contracts to provide public defense would have to work over 26 hours every day of the year to provide adequate assistance of counsel based on the number of cases they are currently handling" and would need to hire an *additional* 1,296 full-time equivalent attorneys "to have an indigent defense system that ensures adequate representation" (Gross 2023). Workload analysis in other states shows similar results, so "in almost three-quarters of county public defender offices, attorney caseloads are greater than the maximum recommended" (Gottlieb 2021). When public defender offices have refused to take more cases because of overwork, they have received little support from judges or legislators. Some underresourced public defender offices have been punished by being held in contempt of court for refusing to take additional cases. In addition, while prosecutors' offices have investigation help from the police, less than two-thirds of public defender offices employ investigators (Gottlieb 2021).

The vast majority of judges at the state level oversee trial courts of general jurisdiction, with substantially fewer sitting on appellate courts or state supreme courts. Judges who oversee most felony cases sit on the benches of what are variously called "district," "superior," or "circuit" courts. There are more than three thousand such courts, which have the authority to try both civil and criminal matters. They also hear appeals from trial courts of limited jurisdiction (i.e., city courts, municipal courts, county courts, justice-of-the-peace courts, magistrate courts) that primarily handle misdemeanors, traffic violations, and ordinance offenses.

In most jurisdictions, before being elected or appointed to office, the judges will have practiced law, but many of them will have no background in criminal law before joining the judiciary. In jurisdictions where judges are elected to office, these may be partisan or nonpartisan elections. Where city councils, mayors, legislatures, or governors appoint judges, they are subject to the politics of local and state bar associations. Like prosecutors, then, whether elected or appointed, judges are also sensitive to the political process that generally serves the interests of the privileged people who elected or appointed them rather than the goals of justice for the marginalized.

Compared to prosecutors and defenders, trial judges command more respect, status, and deference from citizens at large. According to imagery, judges are presumed to have enormous power, although judicial discretion is far more limited than prosecutorial discretion because judges are subject to appeal and legal review by higher courts. Sentencing guidelines, while technically "advisory," exert a great deal of control over the outcome. Since more than 95 percent of criminal cases are resolved by plea bargains, a judge's principal role becomes that of a "bureaucratic stamp" for negotiated deals, and this description from more than forty years ago is still accurate:

> Judges, like many factory workers, sit on an assembly line. They repeatedly perform routine tasks, with each task consuming only a fraction more than a minute. For such judges, the role is exactly the opposite of the intellectual challenge a judgeship is presumed to pose. (Jacob [1973] 1980: 67)

The levels of diversity in federal and state courts continues to expand, but table 9.1 shows that whites and men are still disproportionately overrepresented. State courts and state supreme courts vary greatly in diversity. In several states, more than 40 percent of the state supreme court identify as a person of color. But "in 20 states, no state supreme court justices publicly identify as a person of color, including in 12 states where people of color make up at least 20 percent of the population. Notably, 15 states have never had a Black supreme court

**TABLE 9.1  Demographics of the Federal Judiciary and State Supreme Courts**

|  | Federal Courts (All Levels) (%) | State Supreme Court (%) |
| --- | --- | --- |
| Male | 68.0 | 59 |
| Female | 32.0 | 41 |
| White | 75.7 | 83.5 |
| Black | 11.5 | 9.4 |
| Hispanic | 7.3 | 5.8 |
| Asian American | 3.6 | 2.6 |
| Native American | 0.3 | 1.2 |

*Sources:* American Bar Association 2023; Powers and Bannon 2022.

*Note:* Federal data is for October 1, 2023, and state data is for May 2022. Because of overlapping racial categories, totals exceed 100 percent. For the federal courts, 1.7 percent identify as "mixed race or ethnicity or other."

**TABLE 9.2  Demographics of Federal Judicial Confirmations by the Past Four Presidents**

|  | Biden | Trump | Obama | Bush II |
| --- | --- | --- | --- | --- |
| Male | 37% | 76% | 58% | 78% |
| Female | 63% | 24% | 42% | 22% |
| White | 39% | 84% | 64% | 82% |
| African American | 29% | 4% | 19% | 7% |
| Hispanic | 18% | 4% | 11% | 9% |
| Asian, Hawaiian, Pacific Islander | 18% | 6% | 7% | 1% |
| Native American | 2% | 0% | 0.3% | 0% |
| Openly gay and lesbian | 6% | 0.1% | 3% | 0% |
| TOTAL CONFIRMED JUDGES | 188 | 229 | 324 | 324 |

*Sources:* American Bar Association 2023; Avery 2019; Chavez and Choi 2024; analysis of Federal Judicial Center, n.d.; Samuels 2023.

*Note:* Because people of mixed race are counted in more than one category, totals exceed 100 percent.

justice" (Powers and Bannon 2022). With the federal courts, diversity expands under Democratic presidents, as shown in table 9.2. For example, from January 1, 2021, to October 1, 2023—the Senate confirmed 140 federal judges appointed by President Biden, and "only 14 (10% of new federal judges) were white men" (ABA 2023).

## Class and the Judicial Process

As with class bias in policing, class bias in prosecution and the judicial process takes two main forms. The first is that for street crimes and drugs, poor people are more likely to be charged and to be carried further into the system than wealthy people. The second is that for many corporate crimes, historic norms of weak enforcement have been further eroded. Corporations are more likely to face civil than criminal suits, and individual executives are rarely charged criminally. Settlements involve regulatory theater, with large-sounding fines that represent a small amount of the gains from wrongdoing; corporations promise not to break the law again . . . and break the law again . . . and promise not to break the law again . . . and break the law again.

The last chapter on policing discussed how the wealthy students in *Dorm Room Dealers* were the "anti-targets" of the drug war. In spite of their "brazen" illegality, only a few dealers ended up in the criminal justice system (Mohamed and Fritsvold 2011: 173). One large-scale marijuana dealer, operating before the drug became legal, was charged with what the authors call "relatively serious drug and weapons offenses." He ended up with a "possession ticket" and no weapons charges because "I got real good lawyers [laughs]" (2011: 159). Another dealer was caught with over one hundred marijuana plants and $30,000 in growing equipment, but his parents hired a "high-profile private defense attorney" and horticultural and biological sciences experts plus "various psychiatrists." He ended up with an eighteen-month "diversion program" that resulted in no jail time, and all records were expunged when he successfully completed the program, so someone running a criminal history check would find nothing about this incident (Mohamed and Fritsvold 2011: 161, 167).

For drug offenses, these students had better representation than poor people facing murder charges. For example, Robert Wayne Holsey was convicted of murder, and his "trial lawyer later admitted that at the time he [the lawyer] was drinking up to a quart of vodka daily and facing theft charges that would land him in prison. He said he should not have been representing a client" (Eckholm 2014). Even though he was later disbarred and criminally convicted, the lawyer's defense was found to be adequate and Holsey was executed. While this case seems extreme, it was not considered an exceptional one rising to the level of ineffective assistance of counsel because serious problems are widespread. For example, "some judges have ruled that taking illegal drugs, driving to court drunk or briefly falling asleep at the defense table—even during critical testimony—did not make a lawyer inadequate" (Oppel and Patel 2019). Although this "uncontained crisis" should call into "question the legitimacy of our justice system [and] our commitment to our constitution" (Gross 2023), it does not because cheap and efficient processing of the poor is the primary value.

The liberal perspective on this problem celebrates *Gideon v. Wainwright* (which gave the poor the right to an attorney) and wants to fix the public defender system. In contrast, a critical legal theory perspective tries to make sense of how "fifty years after *Gideon*, poor people have both the right to counsel and the most massive level of incarceration in the world" (Butler 2013: 2191). Perhaps the "reform" mandated by *Gideon* helped legitimate mass incarceration because providing lawyers for the poor created the illusion the system was fair:

> If prosecutors had brought most of their cases against the poor during the
> pre-*Gideon* era when most indigent defendants did not have lawyers, prosecutors
> would have looked like bullies. Since *Gideon*, the percentage of prosecutions against
> the poor has increased from 43% to 80% . . . but now, because of *Gideon*, they
> look less like bullies. (Butler 2013: 2197–98)

Both the rich and poor have criminal defense attorneys, and with this appearance
of equality, "the vast overrepresentation of the poor in America's prisons appears
more like a narrative about personal responsibility than an indictment of criminal
justice" (Butler 2013: 2197). According to the critical perspective, the larger issue
is that prisons are filled with poor people "because prison is for the poor, and not
the rich":

> Poor people lose, most of the time, because in American criminal justice, poor peo-
> ple are losers. Prison is designed for them. This is the real crisis of indigent defense.
> *Gideon* obscures this reality, and in this sense stands in the way of the political
> mobilization that will be required to transform criminal justice. (Butler 2013: 2178)

While the critical analysis of *Gideon* recognizes that increasing the quality of
public defenders will make a difference to some individuals (Butler 2013), the larger
perspective must also recognize that corporate criminals face record low rates of
criminal prosecution, and they have experienced former prosecutors working as
their defense lawyers for other types of charges. Indeed, a site that compiles federal
statistics proclaimed that "Corporate and White-Collar Prosecutions Hit New All-
Time Lows in FY [fiscal year] 2022" (TRAC 2023), which is similar to headlines of
the last several years noting all-time low prosecutions since record keeping began
in the 1980s. Prosecutions hit an all-time high of 10,162 in 2011, and they have
fallen to 4,180 white-collar defendants in 2022 (TRAC 2023), out of almost 72,000
federal criminal cases that year (Gramlich 2023). While 96 percent of immigration
referrals to federal prosecutors resulted in a prosecution, only 38 percent of white-
collar and corporate referrals did.

Eisinger's creatively titled book *The Chickenshit Club: Why the Justice Department Fails to Prosecute Executives* (2017) refers to prosecutors who proudly raised
their hands when asked who had a record of no acquittals or hung juries. Rather
than being celebrated for their no-loss record, they were called out for not taking on
tough cases that should have been prosecuted. Eisinger and others trace the decline
in prosecutions to a few high-profile losses by the DOJ, which made them more risk
averse. Funding also declined for white-collar crime prosecution—moving to anti-
terrorism, immigration, and drug cases—making it harder to bring complex cases.
In contrast to how courts have expanded police powers over the poor, they have
been "broadening corporate and executive rights and privileges, narrowing white-
collar criminal statutes and repeatedly overturning federal prosecutors in notable
white collar cases." In the face of these pressures, "prosecutors switched to a regime
of almost exclusively settling with corporations for money" (Eisinger 2017: xviii).

The lack of prosecutions is not the result of an absence of criminal activity
by financial institutions and their executives. Judge Rakoff (2013) notes that the
final report of the bipartisan Financial Crisis Inquiry Commission "uses variants
of the word 'fraud' no fewer than 157 times in describing what led to the crisis."

Big financial institutions each paid billions in fines, so "how is it possible that you can have this much fraud and not a single person has done anything criminal?" (Ramirez and Ramirez 2017: 207).

Also, the global financial institution HSBC was caught helping Mexican drug traffickers, rogue regimes, and terrorist organizations launder money—and they actively worked to enable billions in transactions in violation of the Trading with the Enemy Act (Senate Permanent Subcommittee on Investigations 2012). HSBC deliberately understaffed anti–money laundering positions so they could save on labor costs while profiting from the financial services they offered to big-time global criminals. HSBC received a fine of $1.9 billion, although their annual profits around that time were $22 billion. Under the Deferred Prosecution Agreement, the DOJ agreed to drop all criminal charges in exchange for organizational reforms, and no executives went to jail for profiting from and helping out drug traffickers, organized crime syndicates, and terrorist organizations (Smythe 2013). Indeed,

> the stiffest penalty doled out to any individual for the biggest drug-money-laundering case in history—during which time HSBC had become the "preferred financial institution" of drug traffickers, according to the Justice Department—involved an agreement to "partially defer bonus compensation for its most senior executives." If bankers can't get time for washing money for people who put torture videos on the internet, what can they get time for? (Taibbi 2020)

Consider, too, this comment from a police officer at the shareholder's meeting of a firm investing in Wells Fargo:

> The Star Performers Investment Club has 30 partners, all of whom are active or retired San Francisco police officers. Several of our members have worked in the fraud detail, and have often commented after the yearslong fraudulent behavior of Wells Fargo employees—should have warranted jail sentences for several dozen, yet Wells just pays civil penalties and changes management. (Bustillos 2020)

Indeed, Wells Fargo's 2020 deferred prosecution agreement was a multibillion-dollar settlement that covered *fifteen years* of wrongdoing (Department of Justice 2020c). It also came after numerous other consent decrees, including four other significant ones, each covering multiple years of wrongdoing, containing commitments not to break the law again, and requiring the bank to have better oversight to prevent further violations (Bustillos 2020).

The pattern of promising not to break the law again, but breaking the law again without prosecution, is unfortunately common among corporations and stands in contrast to the tough-on-crime, zero-tolerance policies prosecutors apply against the poor. For example, Judge Rakoff rejected a proposed settlement involving the SEC and Citicorp, noting that Citigroup's promise not to violate the law in the future was the kind of relief that "Citigroup (a recidivist) knew that the S.E.C. had not sought to enforce against any financial institution for at least the last 10 years" (*U.S. Securities and Exchange Commission v. Citigroup Global Markets* 2011: 11). Further, a *New York Times* investigation found that Citigroup "agreed not to violate the very same antifraud statute in July 2010. And in May 2006. Also as far as back as March 2005 and April 2000" (Wyatt 2011). The *Times* found that nineteen companies were repeat offenders who had promised not to do it again.

Although prosecutors do not care about the financial impact of fines and fees on poor street criminals (and their families), Obama's assistant attorney general for the Criminal Division noted in one post–financial crisis settlement: "Our goal here is not to destroy a major financial institution" (Taibbi 2020). A white-collar crime columnist said "regulators spoke often about the need to carefully construct settlements, so that even repeat offenders might remain viable" (Taibbi 2020). This means that rather than being adversarial, the system "ends up serving as a de facto partner for banks that all but admit they're taking in money from Ponzi schemers, mobsters, drug lords, and rogue states" (Taibbi 2020; Douglas 2013).

These problems are likely to persist and become more significant. The mergers that happened in the aftermath of the financial crisis, and growth since then, have made large firms even larger—thus too big to fail and too big to jail (Taibbi 2011). Nonfinancial firms also have been getting larger. Concentrated power works in its own interest, and "the essential purpose of law is to curb and channel the exercise of power as productively as possible for the benefit of society as a whole." The consistent "core problem is that financial elites dominate the law and can subvert it for profit" (Ramirez and Ramirez 2017: 204)—only it is not just financial elites.

## Race and the Judicial Process

Michelle Alexander notes that "immunizing prosecutors from claims of racial bias and failing to impose any meaningful check on the exercise of their discretion . . . has created an environment in which conscious and unconscious biases are allowed to flourish" (2012: 117). This is contrary to prosecutorial discretion in countries such as France and Italy; in Germany, judges, victims, and defendants may legally challenge the prosecutor's discretion in individual cases (Ma 2008).

This discretion leads to harsher outcomes for racial and ethnic minorities. An overview of research about disproportionate minority contact (DMC) stated that "79 percent of the [107] studies found at least some race effect disadvantaging minority youth" at some stage of processing (Spinney et al. 2018). The National Research Council's extensive review found that "blacks were treated less favorably than whites at a number of stages—for example, in pretrial detention decisions, prosecutorial charging decisions, and decisions to impose community rather than incarcerative punishments—and that the cumulative effect of small differences at each stage was substantial" (2014: 98). In addition to highlighting the importance of *cumulative disadvantage* as bias accumulates through the stages of the criminal legal system, the panel noted an "*increasing disjunction* between racial patterns in crime and imprisonment" (National Research Council 2014: 96, emphasis added). The increasing punishment of Black people happened—and continues to happen—in spite of policies like sentencing guidelines that were supposed to help minimize the effects of race. Further, Spohn (2017: 182; 2000) has been doing high-level reviews of the literature on discrimination and observes:

> Studies of sentences imposed under federal and state guidelines reveal that blacks and Hispanics continue to receive harsher outcomes than whites, and research focusing on mandatory minimum sentences, three-strikes provisions, and habitual offender laws also find that the application of these provisions disadvantages racial

minorities. These findings imply that prosecutors and judges are reluctant to base sentences on only crime seriousness and prior criminal record and that statutorily irrelevant factors such as race and ethnicity (as well as sex, age, and social class) may be factually relevant to criminal justice officials' assessments of dangerousness, threat, and culpability.

Such overviews are important because there is a great deal of research on racial disparities in each of these stages, and it takes someone who is widely read to sort out the larger patterns from idiosyncratic findings. In general, the bias found in studies is attributed to how the courtroom work group deals with the "focal concerns" of case processing: "defendant 'blameworthiness,' community protection, and practical constraints and considerations" (Lanuza et al. 2023: 279). From bail and charging decisions to guilt and punishment, "judges, prosecutors, and other relevant courtroom actors rely on racialized notions of 'blameworthiness,' 'dangerousness,' and recidivism as 'perceptual shorthands' to inform their discretion in making punishment decisions, particularly in cases with a lack of complete information and in organizational contexts where decisions must be made quickly" (Lanuza et al. 2023: 279).

Within this larger context, a few more specific points are worth highlighting. First, an earlier part of the chapter noted the importance of pretrial detention (not making bail), and research finds disparities in the "gray areas" rather than high-risk defendants (Skeem et al. 2023). Jurisdictions that detain many people have low levels of disparity because all defendants are treated harshly. But a review by the Urban Institute states: "People of color are not only more likely to be denied bail altogether, but are also more likely to receive higher bail amounts than white people and are often less likely to be able to afford it" (Nembhard and Robin 2021: 5) because of job employment discrimination.

Second, some research finds that prosecutors are most likely to drop the charges of Black people, but this action is correcting police officers who made arrests for reasons that were not solid; it is not leniency. When federal prosecutors have charges they can work with, they "are more likely to charge Black people with offenses that carry higher mandatory minimums than white people who are similarly situated, and in state courts, prosecutors are more likely to charge Black people under habitual-offender laws than white people" (Nembhard and Robin 2021: 5).

Third, in addition to racial bias, colorism—the relative privilege afforded to lighter-skinned people in all racial groups—applies to charging, bail, plea bargaining, and sentencing. Colorism also means that darker skin tones and more stereotypical African American features are associated with "severity of prison terms, and likelihood of receiving a death sentence" (Lanuza et al. 2023: 277). Most of the research about colorism in the U.S. criminal justice system discussed in previous chapters of this book has been based on skin color differences within African Americans; however, the same patterns apply to the Latino/a/x population. For example, a study in Miami found that the likelihood of conviction increased by 17.5 percentage points when comparing the lightest to darkest defendants. When applying this to the larger sample of 15,720 people, "an estimated 2,751 additional people would be convicted if the lightest-skinned defendants (skin tone 1) were punished at the same rate as those with the darkest skin (skin tone 7)" (Lanuza et al. 2023: 284).

A similar percentage point gap appeared between lighter and darker defendants with the decision to incarcerate, so "an estimated 721 additional defendants would be incarcerated" if the lightest-skinned defendants were punished like the darkest-skinned ones (Lanuza et al. 2023: 284). That is just in Miami.

Fourth, while racially disproportionate prosecutions and sentencing for drugs receive a great deal of attention, Second Amendment issues with prosecutions for gun ownership receive little attention (Anderson 2021). Many poor minorities live in neighborhoods where they carry guns for protection, even if they are legally prohibited because of past criminal convictions or do not have hundreds of dollars for licensing fees. But conviction of a weapons offense in such circumstances is considered a violent crime, even if the gun is not actually used, and carries significant consequences. Indeed, in a Supreme Court case involving New York's licensing requirement, a brief by the Black Attorneys of Legal Aid (2021: 5) noted that the requirement and selective prosecution of minorities "renders the Second Amendment a legal fiction" for them. They tell the story of Sophia Johnson, a single parent who had experienced domestic violence and sexual assault, who legally purchased a firearm for protection that she kept locked and unloaded. After she moved to New York, she was in an abusive relationship with a man who stole her gun. She reported it to the police, who

> arrested her. The prosecution charged her with a felony for owning the gun. They prosecuted her using her own statement to the police, where she affirmed that the gun was hers and that she had bought it out-of-state for her own protection. (Black Attorneys of Legal Aid 2021: 26)

The end result of these processes is that minorities—especially darker-skinned ones—are more likely to have a criminal history and a more serious one, which has several important additional impacts. In *The New Jim Crow*, Alexander (2012) argues that illegal discrimination against Black people has been replaced by legal discrimination against Black criminals. Once Black people are labeled as "criminals," then various agencies can "engage in all the discriminatory practices we supposedly left behind." Black people with criminal records are subject to "legalized discrimination in employment, housing, education, public benefits and jury service, just as their parents, grandparents and great-grandparents once were" (Alexander 2012: 1–2). Also, the criminal record and its severity impacts possible future charging, bail, and sentencing decisions. Programs to divert people from prison into community-based alternatives have "eligibility criteria, like having a clean record, [which] already favors white defendants, since decades of research indicates people of color are more likely to accumulate prior records" (TCR Staff 2021). With both structured questionnaires and algorithms, criminal history may generate racial and color disparities because it is accorded too much weight given its limited ability to predict serious reoffending and failure to appear (Skeem et al. 2023).

Structured questionnaires to help criminal justice workers and judges with decisions are being replaced by algorithms, raising concerns that data reflecting racial bias and colorism are being used to train algorithms in ways that replace existing discrimination with "algorithmic discrimination" (Huq 2019: 4). Algorithms are the equations that help rank search results, recommend movies and songs—and also provide criminal justice risk assessments for bail and sentencing recommendations.

Algorithms are often discussed as artificial intelligence (AI) because computers can scour large data sets and engage in "deep learning" to figure out patterns. But if the data contain patterns of discrimination, the algorithm "learns" these patterns, which become the basis for a supposedly "objective" recommendation. When white engineers first developed Google's algorithm for tagging family photos, there was "a consistent problem whereby black people were being labelled gorillas" (O'Neil 2017). AI still has an "inability to recognize let alone distinguish between dark-skinned faces," which leads to harmful consequences for Black and Brown people, "ranging from everyday inconveniences to wrongful arrests" (Dias 2023).

Further, "Google searches for names perceived to be black generated ads associated with criminal activity," like for criminal background checks. Also, "the Google image search result for 'unprofessional hair,' which returned almost exclusively black women, is similarly trained by the people posting or clicking on search results throughout time" (O'Neil 2017). AI-based chatbots used by doctors were trained on material that had racial biases in it, so the chatbots "could potentially cause harm by perpetuating debunked, racist ideas" (Omiye at al. 2023). Both within and outside of criminal justice, algorithms and AI are trained on data reflecting racism and by people who have conscious or unconscious bias, which "embed[s] discrimination leading to disproportionate harms for minoritized social identities" (Dias 2023).

Criminologists generally recognize that the criminal justice system reflects racial bias—the question is how much. So training algorithms on criminal justice data to see who is likely to be rearrested in the future builds the racism of the existing system into terrorist profiles, risk assessments for bail, predictive policing software, and sentencing tools. Even if such algorithms are told not to use race, they may "pinpoint reliable proxies" because "machine-learning tools are powerful and useful precisely because they can detect regularities in a data-set" (Huq 2019: 37). Further, the data behind algorithms and the weighing for each factor are considered a commercial secret that cannot be disclosed to defendants: "A secret risk assessment algorithm that offers a damning score is analogous to evidence offered by an anonymous expert, whom one cannot cross-examine" (Pasquale 2017; Huq 2019). This also prevents a judge from creating a full public record of their reasoning, which is necessary for a meaningful appeal. Challenges under the equal protection clause require proof of discriminatory intent, but algorithms simply make recommendations based on patterns in data and do not have intent, so "constitutional law does not contain effectual tools to meet these problems" of algorithm discrimination (Huq 2019: 54).

Finally, for some immigrants, deportation is part of the collateral consequences of a criminal conviction. That is, the criminal court judge does not sentence a defendant to deportation, but a guilty plea to certain charges can mean that the federal government will file a removal petition and start deportation hearings. The Supreme Court has recognized that deportation may be more consequential than other aspects of the criminal sentence, and thus that effective assistance of counsel requires the attorney to provide some basic advice to a noncitizen about the possibility of deportation. The case involved a man named Padilla, who had been in the United States for forty years and served "with honor" in the military during the Vietnam War (*Padilla v. Kentucky* 559 U.S. 356 [2010]). He was caught with a "large amount" of marijuana, and his attorney advised him that he "did not have to worry about immigration status since he had been in the country so long," but the drug charges made his deportation virtually mandatory. The Supreme Court, while not using the term "crimmigration," based its opinion on the increased toughness of the laws and the dramatic expansion of the number and types of offenses triggering mandatory deportation: "The 'drastic measure' of deportation or removal is now virtually inevitable for a vast number of noncitizens convicted of crimes" (*Padilla v. Kentucky* 2010).

That deportation is "virtually inevitable" reinforces a key point about the limits of public defenders given the coercion of plea bargaining: they can advise, but there is little they can do about the ultimate "criminal-conviction-based deportation" (Tosh 2023). Under immigration law, deportation is especially likely for "aggravated felonies," although this serious-sounding category includes misdemeanors like check fraud and shoplifting. Immigration lawyers call this the "immigration death penalty" because people—whether documented or not—when convicted of an "aggravated felony" become ineligible for legal relief from removal/deportation proceedings (Tosh 2023). Even immigrants applying for asylum because they fear violence, death, or torture if they are returned to their country lose the right to apply for asylum and are deported, making this process a "death penalty."

More generally, in the immigration courts, immigrants—whether they have been convicted of a crime or not—have no rights to counsel or even people to translate for them. Virtual hearings are often mandatory, without detailed guidelines for judges about how to protect the rights of those appearing virtually and who may not be seen in the same way as if they appeared in person (American Immigration Lawyers Association 2022). Further, Barak (2023), among other contemporary scholars, finds that case backlogs and underresourced court systems result in asylum claims and stays of removal (i.e., appeals that prevent someone from being deported) being given insufficient attention (Kanno-Youngs 2023).

A report on New York's Asylum Office, for example, found "asylum officers rejecting legally sound asylum claims, simply because granting a case takes more time," and "Asylum Officers claimed that they worked under the constant threat of losing their jobs, or fac[ed] other retaliation from upper management, if they could not sustain a pace that they described as unrealistic and punishing" (in Oakre 2023). One former New York asylum officer noted that one impact of their experience at the asylum office "is how cynical it made me about the system in its entirety. . . . It really just undermined a lot of my faith in the rule of law . . . and in the legitimacy of American institutions" (Oakre 2023).

## Gender and the Judicial Process

The Supreme Court in *Gideon* decided that a poor (white) man having an attorney to represent him in a criminal case was a matter of fundamental fairness, in part because of the resources the government had to prosecute him. But when the state, represented by an experienced prosecutor, sought to permanently cut the parental bond between Abby Lassiter and her son, the Supreme Court said the (Black) woman had no right to an attorney provided by the state. To the Court, "fundamental fairness" required providing a lawyer only "where the litigant may lose his physical liberty if he loses the litigation" (*Lassiter v. Dep't of Soc. Servs.*, 452 U.S.

18 at 25 [1981]). Why isn't the termination of parental rights, where women are the vast majority of defendants, considered as serious as, say, a misdemeanor punished by thirty days in jail, where men are the vast majority of defendants? Apparently, "a man's physical liberty is the only interest important enough to trigger a right to counsel" (Sabbeth and Steinberg 2023: 1174).

The denial of an appointed attorney also applies in cases of eviction and debt collection, where women are also disproportionately defendants because of their lower pay and where landlords and debt holders are represented by attorneys (Sabbeth and Steinberg 2023). Because public defenders enforce their client's procedural rights and guard against government abuses of power, their absence in cases involving eviction, debt, and the termination of parental rights means "civil courts routinely disregard the rights of the unrepresented parties—a large percentage of whom are women" (Sabbeth and Steinberg 2023: 1188). Further, lawyers are not in court on the side of defendants to witness injustice and publicize problems, as with public defenders who play a role in criminal justice reform.

The marginalization of women and sexual minorities in the political sphere, which leads to the lack of mandatory legal aid in the cases above, also impacts how they experience the criminal legal system. About 90 percent of criminal cases are tried at the state level, where women of color make up 8 percent of state court judges and white women make up 22 percent—a "gavel gap" because they are underrepresented at that level compared to their percentage in the U.S. population (George and Yoon 2023). This lack of representation impacts women of color (Buist and Stone 2014), trans, and nonheterosexual women in terms of charging decision, plea bargaining, and the collateral consequences of the inequitable decisions. For example, women are still most often the primary caregivers to their children and families, often working inside the home because of gender stereotypes and facing gender/sexuality discrimination with wage labor outside the home. Black women and the LGBTQ+ community experience disproportionately high rates of sexual violence, which is seldom prosecuted, while being disproportionately criminalized for sex work and certain reproductive choices.

Some scholars have suggested a "chivalry hypothesis," whereby prosecutorial discretion will result in fewer and less serious charges against women. But to the extent this applies, it is mostly for white, cisgender, middle-class women. In some cases, however, criminal prosecution can be explicitly patriarchal and sexist. A robust literature exists on patriarchal and sexist violence (like intimate partner violence), and this form of gender-based violence is often underemphasized in the courts. The policing of women's sexuality, reproductive health choices, and patriarchal notions of "modesty" can create scenarios where women and girls face criminal scrutiny and punishment in ways that men and boys do not.

For example, pregnant, drug-using women are subjected to vigorous prosecution that goes way beyond the potential harm done by the behavior (Beety and Oliva 2023; Flavin 2009). Moreover, the response has been an increased willingness to criminalize the woman's behavior rather than expand the availability of drug treatment and prenatal care. The criminalization has included "cases in which despite the fact that medical marijuana, or marijuana in general, has been legalized, states are finding a way to target and subject people who are pregnant" (in Nowell 2021; Kavattur et al. 2023: 4). Even women on anti–substance abuse drugs are prosecuted when their newborns seem to show neonatal abstinence syndrome (signs of withdrawal), which are short-term difficulties and do not result in long-term harm (Bach 2019: 832). Indeed, multiple prestigious medical associations say that ending medication-assisted therapy using synthetic opioids "could trigger withdrawal and contractions that could result in a miscarriage, premature birth or cause a person to relapse" (Walter 2023; Bach 2019: 865). In the face of such criminalization, women "feared that seeking care could lead not to care but to punishment," so they did not seek care (Bach 2019: 862).

In addition, courts have expanded the definitions of child welfare and criminal child abuse to include fetuses (Pregnancy Justice 2022: 13–16), among other areas where prosecutors and courts have increasingly found pregnant women liable for harm to the fetus. Some of these cases involve newborns suing their mothers, such as the case of a pregnant woman hit by a car. She delivered prematurely the next day, and "the court permitted the child to sue her mother for negligence for 'failing to use reasonable care in crossing the street and failing to use a designated crosswalk'" (Pregnancy Justice 2022: 19). The dissent in that case noted that the principle could extend to "her diet, sleep, exercise, sexual activity, work and living environment, and, of course, nearly every aspect of her health care"—indeed, "the mother's every waking and sleeping moment."

With intimate partner violence and rape, courtrooms often reflect stereotypes and the devaluation of women's viewpoints rather than chivalry in the face of assaults. For example, Fersch (2023) indicates four common misperceptions of court personnel and experts:

- Misperception 1: "I would immediately leave a partner who abused me."

The reality is that abusers seek power and control, so leaving—trying to break their control—is the most dangerous time because abusers escalate their tactics to reestablish control ("If I can't have her, no one can"). Many communities do not have the resources to support abused women and keep them safe while they end the relationship and establish a life free of abuse.

- Misperception 2: "I can tell if someone experienced interpersonal violence by the way they act when discussing the abuse."

The reality is that people react to trauma in a variety of ways, and not all of them are predictable (Wadsworth and Records 2013). One extensive review of the literature on sexual victimization noted that "sexual violence victimization is an idiosyncratic experience and generalization of impacts should be conducted with caution, particularly against the background of recent research indicating that posttraumatic growth, defined . . . as 'personal transformation that improves quality of life,' is possible" (Guggisberg et al. 2021). While posttraumatic growth does not negate the trauma felt by most people who experience sexual violence, for some it can result in increased personal strength from adversity, deeper spirituality, and a deeper appreciation for life and relationships.

- Misperception 3: "It is easy to detect if someone is lying based on where they are looking and what they are saying."

The reality is that for many years police dismissed stories of rape survivors as "unfounded" because the stories did not fit what the police—people trained to do interrogations—thought of as a truthful narrative. Campbell's (2012) work on the neurobiology of sexual assault points out how trauma affects the encoding and recall of those memories. Campbell suggests that the body's response to trauma is helpful for the person in the moment, but it alters the encoding process so that it is like taking lecture notes on small Post-it notes of various colors that get put in different folders. Recall is difficult and fractured, and someone may say "this doesn't make any sense" if they were expecting a recounting of the lecture that starts at the beginning; continues in a linear, chronological way; and does not keep adding significant new information when it is retold. Further, the brain processes a sexual assault "much like an attempted murder," so it releases natural painkillers that mean the victim's communications about an assault "may be very flat, incredibly monotone—like seeing no emotional reaction, which again sometimes can seem counterintuitive to both the victim and other people" (Campbell 2012). Responses of sexual assault victims like "freezing" can be because of biochemical reactions leading to "tonic immobility," but people think that her testimony about the sex being unwanted is false: "Well she just laid there, so she must have wanted it. No one wants to have a train pulled on them, so if she just laid there and took it she must have wanted it" (Campbell 2012).

• Misperception 4: "I know what happened and the evidence supports me."

The reality is that people overestimate their ability to see the truth in cases of trauma, especially when combined with various types of privilege. People imagine how they would behave or react in a situation and judge others by that standard, but without considering how class, race, sexuality, and other privileges can affect their imagined "normal" response. "Gut" feelings can lead to improper investigations and prosecutions; leads are not followed and contradictory evidence is ignored, so cases are dismissed or involve wrongful convictions.

Another area of legal discrimination involves "gay panic" or "trans panic" defenses. They have been used to lessen the punishment that the accused may receive if found guilty of homicide or assault when they allege that the victim was transgender or LGB and made a sexual advance at them. This defense essentially blames the victim for their own victimization for allegedly making a sexual advance, usually at a heterosexual male (Movement Advancement Project [MAP] 2023c). There are numerous examples of this phenomenon found in practice in the court system even though "no state recognizes gay and trans panic defenses as freestanding defenses under their respective penal codes" (in MAP 2023c). Instead of having a defined excuse in the self-defense statute, "defendants have used panic defenses in conjunction with other defense strategies to attempt to reduce the severity of their charges or sentencing" (MAP 2023c).

A study of 104 cases that used this defense found that "defense attorneys who enter gay panic defenses can reduce a defendants' murder charges 32% of the time, even though the majority of these homicides involve incredible violence" (Andresen 2020). When there is a conviction, the sentence—including prison time—is also lower. Because the gay panic defense is not written into law, it is indirectly introduced in several ways (LGBTQ+ Bar, n.d.):

• **Defense of insanity or diminished capacity:** The defendant alleges that a sexual proposition by the victim—due to their sexual orientation or gender identity—triggered a nervous breakdown in the defendant, causing an LGBTQ+ "panic."

This defense is based on an outdated psychological term, "gay panic disorder," which was debunked by the American Psychiatric Association and removed from the *Diagnostic and Statistical Manual* (DSM) in 1973.

- **Defense of provocation:** The defense of provocation allows a defendant to argue that the victim's alleged proposition, sometimes termed a "nonviolent sexual advance," was sufficiently "provocative" to induce the defendant to kill the victim. Such advances coming from a heterosexual man to a heterosexual woman or lesbian is not illegal or harmful and would not be a legal excuse for violent retaliation. But the advance is considered "provocative" when it comes from an LGBTQ+ individual.

- **Defense of self-defense:** Defendants claim they believed that the victim, because of their sexual orientation or gender identity/expression, was about to cause the defendant serious bodily harm. Rather than the threat of harm being based on aspects of the behavior that accompanied the sexual advance, the basis for belief about harm is that the person's gender or sexual identity makes them more of a threat to safety. This tactic is often deployed when the defendant used a greater amount of force than reasonably necessary to avoid danger, such as using weapons when their attacker was unarmed.

## Intersectionality and the Judicial Process

Because prosecutorial power is exercised in ways that fall harshly on minorities, some individuals have sought to reform the position by becoming a "progressive prosecutor" and trying to reform the system from the inside. Prosecutors can use their discretion to *not* charge in, say, minor drug cases; they can decide *not* to charge under laws that have mandatory minimums and use discretion to *not* invoke long mandatory terms for repeat minor offenses (see opening narrative in chapter 7). They can create diversion programs so fewer offenders receive criminal records and sentences of incarceration. They can also end cash bail or seriously restrict the number of people held in local jails who are not a public safety or flight risk.

While not all progressive prosecutors are from the Black community, many are Black women (Butler 2023; Davis 2019). Their background shapes their philosophy about prosecution, such as with Kim Foxx, who was twice elected prosecutor in Cook County and was the first African American woman elected as a prosecutor in Illinois. Foxx grew up in public housing—a "daughter of the projects," she says (in Butler 2023: 10180)—and her "mother suffered from mental illness and drug addiction" (Davis 2019). Foxx has publicly discussed her upbringing, including being sexually assaulted twice before she was seven years old. "She has cousins who have done time in prison and cousins who have been shot" (Davis 2019: 8). She hid in the bathtub with her brother when there were gunshots in the neighborhood. And "Foxx learned early on that 'people who perpetrated sinister acts of violence . . . could also be profoundly kind and generous,' like the local drug seller who provided food and protection to the elders in her community" (Butler 2023: 1081).

Reforms to reduce class and racial bias are controversial because "tough on crime" is still at or just below the surface of public sentiment, and leadership by Black women is most likely to cause backlash as a "response to both their progressive policies and their identities" (Butler 2023: 1079). Foxx reformed cash bail, which angered that profitable industry. She charged people with misdemeanors rather than felonies for theft of less than $1,000, which angered retail businesses who wanted to see shoplifters dealt with harshly. She angered police by prosecuting some officers involved in fatal shootings and establishing a Conviction Integrity Unit to investigate claims of wrongful conviction (which led to dropped and dismissed charges because of police misconduct) (Davis 2019).

So, while the prosecutor may be a powerful actor in the judicial process, claiming that power in the interests of racial justice is difficult—even when white men attempt it (Davis 2019). Many advocates of progressive prosecution see the limits of incremental change from having a few of the 3,144 county prosecutors be progressive (Butler 2023; Pfaff 2017). But many still support this small movement because it can make a big difference to some individuals in those jurisdictions. Others support it as a necessary short-term step for "gradual decarceration" within an abolitionist framework (Butler 2023: 1077). But there is only so much reform that can happen when "the reality is that the main day-to-day work of prosecutors, progressive or otherwise, is locking people up—particularly people of color and poor people" (Butler 2023: 1079). Foxx herself notes that in a meeting of Black prosecutors after the police killing of George Floyd, "we were all aware that as individuals there was only so much we could do in a system that by its very design is broken" (in Butler 2023: 1082).

Saying that the system is broken by design is another way of saying that the system is functioning as it is supposed to in upholding class, race, and gender/sexuality privileges. As chapter 10 notes, Black men are disproportionately incarcerated. And "male Latino immigrants have been especially subjected to criminal stereotypes and scapegoating; nearly 90% of detained individuals are men, and more than 97% are Latin American or Caribbean" (Saadi et al. 2020: 190). Indeed, deportation is a "gendered racial removal program" (Golash-Boza and Hondagneu-Sotelo 2013).

Further, just as immigration has become more intertwined with the harsh administration of criminal justice, many of the systems allegedly helping poor women have come to be about surveillance and dispensing harsh penalties. Indeed, just as criminology has neglected the study of immigration and crimmigration, it has also not developed a full understanding of how social control operates in the lives of poor, and especially minority, women through systems of welfare, public housing, child protective services, school, juvenile justice, and health care. All of these systems are increasingly linked, necessitating an understanding of "regulatory intersectionality: the means by which social welfare systems collect and transmit evidence of purportedly deviant conduct from social welfare systems to child welfare and criminal systems, resulting in escalating risk of harm and escalating harms for poor women who seek support" (Bach 2019: 819).

Any provision of services and care increasingly happens through specialty "problem-solving" courts, like drug and mental health courts. However, advocacy for such courts often does not seek to challenge the current environment's high levels of criminalization and low levels of services that people can voluntarily use. Indeed, services are often transferred from the community to support specialty courts, which require a guilty plea—and the accompanying fines and fees—to access them (Bach 2019: 828–29). Many people are not successful with drug treatment, even if they are improving, and with relapse "the punishment is far more severe than the person would have received had they not participated in the drug court" (Bach 2019: 828–29).

Of course most women who have had their pregnancies criminalized have been prosecuted in traditional, punitive ways where "care" and services were not a consideration. Indeed, medical societies oppose criminalization because it drives women away from medical services that support the health of the pregnant woman (Kavattur et al. 2023). A study of almost 1,400 cases from 2006 to 2022 (just before the Supreme Court allowed states to restrict abortion) found an increase in the number of cases over time (Kavattur et al. 2023). They also found that the cases were almost exclusively against *poor* women. While the report noted the significant criminalization of women of color, "the racist carceral tactics established during the war on drugs . . . are now being extended to target poor white communities in the midst of the opioid and methamphetamine epidemics" (Kavattur et al. 2023: 4).

The June 2022 Supreme Court decision in *Dobbs*, which reversed fifty years of precedent supporting the right to an abortion, will increase problems with reproductive justice and the prosecution of poor pregnant women. The ruling almost immediately limited the availability of safe, legal reproductive choice for women in many states, which will disproportionately impact poor women of color (who have the lowest incomes and are least able to travel). The director of health equity at the National Women's Law Center noted that with restricted "access to abortion care and increases [in] unwanted pregnancies, you are potentially cycling more Black and brown women into a system that is already failing them" (in Ollove 2022).

However, chapter 3 noted that whiteness did not protect poor women from involuntary sterilization, and there are limits to how much whiteness can protect poor women when "women getting abortions today are far more likely to be poor than those who had the procedure done 20 years ago" (Tavernise 2019). And the implications of *Dobbs* go far beyond abortion rights because the 1973 decision in *Roe* creating abortion rights "was central to upholding the civil and human rights not only of those seeking abortions but also of all six million people who become pregnant annually in the United States, including the four million who continue their pregnancies to term and the one million who have the dishearteningly common experience of pregnancy loss" (Kavattur et al. 2023: 11).

Beyond issues of reproductive justice, issues of intersectional justice can be seen in the contrast between the immunity of those claiming a gay or trans panic defense and the lack of excuses accorded gay and trans people who fight back against attackers. For example, CeCe McDonald, a trans Black woman, was originally charged with two counts of second-degree murder after she was assaulted verbally and physically outside a Minneapolis bar. Although her actions have been considered as self-defense by many, including actress Laverne Cox of *Orange Is the New Black* fame, McDonald eventually took a plea deal and spent forty-one months in prison—a men's prison, even though CeCe identifies as a woman.

During her trial, CeCe's past criminal record was introduced, yet the original attacker's racist and homophobic history was not included. Also not included at trial were Schmitz's shouts that McDonald and her friends were "faggots" and "niggers" while threatening them with physical violence. Schmitz's girlfriend slashed McDonald's face with broken glass (requiring eleven stitches) while yelling misogynistic obscenities. There was no discussion permitted in court about Schmitz's swastika tattoo or that he was on methamphetamine at the time of the incident or that he had served prison time (Buist and Stone 2014; Erdely 2014). At the trial, court officials misgendered and deadnamed (used their pre-transition name) McDonald and her friends, while the defense essentially blamed them for their own harassment.

## Implications

When it comes to crime, criminals, and class control, the old legal axiom still stands: while rich people don't hold up Dairy Queens (DQs) and poor people don't price-fix or swindle the consumer, police and prosecutors seem to pursue only those who do, in fact, hold up DQs—namely, the poor and marginal. As for the rich, like in the game of Monopoly, they seem to have no need for the "get out of jail free" cards, since very few resources are earmarked for the task of reducing white-collar and corporate crime. But even when they are prosecuted, they can hire attorneys to help them escape or minimize the charges.

While poor people—including disproportionate numbers of women and racial and sexual minorities—have a right to a public defender, that system has been dysfunctional for decades. But equally important, justice is skewed when the wealthy can buy the best lawyers. High-priced lawyers are more expensive because they are more likely to get a better outcome given the same set of facts. When the wealthy can buy the best legal talent, they are not just more likely to escape the consequences of criminal charges, but in other areas of law it "increases the risk of might trumping right" (Higgins 2022). Because the wealthy buy the best legal talent, there is a risk of increased inequality because "the rich are able to enforce their rights when they choose, whilst avoiding their obligations without sanction" (Higgins 2022). Resolving this problem raises many practical issues, but there is little disagreement that the current marketplace for legal talent makes a parody of "equal protection," and it privileges the wealthy and corporations at the expense of everyone else (Wilmot-Smith 2019).

The situation is more troubling when there is no state guarantee for an attorney in cases involving asylum, unaccompanied children in immigration cases, eviction, or termination of parental rights. In those cases, regular people are up against smart career prosecutors and lawyers for corporate landlords. Those "repeat players" (Sabbeth and Steinberg 2023: 1199) have greater credibility in the eyes of judges, so the lawyers can easily "steamroll" over even well-established rights (Sabbeth and Steinberg 2023: 1191).

## Review and Discussion Questions

1. How is the reality of the courtroom work group different from popular and media depictions of the judicial process? Why does it matter?
2. Why is the prosecutor the most powerful actor?
3. Why do the authors argue that immigration enforcement needs to be studied and understood? What does "immigration regime" refer to, and what concerns do the authors raise about it?

4. How prevalent is plea bargaining and what are the concerns about the unfairness and downsides of this common practice?
5. What are the problems with public defenders? What is the critique of the *Gideon* case that created them?
6. How would you describe the efforts to prosecute corporations and executives? What are the lessons from the financial crisis, HSBC, and Wells Fargo?
7. What are the general findings about how race affects each stage of the judicial process? What are the promises and problems with using algorithms and AI to fix bias?
8. What is the critique about the outcome of *Gideon* as opposed to *Lassiter*?
9. What are the concerns about gender/sexuality bias that are raised in the chapter? Which issues concerned you the most? Why?
10. What are progressive prosecutors and what are their promises and limitations?
11. What is regulatory intersectionality? What understandings does it include that mainstream criminology ignores?

## Note

1. We published the first edition of this book in 2001, and all editions have pointed out the limitations and problems of policies by both Democrats and Republicans. In this spirit, we have discussed some of former president Trump's policies, like the executive orders on immigration, while also noting that former president Obama has been called the "deporter in chief" (chapter 1) for his actions after the financial crisis. However, we believe that an extended discussion of the charges against Trump invites partisan arguments that would detract from our focus on critical thinking about class, race, gender/sexuality, and justice. For interested readers, one of the coauthors has documented Trump's long history of criminal activities as a businessman and politician, and he argues that, far from being persecuted, Trump has long been the beneficiary of policies that allow the wealthy to be unaccountable for their wrongdoing (Barak 2022). And Barak's (2024) *Indicting the 45th President* is the "next chapter on the world's most successful outlaw."

# CHAPTER 10

# Punishment

*Sentencing guidelines are a grid that judges use to calculate sentences. The crime a defendant is convicted of is translated into an offense score, and the defendant's criminal history provides another score. The intersection of these scores on the guidelines grid is the appropriate sentencing range. Individual factors about the case and defendant can provide reasons for the judge to sentence in the lower or upper part of that range, or more extensive upward or downward departures. In the federal system, the resulting sentence should, among other concerns,*

1. *reflect the seriousness of the offense, promote respect for the law, and provide just punishment for the offense;*
2. *afford adequate deterrence to criminal conduct; and*
3. *protect the public from further crimes of the defendant.*

*How to apply the guidelines was the question in U.S. v. Deegan (08-2299 [2010]) and whether the ten-year sentence for Dana Deegan for second-degree murder should be upheld. Deegan is a Native American and gave birth to a live baby in her home on a reservation. According to the court:*

> *Deegan fed, cleaned, and dressed him, and then placed him in a basket. She then left the house with her three other children, intentionally leaving the baby alone without food, water, or a caregiver. Deegan did not return to her home for approximately two weeks. When she returned, she found the baby dead in the basket where she had left him. (U.S. Sentencing Commission 1991)*

*The sentencing court heard testimony from Dr. Resnick, an expert in "neonaticide," or killing a newborn in the first twenty-four hours after birth. His report noted that Deegan suffered from extensive abuse and depression. He argued that Deegan, like other women who committed neonaticide, presented a low risk of reoffending. Harsh punishment was unlikely to deter others from committing the offense because women who commit this type of offense are usually overwhelmed and have few resources.*

*Also, similar cases in state court typically resulted in probation or a sentence of not more than three years.*

*The sentencing judge remarked that he had "spent many, many days and nights thinking about the case" and read Resnick's report "at least three times." He noted that Deegan's life had not been "easy." An appeals court, in upholding the ten-year sentence, noted the sentencing judge had said he had "'real compassion for [her] and [her] family and what [she had] gone through,' including the fact that she had three children and that her brother had been murdered. The court said that it 'underst[ood] why [Deegan] took the steps that she did.'"*

*But both courts felt ten years was necessary to "ensure that justice is done," to "reflect the seriousness of the offense, to promote respect for the law and to provide just punishment for the offense." The guidelines in effect were "reasonable": "The sentencing guidelines have been in effect for almost 20 years, and they are designed to provide some honesty in sentencing and to achieve some consistency in the federal system, and they're based upon an analysis of hundreds of thousands of cases."*

*Because Deegan's crime occurred on a reservation, she was subject to federal sentencing guidelines, so the appeals court did not see the relevance of state court sentences, including a neonaticide by a North Dakota State University student who received probation. The concern about "sentencing disparities among defendants with similar records who have been found guilty of similar conduct" refers "only to disparities among federal defendants." The court would have committed an "error" in considering disparities between federal and state sentences.*

*Judge Bright dissented, saying this "represents the most clear sentencing error that this dissenting judge has ever seen." He provided a fuller account of Deegan's "history of extensive and cruel abuse," starting with the fact that "her alcoholic father beat her on an almost daily basis." Some of the beatings were so bad that she was kept from school to avoid reports to Child Protective Services. But all the children were eventually sent to foster homes, "where she experienced physical abuse from some of her foster family members." Further,*

> *at five years of age, her father's drinking buddies began sexually abusing her. By age nine, five or six perpetrators had forced her to participate in oral, vaginal, and anal sex. One of the perpetrators held her head under water several times to make her submissive. (U.S. Sentencing Commission 1991)*

*In spite of this abuse, Deegan cared for and protected her siblings, even if it meant she suffered additional abuse.*

*Deegan began a relationship with the son of one of her foster parents, but "Mr. Hale acknowledged in an interview with the FBI that he had physically, emotionally and verbally abused Ms. Deegan on a regular basis." After their third child was born, Deegan became depressed. Hale was abusing her "two to three times* per week, forcing her to have sexual intercourse with him, and refusing to care for their children." When she became pregnant with a fourth child—the victim in this case—she was "so depressed that she could barely take care of herself and her three children." They were poor, unemployed, and "when Ms. Deegan obtained any money, Mr. Hale took it and bought methamphetamine."

The dissent noted that Resnick, the neonaticide expert, described the mothers who commit this crime as having poor coping skills and inadequate resources. For example, the reservation had few resources, no outreach services, and no domestic violence shelters. North Dakota had no "safe haven law"—allowing parents to drop off babies at hospitals or police stations without question or criminal punishment. (In the years after North Dakota passed such a law, more than one thousand babies were dropped off; all states now have such a law.)

While Deegan's situation was typical for neonaticide, the dissent noted that neonaticide was not included in the sentencing guidelines for second-degree murder—and the guidelines were to create a standard for similar cases and similarly situated offenders. The guidelines "carve out a 'heartland' of typical cases" and provide an approach for sentencing ordinary cases that fall within that heartland. But, in response to his query, the U.S. Sentencing Commission did some research, and of 157,000 cases it could examine electronically, the only case of neonaticide was Deegan's. The dissent's own research went back to federal cases since 1975 and found only one other case. "This case falls so far from the heartland of guidelines sentencing that it is a complete stranger to crimes ordinarily charged and considered as second-degree murder." Thus, any presumption of reasonableness that ordinarily applied to a guidelines sentence did not apply here, the judge argued.

Further, Deegan was not likely to reoffend because she had had her tubes tied and thus could not have another baby. Resnick's testimony was that women who committed neonaticide go on to marry and be good mothers, making this a crime "based on circumstances as opposed to bad character." And her circumstances had changed. Indeed, in the nine years between the act and the trial, "she has got her life together, been a good mother and not been a risk to the community."

While the sentencing judge noted he had considered testimony from Deegan's family, the dissent reproduced a letter from Deegan's sister, noting that "our childhood home was a war zone." Further,

> our family has taken great lengths to reconcile the pain and scars that have been left on our souls. Understanding the intergenerational historical trauma of our American Indian Grandfathers and Grandmothers that came before us, has helped my family to forgive and love our father, knowing that he too suffered. Non-Indian people may not easily internalize this sense of loss and powerlessness so deeply ingrained by American Indian people still today. The cultural deprivations

*and discriminations of our people merely because of our heritage has contributed
to the psychological deficits that Dana, at that particular low time in her life, was
unable to overcome. I fear that these same cultural factors may also contribute to
harsher penalties of an already oppressed woman. (U.S. Sentencing Commission
1991)*

*If neonaticide is understood in the state court—and in twenty-six other coun-
tries that have infanticide laws that cover neonaticide—as deserving probation or
less than three years in prison, then "the sentence here is unjust, excessive, and
treats a woman on the reservation disparately with a woman off the reservation.
Does this disparity not indicate another example of unfair treatment of an American
Indian living on a reservation?"*

*Because of the sentence, Deegan's children were removed from her care. The
prosecutor said this was Deegan's fault—"basically, it was her choice that caused
all of this"—and the family separation should not be considered when sentencing.
But the dissent noted, "There is plenty of blame to go around. Ms. Deegan's father
is dead. But what blame should be placed on Mr. Hale who did not support the
children he fathered and consistently abused Ms. Deegan? And what about the
failures of society to assist Ms. Deegan in her travail?" A number of modest interventions could have prevented the crime. As this dissenting judge argued, "Ms.
Deegan has suffered immense cruelty at the hands of her father, his male friends,
and the father of her children. Now her lifetime of travail becomes magnified by an
unjust and improper prison sentence."*

## Introduction

Punishment is an important aspect of the administration of justice because it
involves a state decision to intentionally inflict suffering and deprivation. The sometimes contradictory rationales for punishment include retribution, deterrence, rehabilitation, incapacitation, and restoration. The dominant justification of punishment
has been retribution, whose essential idea is that the harm of the punishment should
fit the harm done by the crime. Retribution implies some kind of repayment for an
offense committed, with variations in terms of the more emotional revenge and the
supposedly more limited just deserts. Unlike the other rationales for punishment,
retribution is the only one that focuses exclusively on the past criminal offense without consideration given to future criminality.

The classical school of criminology (see chapter 2) introduced the rationale of
deterrence. Eighteenth-century classical theorists believed that retribution by itself
was a waste of time and that the only legitimate purpose for punishment was the
prevention (or deterrence) of crime. Classical theorists were informed by a utilitar-
ian philosophy of "the greatest good for the greatest number," under which the
pain of punishment was only morally valid if it produced a larger good, such as a
reduction in criminal victimization through deterrence or rehabilitation. Sentencing actual offenders so that the punished individual will not engage in future crime

involves specific deterrence; general deterrence refers to preventing other potential offenders from engaging in crime by the example set by punishing specific offenders.

Rehabilitation involves the attempt to "correct" the personality and behavior of offenders through educational, vocational, and therapeutic intervention. Thinkers going back to Plato have suggested that a person being punished should emerge "a better man, or failing that, less of a wretch" (in Johnson 2002: 3). The goal of rehabilitation is not based on fear of punishment but treatments to modify the character of the offender so that they find crime to be morally unacceptable or give the offender skills (education, job training, etc.) so that they have more options for legitimate employment (Leighton 2014). While many deride rehabilitation as being soft on crime, "the rehabilitative ideal draws its power from its nobility and its rationality—from the promise that compassionate science, rather than vengeful punishment, is the road to reducing crime. Rehabilitation allows us to be a better and safer people" (in Leighton 2014: 12).

Incapacitation refers to the removal of those who have been convicted of a criminal violation from the community. This rationale emphasizes public safety in that incarcerated offenders, during their period of punishment, are unable to commit further crimes in the free world. Collective incapacitation refers to sanctions applied to offenders without regard to their personal characteristics. Belonging to the offending crime categories such as violent offender, drug dealer, or child molester would qualify one for a lengthy prison sentence regardless of the circumstances involved in the offense. Selective incapacitation refers to efforts to identify high-risk offenders based on their criminal histories, drug use, schooling, employment records, and so on, and to set them apart from other offenders of the same group.

Another rationale for punishment, restoration, refers to making victims of crime whole through various forms of victim compensation programs and reintegrating offenders with their communities. Unlike the other forms of punishment, which focus almost exclusively on offenders and their punishments, restorative justice seeks to restore or repair the health of the community, meet the needs of victims, and involve the offender in the processes of restoration. Restitution and community service are two common forms of restorative practice by which convicted offenders, as part of their sentences, are required to pay money or provide services to their victims, their victims' survivors, or their community.

Currently, all of these punishment rationales are in use, although more than fifty years of "tough on crime" rhetoric and practice indicate that retribution and deterrence play primary roles. Some increases in sentences were done in the name of "victims' rights," although these efforts neglected victims of white-collar and corporate crime. Efforts to scare potential offenders into obedience included general increases in sentences, more death-penalty-eligible offenses, mandatory sentences, truth in sentencing (mandating that federal offenders serve a minimum of 85 percent of their sentence), "habitual offender" laws (requiring enhanced prison terms for repeat felony offenders, in some cases regardless of the pettiness of the offense), "three strikes and you're out" (mandatory life sentences after repeat convictions), and moves to increase the number of offenses that count as strikes (see the opening narrative of chapter 7). As a result of more people going to prison and those going to prison serving longer sentences, state and federal incarceration rates increased dramatically from the 1970s until 2009.

As the financial crisis hit, a number of states started to reduce their prison population and opened an era of "cheap on crime," which should not be understood as criminal justice reform or a significant change in the punitive mentality (Aviram 2015). Indeed, the decline in the number of people imprisoned—by about four hundred thousand since its peak in 2009—is mostly because COVID reduced arrests and convictions, which impacted admissions to facilities. The impact of COVID was substantially larger than the "brutal timidity" (Osler 2020) of sentencing reform in the decade of cheap on crime. Compassionate releases from prisons and jails, which were well-known COVID hotspots, were minimal (National Academies of Sciences, Engineering, and Medicine 2020: 3). By 2022, the number of incarcerated people was down to about 1.9 million: 663,000 in jail and more than 1.2 million in state and federal prison (Bureau of Justice Statistics 2023b). In addition, about 3,750,000 adults were still under "community supervision," which means parole or probation (Bureau of Justice Statistics 2023c: 4). So about 5.6 million people are under some form of "supervision"/punishment.

While incarceration rates from other countries are not always perfectly comparable, the picture still emerges that the United States leads the developed world—and many developing nations—with the highest incarceration rates. This is not a new phenomenon and dates back to at least the 1990s. Incarceration rates per one hundred thousand are as follows for the United States and selected developed nations (International Centre for Prison Studies 2023):

- United States, 531
- Brazil, 390
- Russian Federation, 300
- South Africa, 258
- Mexico, 176
- Australia, 158
- United Kingdom: England and Wales, 146
- Canada, 88
- Denmark, 69
- India, 41
- Japan, 36

Importantly, criminologists have never been able to draw a connection between increases in incarceration and fluctuating crime rates (Currie 1998; Reiman and Leighton 2023). Indeed, the United States is unique in having both the highest level of incarceration and the highest rate of violent crime among peer developed nations. A review of the extensive literature on the effects of imprisonment on reoffending noted that "every review" of has "reached nearly the same conclusion: compared with noncustodial sanctions, custodial sanctions, including imprisonment, have no appreciable effect on reducing reoffending" (Petrich et al. 2021: 401). The authors conducted a meta-analysis, in which they pooled the samples from many individual studies in ways that allow for more powerful analysis. They conclude that "based on past research and the findings of this meta-analysis, the limited effects of custodial sanctions on reoffending should be viewed as a criminological fact" (Petrich et al. 2021: 401).

In spite of many studies over decades showing that imprisonment had basically no effect on crime rates, many policy makers advocated—and still advocate—for "getting tough" in order to control crime. This lack of correlation between incarceration rates and crime rates is because of the negative effects prison has on offenders, their children, and communities. To the extent that prisons function as "schools for crime," building more of them negates some of the public safety benefits from incapacitation and deterrence. Going on an incarceration binge and building a massive number of schools for crime does not bring down the crime rate.

Prisons function as schools for crime because people in prison deepen ties to others there, and the prison environment offers little rehabilitation (Reiman and Leighton 2023). Prison can be psychologically destructive, and the National Research Council report on incarceration noted that people in prison could "become psychologically scarred in ways that intensify their sense of anger and deepen their commitment to the role of an outsider, and perhaps a criminal lifestyle" (2014: 178). Transition back to the community is difficult because people in prison acquire "a tough veneer that precludes seeking help for personal problems, the generalized mistrust that comes from the fear of exploitation, and the tendency to strike out in response to minimal provocations [that] are highly functional in many prison contexts and problematic virtually everywhere else" (National Research Council 2014: 178).

Further, former prisoners have reduced job possibilities because of their criminal record, and cynicism about the law and justice may reduce their commitment to obey the law. Prisons also have criminogenic (crime-producing) effects on family formation and community well-being. For example, the children of people in prison do less well in school, are more likely to be expelled, face economic hardship, abuse substances, and become involved in the juvenile or criminal justice system. Under conditions of mass incarceration, moving offenders back and forth between prison and home leads to community disorganization and the erosion of informal social controls that prevent crime (Petersilia 2010).

Thus, there are well-established criminogenic effects of incarceration that counteract the crime-reducing effect of incapacitation (Useem and Piehl 2008: 52; Reiman and Leighton 2023). The relative weight of the positive and negative effects changes over time: increasing the number of people incarcerated is most effective when relatively few people are in prison, but further increases have declining effectiveness for crime control—and at some point further increases can cause more crime than they prevent.

One comprehensive study by the Brennan Center for Justice reviewed research on the crime decline to create estimates of the effect of incarceration on crime. They concluded that during the 1990s, incarceration had no effect (0 percent) on violent crime and reduced property crime by 6 percent; from 2000 to 2013, incarceration had no effect (0 percent) on violent crime and reduced property crime by 0.2 percent (Roeder et al. 2015: 22). This is consistent with the findings of the National Research Council on incarceration, which found that "mandatory minimum sentence and three-strike laws have little or no effect on crime rates," and with respect to the effect of the overall increase in incarceration, "the evidence suggests it was unlikely to have been large" (National Research Council 2014: 85, 155).

Running oversized and ineffective prisons cost the United States over $89 billion in 2017, the most recent year with data (Bureau of Justice Statistics 2021d: 4). This number substantially underestimates corrections spending because it does not include an estimated $2.2 billion in prison construction costs (2021d: 5) and another $3 billion in costs to inmate families for commissary and phone calls (Wagner and Rabuy 2017). All this corrections spending comes with what economists call an opportunity cost: money spent here cannot fund other programs. Some trade-offs are inevitable, but increasingly states are cutting budgets for schools, education, drug and alcohol treatment, and crime prevention programs that seek to create law-abiding citizens rather than simply punish them after a criminal act. One criminologist likens this tactic to "mopping the water off the floor while we let the tub overflow. Mopping harder may make some difference in the level of the flood. It does not, however, do anything about the open faucet" (Currie 1985: 85).

Because prisons do little to rehabilitate, this chapter calls them prisons rather than "correctional institutions." Also, punishment more accurately describes the purpose of jails, prisons, parole, and probation than "corrections." Any stories about rehabilitation tend to be ones about individuals, and any successful programs are short-lived; they are celebrated for their success but not continued or scaled up. Indeed, aside from a few periods in history that experimented with rehabilitation, Foucault (1979: 277) noted that "after a century and a half [now almost two centuries] of 'failures,' the prison still exists, producing the same results." The first prisons generated a prison reform movement, and, "word for word, from one century to the other, the same fundamental propositions are repeated" (Foucault 1979: 270).

The large and poor prison system has a negative impact not only on the people sentenced to serve time there but also on the guards and officers working there. Prisons designed to be harsh and miserable for those sentenced there will not be good places to work. The next section explores this dynamic while also providing demographic information about the people who work in prisons. The subsequent sections of this chapter explore the effects of class, race, gender/sexuality, and their intersections. Consistent with previous chapters, this one also covers immigration by discussing detention facilities, which hold immigrants who are denied bail or release while they are awaiting hearings and deportation.

## Corrections Workers

Within the system of punishment, most jobs are in the form of guards and officers, although a small army of probation and parole agents are necessary to supervise the 3.75 million people under supervision. Overall, prison "officers generally have considerable discretion in discharging their duties within the constraints of rules, regulations, and policies. Yet, because they lack clear and specific guidelines on how to exercise their discretion, they feel vulnerable to second-guessing by their superiors and the courts" (Bohm and Haley 2005: 405).

Sykes's classic study, *The Society of Captives* (1958), pointed to some ambiguities in officers' power and discretion because they are outnumbered by people sentenced to do time and depend on their compliance to keep the daily routine of prison functional—what Sykes referred to as the "defects of total power." Officers tend to develop one of three responses to their working conditions (Hawkins and Alpert 1989). First, officers may become alienated and cynical and withdraw into some relatively safe niche within the prison. Second, some officers in their efforts to control inmates become overly authoritarian, confrontational, or intimidating. Finally, there are those officers who adopt a human services/community policing orientation, seeking to make prisons a constructive place for themselves and for inmates (Johnson 2002).

While correctional officers are most directly engaged with inmates, there is a larger prison bureaucracy that accounts for many jobs. By 2017, correctional agencies employed about 758,445 people: 447,800 of these jobs were in state correctional facilities, about 39,100 in federal institutions, and an unknown number in privately owned and managed prisons (Bureau of Justice Statistics 2021d: table 4). Median earnings in 2022 for correctional officers and jailers were $49,600, and $54,700 if the figure includes law enforcement who spend the majority of their time guarding people in confinement (Bureau of Labor Statistics 2023a, 2023b). Pay is higher for federal employees, less for state and local workers, and lower still for private prisons.

Corrections workers for the Federal Bureau of Prisons are required to have a bachelor's degree or three years of related work experience, which can include "persuasive sales work or commissioned sales work" (Federal Bureau of Prisons, n.d.). Applicants for state correctional systems need only be eighteen or twenty-one years of age and possess a high school diploma or GED (Bureau of Labor Statistics 2023b). Efforts to upgrade prison work from that of a mere job to that of a professional career run into constraints because of low pay, the nature of the work, the lack of prestige associated with it, and the remote or rural location of many prisons.

A journalist named Bauer (2016, 2019), for example, applied for a job as a guard in a private prison and was told: "I should tell you upfront that the job only pays $9 an hour, but the prison is in the middle of a national forest . . . there is plenty of fishing, and people around here like to hunt squirrels." The recruiter also noted: "I know it's not a lot of money, but they say you can go from a CO [corrections officer] to a warden in just seven years!" Another journalist who spent time as a CO in a big state prison wrote about a conversation he had with a fellow officer:

> "Officer after officer will tell you: there's no way in hell you'd want your kid to be a [correctional officer]." He said that probably ninety percent of the officers he knew would tell a stranger they met on vacation that they worked at something else—carpentry, he liked to say for himself—because the job carried such a stigma. Sure it had its advantages, like the salary, the benefits, the job security, and with seniority, the schedule: starting work at dawn, he had afternoons free to work on his land . . . but mainly, he said, prison work was about waiting. The inmates waited for their sentences to run out and the officers waited for retirement. It was "a life sentence in eight-hour shifts." (Conover 2000)

Work in prison, like that in other areas of criminal justice, is still dominated by white males—68 percent male and 58 percent white (Zippia 2023). The first women hired to work in a men's high-security institution was in 1978, and progress has been slow because people see necessary qualifications as involving toughness and an authoritarian demeanor—qualities not traditionally associated with women. However, as with policing, interpersonal skills are often better than force, and in the prison setting, "gender diversity among officers is associated with a reduction in the rate of prison suicide" (Carter and Whittle 2023). The percentage of female officers had more of an impact on suicide rates of those sentenced to prison than the number of suicide programs and amount of training officers had.

Many people also work as probation and parole officers, and the field known as "community corrections" has grown dramatically over the past several decades. For example, between 1980 and 2021, the number of people subject to probation rose from 1.1 million to 2.9 million, and parole increased from 250,000 to about 800,000 (Bohm and Haley 2005; Bureau of Justice Statistics 2023c: table 1). White people made up 78 percent of "probation officers and correctional treatment specialists" in 2022, Black or African Americans were 21 percent, and Hispanic or Latino workers were 26 percent. Unlike prison workers, where the majority are male, 53 percent of probation officers were women (Bureau of Labor Statistics 2024a).

## Class and the Punishment of Offenders

Prisons and jails confine mostly poor criminals. As far back as 1967, the President's Commission on Law Enforcement and Administration of Justice noted: "The offender at the end of the road in prison is likely to be a member of the lowest social and economic groups in the country" (in Reiman and Leighton 2023: 74). Contemporary research finds that "two years prior to the year they entered prison, 56 percent of individuals have essentially no annual earnings (less than $500)" (Looney and Turner 2018).

We have tried to show in this book that the concentration of the poor and marginalized in prison happens because the processes described in the last several chapters "weed out the wealthy" (Reiman and Leighton 2023). This process starts with the exclusion from the criminal law of morally blameworthy harms committed by the wealthy and continues through prosecution and sentencing. Who is in prison thus does not reflect who is dangerous so much as the cumulative disadvantage for the poor and cumulative advantage for the wealthy and corporations. Indeed, "boys who grew up in families in the bottom 10 percent of the income distribution—families earning less than about $14,000—are 20 times more likely to be in prison on a given day in their early 30s than children born to the wealthiest families—those earning more than $143,000" (Looney and Turner 2018).

At the sentencing stage, this inequality can be seen represented in table 10.1. Basically, the median sentence is the same for a burglary of less than $4,000 and a case of fraud of $160,000. The table only compares individuals and does not include fraud by organizations. According to the U.S. Sentencing Commission (2022: table O-1), there were only forty organizations—corporations, partnerships, and LLCs—convicted of fraud in 2022. Unlike with individual cases, losses from fraud by organizations are not listed. However, 55 percent of organizations convicted of fraud were sentenced to pay restitution only, meaning there was no fine for wrongdoing (U.S. Sentencing Commission 2022: table O-1), yet the median restitution amount was almost $14 million (U.S. Sentencing Commission 2022: table O-2).

**TABLE 10.1 Federal Sentences Served for Different Classes of Crimes**

|  | Median Loss* | Percentage of Convicted Offenders Sentenced to Prison | Median Prison Sentence |
| --- | --- | --- | --- |
| Crimes of the poor (burglary) | $3,865 | 74 | 18 years |
| Crimes of the affluent (fraud/theft/ embezzlement) | $160,737 | 76 | 21 years |

*Source:* U.S. Sentencing Commission 2022: calculated from tables 13, 15, and E-6 and rounded off.

*Note:* Burglary also includes trespassing offenses. Amount of loss is for "Theft, Property Destruction, Fraud."

* Mean (average) value for burglary was $42,000 and $6.4 million for theft, property destruction, fraud.

The average restitution without a fine for wrongdoing was $401 million, meaning there were some very large frauds (that pulled the average way above the median) that were only punished by restitution.

Sentencing is also different when wealthy individuals and corporations cause death, such as the epidemic of overdose deaths related to prescription opioids. From 1999 to 2021, there were 280,000 overdose deaths linked to prescription opioids, although many people became addicted because of prescriptions and later joined the 645,000 overdose deaths linked to fentanyl and other forms of opiates (Centers for Disease Control and Prevention 2023). This epidemic has been called "a for-profit slaughter" that was "predictable and tremendously lucrative" (Bruder 2018).

The executives of Purdue Pharma, makers of Oxycontin, had knowledge in the first years of the drug's release in 1996 that it was being abused, but they continued to market the drug aggressively, saying falsely that it was less likely to result in addiction and abuse than other prescription opioids (Meier 2018). In 2007, the company hired two former U.S. attorneys, Rudy Giuliani and Mary Jo White, who used their contacts at the DOJ to have felony charges dropped. Under the plea deal, Purdue and three executives pleaded guilty to misdemeanor "misbranding" (Keefe 2021) for false information on labels, and the indictment did not claim that the leaders of the company had knowledge of the wrongdoing. The company paid a fine, and when the government agreed not to ask for imprisonment, the executives agreed to pay $34 million (*U.S. v. Purdue Frederick Company* 2007: 6) along with three years' probation and community service (Meier 2007). The federal court's written opinion to accept the plea noted that the government is "convinced that the nature of the convictions" of individual defendants "will send a strong deterrent message to the pharmaceutical industry" (*U.S. v. Purdue Frederick Company* 2007: 15).

But Purdue was undeterred, and the company escalated payments to doctors as an incentive to prescribe a high volume of pills that the executives knew were being funneled into illicit uses (DOJ 2020a: addendum A 6, 8–10 and 19–32). They also paid pharmacies to keep dispensing the company's drugs in the face of increased regulatory scrutiny (DOJ 2020a: addendum A 2, 32–36). In 2020, Purdue pleaded guilty to three felony counts that covered wrongdoing from 2007 (the date of the settlement that would send a "strong deterrent message") to 2017 (DOJ 2020a). No individuals were charged, even though an internal memo noted that, historically, certain members of the Sackler family functioned as "executives, management, board, and shareholders all-in-one [and] worked collaboratively with other managers on a daily basis" (DOJ 2020b: addendum A 4).

Meanwhile, the poor and some middle-class people have faced serious felony charges under laws that were designed to hold drug dealers accountable for overdose deaths of clients but have been used to go after "friends, partners and siblings" (Goldensohn 2018). "Drug-induced homicide" (DIH) laws were a product of the 1980s war on drugs but have received renewed usage during the opiate crisis. About half of the states have such laws, with the majority imposing sentences of more than ten years, with six states having a maximum of life imprisonment and two states allowing the death penalty (Phillips 2020: 661–62). Unlike murder statutes that require proof of intent, DIH laws impose criminal liability on someone who (in the language of Louisiana's law) "distributes or dispenses a controlled dangerous substance" that results in another person's death (in Phillips 2020: 661). The law is easiest to apply to the last person in the chain who gave drugs to the person who overdosed, although the laws were meant (in the words of New Jersey's law) to deter "the most culpable and dangerous" drug dealers through tough sentences (Phillips 2020: 664).

Although the era of holding individual corporate executives accountable seems to be over, sentences for certain financial criminals are worth exploring to see how the guidelines applied for certain outcomes seemed "too tough" or went "too far" (Leighton and Reiman 2004). For example, Bernard Ebbers received twenty-five years for his role as CEO of WorldCom, which became known as "WorldCon" after it replaced Enron as the largest corporate bankruptcy in American history (at that point in time). How could a nonviolent, first-time criminal get so many years? Chapter 9 mentioned the progressive prosecutor who charged people with misdemeanors rather than felonies for theft of less than $1,000 (angering businesses that wanted to see theft dealt with harshly), which raises the question: if people are charged with a felony for theft of $1,000, then what should be the punishment for stealing millions? The court described the calculation for Ebbers:

> The pre-sentence report ("PSR") recommended a base offense level of six, plus sentencing enhancements of 26 levels for a loss over $100 million, of four levels for involving more than 50 victims, of two levels for receiving more than $1 million from financial institutions as a result of the offense, of four levels for leading a criminal activity involving five or more participants, and of two levels for abusing a position of public trust. With Ebbers' criminal history category of I, the Guidelines range calculated in the PSR was life imprisonment. (in Reiman and Leighton 2010: 96–97)

Ebbers's sentence was longer than some people get for murder, but it is not outrageous to say that causing $100 million in losses to more than fifty victims while leading a criminal activity involving others and a breach of public trust can be worse than taking one life. (The court's opinion also notes that the sentence is based on a $100 million loss estimate, when "a loss calculation of $1 billion is therefore almost certainly too low" [in Reiman and Leighton 2010: 100].) It is also true that his sentence was less than what Andrade received for two residential burglaries and two shoplifting charges over the course of decades (see chapter 8).

Further, punishments should become greater as losses become larger. Companies are now bigger and more powerful, and fraud—especially when it leads to a company's collapse—leaves a much larger financial crater. There are more powerful ripple effects (including unemployment) through associated businesses and the economy in general (Reiman and Leighton 2010: 99). The relatively small number of Enron-era sentences that are in the range of fifteen to thirty years were not run-of-the-mill white-collar crimes; they were systemic and widespread frauds that undermined the public's faith in the financial system and caused extensive harm to employees, communities, and shareholders. For example, the judge sentencing Enron's Jeffrey Skilling noted that he had "imposed on hundreds if not thousands of people a life sentence of poverty" (Johnson 2006).

The financial crisis of 2008 brought no criminal punishments of major financial institutions or their executives because there were no criminal charges. Civil settlements had large-sounding fines, but Nobel Prize–winning economist Joseph Stiglitz notes: "Yeah, we fine them, and what is the big lesson? . . . You're still sitting home pretty with your several hundred million dollars that you have left over after paying fines that look very large by ordinary standards but look small compared to the amount that you've been able to cash in." Ultimately, "the fine is just a cost of doing business" (Stiglitz 2010), with Ritholtz (the author of *Bailout Nation*) suggesting that the government played the role of a "meter maid" giving out parking tickets (Ritholtz 2013).

Because the poor are disproportionately punished for crime, they bear the disproportionate impact of court fines and fees. These "criminal justice financial obligations" are piled on poor defendants without consideration of their ability to pay (although fines are assessed with concern for not destabilizing companies). The Department of Justice (2023) noted: "When fines and fees are assessed without consideration of ability to pay, they can have a devastating impact on a person's life. Individuals who are unable to pay court-assessed fines and fees can face snowballing financial penalties, extended justice-system involvement, suspended driver's licenses and unnecessary incarceration."

The worst abuses happen with private probation services that charge monthly fees on top of court fees, restitution, and even fees charged to poor people to offset the cost of their incarceration. According to a Marshall Project investigation, when people did not, or could not, pay, the private probation company "sought to have them arrested and hauled back into court, where a new order of restitution would be issued and additional fines would be levied" (Cohen 2017). "A defendant would get docked for failing to make a required meeting or other appointment because the defendant was at work trying to earn money to pay a fine that would only get higher because of the missed appointment" (Cohen 2017). Fines that started as hundreds of dollars could grow into more than $10,000. When two judges in one jurisdiction tried to reduce debt and reform the system, the private probation company, the Justice Network, sued for reducing the value of its contracts.

# Race and the Punishment of Offenders

The exceptionally high rate of incarceration in the United States disproportionately affects racial and ethnic minorities. Those rates do not include people detained in immigration facilities, who are mostly Latino. The disparities between whites and minorities are glaring because they reflect the cumulative biases from all stages of criminal justice administration in addition to other contributing factors highlighted in figure 10.1. The disproportionate rates of being in prison are shown in table 10.2, which also highlights that almost 60 percent of the prison population are minorities. Officially, "Community Supervision" is probation and parole, where Black people are also overrepresented in these coercive forms of surveillance.

This overrepresentation in prison matters because of the harm prison does to individuals, families, and communities. The National Research Council noted that the body of credible evidence on the effect of the experience of imprisonment on recidivism (the likelihood of rearrest) "consistently points either to no effect or to an increase rather than a decrease in recidivism" (2014: 155). Its report discusses a number of concerns with current U.S. prisons and their negative effects on inmates. Juveniles, especially those of color, are often put in adult prisons, where they have to deal with greater stress, violence, and predation of adults. Solitary confinement is more likely to be used, and it is imposed with fewer restrictions than other developed nations have on the number of consecutive days a person can spend in solitary

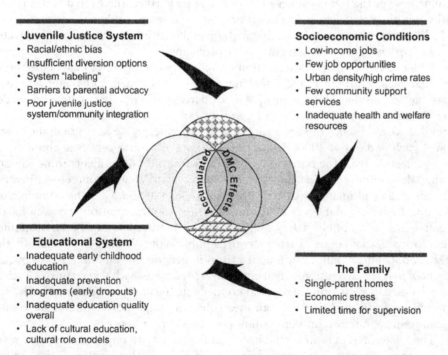

**FIGURE 10.1** Underlying Factors That Contribute to Minority Overrepresentation

*Source:* OJJDP (Office of Juvenile Justice and Delinquency Prevention) 2006.

### TABLE 10.2   PUNISHMENT RATES BY RACE AND ETHNICITY

| | Percent of Prison Population | Incarceration Rate | Community Supervision Rate |
|---|---|---|---|
| White | 31 | 229 | 1,240 |
| Black | 32 | 1,196 | 3,560 |
| Hispanic | 23 | 603 | 1,160 |
| American Indian/Alaskan Native | 2 | 1,042 | — |
| Asian | 1 | 88 | — |
| Other | — | — | 480 |

*Sources:* Bureau of Justice Statistics 2023b: page 1 and table 6; BJS 2023c: table 8.

*Note:* Incarceration rate is only for state and federal prisons, not jails, and is stated per one hundred thousand population eighteen and over. Percent of prison population of each racial group is based on only those cases where race was recorded. "Asian" includes Native Hawaiians and other Pacific Islanders. For community supervision rate, "Other" includes Asians, Native Hawaiians, and Other Pacific Islanders; persons of two or more races; and persons of other races that are not shown separately.

confinement or the total number of days per year. Further, the United States is generally less likely than other developed nations to have mental health screenings and guidelines that would prevent people with mental health issues from being subjected to an experience that will aggravate their problems.

Other effects of mass incarceration on minority communities include the problem that incarceration "reduces the marriageability of men and thereby reduces marriage formation. This, in turn, would increase the number of female-headed households in areas with high incarceration rates and, ultimately, increase crime rates due to an absence of supervision for young males in" areas of high incarceration (Lynch and Sabol 2000: 15). Criminologists also raise concerns about social disorganization from the removal ("coerced migration") of residents to prison and having them dumped back into the community with few resources—either not rehabilitated or ultimately worse off for their time in prison. Clear has summarized the point by stating that "very high concentrations of incarceration may well have a negative impact on public safety by leaving communities less capable of sustaining the informal social control that undergirds public safety" (2002: 181–82; see also Clear 2008). This is not a critique of prison in general but an analysis of how the effects of mass incarceration, when concentrated in areas with few resources such as inner cities, can erode informal social controls such as family, neighborhoods, and community groups. The results can mean that the high incarceration rate creates criminogenic conditions and undermines public safety in those areas.

The overrepresentation with parole and probation are important because revocations are an important source of prison admissions. The tough-on-crime movement has meant the proliferation of conditions for remaining out of prison and a zero-tolerance attitude toward violations (Blackwell 2021; Ortiz and Jackey 2019; Rakia 2019). For example, people on probation and parole are usually required to work, meet their parole or probation office, and report for drug tests; many also have a curfew (home 7 p.m. to 8 a.m.), cannot socialize with people who have a record, and are not allowed to leave the state (even to see family who may be a source of support). While individually some of the conditions make sense, when put together it becomes challenging not to violate one of them. The curfew, for example, limits many job opportunities, so people need to find jobs during the day but then take off from work hours to meet during the day with their parole officer and do drug tests without getting fired for missing work. The type of housing available to people released from prison often has others with a criminal record in the building or nearby. A violation that results in even a short stay in jail can result in the loss of work and housing.

Further, minorities, especially Black people released from prison, experience what is called racialized reentry (Western and Sirois 2019). The stigma of a criminal record and incarceration seems to be stronger for Black people, so job prospects in the legitimate economy are even more limited than for other people released from prison with a criminal record. Indeed, white people released from prison "had higher rates of physical disability and drug addiction, were less ready for employment, and more socially isolated immediately after prison release. Despite these disadvantages, their employment rates were higher and their earnings were nearly double those of formerly incarcerated blacks and Hispanics" (Western and Sirois 2019: 1357). More of the Black people who were employed after prison were forced to take jobs that involved crime and exposed them to higher rates of rearrest and reincarceration. Ultimately, "with the highest incarceration rates and returning to the most adverse economic environments, African Americans have the lowest earnings and bear the greatest weight of the compounded disadvantages of mass incarceration" (Western and Sirois 2019: 1358).

In addition, people released from prison experience ongoing punishments because of the collateral consequences of conviction (Government Accountability Office [GAO] 2017). For example, those convicted of certain types of crime lose their right to vote, hold certain professional licenses, and receive benefits such as access to public housing, unemployment benefits, food stamps, and student loans (Travis 2002; see also Alexander 2012). A review of an American Bar Association database found that "roughly 46,000 collateral consequences existed in federal and state laws and regulations" (GAO 2017: 1). Just at the federal level, "there are 641 collateral consequences that can be triggered by nonviolent drug convictions, and 78 percent of those could potentially last a lifetime" (GAO 2017: 1). These policies make it much more difficult for people released from prison—who have supposedly "done their time"—to reenter society by denying access to affordable housing and sources of legitimate income, as well as erecting barriers to education and the professional credentials necessary for many better jobs.

Another impact of mass incarceration has been massive prison construction in white, rural areas to house inner-city minorities. Indeed, from 1980 to 2000, the United States built more prisons than it had in all the rest of its history (Vieraitis et al. 2007). The "largest prison expansion the world has ever known" (Dyer 2000: 2) occurred in white rural areas, with important racial consequences. Having rural white guards oversee largely minority inner-city inmates creates problems with racial harassment. Also, for purposes of the census, inmates are counted as residents where they are incarcerated, not where their home is. As a result, the population of largely white rural areas gets a boost, while cities show lower numbers of residents. Using the census figures to allocate legislators to state legislatures and the U.S. Congress, as well as to distribute large amounts of government aid, therefore works against minority populations.

Collectively, higher rates of imprisonment for Black and Hispanic people also limit their abilities to participate in the political process and to effect changes in the system, criminal justice or otherwise. Several million Americans are currently or permanently disenfranchised from voting, including one in eight Black males of voting age. Forty-eight states and the District of Columbia prohibit offenders from voting while on parole or probation, and fourteen states have reserved the right to permanently ban felons from voting (Porter 2010). When combined with population counts that affect legislators and financial aid, the sum total of these dynamics is to disadvantage racially diverse cities with large numbers of minority residents who have committed no crimes while economically and politically privileging white areas.

Another important aspect of racialized captivity is immigrant detention. Although it is not usually considered in the context of racialized incarceration patterns, we have argued in this book that the immigration regime is intertwined with the criminal justice system to serve the larger purpose of coercive social control. Earlier chapters have documented how the tough-on-crime movement also changed immigration policies and enforcement, and that crimmigration process means high levels of punitiveness and deplorable conditions of migrant detention facilities. As of early 2024, about 38,500 immigrants were detained—about 11,000 in Immigration and Customs Enforcement (ICE) and 27,500 in Customs and Border Patrol (CBP) facilities (TRAC 2024). However, in 2023, 190,000 immigrants were admitted to both agencies' facilities, better illustrating the number of people subjected to this form of control. Also, as of early 2024, another 190,000 people were subject to the Alternatives to Detention Program that includes GPS monitoring programs (TRAC 2024).

With migrant detention, people are bused and flown around the country without any advance warning. More frequently than those confined to prisons, immigrant detainees are moved across state lines and are denied the ability to regularly communicate with their loved ones or advocates. The network of private contractors, collectively referred to as "ICE Air," has been regularly critiqued by government oversight agencies as lacking in accountability.

Recent detention conditions pre-COVID were deeply problematic. Investigative journalists suing under the Freedom of Information Act obtained more than 1,600 pages of inspection reports covering more than two dozen facilities from 2017 to 2019 (Dreisbach 2023). The Department of Homeland Security's Office for Civil Rights and Civil Liberties hired experts whom the journalists say "found 'negligent' medical care (including mental health care), 'unsafe and filthy' conditions, racist abuse of detainees, inappropriate pepper-spraying of mentally ill detainees and other problems that, in some cases, contributed to detainee deaths" (Dreisbach 2023). The Department of Homeland Security Office of Inspector General (2019) found similar problems. Their review found "nooses in detainee cells, overly restrictive segregation, inadequate medical care, unreported security incidents, and significant food safety issues." New reports have also noted conditions "ranging from dangerous overcrowding and poor sanitation, to allegations of sexual assault and forced mass hysterectomies by U.S. officials" (Mendoza 2016; H. T. Nguyen 2021). Not surprisingly, the conditions of detention coupled with the threat of deportation to extremely violent communities have led to an alarming number of suicides in recent years (Berg et al. 2022; Marquez et al. 2021).

## Gender and the Punishment of Offenders

The environments of women's prisons are generally less oppressive than those of men's because there is less violence, conflict, interracial tension, and hostility toward staff. But women may experience imprisonment more negatively than men because of their separation from their family, especially children. Other contributing factors to this negativity are scarcity of resources, including a lack of work programs, vocational curriculum, and health services (compared with men's facilities); sexual harassment and abuse from prison staff; and fewer distinctions or classifications when it comes to custody and security levels (i.e., many states operate only one major prison for women). In addition, "rates of mental illness are substantially higher among female than male inmates, particularly because they have high rates of childhood sexual abuse and PTSD" (National Research Council 2014: 212).

As of year-end 2022, women made up about 7 percent of prison inmates (Bureau of Justice Statistics 2023b: 5). There were 87,784 female inmates in state and federal prisons compared with 1,142,359 males (Bureau of Justice Statistics 2023b: table 1), which table 10.3 shows as incarceration rates. Although the numbers and rates are lower, incarceration rates for women have grown faster than for men when incarceration was growing, and they have declined less than men's rates more recently.

Because there are fewer women in prison does not mean the sentencing system is fair with respect to gender. Indeed, compared with men, women are differently situated with respect to crime, most notably in that they typically commit less serious crimes than men do, engage in less violent crime, and are less likely to have a prior record. Women are typically arrested for "survival" crimes, including sex work, property crime, and drug-related crimes. Property crimes include bad checks, welfare fraud, and credit card abuse (sometimes charged as identity theft). Mirroring

### TABLE 10.3 Incarceration Rates by Gender, 2022

|  | Incarceration Rate (per 100,000) | Percentage Incarcerated for Violent Crime* |
| --- | --- | --- |
| Male | 666 | 64.2 |
| Female | 49 | 45.5 |

*Source:* BJS 2023b, tables 13 and 16.

*State correctional facilities only.

gender discrimination in the legitimate economy that keeps women in jobs with lower wages, criminal opportunities have a similar gender inequality; women do not tend to be drug kingpins or white-collar criminals to nearly the extent that men are. Histories of abuse and trauma lead to substance abuse, which in turn leads to crime and prison.

Further, women are disproportionately represented among those incarcerated for public order violations, such as solicitation (of sex for money), begging, and driving under the influence. While there are some violent women, reading the statistics about the increasing number of women incarcerated for assault requires caution because of the effect of mandatory arrest laws discussed in previous chapters.

Indeed, an analysis by the Office of Juvenile Justice and Delinquency Prevention (OJJDP) Girls Study Group found that much of girls' assaultive behavior occurred at home among family members. At an earlier time, such behavior might have resulted in a referral to family services, but criminal justice practices have changed: "Charging girls for behavior arising from family chaos sweeps girls with trauma histories and chaotic families into secure juvenile justice confinement" (Sherman 2012: 1593). Historically, "expectations that girls behave obediently, modestly, and cautiously" were

> behind the proliferation of training schools for immigrant girls who were perceived to be immoral and in need of guidance that would enable them to marry and to become responsible mothers. In the mid- and late twentieth century, these expectations supported detention and incarceration of girls for status offenses, for technical probation violations, and particularly for running away. Now, these same expectations result in the detention and incarceration of girls who fight back at home or in intimate relationships and who are victims of sexual exploitation. (Sherman 2012: 1586)

Unlike male prison inmates, who are usually incarcerated according to different levels of security (i.e., maximum, medium, minimum) and classification by type of offense, women prisoners are likely to be incarcerated at a facility with a diverse population of offenders. As measured on a per-inmate basis, expenditures for women for education, vocational, and other programs have been less than for men. The one notable exception has been for monies spent on health care, where women have received 60 percent more than men do. "Reproductive issues are one reason, as 5 to 6 percent of women entering prisons and jails are pregnant" (National Research Council 2014: 212). But even with the seemingly higher expenditures, the critical needs associated with pregnancy, birth, lactation, and caring for an infant are woefully underresourced and understudied, so women who are pregnant and who give birth within correctional settings experience worse health-care outcomes (Alirezaei and Roudsari 2022; Clarke and Simon 2013; Sapkota et al. 2022; Wang 2021). The greater expenditures are also likely related to the greater incidences of HIV and AIDS and with greater needs for mental health services. But even with greater expenditures, female inmates sometimes do not have a mammogram or Pap smear for years.

Also, for many decades, women's prisons were more likely than men's to have a cottage-style design and are less likely to have intimidating features such as gun towers, high concrete walls, and armed guards. This cottage form of imprisoning inmates dates back to the early twentieth century, when cottages were used to house small groups of women so that they could "live with a motherly matron in a family setting" (Rierden 1997: 7). The legacy of this era has meant that women's prisons are still tending to infantilize and domesticize women while reinforcing gender stereotypes (Belknap 2007). Over time, accommodation has moved toward the confinement model used in men's prisons. This development, however, is another example of seeming gender neutrality that is actually based on a male standard (see chapter 5) rather than a genuine effort to address the actual needs of women.

For example, McCorkel's study of a New England women's prison found that "equal treatment" meant that women "received a much-needed law library" but also isolation cells, "boot camps, razor wire fences, and body cavity searches" (2013: 28). This did not make the prison system gender neutral or gender responsive; "it universally masculinized the physical structure of incarceration. In designing the new prison the way that they had, the Department of Corrections made men's prisons the model for all prisons" (McCorkel 2013: 28).

The problem of seeming gender neutrality can be compounded when classification, risk assessment surveys, and drug and alcohol programs designed for men are used for women, as well as when staff are not given training about the different needs and expectations of women. Women are likely to have experienced sexual assault and domestic violence. This problem extends further to LGBT+ inmates, who as youth and adults had experiences like "being kicked out of their homes, schools, being fired from their jobs, evicted by their landlords, denied health care" (Buist and Lenning 2016: 92).

Another important difference with female inmates is their relationship with children. While a large number of incarcerated men are fathers, 70 percent of female offenders have a child under eighteen and are likely to be the primary caretaker. However, women in prison tend to be isolated because of geography, transportation, economic resources, the termination of parental rights, and the lack of institutional support (access to telephones, visiting space for children, staff attitudes, etc.). One nineteen-year-old woman explained: "I was locked in this horrible lonely, scary place with leaking breasts and no baby. . . . I held my pillow like it was my child, and it was soaked with my milk and my tears. . . . I felt bereft, I have never felt grief or pain like it" (Walsh et al. 2023).

Although many women committed crimes in order to support their children—single women with children are the group most likely to experience significant poverty—they were labeled as "bad mothers" because they violated the law and thus "chose" to be absent from their children's lives. Just as a woman's ability to perform motherhood "in a socially acceptable way increases a sense of belonging and competence," being labeled a bad mother and having barriers to being a supportive mother increase depression and anxiety (Walsh et al. 2023). These feelings and the related stress can lead to somatic symptoms, which means the conversion of psychological states to physical ailments like headaches, chest pain, back pain, nausea, or fatigue.

Further, the labeling and lack of support increases women's likelihood of further criminality because "there is significant evidence that the mother-child relationship may hold significant potential for community reintegration" (Subramanian and

Shames 2013). A limited number of mother-child prison units allow newborns and infants to stay with mothers for up to several years. As the Vera Institute explains,

> research conducted on U.S. programs has found that these programs have a positive impact for both mothers and children. Evaluations of prison nursery programs have shown lower rates of recidivism, an increased likelihood of obtaining child custody post-release, higher rates of mother and child bonding, and self-reported increases in self-esteem and self-confidence. (Subramanian and Shames 2013: 16)

Such programs need to be complemented with other programs that help women with job skills so that they are in a better economic position to support children and enhance their capacity in other ways to set up a life that would involve reunification with children.

Another important issue is sexual abuse in prison. Sexual and other abuses of incarcerated people, including juveniles, by (often male) prison staff are problems that have persisted in spite of reforms and lawsuits won by people in prison. Further, people identified as LGBTQ+ "experience sexual violence in prison at devastatingly higher rates, up to ten times higher, than heterosexual inmates" (Buist and Lenning 2016: 108). A recent survey of several hundred trans people in prison found that "more than half (53 percent) said they had experienced a nonconsensual sexual encounter—in other words, a sexual assault—at some point during their current prison sentence" (Chesnut and Peirce 2024: 10).

Victimization of women in prison has tended to come from male staff members who use the power differences to coerce or exploit female inmates. International standards provide that female prisoners should be supervised only by female guards, but sex discrimination laws in the United States mean that men can work in women's prisons and women can work in men's prisons. In popular culture, sex in women's prison is eroticized, as evidenced by the "chicks in chains" film genre (Faith 1993). But the reality is very different, and "women prisoners with histories of abuse may be re-traumatized by sexual harassment and abuse in prison" at the hands of corrections employees (Bloom et al. 2003: 26). The results include post-traumatic stress disorder, depression, "and decreased ability to participate in rehabilitative programs," which ultimately affect reintegration and recidivism (Bloom et al. 2003: 26).

For example, a 2022 Senate subcommittee's report on the sexual abuse of women inmates in federal prisons found numerous issues of abuse by Bureau of Prisons (BOP) employees. The report found evidence that BOP employees were responsible for sexually abusing incarcerated women in nineteen of twenty-nine facilities (two-thirds). Further, the report found that the BOP has failed to implement the Prison Rape Elimination Act (PREA) by failing to protect women from being sexually abused. Indeed, the report revealed that in the FCI Dublin facility (dubbed the "rape club" [Druker 2022]), a minimum security prison in California, the prison's former warden and chaplain sexually abused women incarcerated in the facility. Finally, the report found that in the last ten years, the Bureau of Prisons opened over five thousand cases of sexual assault from both incarcerated men and women (Ossoff and Johnson 2022).

In men's prisons, sexual violence tends to be between men who have been sentenced to prison. Rape functions as a violent rite of passage to convert "men" into "punks" and create hierarchies of power and control, to meet part of the demand for sexual partners, and to establish claims to masculinity. Sykes (1958) noted that one of the pains of imprisonment was a deprivation of heterosexual contact. In this situation, men have to define "manhood" without women and do so by emphasizing the worst aspects of the male gender role—aggression, domination, and emotional coldness. The victims are symbolically transformed into women and even take on the "womanly" functions of the relationship. "Punks" will often do household chores that mimic those of the traditional female, such as doing the laundry, making the bunk, making coffee, or cleaning the cell. Prisoner subculture dictates that aggressive penetrative activity is heterosexual, while receptive penetrated activity is not. The phrase "homosexual rape" is thus misleading since the overwhelming majority of prison perpetrators and victims are heterosexual and resume heterosexual behavior when they are released from incarceration. (In addition, chapter 5 noted that "homosexual" is an outdated term that should not be used.)

One strategy some men use to avoid sexual victimization is to "hook up" with another man in prison. In exchange for sexual favors, men who fear victimization can pair off with a "Man" for protection from gang rapes or repeated threats of rape. The resulting relationships do not reflect consensual gay activity as much as survival-driven behavior. Men who wish to avoid being turned out or who desire to undo its effect must often use violence. One man explained, "It's fixed where if you're raped, the only way you [can stop the abuse is if] you rape someone else. Yes I know that's fully screwed, but that's how your head is twisted. After it's over you may be disgusted with yourself, but you realize you're not powerless and that you can deliver as well as receive pain. Then it's up to you to decide whether you enjoy it or not" (Human Rights Watch 2001).

The violence against LGBTQ+ people in prison goes well beyond sexual violence. Other people in prison assault them as well as direct verbal and psychological abuse against them. When staff do try to provide safety, the targets of violence are usually put in administrative segregation cells, which are the same ones used for punitive solitary confinement. To put the matter bluntly, "keeping someone safe should never mean trapping them alone in a cinderblock cell the size of a bathroom for 23 hours a day" (Bryant 2022). For trans people in prison, other issues include the denial of gender-affirming care, inappropriately gendered officers to supervise showers and do pat-down searches, as well as greater deficits with physical and mental health care (Chesnut and Peirce 2024). Another problem is inappropriate placement in a men's or women's facility: if a transgender woman who was born male commits a crime and she has yet to receive complete gender-confirming surgery, that woman will likely be housed in an all-male facility where the chances of violence and overall harm increase greatly (Buist and Lenning 2023).The same issues occur with LGBTQ+ people held in Immigration and Customs Enforcement (ICE) and Customs and Border Protection (CBP) facilities (Carrillo 2023).

## Intersections and the Punishment of Offenders

The overall rate at which the United States incarcerates groups is shown in table 10.4. (BJS does not publish intersectional data about the jail population or people on probation and parole.) The incarceration rate for white men is 337 per

100,000 population, compared with 1,826 for Black men, and with Hispanic men in between. There is a similar pattern for women, with the rate for white women less than half of that for Black women. At this time, there is growing awareness that more attention should be paid to LGBTQ+ people in prison, officers, and workers in both institutional and community corrections (Buist and Lenning 2023). For all groups, though, the National Research Council concludes that prison does a great deal of harm, and "the most negative of these consequences can undermine post-prison adjustment and linger long after formerly incarcerated persons have been released back into society" (2014: 157). However, the burden of those negative consequences is not evenly distributed across social groups.

Furthermore, to get the full picture requires stepping back from prison to examine those who commit serious harms but are never incarcerated. For example, the A. H. Robins Company manufactured and distributed the Dalkon Shield, a birth control device. The company started selling the intrauterine device (IUD) as a safe, modern, and effective product. Although A. H. Robins had performed few tests on the device, marketing and promotion went ahead quickly, and some 4.5 million IUDs were distributed. Early reports indicated many problems, including that the tail string from the device hung outside the vagina and wicked bacteria up into the woman's body, and the device was not especially effective at preventing pregnancy either. Even worse, women suffered from a variety of crippling and life-threatening infections, some of which required emergency hysterectomies; others had unwanted pregnancies that resulted in miscarriages or spontaneous abortions; or, because of infections, they gave birth to children with severe birth defects. Conservative estimates indicated that some two hundred thousand women were injured (Clinard 1990).

Two court-appointed examiners found that Robins had engaged "in ongoing fraud by knowingly misrepresenting the nature, quality, safety and efficacy" of its IUD. The fraud also "involved the destruction and withholding of relevant evidence" (in Clinard 1990: 104). In spite of these facts, no prosecutor brought criminal charges against the company or its executives. Women were left on their own to file a variety of civil product liability suits. In response, Robins tried to file for bankruptcy in order to avoid liability. However, a judge required the company

**TABLE 10.4 Imprisonment Rates of Sentenced State and Federal Prisoners, Year-End 2022 (per 100,000 U.S. Residents)**

|  | All[a] | White[b] | Black[b] | Hispanic | Other[a,b] |
|---|---|---|---|---|---|
| Males | 666 | 337 | 1,826 | 794 | 2,831 |
| Females | 49 | 40 | 64 | 49 | 269 |

*Source:* BJS 2023b: table 13.

[a] Includes persons of two or more races and other races that are not broken out.

[b] Excludes persons of Hispanic origin.

to establish a trust fund to compensate victims, and he had to reprimand Robins for giving substantial bonuses to its top executives in violation of the bankruptcy laws.

Judge Miles Lord, who heard some four hundred civil law cases, in a famous plea for corporate conscience, pointed out the class bias:

> If some poor young man was, by some act of his—without authority or consent—to inflict such damage on one woman, he would be jailed for a good portion of the rest of his life. And yet your company, without warning to women, invaded their bodies by the millions and caused them injury by the thousands. And when the time came for these women to make claims against your company, you attacked their characters. You inquired into sexual practices and into the identity of their sex partners. You exposed these women—and ruined families and reputation and careers—in order to intimidate those who would raise their voice against you. You introduced issues that had no relationship whatsoever to the fact that you planted in the bodies of these women instruments of death, of mutilation, of disease. (in Hills 1987: 42)

Judge Lord also noted that the consequences might have been harsher had the injured parties been men rather than women, who Judge Lord noted "seem through some strange quirk in our society's mores to be expected to suffer pain, shame and humiliation" (in Hills 1987: 42). The executives from Robins ultimately had to listen to a lecture and return some bonus pay as punishment, whereas offenders who engage in other assaults face prison time.

In a different but powerful way, McCorkel's *Breaking Women* illustrates the importance of examining intersections. The book uses the author's four years of observation of a drug program in a women's prison to analyze gender, race, and privatization. As noted earlier, "gender neutrality" means a male model of getting tough, which happens as increasing numbers of African American women arrive in prison. "The rehabilitative ideal died at the very same moment when the number of African Americans behind bars surpassed the number of incarcerated whites" (McCorkel 2013: 13). At this point in time, "staff began to distinguish between prisoners of old ('good girls') and the incoming tide of 'real criminals'" (McCorkel 2013: 16). McCorkel argues that "racial stereotypes of Black women, particularly as welfare dependent, crime prone, and drug addicted, became galvanizing symbols for abandoning the rehabilitative ideal and replacing it with control strategies that were both more coercive and more intrusive than earlier practices" (2013: 13; Ritchie 2017).

One entity seizing on this new perspective was a for-profit company, which introduced a drug treatment plan that was accepted because it is also "tough": it "breaks down" women so that they accept that addiction is caused by their diseased "self," which is a "permanent condition" that could be "treated but not cured" with a "lifetime of external management and control" (McCorkel 2013: 56). The program, billed as "habilitation" (not "rehabilitation"), consists of verbal abuse of the inmates' mothering, sexuality, and (co)dependence on men and welfare. McCorkel notes that in the Canadian prison system, "prisoners are encouraged to deal with structural issues like poverty and violence by taking responsibility for their own choices and actions, and, ultimately, their own reform" (2013: 151). They seem to take more responsibility for their actions than the state does for social problems, but the goal is "self-governing, rational and autonomous subjects." But with habilitation, there is no building back up, because prisoners are seen as broken beyond repair, which McCorkel argues leads to disempowerment and confusion over their experiences with poverty, violence, and sexual abuse.

The realities of the disproportionate number of poor, Blacks, and Hispanic people in prison do not necessarily capture how the experience of being incarcerated breeds feelings of despair and hopelessness, and often anger and rage, for those individuals imprisoned. For example, these feelings in combination with the stigma of having been incarcerated often make it difficult to find anything other than minimum-wage employment, if that, on release. Moreover, businesses are less likely to locate in areas with large numbers of poor people, especially those areas with high concentrations of Black men, because of concerns about the pool of labor, so these communities find it difficult, if not impossible, to build any type of economically viable base.

Higher rates of incarceration for Black men and women weaken both the economic and familiar stability of Black and other poor communities. Specifically, these correctional practices that disproportionately affect African Americans and other poor minorities have an impact on noncriminal impoverished women and their children. In other words, as corrections budgets have increased nationwide, state funds to support poor and low-income families have been slashed, along with other social services and social service positions disproportionately staffed by women. These connections show problems with conventional discussions of punishment that tend to treat corrections as if it were a discrete and independent social institution. Far from being an entity separate unto itself, the entire criminal justice system, especially the correctional system, has become inextricably intertwined with the welfare system, the political system, and—with the increasing privatization of corrections—the economic system. For example, the impact of having one in three Black men under the control of the criminal justice system cannot be separated from the welfare system's Temporary Assistance to Needy Families (TANF) program or the high percentage of single-female Black households. Similarly, the secondary impact of incarceration of poor women on their children cannot be underestimated with respect to the increased likelihood of the children's delinquency.

Further, TANF prohibits individuals who violate probation or parole orders and their families from receiving TANF or food stamps. The act does not distinguish between minor technical violations such as missing an appointment with a probation or parole officer and committing a new crime. Another provision bans persons convicted of drug felonies from receiving TANF or food stamps for the rest of their lives. Consequently, critics of the act creating TANF were quick to express concern that children would feel the repercussions of provisions intended to punish their mothers and promote "personal responsibility." Hence, children of a poor woman suffer consequences for their mother's behavior in a way that middle-class children would not, should either of their parents be busted for using drugs.

Another important addition to the understanding of intersections comes from examining private prisons. While chapter 1 discussed privatization in more detail, of interest here is that the dramatic growth in incarceration has attracted the interest of numerous business owners who saw—and see—prison as a "big business" that they can cash in on by providing supporting goods and services. The most visible of these industries are for-profit companies, traded on the stock market, that build and run prisons. Privatization is an intersectional issue because, in a variation of *The Rich Get Richer and the Poor Get Prison* (Reiman and Leighton 2023), rich white males get richer because poor minorities go to prison. As noted in chapter 3, stock ownership is concentrated in the hands of relatively few wealthy families who are mostly white, and others who make money support private prisons through financial services (which underwrite loans) or corporate law. Some of the same private prison companies are also involved with migrant detention, which adds to the same flow of capital and profits to a relatively small and privileged group, while racialized persons with relatively less financial and material resources are increasingly held in detention facilities.

For context, remember that chapter 1 identified privatization as one of the major trends that continues to exert an influence on the criminal justice enterprise as a core value of neoliberalism. Privatization refers to the practice of converting government functions and services into private, for-profit business models where government contracts enable the transfer of public tax dollars toward private profiteering and wealth extraction. Punishment and incarceration may seem like odd functions to privatize, but private prisons are a multibillion-dollar-a-year business, and the two largest firms—CoreCivic (formerly Corrections Corporation of America [CCA]) and the GEO Group—are multinational businesses that trade on Wall Street (Selman and Leighton 2010). Outside of private prisons is a larger prison-industrial complex that is composed of businesses that profit from prisons and prisoners. Businesses need to finance and build prisons, and they lend to others in the prison-industrial complex to supply cameras, drug tests, uniforms, food, medical and health-care services, payment systems, commissary, telephone calls, and much more. Economies of scale incentivize builders to have more people in prison, so there is a financial incentive to continue the practice of incarceration and ensure that sentencing reform does not hurt their business.

The captive body becomes the product, with the goal of having the greatest number of "bodies destined for profitable punishment" (Leighton and Selman 2018). This observation also applies to migrant detention, where numerous contractors profit from partnering with ICE, CBP, and Homeland Security. Securities and Exchange Commission (SEC) forms provide a window into the business model of private prisons, which must disclose their risk factors in filings. Risk factors include not getting enough inmates from the government to be profitable, sentencing reform (like the repeal of certain mandatory minimum sentences), steps toward the legalization of drugs, and immigration reform (Selman and Leighton 2010; Reiman and Leighton 2023). While these are controversial topics, the debate over justice policy needs to be on the merits of reform, not based on the financial interests of wealthy shareholders and Wall Street. (Chapter 6 on intersections noted that decisions about a city should not be based on the views and interests of those in the penthouse of a particular part of that area.) Indeed, research demonstrates that private prison firms have already influenced public policy to their own benefit through campaign donations and lobbying. The National Research Council found that "by the mid-1990s, the new economic interests—including private prison companies, prison guards' unions, and the suppliers of everything from bonds for new prison construction to Taser stun guns—were playing an important role in maintaining and sustaining the incarceration increase" (2014: 126).

Private prisons were born from two trends, and the path to the highest profitability is the continuation of them. First, the relentless war on crime and war on drugs caused massive prison overcrowding. But politicians' favorite lines were about lower taxes and less government. Second, President Ronald Reagan declared that "government is the problem," and he set the stage for antigovernment politicians to privatize a range of services. The historical moment was ripe for several politically well-connected individuals, backed by the same venture capital that facilitated the expansion of Kentucky Fried Chicken, to use private funds to build their own prison and collect money from the government to house people in prison (Selman and Leighton 2010). And, although the incarceration binge has been costly and ineffective, it has contributed to social injustice (especially racial); it also means that the for-profit nature of the prison business depends on the continuation of that injustice (Selman and Leighton 2010).

One area of prison privatization that especially deserves consideration is for-profit prison health care. For example, a *New York Times* article was titled "As Health Care in Jails Goes Private, 10 Days Can Be a Death Sentence" (von Zielbauer 2005: A1). The exposé of a company called Prison Health Services revealed that as governments try to reduce the burden of soaring medical costs—due to expanding and aging prison populations and exacerbated by the exploding problems of AIDS and mental illness among inmates—this new for-profit field has become a multibillion-dollar-a-year industry.

The yearlong examination of Prison Health Services (the leader in the field) revealed repeated instances of medical care that were flawed and sometimes lethal: "The company's performance around the nation has provoked criticism from judges and sheriffs, lawsuits from inmates' families and whistle-blowers, and condemnations by federal, state, and local authorities. The company has paid millions of dollars in fines and settlements" (von Zielbauer 2005: A1). Despite similar patterns of abuse found across the nation, like the ones in New York described below, Prison Health has been an ongoing concern:

> In the two deaths, and eight others across upstate New York, state investigators say they kept discovering the same failings: medical staffs trimmed to the bone, doctors underqualified or out of reach, nurses doing tasks beyond their training, prescription drugs withheld, patient records unread and employee misconduct unpunished. Not surprisingly, Prison Health, which is based outside of Nashville, is no longer working in most of those upstate jails. But it is hardly out of work. Despite a tarnished record [from coast to coast], Prison Health has sold its promise of lower costs and better care, and become the biggest for-profit company providing medical care in jails and prisons. It has amassed 86 contracts in 28 states, and now cares for 237,000 inmates, or about 1 in every 10 people behind bars. (von Zielbauer 2005: A26)[1]

## Implications

Crime control policies constantly reward financial white-collar criminals who line their pockets millions of times over at the expense of the general public and well-being of the world. At the same time, crime control policies overwhelmingly penalize the poor and people of color, especially Black and Hispanic or Latino persons, often for relatively harmless acts. Those who become incarcerated face abuse, violence, and victimization in a variety of forms. Penal violence, however, is pretty much hidden from public scrutiny, much like the disproportionate numbers of minority citizens contained in prisons. For example, Sykes and Piquero (2009: 214) have found with respect to contracting HIV inside and outside of prison as well as with other health testing in general that "the penal institution is an active agent in structuring and re-creating health inequalities within prisons, thereby exacerbating existing community health inequities when inmates are released."

Recent changes in state laws have been in the process of overturning a century-old juvenile justice system whose very reason for existence was to protect children from contact with adult prisoners. Despite the fact that whites commit most juvenile crimes, three out of four youths admitted to adult courts, jails, and prisons are children of color. In spite of the fact that penologists and criminologists almost all agree that these children are more likely to be physically and sexually abused in these institutions than in juvenile institutions and that they are more likely to continue committing crimes after their release, more and more prosecutors are moving young offenders into the adult system with little if any regard for the children's age or circumstances.

Ultimately, the institutionalization of penal violence cannot be separated from the structural conditions outside the confining walls. Angela Davis (1998: 2) has reflected, the "prison industrial system materially and morally impoverishes its inhabitants and devours the social wealth needed to address the very problems that have led to spiraling numbers of prisons." The focus should thus not be only on a criminal justice system in need of reform but also on the "Perpetual Prisoner Machine" (Dyer 2000) that has been increasing its size and proportion of state and federal fiscal budgets relative to the declining dollars spent on education and social services since the 1990s.

## Review and Discussion Questions

1. How would you sentence Deegan? In making your decision, explain whether (and why) it is important to focus on the crime already committed or the future benefit to deterring the individual or others. How should the punishment weigh individual responsibility given the total failure of supports? What might a rehabilitative or restorative sentence look like?
2. What is the link between incarceration rates and crime rates? Does getting tough on crime lower crime rates? Why or why not?
3. Why does this chapter use the terms *punishment* and *prison* rather than *corrections*? Why do we refer to the Department of Corrections if rehabilitation is not a goal and most people believe in harsh punishments in warehouse prisons?
4. What are some of the barriers to upgrading prison work into a desirable career?
5. The chapter argues that prisons are filled with poor people because the system weeds out the wealthy, not because they are the largest or worst group of

criminals. What evidence from sentences and sentencing presented here supports that view?

6. In what ways does the disproportionate punishment inflicted on minorities, especially Black people, hurt them and recreate/worsen inequality?

7. How are women differently situated from men with respect to the types of crimes they commit and the impact of incarceration on them?

8. What are private prisons? Why are they and the prison-industrial complex an intersectional issue?

## Note

1. We recognize that many readers have experiences with health care that is limited, hard to access, and expensive. Rather than being a call to make sure people in prison have worse health care, the situation should be a motivation to do better for everybody. After all, *every* other developed nation has managed to figure out a national health care system that does better for the average person.

# Conclusion

*Coauthored with Kaitlyn Selman*

Hard times are coming, when we'll be wanting the voices of writers who can see alternatives to how we live now . . . to other ways of being, and even imagine real grounds for hope. We'll need writers who can remember freedom—poets, visionaries—realists of a larger reality.

—Ursula K. Le Guin

## Introduction

In writing this book, we have documented some of the ways that the United States comes up short on its promises of equality and explained how these inequalities are tied to larger systems of privilege and oppression. Criminology and the criminal "justice" system are part of the systems of class-, race-, and gender/sexuality-based privileges and oppressions. While many people may not appreciate the full extent of problems with the current system, public opinion polls reveal that "both [white and Black] groups distrusted the criminal justice system, with only 17% of white people and 11% of black people reporting confidence in it" (Washburn 2023; Jones 2022). Overall, only 14 percent of people had "a great deal" or "quite a lot" of confidence in the criminal justice system. That is a stunning rejection of current practices, what has passed for reform, and mainstream criminology and criminal justice (which studies crime and educates criminal justice workers). Doing more of the same with some minor tweaks should not be an acceptable option.

However, many people working in the system and profiting from it generally do not see the need for major changes. Many readers who hope for jobs in the system may also be skeptical of major reforms that could reduce the value of their education about the current system or upset established career paths. Further, ideology is important to understand because it plays a role in our ability to see injustice and imagine alternative worlds, and it limits our willingness to take action against injustice. Because the purpose of this book has been to examine injustices, and the conclusion should discuss what can be done about them, ideology is worth exploring briefly.

People often do not see the full intensity of oppression because of ideology, which consists of beliefs that justify inequality and exploitation as natural, inevitable, and ultimately fair (Reiman and Leighton 2023). While people often think of ideology as a more general belief system or worldview, we are using the concept more narrowly to highlight the problem animating the original discussions of ideology: "how people are blinded from seeing—and acting to resist—the full extent of injustice in society" (Reiman and Leighton 2023: 179). Ideology is present "when ideas, however unintentionally, distort reality in a way that justifies the prevailing distribution of power and wealth, hides society's injustices, and thus secures uncritical allegiance to the existing social order." Many of these ideas are broadcast by the corporate- and billionaire-owned media, for which the social, economic, and political systems seem just because of all the privileges corporate executives and billionaires have.

Early work on ideology focused on how unequal societies secured the consent and allegiance of the oppressed through the creation and dissemination of beliefs that society was just. The problem of ideology was why people bought into these ideas and did not see reality, but recent scholarship from the ultrarealists suggests that people are aware of "capitalism's dark side": people basically know that "the pleasures of consumerism will quickly fade—and that we are all, in various ways, forced along a conveyor belt that requires us to buy, discard and then buy again in an endless, environmentally destructive cycle that enriches a tax avoiding oligarchic elite and immiserates low wage production workers" (Winlow et al. 2021: 39). The deeper question, then, is, "Why—rather than joining with others to pursue our mutual betterment—do we routinely visit harm on one another and the natural world?" (Davies 2021).

While part of ideology serves to blind people to such knowledge, it also works so that people can "know" such truths and also "not know." In addition, ideology can make people believe they are not complicit in such oppressive dynamics. It can also make people feel that if society does make changes, they will be for the worse rather than the better—so it seems like "there is no alternative." After all, "if you can convince people that nothing can be done, they won't try to do anything" (Doctorow 2023). Finally, ideology undermines people's ability to imagine better alternatives (Reiman and Leighton 2023; Winlow et al. 2021) and can lead people to accepting "a better kind of wrongness" (in Rothe and Kauzlarich 2022: 248).

The focus on trying to imagine a better world and build a better discipline of criminology is not a new task for this book. In previous editions, the conclusion has detailed a number of possible reforms. Since our basic point is that the criminal justice system can be no fairer than the society for which it supplies "law and order," reform proposals included larger class-, race-, and gender/sexuality-based proposals in addition to criminal justice–based ones. With each new edition over twenty years, the list of proposals was largely unchanged from one edition to the next because there has been so little meaningful reform; and unfortunately the list of proposals grew in response to emerging issues and research.

While we still believe in the need to build a fairer society, we no longer want the conclusion to be a laundry list of reforms. Instead, the conclusion has been redone to help readers imagine alternatives and to consider what can be done now in order to be able to do tomorrow what we are unable to do today. Whether readers at this point see the need for minor changes or far-reaching ones, the following sections provide critical thinking and alternative ways to imagine what criminology is, what it does, and who it does it to. We also discuss some work being done to build community safety outside of criminal justice and with broader concerns than just crime. The discussion here is to help readers choose for themselves how they would envision criminal justice and the type of society they want to create for themselves and future generations.

In that spirit, section 2 focuses on the discipline of criminology and how to introduce more disruptive elements to criminology. It assumes that criminology will continue to largely focus on acts that are defined as crimes (rather than other harms), but how it can do so in ways that do not recreate inequalities. Section 3 also focuses on criminology, but in a way that is centered on the problem of serious harms that are considered noncriminal. To what extent should criminology examine human rights violations and other harms, or would it be better to shift it to the larger study of social harm (zemiology)? Section 4 provides an overview of abolition, which involves building a safer community and society as well as dismantling punitive impulses and the criminal legal system. Even though many criminology students want a career in a fairer criminal justice system rather than abolishing it, abolition is an idea that has taken root for discussion and is something criminology students should understand.

## Disrupting Criminology

Criminology and criminal justice are fields of academic study that are intertwined with fundamental aspects of what it means to be human and how to exist as social and interdependent beings. After all, throughout all of human history, societies have grappled with questions of justice, fairness, retribution, and responses to (real and perceived) acts of harm or deviance. But as chapter 2 discussed, criminological research takes a narrow—sometimes overly narrow—slice of those larger questions to understand what the "crime problem" is, who is causing it, why they are criminals, and what responses society should take to it. The chapter also noted that criminology is embedded in the criminal justice enterprise, so it does not always see the problems it causes or appreciate their seriousness.

As a reminder of what needs disrupting, chapter 2 provided a general critique that was fleshed out in the sections on class, race, gender/sexuality, and intersections. The general problems are that mainstream criminology emphasizes individual-level theories (Pratt and Cullen 2005) rather than structural factors; it is more likely to control for class and race than to explore how a society with inequality and racism can generate crime in people who are oppressed. Further, theorists and researchers create ideas and "knowledge" without an awareness of their own class, race, and gender/sexuality privilege, which can recreate those privileges and oppress others. Different groups of mainstream criminologists then tend to cite each other, leading not to the development of new ideas and the "turnover of central ideas in a field, but rather to ossification of canon" (Chu and Evans 2021). ("Ossification" refers to the process of bone formation, and in this context to an idea becoming fixed or unable to change.) The discipline was in need of "structures fostering disruptive scholarship and focusing attention on novel ideas."

The chapter also critiqued "general theories," because by definition they deny that inequality, racism, patriarchy, and so forth, play any role in crime. We specifically noted the development of Latinx general strain theory and feminist strain theories. We would encourage faculty to include these in class discussion even if the textbooks do not. Depending on the professor, students can try to raise questions or start discussions about these variations. (A safe way to feel out a professor would be to send an email saying, "I found this idea to be interesting and I wonder what you think." Consider also including a link or a citation to what you read.) If the professor seems resistant, then students can at least share information in student-led informal discussion groups. Students can also try to explore these ideas—and what has been discussed elsewhere in this book—in projects and papers, again depending on the professor. (Some mainstream professors will be willing to entertain discussion, but others may want to stick with "the canon" ["sacred texts"].)

Along these same lines, chapter 2 discussed feminist criminology, Black criminology, and queer criminology. There is also LatCrim (Latino/a/x criminology [León 2021]), Asian criminology, and postcolonial criminology (Agozino and Pfohl 2003; Monchalin 2016). The idea here is not just for women, LGBTQ+, and members of minority groups to be able to find research about their communities, but chapter 2 noted that students generally "want to increase their awareness and understanding of a range of perspectives for personal growth as well as to have a more rounded world view" (Stockdale et al. 2021). That range of perspectives can also include critical race theory (Delgado and Stefancic 2012), which has been the subject of heated political controversy. Some of the commentary distorts the fundamental tenets of the theory, and students interested in the legal aspects of criminology can investigate it for themselves. The journal *Critical Criminology* is one source that publishes a variety of disruptive ideas, and students can browse the table of contents of several issues to see what may be of interest in these and other areas.

To be clear, professors should take responsibility for teaching in inclusive ways that allow students to see the repressive impacts of law and criminology on their community as well as its strengths. But the readers of this book are the future of criminology, and changing the discipline may also require initiative from them (you). Gandhi's quote, "Be the change you wish to see in the world," applies here too.

As we have noted throughout the current edition of this book, increasing awareness of intersectional issues and learning the importance and application of critical thinking in research, pedagogy, and praxis are needed. One book that we believe has the potential for positive disruption is *Survivor Criminology: A Radical Act of Hope* (Cook et al. 2022). It focuses on the lived experiences of crime survivors and is groundbreaking in its exploration of survivor narratives and the application of trauma-informed approaches within criminology and criminal legal systems. The book highlights the importance of recognizing the dangers of institutional-level oppression such as racism, heterosexism, sexism, and poverty. Its authors argue for further inclusion of queer criminology, intersectional criminology, convict criminology, and more (Cook et al. 2022). They articulate the impact that feminist criminology has had on many developing subdisciplines, and they urge readers to consider a more nuanced understanding of each other, including students and professors.

For those who want to go further down the path of disruptive criminological ideas, criminologists can be more critical of individual-level theories by adding back in the missing social structure, even "inverting" them (Henson et al. 2023). The starting point is critical thinking, which in this case is about making visible the power and privilege that individual-level theories deny. For example, why does criminology discuss strain theory without spending time talking about the sources of blocked opportunities? The blocked opportunities are taken as a given, and the theory points to adaptations—but it could also explore sources of stratification, inequality, concentrated disadvantage, racism, and so forth, and what people should do about them. Likewise, in addition to individual-level theories of social control, criminologists can also explore the "chronic temptation structures"

(Tonry 2020: 2) facing poor people in a society that equates success with material wealth. Within the existing theory, many versions "place the onus on parents and the institution of school to effectively socialize youth, without considering how the structure of society undermines the function of those domains" (Henson et al. 2023: 22).

Social disorganization theory, too, focuses on the breakdown of informal social control in neighborhoods without asking about the labor, economic development, tax, welfare, education, and other policies that impact those neighborhoods (Henson et al. 2023; Reiman and Leighton 2023: 36). Recognizing that people lead their life "in social structures which are largely not of their own making" (Young 2011: 222), criminologists can recognize that those who engage in street crime "are marginalized people that have grown up with and been shaped by oppressive structures." This is not intended to deny the responsibility people have for their choices, but it allows questions and conversation about who created the oppressive structures. Theory must recognize "the role of the state, dominant classes, and macro-social forces in the production of illegal behavior and the fear of crime" (Henson et al. 2023: 26). Within this perspective,

> social disorganization theory is better conceived as a theory of consequence that explains the impact of structural inequality, racial/ethnic discrimination, and racial/ethnic inequities. What criminologists measure are the behavioral responses to structural stressors with crime as the main outcome of interest. (Henson et al. 2023: 21)

Henson et al. (2023) go on to "invert" social disorganization theory into what they call "critical environmental adaptation theory." The theory looks at "adaptation as acts of resistance and survival" in response to "deliberate legal, social, and economic exclusion" (Henson et al. 2023: 25).

In a different way, a mainstream theory like Hirschi's social bond can be turned "upside down by arguing that bonds to conventional institutions can increase woman abuse in a variety of circumstances because gender inequality is an unacknowledged norm" (DeKeseredy and Schwartz 2013: 72). Male peer-support theory is not trying to validate Hirschi, but it uses ideas about peer support for conventional behavior while recognizing, "depending on the question, that between 25 percent and 60 percent of male college students reported some likelihood that they would rape a woman if they could get away with it" (DeKeseredy and Schwartz 2013: 73). Many men supporting conventional gender roles encourage and shame other men into being dominant with women, aggressive, and feeling entitled to sexual access regardless of consent. The bonding to "conventional" peers can produce pro-abuse support. The larger, and more important, question is: "What if some behaviors criminologists define as deviant are actually acts of conformity to conventional norms—like gender inequality—that are naturalized by the prevailing ideology?" (DeKeseredy and Schwartz 2013: 73).

Finally, unlike most texts on intersections and injustice, this book has given equal attention to class and the problems with economic inequality. It highlighted substantial delinquency in middle-class and affluent teens (chapter 2) as well as rampant criminality by corporations. We noted, for example, Currie discussing that the "long tradition of research on juvenile delinquency had shown us again and again that the problems of drugs and violence among middle-class youth were both widespread and surprisingly severe, though mostly absent from our official statistics" (2005b: 5).

The omission of this subject from criminology is inexcusable, and it holds great potential to transform stereotypes of troubled poor and minority youth. How is it that a discipline trying to understand delinquency ignores youth that Currie calls "children of the American 'mainstream' who shot heroin and speed, drank themselves into emergency rooms, tried to kill themselves with prescription drugs, flirted with death on the highway or in gang fights" (2005b: 8)? Others had mental health problems and/or lived on the street, and Currie notes that many had almost died of overdoses. Females in Currie's sample had behavioral problems from abuse-related trauma, and "several of the women had gotten into violent or degrading relationships with men, often much older men" (2005b: 10).

For many students from middle-class and affluent backgrounds, the list of problems is likely not a surprise. But criminology continues to study the issue in a way implying that poor and minority youth are the troubled. The association of inner cities with "real" delinquency is so strong that Currie relates the following story:

> She had heard that I was interested in the problems of teenagers, and she wanted to talk with me about her own harrowing suburban history, which included heavy drinking and drug use, self-mutilation and attempted suicide. But she wasn't sure that her experience would be useful to me—that it would be sufficiently serious to be of interest—because it was "more of a white kind of messing up." (2005b: 5)

The point here is not that middle-class and affluent teens have it worse than inner-city youth struggling with concentrated disadvantage. But the seriousness of the acts speaks for itself, and Currie notes that as he started talking to his classes about this research, "there were a surprising number of similar students in my classes, even if I counted only those who came of their own accord to tell me about their experiences—there were surely plenty of others" (2005b: 9). It's hard to imagine that with the financial crisis of 2008–2009, the opiate overdose epidemic, climate change concerns, and COVID, the situation is any better or less prevalent. Indeed, one of the authors (Leighton) uses Currie's book in a class and finds that it still resonates, and a steady stream of students use their reflection papers to connect the book to their own experiences, or that of family, friends, relatives, and neighbors.

Chapter 2 critiqued criminology because many groups find little helpful knowledge about their communities in it. The troubles of middle-class and affluent youth may be an odd example of this, but the idealized world of suburbs and gated communities means that many individuals and families find it difficult to get help (even while others enjoy the privilege of assumptions that nonpoor youth are more stable and together). Maybe if some criminology classes had a module or two about the troubles of nonpoor youth, people from those communities could have more discussions about what is happening in them, the distress of youth, and what should be done about it.

A small glimpse of the possible disruption from talking about the delinquency of nonpoor youth is evident from the recent movement of survivors of the troubled teen industry (TTI) speaking out about the trauma and abuse they experienced. Rather than entering the regular juvenile justice system, more affluent teens end up in TTI institutions, which also ensnare youth who were "hanging out with the wrong crowd" and were not acting in ways that parents thought were appropriate for class-based appearances (Mooney and Leighton 2019). The TTI institutions include "therapeutic" boarding schools, last-chance ranches, wilderness therapy, and Christian institutions to help promote heterosexuality for LGBTQ+ youth.

Teens are forcibly removed from their homes at 2 or 3 a.m. by several paramilitary figures in what the industry calls "escorting" and what others refer to as "legalized kidnapping" (Robbins 2014). Youth describe the ordeal as "terrifying and violent" and a source of trauma (Mooney and Leighton 2019). The institutions they end up in are secure facilities, conducting attack therapy and "strong-arm rehabilitation" (Gowan and Whetstone 2012: 76) that many found inappropriate and counterproductive (Mooney and Leighton 2019). Such institutions are very lightly regulated, so survivors also recount significant physical, psychological, and sexual abuse (Government Accountability Office 2008a, 2008b; Szalavitz 2006).

"Code silence" is a common punishment involving forced isolation, so people who have been through the TTI started posting on social media using #BreakingCodeSilence (as well as #ISeeYouSurvivor). The already growing movement received substantial publicity when socialite and entrepreneur Paris Hilton told of her own experiences of physical and emotional abuse in a facility in her freely available documentary, *This Is Paris* (Hilton et al. 2020; Harris 2021). Survivor scholars and others are publishing academic articles (Chatfield 2023; Golightley 2020; Magnuson et al. 2022). While the lives of Hilton and some others may not be readily relatable for most students, the lesson is that there are some limits to how much white and class privilege can protect youth in the United States, which (along with Somalia) is one of the only countries not to ratify the United Nations Convention on the Rights of the Child.

The other aspect of class that needs to be disrupted is the lack of attention to crimes of the powerful, especially corporate crimes. Part of the problem, admittedly, is that because of lobbying, some seriously harmful behaviors are not illegal, although the lack of enforcement contributes in a substantial way to the perception that corporations do not engage in criminal activities (Ramirez and Ramirez 2017; Will et al. 2013). But more than forty years ago, a criminologist called on the discipline to rethink its focus, and that call is still largely unheeded:

> The possible clue to our understanding most serious crimes can be located in power, not weakness, privilege, not disadvantage, wealth, not poverty. This is not an idea that has found much elbow room within traditional criminology. (Box 1983: 202; see also Scott and Sim 2023)

The overemphasis on studying crimes by poor minorities and reinforcing that the threat for Americans is from below is a lost opportunity for criminology to help students acquire knowledge and skills they need to negotiate life in a corporate-dominated world. For example, wage theft involves the nonpayment of wages due under law, and it includes paying for fewer hours than the person worked, not paying time and a half for overtime, working unpaid before or after the shift (or other work "off the clock"), failure to pay minimum wage (especially to servers), and many more (Leighton 2018). But how often are a state's fraud, theft, or grand larceny laws used to prosecute wage theft—especially in comparison to how they would be used to handle an employee stealing a similar amount from the employer? Where can students go to find information on wage and hour laws? (State departments of labor usually have a wage and hour division.) Where can an employee victimized by wage theft get help? Why do so many universities say they want to prepare students for the job market but not talk about wage theft and illegal wage suppression tactics?

## Studying Social Harm (in Addition to, or Instead of, Criminology)

Most people get into criminology because they want to help others. That help is with the harms of street crime—and often with an eye to reforming the system so it does less harm to those going through it. But "perhaps the next, crucial, step—a challenge for all of us" is to "transcend the fascination with crime harms and to determine the harms that really blight the lives of children, women and men on a daily basis: those actions, omissions, policies, processes, conditions, states of affairs, assumptions, ways of doing things and dominant structures which contribute to the absence of or distortions in human self-actualization" (Tombs 2023).

While some people embrace the study of street crime, those who have a broader view have two routes. One path is continuing the long-running "reformation project" (Davies 2021: 467) of criminology to get it to study harms not defined as crimes. This reformation might be as modest as extending criminology to cover more acts of corporations and problems like climate change. The reformation may also be more expansive in getting criminology to not just recognize *acts* of violence but also *states* of violence—slow violence—like poverty, racism, sexism, heteronormativity, and other forms of oppression. The other path lies in realizing that criminology will always favor studying the acts of the poor that are defined as crime, so instead we should embrace the idea that "harm provides a more comprehensive starting point for understanding *victimization* than crime does" (Davies 2021: 455). The starting point for discussion with zemiology—the study of social harm—does not need to be the criminal law, and the solution does not necessarily need to involve law, police, or punishment.

Victimology is the scientific study of victims and victimization, and as a subfield of criminology the debates around its scope illustrate the problem. Victimology can be traced back to 1937, when Mendolsohn began gathering information about victims for his law practice. He subsequently conducted research on victims, and Mendolsohn and others "formulated a broad-based victimology that considered not merely crime victims, but all victims, including those produced by politics, by technology, by accidents, as well as by crime" (Elias 1986: 18).

The field, research, and applications of victimology have continued to develop, but the struggle to maintain the broader perspective (beyond formal victims of street crime) envisioned by Mendolsohn has been a difficult one. Indeed, victimology has tended to focus narrowly on criminal victimization, victim-offender relationships, and victim precipitation (the contribution a victim makes to their victimization). Thus, much victimology is limited to victims based on existing criminal law—especially street crime rather than corporate crime. The "victims' rights" movement of the 1990s largely ignored victims of corporate crime. Victimology, like criminology, too often excludes structural sources and context for better understanding victimization.

In his treatise *The Politics of Victimization*, Elias captured the dilemma in victimology in a way that is still relevant more than forty years later:

> Americans are a frightened people. We anticipate victimization even more than we experience it, although much actual victimization does occur. We mostly fear being robbed, raped, or otherwise assaulted, or even killed. Yet, while these crimes have captured our imaginations, they comprise only part of the victimization we suffer. We face not only the danger of other crimes, but also countless other actions that we often have not defined or perceived as criminal, despite their undeniable harm. We may have a limited social reality of crime and victimization that excludes harms such as consumer fraud, pollution, unnecessary drugs and surgery, food additives, workplace hazards and diseases, police violence, censorship, discrimination, poverty, exploitation, and war. We suffer victimization not only by other individuals, but also by governments and other social institutions, not to mention the psychological victimization bred by our own insecurities. (Elias 1986: 3–4)

He suggests that the pathway to a more comprehensive victimology lies in the wedding of victimology with human rights, which can

> dissolve the "mental prison" that often characterizes how we think about victimization, and substitute a . . . broader conception that considers not only common crime but also corporate and state crime, that examines not only individual criminals but also institutional wrong-doing, and that encompasses not merely traditional crime but all crimes against humanity. (Elias 1986: 7)

While the idea of the criminal law and criminology being a "mental prison" is amusing in an ironic way, the idea is that the "criminal law may provide the first narrowing of our consciousness of both crime and victimization, a process that continues in enforcement and subsequent stages of the criminal process" (Elias 1986: 32). The penal code thus creates "an 'official' or 'social' reality of victimization which, among those harms it defines as criminal, stresses acts mostly committed by less privileged people, de-emphasizes and softens the acts committed by more privileged people, and then excludes from its definition other, extensive, and (usually more) harmful acts altogether, such as corporate crimes, state crimes, and what human rights advocates would call 'crimes against humanity'" (1986: 33). Indeed, one of the most influential papers in zemiology goes further to argue that the label of "crime" gives "undue attention" to certain harms and "distracts attention away from more serious harm" (Hillyard and Tombs 2021: 14). For example, shoplifting even small items for survival is a crime, and the victimization of businesses gets attention more so than predatory finance and "financial violence"—"the intentional and strategic exploitation of vulnerable communities for profit" (Sugata 2019: 8).[1]

Another consequence of the "mental prison" is that most attempts at criminal justice reform are "reformist" rather than "structural" in nature; that is, they do not upset or challenge existing power relations, nor do they address the larger social and cultural roots of these patterns of victimization. Instead, these efforts at criminal justice reform or victimization reduction are aimed almost exclusively at controlling or changing the individual perpetrators ("bad apples"). In addition to structural reforms, options for responding to harm focus on police and punitive measures. What's needed, in contrast, are much wider strategies of recovery that include an array of diverse services, programs, and resources that revolve around "restorative" and redemptive practices of justice, focusing more broadly on the causes of victimization. Such policies strive to reconcile the collective interests of perpetrators, victims, and bystanders alike by rehabilitating, reaffirming, and reconstructing their personal and social well-being. These strategies of intervention are also aimed at strengthening community, and they are designed in the spirit of establishing community efficacy (Barak 2003).

For decades, critical criminologists have cautioned about the consequences of defining criminology based on state definitions of crime, which are the outcome of a political process. If criminologists are limited to whatever the state defines as a felony or misdemeanor, they end up ignoring or deprioritizing a range of harms and systemic injustices that are *technically* noncriminal and therefore beyond the scope of the field. No major financial institution or its executives were criminally indicted for causing the financial crisis of 2008–2009, so is it not a concern for criminologists? Climate change threatens human extinction, but no laws are being broken, so is it a concern for another field (Kramer 2020)?

Returning to the theme of this section, one option is to keep working on mainstream criminology to be more open to studying, theorizing, and working to reduce harms that are not defined as criminal. This option is challenging because criminology has held tightly to its focus on acts by the poor that have been formally defined as crime. However, as chapter 7 noted, the point of prohibiting an act by the criminal law is to protect society from injurious or dangerous actions. Criminological theorist Agnew explains that there are "unrecognized blameworthy harms," meaning that they are not recognized as crimes, but perhaps they should be, or at least be of interest to criminologists. Further, "much state and corporate harm falls into this category" (Agnew 2011: 38), and, making "the public and state aware of unrecognized blameworthy harms" should be "a major mission" of criminologists (Agnew 2011: 43, emphasis added).

The other option is to recognize that criminology will always focus on the harms that are defined as crimes, so is it better to read, study, publish, and do advocacy in a different field? In "Beyond Criminology?," the authors suggest that "the deleterious activities of local and national states, and of corporations, upon people's lives, whether in respect of lack of wholesome food, inadequate housing or heating, low income, exposure to various forms of danger, violations of basic human rights, and victimization to various forms of crime, produces the need for a disciplinary home which could embrace a range of harms that affect many people throughout their life cycle" (Hillyard and Tombs 2021: 23).

Criminology focuses mostly on individual victims, but there is a need to be able to discuss "harmed communities" (Hillyard and Tombs 2021: 23) and to understand victimology in a way that "captures the myriad ways in which the abuse of power is injurious and impacts at various levels" (Davies 2021: 465). Currently, there is a "substantial amount of time and intellectual effort in the exercises of setting out, and then justifying, how and why certain activities of states and corporations can and should be treated through criminology" (Hillyard and Tombs 2021:

15). Perhaps there would be more progress on understanding and responding to the harm if the justifications and explanations to criminologists were not necessary.

This issue of how to deal with substantial and serious harms that are not recognized as crimes is an important question because the government and corporations can use their power to make sure their actions are not criminalized while using that same power to commit mass victimization. To give up on criminology means that the criminal law fixes the boundaries of criminology, so "the *existent ethical standpoint of the State* is taken as a given" (Schwendinger and Schwendinger 2001: 78, emphasis in the original). And someone needs to keep reminding criminology that the field should be based on "a moral theory about what human beings owe to their fellows in the way of conduct" (in Reiman and Leighton 2023: 262).

Although this section presented a decision as to whether to make criminology a "reformation project" (Davies 2021: 467) or to switch gears for zemiology and a broader conception of social harm, doing both may be an effective path forward (Hillyard and Tombs 2021: 33). The ineffectiveness of the criminal justice system and the harm it produces are both reasons to try to reform it and reasons to leave criminology for something that may be more successful in dealing with social problems and harms.

## Abolition and Building a New World

Chapter 2 noted that readers need to think through how they feel about "criminal justice logic" and ask, "Is criminology a discipline of freedom or one of captors?" (Friedman 2021: 1). While many may respond that they would like to see violent and dangerous people locked up, there is nevertheless a problem of mass incarceration—and the aggressive policing and prosecution necessary to maintain it—that must be studied and challenged. Understanding abolition is one of the best ways to do this because it involves both a critique of the current system and advocacy for building better communities. (Abolition is not about releasing all the prisoners and closing police stations at the end of the month, but instead it is about building communities that have less crime and more non–criminal justice institutions to deal with social problems.)

Most people studying criminology and criminal justice see the need for some reforms and stopping certain practices. Reading about what abolition is and what it proposes is a way for readers to think through how deep the problems of criminal justice go—and how much needs to be changed. Further, the police killing of George Floyd in 2020 brought increased attention to abolitionism, which stretches back decades. So even readers who do not embrace abolition should understand what it is about so they can meaningfully engage in the public debates about criminal justice in the years ahead.

### A: Abolition in Context

Abolition is not about reform in the way most people think about criminal justice reform. The usual call for reform rests on a belief that the system can be fixed with the right policies, the right people, and, of course, the right amount of money. But the interest in Vitale's (2021) *End of Policing* is not because he has a good proposal for diversity, equity, and inclusion training of police to stop the killing of minorities. It is because of the sentiments we quoted in chapter 8 that "there is not a single era in the United States history in which the police were not a force of violence against Black people" (in Pickett et al. 2022: 295). The interest is also because of the growing awareness that "after decades of attempts to tinker with the institution of policing, it is becoming impossible to ignore that no amount of police reform seems capable of stopping cops from killing Black people" (Shanahan and Kurti 2022: 24). If reforms do not work, then maybe the system is not "broken." If it is not broken, then maybe it should be replaced with other institutions to promote public safety within communities, and for those communities to exist within less criminogenic social structures.

Further, abolition warns that reform can fail to fix a problem substantially while legitimating the larger system. Chapter 9, for example, discussed the critique of *Gideon v. Wainwright* (that gave the poor the right to an attorney): "fifty years after *Gideon*, poor people have both the right to counsel and the most massive level of incarceration in the world" (Butler 2013: 2191). Perhaps the "reform" mandated by *Gideon* helped legitimate mass incarceration because providing lawyers for the poor created the illusion that the system was fair:

> If prosecutors had brought most of their cases against the poor during the pre-*Gideon* era when most indigent defendants did not have lawyers, prosecutors would have looked like bullies. Since *Gideon*, the percentage of prosecutions against the poor has increased from 43% to 80% . . . but now, because of *Gideon*, they look less like bullies. (Butler 2013: 2197–98)

So the following overview of abolition is based on a recognition that (1) the criminal justice–industrial complex is expensive, (2) the system is failing to deliver justice, (3) the system is failing to keep people safe and prevent crime, and (4) the system is failing in these ways in spite of serious, ongoing efforts since the 1960s to improve it. For some people, abolition just means prisons, but we are describing a broader "carceral abolitionism," which seeks to abolish all forms of punitive control. It tries to critique and create alternatives to "the control and punishment mindset that suggests criminalization is the best paradigm to organize human life and to solve social problems" (in Stephens-Griffin 2023; Meiners 2017). While often seen as a leftist, anarchist project, abolition also has roots in religious traditions, for example, Griffith's (1993) *The Fall of the Prison: Biblical Perspectives on Prison Abolition* (for more contemporary takes, see Herskind, n.d.; christiansforab olition.org).

As further context, the term "abolition" is meant to invoke connections to the movement to abolish slavery in the southern United States. That earlier movement sought to abolish the kidnapping of, forced laboring of, and violence inflicted upon African and Indigenous peoples. Those fighting for the abolition of chattel slavery demanded the full emancipation of enslaved people from conditions of ownership, as well as the provision of reparations to ensure the ability to make a life here. And while "emancipation" was announced in 1863, the discussion of race across earlier chapters has illustrated that with the end of formalized slavery came the introduction of the Black codes, convict leasing, and eventually disproportionate mass incarceration of minorities (Alexander 2012). Indeed, W. E. B. Du Bois

([1935] 2017) noted that new, truly democratic institutions aimed at incorporating Black people into the social order were not created, and the space left by slavery was filled by laws like the Black codes, policing, and prisons. So, what binds the fight for the abolition of chattel slavery to the contemporary abolitionist movement is a desire to end the coercive structures aimed at the social control of minorities and the poor.

Because the emphasis with the term "abolition" is what is ending, we would like to emphasize that abolition is a project of both dismantling *and* building:

> Abolition is not about arguing for the mere *absence* of something, but for the *presence* of something transformative, emancipatory, and consistent with our most aspirational values. . . . What the world will become already exists in fragments and pieces, experiments and possibilities. So those who feel in their gut deep anxiety that abolition means knock it all down, scorch the earth and start something new, let that go. Abolition is building the future from the present, in all of the ways we can. (Lambert and Gilmore 2018)

In this way, abolition must be thought of as a "both/and project" in that it is *both* about dismantling "institutions that advance the dominance of any one group over any other" (Mendieta 2005: 14) *and* about "building a new world where we work together to meet one another's needs" (Hill 2021). Fortunately, so much of what we think is "fixed" and "deeply entrenched" about criminal justice is actually very young and entirely country specific in practice (Saleh-Hanna et al. 2023).

The rest of the material on abolition is divided into three sections. Section B provides a deeper understanding of why abolition is not about reform. Most readers probably still believe in fixing the system and have a list of pet reforms they would like to see happen. While they may not change their view, it is important to understand the concerns abolitionists have about the outcomes of reform. Section C discusses the punitive mindset, the variety of ways it is activated, and how to resist it. Section D explores transforming communities and being "fractal"—working through our interpersonal relationships and the conditions in our communities to create patterns that can spiral upward (brown 2017).

Sections C and D describe "everyday abolition," where "efforts toward structural change" are connected "with our everyday cultures and practices" (Lamble 2021). Because abolition is a project of both dismantling *and* building, living abolition in daily life also necessitates a dual approach: resisting punitive responses to people and experiences in our lives and building relationships based in care. As such, while the examples given here will not directly apply to the specific situations every reader might encounter, they will hopefully at least incite the reader's imagination about different, safer, and more just ways to live.

## B: The Limits of Reform

Criminal justice reform has been strikingly infrequent since the recognition of mass incarceration and all of its problems. But the abolitionist critique is that even when reform happens, it is problematic. Reform often appears to make changes while allowing deeper problems to fester, and at times even well-meaning reform can have counterproductive effects. Murakawa (2014), for example, contends that the efforts of postwar racial liberals provided the scaffolding from which the prison nation was built. She notes that one of the first statements of liberal law and order, President Truman's 1947 report "To Secure These Rights," argued that racial violence was the product of individual biases and too much local discretion (a view that is still popular because it allows people to deny structural and institutional racism). Too much discretion allowed prejudice to be turned into discriminatory acts, so the solution to curbing racism and civil unrest was eliminating discretion through greater federal management of laws, policies, and punishment. The policies and programs that such an argument informed ended up institutionalizing rather than disrupting racism but gave the appearance of a "color-blind" system. Federal power in criminal justice increased in order to fight racism, resulting in a stronger but still racist criminal justice system.

Further, the Sentencing Reform Act of 1984 was designed to mitigate the impact of discretion in sentencing and parole decisions, but it allowed for longer and harsher sentences. Similarly, electronic monitoring (EM), or "e-carceration," is supposed to temper mass incarceration, but instead it expands the scope of the prison into one's home and neighborhood (Kilgore 2015, 2022). It is experienced, disproportionately by minorities, as a form of "control and humiliation which often comes with serious financial penalties and the constant threat of re-incarceration" (Kilgore 2015: 5). Programs intended to be "diversion" result in "net widening" as the new option claims jurisdiction over more people who would have gone free than people diverted from prison.

Practices like diverting offenders to drug courts and doling out "alternative" treatment to offenders through "problem-solving courts" (Whitlock and Heitzeg 2021) have also contributed to the growth of the criminal justice–industrial complex, but rooted in the language of reform and alternatives. Chapter 9 noted that advocacy for "problem-solving" courts (like drug and mental health courts) often does not challenge the high levels of criminalization and low levels of services that people can voluntarily use. The limited services are often transferred from the community to support specialty courts, which require a guilty plea—and the accompanying fines and fees—to access them (Bach 2019: 828–29). For people who relapse, "the punishment is far more severe than the person would have received had they not participated in the drug court" (Bach 2019: 828–29).

Another area with a long history of failed reform is policing. Police reform has been in the spotlight as Black Lives Matter called attention to ongoing police shootings of unarmed minorities. The public and politicians assume that policing can be reformed—that with enough funding, energy, creativity, and public buy-in, policing can change for the better. Much of this reformist energy has been dedicated to specialized technology and training and community oversight of the police. The Obama administration, for example, dedicated $43 million to arming police with body-worn cameras, but "body cameras have not delivered on early promises to reduce force and increase accountability" (Murakawa 2021: 165; Pang and Pavlou 2017). Instead, "they have expanded police surveillance powers, especially when equipped with facial recognition" (Murakawa 2021: 165). Proposals for more police training mean that police have larger budgets, but training regarding "fair and impartial policing" (in particular) has "no impact on problems like racial disparities in traffic stops or marijuana arrests" (Vitale 2021: 8; Worden et al. 2020). More generally, there is little support for the transformative power of training (Minnesota Advisory Committee 2018).

Civilian review boards have also been proposed as a way to hold police accountable, based on a belief that they will deter behavior that violates policy. Major cities like Boston, New York, Berkeley, and Pittsburgh have tried variations of police review boards that task community members with setting policies, investigating civilian complaints, disciplining officers, and controlling police budgets (Adams and Rameau 2016). The research assessing the impact of civilian review and oversight boards on various outcomes is limited, largely due to the varied structure and role these boards may adopt (Council on Criminal Justice 2021). However, there is some support for the relationship between review boards and reduced racial disparity in disorderly conduct arrests and police homicides of community members (Ali and Pirog 2019). Taken together, however, "the evaluative research on civilian oversight effectiveness suggests that bodies with more authority are more likely to yield desired impacts" (Council on Criminal Justice 2021: 3), but it is rare for a review board to have the necessary authority to produce these outcomes (Ofer 2016). Indeed, the national abolitionist organization Critical Resistance (n.d.) notes that "some argue for civilian review boards 'with teeth,' the power to make decisions and take away policing tools and tactics. However, a board with that level of power has never existed despite 50+ years of organizing for them."

The review of reforms may seem harsh, but it sets the stage for abolitionists wanting "nonreformist reforms" and the dismantling of the criminal justice–industrial complex—not more reforms like those of the past fifty years. In this view, the system is not broken and in need of mending—it is working as it was meant to, which is to manage potentially disgruntled poor and minority people (Davis 2005). While the 1960s Great Society programs sought to respond to the civil rights movement and urban riots by trying to better distribute the benefits of the American economy, it quickly ended in favor of policies to get tough on crime. The criminal justice system kept expanding (despite its obvious failures) because "police and prisons have proven cheaper for the ruling class than guaranteeing free health care, housing, and education, and other minimum demands for a comfortable life" (Shanahan and Kurti 2022: 165). So the United States "has become an open-air theater of punishment and control" (Shanahan and Kurti 2022: 70), where the ("reformed") criminal justice system "has been deployed, not as a response to crime but to manage daily life, tightly regulating how they [poor and minorities] are allowed to congregate, support themselves when consigned to informal economies, shop, and even drive their cars" (Shanahan and Kurti 2022: 74). Reform, then, would involve simply "tinkering" at the edges of this system, helping it to more efficiently capture more poor and minority people destined for "profitable punishment" (Leighton and Selman 2018; Schenwar and Law 2020; Whitlock and Heitzeg 2021).

## C: Resisting Punitive Responses

Central to the work of abolition is "undoing the cultural norms and mindsets that trap us within punitive habits and logics" (Lamble 2021; Purnell 2022). Because the police are armed and are the entry point to the criminal justice system, calling the police is an important area for change. There are situations in which the police may be the only available body to respond, but police do not have to be called for almost every real or perceived social problem. A study by the Vera Institute of Justice (Dholakia 2022) analyzed 9-1-1 calls for two years across nine U.S. cities, and the researchers concluded that in most of these cities, fewer than 3 percent of the calls were related to violent crime, and an average of 62.6 percent of the calls involved "noncriminal" situations.

Understanding this naturalized tendency to involve the police requires thinking through the *reasons* for calling the police in the first place: is it because an official record of an event/experience is needed, such as for insurance or financial compensation purposes? Is it based on a perceived need to surveil others for one's own protection? Or is it out of concern for the safety of others? Factors such as race, class, gender, and sexuality can impact people's interpretation of whether something is "suspicious" or "threatening"—and those interpretations can result in community members being brutalized or shot in response. Often, calling the police is a default because it seems there is no one else to call.

Witnessing someone urinating in public or engaging in harmless graffiti, for example, might not deserve an intervention. However, if someone is in danger or seems like they need assistance, then it is helpful to have a "toolkit" of responses that provides meaningful help but does not rely on the police. Becoming knowledgeable about the community resources and organizations that offer support makes it possible to avoid calling the police while still receiving aid. For example, 3-1-1 can be used in nonemergency situations, street medics can provide medical treatment, domestic violence organizations employ workers trained in supporting victims, and mental health organizations often have trained professionals who can directly respond to crises.

For areas that do not have these resources, some cities have organizations and offices explicitly dedicated to functioning as an alternative to the police that can serve as models. For example, Eugene, Oregon's CAHOOTS is a mobile crisis intervention program, and Minneapolis has an Office of Violence Prevention. Programs like these have been found to successfully reduce police intervention (Beck et al. 2020). Indeed, many abolitionist organizations focus at least some of their work on developing alternatives to calling the police. These alternatives provide people with a direct response to a crisis or their feelings of unsafety in the moment. For example, the organization Raheem (n.d.) is currently developing an emergency dispatch app that will allow people who need help to bypass police involvement that generally comes with calling 9-1-1. Similarly, the Oakland Power Projects (OPP) has worked to create community-based responses to harm that make safety outside of state systems possible. An impressive feature here is that "safety" extends to include more than just interpersonal violence (the next section will more fully discuss this topic). Through their discussions with community members, OPP has developed resources for preventative health needs, including developing first-aid medical kits and "Know Your Options" workshops that train people in responding to medical and mental health emergencies without calling the police. From these workshops, OPP members constructed questions, guidelines, and potential strategies for practicing collective safety in other communities, including strategies for assessing potentially dangerous situations, assigning support roles to those involved, and reducing harm if someone needs to be taken to the hospital; recognizing and responding to an opiate overdose;

and assessing and providing support in a psychosocial crisis (Oakland Power Projects 2020).

Keeping people out of jail and prison is also a crucial part of resisting carcerality. Community bail funds provide a variety of services, but their primary role is to collect money that can be used to post the bail of people who cannot afford it themselves. As chapter 9 noted, not being able to make bail means a person who has not been convicted continues to experience the horrors of jail. Remaining behind bars means they may lose their job, which can also mean losing the place where they live and custody of their children. Also, people who do not make bail cannot help out with their defense by contacting witnesses and gathering evidence, so they are more likely to be convicted or take a bad plea offer (Jones 2013). They were also more likely to commit future crimes (Heaton et al. 2017: 717–18), since "even short-term detention has criminogenic effects" because of jail conditions and reduced employment options (Heaton 2020: 369). In 2020, four community bail funds—Chicago, Colorado, Connecticut, and Massachusetts—reported that they were able to pay the bails of over four thousand people (Davidson et al. 2020), while the national coalition of bail funds, the Bail Project, funded the release of over 17,500 people (Bail Project 2021).

Other ways that abolitionists have worked to resist punitive impulses have included challenging police requests for additional funds and advocating that the money be used for other community needs. For example, in 2019, Durham's city council rejected a $1.2 million request made by the Durham police department to fund eighteen new police officers. Members of the Beyond Policing Coalition analyzed city budget data, canvassed residents, and lobbied council members to make the case that the money should be used to support affordable housing, jobs, living wages, and harm reduction initiatives. As a result, the funds have officially been directed away from policing and toward raising the minimum wage for part-time city workers to $15 an hour (Alsous 2019). Additionally, in response to the efforts of organizations including Black Youth Project 100 Atlanta, the Fulton County commissioners agreed to reject any further consideration of expanding the Fulton County Jail using federal COVID-19 relief money (BYP100 Atlanta 2020).

Schools have also been strong sites for challenging the presence of carceral logics. In response to the torture inflicted on over 120 mostly Black men by former Chicago Police commander Jon Burge and his officers, a campaign emerged spearheaded by Chicago Justice Torture Memorials and We Charge Genocide and supported by various abolitionist organizations like Project NIA, Assata's Daughters, and BYP100. The reparations package requires that the official curriculum for Chicago Public Schools include at least one lesson about the Burge case and its legacy to be delivered to eighth and tenth graders (Chicago Torture Justice Memorials 2020). Among other groups, abolitionists have also been involved in efforts to remove police from schools, as organizers cite the harm caused by the school-to-prison pipeline and various instances of police violence on students, especially Black, Brown, poor, queer, and disabled students. For example, school districts in Minneapolis, Seattle, Oakland, Denver, and Portland have voted to suspend or completely revoke their contracts with local police departments, some choosing instead to divert the funding toward social workers, mental health professionals, and restorative justice training (Goldstein 2021).

## D: Cultivating Safety and Building a New World

The physical cages of prison and jail are not the only ones trapping marginalized populations, nor is crime victimization the only threat to people's safety. Widespread poverty; low-wage, precarious (un)employment; unequal access to adequate health care; and underresourced schools also harm and limit them. For this reason, contemporary abolitionists argue that this work is not simply about addressing prisons and police, nor is it primarily concerned with acts formally defined as crime (Abolition Collective 2020; Brown and Schept 2017). Abolitionists recognize that not everything that is legally defined as a crime is harmful, and not everything that is harmful is legally defined, policed, or processed as a crime. Instead, there is a shared understanding that the category "crime" has been socially constructed, and in a society defined by conflict and inequality, it is often leveraged as a tool to maintain the marginalized status of the many for the benefit of the powerful few (Shelden and Vasiliev 2018). As such, abolitionists tend to invoke the language of "harm" to describe what they are fighting against and "safety" to describe what they are fighting for.

As the previous section discussed, "harm" is a more expansive term that can include interpersonal violence but also violence enacted by corporations and governments. It also includes conditions of deprivation and marginalization like poverty, heterosexism, ableism, and racism, as well as the denial of self-determination. In contrast, safety can be thought of as "a set of resources, relationships, skills, and tools that can be developed, disseminated, and deployed to prevent, interrupt, and heal from harm" (Kaba and Ritchie 2022). A safe society is not just measured by the crime rate but is one in which "we have everything we need: food, shelter, education, health, art, beauty, clean water, and more. Things that are foundational to our personal and community safety" (Kaba 2021: 2).

Because harm is not limited to violations of the law, and because the criminal legal system has been complicit in causing harm, safety should be cultivated *outside* of it. And because safety is an inherent goal of abolition, that also means that abolition is necessarily a project of *building*. It requires creating the conditions for safety and continuously tending to those conditions so that those relationships and tools for preventing, intervening in, and healing harm can grow, thrive, and evolve.

There is a long history of this work. For example, in response to the systematic exclusion of Black and Brown people from social institutions, the Black Panthers and later the Young Lords set out to provide resources for the most marginalized members of society. The Black Panther Party's Breakfast for Children program fed more than twenty thousand schoolchildren across twenty-three cities by the end of 1969 (Pien 2010). It complemented their larger Free Food Program, which supplemented "the groceries of Black and poor people until economic conditions allow them to purchase good food at a reasonable price" (Hilliard 2010: 35). Members were also trained in first aid, with some becoming certified emergency technicians as part of their Free Ambulance Service (Nelson 2011). Inspired by this work, the Young Lords, a radical group of poor and working-class Puerto Rican youth in New York City, opened a free medical clinic, drug rehabilitation program, and child-care center for community members in the basement of a church they had occupied (Fernández 2019). While not solutions to the ravages of global capitalism, these programs were developed to ensure that people could survive day to day while fighting those forces of oppression.

Many current abolition groups continue to recognize these needs and provide mutual aid. These programs involve

> the work we do in social movements to directly support each other's survival needs, based on a shared understanding that the crises we are facing are caused by the system that we're living under, and are worsened by those systems. Mutual aid focuses on helping people get what they need right now, as we work to get to the root causes of these problems. (Fernandez 2020)

Unlike charity, mutual aid does not come with long lists of eligibility requirements, and it is not just for people the government or nonprofits (funded by the wealthy) consider the "deserving poor" (Spade 2020). The provision of aid in this way allows abolitionists to ask: "What are you mad about? What do you want to do?" (Fernandez 2020). And through those connections and discussions, abolitionists try to build the "capacity to meet our own needs in our own communities, to decide for ourselves, together, how our lives work rather than having rich people and their puppets decide" (Fernandez 2020).

Current mutual aid and abolitionist work still focuses on access to food—especially healthy food—and clean water. The problem identified by the Panthers and Young Lords has become food apartheid, "a system of segregation that divides those with access to an abundance of nutritious food and those who have been denied that access due to systemic injustice" (Project Regeneration, n.d.). In response, the St. Louis chapter of Youth Undoing Institutional Racism created a community garden to place people in direct connection with the earth and their neighbors. It promotes health and vitality, provides free or affordable food, and cultivates relationships, thus "countering the global capitalist structure" (Vidovic and Brown 2015) of isolation and deprivation.

Similarly, through Assata's Daughter's environmental justice program, young Black Chicagoans (who receive stipends) are trained in basic gardening and urban farming while learning about land conservation, food justice, and the importance of self-sustainability as a tool of resistance. This knowledge is then put to work in the community garden, "which not only provides local community members with affordable produce but is also a source of income for those who choose to work there" (Selman 2021: 42). Community fridges can also provide food for neighbors who need it. Designed to respond to the conditions of poverty and systemic racism that fuel food insecurity, this food is given with no surveillance and no strings attached—anyone who needs food, for whatever reason, can take as much as they need, when they need it. This can not only reduce the potential reliance on and police detection of "survival crime" but increase the overall well-being of a community (Evans 2020; Morrow 2019).

Health care and housing similarly pose threats to one's sense of safety. Founding members of the Ujimaa Medics explain that after a young person was shot in their neighborhood and died on the way to the hospital, they recognized that "our people needed immediate skills to help until a higher level of care could arrive" (Spade and Sirvent 2020). So the UMedics set out to identify, build on, and provide training in community health care. First-aid training can enable a person to dispense immediate care to another—in the most extreme cases, stabilizing the wounded enough to get to the nearest hospital and thus decreasing the reliance on 9-1-1 and potential police presence. Other organizations work outside urban areas. For example, Holler Health Justice provides support for "Appalachian communities and individuals most disproportionately affected by health inequities" (Holler Health Justice, n.d.), including but not limited to reproductive health.

Other noteworthy efforts include the Gworls, a Black, trans-led collective that helps fund-raise for housing, gender-affirming care, medical bills, and travel assistance for trans people who need support. Their work involves an explicit understanding that in a racial capitalist cis-heteropatriarchy, trans people are systematically blocked from accessing such resources (For the Gworls, n.d.). Relatedly, tenant and neighborhood councils (TANCs) popped up during the COVID-19 pandemic to help tenants fight abusive landlords and gentrifying companies. As the Bay Area TANC explains, "We are fed up with our neighbors having no option but to live unsheltered and at constant risk of police harassment. We want to stop landlords, developers, and cops from looting our communities" (Tenant and Neighborhood Councils, n.d.). Programs like these, much like the work of the Black Panthers and Young Lords, are deeply rooted in the understanding that "the only way we can make it is to rely on each other" (Willingham 2022).

LGBTQ+ people are not only overrepresented at every stage of the criminal justice system (Buist and Lenning 2023; Jones 2021) but see their liberation tied to abolition: "Queerness requires imagining a world that has never existed," and thus "abolition and queerness are intrinsically linked in their exploration and dismissal of the impossible" (Nwanne 2020). Black and Pink, a national prison abolitionist organization, is dedicated to abolishing prisons *because of* the fundamental understanding that queer liberation is intertwined with freedom from the cages of the carceral state. They coordinate a pen-pal network that facilitates connection and support between LGBTQIA2S+[2] prisoners and those on the outside. Black and Pink also raises funds for "Opportunity Campus," a housing and community space in Omaha, Nebraska, for youth and young adults who have interacted with the criminal justice/juvenile justice systems. Opportunity Campus will "provide housing, wrap around support services, mental health support, daily drop-in services (such as hot meals, showers, food pantry, and laundry), and community programming to system-impacted LGBTQIA2S+ youth, young adults, and their families" (Black and Pink, n.d.)—all at no cost to those who need the services.

While many projects involve sexual and racial minorities, abolition is not a project that solely focuses on, or benefits, just those groups: "There are no single-issue struggles because we don't live single-issue lives" (Lorde [1982] 2012). Much as the criminal justice–industrial complex perpetuates inequality along intersecting lines of race, class, gender/sexuality, and ability, resistance to such oppression similarly reckons with all forms of marginalization. While this book has focused on class, race, gender/sexuality, and their intersections, there are numerous other types of oppression. For example, disability justice "is a requisite for abolition because carceral systems medicalize, pathologize, criminalize, and commodify survival, divergence, and resistance" (Lewis 2021: 62). Put another way, any abolitionist work must be rooted in a commitment to disability justice: to "radically transform social conditions and norms in order to affirm and support all people's inherent right to live and thrive" (Lewis 2021: 65). This undergirds the work of organizations like the Fireweed Collective, which provides education and mutual aid through a disability justice lens in order to "disrupt the harm of systems of abuse and oppression, often reproduced by the mental health system" (Fireweed Collective, n.d.). They provide workshops on how to build a "care team" for times of crisis that do not rely on the police or formal mental health systems. Similarly, Project LETS is a collective to "advocate for the liberation of our community members globally" (Project LETS, n.d.) by offering a global network of peer support for those who have lived experience with mental illness.

The point of not leading single-issue lives is also evident in the experiences of Michael Zinzun, a member of the Black Panther Party who, after being brutally attacked by a police officer, funneled the financial settlement from the city into the Coalition Against Police Abuse. In working with victims of police violence, he also became acutely aware of the other violent conditions people were exposed to—one being the increased risk of death for public housing project residents from asthma due to the presence of roach and mouse droppings and the frequent use of pesticides by landlords (Kumanyika and Gilmore 2020). Zinzun became "a model" for what abolition can mean: "He was against the police because police were shortening lives. He became an environmental justice activist because the environment within the living spaces for these young people was literally killing them" (Kumanyika and Gilmore 2020).

Other abolitionists have formed alliances with environmental justice activists because of the environmental harms of prison or police academy buildings. This was the case in Letcher County, Kentucky, when members of the Letcher Governance Project, the Campaign to Fight Toxic Prisons, and the Center for Biological Diversity, among others, joined forces to defeat the building of a new federal prison—citing not only the environmental impact of building on a toxic mountaintop-removal mining site, but also the negative social and psychological effects of a local economy dependent on a prison (Schept 2022).

Similar points are being made in Atlanta, Georgia, where protestors have organized against the building of "Cop City" (discussed at the end of chapter 8). The center, serving as a "mock city" for police, fire, and emergency responder training, will, according to activists, further militarize the police while also destroying eighty-five acres of one of the largest remaining urban forests in the United States—and some of the limited green space available to poorer and minority residents (Fatica 2022). In 2023, a forest defender named Manuel Terán (Tort/Tortuguita) was killed by police, further demonstrating the point that "abolition has to be 'green.' It has to take seriously the problem of environmental harm, environmental racism, and environmental degradation" (Gilmore 2022: 22).

Finally, abolition is not a uniquely U.S. project, as neoliberalism has carried the same problems and versions of the criminal justice–industrial complex to other areas of the world. While abolition embraces and connects a variety of issues in the United States, "it has to be international. It has to stretch across borders so that we can consolidate our strength, our experience, and our vision for a better world" (Gilmore 2022: 22; Davis 2015). Gilmore and other abolitionists emphasize that the work of abolition is a better *world*, not simply a better United States. Thus, abolitionists engage in global actions against police (Maher 2021: 159). Indeed, the police killing of George Floyd led to "more than 11,000 protests in over 3,000 different places throughout the U.S." and another "8,700 demonstrations in 74 countries, bridging BLM [Black Lives Matter] solidarity with local struggles around police violence and racism" (Shanahan and Kurti 2022: 31).

The global nature of the protests over police treatment of the poor points to global issues that create the same problems with multiple criminal justice systems. Thus, abolition requires a confrontation with and a contestation of interconnected systems of oppression, including global capitalism and the global systems of class, race, gender/sexuality, and intersectional concerns connected with it. As such, advocates for abolition say that it is a project for everyone, everywhere. But tackling such problems can seem like an immense task and that there's "nothing we can do" (so we will do nothing). Indeed, capitalism is also behind problems of climate change and ecological destruction, with the idea that "it's easier to imagine an end to the world than an end to capitalism" (in Dean 2019). But science fiction writer Ursula K. Le Guin (2014) argued, "We live in capitalism. Its power seems inescapable. So did the divine right of kings. Any human power can be resisted and changed by human beings."

\* \* \*

While undermining global capitalism is not a project all readers will want to embark on, there are important connections between inequality, crime, and crime control. An economic system that generates high levels of exploitation and insecurity will also generate high levels of crime and violence. Chapter 2 noted Currie's analysis that crime and violence are caused by "the experience of life year in, year out at the bottom of a harsh, depriving, and excluding social system [that] wears away at the psychological and communal conditions that sustain healthy human development" (1998: 134). The types of concerns Currie was calling out more than twenty-five years ago have not changed for the better. Indeed, "compared to other developed nations, America's political economy exposes communities, families, and individuals to greater market-generated risks—economic insecurity, unemployment, poverty, inadequate housing, inadequate healthcare, food insecurity, and so on." Because of a "politics of abandonment" made worse by neoliberalism, the American "welfare state provides them with fewer social protections—such as social insurance, income support, public goods, and social rights" (Garland 2023: 51). Reform, then, should be driven by "a broadly class-based movement for economic justice" (Garland 2023: 58). The greater equality will lead to less desperation, frustration, aggression, and crime—and thus less need for a large and militarized criminal justice response.

The criminological research demonstrating "that nations with higher levels of equality have lower levels of violence and fewer social problems than more unequal nations" (Garland 2023: 51) supports the basic ideas of abolition: changing society to better support people's needs will result in less crime and less need for a criminal justice system. The scale of change is significant, but it is consistent with the scope of the problem. The United States has one of the highest rates of crime and violence in the developed world, the highest incarceration rate and most militarized police, and low confidence in the criminal justice system.

What's written in this chapter is clearly not a full blueprint for reform, and the point was not that the reader would believe all the ideas here; it was rather to present ideas to stimulate the reader's critical thinking and imagination. We hope you have arrived at this point with a deeper appreciation of the limitations of justice in the United States and at the same time that "there *is* an alternative" to a criminal justice system that lacks the public's confidence—and to the field of criminology currently training people to work in it and providing ideas for its development. We hope that you can reflect on the question, "Why—rather than joining with others to pursue our mutual betterment—do we routinely visit harm on one another and the natural world?" (Davies 2021). Simple steps are starting points for change, and simple acts of contesting that "there is no alternative" will not make the world worse than it is.

## Review and Discussion Questions

1. What is ideology? What does it have to do with concluding a book about injustice and the problems of the criminal justice system?
2. The introduction of this chapter included the quote, "Why—rather than joining with others to pursue our mutual betterment—do we routinely visit harm on one another and the natural world?" (Davies 2021). What do you think the answer is?
3. This conclusion noted that it had dropped a list of proposals that earlier editions of this book had. Do you think that a list of proposals—including reform ideas that are twenty years old—has value? Why or why not?
4. What does it mean to "disrupt" criminology? Why do the authors feel it is necessary? How do the ideas in that section accomplish "disruption"? Which, if any, would you like to follow up on in your criminology studies?
5. Why do the authors feel like criminology needs to think about social harm beyond what the criminal law defines as crime? Why do you agree or disagree? What is zemiology and why is it presented as an alternative?
6. How would you describe abolition to someone? What are the points you agree with? What do you disagree with?
7. Why do abolitionists argue that the system cannot be reformed? Why do you agree or disagree?
8. Are there alternatives to the police in your community that could reduce the "carceral mind-set"? Are there any being developed? Are there examples of abolitionist work in your local community?

## Notes

1. In a further defense of the term "financial violence" rather than "predatory finance," the author writes:

> I find that the language of financial violence draws attention to three additional factors regarding instruments such as title loans. First, the literature shows that the core customer base is utilizing these loans to pay for daily needs such as groceries, child care, utilities, and rent. Thus, such practices are not only predatory but they serve to violently disrupt almost every aspect of life as one's daily subsistence becomes tethered to high-interest debt. Second, financial violence

moves us past the problematic misconception of individual bad actors. While the term predatory lender remains useful in certain contexts, it can also deflect attention onto so-called bad apples rather than addressing the violence that is endemic to the financial system as a whole. Third, the concept of violence draws explicit attention to the political power that holds the system in place. Taking seriously Ruth Wilson Gilmore's insight that it is "the application of violence [that] produces political power in a vicious cycle" (2022, p. 16), we can begin to untangle the nexus of finance, politics, profit, and vulnerability. (Sugata 2019: 8)

2. Instead of LGBTQ+, this organization uses LGBTQIA2S+: lesbian, gay, bisexual, transgender and/or gender expansive, queer and/or questioning, intersex, asexual, and two-spirit.

# References

References for several common sources of data are referenced here rather than through multiple similar entries for different years of the same publication:

**BJS**: Bureau of Justice Statistics, a source of many reports cited in this book. The BJS is an agency of the U.S. Department of Justice. Reports of the BJS are published by the U.S. Government Printing Office in Washington, DC, and can be accessed online at https://www.bjs.gov or https://www.ojp.usdoj.gov/bjs. Most of the publications are listed below, although some text references to BJS that include the name of the publication are not.

**FBI** or **UCR**: U.S. Department of Justice, Federal Bureau of Investigation, *Crime in the United States* (the publication that contains data from the Uniform Crime Reports). References to this annual report will be indicated by *UCR*, followed by the year for which the statistics are reported. Data back to 1995 can be accessed through https://www.fbi.gov/about-us/cjis/ucr/ucr. After 2019, the FBI no longer published *Crime in the United States* and moved to uploading data into Crime Data Explorer tools. References like UCR data for 2020 and later will be to UCR data drawn from the Crime Data Explorer at https://cde.ucr.cjis.gov/LATEST/webapp/#/pages/home. The expanded homicide and hate crimes data are from the Documents and Downloads section, from which users can scroll down to data categories and select a year and specific tables that can be downloaded in a zip format.

Abolition Collective. 2020. *Making Abolitionist Worlds: Proposals for a World on Fire*. Brooklyn, NY: Common Notions.

Adams, M., and M. Rameau. 2016. "Black Community Control over Police." *Wisconsin Law Review* 515.

Agnew, R. 2011. *Toward a Unified Criminology: Integrating Assumptions about Crime, People and Society*. New York: New York University Press.

Agozino, B., and S. Pfohl. 2003. *Counter-Colonial Criminology: A Critique of Imperialist Reason*. Sterling, VA: Pluto Press.

Ahrens, Deborah. 2020. "Retroactive Legality: Marijuana Convictions and Restorative Justice in an Era of Criminal Justice Reform." *Journal of Criminal Law and Criminology* 110(3): 379–440.

Akins, S. 2013. "287(g)." *Criminology & Public Policy* 12(2): 227–36. https://doi.org/10.1111/1745-9133.12042.

Alexander, Michelle. 2012. *The New Jim Crow: Mass Incarceration in the Age of Colorblindness*. New York: New Press.

Ali, Amir. 2017. "Judge Konzinski Asked the Wrong Question and Got the Wrong Answer." *Take Care*, March 20. https://takecareblog.com/blog/judge-kozinski-asked-the-wrong-question-and-got-the-wrong-answer.

Ali, M. U., and M. Pirog. 2019. "Social Accountability and Institutional Change: The Case of Citizen Oversight of Police." *Public Administration Review* 79(3): 411–26.

Alirezaei, S., and R. Latifnejad Roudsari. 2022. "The Needs of Incarcerated Pregnant Women: A Systematic Review of Literature." *International Journal of Community Based Nursing and Midwifery* 10(1): 2–17. https://doi.org/10.30476/IJCBNM.2021.89508.1613.

Allen, Dan. 2023. "'The Stroll' Puts Trans Sex Workers on the Map of NYC's Queer History." NBC News, June 20. https://www.nbcnews.com/nbc-out/out-pop-culture/-stroll-puts-trans-sex-workers-map-nycs-queer-history-rcna89835.

Alsous, Z. 2019. "'Starve the Beast': Southern Campaigns to Divest, Decarcerate, and Re-Imagine Public Safety." *Scalawag*, November 4. https://www.rjactioncenter.org/post/media-starve-the-beast-southern-campaigns-to-divest-decarcerate-and-re-imagine-public-safety.

Alter, A., and E. A. Harris. 2023. "Asked to Delete References to Racism from Her Book, an

Author Refused." *New York Times*, May 11. https://www.nytimes.com/2023/05/06/books/scholastic-book-racism-maggie-tokuda-hall.html.

Álvarez, Sophia E., and Martin G. Urbina. 2015. "Bridging the Gaps and Future Research." In *Latino Police Officers in the United States*, edited by Martin Guevara Urbina and Sofia Espinoza Álvarez, 148–72. Springfield, IL: Charles C. Thomas.

American Bar Association. 2023. "Profile of the Legal Profession." https://www.abalegalprofile.com/index.html.

American College of Obstetricians and Gynecologists. 2022. "Ectopic Pregnancy." https://www.acog.org/womens-health/faqs/ectopic-pregnancy.

American Immigration Lawyers Association. 2022. "Policy Brief: Use of Virtual Hearings in Removal Proceedings." Doc No. 22050500. AILA, May 3. https://www.aila.org/library/policy-brief-use-of-virtual-hearings-in-removal.

———. 2023. *Featured Issue: America Needs a Fair and Independent Immigration Court.* AILA, October 20. https://www.aila.org/advo-media/issues/immigration-courts.

American Society of Criminology. n.d. "Statement of the American Society of Criminology Executive Board Concerning the Trump Administration's Policies Relevant to Crime and Justice." https://www.asc41.com/policies/ASC_Executive_Board_Statement_on_Trump_Administration_Crime_and_Justice_Policies.pdf.

Andersen, Margaret L., and Patricia Hill Collins. 1998. *Race, Class and Gender: An Anthology.* 3rd ed. Belmont, CA: Wadsworth.

Anderson, Carol. 2021. *The Second: Race and Guns in a Fatally Unequal America.* New York: Bloomsbury.

Anderson, Charles H. 1974. *The Political Economy of Social Class.* Englewood Cliffs, NJ: Prentice-Hall.

Anderson, N., D. G. Robinson, E. Verhagen, K. Fagher, P. Edouard, D. Rojas-Valverde, O. H. Ahmed, et al. 2023. "Under-representation of Women Is Alive and Well in Sport and Exercise Medicine: What It Looks Like and What We Can Do about It." *BMJ Open Sport & Exercise Medicine* 9(2).

Andresen, W. C. 2020. "I Track Murder Cases That Use the 'Gay Panic Defense,' a Controversial Practice Banned in 9 States." *The Conversation*, January 29. https://theconversation.com/i-track-murder-cases-that-use-the-gay-panic-defense-a-controversial-practice-banned-in-9-states-129973.

Androff, David. 2014. "Human Rights and the War on Immigration." In *The Criminalization of Immigration: Contexts and Consequences*, edited by Alissa R. Ackerman and Rich Furman, 147–62. Durham, NC: Carolina Academic Press.

Angehrn A., A. J. Fletcher, and R. N. Carleton. 2021. "'Suck It Up, Buttercup': Understanding and Overcoming Gender Disparities in Policing." *International Journal of Environmental Research and Public Health* 8(14): 7627. https://doi.org/10.3390/ijerph18147627.

Aragao, C. 2023. "Gender Pay Gap in U.S. Hasn't Changed Much in Two Decades." Pew Research Center, March 1. https://www.pewresearch.org/short-reads/2023/03/01/gender-pay-gap-facts/#:~:text=Family%20caregiving%20responsibilities%20bring%20different,fatherhood%20can%20increase%20men%27s%20earnings.

Arford, T., and E. Madfis. 2022. "Whitewashing Criminology: A Critical Tour of Cesare Lombroso's Museum of Criminal Anthropology." *Critical Criminology* 30:723–40. https://doi.org/10.1007/s10612-021-09604-x.

Arrigo, B., B. Sellers, H. Copes, and J. Paz. 2021. "New Qualitative Methods and Critical Research Directions in Crime, Law, and Justice: Editors' Introduction." *Journal of Criminal Justice Education* 33(2): 145–50. https://doi.org/10.1080/10511253.2022.2027484.

Arrigo, B. A., and B. D. Sellers, eds. 2021. *The Precrime Society: Crime, Culture, and Control in the Ultramodern Age.* Bristol: Bristol University Press and Policy Press.

Arthur, Charles. 2013. "Symantec Discovers 2005 US Computer Virus Attack on Iran Nuclear Plants." *Guardian*, February 26. https://www.guardian.co.uk/technology/2013/feb/26/symantec-us-computer-virus-iran-nuclear.

Associated Press. 2022. "U. of Michigan Reaches $490M Settlement Over Sexual Abuse by A Former Sports Doctor." National Public Radio, January 19. https://www.npr.org/2022/01/19

/1074071024/university-michigan-sexual-abuse-sports-doctor.

Atwoli, Lukoye, Abdullah H. Baqui, Thomas Benfield, Raffaella Bosurgi, Fiona Godlee, Stephen Hancocks, Richard Horton, et al. 2021. "Call for Emergency Action to Limit Global Temperature Increases, Restore Biodiversity, and Protect Health." *New England Journal of Medicine* 385:1134–37. https://doi.org/10.1056/NEJMe2113200.

Auerbach, Jerold S. 1976. *Unequal Justice: Lawyers and Social Change in Modern America.* New York: Oxford University Press.

Austen, I. 2021. "Two Years after Legalizing Cannabis, Has Canada Kept Its Promises?" *New York Times*, April 18. https://www.nytimes.com/2021/01/23/world/canada/marijuana-legalization-promises-made.html.

Austin, A. 2023. "On the Interrelationship of Race and Class." Center for Economic and Policy Research, March 14. https://cepr.net/on-the-interrelationship-of-race-and-class.

Austin, Regina, and Michael Schill. 1991. "Black, Brown, Poor and Poisoned: Minority Grassroots Environmentalism and the Quest for Eco-Justice." *Kansas Journal of Law and Public Policy* 17(2): 69–82.

Avery, Daniel. 2019. "Donald Trump's First Openly Gay Judicial Nominee Was Just Approved by the Senate. Here's Why LGBT Groups Aren't Thrilled." *Newsweek*, August 8. https://www.newsweek.com/mary-rowland-lesbian-judge-trump-nominee-1452856.

Aviram, Hadar. 2015. *Cheap on Crime: Recession-Era Politics and the Transformation of American Punishment.* Oakland, CA: University of California Press.

Baca Zinn, Maxine, Pierrette Hondagneu-Sotelo, and Michael Messner, eds. 2005. *Gender through the Prism of Difference.* 3rd ed. New York: Oxford University Press.

Bach, Wendy. 2019. "Prosecuting Poverty, Criminalizing Care." *William and Mary Law Review* 60(3): 809–89. https://scholarship.law.wm.edu/wmlr/vol60/iss3/3.

Bacigalupi, P. 2016. *The Water Knife.* New York: Vintage.

Bail Project. 2021. "Annual Report." https://bailproject.org/wp-content/uploads/2021/11/the_bail_project_annual_report_2021_web.pdf.

Bakan, Joel. 2004. *The Corporation: The Pathological Pursuit of Profit and Power.* New York: Free Press.

Balko, Radley. 2013. "Rise of the Warrior Cop." *Wall Street Journal*, August 7. https://online.wsj.com/news/articles/SB10001424127887323848804578608040780519904.

Ball, M. 2014. "What's Queer about Queer Criminology?" In *Handbook of LGBT Communities, Crime, and Justice*, edited by Dana Peterson and Vanessa R. Panfil, 531–55. New York: Springer. https://doi.org/10.1007/978-1-4614-9188-0_24.

Barak, Gregg. 1980. *In Defense of Whom? A Critique of Criminal Justice Reform.* Cincinnati, OH: Anderson.

———, ed. 1991. *Crimes by the Capitalist State: An Introduction to State Criminality.* Albany: State University of New York Press.

———. 1998. *Integrating Criminologies.* Boston, MA: Allyn & Bacon.

———. 2003. *Violence and Nonviolence: Pathways to Understanding.* Thousand Oaks, CA: Sage.

———. 2012. *Theft of a Nation: Wall Street Looting and Federal Regulatory Colluding.* Lanham, MD: Rowman & Littlefield.

———. 2013. "The Flickering Desires for White-Collar Crime Studies in the Post-Financial Crisis: Will They Ever Shine Brightly?" *Western Criminology Review* 14(2): 61–71.

———, ed. 2015. *The Routledge International Handbook of the Crimes of the Powerful.* New York: Routledge.

———. 2017. *Unchecked Corporate Power: Why the Crimes of Multinational Corporations Are Routinized Away and What We Can Do about It.* New York: Routledge.

———. 2022. *Criminology on Trump.* Routledge.

———. 2024. *Indicting the 45th President: Boss Trump, the GOP, and What We Can Do about the Threat of American Democracy.* New York: Routledge.

Barak, M. P. 2023. *The Slow Violence of Immigration Court: Procedural Justice on Trial.* New York: New York University Press.

Barak, M., and P. Leighton. 2013. "Immigrants as Victims." In *Encyclopedia of Street Crime in America*, edited by Jeffery Ian Ross. Thousand Oaks, CA: Sage.

Barak, M. P., K. L. León, and E. R. Maguire. 2020. "Conceptual and Empirical Obstacles in

Defining MS-13." *Criminology & Public Policy* 19(2): 563–89. https://doi.org/10.1111/1745-9133.12493.

Barideaux, K., Jr., A. Crossby, and D. Crosby. 2021. "Colorism and Criminality: The Effects of Skin Tone and Crime Type on Judgements of Guilt." *Applied Psychology in Criminal Justice* 16(2): 181–99.

Barstow, David. 2003. "When Workers Die: U.S. Rarely Seeks Charges for Deaths in Workplace." *New York Times*, December 22. https://www.nytimes.com/2003/12/22/national/22OSHA.html.

Batalova, J., M. Hanna, and C. Levesque. 2021. "Frequently Requested Statistics on Immigrants and Immigration in the United States." Migration Policy Institute, February 11. https://www.migrationpolicy.org/article/frequently-requested-statistics-immigrants-and-immigration-united-states-2020.

Bateman-House, A., and A. Fairchild. 2008. "Medical Examination of Immigrants at Ellis Island." *AMA Journal of Ethics*, April. https://journalofethics.ama-assn.org/article/medical-examination-immigrants-ellis-island/2008-04.

Bauer, Shane. 2016. "My Four Months as a Private Prison Guard." *Mother Jones*, July/August. https://www.motherjones.com/politics/2016/06/cca-private-prisons-corrections-corporation-inmates-investigation-bauer.

Bauer, S. 2019. *American Prison: A Reporter's Undercover Journey into the Business of Punishment*. New York: Penguin.

BBC News. 2018. "Elliot Rodger: How Misogynist Killer Became 'Incel Hero.'" April 25. https://www.bbc.com/news/world-us-canada-43892189.

Beck J., M. Reuland, and L. Pope. 2020. "Behavioral Health Crisis Alternatives: Shifting from Police to Community Responses. *Vera*, November. https://pceinc.org/wp-content/uploads/2020/12/20201100---Behavioral-Health-Crisis-Alternatives---Vera---Beck-Reuland-Pope.pdf.

Beety, V. E., and J. D. Oliva. 2023. "Policing Pregnancy 'Crimes.'" *New York University Law Review* 98:29–54.

Beirne, P., and J. Messerschmidt. 1991. *Criminology*. San Diego, CA: Harcourt Brace Jovanovich.

———. 2000. *Criminology*. 3rd ed. Boulder, CO: Westview.

Belknap, J. 2004. "Meda Chesney-Lind." *Women & Criminal Justice* 15(2): 1–23. https://doi.org/10.1300/J012v15n02_01.

———. 2007. *The Invisible Woman: Gender, Crime, and Justice*. 3rd ed. Belmont, CA: Wadsworth.

———. 2020. *The Invisible Woman: Gender, Crime, and Justice*. 5th ed. Los Angeles, CA. Sage Publications.

Bell, Derrick. 1989. "Racism: A Prophecy for the Year 2000." *Rutgers Law Review* 42:93–108; revised and expanded version in "After We're Gone: Prudent Speculations on America in a Post-Racial Epoch." *St. Louis Law Review* 34(1990): 1–8.

Bellafonte, Ginia. 2023. "Here's What Happens as the Era of Mass Incarceration Winds Down." *New York Times*, March 31. https://www.nytimes.com/2023/03/31/nyregion/mass-incarceration-ny.html.

Benjamin, Ruha. 2019. *Captivating Technology: Race, Carceral Technoscience, and Liberatory Imagination in Everyday Life*. Durham, NC: Duke University Press.

Bennett, M. 2020. "In Their Words: Black Leaders on Food and Racial Justice." Greater Chicago Food Depository, June 5. https://www.chicagosfoodbank.org/blog/in-their-words-black-leaders-on-food-and-racial-justice.

Bennett, Neil, et al. 2022. "Wealth Inequality in the U.S. by Household Type." United States Census Bureau, August 1. https://www.census.gov/library/stories/2022/08/wealth-inequality-by-household-type.html.

Berg, U. D., S. Tosh, and S. K. León. 2022. "Carceral Ethnography in a Time of Pandemic: Examining Migrant Detention and Deportation during COVID-19." *Ethnography*, February 28. https://doi.org/10.1177/14661381211072414.

Bergner, D. 2020. "'White Fragility' Is Everywhere. But Does Antiracism Training Work?" *New York Times*, July 15. https://www.nytimes.com/2020/07/15/magazine/white-fragility-robin-diangelo.html.

Berkowitz, Deborah. 2019. "Workplace Safety Enforcement Continues to Decline in Trump Administration." National Employment Law Project. https://www.nelp.org/publication/workplace-safety-enforcement-continues-decline-trump-administration.

Berman, M., and S. Clement. 2023. "Post-ABC Poll: Confidence in Police Drops after Tyre Nichols Beating." *Washington Post*, February 3. https://www.washingtonpost.com/nation/2023/02/03/post-abc-poll-police-tyre-nichols.

Bethea, C. 2022. "The New Fight over an Old Forest in Atlanta." *New Yorker*, August 3. https://www.newyorker.com/news/letter-from -the-south/the-new-fight-over-an-old-forest-in -atlanta.

Bhutta, N., A. C. Chang, L. J. Dettling, and J. W. Hsu. 2020. "Disparities in Wealth by Race and Ethnicity in the 2019 Survey of Consumer Finances." Board of Governors of the Federal Reserve System, September 28. https:// www.federalreserve.gov/econres/notes/feds -notes/disparities-in-wealth-by-race-and-ethnic ity-in-the-2019-survey-of-consumer-finances -20200928.htm.

Bickel, Karl. 2013. "Will the Growing Militarization of Our Police Doom Community Policing?" *Community Policing Dispatch* 6 (December 12). https://cops.usdoj.gov/html/ dispatch/12-2013/will_the_growing_militari zation_of_our_police_doom_community_polic ing.asp.

Binstein, Michael, and Charles Bowden. 1993. *Trust Me: Charles Keating and the Missing Billions*. New York: Random House.

Bird, J. 2017. "How to Talk (and Listen) to Transgender People." TED, June. https://www .ted.com/talks/jackson_bird_how_to_talk_and _listen_to_transgender_people/transcript?lan guage=en.

Black, Donald. 1976. *The Behavior of Law*. New York: Academic Press.

Black and Pink. n.d. "Opportunity Campus." https://www.blackandpink.org/programs/ opportunity-campus-capital-campaign.

Black Attorneys of Legal Aid, The Bronx Defenders, Brooklyn Defender Services, Et Al. as *Amici Curiae* Brief in Support of Petitioners, New York State Rifle & Pistol Association, Inc., *Robert Nash and Brandon Koch v. Keith M. Corlett and Richard J. McNally, Jr.* 2021. No. 20-843. U.S. Supreme Court. https://www.supremecourt.gov/DocketPDF/20 /20-843/184718/20210723101034102_20-843 %20Amici%20Brief%20revised%20cover.pdf.

Black Feminist Future. n.d. "What Is Patriarchal Violence? A Working Definition from the Abolishing Patriarchal Violence Innovation Lab." https://blackfeministfuture.org/resources/what -is-patriarchal-violence-a-working-definition -from-the-abolishing-patriarchal-violence-inno vation-lab.

Blackwell, S. 2021. "'Guys, Get Your Guns Out!': An Autobiographical Account of a US Community Corrections Training Academy." *Probation Journal* 68(3): 330–46.

Blitstein, Ryan. 2009. "Racism's Hidden Toll." *Miller-McCune*, July–August, 48–57.

Bloom, Barbara, Barbara Owen, and Stephanie Covington. 2003. *Gender-Responsive Strategies: Research, Practice, and Guiding Principles for Women Offenders*. Report, National Institute of Corrections/U.S. Department of Justice, Washington, DC. https://www.nicic.org /pubs/2003/018017.pdf.

Blumstein, Alfred. 1995. "Interview with Professor Alfred Blumstein of Carnegie Mellon University." *Law Enforcement News* 422:10.

Boddupalli, A., and L. Mucciolo. 2022. "Following the Money on Fines and Fees." Tax Policy Center, January 13. https://www.taxpolicy center.org/publications/following-money-fines -and-fees/full.

Bohm, Robert M., and Keith N. Haley. 2004. *Introduction to Criminal Justice*. 3rd ed. Boston, MA: McGraw-Hill.

———. 2005. *Introduction to Criminal Justice*. 4th ed. Boston, MA: McGraw-Hill.

Bonilla-Silva, E. 2018. *Racism without Racists: Color-Blind Racism and the Persistence of Racial Inequality in America*. 5th ed. Lanham, MD: Rowman & Littlefield.

Box, S. 1983. *Power, Crime and Mystification*. London: Routledge.

Braithwaite, John. 1992. "Poverty, Power and White-Collar Crime: Sutherland and the Paradoxes of Criminological Theory." In *White Collar Crime Reconsidered*, edited by Kip Schlegel and David Weisburd, 78–107. Boston, MA: Northeastern University Press.

Brayne, Sarah. 2017. "Big Data Surveillance: The Case of Policing." *American Sociological Review* 82(5): 977–1008.

Brouwer, Steve. 1998. *Sharing the Pie: A Citizen's Guide to Wealth and Power in America*. New York: Henry Holt.

Brown, A. 2020. "The Changing Categories the U.S. Census Has Used to Measure Race." Pew Research Center, February 25. https:// www.pewresearch.org/short-reads/2020/02/25 /the-changing-categories-the-u-s-has-used-to -measure-race.

brown, a. m. 2017. *Emergent Strategy: Shaping Change, Shaping Worlds*. Oakland, CA: AK Press.

Brown, M., and J. Schept. 2017. "New Abolition, Criminology and a Critical Carceral Studies." *Punishment & Society* 19(4): 440–62.

Brown, Robert McAfee. 1987. *Religion and Violence*. 2nd ed. Philadelphia, PA: Westminster.

Bruder, Jessica. 2018. "The Worst Drug Crisis in American History." *New York Times*, July 31. https://www.nytimes.com/2018/07/31/books/review/beth-macy-dopesick.html.

Brune, Tom. 1999. "Census Will for First Time Count Those of Mixed Race." *Seattle Times*, August 17. https://community.seattletimes.nwsource.com/archive/?date=19990817&slug=2977786.

Brunskell-Evans, Heather. 2017. "Book Review: The End of Patriarchy: Radical Feminism for Men by Robert Jensen." *Dignity: A Journal on Sexual Exploitation and Violence* 2(2): 1–3. https://doi.org/10.23860/dignity.2017.02.02.04.

Bryant, Erica. 2022. "Violence, Torture and Isolation: What It's Like to Be Trans in Prison." *Vera*, November 17. https://www.vera.org/news/violence-torture-and-isolation-what-its-like-to-be-trans-in-prison.

Buckley, C. 2022. "At 75, the Father of Environmental Justice Meets the Moment." *New York Times*, November 10. https://www.nytimes.com/2022/09/12/climate/robert-bullard-environmental-justice.html.

Budds, D. 2023. "Designing Cop City: What the Evolution of the Tactical Village, from Riotsville to Atlanta, Reveals about Policing." *Curbed*, June 21. https://www.curbed.com/2023/06/atlanta-cop-city-design-architecture-tactical-village.html.

Buist, Carrie L., and Paul Leighton. 2015. "Corporate Criminals Constructing White Collar Crime—Or Why There Is No Corporate Crime on USA Network's *White Collar* Series." In *The Routledge International Handbook of Crimes of the Powerful*, edited by G. Barak, 73–86. New York: Routledge.

Buist, C., and E. Lenning. 2016. *Queer Criminology*. New York: Routledge.

———. 2023. *Queer Criminology*. 2nd ed. New York: Routledge.

Buist, C., and L. Kahle Semprevivo, eds. 2022. *Queering Criminology in Theory and Praxis: Reimagining Justice in the Criminal Legal System and Beyond*. Bristol: Bristol University Press.

Buist, C. L., and C. Stone. 2014. "Transgender Victims and Offenders: Failures of the United States Criminal Justice System and the Necessity of Queer Criminology." *Critical Criminology* 22:35–47.

Bullard, Robert. 1994. *Unequal Protection: Environmental Justice and Communities of Color*. San Francisco, CA: Sierra Club.

Bullard, R. D., R. A. Chapman, C. M. Kabel, N. Mallett, and J. Q. Schaeffer. 2022. "Climate Crisis, Environmental Justice, and Racial Justice." In *Necessary Conversations: Understanding Racism as a Barrier to Achieving Health Equity*, edited by A. L. Plough. New York: Oxford University Press.

Bureau of Indian Affairs. n.d. "Missing and Murdered Indigenous People Crisis." https://www.bia.gov/service/mmu/missing-and-murdered-indigenous-people-crisis#:~:text=In%20the%20year%20leading%20up,experienced%20violence%20in%20their%20lifetime.

Bureau of Justice Statistics (BJS). 2001. "Federal Drug Offenders, 1999, with Trends 1984–1999." NCJ 187285.

———. 2005. "Contacts between Police and the Public: Findings from the 2002 National Survey." NCJ 207845.

———. 2011. "Criminal Victimization in the United States, 2008—Statistical Tables." NCJ 231173.

———. 2021a. "Criminal Victimization, 2021." NCJ 305101.

———. 2021b. "Stalking Victimization, 2019." NCV 301735.

———. 2021c. "State and Local Law Enforcement Training Academies, 2018—Statistical Tables." NCJ 255915.

———. 2021d. "Justice Expenditures and Employment in the United States, 2017." NCJ 256093.

———. 2022a. "Violent Victimization by Sexual Orientation and Gender Identity, 2017–2020." NCJ 304277.

———. 2022b. "Local Police Departments Personnel, 2020." NCJ 305187.

———. 2022c. "Federal Law Enforcement Officers, 2020—Statistical Tables." NCJ 304752.

———. 2023a. "Jail Inmates in 2022—Statistical Tables." NCJ 307086.

———. 2023b. "Prisoners in 2022—Statistical Tables." NCJ 307149.

———. 2023c. "Correctional Populations in the United States, 2021—Statistical Tables." NCJ 305542.

———. 2023d. "Capital Punishment, 2021—Statistical Tables." NCJ 305534.

———. 2023e. "Criminal Victimization, 2022." NCJ 307089.

Bureau of Labor Statistics. 2016. *Occupational Outlook Handbook, 2016–17 Edition*. Washington, DC: U.S. Department of Labor.

———. 2023a. *Occupational Employment and Wages Statistics, May 2022: Correctional Officers and Jailers*. Washington, DC: U.S. Department of Labor. https://www.bls.gov/oes/current /oes333012.htm.

———. 2023b. *Occupational Outlook Handbook: Correctional Officers and Bailiffs*. Washington, DC: U.S. Department of Labor. https://www.bls .gov/ooh/protective-service/correctional-officers .htm#tab-4.

———. 2024a. "Labor Force Statistics from the Current Population Survey: Household Data, Annual Averages." https://www.bls.gov/cps/ cpsaat11.htm.

———. 2024b. "Occupational Outlook Handbook, Police and Detectives." Washington, DC: U.S. Department of Labor. https://www .bls.gov/ooh/protective-service/police-and -detectives.htm.

Burris, S., E. D. Anderson, and A. C. Wagenaar. 2021. "The 'Legal Epidemiology' of Pandemic Control." *New England Journal of Medicine* 384(21): 1973–75. https://www.nejm.org/doi/ full/10.1056/NEJMp2103380.

Bustillos, M. 2020. "The Robber Bank: Can America Ever Rid Itself of Wells Fargo?" *Slate*, March 9. https://slate.com/news-and-politics /2020/03/wells-fargo-fines-penalties-never-stop .html.

Butler, Anne. 1997. *Gendered Justice in the American West: Women Prisoners in Men's Penitentiaries*. Urbana: University of Illinois Press.

Butler, P. D. 2013. "Poor People Lose: *Gideon* and the Critique of Rights." *Yale Law Journal* 122:2176–204.

Butler, Paul. 2017. *Chokehold: Policing Black Men*. New York: New York University Press.

Butler, P. 2021. "The Prosecutor Problem." Brennan Center for Justice, August 23. https://www .brennancenter.org/our-work/analysis-opinion/ prosecutor-problem.

———. 2023. "Sisters Gonna Work It Out: Black Women as Reformers and Radicals in the Criminal Legal System." *Michigan Law Review* 121(6). https://repository.law.umich.edu/cgi/ viewcontent.cgi?article=11844&context=mlr.

Byju, A. S. 2021. "Eating Endangered." *Current Affairs*, July 9. https://www.currentaffairs.org /2021/07/eating-endangered.

BYP100 Atlanta. 2020. "Stop $23 Million Jail Expansion." Facebook, June 3. https:// www.facebook.com/BYP100/photos/a .683777715006896/3154103897974253.

Cahn, Albert Fox, and Eleni Manis. 2022. "Pregnancy Panopticon." Surveillance Technology Oversight Project, May 24. https://www .stopspying.org/pregnancy-panopticon.

Calavita, Kitty, Henry Pontell, and Robert Tillman. 1997. *Big Money Crime: Fraud and Politics in the Savings and Loan Crisis*. Berkeley: University of California Press.

Cameron, C. 2022. "Homeland Security Watchdog Omitted Damaging Findings from Reports." *New York Times*, April 7. https://www.nytimes .com/2022/04/07/us/politics/homeland-security -inspector-general.html.

Campbell, Rebecca. 2012. *The Neurobiology of Sexual Assault: Implications for Law Enforcement, Prosecution, and Victim Advocacy*. Transcript, National Institute of Justice. Washington, DC: U.S. Department of Justice. https:// nij.ojp.gov/media/video/24056#0-0.

Cantor, Nathaniel E. 1932. *Crime: Criminals and Criminal Justice*. New York: Henry Holt.

Carceral, K. C. 2005. *Prison, Inc.* New York: New York University Press.

Carmichael, Stokely, and Charles Hamilton. 1967. *Black Power: The Politics of Liberation in America*. New York: Vintage.

Carrillo, A. 2023. "ICE(D) Out: Exploration of Media Coverage of the Death and Mistreatment of Trans Women in ICE Detention Facilities." In *The (Mis)Representation of Queer Lives in True Crime*, edited by A. E. Goldberg, C. D. Slackoff, and C. L. Buist. New York: Routledge.

Carter, T. J., and Jasmine Talley. 2022. "'Fucked up': Examining Skin Tone and Student Perceptions of the U.S. Criminal Justice System."

*Journal of Criminal Justice Education* 35(1): 37–55. https://doi.org/10.1080/10511253.2022.2142625.

Carter, T. J., and Tanya Whittle. 2023. "The Impact of Correctional Officer Gender on Prison Suicide." *Health Justice* 11(10): 1–14. https://doi.org/10.1186/s40352-023-00214-z.

Castle, T. 2021. "'Cops and the Klan': Police Disavowal of Risk and Minimization of Threat from the Far-Right." *Critical Criminology* 29:215–35. https://doi.org/10.1007/s10612-020-09493-6.

CCCSE (Center for Community College Student Engagement). 2022. "Mission Critical: The Role of Community Colleges in Meeting Students' Basic Needs." https://www.cccse.org/NR22.

Center for Constitutional Rights. 2023. "Crimes against Nature by Solicitation Litigation." https://ccrjustice.org/home/what-we-do/our-cases/crimes-against-nature-solicitation-cans-litigation.

Center for Reproductive Rights. n.d. "After Roe Fell: Abortion Laws by State." https://reproductiverights.org/maps/abortion-laws-by-state.

Center for Research on Criminal Justice. 1975. *The Iron Fist and Velvet Glove.* Berkeley, CA: CRCJ.

Center on Extremism. 2023. "Incels (Involuntary Celibates)." Anti-Defamation League, March 14. https://www.adl.org/resources/backgrounder/incels-involuntary-celibates.

Centers for Disease Control and Prevention. 2023. "Opioid Overdose." National Center for Injury Prevention and Control, August 23. https://www.cdc.gov/drugoverdose/deaths/opioid-overdose.html.

Chambliss, William. 1973. "The Saints and the Roughnecks." *Society* 11(1): 24–31.

Chambliss, William J., and Milton Mankoff. 1976. *Whose Law? What Order? A Conflict Approach to Criminology.* New York: Wiley.

Chambliss, William, and R. B. Seidman. 1982. *Law, Order and Power.* 2nd ed. Reading, MA: Addison-Wesley.

Chammah, M. 2020. "The Rise of the Anti-Lockdown Sheriffs." The Marshall Project, May 18. https://www.themarshallproject.org/2020/05/18/the-rise-of-the-anti-lockdown-sheriffs.

Chang, A. 2020. "In 'Sexual Citizens,' Students Open Up about Sex, Power and Assault on Campus." National Public Radio, January 23. https://www.npr.org/transcripts/798545780.

Chatfield, M. M. 2023. "'That Hurts You Badder Than Punchin'': The Troubled Teen Industry and Therapeutic Violence in Group Rehabilitation Programs since World War II." *Social History of Alcohol and Drugs* 37(2): 268–92.

Chavez, N., and A. Choi. 2024. "Biden Administration Ties Record for Number of Confirmed LGBTQ Judges in Federal Courts." CNN, March 19. https://www.cnn.com/2024/03/19/us/biden-record-lgbtq-judges-reaj/index.html.

Cheney-Rice, Z. 2023. "How 'Cop City' Trumped Justice." *Intelligencer*, March 9. https://nymag.com/intelligencer/2023/03/atlanta-cop-city-arrests-domestic-terrorism-charges.html.

Chesney-Lind, Meda. 1996. "Sentencing Women to Prison: Equality without Justice." In *Race, Gender, and Class in Criminology: The Intersections*, edited by Martin D. Schwartz and Dragan Milovanovic, 127–40. New York: Garland.

———. 2006. "Patriarchy, Crime, and Justice: Feminist Criminology in an Era of Backlash." *Feminist Criminology* 1(1): 6–26.

Chesney-Lind, Meda, and Joycelyn M. Pollock. 1995. "Women's Prisons: Equality with a Vengeance." In *Women, Law, and Social Control*, edited by Alida V. Merlo and Joycelyn M. Pollock, 155–75. Boston, MA: Allyn & Bacon.

Chesnut, Kelsie, and Jennifer Peirce. 2024. "Advancing Transgender Justice: Illuminating Trans Lives behind and beyond Bars." Vera Institute of Justice, February. https://www.vera.org/downloads/publications/advancing-transgender-justice.pdf.

Chetty, R., J. N. Friedman, N. Hendren, M. R. Jones, and P. R. Sonya 2020. "The Opportunity Atlas: Mapping the Childhood Roots of Social Mobility." https://opportunityinsights.org/wp-content/uploads/2018/10/atlas_paper.pdf.

Cheung, K. 2022. "'Fetal Personhood.' Questions to Ketanji Brown Jackson Should Terrify Us." *Jezebel*, March 24. https://jezebel.com/fetal-personhood-questions-to-ketanji-brown-jackson-sho-1848698963.

Chicago Torture Justice Memorials. 2020. "The Reparations Ordinance." https://chicagotorture.org/reparations/ordinance.

Choi, A. 2023. "Record Number of Anti-LGBTQ Bills Have Been Introduced This Year." CNN,

April 6. https://www.cnn.com/2023/04/06/politics/anti-lgbtq-plus-state-bill-rights-dg/index.html.

Chouhy, C., and A. Madero-Hernandez. 2019. "'Murders, Rapists, and Bad Hombres': Deconstructing the Immigration-Crime Myths." *Victims & Offenders* 14(8): 1010–39. https://doi.org/10.1080/15564886.2019.1671283.

Chow, K. 2018. "So What Exactly Is 'Blood Quantum'?" National Public Radio, February 9. https://www.npr.org/sections/codeswitch/2018/02/09/583987261/so-what-exactly-is-blood-quantum.

Christianson, Scott. 1998. *With Liberty for Some: 500 Years of Imprisonment in America*. Boston, MA: Northeastern University Press.

Chu, J. S. G., and J. A. Evans. 2021. "Slowed Canonical Progress in Large Fields of Science." *Proceedings of the National Academy of Sciences* 118(41). https://doi.org/10.1080/10511253.2021.2019290.

Clarke, J. G., and R. E. Simon. 2013. "Shackling and Separation: Motherhood in Prison." *AMA Journal of Ethics* 15(9): 779–85. https://doi.org/10.1001/virtualmentor.2013.15.9.pfor2-1309.

Clear, Todd. 2002. "The Problem with 'Addition by Subtraction.'" In *Invisible Punishment: The Collateral Consequences of Mass Imprisonment*, edited by Meda Chesney-Lind and Marc Mauer, 181–93. New York: New Press.

———. 2008. "The Great Penal Experiment: Lesson for Social Justice." In *After the War on Crime: Race, Democracy, and a New Reconstruction*, edited by M. L. Frampton, I. H. López, and J. Simon, 61–72. New York: New York University Press.

Clinard, Marshall. 1990. *Corporate Corruption: The Abuse of Power*. New York: Praeger.

Cohen, Andrew. 2017. "Is There a Constitutional Right to Cash in on the Poor?" The Marshall Project, September 11. https://www.themarshallproject.org/2017/09/11/is-there-a-constitutional-right-to-cash-in-on-the-poor.

Cohn, Samuel K. 2012. "Pandemics: Waves of Disease, Waves of Hate from the Plague of Athens to A.I.D.S." *Historical Journal (Cambridge, England)* 85(230): 535–55. https://doi.org/10.1111/j.1468-2281.2012.00603.x.

Coker, T. R., T. L. Cheng, and M. Ybarra. 2023. "Addressing the Long-term Effects of the COVID-19 Pandemic on Children and Families: A Report from the National Academies of Sciences, Engineering, and Medicine." *Journal of the American Medical Association* 329(13): 1055–56.

Cole, David. 1999. *No Equal Justice: Race and Class in the American Criminal Justice System*. New York: New Press.

Coleman, C. 2023. "'Excuse after Excuse': Black and Latino Developers Face Barriers to Success." *New York Times*, March 3. https://www.nytimes.com/2023/03/03/realestate/real-estate-developers-black-latino.html.

Colias, Mike. 2016. "How GM Saved Itself from Flint Water Crisis." *Automotive News*, January 31. https://www.autonews.com/article/20160131/OEM01/302019964/how-gm-saved-itself-from-flint-water-crisis.

Collins P. H. 1990. *Black Feminist Thought: Knowledge Consciousness and the Politics of Empowerment*. Boston, MA: Unwin Hyman.

Columbia Law School. 2017. "Kimberlé Crenshaw on Intersectionality, More than Two Decades Later." June 8. https://www.law.columbia.edu/news/archive/kimberle-crenshaw-intersectionality-more-two-decades-later.

Combahee River Collective Statement. (1977) 2015. https://www.loc.gov/item/lcwaN0028151.

Community Peacemaker Teams. n.d. "The Cisgender Privilege Checklist." https://cpt.org/wp-content/uploads/Undoing20Heterosexism20-20The20Cisgender20Privilege20Checklist-11.pdf.

Conference of State Court Administrators. 2011. "Courts Are Not Revenue Centers." Policy paper, Conference of State Court Administrators. https://csgjusticecenter.org/wp-content/uploads/2013/07/2011-12-COSCA-report.pdf.

Conley, John, ed. 1994. *The 1967 President's Crime Commission Report: Its Impact 25 Years Later*. Cincinnati, OH: Anderson.

Conover, Ted. 2000. "Guarding Sing Sing." *New Yorker*, April 3. https://www.tedconover.com/2010/01/guarding-sing-sing.

Conway, Katherine. 2017. "Fundamentally Unfair: Databases, Deportation, and the Crimmigrant Gang Member Comments." *American University Law Review* 67:269–332.

Cook, K. J. 2016. "Has Criminology Awakened from Its 'Androcentric Slumber'?" *Feminist Criminology* 11(4): 334–53.

Cook, K. J., J. M. Williams, R. D. Lamphere, S. L. Mallicoat, and A. R. Ackerman, eds. 2022. *Survivor Criminology: A Radical Act of Hope.* Lanham, MD: Rowman & Littlefield.

Cook, P. J. 2020. "Thinking about Gun Violence." *Criminology & Public Policy* 19(4): 1371–93. https://doi.org/10.1111/1745-9133.12519.

Corak, Miles. 2013. "Income Inequality, Equality of Opportunity, and Intergenerational Mobility." *Journal of Economic Perspectives* 27(3): 79–102.

———. 2020. "Intergenerational Mobility: What Do We Care About? What Should We Care About?" *Australian Economic Review* 53(2): 230–40.

Cortez, D. 2019. "I Asked Latinos Why They Joined Immigration Law Enforcement. Now I'm Urging Them to Leave." *USA Today*, July 11. https://www.usatoday.com/story/opinion/voices/2019/07/03/latino-border-patrol-ice-agents-immigration-column/1619511001.

———. 2020. "Latinxs in La Migra: Why They Join and Why It Matters." *Political Research Quarterly* 74(3). https://doi.org/10.1177/1065912920933674.

Cottom, Tressie McMillian. 2017. "How We Make Black Girls Grow Up Too Fast." *New York Times*, July 29. https://www.nytimes.com/2017/07/29/opinion/sunday/how-we-make-black-girls-grow-up-too-fast.html.

Cotton, James A. 1997. "Toward a Fairness in Compensation of Management and Labor: Compensation Ratios, a Proposal for Disclosure." *Northern Illinois University Law Review* 18(1): 157–96.

Council on Criminal Justice. 2021. "Civilian Oversight: Policy Assessment." Task Force on Policing, April. https://assets.foleon.com/eu-central-1/de-uploads-7e3kk3/41697/civilian_oversight.2690411fd370.pdf.

Cowley, Stacy, and Jessica Silver-Greenberg. 2017. "De-Cos Halts Obama-Era Plan to Revamp Student Loan Management." *New York Times*, April 14. https://www.nytimes.com/2017/04/14/business/dealbook/education-department-federal-student-loan-program.html.

Coyle, M. J., and J. Schept. 2018. "Penal Abolition Praxis." *Critical Criminology* 26(3): 319–23. https://doi.org/10.1007/s10612-018-9407-x.

Crenshaw, Kimberlé Williams, and Andrea J. Richie. 2015. *Say Her Name: Resisting Police Brutality against Black Women.* Report, African American Policy Forum. New York: Center for Intersectionality and Social Policy Studies. https://static1.squarespace.com/static/53f20d90e4b0b80451158d8c/t/560c068ee4b0af26f72741df/1443628686535/AAPF_SMN_Brief_Full_singles-min.pdf.

Critical Resistance. n.d. "Reformist Reforms vs. Abolitionist Steps in Policing." https://static1.squarespace.com/static/59ead8f9692ebee25b72f17f/t/5b65cd58758d46d34254f22c/1533398363539/CR_NoCops_reform_vs_abolition_CRside.pdf.

Crosley-Corcoran, G. 2017. "Explaining White Privilege to a Broke White Person." *HuffPost*, December 6. https://www.huffpost.com/entry/explaining-white-privilege-to-a-broke-white-person_b_5269255.

Cunneen, C. 2014. "Colonial Processes, Indigenous Peoples, and Criminal Justice Systems." In *The Oxford Handbook of Ethnicity, Crime, and Immigration*, edited by Sandra M. Bucerius and Michael Tonry, 386–407. New York: Oxford University Press. https://doi.org/10.1093/oxfordhb/9780199859016.013.018.

Currie, Elliott. 1985. *Confronting Crime: An American Challenge.* New York: Pantheon.

———. 1998. *Crime and Punishment in America.* New York: Henry Holt.

———. 2005a. "Inequality, Community, and Crime." In *The Essential Criminology Reader*, edited by Stuart Henry and Mark Lanier, 299–306. Boulder, CO: Westview.

———. 2005b. *The Road to Whatever: Middle-Class Culture and the Crisis of Adolescence.* Macmillan.

Cushing, Tim. 2021. "Private Security Company Thinks It Should Be Able to Take People to Jail Just Like Real Cops." *Techdirt*, May 27. https://www.techdirt.com/articles/20210526/10185346876/private-security-company-thinks-it-should-be-able-to-take-people-to-jail-just-like-real-cops.shtml.

Dank, Meredith, Lilly Yu, Jennifer Yahner, Elizabeth Pelletier, Mitchyll Mora, and Brendan Conner. 2015. *Locked In: Interactions with the Criminal Justice and Child Welfare Systems for LGBTQ Youth, YMSM, and YWSW Who Engage in Survival Sex.* Report, Urban Institute. https://www.urban.org/research/publication/locked-interactions-criminal-justice-and-child

-welfare-systems-lgbtq-youth-ymsm-and-ywsw
-who-engage-survival-sex/view/full_report.

Davidson, B., E. Epps, S. Grace, and A. Rich-Shea. 2020. "Community Bail Funds as a Tool for Abolition." LPE Project, February 13. https:// lpeproject.org/blog/community-bail-funds-as-a -tool-for-prison-abolition.

Davies, P. 2021. "Why Social Harm Matters: Five Reasons from a Feminist Influenced Victim Perspective." In *The Palgrave Handbook of Social Harm*, edited by P. Davies, P. Leighton, and T. Wyatt. Cham: Palgrave Macmillan. https://doi .org/10.1007/978-3-030-72408-5_18.

Davis, A. J. 2019. "Reimagining Prosecution: A Growing Progressive Movement." *UCLA Criminal Justice Law Review* 3(1). https://escholarship .org/content/qt2rq8t137/qt2rq8t137.pdf.

Davis, A. Y. 2005. *Abolition Democracy: Beyond Empire, Prisons, and Torture*. New York: Seven Stories Press.

———. 2015. *Freedom Is a Constant Struggle: Ferguson, Palestine, and the Foundations of a Movement*. Chicago: Haymarket Books.

Davis, Angela. 1998. "What Is the Prison Industrial Complex? Why Does It Matter?" *Colorlines Magazine*, September 10, 1–8.

Dawson, A. 2018. "Police Legitimacy and Homicide: A Macro-Comparative Analysis." *Social Forces* 97(2): 841–66. https://doi.org/10.1093/ sf/soy043.

Day, Kathleen. 1993. *S&L Hell: The People and the Politics behind the $1 Trillion Savings and Loan Scandal*. New York: Norton.

Dean, J. 2019. "Capitalism Is the End of the World." *Mediations* 33(1–2): 149–58. https:// mediationsjournal.org/articles/end-of-world.

De Coster, S., and K. Heimer. 2018. "Gendering Traditional Theories of Crime." In *Encyclopedia of Criminology and Criminal Justice*, edited by G. Bruinsma and D. Weisburd, 1883–92. New York: Springer. https://doi.org/10.1007 /978-1-4614-5690-2_69.

DeKeseredy, W. S., and M. D. Schwartz, eds. 2013. *Male Peer Support and Violence against Women: The History and Verification of a Theory*. Boston, MA: Northeastern University Press.

Delaney, Kevin. 1999. *Strategic Bankruptcy: How Corporations and Creditors Use Chapter 11 to Their Advantage*. Berkeley: University of California Press.

Delgado, Richard, ed. 1995. *Critical Race Theory: The Cutting Edge*. Philadelphia, PA: Temple University Press.

Delgado, Richard, and Jean Stefancic. 1991. "Derrick Bell's Chronicle of the Space Traders: Would the U.S. Sacrifice People of Color if the Price Were Right?" *University of Colorado Law Review* 62:321–29.

———. 1997. *Critical White Studies: Looking behind the Mirror*. Philadelphia, PA: Temple University Press.

———. 2012. *Critical Race Theory: An Introduction*. 2nd ed. New York: New York University Press.

Department of Health and Human Services. n.d. "HHS Poverty Guidelines for 2023." https:// aspe.hhs.gov/topics/poverty-economic-mobility/ poverty-guidelines.

Department of Homeland Security. 2019. "RAIO Directorate—Officer Training. Guidance for Adjudicating Lesbian, Gay, Bisexual, Transgender, and Intersex (LGBTI) Refugee and Asylum Claims." U.S. Citizenship and Immigration Services. https://www.uscis.gov/sites/default/files/ document/foia/LGBTI_Claims_LP_RAIO.pdf.

———. 2023. "Humanitarian: Refugees and Asylum." U.S. Citizenship and Immigration Services. https://www.uscis.gov/humanitarian/ refugees-and-asylum/asylum.

Department of Homeland Security Office of Inspector General. 2019. "Concerns about ICE Detainee Treatment and Care at Four Detention Facilities, OIG-19-47." https://www.oig.dhs .gov/sites/default/files/assets/2019-06/OIG-19 -47-Jun19.pdf.

Department of Justice (DOJ). 2015. "Investigation of the Ferguson Police Department." Report from the Civil Rights Division, March 4. https:// www.justice.gov/sites/default/files/opa/press -releases/attachments/2015/03/04/ferguson _police_department_report.pdf.

———. 2020a. "Justice Department Announces Global Resolution of Criminal and Civil Investigations with Opioid Manufacturer Purdue Pharma and Civil Settlement with Members of the Sackler Family." Office of Public Affairs, Press Release 20-1136, October 21, 2020. https://www.justice.gov/opa/pr/justice-department-announces-global-resolution-criminal-and -civil-investigations-opioid.

———. 2020b. "USA v. Purdue Pharma Settlement Agreement." https://www.justice.gov/opa/press-release/file/1329736/download.

———. 2020c. "Wells Fargo Agrees to Pay $3 Billion to Resolve Criminal and Civil Investigations into Sales Practices Involving the Opening of Millions of Accounts without Customer Authorization." Press release, February 21. https://www.justice.gov/opa/pr/wells-fargo-agrees-pay-3-billion-resolve-criminal-and-civil-investigations-sales-practices.

———. 2023. "In Celebration of 2nd Anniversary, Justice Department's Office for Access to Justice Publishes Report on Economic Justice Policies That Reduce Reliance on Fines and Fees." Office of Public Affairs, Press Release 23-1222, November 2. https://www.justice.gov/opa/pr/celebration-2nd-anniversary-justice-departments-office-access-justice-publishes-report.

Department of Labor. 2023. "5 Fast Facts: The Gender Wage Gap." *U.S. Department of Labor Blog.* https://blog.dol.gov/2023/03/14/5-fast-facts-the-gender-wage-gap#:~:text=Women%27s%20labor%20is%20undervalued.,jobs%20that%20offer%20fewer%20benefits.

Deutsch. n.d. "The Male Privilege Checklist." https://cpt.org/wp-content/uploads/US20-20Male20Privilege20Checklist-11.pdf.

Dholakia, N. 2022. "Most 911 Calls Have Nothing to Do with Crime. Why Are We Still Sending Police?" *Vera*, April 22. https://www.vera.org/news/most-911-calls-have-nothing-to-do-with-crime-why-are-we-still-sending-police.

DiAngelo, R. 2018. *White Fragility. Why It's So Hard for White People to Talk about Racism.* Boston, MA: Beacon Press.

Dias, Beatrice. 2023. "The Dystopian AI Future Some Fear Is the Present-Day Reality Others Live." FAIR (Fairness & Accuracy in Reporting), November 21. https://fair.org/home/the-dystopian-ai-future-some-fear-is-the-present-day-reality-others-live.

Diaz, Jaclyn. 2021. "New York Repeals 'Walking While Trans' Law." National Public Radio, February 3. https://www.npr.org/2021/02/03/963513022/new-york-repeals-walking-while-trans-law.

Dickerson, Caitlin. 2022. "The Secret History of Family Separation." *The Atlantic*, August 7. https://www.theatlantic.com/magazine/archive/2022/09/trump-administration-family-separation-policy-immigration/670604.

Dittmar, K., K. Sanbonmatsu, S. J. Carroll, D. Walsh, and C. Wineinger. 2017. *Representation Matters: Women in the U.S. Congress.* New Brunswick, NJ: Center for American Women and Politics, Eagleton Institute of Politics, Rutgers, The State University of New Jersey.

Dittmar, K., C. Wineinger, and K. Sanbonmatsu. 2022. "Studying Legislatures at the Intersection of Gender and Race: The View from the 114th Congress." *PS: Political Science and Politics* 55(2): 277–79. https://doi.org/10.1017/S1049096521001608.

Doctorow, Cory. 2023. "There Is Always an Alternative." *Medium*, June 24. https://doctorow.medium.com/there-is-always-an-alternative-e55fd414d1fd.

Doerer, K. 2022. "Hate Leader Nick Fuentes Is Recruiting Incels." *Mother Jones*, December 22. https://www.motherjones.com/politics/2022/12/hate-leader-nick-fuentes-is-recruiting-incels.

Domestic Abuse Intervention Programs. n.d. "Understanding the Power and Control Wheel." https://www.theduluthmodel.org/wheels/understanding-power-control-wheel.

Dorf, M. 2023. "Did SCOTUS Finally Wake Up to the Threat of State Nullification of Federal Law?" *Verdict*, October 25. https://verdict.justia.com/2023/10/25/did-scotus-finally-wake-up-to-the-threat-of-state-nullification-of-federal-law.

Douglas, Danielle. 2013. "Attorney General Says Big Banks' Size May Inhibit Prosecution." *Washington Post*, March 6. https://www.washingtonpost.com/business/economy/holder-concerned-megabanks-too-big-to-jail/2013/03/06/6fa2b07a-869e-11e2-999e-5f8e0410cb9d_story.html.

Douglas, William O. 1954. *An Almanac of Liberty.* Garden City, NY: Doubleday.

Dreisbach, Tom. 2023. "Government's Own Experts Found 'Barbaric' and 'Negligent' Conditions in ICE Detention." National Public Radio, August 16. https://www.npr.org/2023/08/16/1190767610/ice-detention-immigration-government-inspectors-barbaric-negligent-conditions.

Druker, S. 2022. "Senate Report Details Rampant Sexual Abuse of Federal Female Prisoners." United Press International, December 13.

https://www.upi.com/Top_News/US/2022/12/13/senate-report-female-prisoner-sexual-abuse/5561670969285.

Drury, J. 2002. "'When the Mobs Are Looking for Witches to Burn, Nobody's Safe': Talking about the Reactionary Crowd." *Discourse & Society* 13(1): 41–73. https://doi.org/10.1177/0957926502013001003.

DuBois, Ellen Carol, and Lynn Dumenil. 2005. *Through Women's Eyes: An American History*. Boston, MA: Bedford/St. Martin's.

Du Bois, W. E. B. (1935) 2017. *Black Reconstruction in America: Toward a History of the Part Which Black Folk Played in the Attempt to Reconstruct Democracy in America, 1860–1880*. New York: Routledge.

Duffee, David. 1980. *Explaining Criminal Justice: Community Theory and Criminal Justice Reform*. Prospects Heights, IL: Waveland Press.

Dunn, T. R. 2019. *Talking White Trash: Mediated Representation and Lived Experiences of White Working-Class People*. New York: Routledge.

Duran, Robert. 2013. *Gang Life in Two Cities: An Insider's Journey*. New York: Columbia University Press.

Dwyer, Angela, Matthew Ball, and Thomas Crofts. 2016. *Queering Criminologies*. Basingstoke: Palgrave Macmillan.

Dyer, Joel. 2000. *The Perpetual Prisoner Machine: How America Profits from Crime*. Boulder, CO: Westview.

Dyer, Richard. 2005. "The Matter of Whiteness." In *White Privilege: Essential Readings on the Other Side of Racism*, edited by Paula Rothenberg, 9–14. New York: Worth.

Eagly, Ingrid. 2017. "Reforming Criminal Justice in an Era of Mass Deportation." *Harvard Law Review Blog*, October 17. https://blog.harvardlawreview.org/reforming-criminal-justice-in-an-era-of-mass-deportation.

Earp, B. D., J. Lewis, C. L. Hart, and Bioethicists and Allied Professionals for Drug Policy Reform. 2021. "Racial Justice Requires Ending the War on Drugs." *American Journal of Bioethics* 21(4): 4–19. https://doi.org/10.1080/15265161.2020.1861364.

Eckholm, Erik. 2014. "Robert Wayne Holsey Faces Lethal Injection in Georgia." *New York Times*, December 8. https://www.nytimes.com/2014/12/09/us/robert-wayne-holsey-faces-lethal-injection-in-georgia.html.

*Economist*. 2014. "Cops or Soldiers?" March 20. https://www.economist.com/news/united-states/21599349-americas-police-have-become-too-militarised-cops-or-soldiers.

Edelstein, Charles D., and Robert J. Wicks. 1977. *An Introduction to Criminal Justice*. New York: McGraw-Hill.

EEOC (U.S. Equal Employment Opportunity Commission). n.d. "What You Should Know about EEOC and the Enforcement Protections for LGBT Workers." https://www.eeoc.gov/eeoc/newsroom/wysk/enforcement_protections_lgbt_workers.cfm.

Eichstaedt, Peter. 1994. *If You Poison Us: Uranium and Native Americans*. Santa Fe, NM: Red Crane Books.

Eisenhower, Dwight. 1961. "Farewell Address." Transcript. https://en.wikisource.org/wiki/Eisenhower%27s_farewell_address.

Eisinger, J. 2017. *The Chickenshit Club: Why the Justice Department Fails to Prosecute Executives*. New York: Simon & Schuster.

Ekins, Emily. 2016. "Policing in America: Understanding Public Attitudes toward the Police. Results from a National Survey." Report, Cato Institute. https://www.cato.org/survey-reports/policing-america.

Elias, Robert. 1986. *The Politics of Victimization: Victims, Victimology and Human Rights*. New York: Oxford University Press.

Engel, R. S., and J. M. Calnon. 2004. "Examining the Influence of Drivers' Characteristics during Traffic Stops with Police: Results from a National Survey." *Justice Quarterly* 21(1): 49–90.

Enke, A., ed. 2012. *Transfeminist Perspectives in and Beyond Transgender and Gender Studies*. Philadelphia, PA: Temple University Press.

Enos, T. 2018. "8 Things You Should Know about Two Spirit People." *ICT News*, September 13. https://ictnews.org/archive/8-misconceptions-things-know-two-spirit-people.

Equality Act. 2021. "H.R.5—Equality Act." Congress.gov. https://www.congress.gov/bill/117th-congress/house-bill/5.

Equality Federation. 2023. "State Legislation Tracker." https://www.equalityfederation.org/state-legislation.

Erdely, S. R. 2014. "The Transgender Crucible." *Rolling Stone*, July 30. https://www.rollingstone.com/culture/culture-news/the-transgender-crucible-114095.

Etzioni, Amitai. 1990. "Going Soft on Corporate Crime." *Washington Post*, April 1.

Evans, D. 2020. "Give Some, Take Some: How the Community Fridge Fights Food Insecurity. *Eater*, June 17. https://www.eater.com/2020/6/17/21291849/community-fridges-food-insecurity-coronavirus-covid-19-impact.

Executive Office for Immigration Review. n.d. *Immigration Court Practice Manual*. U.S. Department of Justice. https://www.justice.gov/eoir/reference-materials/ic/chapter-1/4.

Faith, Karlene. 1993. "Gendered Imaginations: Female Crime and Prison Movies." *Justice Professional* 8(1): 53–70.

Fasenfest, D. 2017. "A Neoliberal Response to an Urban Crisis: Emergency Management in Flint, MI." *Critical Sociology* 45(1): 33–47. https://doi.org/10.1177/0896920517718039.

Fatica, R. 2022. "Atlanta Fights to Save Its Forest." *Unicorn Riot*, May 14. https://unicornriot.ninja/2022/atlanta-fights-to-save-its-forest.

Feagin, Joe, and Clairece Booher Feagin. 1996. *Racial and Ethnic Relations*. Upper Saddle River, NJ: Prentice-Hall.

Feagin, Joe, and Hernan Vera. 1995. *White Racism: The Basics*. New York: Routledge.

Federal Bureau of Prisons. n.d. *Correctional Officer: Job Series Number 0007*. U.S. Bureau of Prisons. https://www.bop.gov/jobs/positions/index.jsp?p=Correctional%20Officer.

Federal Judicial Center. n.d. "Biographical Directory of Article III Federal Judges: Export." Downloaded May 30, 2024. https://www.fjc.gov/history/judges/biographical-directory-article-iii-federal-judges-export.

Federal Reserve Board. n.d. "Distribution of Household Wealth in the U.S. since 1989." https://www.federalreserve.gov/releases/z1/dataviz/dfa/distribute/chart.

Fedina, Lisa, et al. 2018. "Police Violence among Women in Four U.S. Cities." *Preventive Medicine* 106:150–56. https://doi.org/10.1016/j.ypmed.2017.10.037.

Fernandes, F. 2023. "Ranked: The Highest Paid CEOs in the S&P 500." *Visual Capitalist*, September 19. https://www.visualcapitalist.com/the-highest-paid-ceos.

Fernandez, D. 2020. "Dean Spade on the Promise of Mutual Aid." *The Nation*, December 18. https://www.deanspade.net/2020/12/18/interview-with-the-nation-about-mutual-aid.

Fernández, J. 2019. *The Young Lords: A Radical History*. Chapel Hill: University of North Carolina Press.

Fersch, Patricia. 2023. "Gender Bias in the Courts: Women Are Not Believed." *Forbes*, April 5. https://www.forbes.com/sites/patriciafersch/2023/04/05/gender-bias-in-the-courts-women-are-not-believed.

Feuer, A., and M. Haberman. 2024. "Trump Wants to Prosecute Biden. He Also Thinks Presidents Deserve Immunity." *New York Times*, April 30. https://www.nytimes.com/2024/04/30/us/politics/trump-biden-president-immunity.html.

Fieldstat, E. 2019. "James Alex Fields, Driver in Deadly Car Attack at Charlottesville Rally, Sentenced to Life in Prison." NBC News, June 28. https://www.nbcnews.com/news/us-news/james-alex-fields-driver-deadly-car-attack-charlottesville-rally-sentenced-n1024436.

Figliuzzi, F. 2021. "FBI Called in to Help Teachers as Extremist Violence Gets Personal." MSNBC, October 8. https://www.msnbc.com/opinion/fbi-called-help-teachers-extremist-violence-gets-personal-n1281044.

Fireweed Collective. n.d. "Mission and Vision." https://fireweedcollective.org/mission-vision-values.

Flagg, A. 2021. "The Black Mortality Gap, and a Document Written in 1910." *New York Times*, August 30. https://www.nytimes.com/2021/08/30/upshot/black-health-mortality-gap.html.

Flavelle, C. 2021. "Forced Relocation Left Native Americans More Exposed to Climate Threats, Data Show." *New York Times*, October 28. https://www.nytimes.com/2021/10/28/climate/native-americans-climate-change-effects.html.

———. 2023. "As the Colorado River Shrinks, Washington Prepares to Spread the Pain." *New York Times*, January 27. https://www.nytimes.com/2023/01/27/climate/colorado-river-biden-cuts.html.

Flavin, Jeanne. 2009. *Our Bodies, Our Crimes: The Policing of Women's Reproduction in America*. New York: New York University Press.

Florido, A., S. Handel, and M. Lim. 2022. "How Black Activities Used Lynching Souvenirs to Expose American Violence." National Public Radio, February 8. https://www.npr.org/2022/02/08/1078977454/race-racism-lynching-postcards-ahmaud-arbery-george-floyd.

Foley, Neil. 2005. "Becoming Hispanic: Mexican Americans and Whiteness." In *White Privilege: Essential Readings on the Other Side of Racism*, edited by Paula Rothenberg, 55–66. New York: Worth.

*Forbidden America*. 2022. Directed by Louis Theroux. Mindhouse Productions & BBC.

Forell, Caroline, and Donna Matthews. 2000. *A Law of Her Own*. New York: New York University Press.

For the Gworls. n.d. "Home." https://www.forthegworls.party/home.

*Fortune*. 2022. "Fortune 500." https://fortune.com/ranking/fortune500/2022/search.

Foucault, Michel. 1979. *Discipline and Punish: The Birth of the Prison*. New York: Random House.

———. 1980. *The History of Sexuality*. Vol. 1, *An Introduction*. New York: Vintage.

Frankenberg, Ruth. 1993. *White Women, Race Matters: The Social Construction of Whiteness*. Minneapolis: University of Minnesota Press.

Franklin, H. B. 1989. *Prison Literature in America*. New York: Oxford University Press.

Franta, Benjamin. 2018. "Early Oil Industry Knowledge of CO2 and Global Warming." *Nature Climate Change* 8(12).

———. 2021. "Early Oil Industry Disinformation on Global Warming." *Environmental Politics* 30(4): 663–68.

Free, Marvin D., Jr., and Mitch Ruesink. 2012. *Race and Justice: Wrongful Convictions of African American Men*. Boulder, CO: Lynne Rienner.

Friedman, B. 2021. "Disciplinary Innovation: Carcerality, Captivity, and Historicizing the Carceral State." *American Society of Criminology: The Criminologist* 46(6): 1–4. https://asc41.com/wp-content/uploads/ASC-Criminologist-2021-11.pdf.

Friedman, L. 2022. "White House Takes Aim at Environmental Racism, but Won't Mention Race." *New York Times*, February 15. https://www.nytimes.com/2022/02/15/climate/biden-environment-race-pollution.html.

Friedrichs, D. O. 2010. *Trusted Criminals: White Collar Crime in Contemporary Society*. Belmont, CA: Cengage Learning.

Fullwiley, Duana. 2014. "The 'Contemporary Synthesis': When Politically Inclusive Genomic Science Relies on Biological Notions of Race." *Isis* 105(4): 803–14.

Future of Media Project. 2022. "Index of US Mainstream Media Ownership." Institute for Quantitative Social Science at Harvard University. https://projects.iq.harvard.edu/futureofmedia/index-us-mainstream-media-ownership.

Gabbidon, Shaun, and Helen Taylor Greene. 2005. *Race and Crime*. Thousand Oaks, CA: Sage.

Gamble, Sarah, ed. 1999. *The Routledge Critical Dictionary of Feminism and Postfeminism*. New York: Routledge.

Garland, D. 2023. "The Current Crisis of American Criminal Justice: A Structural Analysis." *Annual Review of Criminology* 6:43–63.

Geller, Eric. 2017. "Trump Signs Long-Awaited Cyber Order, Launching Hacking Defense Review." *Politico*, May 11. https://www.politico.com/story/2017/05/11/trump-cyber-executive-order-238273.

George, T. E., and A. H. Yoon. 2023. "Gavel Gap: The Differences between the Race & Gender Composition of the Courts & the Communities They Serve." American Constitution Society. https://www.acslaw.org/analysis/reports/gavel-gap.

Georgia Bureau of Investigation. 2023. "Five Arrested for Domestic Terrorism Charges at Site of Future Atlanta Public Safety Training Center." https://gbi.georgia.gov/press-releases/2023-06-23/five-arrested-domestic-terrorism-charges-site-future-atlanta-public.

German, M. 2020. "The FBI Targets a New Generation of Black Activists." Brennan Center for Justice, June 26. https://www.brennancenter.org/our-work/analysis-opinion/fbi-targets-new-generation-black-activists.

Geronimus, Arline, Cynthia Colen, Tara Shochet, Lori Barer Ingber, and Sherman James. 2006a. "Urban-Rural Differences in Excess Mortality among High-Poverty Populations: Evidence from the Harlem Household Survey and the Pitt County, North Carolina, Study of African American Health." *Journal of Health Care for the Poor and Underserved* 17(3): 532–58.

Geronimus, Arline, Margaret Hicken, Danya Keene, and John Bound. 2006b. "Weathering and Age-Patterns of Allostatic Load Scores among Blacks and Whites in the United States." *American Journal of Public Health* 96:826–33.

Gezinski, L. B. 2022. "'It's Kind of Hit and Miss with Them': A Qualitative Investigation of Police Response to Intimate Partner Violence in a Mandatory Arrest State." *Journal of Family Violence* 37:99–111. https://doi.org/10.1007/s10896-020-00227-4.

Ghandnoosh, Nazgol, and Josh Rovner. 2017. *Immigration and Public Safety.* Report, Sentencing Project, Washington, DC. https://www.sentencingproject.org/publications/immigration-public-safety.

Gilbert, Dennis. 1998. *The American Class Structure.* 5th ed. Belmont, CA: Wadsworth.

Gilmore, R. W. 2022. *Abolition Geography: Essays towards Liberation.* New York: Verso.

Glasmeier, Amy. 2017. "Findings from Latest Living Wage Data Update." Living Wage Calculator. https://livingwage.mit.edu.

Glennon, L. 2020. "Raising Strong Sexual Citizens." *Columbia Magazine,* Spring/Summer. https://magazine.columbia.edu/article/raising-strong-sexual-citizens.

Golash-Boza, Tanya Maria. 2015. *Deported: Immigrant Policing, Disposable Labor, and Global Capitalism.* New York: New York University Press.

———. 2016a. "A Critical and Comprehensive Sociological Theory of Race and Racism." *Sociology of Race and Ethnicity* 2(2): 129–41. https://doi.org/10.1177/2332649216632242.

———. 2016b. *Immigration Nation: Raids, Detentions, and Deportations in Post-911 America.* Boulder, CO: Paradigm.

Golash-Boza, Tanya, and Pierrette Hondagneu-Sotelo. 2013. "Latino Immigrant Men and the Deportation Crisis: A Gendered Racial Removal Program." *Latino Studies* 11(3): 271–92.

Goldensohn, Rosa. 2018. "They Shared Drugs. Someone Died. Does that Make Them Killers?" *New York Times,* May 25. https://www.nytimes.com/2018/05/25/us/drug-overdose-prosecution-crime.html.

Goldrick-Rab, Sara. 2016. *Paying the Price: College Costs, Financial Aid, and the Betrayal of the American Dream.* Chicago: University of Chicago Press.

Goldrick-Rab, Sara, Jed Richardson, and Anthony Hernandez. 2017. *Hungry and Homeless: Results from a National Study of Basic Needs Security in Higher Education.* Report, Wisconsin Hope Lab, March 2017. https://wihopelab.com/publications/hungry-and-homeless-in-college-report.pdf.

Goldstein, D. 2021. "Do Police Officers Make Schools Safer or More Dangerous?" *New York Times,* October 28. https://www.nytimes.com/2020/06/12/us/schools-police-resource-officers.html.

Goldstein, Joseph. 2013. "Judge Rejects New York's Stop-and-Frisk Policy." *New York Times,* August 12. https://www.nytimes.com/2013/08/13/nyregion/stop-and-frisk-practice-violated-rights-judge-rules.html.

Golightley, S. 2020. "Troubling the 'Troubled Teen' Industry: Adult Reflections on Youth Experiences of Therapeutic Boarding Schools." *Global Studies of Childhood* 10(1): 53–63.

Gomes, C. M. 2021. "Notes on Gender, Race and Punishment from a Decolonial Perspective to a Southern Criminology Agenda." *International Journal for Crime, Justice and Social Democracy* 10(4): 90–101.

Goodman, Marc. 2016. *Future Crimes.* New York: Anchor.

Gorman, Tessa. 1997. "Back on the Chain Gang: Why the 8th Amendment and the History of Slavery Proscribe the Resurgence of Chain Gangs." *California Law Review* 85(2): 441–78.

Gottlieb, A. 2021. "Making Gideon Count? Public Defender Resources and Felony Case Outcomes for Black, White, and Latinx Individuals." *Race and Justice* 13(4). https://doi.org/10.1177/21533687211006456.

Gould, Jon B., and Maya Barak. 2019. *Capital Defense: Inside the Lives of America's Death Penalty Lawyers.* New York: New York University Press.

Gould, Jon, and Kenneth S. León. 2017. "A Culture That Is Hard to Defend: Extralegal Factors in the Defense of Federal Death Penalty Cases." *Journal of Criminal Law & Criminology* 107(4): 643–86. https://scholarlycommons.law.northwestern.edu/jclc/vol107/iss4/3.

Gover, A. R., S. B. Harper, and L. Langton. 2020. "Anti-Asian Hate Crime during the COVID-19 Pandemic: Exploring the Reproduction of Inequality." *American Journal of Criminal Justice* 45:647–67.

Government Accountability Office (GAO). 2007. *Residential Treatment Programs: Concerns regarding Abuse and Death in Certain Programs for Troubled Youth. Testimony before* the Committee on Education and Labor, House of Representatives. Report, GAO-08-146T. https://www.gao.gov/assets/gao-08-146t.pdf.

———. 2008a. *Residential Facilities: State and Federal Oversight Gaps May Increase Risk to Youth Well-Being*. Report, GAO-08-696T. https://www.gao.gov/products/gao-08-696t.

———. 2008b. *Residential Facilities: Improved Data and Enhanced Oversight Would Help Safeguard the Well-Being of Youth with Behavioral and Emotional Challenges*. Report, GAO-08-346. https://www.gao.gov/products/gao-08-346.

———. 2009. *Corporate Crime: DOJ Has Taken Steps to Better Track Its Use of Deferred and Non-Prosecution Agreements, but Should Evaluate Effectiveness*. Report, GAO-10-110. https://www.gao.gov/assets/300/299781.pdf.

———. 2017. *Nonviolent Drug Convictions: Stakeholders' Views on Potential Actions to Address Collateral Consequences*. Report, GAO-17-691. https://www.gao.gov/assets/690/687003.pdf.

Gowan, T., and S. Whetstone. 2012. "Making the Criminal Addict: Subjectivity and Social Control in a Strong-Arm Rehab." *Punishment & Society* 14(1): 69–93.

Gramlich, J. 2023. "Fewer than 1% of Federal Criminal Defendants Were Acquitted in 2022." Pew Research Center, June 14. https://www.pewresearch.org/short-reads/2023/06/14/fewer-than-1-of-defendants-in-federal-criminal-cases-were-acquitted-in-2022.

Grewcock, M. 2018. "Introduction: Mapping the Contours of State Crime and Colonialism." *State Crime* 7(2): 167–72. https://doi.org/10.13169/statecrime.7.2.0167.

Griffith, L. 1993. *The Fall of the Prison: Biblical Perspectives on Prison Abolition*. Grand Rapids, MI: Eerdmans.

Grinberg, D. 2019. "Tracking Movements: Black Activism, Aerial Surveillance, and Transparency Optics." *Media, Culture & Society* 41(3): 294–316. https://doi.org/10.1177/0163443718810921.

Gross, J. 2023. "Reframing the Indigent Defense Crisis." *Harvard Law Review*, March 18. https://harvardlawreview.org/blog/2023/03/reframing-the-indigent-defense-crisis.

Gross, Kali Nicole. 2015. "African American Women, Mass Incarceration, and the Politics of Protection." *Journal of American History* 102(1): 25–33. https://doi.org/10.1093/jahist/jav226.

Grossman, Lev, and Jay Newton-Small. 2013. "The Secret Web: Where Drugs, Porn and Murder Live Online." *Time*, November 11, 26–33.

Grossman, Ron. 2014. "Fatal Black Panther Raid in Chicago Set Off Sizable Aftershocks." *Chicago Tribune*, December 4. https://www.chicagotribune.com/news/history/ct-black-panther-raid-flashback-1207-20141206-story.html.

Grover, C. 2018. "Violent Proletarianisation: Social Murder, the Reserve Army of Labour and Social Security 'Austerity' in Britain." *Critical Social Policy* 39(3): 335–55. https://doi.org/10.1177/0261018318816932.

Guadalupe-Diaz, X. L. 2019. *Transgressed: Intimate Partner Violence in Transgender Lives*. New York: New York University Press.

Guggisberg, Marika, Simone Bottino, and Christopher M. Doran. 2021. "Women's Contexts and Circumstances of Posttraumatic Growth after Sexual Victimization: A Systematic Review." *Frontiers in Psychology* 12:1–13. https://doi.org/10.3389/fpsyg.2021.699288.

Gupta, A. H. 2023. "How 'Weathering' Contributes to Racial Health Disparities." *New York Times*, April 14. https://www.nytimes.com/2023/04/12/well/live/weathering-health-racism-discrimination.html.

Gurusami, S. 2019. "Mother under the State: The Maternal Labor of Formerly Incarcerated Black Women." *Social Problems* 66(1): 128–43. https://doi.org/10.1093/socpro/spx045.

Gutin, Iliya. 2019. "Essential(ist) Medicine: Promoting Social Explanations for Racial Variation in Biomedical Research." *Medical Humanities* 45(3): 224–34. https://doi.org/10.1136/medhum-2017-011432.

Guzman, Gloria, and Melissa Kollar. 2023. *Income in the United States: 2022*. Current Population Reports, P60-276. Washington, DC: U.S. Census Bureau/U.S. Government Publishing Office.

Hacker, Andrew. 1995. *Two Nations: Black and White, Separate, Hostile, Unequal*. New York: Ballantine.

Hadley, M. 2018. "Female Cops: Fighting for Respect in a 'Boys Club' Culture." *The Crime Report*, May 14. https://thecrimereport.org

/2018/05/14/female-cops-fighting-for-respect-in-a-boys-club-culture.

Hampton, S. C. 2023. "The 2020 US Census: Where Did All the New Native Americans Come From?" *Memories of the People*, April 5. https://memoriesofthepeople.blog/2023/04/05/the-2020-us-census-where-did-all-the-new-native-americans-come-from/90io.

Hanauer, N., and D. M. Rolf. 2020. "The Top 1% of Americans Have Taken $50 Trillion from the Bottom 90%—And That's Made the U.S. Less Secure." *Time*, September 14. https://time.com/5888024/50-trillion-income-inequality-america.

Hannah-Jones, N. 2019. "Our Democracy's Founding Ideals Were False When They Were Written. Black Americans Have Fought to Make Them True." *New York Times*, August 14. https://www.pulitzer.org/winners/nikole-hannah-jones-new-york-times.

Hardcastle, J. L. 2023. "Police Use of PayPal Records under Fire after Raid on 'Cop City' Protest Fund Trio." *The Register*, June 6. https://www.theregister.com/2023/06/06/cop_city_paypal.

Hare, R. M. 1990. "Public Policy in a Pluralist Society." In *Embryo Experimentation*, edited by Peter Singer, Helga Kuhse, Stephen Buckle, Karen Dawson, and Pascal Kasimba, 183–94. Cambridge: Cambridge University Press.

Hargrove, T., and S. M. Gonzalez. 2022. "A Conversation on Race and Colorism in *Social Forces*." *Social Forces* 101(1): 102–10. https://doi.org/10.1093/sf/soac045.

Harring, Sidney L. 1983. *Policing a Class Society: The Experience of American Cities, 1865–1915*. New Brunswick, NJ: Rutgers University Press.

Harris, Angela P. 1997. "Race and Essentialism in Feminist Legal Theory." In *Critical Race Feminism: A Reader*, edited by Adrien K. Wing, 11–18. New York: New York University Press.

Harris, A., and Z. Leonardo. 2018. "Intersectionality, Race-Gender Subordination, and Education." *Review of Research in Education* 42(1): 1–27. https://doi.org/10.3102/0091732X18759071.

Harris, David. 1999. "The Stories, the Statistics, and the Law: Why 'Driving While Black' Matters." *Minnesota Law Review* 84(2): 265–326. https://scholarship.law.umn.edu/cgi/viewcontent.cgi?article=2132&context=mlr.

Harris, Kirby. 2021. "Why Paris Hilton Is #BreakingCodeSilence." *Queen's University Journal*, April 8. https://www.queensjournal.ca/why-paris-hilton-is-breakingcodesilence.

Hart, Lynda. 1994. *Fatal Women: Lesbian Sexuality and the Mark of Aggression*. Princeton, NJ: Princeton University Press.

*Harvard Law Review*. 1988. "Developments in the Law: Race and the Criminal Process." *Harvard Law Review* 101:1472.

Hausman, David K. 2020. "Sanctuary Policies Reduce Deportations without Increasing Crime." *Proceedings of the National Academy of Sciences* 117(44): 27262–67.

Hawkesworth, M. E. 2018. *Globalization and Feminist Activism*. 2nd ed. Lanham, MD: Rowman & Littlefield.

Hawkins, Darnell. 1995. *Ethnicity, Race and Crime*. Albany: State University of New York Press.

Hawkins, Richard, and Geoffrey Alpert. 1989. *American Prison Systems: Punishment and Justice*. Englewood Cliffs, NJ: Prentice-Hall.

Heaton, P. 2020. "The Expansive Reach of Pretrial Detention." *North Carolina Law Review* 98:369–79.

Heaton, P., S. Mayson, and M. Stevenson. 2017. "The Downstream Consequences of Misdemeanor Pretrial Detention." *Stanford Law Review* 69(711): 717–18.

Henson, A., T. T. Nguyen, and A. Olaghere. 2023. "Revising the Critical Gaze: An Inversion of Criminological Theories to Center Race, Racism, and Resistance." *Critical Criminology* 31(1): 17–33. https://doi.org/10.1007/s10612-022-09665-6.

Hernández, David Manuel. 2008. "Pursuant to Deportation: Latinos and Immigrant Detention." *Latino Studies* 6(1–2): 35–63. https://dx.doi.org/10.1057/lst.2008.2.

Herskind, M. n.d. "Christianity and Prison Abolition." https://micahherskind.com/abolition-resource-guide/christianity-and-prison-abolition.

Hessick, C. B. 2021a. *Punishment without Trial: Why Plea Bargaining Is a Bad Deal*. New York: Abrams Press.

———. 2021b. "The Constitutional Right We Have Bargained Away." *The Atlantic*, December 24. https://www.theatlantic.com/ideas/archive/2021/12/right-to-jury-trial-penalty/621074.

Hickman, Caroline, Elizabeth Marks, Panu Pih-kala, Susan Clayton, R. Eric Lewandowski, Elouise E. Mayall, et al. 2021. "Climate Anxiety in Children and Young People and Their Beliefs about Government Responses to Climate Change: A Global Survey." *Lancet Planetary Health* 5(12): e863–e873. https://doi.org/10.1016/S2542-5196(21)00278-3.

Higgins, A. 2022. "What Price Are We Willing to Pay for the Dream of Equal Justice?" *Oxford Journal of Legal Studies* 42(1): 325–44. https://doi.org/10.1093/ojls/gqab002.

Hightower, Jim. 1998. *There's Nothing in the Middle of the Road but Yellow Stripes and Dead Armadillos*. New York: Harper Perennial.

Hill, M. L. 2021. "Anything Is Possible: Toward an Abolitionist Vision." *ROAR*, January 23. https://roarmag.org/essays/marc-lamont-hill-abolitionist-vision.

Hilliard, D. 2010. *The Black Panther Party: Service to the People Programs*. Albuquerque: University of New Mexico Press.

Hills, Stuart, ed. 1987. *Corporate Violence: Injury and Death for Profit*. Savage, MD: Rowman & Littlefield.

Hillyard, P., and S. Tombs. 2021. "Beyond Criminology?" In *The Palgrave Encyclopedia of Social Harm*, edited by P. Davies, P. Leighton, and T. Wyatt. Cham: Palgrave.

Hilton, P., and A. Saidman. (producers), and Dean, A. (director). 2020. *This Is Paris*. [Video]. https://youtu.be/wOg0TY1jG3w.

Hinojosa, Ricardo. 2008. "Statement of Ricardo Hinojosa, Chair, United States Sentencing Commission, before the Senate Judiciary Committee." Office of the U.S. Government, February 12.

Hinton, E. 2021. *America on Fire: The Untold History of Police Violence and Black Rebellion since the 1960s*. New York: Liverlight.

Hitt, Jack. 2005. "The Newest Indians." *New York Times Magazine*, August 21. https://www.nytimes.com/2005/08/21/magazine/21NATIVE.html.

Hodges, C. 2021. "From Abuse to Arrest: How America's Legal System Harms Victims of Domestic Violence." *Brown Political Review*, August 23. https://brownpoliticalreview.org/2021/08/abuse-to-arrest.

Hoffman, Jan. 2017. "Sick and Afraid, Some Immigrants Forgo Medical Care." *New York Times*, June 26. https://www.nytimes.com/2017/06/26/health/undocumented-immigrants-health-care.html.

———. 2023. "Addiction Treatment Medicine Is Vastly Underprescribed, Especially by Race, Study Finds." *New York Times*, May 10. https://www.nytimes.com/2023/05/10/health/addiction-treatment-buprenorphine-suboxone.html.

Holler Health Justice. n.d. "Who We Are and What We Do." https://www.hollerhealthjustice.org/about.

Hufstader, Rebecca A. 2015. "Immigration Reliance on Gang Databases: Unchecked Discretion and Undesirable Consequences Notes." *New York University Law Review* 90:671–709.

Hull, Gloria T., Patricia Bell Scott, and Barbara Smith, eds. 1982. *All the Women Are White, All the Blacks Are Men, but Some of Us Are Brave: Black Women's Studies*. New York: Feminist Press.

Human Rights Campaign. n.d. "The Wage Gap among LGBTQ+ Workers in the United States." https://www.hrc.org/resources/the-wage-gap-among-lgbtq-workers-in-the-united-states.

Human Rights Watch. 2001. *No Escape: Male Rape in U.S. Prisons*. Report, April 1. https://www.hrw.org/reports/2001/prison.

———. 2022. "Qatar World Cup Ambassador's Homophobic Comments Fuel Discrimination." Human Rights Watch, November 10. https://www.hrw.org/news/2022/11/10/qatar-world-cup-ambassadors-homophobic-comments-fuel-discrimination.

Humm, Maggie. 1990. *The Dictionary of Feminist Theory*. Columbus: Ohio State University Press.

Huq, Aziz Z. 2019. "Racial Equity in Algorithmic Criminal Justice." *Duke Law Journal* 68:1–71. https://ssrn.com/abstract=3144831.

Ignatiev, N. 2008. *How the Irish Became White*. New York: Routledge.

Immigration Equality. 2020. "Legal Help: Asylum." https://immigrationequality.org/legal/legal-help/asylum.

Indian Law and Order Commission. 2013. *A Roadmap for Making Native America Safer: Report to the President and Congress of the United States*. https://www.aisc.ucla.edu/iloc/report/index.html.

Institute for Criminal Justice Training Reform. n.d. "Not Enough Training." https://www.trainingreform.org/not-enough-training.

Intergovernmental Panel on Climate Change (IPCC). 2022. *Climate Change 2022: Impacts, Adaptation and Vulnerability*. Working Group II contribution to the Sixth Assessment Report of the Intergovernmental Panel on Climate Change. https://www.ipcc.ch/report/ar6/wg2.

International Association of Chiefs of Police. n.d. "Responding to Sexual Violence in LGBTQ+ Communities."

International Centre for Prison Studies. 2023. "World Prison Brief." Accessed December 22, 2023. https://www.prisonstudies.org.

Intersex Society. n.d. "What Is Intersex?" https://www.isna.org/faq/what_is_intersex.

Introcaso, D. 2021. "Deaths of Despair: The Unrecognized Tragedy of Working Class Immiseration." *Stat News*, December 29. https://www.statnews.com/2021/12/29/deaths-of-despair-unrecognized-tragedy-working-class-immiseration.

Irwin, John, and James Austin. 1997. *It's About Time: America's Imprisonment Binge*. Belmont, CA: Wadsworth.

Isenberg, Nancy. 2016. *White Trash: The 400-Year Untold History of Class in America*. New York: Penguin.

Isom Scott, D. 2020. "The New Juan Crow? Unpacking the Links between Discrimination and Crime for Latinxs." *Race and Justice* 10(1): 20–42. https://doi.org/10.1177/2153368717721613.

Isom Scott, D. A., S. Whiting, and J. M. Grosholz. 2020. "Examining and Expanding Latinx General Strain Theory." *Race and Justice* 13(2). https://doi.org/10.1177/2153368720930409.

Jackson, A. N., L. Fedina, J. DeVylder, and R. P. Barth. 2021. "Police Violence and Associations with Public Perceptions of the Police." *Journal of the Society for Social Work and Research* 12(2): 303–26. https://doi.org/10.1086/711683.

Jacob, Herbert. (1973) 1980. *Urban Justice: Law and Order in American Cities*. Reprint; Englewood Cliffs, NJ: Prentice-Hall.

Jacobs, James B. 2009. "Gang Databases." *Criminology & Public Policy* 8(4): 705–9. https://doi.org/10.1111/j.1745-9133.2009.00586.x.

Jaffe, Sarah. 2016. "Standing Firm at Standing Rock: Why the Struggle Is Bigger Than One Pipeline." *Moyers and Company*, September 28. https://billmoyers.com/story/standing-firm-standing-rock-pipeline-protesters-will-not-moved.

Janney, T., and J. Lutz. 2022. "2022 CEO Pay Ratio among S&P 500 Companies." *FW Cook*, August 25. https://www.fwcook.com/Blog/2022-CEO-Pay-Ratio-Among-SP-500-Companies.

Jim Crow Museum. 2007. "TV's First Interracial Kiss." Jim Crow Museum, November. https://jimcrowmuseum.ferris.edu/question/2007/november.htm.

Jiménez, J. 2022. "6 Takeaways from the Report on Abuse in Women's Soccer." *New York Times*, October 3. https://www.nytimes.com/2022/10/03/sports/soccer/soccer-abuse-report-takeaways.html.

Johnson, B. D. 2019. "Trials and Tribulations: The Trial Tax and the Process of Punishment." *Crime and Justice* 48:313–63. https://doi.org/10.1086/701713.

Johnson, Carrie. 2006. "Skilling Gets 24 Years for Fraud at Enron." *Washington Post*, October 24, A1.

Johnson, Jenna. 2015. "Trump Calls for 'Total and Complete Shutdown of Muslims Entering the United States.'" *Washington Post*, December 7. https://www.washingtonpost.com/news/post-politics/wp/2015/12/07/donald-trump-calls-for-total-and-complete-shutdown-of-muslims-entering-the-united-states.

Johnson, M. 2020. "The Dangerous Consequences of Florida's 'Don't Say Gay' Bill on LGBTQ+ Youth in Florida." *Georgetown Journal of Gender and the Law* 23(3). https://www.law.georgetown.edu/gender-journal/online/volume-xxiii-online/the-dangerous-consequences-of-floridas-dont-say-gay-bill-on-lgbtq-youth-in-florida.

Johnson, Robert. 2002. *Hard Time: A Fresh Look at Understanding and Reforming the Prison*. Belmont, CA: Wadsworth.

Johnson, Robert, and Paul Leighton. 1999. "American Genocide: The Destruction of the Black Underclass." In *Collective Violence: Harmful Behavior in Groups and Governments*, edited by Craig Summers and Eric Markusen, 95–140. Lanham, MD: Rowman & Littlefield. https://paulsjusticepage.com.

Johnson, S. B., R. W. Blum, and J. N. Giedd. 2009. "Adolescent Maturity and the Brain: The Promise and Pitfalls of Neuroscience Research in Adolescent Health Policy."

*Journal of Adolescent Health* 45(3): 216–21. https://doi.org/10.1016/j.jadohealth.2009.05.016.

Jones, C. 2013. "'Give Us Free': Addressing Racial Disparities in Bail Determinants." *N.Y.U. Journal of Legislation & Public Policy* 16(4).

Jones, J. 2023. "Activists Denounce Atlanta's Plan for 'Cop City' after Police Clash." MSNBC, March 6. https://www.msnbc.com/the-reidout /reidout-blog/atlanta-cop-city-police-protesters -rcna73666.

Jones, J. M. 2021. "LGBT Identification Rises to 5.6% in Latest U.S. Estimate." *Gallup News*, February 24. https://news.gallup.com/poll /329708/lgbt-identification-rises-latest-estimate .aspx.

———. 2022. "Confidence in U.S. Institutions Down; Average at New Low." *Gallup News*, July 5. https://news.gallup.com/poll/394283/ confidence-institutions-down-average-new-low .aspx.

Jones, N. A., and J. J. Bullock. 2013. "Understanding Who Reported Multiple Races in the U.S. Decennial Census: Results from Census 2000 and the 2010 Census." *Family Relations* 62(1): 5–16.

Jones, Nikki. 2011. "Something Smells Like a Pig, You Say?" *Public Intellectual*, May 2. https:// thepublicintellectual.org/2011/05/02/if-it-smells -like-a-pig.

Kaba, M. 2021. "So You're Thinking about Becoming an Abolitionist." In *Abolition for the People: The Movement for a Future without Policing & Prisons*, edited by C. Kaepernick. New York: Kaepernick Publishing.

Kaba, M., and A. Richie. 2022. "Reclaiming Safety." *Inquest*, August 30. https://inquest.org/ reclaiming-safety.

Kahle, L. 2020. "Are Sexual Minorities More at Risk? Bullying Victimization among Lesbian, Gay, Bisexual, and Questioning Youth." *Journal of Interpersonal Violence* 35(21–22): 4960–78. https://doi.org/10.1177/0886260517718830.

Kandal, Terry. 1988. *The Woman Question in Classical Sociological Theory*. Miami: Florida International University Press.

Kanno-Youngs, Z. 2023. "Backlogged Courts and Years of Delays Await Many Migrants." *New York Times*, May 12. https://www.nytimes .com/2023/05/12/us/politics/immigration-courts -delays-migrants-title-42.html.

Kaplan, J. 2021. "The Number of Billionaires grew by 1304% in 2020—Making the Pandemic a 'Windfall to Billionaire Wealth.'" *Markets Insider*, September 20. https://markets .businessinsider.com/news/stocks/number-of-bil lionaires-in-world-grew-pandemic-wealth-tax -2021-9.

Karlamangla, S. 2022. "Anna May Wong Will Be the First Asian American on U.S. Currency." *New York Times*, October 18. https://www .nytimes.com/2022/10/18/us/anna-may-wong -quarter.html.

Katyal, Neal. 2011. "Confession of Error: The Solicitor General's Mistakes during the Japanese-American Internment Cases." Statement, Office of the Solicitor General. https://www .justice.gov/archives/opa/blog/confession-error -solicitor-generals-mistakes-during-japanese -american-internment-cases.

Katz, R. S. 2022. "The Color of Queer Theory in Social Work and Criminology Practice: A World without Empathy." In *Queering Criminology in Theory and Praxis: Reimagining Justice in the Criminal Legal System and Beyond*, edited by C. Buist and L. Kahle Semprevivo, 250–62. Bristol: Bristol University Press.

Kavattur, Purvaja S., Somjen Frazer, Abby El-Shafei, Kayt Tiskus, Laura Laderman, Lindsey Hull, Fikayo Walter-Johnson, Dana Sussman, and Lynn M. Paltrow. 2023. *The Rise of Pregnancy Criminalization: A Pregnancy Justice Report*. New York: Pregnancy Justice. https://www .pregnancyjusticeus.org/wp-content/uploads /2023/09/9-2023-Criminalization-report.pdf.

Keefe, Patrick R. 2021. "How Did the Sacklers Pull This Off?" *New York Times*, July 14. https:// www.nytimes.com/2021/07/14/opinion/sackler -family-opioids-settlement.html.

Kemp, Luke, Chi Xu, Joanne Depledge, Kristie L. Ebi, Goodwin Gibbins, Timothy A. Kohler, Johan Rockström, et al. 2022. "Climate Endgame: Exploring Catastrophic Climate Change Scenarios." *Proceedings of the National Academy of Sciences* 119(34): e2108146119. https:// doi.org/10.1073/pnas.2108146119.

Kendall, M. 2020. *Hood Feminism: Notes from the Women White Feminists Forgot*. New York: Bloomsbury.

Kennedy, Marc C. 1970. "Beyond Incrimination: Some Neglected Facets of the Theory of Punishment." *Catalyst* 5 (Summer): 1–30.

Kent, A. H., and L. R. Ricketts. 2021. "Gender Wealth Gap: Families Headed by Women Have Lower Health." Federal Reserve Bank of St. Louis, January 12. https://www.stlouisfed.org/en/publications/in-the-balance/2021/gender-wealth-gap-families-women-lower-wealth.

Kent, L., and H. Ritchie. 2021. "Plymouth Shooter Made Misogynistic Remarks Echoing the 'Incel' Ideology." CNN, August 15. https://www.cnn.com/2021/08/14/uk/plymouth-shooting-incel-jake-davison-profile-intl/index.html.

Khan, Lina M. 2017. "Amazon's Antitrust Paradox." *Yale Law Journal* 126(3): 710–805.

Kilgore, J. 2015. "Electronic Monitoring Is Not the Answer: Critical Reflections on a Flawed Alternative." *Media Justice*, October. https://mediajustice.org/wp-content/uploads/2015/10/EM-Report-Kilgore-final-draft-10-4-15.pdf.

———. 2022. *Understanding E-Carceration: Electronic Monitoring, the Surveillance State, and the Future of Mass Incarceration.* New York: New Press.

Killermann, S. 2011. "30+ Examples of Cisgender Privileges." https://www.itspronouncedmetrosexual.com/2011/11/list-of-cisgender-privileges.

Killingbeck, Donna. 2005. "A Sociological History of Prison Privatization in the Contemporary United States." PhD diss., Western Michigan University, Kalamazoo.

Kim, J. J. 2021. "Violations of the U.S. Minimum Wage Laws: A Method of Wage Theft." *Journal of Economic Issues* 55(4): 977–98. https://doi.org/10.1080/00213624.2021.1982346.

Kim, J. J., and S. Allmang. 2021. "Wage Theft in the United States: Towards New Research Agendas." *Economic and Labor Relations Review* 32(4). https://doi.org/10.1177/10353046211025.

Kimani, A. 2022. "Big Oil Is No Longer 'Unbankable.'" Oilprice.com, March 22. https://oilprice.com/Energy/Crude-Oil/Big-Oil-Is-No-Longer-Unbankable.html.

King, S. 2018. "Despite Liberalizing Marijuana Laws, the War on Drugs Still Targets People of Color." *The Intercept*, January 25. https://theintercept.com/2018/01/25/marijuana-legalization-weed-drug-arrest.

Kipnis, Kenneth. 2001. "Criminal Justice and the Negotiated Plea." In *Criminal Justice Ethics*, edited by Paul Leighton and Jeffrey Reiman, 362–71. Upper Saddle River, NJ: Prentice-Hall.

Klein, Dorie. (1973) 1995. "The Etiology of Female Crime: A Review of the Literature." In *The Criminal Justice System and Women*, 2nd ed., edited by Barbara Raffel Price and Natalie J. Sokoloff, 30–53. New York: McGraw-Hill.

Kochhar, R. 2023. "The Enduring Grip of the Gender Pay Gap." Pew Research Center, March 1. https://www.pewresearch.org/social-trends/2023/03/01/the-enduring-grip-of-the-gender-pay-gap.

Kochhar, R., and S. Sechopoulos. 2022. "COVID-19 Pandemic Pinches Finances of America's Lower- and Middle-Income Families." Pew Research Center, April 20. https://www.pewresearch.org/social-trends/2022/04/20/covid-19-pandemic-pinches-finances-of-americas-lower-and-middle-income-families.

Kopan, T. 2017. "MS-13 Is Trump's Public Enemy No.1, but Should It Be?" CNN, April 29. https://www.cnn.com/2017/04/28/politics/ms13-explained-immigration-sessions.

Kornya, A., D. Rodarmel, B. Highsmith, M. Gonzalez, and T. Mermin. 2019. "Crimsumerism: Combating Consumer Abuses in the Criminal Legal System." *Harvard Civil Rights–Civil Liberties Law Review* 54(3).

Kosciw, J. G., C. M. Clark, and L. Menard. 2022. *The 2021 National School Climate Survey.* GLSEN. https://www.glsen.org/sites/default/files/2022-10/NSCS-2021-Full-Report.pdf.

Kramer, R. C. 2020. *Carbon Criminals, Climate Crimes.* New Brunswick, NJ: Rutgers University Press.

Kraska, Peter. 2004. *Theorizing Criminal Justice: Eight Essential Orientations.* Long Grove, IL: Waveland Press.

———. 2007. "The Blurring of War and Law Enforcement." In *Violence, Conflict, and World Order: Critical Conversations on State-Sanctioned Justice*, edited by G. Barak, 161–87. Lanham, MD: Rowman & Littlefield.

Kravitz-Wirtz, N., A. Aubel, J. Schleimer, R. Pallin, and G. Wintemute. 2021. "Public Concern about Violence, Firearms, and the COVID-19 Pandemic in California." *JAMA Network Open*

4(1): e2033484. https://doi.org/10.1001/jama networkopen.2020.33484.

Krieger, S. 2023. *Incentivizing Injustice: The 2008 Financial Crisis and Prosecutorial Indiscretion.* Lanham, MD: Rowman & Littlefield.

Krivo, Lauren, and Ruth Peterson. 2009. Introduction to the special issue, "Race, Crime, and Justice: Contexts and Complexities." *Annals of the American Academy of Political and Social Science* 623 (May): 7–10.

Kubrin, Charis E. 2014. "Secure or Insecure Communities?" *Criminology & Public Policy* 13(2): 323–38. https://doi.org/10.1111/1745-9133 .12086.

Kumanyika, C., and R. W. Gilmore. 2020. "Ruth Wilson Gilmore Makes the Case for Abolition." *The Intercept*, June 10. https://theintercept.com /2020/06/10/ruth-wilson-gilmore-makes-the -case-for-abolition.

Kurdyla, V., A. M. Messinger, and X. L. Guadalupe-Diaz. 2022. "Health Covariates of Intimate Partner Violence in a National Transgender Sample." In *Queering Criminology in Theory and Praxis: Reimagining Justice in the Criminal Legal System and Beyond*, edited by C. L. Buist and L. K. Semprevivo, 129–43. Bristol: Bristol University Press.

Lambert, L., and R. W. Gilmore. 2018. "Making Abolition Geography in California's Central Valley." *The Funambulist* 21. https://thefunam bulist.net/magazine/21-space-activism/interview -making-abolition-geography-california-central -valley-ruth-wilson-gilmore.

Lamble, S. 2021. "Practicing Everyday Abolition." Abolitionist Futures. https://abolitionistfutures .com/latest-news/practising-everyday-abolition.

Lanier, Mark M., and Stuart Henry. 2004. *Essential Criminology.* Boulder, CO: Westview.

Lanuza, Y. R., N. Petersen, and M. Omori. 2023. "Colorism in Punishment among Hispanics in the Criminal Justice System." *Social Problems* 70:275–96. https://doi.org/10.1093/socpro /spab044.

Lauritsen, Janet. 2004. "Searching for a Better Understanding of Race and Ethnic Differences in Violent Crime." *Criminal Justice Ethics* 24(1): 68–73.

Lazarus, Edward. 1991. *Black Hills, White Justice: The Sioux Nation versus the United States, 1775 to the Present.* New York: HarperCollins.

Leaf, Clifton. 2005. "Enough Is Enough: White-Collar Criminals; They Lie They Cheat They Steal and They've Been Getting Away with It for Too Long." In *Annual Editions: Criminal Justice*, 29th ed., edited by Joseph L. Victor and Joanne Naughton, 35–42. Dubuque, IA: McGraw-Hill/Dushkin. Reprinted from *Fortune*, March 18, 2002, 62–65.

Lee, Charles. 1992. "Toxic Waste and Race in the United States." In *Race and the Incidence of Environmental Hazards: A Time for Discourse*, edited by Bunyan Bryant and Paul Mohai, 10–27. Boulder, CO: Westview.

Lee, Jennifer J., and Annie Smith. 2019. "Regulating Wage Theft." *Washington Law Review* 94(2): 759–822.

Le Guin, Ursula K. 2014. "National Book Foundation Speech." *Rulerless*, November 19. https://www.rulerless.org/le-guin-speech.

Legum, J. 2021. "A Tale of Two Thefts." *Popular Information*, November 29. https://popular.info /p/a-tale-of-two-thefts.

Leighton, Paul. 2013. "Corporate Crime and the Corporate Agenda for Crime Control: Disappearing Awareness of Corporate Crime and Increasing Abuses of Power." *Western Criminology Review* 14(2): 38–51. https://wcr .sonoma.edu/v14n2/Leighton.pdf.

———. 2014. "'A Model Prison for the Next 50 Years': The High-Tech, Public-Private Shimane Asahi Rehabilitation Center." *Justice Policy Journal* 11(1). https://www.cjcj.org/ media/import/documents/leighton_model_pris ons_final_formatted.pdf.

———. 2018. "No Criminology of Wage Theft: Revisiting 'Workplace Theft' to Expose Capitalist Exploitation." In *Revisiting Crimes of the Powerful: Marxism, Crime, and Deviance*, edited by S. Bittle, L. Snider, S. Tombs, and D. Whyte. New York: Routledge.

Leighton, Paul, and Jeffrey Reiman, eds. 2001. *Criminal Justice Ethics.* Upper Saddle River, NJ: Prentice-Hall.

———. 2002. *Getting Tough on Corporate Crime? Enron and a Year of Corporate Financial Scandals.* Boston, MA: Allyn & Bacon. https:// www.paulsjusticepage.com/RichGetRicher/ fraud.htm.

———. 2004. *A Tale of Two Criminals: We're Tougher on Corporate Criminals, but They Still Don't Get What They Deserve.* Boston, MA:

Allyn & Bacon. https://paulsjusticepage.com/RichGetRicher/fraud2004.htm.

———. 2014. "A Suitable Amount of Street Crime and a Suitable Amount of White Collar Crime: Inconvenient Truths about Inequality, Crime and Criminal Justice." In *Routledge Handbook of International Crime and Justice Studies*, edited by B. Arrigo and H. Berscot, 331–42. New York: Routledge.

Leighton, P., and D. Selman. 2018. "Private Prisons, the Criminal Justice–Industrial Complex and Bodies Destined for Profitable Punishment." In *Routledge Handbook of Critical Criminology*, 2nd ed., edited by W. S. DeKeseredy and M. Dragiewicz, 260–68. New York: Routledge.

León, K. S. 2021. "Critical Criminology and Race: Re-examining the Whiteness of US Criminological Thought." *Howard Journal of Crime and Justice* 60(3): 388–408. https://doi.org/10.1111/hojo.12441.

León, K. S., and M. Barak. 2023. "MS-13, Gang Studies, and Crimes of the Powerful." In *Critical and Intersectional Gang Studies*, edited by J. M. Ortiz, 84–99. New York: Routledge. https://doi.org/10.4324/9781003159797-8.

León, Kenneth Sebastian, and Andrea Gómez Cervantes. 2022. "Techno-Bureaucratic Race-Making: Latino (Mis)Representation in Criminology and Criminal Justice Knowledge Claims." *Journal of Criminal Justice Education* 34(3). https://doi.org/10.1080/10511253.2022.2155204.

Levenson, E. 2018. "Michigan State University Reaches $500 Million Settlement with Larry Nassar Victims." CNN, May 17. https://www.cnn.com/2018/05/16/us/larry-nassar-michigan-state-settlement/index.html.

Levine, P., and R. McKnight. 2020. "Three Million More Guns: The Spring 2020 Spike in Firearm Sales." Brookings Institution, July 13. https://www.brookings.edu/blog/up-front/2020/07/13/three-million-more-guns-the-spring-2020-spike-in-firearm-sales.

Levy, R., and M. Mattsson. 2022. "The Effects of Social Movements: Evidence from #MeToo." https://dx.doi.org/10.2139/ssrn.3496903.

Lewis, T. L. 2021. "Disability Justice Is an Essential Part of Abolishing the Police." In *Abolition for the People: The Movement for a Future without Policing & Prisons*, edited by C. Kaepernick. New York: Kaepernick Publishing.

LGBTQ+ Bar. n.d. "LGBTQ+ 'Panic' Defense." https://lgbtqbar.org/programs/advocacy/gay-trans-panic-defense.

Library of Congress. n.d. "The U.S. Mainland: Growth and Resistance." https://www.loc.gov/classroom-materials/immigration/japanese/the-us-mainland-growth-and-resistance.

Lichtblau, Eric, David Johnston, and Ron Nixon. 2008. "FBI Struggles to Handle Financial Fraud Cases." *New York Times*, October 18. https://www.nytimes.com/2008/10/19/washington/19fbi.html.

Light, M. T., J. He, and J. P. Robey. 2020. "Comparing Crime Rates between Undocumented Immigrants, Legal Immigrants, and Native-Born US Citizens in Texas." *Proceedings of the National Academy of Sciences* 117(51): 32340–47. https://doi.org/10.1073/pnas.2014704117.

Light, M. T., and T. Miller. 2017. "Does Undocumented Immigration Increase Violent Crime?" *Criminology* 56(2): 370–401. https://doi.org/10.1111/1745-9125.12175.

Lipsitz, George. 2005. "The Possessive Investment in Whiteness." In *White Privilege: Essential Readings on the Other Side of Racism*, 2nd ed., edited by Paula S. Rothenberg, 67–90. New York: Worth.

Liptak, A. 2022. "The Persistent Gender Gap at the Supreme Court Lectern." *New York Times*, June 22. https://www.nytimes.com/2022/01/17/us/supreme-court-gender-gap.html.

Littman, A. 2021. "Jails, Sheriffs, and Carceral Policymaking." *Vanderbilt Law Review* 74(4).

Liu, Grace S., Brenda L. Nguyen, Bridget H. Lyons, Kameron J. Sheats, Rebecca F. Wilson, Carter J. Betz, and Katherine A. Fowler. 2023. "Surveillance for Violent Deaths: National Violent Death Reporting System, 48 States, the District of Columbia, and Puerto Rico, 2020." *Surveillance Summaries* 72(5): 1–38.

Looney, Adam, and Nicholas Turner. 2018. "Work and Opportunity before and after Incarceration." Brookings Institution, March. https://www.brookings.edu/wp-content/uploads/2018/03/es_20180314_looneyincarceration_final.pdf.

Lopez, G., and A. Wu. 2022. "Covid's Toll on Native Americans." *New York Times*, September 8. https://www.nytimes.com/2022/09/08/briefing/covid-death-toll-native-americans.html.

Lopez, M. H., J. M. Krogstad, and J. S. Passel. 2022. "Who Is Hispanic?" Pew Research Center, September 15. https://www.pewresearch.org/short-reads/2022/09/15/who-is-hispanic.

Lorde, A. (1982) 2012. *Sister Outsider: Essays and Speeches*. Berkeley, CA: Crossing Press.

Loudin, A. 2023. "After Decades of Neglecting Women Athletes, Sport and Exercise Medicine Is Finally Catching Up." *Stat News*, May 19. https://www.statnews.com/2023/05/19/sports-medicine-women-athletes.

Lowell, A. D. 2022. "Biden's Supreme Court Nominee Should Be a Criminal Defense Lawyer." *Washington Post*, February 2. https://www.washingtonpost.com/opinions/2022/02/02/biden-supreme-court-pick-should-be-criminal-defense-lawyer.

Ludwig, J. 2021. "Data Points: Illegal Gun Carrying in Chicago Spiked in 2020—and Deadly Violence." Chicago Tribune, April 2. https://www.chicagotribune.com/opinion/commentary/ct-opinion-data-points-gun-carrying-crime-lab-20210403-5iz6blr6urhlji7hxwyjwrnhc4-htmlstory.html.

Lusane, Clarence. 1991. *Pipe Dream Blues: Racism and the War on Drugs*. Boston, MA: South End Press.

Luthar, S. S. 2013. "The Problem with Rich Kids." *Psychology Today*, November 5. https://www.psychologytoday.com/us/articles/201311/the-problem-rich-kids.

Lynch, James, and William Sabol. 2000. "Prison Use and Social Control: Policies, Processes, and Decisions of the Criminal Justice System; Criminal Justice 2000." NCJ 182410. Washington, DC: U.S. Department of Justice.

Lynch, Michael J., and Nancy K. Frank. 1992. *Corporate Crime, Corporate Violence*. Albany, NY: Harrow & Heston.

Lynch, Michael, Ray Michalowski, and W. Byron Groves. 2000. *The New Primer in Radical Criminology*. 3rd ed. Monsey, NY: Willow Tree.

Lynch, Michael, and Paul Stretesky. 1998. "Uniting Class, Race and Criticism through the Study of Environmental Justice." *Critical Criminologist* 9(1): 1, 4–6.

Ma, Yue. 2008. "Prosecutorial Discretion and Plea Bargaining in the United States, France, Germany, and Italy: A Comparative Perspective." In *Global Criminology and Criminal Justice: Current Issues and Perspectives*, edited by Nick Larsen and Russell Smandych, 281–310. Buffalo, NY: Broadview.

MacFarquhar, N. 2021. "With Homicides Rising, Cities Brace for a Violent Summer." *New York Times*, June 1. https://www.nytimes.com/2021/06/01/us/shootings-in-us.html.

Mackay, C. (1841) 1932. *Extraordinary Popular Delusions and the Madness of Crowds*. New York: Farrar, Straus & Giroux.

MacKinnon, Catharine A. (1984) 1991. "Difference and Dominance: On Sex Discrimination." In *Feminist Legal Theory*, edited by Katharine T. Bartlett and Rosanne Kennedy, 81–94. Boulder, CO: Westview.

MacLeod, A. 2019. "The Homeless 8-Year-Old Chess Champion and Other Horrific 'Uplifting' Stories." FAIR (Fairness & Accuracy in Reporting), March 25. https://fair.org/home/the-homeless-8-year-old-chess-champion-and-other-horrific-uplifting-stories.

Magnuson, D., W. Dobud, and N. J. Harper. 2022. "Can Involuntary Youth Transport into Outdoor Behavioral Healthcare Treatment Programs (Wilderness Therapy) Ever Be Ethical?" *Child and Adolescent Social Work Journal* 41(6): 1–9.

Maher, G. 2021. *A World without Police: How Strong Communities Make Cops Obsolete*. New York: Verso.

Maldonado-Torres, N. 2007. "On the Coloniality of Being: Contributions to the Development of a Concept." *Cultural Studies* 21(2–3): 240–70. https://doi.org/10.1080/09502380601162548.

Marier, C. J., and L. A. Fridell. 2020. "Demonstrations, Demoralization, and De-policing." *Criminology & Public Policy* 19(3): 693–719. https://doi.org/10.1111/1745-9133.12492.

Markel, Howard, and Alexandra Minna Stern. 2002. "The Foreignness of Germs: The Persistent Association of Immigrants and Disease in American Society." *Milbank Quarterly* 80(4): 757–88. https://doi.org/10.1111/1468-0009.00030.

Markowitz, Eric. 2015. "Chain Gang 2.0: If You Can't Afford This GPS Ankle Bracelet, You Get Thrown in Jail." *International Business Times*, September 15. https://www.ibtimes.com/chain-gang-20-if-you-cant-afford-gps-ankle-bracelet-you-get-thrown-jail-2065283.

Marquez, Beatriz Aldana, Guadalupe Marquez-Velarde, John M. Eason, and Linda Aldana.

2021. "Pushing Them to the Edge: Suicide in Immigrant Detention Centers as a Product of Organizational Failure." *Social Science & Medicine* 283:114–77. https://doi.org/10.1016/j .socscimed.2021.114177.

Martínez, D. E. 2022. "Escalated Border Enforcement and Migrant Deaths in Southern Arizona." *The Criminologist* 47(2): 1–39. https:// asc41.com/wp-content/uploads/ASC_Criminol ogist_2022_03.pdf.

Martínez, Ramiro. 2008. "The Impact of Immigration Policy on Criminological Research." *Criminology & Public Policy* 7(1): 53–58. https://doi.org/10.1111/j.1745-9133.2008 .00490.x.

Masters, Jeff. 2022. "The Future of Global Catastrophic Risk Events from Climate Change." Yale Climate Connections, July 28. https://yaleclimateconnections.org/2022/07/the -future-of-global-catastrophic-risk-events-from -climate-change.

Matthews, Shanelle, and Miski Noor. 2017. *Celebrating Black Lives Matter: Four Years Report.* https://richmondpledge.org/wp-content/uploads /Module-5-Pre-Session-BLM-Anniversary -Report.pdf.

Matz, Joshua. 2017. "A Deportation That Diminishes Not Only Our Country but Our Courts." *Take Care*, May 31. https://takecareblog.com /blog/a-deportation-that-diminishes-not-only -our-country-but-our-courts.

Maxmen, M. 2021. "Inequality's Deadly Toll." *Nature*, April 28. https://www.nature.com/ immersive/d41586-021-00943-x/index.html.

McCorkel, Jill A. 2013. *Breaking Women: Gender, Race, and the New Politics of Imprisonment.* New York: New York University Press.

McCoy, M., S. Martinelli, S. Reddy, R. Don, A. Thompson, M. Speer, R. Bravo, M. Yudell, and S. Darira. 2022. "Food Insecurity on College Campuses: The Invisible Epidemic." *Health Affairs*, January 31. https://www.healthaffairs .org/do/10.1377/forefront.20220127.264905.

McDiarmid, J. 2019. *Highway of Tears: A True Story of Racism, Indifference and the Pursuit of Justice for Missing and Murdered Indigenous Women and Girls.* Toronto: Anchor Canada.

McFarling, U. L. 2023. "MRI Scans Reveal Disparate Impact of Poverty and Other 'Toxic Stress' on Brains of Black Children." *Stat*, February

1. https://www.statnews.com/2023/02/01/brain -scans-reveal-disparate-impact-of-poverty-toxic -stress-on-black-children.

McGurrin, Danielle, Melissa Jarrell, Amber Jahn, and Brandy Cochrane. 2013. "White Collar Crime Representation in the Criminological Literature Revisited, 2001–2010." *Western Criminology Review* 14(2): 3–19. https://wcr.sonoma .edu/v14n2/McGurrin.pdf.

McIntire, M., and M. H. Keller. 2021. "The Demand for Money behind Many Police Traffic Stops." *New York Times*, November 2. https:// www.nytimes.com/2021/10/31/us/police-ticket -quotas-money-funding.html.

McIntosh, Peggy. (1988) 1997. "White Privilege and Male Privilege: A Personal Account of Coming to See Correspondences through Work in Women's Studies." In *Critical White Studies*, edited by Richard Delgado and Jean Stefancic, 291–99. Philadelphia, PA: Temple University Press.

McKinley, Jesse, and Luis Ferré-Sadurní. 2021. "N.Y. Repeals Law That Critics Say Criminalized 'Walking While Trans.'" *New York Times*, February 3. https://www.nytimes.com/2021/02 /03/nyregion/walking-while-trans-ban.html.

McPhail, Clark. 1991. *The Myth of the Madding Crowd.* New York: Aldine de Gruyter.

Megan, N., and D. L. Brunsma. 2017. "Moving beyond Cis-terhood: Determining Gender through Transgender Admittance Policies at US Women's Colleges." *Gender & Society* 31(2): 145–70.

Meier, Barry. 2007. "In Guilty Plea, OxyContin Maker to Pay $600 Million." *New York Times*, May 10. https://www.nytimes.com/2007/05/10/ business/11drug-web.html.

———. 2018. "Origins of an Epidemic: Purdue Pharma Knew Its Opioids Were Widely Abused." *New York Times*, May 29. https:// www.nytimes.com/2018/05/29/health/purdue -opioids-oxycontin.html.

Meiners, E. R. 2017. "The Problem Child: Provocations toward Dismantling the Carceral State." *Harvard Educational Review* 87(1): 122–46.

Mejia, B. 2018. "Many Latinos Answer Call of the Border Patrol in the Age of Trump." *LA Times*, April 23. https://www.latimes.com/local/lanow/ la-me-ln-citizens-academy-20180323-htmlstory .html.

Mellinger, H. 2022. "Interpretation at the Asylum Office." *Law & Policy* 44(3): 230–54. https://doi.org/10.1111/lapo.12192.

Mendieta, E. 2005. Introduction to *Abolition Democracy: Beyond Empire, Prisons, and Torture*, by A. Davis. New York: Seven Stories Press.

Mendoza, Maria A. 2016. "A System in Need of Repair: The Inhuman Treatment of Detainees in the U.S. Immigration Detention System." *North Carolina Journal of International Law* 41:405–52.

Menjívar, Cecilia, and Leisy Abrego. 2012. "Legal Violence: Immigration Law and the Lives of Central American Immigrants." *American Journal of Sociology* 117(5): 1380–421. https://doi.org/10.1086/663575.

Mercurio, E., E. García-López, L. A. Morales-Quintero, N. E. Llamas, J. Á. Marinaro, and J. M. Muñoz. 2020. "Adolescent Brain Development and Progressive Legal Responsibility in the Latin American Context." *Frontiers in Psychology* 11:627. https://doi.org/10.3389/fpsyg.2020.00627.

Mervosh, S., and D. Goldstein. 2023. "Florida Rejects Dozens of Social Studies Textbooks, and Forces Changes in Others." *New York Times*, May 9. https://www.nytimes.com/2023/05/09/us/desantis-florida-social-studies-textbooks.html.

Messerschmidt, James W. 1997. *Crime as Structured Action: Gender, Race, Class, and Crime in the Making*. Thousand Oaks, CA: Sage.

Messinger, A. M. 2017. *LGBTQ Intimate Partner Violence: Lessons for Policy, Practice, and Research*. Oakland: University of California Press.

Mikell, T. 2023. "Trans Black Women Deserve Better: Expanding Queer Criminology to Unpack Trans Misogynoir in the Field of Criminology." In *Abolish Criminology*, edited by V. Saleh-Hanna, J. M. Williams, and M. J. Coyle, 93–104. New York: Routledge.

Miller, Jerome G. 1996. *Search and Destroy: African-American Males in the Criminal Justice System*. Cambridge: Cambridge University Press.

Miller, Jody. 2008. *Getting Played: African American Girls, Urban Inequality, and Gendered Violence*. New York: New York University Press.

Miller, Robin, and Sandra Lee Browning. 2004. "A Critical Examination of Law and Social Control: Introductory Remarks." In *For the Common Good: A Critical Examination of Law and Social Control*, edited by Robin Miller and Sandra Lee Browning, 3–8. Durham, NC: Carolina Academic Press.

Miller, Susan L. 1998. Introduction to *Crime Control and Women*, edited by Susan L. Miller, xv–xxiv. Thousand Oaks, CA: Sage.

Miller, Susan, and Michelle Meloy. 2006. "Women's Use of Force." *Violence against Women* 12(1): 89–115.

Minnesota Advisory Committee. 2018. "Civil Rights and Policing Practices in Minnesota." U.S. Commission on Civil Rights. https://www.usccr.gov/files/pubs/2018/03-22-MN-Civil-Rights.pdf.

Moffitt, K. 2021. "What Does Intersectionality Mean in 2021? Kimberlé Crenshaw's Podcast Is A Must-Listen Way to Learn." *Columbia News*, February 22. https://news.columbia.edu/news/what-does-intersectionality-mean-2021-kimberle-crenshaws-podcast-must-listen-way-learn.

Mohamed, A. Rafik, and Erik Fritsvold. 2011. *Dorm Room Dealers: Drugs and the Privileges of Race and Class*. Boulder, CO: Lynne Rienner.

Monchalin, L. 2016. *The Colonial Problem: An Indigenous Perspective on Crime and Injustice in Canada*. Toronto: University of Toronto Press.

Mooney, G. 2008. "Explaining Poverty, Social Exclusion and Inequality." In *Understanding Inequality, Poverty and Wealth*, edited by T. Ridge and S. Wright, 61–78. Bristol: Policy.

Mooney, H., and P. Leighton. 2019. "Troubled Affluent Youth's Experiences in a Therapeutic Boarding School: The Elite Arm of the Youth Control Complex and Its Implications for Youth Justice." *Critical Criminology* 27(4): 611–26. https://doi.org/10.1007/s10612-019-09466-4.

Moosavi, L. 2019. "A Friendly Critique of 'Asian Criminology' and 'Southern Criminology.'" *British Journal of Criminology* 59(2): 257–75. https://doi.org/10.1093/bjc/azy045.

Morris, M. W. 2018. *Pushout: The Criminalization of Black Girls in Schools*. New York: New Press.

Morrow, O. 2019. "Community Self-Organizing and the Urban Food Commons in Berlin and New York." *Sustainability* 11(13): 3641.

Movement Advancement Project (MAP). 2023a. "Our Work: Democracy Maps." https://www.lgbtmap.org.

———. 2023b. "Under Fire: Erasing LGBTQ People from Schools and Public Life." https://www.mapresearch.org/file/MAP-Under-Fire-Erasing-LGBTQ-People_2023.pdf.

———. 2023c. "Gay/Trans Panic Defense Bans." https://www.lgbtmap.org/equality-maps/panic_defense_bans.

Mowatt, R. A. 2023. "A People's Future of Leisure Studies: Fear City, Cop City and Other Tales, a Call for Police Research." *Leisure Sciences* 45(5): 497–519. https://doi.org/10.1080/01490400.2023.2183288.

Moyer, M. W. 2020. "Undocumented Immigrants Are Half as Likely to Be Arrested for Violent Crimes as U.S.-Born Citizens." *Scientific American*, December 7. https://www.scientificamerican.com/article/undocumented-immigrants-are-half-as-likely-to-be-arrested-for-violent-crimes-as-u-s-born-citizens.

Mullan, E. H. 1917. "Mental Examination of Immigrants-Administration and Line Inspection at Ellis Island." *Public Health Reports* 32(20): 733–46. https://doi.org/10.2307/4574515.

Murakawa, N. 2014. *The First Civil Right: How Liberals Built Prison America*. New York: Oxford University Press.

———. 2021. "The Three Traps of Police Reform." In *Abolition for the People: The Movement for a Future without Policing & Prisons*, edited by C. Kaepernick. New York: Kaepernick Publishing.

Murdoch, S. C. 2021. *Yellow Bird: Oil, Murder, and a Woman's Search for Justice in Indian Country*. New York: Random House.

Myrdal, Gunnar. 1944. *An American Dilemma: The Negro Problem and Modern Democracy*. New York: Pantheon.

Natapoff, A. 2019. "The High Stakes of Low-Level Criminal Justice." *Yale Law Journal* 128(6): 1478–791.

National Academies of Sciences, Engineering, and Medicine. 2020. *Decarcerating Correctional Facilities during COVID-19: Advancing Health, Equity, and Safety*. Washington, DC: National Academies Press. https://doi.org/10.17226/25945.

National Archives. 2022. "Women's Rights and the Civil Rights Act of 1964." https://www.archives.gov/women/1964-civil-rights-act.

———. 2023. "Chinese Exclusion Act (1882)." https://www.archives.gov/milestone-documents/chinese-exclusion-act.

National Association of Social Workers. 2021. "NASW Code of Ethics." https://www.socialworkers.org/About/Ethics/Code-of-Ethics/Code-of-Ethics-English/Social-Workers-Ethical-Responsibilities-to-Clients.

National Institute of Health. 2013. *Lead and Your Health*. https://www.niehs.nih.gov/health/materials/lead_and_your_health_508.pdf.

National Research Council. 2014. *The Growth of Incarceration in the United States: Exploring Causes and Consequences*. Report, edited by Jeremy Travis, Bruce Western, and Steve Redburn. Washington, DC: National Academies Press.

Nelson, A. 2011. *Body and Soul: The Black Panther Party and the Fight against Medical Discrimination*. Minneapolis: University of Minnesota Press.

Nembhard, S., and L. Robin. 2021. "Racial and Ethnic Disparities throughout the Criminal Legal System: A Result of Racist Policies and Discretionary Practices." Washington, DC: The Urban Institute. https://www.urban.org/sites/default/files/publication/104687/racial-and-ethnic-disparities-throughout-the-criminal-legal-system.pdf.

Newman, Lily Hay. 2022. "The Surveillance State Is Primed for Criminalized Abortion." *Wired*, May 22. https://www.wired.com/story/surveillance-police-roe-v-wade-abortion.

New York State Office of the Attorney General. 1999. *Results of Investigation into NYPD "Stop and Frisk" Practice*. Albany, NY: Office of the Attorney General.

*New York Times*. 2024. "Tracking Abortion Bans across the Country." https://www.nytimes.com/interactive/2024/us/abortion-laws-roe-v-wade.html.

Nguyen, Hannah T. 2021. "Time to Ditch Deliberate Indifference: COVID-19, Immigrant Challenges, and the Future of Due Process." *Georgetown Law Review* 58:17–26.

Nguyen, V. T. 2021. "The Beautiful, Flawed Fiction of 'Asian American.'" *New York Times*, May 31. https://www.nytimes.com/2021/05/31/opinion/culture/asian-american-AAPI-decolonization.html.

Niehaus, Manuela. 2022. "Protecting Whose Children? The Rights of Future Generations in the Courts of Germany and Colombia." *Völkerrechtsblog*, March 23. https://doi.org/10.17176/20220324-000931-0.

Norton, M., and D. Ariely. 2011. "Building a Better America—One Wealth Quintile at a Time." *Perspectives on Psychological Science* 6(1): 9–12.

Nowell, Cecilia. 2021. "A Mom Was Charged with Child Neglect for Using Medical Marijuana While Pregnant. The Arizona Case Could Set a Precedent." *Washington Post*, September 13. https://www.thelily.com/a-mom-was-charged-with-child-neglect-for-using-medical-marijuana-while-pregnant-the-arizona-case-could-set-a-precedent.

Nowrasteh, Alex. 2015. "Immigration and Crime—What the Research Says." Cato Institute, July 14. https://www.cato.org/blog/immigration-crime-what-research-says.

Nwanne, G. 2020. "There Is No Queer Liberation without Prison Abolition." *Them*, June 19. https://www.them.us/story/no-queer-liberation-without-prison-abolition.

Oakland Power Projects. 2020. "Alternatives to Calling the Police." In *Beyond Survival: Strategies and Stories from the Transformative Justice Movement*, edited by E. Dixon and L. Piepzna-Samarasinha. Chico, CA: AK Press.

Oakre, Fisayo. 2023. "New York Asylum Office Rejects Valid Asylum Seekers Just to Save Time." *Documented*, October 27. https://documentedny.com/2023/10/27/new-york-asylum-office-rejections-claims.

Ockerman, E. 2022. "This Is How Much More an S&P 500 CEO Earned Than the Typical Worker Last Year." *MarketWatch*, July 24. https://www.marketwatch.com/story/the-typical-s-p-500-ceo-made-324-times-more-than-the-median-paid-worker-last-year-report-11658253925.

O'Connor, A. 2021. "Excessive Drinking Rose during the Pandemic. Here Are Ways to Cut Back." *New York Times*, April 14. https://www.nytimes.com/2021/04/12/well/mind/covid-pandemic-drinking.html.

Ofer, U. 2016. "Getting It Right: Building Effective Civilian Review Boards to Oversee Police." *Seton Hall Law Review* 46.

OJJDP (Office of Juvenile Justice and Delinquency Prevention). 2006. *Disproportionate Minority Contact Technical Assistance Manual*. 3rd ed. Washington, DC: U.S. Department of Justice.

Ollove, M. 2022. "Critics Fear Abortion Bans Could Jeopardize Health of Pregnant Women." Pew Trusts, June 22. https://www.pewtrusts.org/en/research-and-analysis/blogs/stateline/2022/06/22/critics-fear-abortion-bans-could-jeopardize-health-of-pregnant-women.

Omiye, J. A., J. C. Lester, S. Spichak, V. Rotemberg, and R. Daneshjou. 2023. "Large Language Models Propagate Race-Based Medicine." *NPJ Digital Medicine* 6(1): 195. https://doi.org/10.1038/s41746-023-00939-z.

O'Neil, Cathy. 2017. "How Can We Stop Algorithms Telling Lies?" *The Guardian*, July 16. https://www.theguardian.com/technology/2017/jul/16/how-can-we-stop-algorithms-telling-lies.

OpenSecrets.org. n.d. "Donor Demographics." https://www.opensecrets.org/elections-overview/donor-demographics?cycle=2020&display=A.

Opler, Morris E. 1943. "Interview with . . . an Older Nisei." Manzanar Community Analysis Report 36, RG 210. https://historymatters.gmu.edu/d/5152.

Oppel, R. A., Jr., and J. K. Patel. 2019. "One Lawyer, 194 Felony Cases, and No Time." *New York Times*, January 31. https://www.nytimes.com/interactive/2019/01/31/us/public-defender-case-loads.html.

Oreskes, Naomi, and Erik Conway. 2012. *Merchants of Doubt: How a Handful of Scientists Obscured the Truth on Issues from Tobacco Smoke to Global Warming*. New York: Bloomsbury.

Ortiz, J. M., and H. Jackey. 2019. "The System Is Not Broken, It Is Intentional: The Prisoner Reentry Industry as Deliberate Structural Violence." *Prison Journal* 99(4): 484–503. https://doi.org/10.1177/0032885519852090.

Oshinsky, David. 1996. *Worse Than Slavery: Parchman Farm and the Ordeal of Jim Crow Justice*. New York: Free Press.

Osler, Mark W. 2020. "The First Step Act and the Brutal Timidity of Criminal Law Reform." *New England Law Review* 54(2): 161–98.

Ossoff, J., and R. Johnson. 2022. "Sexual Abuse of Female Inmates in Federal Prisons: Staff Report." U.S. Senate Committee on Homeland Security and Governmental Affairs, December 13. https://www.hsgac.senate.gov/wp-content/uploads/imo/media/doc/2022-12-13

%20PSI%20Staff%20Report%20-%20Sexual%20Abuse%20of%20Female%20Inmates%20in%20Federal%20Prisons.pdf.

Ostler, Jeffrey, and Nick Estes. 2017. "The Supreme Law of the Land: Standing Rock and the Dakota Access Pipeline." *Indian Country*, January 16. https://indiancountrymedianetwork.com/news/opinions/supreme-law-land-standing-rock-dakota-access-pipeline.

Oxfam. 2022. "Ten Richest Men Double Their Fortunes in Pandemic while Incomes of 99 Percent of Humanity Fall." Press release, January 17. https://www.oxfam.org/en/press-releases/ten-richest-men-double-their-fortunes-pandemic-while-incomes-99-percent-humanity.

Packer, Herbert. 1964. "Two Models of the Criminal Process." *University of Pennsylvania Law Review* 113:1–23.

Paik, L. 2017. "Critical Perspectives on Intersectionality and Criminology: Introduction." *Theoretical Criminology* 21(1): 4–10. https://doi.org/10.1177/1362480616677495.

Paltrow, Lynn, and Jeanne Flavin. 2013. "Arrests of and Forced Interventions on Pregnant Women in the United States, 1973–2005: Implications for Women's Legal Status and Public Health." *Journal of Health Politics, Policy and Law* 38(2): 299–343.

Panfil, Vanessa. 2013. "Better Left Unsaid? The Role of Agency in Queer Criminological Research." *Critical Criminology* 22(1): 99–111.

Panfil, V. R. 2017. *The Gang's All Queer: The Lives of Gay Gang Members*. New York: New York University Press.

Pang, M. S., and P. A. Pavlou. 2017. "Armed with Technology: The Impact on Fatal Shootings by the Police." Office of Justice Programs. https://bja.ojp.gov/sites/g/files/xyckuh186/files/bwc/pdfs/SSRN-id2808662.pdf.

Parker, K., J. M. Horowitz, R. Morin, and M. H. Lopez. 2015. "Chapter 1: Race and Multiracial Americans in the U.S. Census." Pew Research Center, June 11. https://www.pewresearch.org/social-trends/2015/06/11/chapter-1-race-and-multiracial-americans-in-the-u-s-census/#mulattos-quadroons-and-octoroons.

Parris, D., E. Fulks, and C. Kelley. 2021. "Anti-LGBTQ Policy Proposals Can Harm Youth Mental Health." *Child Trends*, July 6. https://www.childtrends.org/publications/anti-lgbtq-policy-proposals-can-harm-youth-mental-health.

Pasquale, Frank. 2017. "Secret Algorithms Threaten the Rule of Law." *MIT Technology Review*, June 1. https://www.technologyreview.com/s/608011/secret-algorithms-threaten-the-rule-of-law.

Patterson, William, ed. (1951) 1970. *We Charge Genocide: The Crime of Government against the Negro People*. Reprint; New York: International Publishers.

———. 1971. *The Man Who Charged Genocide: An Autobiography*. New York: International Publishers.

Pearce, F. 1976. *Crimes of the Powerful: Marxism, Crime and Deviance*. London: Pluto Press.

Pease, B. 2010. *Undoing Privilege: Unearned Advantage in a Divided World*. London: Zed.

Persson, L., B. M. C. Almroth, C. D. Collins, S. Cornell, C. A. de Wit, M. L. Diamond, P. Fantke, et al. 2022. "Outside the Safe Operating Space of the Planetary Boundary for Novel Entities." *Environmental Science & Technology* 56(3): 1510–21. https://doi.org/10.1021/acs.est.1c04158.

Petering, Robin. 2015. "The Potential Costs of Police Databases: Exploring the Performance of California's Gang Database (CalGang)." *Journal of Forensic Social Work* 5(1/3): 67–81. https://doi.org/10.1080/1936928X.2015.1109399.

Petersilia, Joan. 2010. "Community Corrections: Probation, Parole, and Prisoner Reentry." In *Crime and Public Policy*, edited by James Q. Wilson and Joan Petersilia, 499–531. Oxford: Oxford University Press.

Peterson-Withorn, Chase. 2022. "The 2022 Forbes 400 List of Richest Americans." *Forbes*, September 27. https://www.forbes.com/sites/chasewithorn/2022/09/27/the-2022-forbes-400-list-of-richest-americans-facts-and-figures.

———. 2023. "The 2023 Forbes 400 List of Richest Americans." *Forbes*, October 3. https://www.forbes.com/sites/chasewithorn/2023/10/03/the-2023-forbes-400-list-of-richest-americans-facts-and-figures/?sh=2a579ee2c4ce.

Petrich, D. M., T. C. Pratt, C. L. Jonson, and F. T. Cullen. 2021. "Custodial Sanctions and Reoffending: A Meta-analytic Review." *Crime and Justice* 50(1): 353–424.

Pfaff, J. 2017. *Locked In: The True Causes of Mass Incarceration—and How to Achieve Real Reform*. New York: Basic Books.

Pfohl, Stephen J. 1985. *Images of Deviance and Social Control*. New York: McGraw-Hill.

Phillips, Kaitlin S. 2020. "From Overdose to Crime Scene: The Incompatibility of Drug-Induced Homicide Statutes with Due Process." *Duke Law Journal* 70:659–704. https://scholarship.law.duke.edu/dlj/vol70/iss3/4.

Phillips, Katherine W. 2014. "How Diversity Makes Us Smarter." *Scientific American*, October 1. https://www.scientificamerican.com/article/how-diversity-makes-us-smarter.

Pickering, Sharon, Mary Bosworth, and Marie Segrave. 2014. "Guest Editor Introduction for Special Issue on Borders, Gender and Punishment." *Punishment & Society* 16(2): 131–34. https://doi.org/10.1177/1462474513517021.

Pickett, J. T., A. Graham, and F. T. Cullen. 2022. "The American Racial Divide in Fear of the Police." *Criminology* 60:291–320.

Pien, D. 2010. "Black Panther Party's Free Breakfast Program (1969–1980)." BlackPast, February 11. https://www.blackpast.org/african-american-history/black-panther-partys-free-breakfast-program-1969-1980.

Pierson, E., C. Simoiu, J. Overgoor, S. Corbett-Davies, D. Jenson, A. Shoemaker, V. Ramachandran, P. Barghouty, C. Phillips, R. Shroff, and S. Goel. 2020. "A Large-Scale Analysis of Racial Disparities in Police Stops across the United States." *Nature Human Behaviour* 4:736–45. https://www.nature.com/articles/s41562-020-0858-1.

Piquero, A. R. 2021. "The Policy Lessons Learned from the Criminal Justice System Response to COVID-19." *Criminology & Public Policy* 20(3): 385. https://doi.org/10.1111/1745-9133.12562.

Pizzo, Stephen, Mark Fricker, and Paul Muolo. 1991. *Inside Job: The Looting of America's Savings & Loans*. New York: Harper Perennial.

Pizzo, Stephen, and Paul Muolo. 1993. "Take the Money and Run: A Rogues Gallery of Some Lucky S & L Thieves." *New York Times Magazine*, May 9.

Platt, Anthony. 1969. *The Child Savers: The Invention of Delinquency*. Chicago: University of Chicago Press.

———. 1974. "Prospects for a Radical Criminology." *Crime and Social Justice* 1 (Fall): 1–14.

Platt, Anthony, and Randi Pollock. 1974. "Channeling Lawyers: The Careers of Public Defenders." *Issues in Criminology* 9(1): 1–31.

Pollak, Otto. 1950. *The Criminality of Women*. Philadelphia: University of Pennsylvania Press.

Pomykala, Joseph. 2000. "Bankruptcy's Origins in Debtor-Perpetrated Crime." Working paper, Department of Economics, Towson University, Towson, MD. https://ssrn.com/abstract=222377.

Porter, Nicole. 2010. *Expanding the Vote: State Felony Disenfranchisement Reform, 1997–2010*. Report, Sentencing Project. https://www.sentencingproject.org/doc/publications/publications/vr_ExpandingtheVoteFinalAddendum.pdf.

Posner, Richard. 1992. *Sex and Reason*. Cambridge, MA: Harvard University Press.

Potok, Mark. 2017. "The Trump Effect." *Intelligence Report*, February 15. https://www.splcenter.org/fighting-hate/intelligence-report/2017/trump-effect.

Potter, Hillary. 2013. "Intersectional Criminology: Interrogating Identity and Power in Criminological Research and Theory." *Critical Criminology* 21:305–18. https://doi.org/10.1007/s10612-013-9203-6.

———. 2015. *Intersectionality and Criminology: Disrupting and Revolutionizing Studies of Crime*. New York: Routledge.

Powers, A., and A. Bannon. 2022. "State Supreme Court Diversity—May 2022 Update." Brennan Center for Justice, May 25. https://www.brennancenter.org/our-work/research-reports/state-supreme-court-diversity-may-2022-update.

Pratt, Travis C., and Francis T. Cullen. 2005. "Assessing Macro-Level Predictors and Theories of Crime: A Meta-Analysis." *Crime and Justice* 32:373–450.

Pregnancy Justice. 2022. "When Fetuses Gain Personhood: Understanding the Impact of IVF, Contraception, Medical Treatment, Criminal Law, Child Support, and Beyond." https://www.pregnancyjusticeus.org/wp-content/uploads/2022/12/fetal-personhood-with-appendix-UPDATED-1.pdf.

Project LETS. n.d. "Our Mission." https://projectlets.org.

Project Regeneration. n.d. "Food Apartheid." https://regeneration.org/nexus/food-apartheid.

Provine, D. M., M. W. Varsanyi, P. G. Lewis, and S. H. Decker. 2016. *Policing Immigrants: Local Law Enforcement on the Front Lines.* Chicago: University of Chicago Press.

Purnell, D. 2022. *Becoming Abolitionists: Police, Protests, and the Pursuit of Freedom.* New York: Astra Publishing House.

Putnam, L. 2022. "Facebook Has a Child Predation Problem." *Wired,* March 13. https://www.wired.com/story/facebook-has-a-child-predation-problem.

Pyrooz, D. C., S. H. Decker, S. E. Wolfe, and Shjarback. 2016. "Was There a Ferguson Effect on Crime Rates in Large US Cities?" *Journal of Criminal Justice* 46:1–8. https://doi.org/10.1016/j.jcrimjus.2016.01.001.

Quinney, Richard. 1977. *Class, State and Crime.* New York: Longman.

Rabe-Hemp, C. 2018. *Thriving in an All-Boys Club: Female Police and Their Fight for Equality.* Lanham, MD: Rowman & Littlefield.

Rabin, A., C. Stough, A. Dutt, and F. Jacquez. 2022. "Anti-immigration Policies of the Trump Administration: A Review of Latinx Mental Health and Resilience in the Face of Structural Violence." *Analyses of Social Issues and Public Policy* 22(3): 876–905. https://doi.org/10.1111/asap.12328.

Radcliffe-Brown, A. R. (1933) 1965. *Structure and Function in Primitive Society: Essays and Addresses.* New York: Free Press.

Rafter, Nicole Hahn. 1990. *Partial Justice: Women, Prisons and Social Control.* New Brunswick, NJ: Transaction.

Raheem. n.d. "Vision." https://www.raheem.ai.

Rakia, Raven. 2019. "'I Had Nothing': How Parole Perpetuates a Cycle of Incarceration and Instability." *Prison Legal News,* July 2, 12.

Rakoff, Jed S. 2013. "Why Have No High Level Executives Been Prosecuted in Connection with the Financial Crisis?" *The Big Picture* (blog), November 14. https://ritholtz.com/2013/11/judge-rakoff-why-have-no-high-level-executives-been-prosecuted-in-connection-with-the-financial-crisis.

Ramirez, Mary Kreiner, and Steven Ramirez. 2017. *The Case for the Corporate Death Penalty: Restoring Law and Order on Wall Street.* New York: New York University Press.

Ramos, J., and M. Wenger. 2018. "Effects in Disguise: The Importance of Controlling for Constructs at Multiple Levels in Macro-level Immigration and Crime Research." *City & Community* 17(4): 1100–18. https://doi.org/10.1111/cico.12343.

Rani Jha, Meeta. 2016. *The Global Beauty Industry: Colorism, Racism, and the National Body.* New York: Routledge.

Rawls, John. 1971. *A Theory of Justice.* Cambridge, MA: Belknap Press.

Rayasam, R., N. D. McCaskill, B. Jin, and A. J. Vestal. 2021. "Why State Legislatures Are Still Very White—and Very Male." *Politico,* February 23. https://www.politico.com/interactives/2021/state-legislature-demographics.

Reagan, Leslie J. 2022. *When Abortion Was a Crime: Women, Medicine, and Law in the United States, 1867–1973.* Berkeley: University of California Press.

Rebouché, Rachel. 2023. "Medication Abortion and the Post-Dobbs Legal Landscape." *Seton Hall Law Review* 53(1633). https://scholarship.shu.edu/cgi/viewcontent.cgi?article=3554&context=shlr.

Redstockings. 1978. *Feminist Revolution.* New York: Random House.

Reel, Monte. 2016. "Secret Cameras Record Baltimore's Every Move from Above." *Bloomberg.* https://www.bloomberg.com/features/2016-baltimore-secret-surveillance.

Reeves, Richard. 2015. *Infamy: The Shocking Story of the Japanese American Internment in World War II.* New York: Henry Holt.

Reference for Business. 2022a. "National Amusements Inc." https://www.referenceforbusiness.com/history2/48/National-Amusements-Inc.html.

———. 2022b. "Viacom Inc." https://www.referenceforbusiness.com/history2/77/Viacom-Inc.html.

Reilly, Peter R. 2015. "Justice Deferred Is Justice Denied: We Must End Our Failed Experiment in Deferring Corporate Criminal Prosecutions." *Brigham Young University Law Review* 2015(2): 307–58.

Reiman, Jeffrey, and Paul Leighton. 2010. *The Rich Get Richer: A Reader.* Boston, MA: Allyn & Bacon.

———. 2023. *The Rich Get Richer and the Poor Get Prison.* 13th ed. New York: Routledge.

Reingold, B., K. L. Haynie, and K. Widner. 2021. *Race, Gender, and Political Representation.* New York: Oxford University Press.

Ren, J., and J. Feagin. 2021. "Face Mask Symbolism in Anti-Asian Hate Crimes." *Ethnic and Racial Studies* 44(5): 746–58.

Renzetti, Claire M. 1998. "Connecting the Dots: Women, Public Policy, and Social Control." In *Crime Control and Women*, edited by Susan L. Miller, 181–89. Thousand Oaks, CA: Sage.

Renzetti, C. M. 2013. *Feminist Criminology.* New York: Routledge.

Rheingold, H. 2002. *Smart Mobs: The Next Social Revolution.* New York: Basic Books.

Rhinehart, L., and C. McNicholas. 2024. "What's behind the Corporate Effort to Kneecap the National Labor Relations Board?" Economic Policy Institute, March 7. https://www.epi.org/blog/whats-behind-the-corporate-effort-to-kneecap-the-national-labor-relations-board-spacex-amazon-trader-joes-and-starbucks-are-trying-to-have-the-nlrb-declared-unconstitutional.

Ricks, A. 2017. "Latinx Immigrant Crime Victims Fear Seeking Help." *Urban Wire*, September 25. https://www.urban.org/urban-wire/latinx-immigrant-crime-victims-fear-seeking-help.

Rierden, Andi. 1997. *The Farm: Life inside a Women's Prison.* Amherst: University of Massachusetts Press.

Rios, Victor. 2011. *Punished: Policing the Lives of Black and Latino Boys.* New York: New York University Press.

Ritchie, Andrea. 2017. *Invisible No More: Police Violence against Black Women and Women of Color.* Boston, MA: Beacon Press.

Ritholtz, Barry. 2008a. "CEO Clawback Provisions in the Bailout?" *The Big Picture* (blog), September 24. https://bigpicture.typepad.com/comments/2008/09/ceo-clawback-pr.html.

———. 2008b. "A Memo Found in the Street: Uncle Sam the Enabler." In *The Rich Get Richer and the Poor Get Prison: A Reader*, edited by Jeffrey Reiman and Paul Leighton, 100–102. Boston, MA: Allyn & Bacon/Pearson.

———. 2008c. "What Is 'Nonfeasance'?" *Seeking Alpha*, August 18. https://seekingalpha.com/article/91465-what-is-nonfeasance.

———. 2008d. "Where's the Ref?" *Forbes*, September 12. https://www.forbes.com/home/2008/09/12/lehman-greenspan-regulation-opinions-cx_br_0912ritholtz.html.

———. 2009a. *Bailout Nation.* Hoboken, NJ: Wiley.

———. 2009b. "Tactical Error: Health Care vs. Finance Regulatory Reform." *The Big Picture* (blog), September 9. https://www.ritholtz.com/blog/2009/09/finance-reform-vs-health-care-reform.

———. 2013. "Meet Uncle Sam, Your Partner in Crime." *Bloomberg*, November 5. https://www.bloomberg.com/news/2013-11-05/meet-uncle-sam-your-partner-in-crime.ht.

———. 2022. "Top 0.1%: How Much Wealth Does It Take?" *The Big Picture* (blog), December 5. https://ritholtz.com/2022/12/top-01-how-much.

Ritzer, G. 2004. *The McDonaldization of Society.* Thousand Oaks, CA: Pine Forge Press.

Roach, Stephen. 2006. "Globalization's New Underclass." Morgan Stanley Global Economic Forum, March 3.

Robbins, I. 2014. "Kidnapping Incorporated: The Unregulated Youth-Transportation Industry and the Potential for Abuse." *American Criminal Law Review* 51(3): 563–600.

Roberts, Dorothy E. 1993. "Crime, Race, and Reproduction." *Tulane Law Review* 67(6): 1945–77.

Robinson, N. 2023. "How DHS Is Fueling Georgia's 'Terrorism' Crackdown on Cop City Protests." *Just Security*, June 15. https://www.justsecurity.org/86944/how-dhs-is-fueling-georgias-terrorism-crackdown-on-cop-city-protests.

Rodrigues, Meghie. 2022. "How Climate Change Could Drive an Increase in Gender-Based Violence." *Nature*, July 13. https://www.nature.com/articles/d41586-022-01903-9.

Roeder, Oliver, Lauren-Brooke Eisen, and Julia Bowling. 2015. *What Caused the Crime Decline?* Report, Brennan Center for Justice. https://www.brennancenter.org/sites/default/files/publications/What_Caused_The_Crime_Decline.pdf.

Rojas, R. 2021. "Homer Plessy's Arrest in 1892 Led to a Landmark Ruling. Now He May Get Justice." *New York Times*, November 12. https://www.nytimes.com/2021/11/12/us/plessy-ferguson-pardon.html.

Rojas, R., and S. Keenan. 2023. "Georgia Officials Target Bail Fund in Crackdown on 'Cop

City' Protests." *New York Times*, June 2. https://www.nytimes.com/2023/06/02/us/cop-city-atlanta-protests.html.

Romo, V. 2021. "USC Agrees to $852 Million Settlement to End Sex Abuse Litigation." National Public Radio, March 25. https://www.npr.org/2021/03/25/981435791/usc-agrees-852-million-settlement-to-end-sex-abuse-litigation.

Rosenfeld, R. 2016. "Documenting and Explaining the 2015 Homicide Rise: Research Directions." National Institute of Justice. https://www.ojp.gov/pdffiles1/nij/249895.pdf.

Rosenfeld, R., and J. Wallman. 2019. "Did De-policing Cause the Increase in Homicide Rates?" *Criminology & Public Policy* 18(1): 51–75. https://doi.org/10.1111/1745-9133.12414.

Ross, L. 1998. *Inventing the Savage: The Social Construction of Native American Criminality*. Austin: University of Texas Press.

Rothe, D., and D. Kauzlarich. 2022. *Crimes of the Powerful: White-Collar Crime and Beyond*. New York: Routledge.

Rothstein, R. 2018. *The Color of Law: A Forgotten History of How Our Government Segregated America*. New York: Norton.

Ruiz, N. G., K. Edwards, and M. H. Lopez. 2021. "One-Third of Asian Americans Fear Threats, Physical Attacks and Most Say Violence against Them Is Rising." Pew Research Center, April 21. https://www.pewresearch.org/fact-tank/2021/04/21/one-third-of-asian-americans-fear-threats-physical-attacks-and-most-say-violence-against-them-is-rising.

Rusche, Georg, and Otto Kirchheimer. (1939) 1968. *Punishment and Social Structure*. Reprint; New York: Russell & Russell.

Rushin, S., and R. Michalski. 2020. "Police Funding." *Florida Law Review* 72:277–330.

Russell, K. 2019. "Black Criminology in the 21st Century." In *Building a Black Criminology*, edited by J. Unnever, S. L. Gabbidon, and C. Chouhy. New York: Taylor & Francis.

Russell K. K. 1992. "Development of a Black Criminology and the Role of the Black Criminologist." *Justice Quarterly* 9(4): 667–83. https://doi.org/10.1080/07418829200091601.

Russell, Katheryn K. 1998. *The Color of Crime: Racial Hoaxes, White Fear, Black Protectionism, Police Harassment, and Other Macroaggressions*. New York: New York University Press.

Saadi, A., M. De Trinidad Young, C. Patler, J. L. Estrada, and H. Venters. 2020. "Understanding US Immigration Detention." *Health and Human Rights* 22(1): 187–97.

Sabbeth, K. A., and J. Steinberg. 2023. "The Gender of Gideon." *UNC Law Review* 69(1130). https://scholarship.law.unc.edu/cgi/viewcontent.cgi?article=1613&context=faculty_publications.

Said, E. W. 1994. *Culture and Imperialism*. New York: Vintage.

Saleh-Hanna, V., J. Williams, and M. J. Coyle, eds. 2023. *Abolish Criminology*. London: Routledge. https://doi.org/10.4324/9780367817114.

SAMHSA (Substance Abuse and Mental Health Administration). 2012. "Results from the 2012 National Survey on Drug Use and Health: Detailed Tables." https://www.oas.samhsa.gov.

Samuels, B. 2023. "Here Are the History-Making LGBTQ Officials in the Biden Administration." *The Hill*, June 6. https://thehill.com/homenews/administration/4030255-here-are-the-history-making-lgbtq-officials-in-the-biden-administration.

Sandoval, E. 2022. "In San Antonio, the Poor Live on Their Own Islands of Heat." *New York Times*, July 26. https://www.nytimes.com/2022/07/26/us/texas-heat-poverty-islands-san-antonio.html.

Sapkota, D., S. Dennison, J. Allen, J. Gamble, C. Williams, N. Malope-Rwodzi, L. Baar, J Ransley, and T. Renae McGee. 2022. "Navigating Pregnancy and Early Motherhood in Prison: A Thematic Analysis of Mothers' Experiences." *Health & Justice* 10:1–15. https://doi.org/10.1186/s40352-022-00196-4.

Savage, C. 2022. "As a Public Defender, Supreme Court Nominee Helped Clients Others Avoided." *New York Times*, March 21. https://www.nytimes.com/2022/02/26/us/politics/ketanji-brown-jackson-supreme-court.html.

Schaeffer, K. 2023. "The Changing Face of Congress in 8 Charts." Pew Research Center, February 7. https://www.pewresearch.org/short-reads/2023/02/07/the-changing-face-of-congress.

Schenwar, M., and V. Law. 2020. *Prison by Any Other Name: The Harmful Consequences of Popular Reforms*. New York: New Press.

Schept, J. 2022. *Coal, Cages, Crisis*. New York: New York University Press.

Schlosser, Eric. 1998. "The Prison-Industrial Complex." *Atlantic*, December 1. https://www.theatlantic.com/doc/199812/prisons.

Schmitt, Richard. 2008. "FBI Saw Threat of Loan Crisis." *Los Angeles Times*, August 25, A1.

Schrag, P. 2010. *Not Fit for Our Society: Immigration and Nativism in America*. Berkeley: University of California Press.

Schweingruber, D. 2000. "Mob Sociology and Escalated Force: Sociology's Contribution to Repressive Police Tactics." *Sociological Quarterly* 41(3): 371–89. https://doi.org/10.1111/j.1533-8525.2000.tb00083.x.

Schweingruber, D., and R. T. Wohlstein. 2005. "The Madding Crowd Goes to School: Myths about Crowds in Introductory Sociology Textbooks." *Teaching Sociology* 33(2): 136–53. https://doi.org/10.1177/0092055X0503300202.

Schwendinger, H., and J. Schwendinger. 2001. "Defenders of Order or Guardians of Human Rights?" In *What Is Crime? Controversies over the Nature of Crime and What to Do about It*, edited by Stuart Henry and Mark Lanier. Lanham, MD: Rowman & Littlefield.

Scott, D. G., and J. Sim, eds. 2023. *Demystifying Power, Crime and Social Harm*. eBook. Palgrave Macmillan.

Scott, D. I. 2018. "Latina Fortitude in the Face of Disadvantage: Exploring the Conditioning Effects of Ethnic Identity and Gendered Ethnic Identity on Latina Offending." *Critical Criminology* 26(1): 49–73.

Scott, J., and D. Leonhardt. 2005. "Class in America: Shadowy Lines That Still Divide." *New York Times*, May 15.

Scully, Diana. 1990. *Understanding Sexual Violence: A Study of Convicted Rapists*. London: HarperCollins.

Segalov, Michael. 2015. "We Spoke to the Activist behind #BlackLivesMatter about Racism in Britain and America." *Vice*, February 2. https://www.vice.com/en_us/article/mv5y3x/patrisse-cullors-interview-michael-segalov-188.

Sellin, Thorsten. 1928. "The Negro Criminal: A Statistical Note." *Annals of the American Academy of Political and Social Science* 140:52–64.

Selman, Donna, and Paul Leighton. 2010. *Punishment for Sale*. Lanham, MD: Rowman & Littlefield.

Selman, K. J. 2021. "Carving the Terrain of Freedom: The Multidimensionality of Youth-Focused Abolition Geography." *Social Justice* 48(3): 31–57.

Senate Appropriations Committee. 2021. "Domestic Violent Extremism in America." May 12. https://www.congress.gov/117/chrg/CHRG-117shrg49554/CHRG-117shrg49554.pdf.

Senate Permanent Subcommittee on Investigations. 2012. *HSBC Exposed U.S. Financial System to Money Laundering, Drug, Terrorist Financing Risks*. U.S. Senate Committee on Homeland Security and Governmental Affairs, July 16. https://www.hsgac.senate.gov/subcommittees/investigations/minority-news/hsbc-exposed-u-s-financial-system-to-money-laundering-drug-terrorist-financing-risks.

Seybold, M. 2017. "Barnum Presidents and Benevolent Monopolists: Mark Twain, Amazon, and the Futility of Antitrust." *Los Angeles Review of Books*, August 30. https://lareviewofbooks.org/article/barnum-presidents-and-benevolent-monopolists-mark-twain-amazon-futility-antitrust/#.

Sforza, L. 2023. "Survey: Nearly Two-Thirds of Americans Are Living Paycheck to Paycheck." *The Hill*, January 30. https://thehill.com/policy/finance/3836902-survey-nearly-two-thirds-of-americans-are-living-paycheck-to-paycheck.

Shah, R. 2021. Editor's introduction to the special issue, "Centering the Margins: Addressing the Implementation Gap of Critical Criminology." *Critical Criminology* 29(1): 3–9. https://doi.org/10.1007/s10612-021-09560-6.

Shanahan, J., and Z. Kurti. 2022. *States of Incarceration: Rebellion, Reform, and America's Punishment System*. London: Reaktion Books.

Shapero, J. 2022. "'Incel' Movement Has Ramped Up Calls for Violence, Report Says." *The Hill*, September 23. https://thehill.com/policy/technology/3658185-incel-movement-has-ramped-up-calls-for-violence-report-says.

Shaw, Clifford R., and Henry D. McKay. 1942. *Juvenile Delinquency and Urban Areas: A Study of Rates of Delinquents in Relation to Differential Characteristics of Local Communities in American Cities*. Chicago: University of Chicago Press.

Sheehan, K. 2017. "Is Living as an Undocumented Immigrant in the U.S. a Crime?" *Politifact*, December 1. https://www.politifact.com

/factchecks/2017/dec/02/kathy-sheehan/being -undocumented-immigrant-us-not-crime.

Shelden, R. G., and P. V. Vasiliev. 2018. *Controlling the Dangerous Classes: A History of Criminal Justice in America.* Waveland Press.

Sherman, Alex. "Sumner Redstone Handed a Media Empire to His Daughter, Shari, Who Now Controls Its Fate." CNBC, August 12, 2020. https://www.cnbc.com/2020/08/12/shari -redstone-now-fully-controls-the-fate-of-via comcbs.html.

Sherman, Amy. 2020. "Yes, Congress Has Disproportionate Share of Millionaires, but Claim's Numbers Are Off." *Politifact*, January 22. https://www.politifact.com/factchecks /2020/jan/22/facebook-posts/yes-congress-has -disproportionate-share-millionair.

Sherman, Francine. 2012. "Justice for Girls: Are We Making Progress?" *UCLA Law Review* 59:1584–627.

Shoalts, D. 2022. "Hockey Canada C.E.O. and Board of Directors Resign amid Controversy." *New York Times*, October 11. https://www .nytimes.com/2022/10/11/sports/hockey/hockey -canada-board-resigns.html.

Silber Mohamed, H., and E. M. Farris. 2020. "'Bad Hombres'? An Examination of Identities in U.S. Media Coverage of Immigration." *Journal of Ethnic and Migration Studies* 46(1): 158–76. https://doi.org/10.1080/1369183X .2019.1574221.

Silva, T. J. 2018. "Straight Identity and Same-Sex Desire: Conservatism, Homophobia, and Straight Culture." *Social Forces* 97(3): 1067–94. https://doi.org/10.1093/sf/soy064.

Simon, David. 1999. *Elite Deviance.* 6th ed. Boston, MA: Allyn & Bacon.

Singer, N. 2024. "Teen Girls Confront an Epidemic of Deepfake Nudes in Schools." *New York Times*, April 8. https://www.nytimes.com/2024 /04/08/technology/deepfake-ai-nudes-westfield -high-school.html.

Skeem, J., L. Montoya, and C. Lowenkamp. 2023. "Understanding Racial Disparities in Pretrial Detention Recommendations to Shape Policy Reform." *Criminology & Public Policy* 22(2): 233–62. https://doi.org/10.1111/1745-9133 .12620.

Skoy, E. 2021. "Black Lives Matter Protests, Fatal Police Interactions, and Crime." *Contemporary*

*Economic Policy* 39(2): 280–91. https://doi.org /10.1111/coep.12508.

Slakoff, D. C., and P. K. Brennan. 2020. "White, Black, and Latina Female Victims in U.S. News: A Multivariate and Intersectional Analysis of Story Differences." *Race and Justice* 13(2): 155–84. https://doi.org/10.1177 /2153368720961837.

Smarsh, Sarah. 2014. "Poor Teeth." *Aeon*, October 23. https://aeon.co/essays/there-is-no-shame -worse-than-poor-teeth-in-a-rich-world.

Smith, E. B., and P. Kuntz. 2013. "CEO Pay 1,795-to-1 Multiple of Wages Skirts U.S. Law." *Bloomberg*, April 29. https://www.bloomberg .com/news/2013-04-30/ceo-pay-1-795-to-1 -multiple-of-workers-skirts-law-as-sec-delays .html.

Smothers, Ronald. 1995. "Wave of Prison Uprisings Provokes Debate on Crack." *New York Times*, October 24, A12.

Smythe, Christie. 2013. "HSBC Judge Approves $1.9 Billion Drug-Money Laundering Accord." *Bloomberg*, July 3. https://www.bloomberg.com /news/articles/2013-07-02/hsbc-judge-approves -1-9b-drug-money-laundering-accord.

Soltes, Eugene F. 2019a. "The Frequency of Corporate Misconduct: Public Enforcement versus Private Reality." *Journal of Financial Crime* 26(4): 923–37. https://doi.org/10.1108/JFC-10 -2018-0107.

———. 2019b. "Where Is Your Company Most Prone to Lapses in Integrity?" *Harvard Business Review* 97(4): 51–54. https://hbr.org/2019/07 /where-is-your-company-most-prone-to-lapses -in-integrity.

Sorensen, A. 2021. "Representation Matters: Women & Working-Class Diversity in Congress." *University of Minnesota: The Gender Policy Report*, October 19. https://genderpoli cyreport.umn.edu/working-class-diversity-in -congress.

South and South. 2021. *City Preparedness for the Climate Crisis: A Multidisciplinary Approach.* Northampton, MA: Edward Elgar.

Spade, D. 2020. *Mutual Aid: Building Solidarity during This Crisis (and the Next).* New York: Verso.

Spade, D., and R. Sirvent. 2020. "BAR Abolition Mutual Aid Spotlight: Ujimaa Medics." *Black Agenda Report*, March 25. https://www

.blackagendareport.com/bar-abolition-mutual-aid-spotlight-ujimaa-medics.

Spencer, C. 2021. "More Than a Third of White Students Lie about Their Race on College Applications, Survey Finds." *The Hill*, October 31. https://thehill.com/changing-america/enrichment/education/577722-more-than-a-third-of-white-students-lie-about-their.

Spinney, E., M. Cohen, W. Feyerherm, R. Stephenson, M. Yeide, and T. Shreve. 2018. "Disproportionate Minority Contact in the U.S. Juvenile Justice System: A Review of the DMC Literature, 2001–2014, Part I." *Journal of Crime and Justice* 41(5): 573–95. https://doi.org/10.1080/0735648X.2018.1516155.

Spivack, C. 2021. "Receptionist? Maître d'? Now You're Also a Vaxx Bouncer." *Curbed*, August 23. https://www.curbed.com/2021/08/nyc-vaccine-mandate-enforcement-bouncers.html.

Spohn, C. 2000. "Thirty Years of Sentencing Reform: The Quest for a Racially Neutral Sentencing Process." *Criminal Justice* 3(1): 427–501.

———. 2017. "Race and Sentencing Disparity." *Reforming Criminal Justice: A Report of the Academy for Justice on Bridging the Gap between Scholarship and Reform* 4:182. https://law.asu.edu/sites/default/files/pdf/academy_for_justice/9_Criminal_Justice_Reform_Vol_4_Race-and-Sentencing-Disparity.pdf.

Standing, Guy. 2014. *The Precariat: The New Dangerous Class*. New York: Bloomsbury.

Starr, Douglas. 1998. *Blood: An Epic History of Medicine and Commerce*. New York: Quill.

Steffen, W., K. Richardson, J. Rockström, S. E. Cornell, I. Fetzer, E. M. Bennett, R. Biggs, S. R. Carpenter, et al. 2015. "Planetary Boundaries: Guiding Human Development on a Changing Planet." *Science* 347(6223): 1259855. https://www.science.org/doi/full/10.1126/science.1259855.

Steffensmeier, D., J. T. Ulmer, B. Feldmeyer, and C. T. Harris. 2010. "Scope and Conceptual Issues in Testing the Race-Crime Invariance Thesis: Black, White, and Hispanic Comparisons." *Criminology* 48(4): 1133–69. https://doi.org/10.1111/j.1745-9125.2010.00214.x.

Steffensmeier, Darrell, Jennifer Schwartz, and Michael Roche. 2013. "Gender and Twenty-First-Century Corporate Crime: Female Involvement and the Gender Gap in Enron-Era Corporate Frauds." *American Sociological Review* 78(3): 448–76.

Stein, B. 2006. "In Class Welfare, Guess Which Class Is Winning." *New York Times*, November 26. https://www.nytimes.com/2006/11/26/business/yourmoney/26every.html.

Stephens-Griffin, N. 2023. "Embracing 'Abolition Ecology': A Green Criminological Rejoinder." *Critical Criminology* 31:433–49. https://doi.org/10.1007/s10612-022-09672-7.

Stephenson, Neal. 1992. *Snow Crash*. New York: Bantam.

Stevens, G., H. Ishizawa, and D. Grbic. 2015. "Measuring Race and Ethnicity in the Censuses of Australia, Canada, and the United States: Parallels and Paradoxes." *Canadian Studies in Population* 42(1–2): 13. https://doi.org/10.25336/P6PW39.

Stiglitz, Joseph E. 2010. Interview with Sam Gustin and Michael Rainey. *Daily Finance*, October 20. https://www.dailyfinance.com/2010/10/22/joseph-stiglitz-interview-transcript.

———. 2012. *The Price of Inequality: How Today's Divided Society Endangers Our Future*. New York: Norton.

Stockdale, K. J., R. Sweeney, and C. McCluskey Dean. 2021. "Exploring the Criminology Curriculum: Using the Intersectionality Matrix as a Pedagogical Tool to Develop Students' Critical Information Literacy Skills." *Journal of Criminal Justice Education* 33(4): 1–19. https://doi.org/10.1080/10511253.2021.2019290.

Stoller, M. 2019. *Goliath: The 100-Year War between Monopoly Power and Democracy*. New York: Simon & Schuster Paperbacks.

———. 2022. "Antitrust Cops Put Handcuffs for CEOs on the Table." *BIG by Matt Stoller*, March 3. https://mattstoller.substack.com/p/antitrust-cops-handcuffs-are-coming.

———. 2023. "All Rise: How Judges Rule America." *BIG by Matt Stoller*, May 3. https://mattstoller.substack.com/p/all-rise-how-judges-rule-america.

Strauss, David. 2007. "Militarization of Policing." In *Battleground: Criminal Justice*, edited by G. Barak, 454–59. Westport, CT: Greenwood.

Strauss, David A. 2023. "Rights, Remedies, and Texas's S.B. 8." *Supreme Court Review* 2022:81–110.

Stumpf, Juliet. 2006. "The Crimmigration Crisis: Immigrants, Crime, and Sovereign Power." *American University Law Review* 56:367–419.

Subramanian, Ram, and Alison Shames. 2013. "Sentencing and Prison Practices in Germany and the Netherlands: Implications for the United States." Report for Vera Institute of Justice, New York, October. https://www.vera.org/sites/default/files/resources/downloads/european-american-prison-report-v3.pdf.

Sugata, M. 2019. "Title Lending as a Predatory Practice: Subprime Populations and Financial Violence." *Sociology Compass* 13(7). https://doi.org/10.1111/soc4.12703.

Sutherland, E. H. 1939. "White-Collar Criminality." *American Sociological Review* 5:1–12. https://doi.org/10.2307/2083937.

———. 1985. *White Collar Crime: The Uncut Version*. New Haven, CT: Yale University Press.

Sutton, T. E., and L. G. Simons. 2021. "A Longitudinal Test of a Feminist Pathways Model among Black Youth: Incorporating Racial Discrimination and School Difficulties." *Feminist Criminology* 16(1): 26–46. https://doi.org/10.1177/1557085120923042.

Swift, Pat. 1997. "At the Intersection of Racial Politics and Domestic Abuse." *Buffalo News*, December 27, B7.

Sykes, Bryan, and Alex Piquero. 2009. "Structuring and Re-Creating Inequality: Health Testing Policies, Race, and the Criminal Justice System." *Annals of the American Academy of Political and Social Science* 623 (May): 214–29.

Sykes, Gresham. 1958. *The Society of Captives: A Study of a Maximum Security Prison*. Princeton, NJ: Princeton University Press.

Szalavitz, M. 2006. *Help at any Cost: How the Troubled-Teen Industry Cons Parents and Hurts Kids*. New York: Penguin.

Taibbi, Matt. 2011. "Why Isn't Wall Street in Jail?" *Rolling Stone*, March 3. https://www.rollingstone.com/politics/news/why-isnt-wall-street-in-jail-20110216.

———. 2014. *The Divide: American Injustice in the Age of the Wealth Gap*. New York: Spiegel & Grau.

———. 2020. *Revenge of the Money Launderers*. Racket News, September 25. https://taibbi.substack.com/p/revenge-of-the-money-launderers-b84.

———. 2022. "Meet the Censored: Cherie DeVille." *TK News* by Matt Taibbi, March 9. https://taibbi.substack.com/p/meet-the-censored-cherie-deville.

Taub, Stephen. 2024. "The 23nd Annual Ranking of the Highest-Earning Hedge Fund Managers." *Institutional Investor*, March 27. https://www.institutionalinvestor.com/article/2d0quhk4ghsahyyia26m8/corner-office/the-23nd-annual-ranking-of-the-highest-earning-hedge-fund-managers.

Tavernise, S. 2019. "Why Women Getting Abortions Now Are More Likely to Be Poor." *New York Times*, July 9. https://www.nytimes.com/2019/07/09/us/abortion-access-inequality.html.

TCR Staff. 2021. "Race Can Determine Who Avoids Prison: Study." *The Crime Report*, July 30. https://thecrimereport.org/2021/07/30/race-can-determine-who-avoids-prison-study.

Tenant and Neighborhood Councils (TANC). n.d. "Who We Are." https://baytanc.com/abolition-now.

Theoharis, Jeanne. 2015. "How History Got the Rosa Parks Story Wrong." *Washington Post*, December 1. https://www.washingtonpost.com/posteverything/wp/2015/12/01/how-history-got-the-rosa-parks-story-wrong.

*This American Life*. 2008. "Giant Pool of Money." April 9, program 355. Transcript available at https://www.thisamericanlife.org/radio-archives/episode/355/The-Giant-Pool-of-Money.

Tippett, Rebecca, Avis Jones-DeWeever, Maya Rockeymoore, Darrick Hamilton, and William Darrity Jr. 2014. "Beyond Broke: Why Closing the Racial Wealth Gap Is a Priority for National Economic Security." Center for Global Policy Solutions, April 21.

Tolnay, S. E., and E. M. Beck. 1995. *A Festival of Violence: An Analysis of Southern Lynchings, 1882–1930*. Urbana: University of Illinois Press.

Tombs, S. 2023. "Assessing the Harms of Crime: A New Framework for Criminal Policy." Book review. *British Journal of Criminology* 63(6). https://doi.org/10.1093/bjc/azad019.

Tonry, Michael. 1995. *Malign Neglect: Race, Crime, and Punishment in America*. New York: Oxford University Press.

———. 2020. *Doing Justice, Preventing Crime*. New York: Oxford University Press.

Toor, A. 2018. "'Our Identity Is Often What's Triggering Surveillance': How Government Surveillance of #BlackLivesMatter Violates the First Amendment Freedom of Association." *Rutgers Computer & Technology Law Journal* 44(2): 286.

Tosh, Sarah. 2019. "Drugs, Crime, and Aggravated Felony Deportations: Moral Panic Theory and the Legal Construction of the 'Criminal Alien.'" *Critical Criminology* 27(2): 329–45. https://doi.org/10.1007/s10612-019-09446-8.

———. 2023. *The Immigration Law Death Penalty: Aggravated Felonies, Deportation, and Legal Resistance.* New York: New York University Press.

Totten, Mark D. 2000. *Guys, Gangs, and Girlfriend Abuse.* Petersborough, ON: Broadview.

TRAC. n.d. *Immigration Court Primer.* TRAC. https://trac.syr.edu/immigration/quickfacts/about_eoir.html.

———. 2023. *Corporate and White-Collar Prosecutions Hit New All-Time Lows in FY 2022.* TRAC-FBI. https://trac.syr.edu/reports/708.

———. *Immigration Detention Quick Facts.* TRAC Immigration. Accessed February 4, 2024. https://trac.syr.edu/immigration/quickfacts.

Travis, Jeremy. 2002. "Invisible Punishment: An Instrument of Social Exclusion." In *Invisible Punishment: The Collateral Consequences of Mass Imprisonment*, edited by Meda Chesney-Lind and Marc Mauer, 15–36. New York: New Press.

Travis, J., and B. Western. 2021. "The Era of Punitive Excess." Brennan Center for Justice, April 13. https://www.brennancenter.org/our-work/analysis-opinion/era-punitive-excess.

Travis, J., B. Western, and S. Redburn, eds. 2014. *The Growth of Incarceration in the United States: Exploring Causes and Consequences.* Washington, DC: National Academies Press.

Tregea, W. S. 2014. *Prisoners on Criminology: Convict Life Stories and Crime Prevention.* Lanham, MD: Lexington Books.

Trevor Project. 2022. "2022 National Survey on LGBTQ Youth Mental Health." https://www.thetrevorproject.org/survey-2022.

Treyger, Elina, Aaron Chalfin, and Charles Loeffler. 2014. "Immigration Enforcement, Policing, and Crime." *Criminology & Public Policy* 13(2): 285–322.

Trump, Donald. 2015. "Full Text: Donald Trump Announces a Presidential Bid." *Washington Post*, June 16. https://www.washingtonpost.com/news/post-politics/wp/2015/06/16/full-text-donald-trump-announces-a-presidential-bid.

Turnbull, Sarah, Monish Bhatia, and Gemma Lousley. 2020. "Editors' Introduction to the Special Issue, 'Critical Engagements with Borders, Racisms and State Violence.'" *Critical Criminology* 28(2): 169–73. https://doi.org/10.1007/s10612-020-09525-1.

Twyman-Ghoshal, A., E. Patten, and E. Ciaramella. 2022. "Exploring Media Representations of the Nexus between Climate Change and Crime in the United States." *Critical Criminology* 30:799–820. https://doi.org/10.1007/s10612-022-09608-1.

Uhlmann, David M. 2013. "Deferred Prosecution and Non-Prosecution Agreements and the Erosion of Corporate Criminal Liability." *Maryland Law Review* 72(4): 1295–344.

Unnever, James, and Shaun Gabbidon. 2011. *A Theory of African American Offending: Race, Racism and Crime.* London: Routledge.

Unnever, J. D., S. L. Gabbidon, K. Russell-Brown, and A. Owusu-Bempah. 2019. "Building a Black Criminology: The Time Is Now." *American Society of Criminology: The Criminologist* 44(1). https://asc41.com/wp-content/uploads/ASC-Criminologist-2019-01.pdf.

Urban Institute. 2021. "Incorporating Racial Equity Analysis in Policymaking: Racial Impact Statements in Justice Reform." https://www.urban.org/events/incorporating-racial-equity-analysis-policymaking-racial-impact-statements-justice-reform.

Urbina, Martin Guevara, Joel E. Vela, and Juan O. Sánchez. 2014. *Ethnic Realities of Mexican Americans: From Colonialism to 21st Century Globalization.* Springfield, IL: Charles C. Thomas.

Urquhart, E. 2020. "J. K. Rowling and the Echo Chamber of TERFs." *Slate*, June 12. https://slate.com/human-interest/2020/06/jk-rowling-trans-men-terf.html.

U.S. Census Bureau. 2022. "Race: About." March 1. https://www.census.gov/topics/population/race/about.html.

———. 2023. "Black Individuals Had Record Low Official Poverty Rate in 2022." https://

www.census.gov/library/stories/2023/09/black-poverty-rate.html.

U.S. Courts. n.d. "The 14th Amendment and the Evolution of Title IX." https://www.uscourts.gov/educational-resources/educational-activities/14th-amendment-and-evolution-title-ix.

U.S. Sentencing Commission. 1991. *Mandatory Minimum Penalties in the Federal Criminal Justice System*. August. Washington, DC: U.S. Sentencing Commission.

———. 2022. *Annual Report and Sourcebook of Federal Sentencing Statistics*. Washington, DC: U.S. Sentencing Commission. https://www.ussc.gov/research/sourcebook-2022.

Useem, Bert, and Anne Morrison Piehl. 2008. *Prison State: The Challenge of Mass Incarceration*. Cambridge: Cambridge University Press.

Valencia, N., D. M. Sayers, and P. Kirkland. 2023. "Climate Activist in 'Cop City' Protest Sustained 57 Gunshot Wounds, Official Autopsy Says, but Questions about Gunpowder Residue Remain." CNN, April 20. https://www.cnn.com/2023/04/20/us/cop-city-activist-killed-dekalb-county-medical-examiner/index.html.

Vera Institute of Justice. 2016. *Overlooked: Women and Jails in an Era of Reform*. https://www.vera.org/downloads/publications/overlooked-women-and-jails-fact-sheet.pdf.

Vidovic, K., and J. Brown. 2015. "Planting Seeds of Change in St. Louis." American Friends Service Committee, June 12. https://www.afsc.org/story/planting-seeds-change-st-louis.

Vieraitis, L. M., T. V. Kovandzic, and T. B. Marvell. 2007. "The Criminogenic Effects of Imprisonment: Evidence from State Panel Data, 1974–2002." *Criminology & Public Policy* 6(3): 589–622.

Vitale, A. 2021. *The End of Policing*. New York: Verso.

Vold, G., and T. Bernard. 1986. *Theoretical Criminology*. 3rd ed. New York: Oxford University Press.

von Zielbauer, Paul. 2005. "As Health Care in Jails Goes Private, 10 Days Can Be a Death Sentence." *New York Times*, February 27, A1, A26.

Wadsworth, Pamela, and Kathie Records. 2013. "A Review of the Health Effects of Sexual Assault on African American Women and Adolescents." *Journal of Obstetric, Gynecologic and Neonatal Nursing* 42(3): 249–73. https://doi.org/10.1111/1552-6909.12041.

Wagner, Peter, and Bernadette Rabuy. 2017. *Following the Money of Mass Incarceration*. Report, Prison Policy Initiative. https://www.prisonpolicy.org/reports/money.html.

Walker, Samuel. 1980. *Popular Justice: A History of American Criminal Justice*. New York: Oxford University Press.

Walsh, Amy, Pauline Adair, Grainne Ward, Bridget Tiernan, and David McCormack. 2023. "Experiences of Mothering from Prison; A Qualitative Evidence Synthesis." *Journal of Forensic Psychiatry & Psychology* 34(2): 216–60. https://doi.org/10.1080/14789949.2023.2201223.

Walter, S. 2023. "They Followed Doctors' Orders. Then Their Children Were Taken Away." *New York Times*, July 1. https://www.nytimes.com/2023/06/29/magazine/pregnant-women-medication-suboxonbabies.html.

Wang, H. L. 2022. "The U.S. Census Sees Middle Eastern and North African People as White. Many Don't." National Public Radio, February 17. https://www.npr.org/2022/02/17/1079181478/us-census-middle-eastern-white-north-african-mena.

———. 2023. "New 'Latino' and 'Middle Eastern or North African' Checkboxes Proposed for U.S. Forms." National Public Radio, April 7. https://www.npr.org/2023/01/26/1151608403/mena-race-categories-us-census-middle-eastern-latino-hispanic.

Wang, L. 2021. "Unsupportive Environments and Limited Policies: Pregnancy, Postpartum, and Birth during Incarceration." *Prison Policy Initiative*, August 19. https://www.prisonpolicy.org/blog/2021/08/19/pregnancy_studies.

Wang, N., A. McDonald, D. Bateyko, and E. Tucker. 2022. "American Dragnet: Data-Driven Deportation in the 21st Century." American Dragnet, May 10. https://americandragnet.org.

Washburn, E. 2023. "America Less Confident in Police Than Ever Before: A Look at the Numbers." *Forbes*, February 3. https://www.forbes.com/sites/emilywashburn/2023/02/03/america-less-confident-in-police-than-ever-before-a-look-at-the-numbers.

Wegner, H. 2022. "Police Play Disney Music to Stop YouTuber from Filming Them in California, Video Shows." *Sacramento Bee*, April

21. https://www.sacbee.com/news/nation-world/national/article260245605.html.

Weisshaar, K., and P. Casey. 2022. "100 Years of Sex and Gender in *Social Forces*." *Social Forces* 101(2): 546–57. https://doi.org/10.1093/sf/soac090.

Welch, Michael. 1996. *Corrections: A Critical Approach*. New York: McGraw-Hill.

Westat, D. C., B. Fisher, S. Chibnall, S. Harps, R. Townsend, G. Thomas, H. Lee, V. Kranz, R. Herbison, and K. Madden. 2020. "Report on the AAU Campus Climate Survey on Sexual Assault and Misconduct." Association of American Universities. https://www.nsvrc.org/sites/default/files/2021-04/aau-report_rev-01-17-2020.pdf.

Western, Bruce, and Catherine Sirois. 2019. "Racialized Re-entry: Labor Market Inequality after Incarceration." *Social Forces* 97(4): 1517–42. https://doi.org/10.1093/sf/soy096.

Weyler, Rex. 1992. *Blood of the Land: The Government and Corporate War against First Nations*. Philadelphia, PA: New Society.

Whitlock, K., and N. A. Heitzeg. 2021. *Carceral Con: The Deceptive Terrain of Criminal Justice Reform*. Oakland: University of California Press.

Whittingdale, E. 2021. "Becoming a Feminist Methodologist while Researching Sexual Violence Support Services." *Journal of Law and Society* 48(S1): S10–S27. https://doi.org/10.1111/jols.12335.

Whyte, D. 2020. *Ecocide: Kill the Corporation before It Kills Us*. Manchester: Manchester University Press.

Wicks, A. 2016. "More Republican Legislators Arrested for Bathroom Misconduct than Trans People." *Complex*, March 29. https://www.complex.com/life/2016/03/republican-legislators-arrested-for-bathroom-misconduct.

Wildman, Stephanie M. (1996) 1997. "Reflections on Whiteness: The Case of Latinos(as)." In *Critical White Studies: Looking behind the Mirror*, edited by Richard Delgado and Jean Stefancic, 323–26. Philadelphia, PA: Temple University Press.

Wildman, Stephanie M., and Adrienne D. Davis. 1997. "Making Systems of Privilege Visible." In *Critical White Studies: Looking behind the Mirror*, edited by Richard Delgado and Jean Stefancic, 314–19. Philadelphia, PA: Temple University Press.

Wilkey, Joshua. 2017. "Blessed Are the White Trash." *This Appalachia Life* (blog), May 5. https://www.thisappalachialife.com/single-post/2017/05/05/Blessed-are-the-White-Trash.

Will, Susan, Stephen Handelman, and David Brotherton, eds. 2013. *How They Got Away with It: White Collar Criminals and the Financial Meltdown*. New York: Columbia University Press.

Williams, E. 2023. "Forbes: These Are the World's 14 Black Billionaires." *Atlanta Journal-Constitution*, February 28. https://www.ajc.com/news/atlanta-black-history/who-are-the-black-billionaires/PRWODTCBXNHZLLSQTZOHU5Y3B4.

Willingham, A. J. 2022. "The Community Fridge Movement Could Change the Way We Think about Helping Each Other." CNN, April 15. https://www.cnn.com/2022/04/15/us/community-fridge-mutual-aid-free99-love-fridge/index.html.

Wilmot-Smith, F. 2019. *Equal Justice: Fair Legal Systems in an Unfair World*. Cambridge, MA: Harvard University.

Wing, Adrien Katherine, ed. 1997. *Critical Race Feminism: A Reader*. New York: New York University Press.

Wingfield, M. 2023. "Coalition of Atlanta Faith Leaders Plans Action to 'Stop Cop City' and Defend a Forest." *Baptist News*, March 3. https://baptistnews.com/article/coalition-of-atlanta-faith-leaders-plans-action-to-stop-cop-city-and-defend-a-forest.

Winlow, S., E. Kelly, and T. Ayres. 2021. "Ideology and Harm." In *The Palgrave Encyclopedia of Social Harm*, edited by P. Davies, P. Leighton, and T. Wyatt. Cham: Palgrave.

Wise, Tim. 2012. *Dear White America: Letter to a New Minority*. San Francisco, CA: City Lights.

Withrow, Brian. 2006. *Racial Profiling: From Rhetoric to Reason*. Upper Saddle River, NJ: Prentice-Hall.

Wolfgang, Marvin, and Bernard Cohen. 1970. *Crime and Race: Conceptions and Misconceptions*. New York: Institute of Human Relations Press.

Women's Sports Federation. 2019. "History of Title IX." https://www.womenssportsfoundation.org/advocacy/history-of-title-ix.

Woods, Jewel. 2008. "The Black Male Privileges Checklist." https://jewelwoods.com/node/9.

Woods, J. B. 2015. "The Birth of Modern Criminology and Gendered Constructions of Homosexual Criminal Identity." *Journal of Homosexuality* 62(2): 131–66. https://doi.org/10.1080/00918369.2014.969053.

Worden, R. E., S. J. McLean, R. S. Engel, H. Cochran, N. Corsaro, D. Reynolds, C. J. Najdowski, and G. T. Isaz. 2020. "The Impacts of Implicit Bias Awareness Training in the NYPD." John F. Finn Institute for Public Safety Inc. and Center for Police Research and Policy at the University of Cincinnati. https://www.nyc.gov/assets/nypd/downloads/pdf/analysis_and_planning/impacts-of-implicit-bias-awareness-training-in-%20the-nypd.pdf.

World Bank. 2022. "GDP: Current US$." https://data.worldbank.org/indicator/NY.GDP.MKTP.CD?most_recent_value_desc=true.

World Health Organization. 2005. "Gender and Reproductive Rights." https://www.who.int/reproductive-health/gender.

Wray, M., and A. Newitz, eds. 1996. *White Trash Studies: Race and Class in America*. New York: Routledge.

Wright, K. A., J. J. Turanovic, and N. Rodriguez. 2016. "Racial Inequality, Ethnic Inequality, and the System Involvement of At-Risk Youth: Implications for the Racial Invariance and Latino Paradox Theses." *Justice Quarterly* 33(5): 863–89. https://doi.org/10.1080/07418825.2014.987310.

Wu, Y., I. Sun, and M. Xie. 2021. "Asian-American Victimization: Expanding Research on Minority Vulnerability." *American Society of Criminology: The Criminologist* 46(5). https://asc41.com/wp-content/uploads/ASC-Criminologist-2021-09.pdf.

Wyatt, Edward. 2011. "Promises Made, and Remade, by Firms in S.E.C. Fraud Cases." *New York Times*, November 7. https://www.nytimes.com/2011/11/08/business/in-sec-fraud-cases-banks-make-and-break-promises.html.

Yavorsky, J. E., L. A. Keister, and Y. Qian. 2020. "Gender in the One Percent." *Contexts* 19(1): 12–17. https://doi.org/10.1177/1536504220902196.

Yee, A. 2023. "New Surveys of Asian Americans Show Persistent Racism and Hardship." *Bloomberg*, May 9. https://www.bloomberg.com/news/articles/2023-05-09/aapi-month-brings-new-research-on-asian-american-communities#:~:text="While%20%27model%20minorities%27%20are,%2C"%20according%20to%20the%20report.

York, J. C. 2022. "Silicon Valley's Sex Censorship Harms Everyone." *Wired*, March 18. https://www.wired.com/story/silicon-values-internet-sex-censorship.

Younes, L., A. Kofman, A. Shaw, and L. Song. 2021. "Poison in the Air." *ProPublica*, November 2. https://www.propublica.org/article/toxmap-poison-in-the-air.

Young, Jock. 2011. *The Criminological Imagination*. Malden, MA: Polity.

Yu, C. 2023. *Up to Speed: The Groundbreaking Science of Women Athletes*. New York: Riverhead Books.

Zatz, M. S., and H. Smith. 2012. "Immigration, Crime, and Victimization: Rhetoric and Reality." *Annual Review of Law and Social Science* 8:141–59. https://doi.org/10.1146/annurev-lawsocsci-102811-173923.

Zaw, Khaing, Jhumpa Bhattacharya, Ann Price, Darrick Hamilton, and William Darity Jr. 2017. *Women, Race and Health*. Report, Samuel DuBois Cook Center on Social Equity and Insight Center for Community Economic Development, January. https://www.insightcced.org/wp-content/uploads/2017/01/January2017_ResearchBriefSeries_WomenRaceWealth-Volume1-Pages.pdf.

Zhang, Y., L. Zhang, and F. Benton. 2022. "Hate Crimes against Asian Americans." *American Journal of Criminal Justice* 47(3): 441–61. https://doi.org/10.1007/s12103-020-09602-9.

Zinn, Howard. 2003. *A People's History of the United States*. New York: HarperCollins.

Zippia. 2023. "Correctional Guard Demographics and Statistics in the US." https://www.zippia.com/correctional-guard-jobs/demographics.

Zuboff, S. 2021. "You Are the Object of a Secret Extraction Operation." *New York Times*, November 12. https://www.nytimes.com/2021/11/12/opinion/facebook-privacy.html.

# Cases

*303 Creative v. Elenis*, No. 21-476. 2023.

*Bordenkircher v. Hayes*, 434 U.S. 357. 1978.

*Bostock v. Clayton County*, 590 U.S. ___. 2020.

*Brown v. Topeka, Kansas, Board of Education*, 347 U.S. 483. 1954.

*Dobbs v. Jackson Women's Health Organization*, 597 U.S., No. 19-1392. 2022.

*Floyd v. City of New York*, 08 Civ. 1034. 2013.

*Gideon v. Wainwright*, 372 U.S. 335. 1963.

*Graham v. Florida*, 560 U.S. 48, No. 08-7412. 2010.

*International Refugee Assistance Project v. Trump*, 17-1351. 2017.

*Juliana v. United States*. 2020. United States Court of Appeals for the Ninth Circuit Court. https://cdn.ca9.uscourts.gov/datastore/opinions/2020/01/17/18-36082.pdf.

——. 2015. First Amended Complaint. https://www.ourchildrenstrust.org/court-orders-and-pleadings.

*Korematsu v. U.S.*, 214 U.S. 220. 1944.

*Lassiter v. Dep't of Soc. Servs.*, 452 U.S. 18 at 25. 1981.

*Lockyer v. Andrade*, 538 U.S. 63. 2003.

*Loving v. Virginia*, 388 U.S. 1. 1967.

*Miller v. Alabama*, 567 U.S. 460, No. 10-9646. 2012.

*Missouri v. Frye*, 566 U.S. 134, No. 10-444. 2012.

*Padilla v. Kentucky*, 130 S. Ct. 1473. 2010.

*Plessy v. Ferguson*, 163 U.S. 537. 1896.

*R.A.V. v. St. Paul*, 507 U.S. 377. 1992.

*Roper v. Simmons*, 543 U.S. 551. 2005.

*Rummel v. Estelle*, 445 U.S. 263. 1980.

*State v. Mitchell*, 485 NW2d 807. 1992.

*Terry v. Ohio*, 392 U.S. 1. 1968.

*Trump v. Hawaii*, 9th Cir. 17-15589. 2017.

*United States of America v. The Purdue Frederick Company, Inc., Et Al.*, Case No. 1:07CR00029. 2007. https://www.vawd.uscourts.gov/OPINIONS/JONES/107CR00029.PDF.

*U.S. v. Deegan*, 08-2299. 2010.

*U.S. Securities and Exchange Commission v. Citigroup Global Markets*, 11 Civ. 7387. 2011.

*Virginia v. Black*, 538 U.S. 343. 2003.

*Whitney v. California*, 274 U.S. 357. 1927.

*Wisconsin v. Mitchell*, 508 U.S. 476. 1993.

# Index

Page numbers in italics refer to boxes, figures, and tables.

climate change and, 16
heteronormativity, 47, 50, 120, 181
incarceration and, 26, 267, 268, 269
intersex people, 187
law enforcement and, 130, 213, 214
LGBTQIA2S+, 296, 300n2
marginalization of, 50
marriage, 183
prison violence against, 270
public accommodations and, 182–83
rights, 182
same-sex marriage, 136
sexual assault, 213
suicide and death, 184
unemployment of, 27
victimization, 50–51, 123, 131
youth, 214–15, 283
living wages, 69
lobbying, 83
Lombroso, Cesare, 38–39
*Louisiana Separate Car Act*, 87
*Loving v. Virginia*, 94
lynching, 111, 173, 215
anti-lynching law, 134

male privilege, 63, 118, 121–25, *126*, 143
Mann Act of 1910, 133–34
Mara Salvatrucha (MS-13), 22, 219
marijuana, 165, 175, 198, 238, 290.
  *See also* drug war
drug war and, 173, 174, 232, 240
legalization and decriminalization, 174–75, 205, 240
marriage, 123, 133, 136, 183, 262
Martin, Trayvon, 157
Marx, Karl, 41, 64, 80
masculinity, 48, 53, 117, 119–20
mass deportations, 21
mass incarceration, 288, 290
mass shootings, 115
McCorkel, Jill, 271–72
McDonald, CeCe, 245
McDonald, Laquan, 190
*The McDonaldization of Society* (Ritzer), 61
media, 73
BLM and, 192, 202
courtroom drama and, 221
crime and, 2
ownership, 74
social, 14–15, 29, 114, 148
women and, 117
MENA. *See* Middle East and North Africa
mental health, 110, 156, 297

mental illness, 14
mergers, 83, 170, 235
Middle East and North Africa (MENA), 93
militarization, of law enforcement, 13, 23–25
military industrial complex, 12
*Miller v. Alabama*, 221
minimum wage, 69
minorities. *See also specific types*
communities of, 109
COVID pandemic and, 109–10, *110*
criminalization of, 107
criminal justice and, 225
DMC, 152
in Hollywood, 112n1
law enforcement and, 143, 192, 203, 206
oppression of, 46
in prison, 156
punishment and, *261*
miscarriage, 184, 212, 214
miscegenation, laws against, 94–95
misogyny, 38, 115, 118, 123, 131
Monero, 29–30
moral panics, 186
mortgages, 73, 171
motherhood, 267–68
MS-13. *See* Mara Salvatrucha
Mulvaney, Dylan, 131
murder
Black women and, *142*
gender/sexuality and, *129*
by law enforcement, 157, 203
sex and, *129*
statutes, 259
women and, 142
workplace and, 78–79
Muslim ban, 176
mutual aid, 294–95

Nasser, Larry, 133
national security, 166
National Women's Party, 134
Native Americans, 105
ancestry of, 95
climate change and, 108
Dakota Access Pipeline, 108–9
exploitation of, 108
land of, 75, 108
stereotypes, 177
victimization of, 154
women, 154
Nazis, 114–15
neoliberalism, 19–20, 273, 297
neonaticide, 248–51
New Deal, 82, 134
New England Abolition Society, 133

*The New Jim Crow* (Alexander), 175, 237
Nineteenth Amendment, 134
Nixon, Richard, 17.3
nonprosecution agreements, 226

Oakland Power Projects (OPP), 292
Obama, Barack, 28, 247n1, 290
Obamacare. *See* Affordable Care Act
opioids, 4, 55, 241, 245, 258
Opportunity Campus, 296
oppression, 277
criminal justice system and, 8
of minorities, 46
PV and, 128
Orientalism, 56
Occupational Safety and Health Administration (OSHA), 169, 200
OxyContin, 258

PACs. *See* political action committees
Parks, Rosa, 111, 112
parole, 262–63, 264, 272
paternalism, 118, 209
patriarchal violence (PV), 115, 116, 127–28
patriarchy, 47, 115
bias and, 147
definition of, 118
gender/sexuality and, 120
radical feminism and, 180
violence and, 127–28
pay gap, 125, 136
Pearl Harbor, 107
Peel, Robert (Sir), 23, 25
petit bourgeoisie, 64
plantations, 106, 172
plea bargains, 219–21, 224–25, 230
alternative to, 226
*Plessy v. Ferguson*, 87–89, 94, 100, 111, 173
police. *See* law enforcement
political action committees (PACs), 80, 82
*The Politics of Victimization* (Elias), 285
pollution, 41, 43, 103–5, 110, 285
positivism, 34, 37, 46
positivist criminology, 36–40, 46
postcolonial criminology, 280
posttraumatic stress disorder (PTSD), 110, 154, 192, 265
poverty, 139. *See also* income
bail and, 224
criminalization of, 27
difficulty of escaping, 76
education and, 20
of felons, 175
inequality and, 41–42

# About the Authors

**Gregg Barak** was the cofounder and former North American editor of the *Journal of White Collar & Corporate Crime* and is the award-winning author of four books including *Criminology on Trump* (2022). His most recent book, *Indicting the 45th President: Boss Trump, the GOP, and What We Can Do about the Threat to American Democracy*, was published April 1, 2024. Barak is a contributing writer for *Raw Story* and *Salon*.

**Carrie L. Buist** is associate professor in the School of Criminology, Criminal Justice, and Legal Studies at Grand Valley State University. Dr. Buist received her PhD from Western Michigan University in sociology with concentrations in criminology and gender and feminism. Dr. Buist's most current research focuses on the experience of justice-involved LGBTQ+ folks, and she has published and presented widely on the topic of queer criminology. Her cowritten book *Queer Criminology* won the Division on Critical Criminology's Book of the Year Award in 2016, and she has been honored with numerous awards in research, teaching, and mentorship. Dr. Buist's publications also include but are not limited to *The (Mis)Representation of Queer Lives in True Crime* (coedited), *Queering Criminology in Theory and Praxis: Reimagining Justice in the Criminal Legal System and Beyond* (coedited), *Queer Criminology* (cowritten) (1st and 2nd eds.), *The Trifecta of Violence: A Sociological Comparison of Lynching and Violence against Transgender Women* (cowritten), and *LGBTQ Rights in the Fields of Criminal Law and Law Enforcement*.

**Allison Cotton** is a professor of criminal justice and criminology at Metropolitan State University of Denver (Colorado, USA). A Colorado native, Dr. Cotton earned a BA in sociology from the University of Colorado at Boulder in 1991, an MA in sociology from Howard University in Washington, DC, in 1995, and a PhD in sociology from the University of Colorado at Boulder in 2002. Dr. Cotton has authored several books on the topics of race, class, gender, and crime; the death penalty; and women and violence. She is a member of the American Society of Criminology. A two-time Fulbright Scholar, Dr. Cotton has served as a board member of the Colorado Fulbright Foundation. She has also served as a member of the board of directors for the American Civil Liberties Union (ACLU) of Colorado. Dr. Cotton is an active member of Delta Sigma Theta Sorority Inc. (a public service organization).

**Paul Leighton** is a professor in the Department of Sociology, Anthropology, and Criminology at Eastern Michigan University. He is a coauthor of *The Rich Get Richer and the Poor Get Prison* (9th to 13th eds., 2023). He is also a founding coauthor of *Class, Race, Gender & Crime* (1st to 6th eds., 2024). Leighton was also a coauthor of *Punishment for Sale: Private Prisons, Big Business and the Incarceration Binge*. He has been an editor of *Critical Criminology: An International Journal* and has delivered invited keynote addresses in the United States, Canada, and Norway. He is a past president of the board of SafeHouse and is currently head of the advisory board of the food pantry serving the university.

**K. Sebastian León** is associate professor of Latino and Caribbean studies and criminal justice at Rutgers University, New Brunswick. He specializes in crimes of the powerful and racialized social control within and beyond criminal justice contexts. León is a former research contractor at the U.S. Department of Justice–National Institute of Justice and has extensive experience studying localized public safety challenges using qualitative and mixed-method approaches. These include medium and large-scale collaborative studies of the Colombian National Police, the Honduran National Police, U.S. jails, and the transnational capacity of MS-13 in the United States and El Salvador. More information about his teaching and research can be found at www.ksebastianleon.com.